AN INTRODUCTION TO
THE CREATION OF
ELECTROACOUSTIC MUSIC

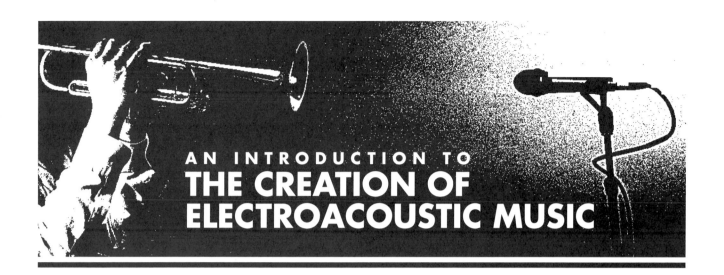

AN INTRODUCTION TO
THE CREATION OF
ELECTROACOUSTIC MUSIC

SAMUEL PELLMAN

HAMILTON COLLEGE

WADSWORTH PUBLISHING COMPANY

BELMONT, CALIFORNIA

A DIVISION OF WADSWORTH, INC.

Music Editor: Katherine Hartlove
Editorial Assistant: Kate Peltier
Production: Cecile Joyner / The Cooper Company
Production Service Coordinator: Debby Kramer
Designer: Janet Bollow
Print Buyer: Karen Hunt
Copy Editor: Peggy Tropp
Cover Designer: William Reuter Design
Compositor: **T:H** Typecast, Inc.
Cover Printer: Phoenix Color Corporation
Printer: Arcata Graphics / Kingsport

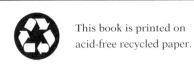

International Thomson Publishing
The trademark ITP is used under license.

4 5 6 7 8 9 10-02 01 00 99

Printed in the United States of America

LIBRARY OF CONGRESS CATALOGING-IN-PUBLICATION DATA

Pellman, Samuel, 1953–
     An introduction to the creation of electroacoustic music / Samuel
Pellman.
             p.   cm.
     Discography: p.
     Includes bibliographical references and index.
     ISBN 0–534–21450–9
     1. Electronic music—History and criticism.   2. Electronic music—
Instruction and study.   3. Music—Acoustics and physics.
     I. Title.
ML1380.P45   1994
786.7—dc20   93-11562

CONTENTS

CHAPTER 6   **ADVANCED MIDI NETWORKS**   181

CHAPTER 7   **TONE COLORS**   209

CHAPTER 8   **ANALOG SOUND SYNTHESIS**   225

PREFACE

Since its origins nearly a half-century ago, the field of electroacoustic music has passed through a remarkable series of changes. New instruments and techniques, based upon the most recent technological innovations, have appeared regularly. These often relegate older electroacoustic instruments to the status of relics. A text for electroacoustic music itself can rather quickly become a historical artifact.

Many practices and techniques have nonetheless proven durable. Other enduring aspects include the challenge of writing meaningful music in a genre for which the technology is so transitory—that is, developing a strategy for coping with change—and the changed relationships among composers, performers, and listeners that have resulted from the application of electronic technology. Issues such as these are among the principal topics addressed in this text.

There is enough material here to occupy a year or more of study. Chapters 1 through 4 describe techniques related to the recording of sound in a variety of media. Chapters 5 and 6 comprise a unit dedicated to the Musical Instrument Digital Interface. Chapters 7, 8, and 9 address more advanced topics of sound sampling and synthesis. The remaining chapters discuss a variety of aesthetic and other issues related to the composition and presentation of electroacoustic music and the future of the medium.

The particular order of topics selected here happens to be one the author has used with the most success with his own classes. Recently, the author presented the material in a different order, with similar success. The first semester began with the Introduction, skipped to Chapter 5, continued with Chapters 1, 2, and 4, then Chapter 3, and finished with the first part of Chapter 10 (up to Advanced Topics in Composition). The second semester commenced with Chapter 6 and proceeded in order to the end of the text. Other orderings are quite feasible as well. A requisite amount of redundancy has been incorporated into the text to facilitate such order swapping.

A significant smattering of knowledge of acoustics is necessary for all accomplished electroacoustic musicians. Acquiring this knowledge, however, can often seem a rather tedious process. Therefore, rather than warehouse all of this information in one, big, ugly chapter, it has been divided into smaller sections that are placed in or near the chapters where the information is most relevant. An important exception to this is Chapter 7, which is dedicated to the subject of tone color. This topic can be regarded as of paramount importance to the understanding of what synthesizers do. Instructors may wish to supplement this and the other sections of information regarding acoustics as necessary.

As with cooking, skiing, gardening, and the other recreations of life, it is not sufficient merely to read about electroacoustic music. Therefore, nearly every chapter in this text includes brief *études,* or "studies," that require involvement in a particular set of technical challenges. These are designed to foster a playful approach to sound by providing glimpses of the amazing universe of possible sounds and textures that can be created with electroacoustic instruments.

Most students, whether undergraduates or graduate students, music majors or nonmajors, have in common a relative unfamiliarity with the intensive application of contemporary technology that is involved in electroacoustic music. It is rather easy—even for professionals, in fact—to be overawed and even somewhat intimidated by the machinery. It is clear that there is no correlation between eventual success with equipment and one's race, gender, creed, virtue, or whatever; there is a direct correlation, however, between success and one's patience and diligence. This text aims to be accessible to students with relatively little experience with electronic musical technology, yet sufficiently detailed to enable them to achieve results of high quality, both technically and musically.

To bridge the difference between the generic descriptions of equipment provided in this text and the challenges of operating a specific device in the studio, it may be helpful to neophyte users for the instructor to prepare summaries of the basic operating procedures described in the owner's manuals. The author of this text has even occasionally prepared videotaped demonstrations of the operation of particular pieces of equipment. These have proven to be very successful as references for new students.

The primary purpose of this text is to provide a broad and secure base of practical knowledge regarding the creation of music with electroacoustic instruments. The technical information, while often fascinating in its own right, is presented as a means to the end of musical accomplishment. This, in essence, is the challenge and the promise of electroacoustic music.

ACKNOWLEDGMENTS

For their most valuable assistance in the preparation of this text, the author would gratefully like to acknowledge Chris Ingersoll, the graphic artist at Hamilton College, and Marianita Peaslee, the college photographer. I would also like to thank George Myers for his help in the preparation of many of the illustrations. My appreciation also goes to the librarians at Hamilton College, the staff at the college's Information Technology Services, and my colleagues in the Department of Music.

Deep gratitude and admiration go to the team at Wadsworth and The Cooper Company, including Suzanna Brabant, Dana Lipsky, Tammy Goldfeld, Katherine Hartlove, Kristina Pappas, Cecile Joyner, Janet Bollow, Peggy Tropp, and all others involved in bringing this project to such a satisfying outcome. For their astute comments and suggestions, I also express much appreciation to the content reviewers, including Burton Beerman, Bowling Green State University; Frederick Bianchi, University of Cincinnati; David Mathew, Georgia Southern University; David Sanders, Center for the Media Arts; Peter Temko, University of Tennessee at Chattanooga; and Don Wilson, University of Miami. Others who contributed valuable information and insights to me as I prepared this text include William Yardley, at the Smithsonian Institution, Reynold Weidenaar, and Tom Rhea.

Information of perhaps the greatest value has been provided by my students at Hamilton College (and those at the Eastman School of Music in the fall of 1987), who graciously served as experimental subjects as this text was prepared. I must also acknowledge the prerequisite contributions of my own teachers at Miami University, in Ohio, and Cornell University.

Finally, I express the deepest gratitude to my wife, Colleen, whose keen comments and belief have sustained this project. Also, I cite the inspiration and assistance provided by my daughter, Emily, and son, John (both of whom graciously provided audio material used for many of the illustrations in Chapter 3). To these three people I dedicate this book.

INTRODUCTION

For thousands of years, the predominant medium of musical expression was the human voice. In the past few centuries, however, musical instruments have become increasingly important. The sophistication of these instruments has paralleled the development of technology in general. Early musical instruments were relatively simple devices constructed of wood or of the horns of animals. By the 19th century, the level of mechanical ingenuity had progressed to the point that remarkably clever instruments made of a wide variety of materials, including metals, could be perfected or invented. The piano is perhaps the best representative of the technology of that time. Modern wind and brass instruments, such as the saxophone and the trumpet, reached maturity during this time as well. One thing that all of these instruments had in common was that they depended on the power of human breath or the muscles of the arms to create the waves of sound that could be heard as music.

The preeminent technology of the 20th century has been electronic. It seems inevitable, therefore, that musical instruments would be developed that would apply the power of electricity and the control capabilities of electronics to the task of creating musical sounds. The field of scientific study that deals with the transformation of energy between electrical forms and acoustical forms is called *electroacoustics*. This term has been borrowed by musicians who use electronic instruments, so that their music has come to be known as *electroacoustic music*. Such music may consist of sounds that are produced naturally and then transformed electronically (as described in detail in Chapters 2, 3, and 4, or of sounds that are created synthetically, by oscillating electrical circuits (as described in Chapters 8 and 9). Most typically, perhaps, it includes both kinds of sounds. Indeed, the array of resources available to contemporary musicians working in the medium of electroacoustic music is an impressively rich and immense one, as will be demonstrated throughout this text.

AN INTRODUCTION TO
THE CREATION OF ELECTROACOUSTIC MUSIC

CHAPTER 1

FROM SOUND TO ELECTRICITY, AND BACK

*S*everal instruments can be found in nearly all contemporary facilities for **electroacoustic music.** Sound synthesizers, samplers, and microphones are typically the sources of the electrical signals that will become musical sound. A mixing console and its associated sound-effects devices (usually located in a nearby equipment rack) prepare and process the signals for immediate listening by the musician and an audience, or for recording.

Although much electroacoustic music is performed live, most is recorded for subsequent listening. Thus, a typical studio for electroacoustic music will include a variety of tape-recording machines. These not only provide a means of storing the accomplishments of the musician in the studio, but (as will be learned from this and the following three chapters) also provide further opportunities for the creative manipulation of the musical sound.

To understand what these instruments can do and how they are used together to produce much of the music we hear today, it is helpful to begin with a good understanding of the nature of sound itself.

THE SCIENCE OF SOUND, PART I

Sound, as you may recall from your favorite high school physics text, begins when an object vibrates. A string is plucked, a bell is struck, lips buzz in the mouthpiece of a trumpet, a reed wails in the mouthpiece of a saxophone—these are some of the ways in which sounds are created.

It may be helpful to imagine what happens when, for example, a string is plucked. The player's hand pulls the string to the side, resulting in a fair amount of lateral tension (see Figure 1.1a). As the string slips away from the player's hand, this tension is released as the string snaps back toward

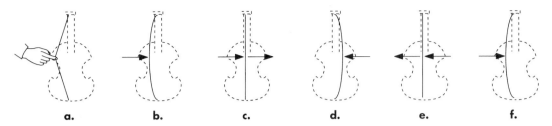

FIGURE 1.1
The motion of a plucked string.

a. b. c. d. e. f.

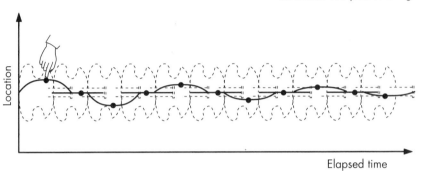

FIGURE 1.2
The location of a plucked string over time. Note that with successive vibrations the string loses some of its energy and does not move quite as far from its rest position. This indicates that the vibration is decaying.

Location

Elapsed time

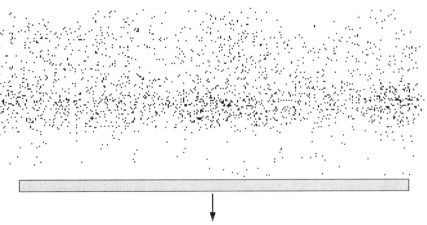

a. a compression of air molecules ahead of an advancing surface

b. a rarefaction of air molecules behind a retreating surface

FIGURE 1.3
Compression and rarefaction of air molecules above the surface of the body of an instrument.

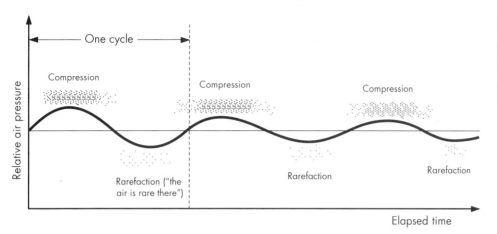

FIGURE 1.4
The fluctuations in the air pressure near a vibrating musical instrument. Note the similarity of this pattern to that of string location, shown in Figure 1.2.

its original, "rest" position (see Figure 1.1b). When it arrives there however, it is moving too fast to stop (see Figure 1.1c). The string continues past its original position until it reaches the point where the lateral tension of the string pulls it to a stop (see Figure 1.1d). This tension again causes it to snap back toward the rest position (see Figure 1.1e). Once again, it is going too fast to stop at this rest position, and it continues until the lateral tension of the string slows it to a stop (see Figure 1.1f). The string has now completed one vibration. The lateral tension on the string causes it to snap back yet again toward the "rest" position, and another cycle of vibration begins.

Each time the motion of the string is stopped by the lateral tension on the string, some of the energy given initially by the musician's pluck is transferred to the body of the instrument, and from there to the surrounding air. Furthermore, as the string moves, some of its energy is lost to the air it encounters along the way. Over time, then, the successive cycles of vibration become progressively weaker, until eventually the vibration is extinguished. Figure 1.2, a graph of the location of the string over time, illustrates this gradual dampening, or **decay,** of the vibrations of the plucked string.

In the meantime, the air surrounding the body of the instrument is agitated and dislocated by the vibrations it has acquired from the string. As the body advances through the air, it pushes the air molecules that are ahead of it, compressing them into something of a shock wave (see Figure 1.3a). Then, as the body reverses direction (see Figure 1.3b), it pulls at the molecules it leaves behind, creating a partial vacuum in its wake. Figure 1.4 is a graph of these fluctuations in air pressure over time in a selected space near the instrument.

These disturbances in the molecules of air surrounding the instrument in turn affect the molecules of air that surround them, and these in turn disturb the molecules further beyond. Thus, ever-widening ripples of **compressions** and **rarefactions** emanate from the instrument.

FREQUENCY

The number of cycles of vibration that occur in one second is the **frequency** of the sound. The amount of time that elapses during one cycle of vibration is called the **period** of the vibration. The period of a vibration is calculated by finding the reciprocal of the frequency:

$$P = \frac{1}{f}$$

where P = the period in seconds
f = the frequency of the sound.

A sound with a frequency of 440 cycles per second (abbreviated **cps**) is commonly used by musicians as a reference when they tune their instruments. This frequency is written as a note A on printed music (see Figure 1.5), and is therefore identified as **A-440.**

The term **hertz** (abbreviated **Hz**) is now in common use as an alternative to cps when the frequency of a sound is specified.[1] One thousand hertz are called a kilohertz (kHz). Engineers and physicists often use a sound with a frequency of 1 kHz when conducting tests or experiments, or when calibrating laboratory instruments. The period of this frequency is .001 seconds, or 1 millisecond (1/1000th of a second).

A sound must have a frequency of approximately 20 Hz or more to be heard by most humans. Frequencies of less than 20 Hz, though perhaps still audible to elephants, are essentially inaudible to humans, and are described as **subsonic** or **infrasonic.**

The upper limit of frequencies audible to humans is less precise. Frequencies higher than the upper limit are described as **ultrasonic.** With young, undamaged ears, it may be possible to hear frequencies of up to 17,000 Hz or more. As people become older, the upper limit of their hearing becomes gradually lower; to an average 50-year-old, for example, the highest audible frequency is approximately 12,000 Hz. This natural decline can be accelerated by damage to the ears caused by infection or by frequent exposure to excessive noise in the workplace. The most preventable cause of deafness to high frequencies is prolonged, frequent exposure to overly loud music.[2] The audio quality of the world's worst "boom box" can be indistinguishable from that of a fine stereo system to a person who has sustained such deterioration in hearing.

FIGURE 1.5
The musical notation for A-440.

---

1. This is named in honor of Heinrich Hertz, the 19th-century German physicist who discovered radio waves.

2. Although it is true that Beethoven continued to write truly great music even after he became totally deaf, most professional musicians recognize that they do not have the innately powerful musical gifts that Beethoven had. Therefore, if they often work in environments where the music is highly amplified, and they want to be able to continue to work and earn a living, they choose to wear some form of hearing protection.

INTENSITY

When an object vibrates to produce sound, it moves back and forth, or **oscillates,** through its rest position. The distance between the rest position and the farthest point to which the object moves is called the **amplitude** of the vibration (see Figure 1.6a). The term *amplitude* can also be used to refer to the extent of the change in air pressure in a wave of sound from the normal level of air pressure (see Figure 1.6b).

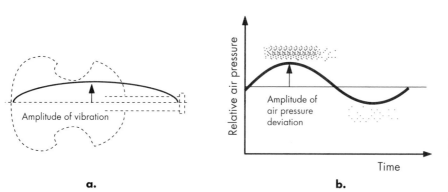

FIGURE 1.6
Two situations to which the concept of amplitude is applied.

The power, or **intensity,** of a sound is directly related to the amplitude of the vibration. This power can be measured in watts, but this is not particularly convenient for most people who work with sound because human ears are sensitive to a tremendous range of sound intensity. This range of intensity is managed more effectively by the use of a logarithmically based unit called the **decibel** (named in honor of Alexander Graham Bell and abbreviated **dB**). The decibel (which incidentally is also used by engineers as a unit for comparing electrical signal levels) provides a means of relating different levels of sound intensity (see Table 1.1). This serves well the needs of technicians and recording engineers, but musicians are more familiar with the set of terms shown in Table 1.2 for describing the relative intensities of musical sounds. Though much less precise than decibels, these terms, which have been in use since the 17th century, have been considered sufficient by musicians.

ENVELOPES

The intensity of a sound is generally not a static quantity, but changes over the duration of the sound. Thus, at the beginning of a sound, the intensity does not change in an instant from silence to peak level; rather, it requires a certain amount of time, called the **attack time** (or simply, the **attack**), to do so. Similarly, at the end of a sound, the intensity does not suddenly plummet to silence. The amount of time required for the intensity of the

	Power (watts/square meter)	dB (sound pressure level)
Threshold of pain	10	130
Passenger jet taking off (as heard from about 500 feet away)	1	120
Very loud, amplified music	.1	110
Power saw	.01	100
Subway	.001	90
Heavy traffic on freeway	.0001	80
Busy street traffic	.00001	70
Friendly conversation	.000001	60
Typical office	.0000001	50
Hushed conversation	.00000001	40
Waiting room at dentist's office	.000000001	30
Very quiet living room	.0000000001	20
Breathing	.00000000001	10
Threshold of hearing	.000000000001	0

TABLE 1.1
Familiar sounds, their power, and their relative intensity in decibels.

Musicians use the term *dynamic markings* to refer to the symbols used to notate these intensity levels. The decibel equivalents are provided here as a general reference. In practice, there is a considerable difference in intensity level between the sound of a violin playing a dynamic marking of *ff*, for example, and that of a trumpet playing *ff!*

fff	*fortississimo*	very, very loud!	100 dB
ff	*fortissimo*	very loud	90
f	*forte*	loud	80
mf	*mezzo-forte*	somewhat loud	72
mp	*mezzo-piano*	somewhat soft	68
p	*piano*	soft	60
pp	*pianissimo*	very soft	50
ppp	*pianississimo*	very, very soft	40

TABLE 1.2
Common levels of intensity used in music.

sound to diminish to nothing is called the **decay time** (or simply, the **decay**), or the **release.**

Piano, guitar, and drum sounds tend to have very short attack times, whereas sounds produced by violins and other bowed-string instruments tend to have longer attack times. Players of woodwind and brass instruments can produce a range of attack times that depend on the placement of the tongue and the pressure of the breath. Cymbals, gongs, and pianos (particularly if the "sustain" pedal is down) have long decay times; most other instruments produce tones with much shorter decay times.

Segments of time during which the intensity of the sound changes, such as attacks and decays, are called transient stages, or just **transients.**

THE DIFFERENCE BETWEEN INTENSITY AND LOUDNESS

*M*usicians tend to use the terms *intensity* and *loudness* interchangeably. For people who work in **acoustics,** the study of the physical properties of sound, and in **psycho-acoustics,** the study of the perception of sound, there is a subtle but important distinction. In 1933, the researchers Harvey Fletcher and W. A. Munson reported that the perception of a sound's loudness, while obviously related to its intensity, is also related to its frequency. The line on the graph in Figure 1.7 is called an **equal loudness contour.** It charts the actual intensity of sounds at various frequencies that were reported by test subjects as having the same apparent loudness.

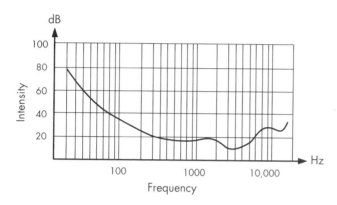

FIGURE 1.7

An equal loudness contour. Sounds with the frequency-intensity combinations found on this curve will seem equally loud to most listeners [after D. W. Robinson and R. S. Dadson, "A Re-determination of the Equal-Loudness Relations for Pure Tones," *British Journal of Applied Physics 7* (1956), pp. 166–181].

The intensity—an objective, acoustical property of the sounds—was measured by a laboratory instrument called a sound pressure meter. The loudness—a subjective, psychoacoustical quantity—was determined by the perception and judgment of the listeners. The graph indicates that human ears are particularly sensitive to sounds in the range of 3–5 kHz in frequency. Sounds that are higher than 5 kHz must be progressively more intense if they are to be heard as being just as loud. It is apparent that we are not very sensitive to low frequencies either. A 50-Hz sound must have an intensity of approximately 55 dB if it is to be heard as being "just as loud" as a 3000-Hz sound that has an intensity of only 15 dB.

This means, among other things, that bass instruments (such as the 'cello, bass guitar, and "kick" drum) must be significantly more powerful than midrange instruments (such as the voice, clarinet, and saxophone) if they are to make the impression of being just as loud. An implication of Fletcher and Munson's work, then, is that most of the power of a stereo amplifier will be consumed by the production of low-frequency sounds from bass instruments.

Many researchers also make a distinction between frequency and pitch. Frequency is an acoustical property of sounds and can be measured by laboratory instruments; pitch is what is perceived of the frequency and is a psychoacoustical attribute. Some research has suggested that high levels of intensity can affect the perception of a sound's frequency; for example, for some listeners, a sound of high frequency at high intensity may seem somewhat lower in pitch than a sound of the same frequency at a lower intensity. The distinction between frequency and pitch is much less obvious, however, than the distinction between intensity and loudness. In any case, with frequency and pitch, as with intensity and loudness, musicians do not feel the need to be precise about the distinction, and tend to use the terms interchangeably.

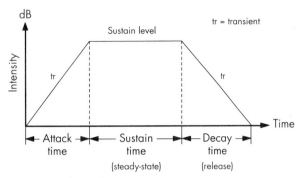

a. a simple envelope

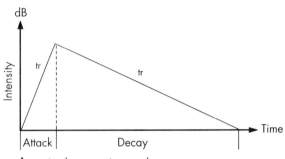

b. a simple percussive envelope

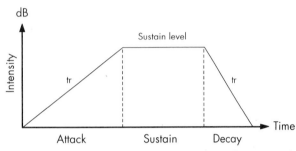

c. a simplified representation of the envelope of a tone produced on a bowed-string instrument

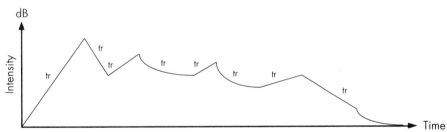

d. a more complex envelope, with many transients, more typical of a naturally produced instrumental sound

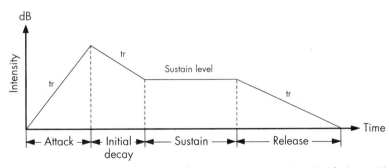

e. an "ADSR" envelope, commonly found on synthesizers (described further in Chapter 8)

FIGURE 1.8
A few examples of intensity envelopes.

Between transients there may be times when the intensity of the sound is fairly steady. Such times are called **sustain** or **steady-state** stages. Tones produced by singing, by woodwind and brass instruments, or by bowed-string instruments can be readily sustained because the musician continues to supply energy to the instrument after the attack. However, tones from the piano or guitar, or sounds from other percussion instruments, do not seem to have such steady-state stages. The energy for such sounds all comes at the beginning, from a single blow of a hammer or mallet, or a pluck of a string.

A graph of intensity through the duration of a sound reveals the contour of its intensity changes. This is called the **envelope** of the sound.[3] Figure 1.8 illustrates a variety of such envelopes.

PHASE

The **phase** of a sound is the point within a cycle of vibration where the sound is at a particular instant. For reference purposes, a cycle of a wave is normally divided into 360 degrees of phase (see Figure 1.9).

The concept of phase is especially useful for describing some of the interactions that can occur when two sounds are combined. If two sounds have the same frequency and have the same phase they are said to be "in phase." The amplitude of one wave combines with the amplitude of the other wave to create the impression of a single sound with even greater amplitude (see Figure 1.10). This phenomenon is called **constructive interference.**

If a sound begins when another sound of the same frequency is half a cycle ahead, then the crests of one wave will coincide with the troughs of the other. In this case, the two sounds are described as being 180° out of phase. The amplitude of one sound will subtract from the amplitude of the other, a phenomenon called **destructive interference.** If the amplitude of the two sounds is equal, then the two sounds will totally cancel each other (see Figure 1.11).

An example of a situation in which destructive interference is a problem is when the cable to one of the loudspeakers in a stereo system is con-

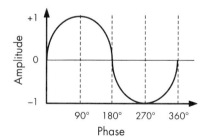

FIGURE 1.9
The division of a cycle of vibration into 360 degrees of phase.

---

3. More specifically, this describes an intensity envelope, or amplitude envelope. The concept of an envelope can also be applied to other kinds of changes that happen over the duration of a sound—for example, changes in pitch or tone color.

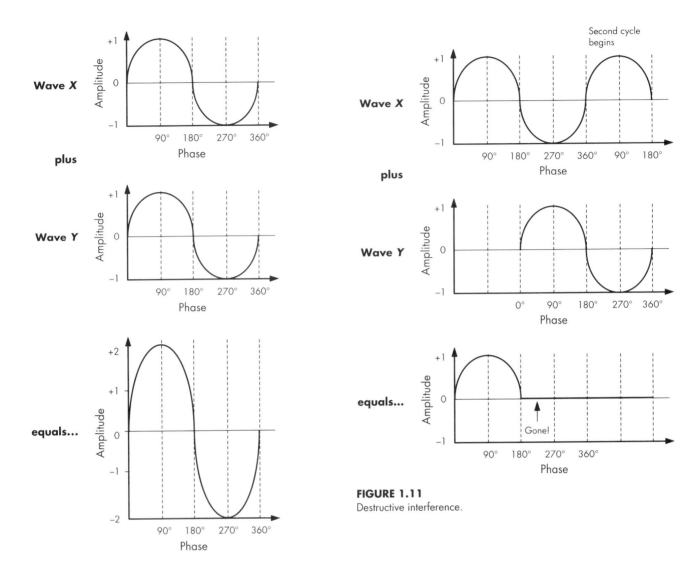

FIGURE 1.10
Constructive interference by two waves of sound.

FIGURE 1.11
Destructive interference.

nected incorrectly, with wires reversed. A listener at a midpoint in front of the loudspeakers will receive sounds that are out of phase from the incorrectly wired loudspeaker. These sounds will at least partially cancel the sounds from the other loudspeaker, resulting in a much less than satisfactory listening experience. Phase is just as significant a factor at all other stages of the recording and playback process, so care must be taken whenever audio components are connected.

OTHER PHENOMENA ARISING FROM COMBINATIONS OF SOUNDS

As described previously, when two sounds of the same frequency and phase are combined, the listener will have the impression of a single sound that is louder than either of the two contributing sounds would be if heard by

Sound *X* has 10 cycles of vibration.

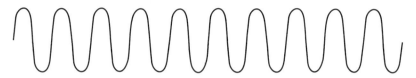

Sound *Y* has 11 cycles of vibration.

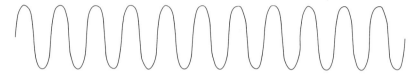

Combine sounds *X* and *Y*...

Constructive interference   Destructive interference   Constructive interference again

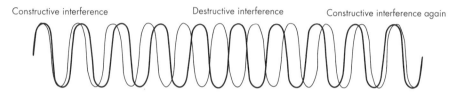

...and this is what you will hear.

A beat   The next beat

The null between beats

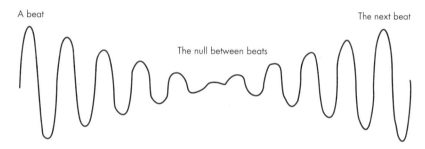

themselves. If the two sounds are slightly *different* in frequency, however, the listener will again have the impression that there is a single sound, but its loudness will pulsate as the contributing sounds are alternately in phase and out of phase. For example, consider the combination of a sound with a frequency of 441 Hz and a sound with a frequency of 440 Hz. The sounds begin together, in phase, and they interfere constructively (see Figure 1.12). After one-half second has elapsed, however, the first sound has vibrated 220.5 times, while the second sound has only vibrated 220 times. The two sounds are a half-cycle apart, or 180° out of phase. At this point, they interfere destructively, and the combined loudness is diminished. The moment of this occurrence is often referred to as a null.

By the end of one full second, however, both sounds have completed full cycles—the 441st cycle for the first sound, the 440th cycle for the second sound. The two sounds are in phase again, and their combined loudness is greater. This alternating pattern of constructive and destructive interference will continue as long as the two sounds are combined. Once each

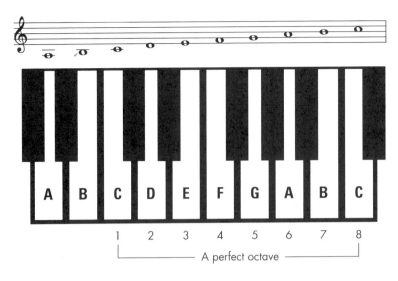

FIGURE 1.13
An octave on a keyboard.

second the loudness will rise, and then it will diminish. (If the difference between the two frequencies is 2 cps, then the loudness will rise and diminish twice each second.) This pulsation of loudness, produced by the combination of two sounds of nearly the same frequency, is called **beating.**

Beating is a phenomenon of great value to musicians when they tune instruments. As an instrument becomes more closely in tune with another instrument, the frequency of the beating produced by the combination of the sounds from the two instruments becomes slower. The frequency of the beating equals the difference between the frequencies of the two sounds. If the two instruments could be exactly in tune, the beating would stop altogether. In the real world of fluctuating room temperatures and humidity levels, however, such precision is practically impossible to achieve; as a result, there will always be some amount of acoustic beating when two or more acoustic instruments attempt to produce the same pitch. In fact, such beating contributes to the liveliness of the tone and is regarded as desirable, up to a point.

As two frequencies are taken out of tune, the frequency of the beating between them increases. Soon, however, when the frequencies have diverged sufficiently, the beating disappears and instead the listener perceives two distinct frequencies. An **interval** is a combination of two such distinct frequencies. The term is also used to describe two frequencies heard in succession.

Intervals are often expressed as the ratios between two frequencies, and these ratios are then related to the distances between the keys on a keyboard. For example, the frequency produced by "middle C" is 261.62 Hz. The frequency produced by the eighth white key above middle C is 523.25 Hz—double the frequency of middle C (see Figure 1.13). The ratio between the higher and lower frequencies is 2:1, and this interval is called a perfect **octave** (Latin for "eighth").[4]

---

4. Frequencies an octave apart are given the same letter name in musical notation. For example, a frequency of 220 Hz, which is one octave lower than A-440, is also called an A—in this case, it is the A below middle C.

A perfect **fifth** is an interval with a ratio of 3:2 between the higher and lower frequencies. The interval between the frequency of middle C (261.62 Hz) and the frequency of G, the fifth white key above (392 Hz), is very nearly a perfect fifth.

A perfect **fourth** has a ratio of 4:3. One example of a perfect fourth is the interval between the F above middle C (349.22 Hz) and middle C (261.62 Hz). A major **third** has a frequency ratio of 5:4 and is exemplified by the interval between the E above middle C (329.62 Hz) and middle C (261.62 Hz).

The intervals just described represent fairly simple numerical ratios and are fairly stable—even pleasant sounding (although these characterizations are also determined somewhat by the context of the music in which the intervals are used and are therefore relative, not absolute). Such combinations of frequencies are **consonant.** Other consonances, besides the perfect octave (2:1), perfect fifth (3:2), perfect fourth (4:3), and major third (5:4), are the minor third (6:5), major sixth (5:3), and minor sixth (8:5).

Other combinations of frequencies—unstable, unpleasant sounding, and represented by more complex numerical ratios—are considered **dissonant.** For example, the interval between the black key above F (called F-sharp) and middle C can be expressed by the ratio 64:45. The relative harshness of this interval, and the difficulty of finding the pitches when singing it, led the musicians of the Middle Ages to call it *diabolus in musica*, or "the devil in music."

Further exploration of this topic is perhaps better pursued in a course on music theory, which among other things seeks to describe how combinations of pitches function within a particular musical style.

TIMBRE

Virtually any sound is actually a combination of many, more or less related frequencies, and typically each frequency component of the sound has an independent envelope of amplitude. The overall perception we have of this aggregation of frequency components is called the **timbre** or **tone color** of the sound.[5] This information provides the primary set of cues that enable us to distinguish among tones produced on different musical instruments —for example, the difference between a clarinet sounding A-440 and a piano sounding A-440.

Timbre is a phenomenon of considerable importance to electroacoustic musicians, because contemporary technology has made precise control of timbre possible for the first time. Therefore, the subject will be explored in great detail later in this text. For now, however, it is time to return to the studio, where the next task for the aspiring electroacoustic musician is to convert acoustical vibrations into electrical ones.

---

5. *Timbre*, a word of French origin, is pronounced "TAM-ber." The expressions *tone color* or *tone quality* are synonymous with timbre and are often found in writings on the subject.

TRANSDUCERS

A **transducer** is a device that converts kinetic energy into electrical energy, or electrical energy into kinetic energy. The most common transducers in studios for electroacoustic music are microphones and loudspeakers. The depth and variety of techniques for the use of microphones and other transducers is most impressive indeed. It should be no surprise that successful electroacoustic musicians approach the use of these tools with the same care and attention that the superb pianist or gifted saxophonist brings to his or her instrument. Because so much of the sound heard in electroacoustic music originates from naturally produced sounds, it is important that these be captured and reproduced as faithfully as possible. Before the piece of music is completed, the musician will come to be quite familiar with these sounds, and any flaws will become increasingly noticeable and troublesome. Skillful technique and awareness are vital, therefore, from the very beginning of the process of producing electroacoustic music.

MICROPHONES

A microphone converts the kinetic energy of sound waves in the air into corresponding patterns of electrical current. Not a great deal of electricity is generated from sound waves by a microphone, of course. In fact, the electrical signal from a microphone is typically quite weak relative to the level of electrical signals, called **line level,** sent and received by other pieces of audio equipment. Therefore, a microphone signal will require **preamplification** to boost it to line level and make it usable by other pieces of equipment. Preamplifier circuits (or preamp circuits, as they are

FIGURE 1.14
Common microphone field patterns.

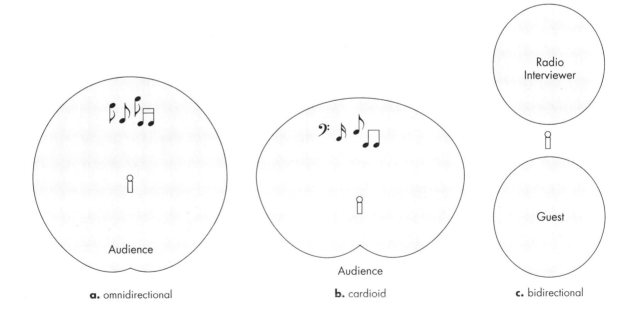

a. omnidirectional   **b.** cardioid   **c.** bidirectional

usually called) are generally included at the inputs of mixing consoles, and often can be found installed as separate microphone inputs on tape recorders and other audio devices as well.

A microphone is often described according to its directional sensitivity, or **field pattern.** An **omnidirectional** microphone, for example, is one that is sensitive to sounds of any frequency coming from any direction (see Figure 1.14a). If it is desirable to include the sounds of the audience or the reverberation of the room in the recording, then an omnidirectional microphone might be chosen.

A **cardioid** microphone, also called a unidirectional microphone, has a heart-shaped field pattern (see Figure 1.14b). For higher frequencies in particular, it is more sensitive to sounds coming from before the microphone than it is to those coming from behind (for low frequencies, the response is essentially omnidirectional). A cardioid microphone is used to pick up sounds from a particular instrument or group of instruments, to the partial exclusion, at least, of sounds from the audience, other instruments, or the reverberation of the room.[6]

A **bidirectional** microphone, also called a "figure-8" microphone, is equally sensitive to sounds coming from the front and coming from behind, but is insensitive to sounds coming from the sides (see Figure 1.14c). Although not used as often as microphones with omnidirectional or cardioid field patterns, bidirectional microphones are sometimes employed for stereo recording of live musicians or for situations in the recording studio where it is important to maintain some degree of isolation between the sounds produced by two or more different instruments. Bidirectional microphones are also in common use for one-on-one interviews on radio programs.

When selecting a microphone for a particular task, it is important to consider not only its field pattern but also its **frequency response**—how uniformly it responds across a range of frequencies. If the response of the microphone is specified as 20 Hz to 20 kHz ± 3 dB, for example, then the entire range of frequencies heard by humans is covered and the relative intensity of a frequency in the signal will not vary by more than 3 decibels from the relative intensity of that frequency in the original sound. This is a very good microphone; it has what is described as a "flat" response.

While a flat response is generally a good thing, there are also occasions when a deviation from flat response can be useful. The graph in Figure 1.15 shows the frequency response of a microphone that is particularly sensitive to frequencies between approximately 3000 and 7000 Hz, a range

---

6. Variants of the cardioid pattern are the supercardioid, which is somewhat less sensitive to sounds coming from the sides, and the hypercardioid, which is even less sensitive to sounds coming from the sides but somewhat more sensitive to sounds from behind. Yet another variant is the ultracardioid pattern (also known as the "shotgun" pattern), which has a very narrow and extended field to the front. It is most likely to be used for location sound recording by naturalists, by television or radio sound crews, or by eavesdroppers!

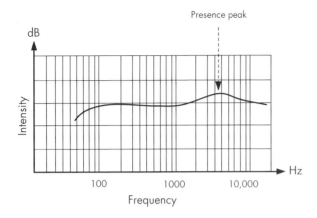

FIGURE 1.15

A graph of the frequency response of a microphone with a presence peak.

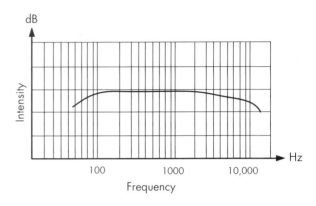

FIGURE 1.16

A graph of the frequency response of a microphone with diminished response to higher frequencies.

in which frequencies important to the intelligibility of speech are located. Enhanced response to frequencies in this range is called a **presence peak.** For recording someone who is speaking or singing, the best choice of microphone might well be one with such a presence peak in its frequency response. The graph in Figure 1.16 shows the frequency response of a microphone that does a poor job with high frequencies. If the task is to record a bass drum, however, this microphone might be a fine choice.

The best frequency response for a microphone generally can be achieved when the microphone is pointed directly at the source of sound (the published specifications of the frequency response of a microphone usually assume this as a test condition). If the microphone is pointed away from the source, then there are likely to be significant differences between the balance of frequencies in the microphone signal and the balance of frequencies in the original sound. This is particularly true for microphones with cardioid or bidirectional field patterns. As mentioned previously, a cardioid microphone is particularly sensitive to higher frequencies coming from the front, but responds equally well to low frequencies coming from any direction. Thus, if the microphone is pointed away from the source, the low frequencies will be unaffected but the high frequencies in the microphone signal will be somewhat weakened. This alteration of the balance between low and high frequencies in a microphone signal is called off-axis coloration.

The balance between low and high frequencies can also be affected by the closeness of the microphone to the source. With cardioid and bidirectional microphones in particular (or with microphones that achieve an omnidirectional pattern by placing two cardioid elements back to back), there is an increasing response to low frequencies when the microphone is brought within approximately two feet of the source. This is called the **proximity effect.** Often this effect is employed deliberately to provide a deeper and more "rounded" quality to the tone of a singing or speaking voice (in fact, it is an essential attribute of the vocal sound of a radio DJ).

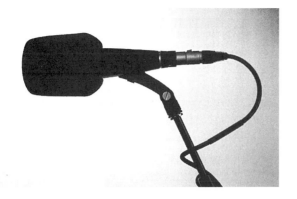

FIGURE 1.17
Microphones with accessories designed to minimize extraneous noises: (left) a windscreen; (right) a shock mount.

However, much of the time the boost of low frequencies that results from proximity to the microphone can obscure or muddy the texture of the sound. It may nonetheless be necessary to place the microphone up close to provide better isolation from the sounds of other instruments in the room, or because the intensity of the sound itself is weak (according to the "inverse square law," at half the distance the sound pressure level received by the microphone is four times as great). Therefore, to facilitate close placement without a proximity effect, many microphones have a bass roll-off switch that reduces the intensity of the low frequencies in the signal, thus restoring some of the balance between low and high frequencies.

Placing a microphone close to the source of the sound can be an advantage not only if the proximity effect is desired or if the sound source is weak, but also if a crispness or "presence" of sound quality is sought. The higher frequencies in a sound are the ones that contribute primarily to this crispness. However, they are highly directional and can be easily blocked by objects in the room or absorbed by carpets, clothing, and other surfaces. Therefore, catching high frequencies before they disappear can be best accomplished by placing the microphone up close. (For further hints regarding microphone placement, see Appendix A.)

However, close placement can be a problem when recording speech or singing (or the performance of a woodwind instrument). The puffs of air associated with the consonants *p, b, k, t,* and *f* (called *plosives*), the hissing of the letters *s* and *z* (called *sibilants*), and even breathing can noticeably rattle the diaphragm of a microphone. To minimize this, the microphone can be placed above, below, or to one side of the mouth and out of harm's way (but still pointed directly at the mouth to avoid off-axis coloration). In addition, a foam cover, called a **pop filter** or **windscreen,** can be placed over the end of the microphone (see Figure 1.17a).

Incidentally, when checking to see if a microphone is live, it is never a good idea to blow into it or even to tap it. Snapping fingers in front of the microphone will work well, as will speaking the phrase "testing, testing, . . ." or counting aloud.

Vibrations from the microphone stand can also intrude into the microphone signal. To reduce the noise caused by floor vibrations or by collisions of big feet with the base of the stand, a microphone should be placed in a **shock mount** (see Figure 1.17b).

LOUDSPEAKERS

Yet another transducer found in a studio for electroacoustic music is the loudspeaker. As the final device in the chain of audio devices used to reproduce sound, its task is to convert the electrical vibrations into acoustical ones. One of the most important matters to consider regarding loudspeakers is their placement in the room relative to the most likely spot for listening and relative to the walls and other surfaces. In a typically rectangular room, the loudspeakers will probably be placed near one of the short walls, as shown in Figure 1.18. The loudspeakers will be angled toward the center of the room, at perhaps an angle of 30° with respect to the wall. (Much experimentation is likely, however, before the best angle of placement relative to the wall and separation distance between the loudspeakers are found.) The optimal listening location is likely to be found around the point in the room that completes an equilateral triangle formed by the loudspeakers and the listener.

The proximity of the loudspeakers to the walls and other surfaces in the room may be largely determined by the design of the particular model of loudspeaker chosen. It is important, therefore, to begin by consulting the owner's manual provided by the manufacturer. Generally, the closer a loudspeaker is to a wall, the more prominent the bass frequencies will be in the reproduced sound. If the loudspeaker is placed in a corner, where two or more surfaces meet, the bass response will seem to be even greater. If the loudspeaker is placed on a thick carpet, or if the room is heavily curtained, the relative presence of high frequencies will be reduced, and again the bass response will seem enhanced in comparison.

Because so many characteristics of the room can affect the sound that is reproduced by the speakers, many musicians who do most of their work alone in a studio prefer working with a near-field monitor speaker system, illustrated in Figure 1.19. In such a system, the loudspeakers and the listener are just a few feet apart and are far removed from the walls of the room. The area of optimal listening is reduced quite a bit, but the effects of the acoustics of the room are also reduced considerably.

Both studio and stage musicians must take great care when using a live microphone and a live loudspeaker system at the same time in the same space. **Feedback,** a ringing (and sometimes howling or screaming) sound, usually of definite frequency, occurs when part of the output of an audio system is picked up and fed back to the input. When a live microphone is placed in front of a loudspeaker that is reproducing the sounds being picked up by the microphone, there is a very strong possibility that the microphone will pick up these reproductions and recycle them through the sound system again and again. Each time the sounds are fed back, particular frequencies will be reinforced by resonances in the system until they are heard at a level that is out of proportion to the rest of the signal. The feedback becomes audible as a ringing of these frequencies.

One way to avoid this problem is to keep the microphone behind and therefore out of the field of the loudspeaker (see Figure 1.20a). Another

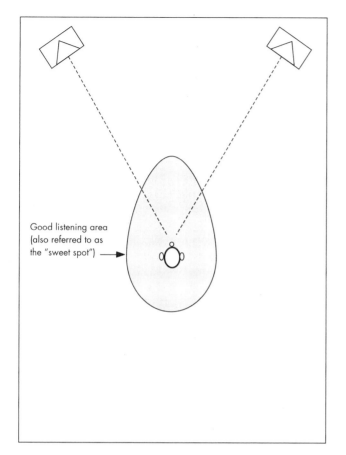

FIGURE 1.18
Loudspeaker placement in a typical room.

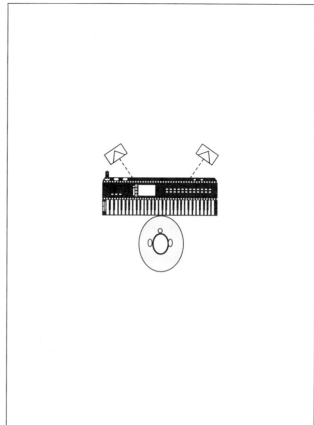

FIGURE 1.19
A near-field monitor set up.

method for minimizing feedback is to use a device called an equalizer to filter out, at least to some extent, the frequencies that are most likely to ring (this is usually done before a sound check for a live performance and is called "ringing out the system"). Still another way to reduce the likelihood of feedback, particularly if it is not possible to avoid placing the microphone in the field of the loudspeaker, is to select a microphone with a cardioid field pattern and to point it away from the loudspeaker (see Figure 1.20b).

When a session in the studio is finished, it is important first to turn off the amplifiers that power the loudspeakers. If other devices, connected to the inputs of the amplifiers, are turned off first, there will be an abrupt change in the signal provided to the loudspeakers. At best, this will produce a rude noise, such as a loud pop or thump; at worst, the loudspeakers can be seriously damaged. For the same reason, care must be taken when powering up the equipment at the beginning of a studio session. The amplifiers that power the loudspeakers should be the last components powered up at the beginning of work. The guiding principle is "amps on last, amps off first."

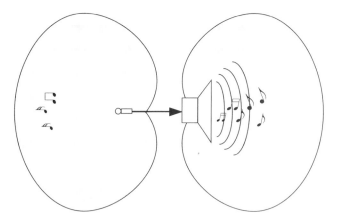

a. The microphone is behind the loudspeaker, out of its field.

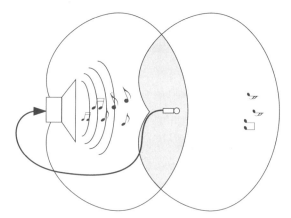

b. The microphone is in front of the loudspeaker, but is pointed away from it. Because the loudspeaker is in a region where the microphone's response is not very great, the sounds from the loudspeaker are less likely to be picked up by the microphone and fed back into the sound system.

FIGURE 1.20
Careful placement of a microphone and its loudspeaker can reduce the possibility of feedback.

OTHER TRANSDUCERS

Another transducer often encountered in the studio for electroacoustic music is the electric guitar pickup. As the strings of the guitar vibrate in the magnetic field of the pickup, corresponding patterns of electrical current are induced that can then be amplified and processed. The output **impedance** of the guitar pickup (the resistance of the circuit to a varying electrical current) is relatively high, and the cords are vulnerable to hum and other forms of electrical interference. Therefore, if the output of a guitar pickup is to be sent to a mixing console, the output signal must be converted to a low impedance level. This is usually accomplished by the use of a direct insertion box, perhaps better known as a **direct box** (see Figure 1.21).

If the direct box does not require electrical power, it is called a passive direct box. There will be some loss of signal level, and the frequency response may be somewhat affected. These drawbacks can be avoided by the use of an active direct box. An active direct box requires power, either from internal batteries or from the mixing console. Power from the mixer, called **phantom power,** is obtained through the cable that connects the direct box to the mixer.

Similar to the electric guitar pickup is the **contact microphone,** which is attached to the body of the instrument and picks up the vibrations directly. This produces a signal with the presence and richness of detail that never quite make the transfer to the air surrounding the instrument. A contact microphone can also provide a signal that is almost completely isolated from the sounds of other instruments in the room. As is the case with a guitar pickup, the output impedance of a contact microphone is likely to

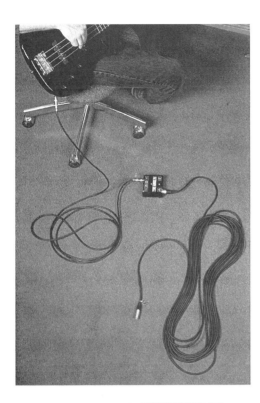

FIGURE 1.21
An electric guitar is patched into a direct box, which then provides a low-impedance, balanced signal to the mixing console.

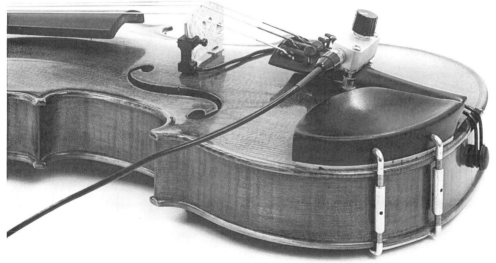

FIGURE 1.22
A contact microphone installed on a violin. (Courtesy of Barcus-Berry.)

be high, and an impedance transformer or direct box will be necessary if the signal is to be fed to a mixing console.

A phono cartridge is a transducer with a needle that "rides the waves" in the groove of a phonograph record and produces an electrical current whose pattern corresponds to the movements of the needle. Because of particular ways in which the balance of low and high frequencies is deliberately altered when producing an LP recording, a phono cartridge requires a preamplifier that not only boosts the signal but also restores this balance. Thus, a phono cartridge will not use the same preamplifier circuits that are used for a microphone, but will require its own inputs instead.

A FEW DETAILS ABOUT HOW MICROPHONES AND LOUDSPEAKERS WORK

*T*here are two principal methods by which microphones accomplish their task of converting sound waves into electrical waves. **Dynamic microphones** are based on the principles of electromagnetic induction. Inside the microphone is a movable plate called the diaphragm. As sound waves reach the microphone, the fluctuations in air pressure first push the diaphragm in and then pull it back (much like what happens to someone swimming in the waves at the seashore). Attached to the back side of the diaphragm is a coil of wire, called the voice coil. Surrounding this voice coil is a stationary magnet. As the coil moves back and forth across the magnet's lines of force, an electrical current is induced in the wire of the coil. The strength and polarity of this current are directly related to the movement of the diaphragm in response to the fluctuations of the air pressure outside the microphone. Thus, acoustical vibrations are transformed into electrical ones (see Figure 1.23).

Capacitor microphones (also known as condenser microphones) are based on the principles of electrical capacitance. An electrical voltage is applied to a circuit that includes the diaphragm and a second, stationary plate behind the diaphragm. As the diaphragm flutters to and fro in response to the ebb and flow of the sound waves that reach the microphone, the gap between the diaphragm and the back plate alternately widens and narrows. As the gap widens,

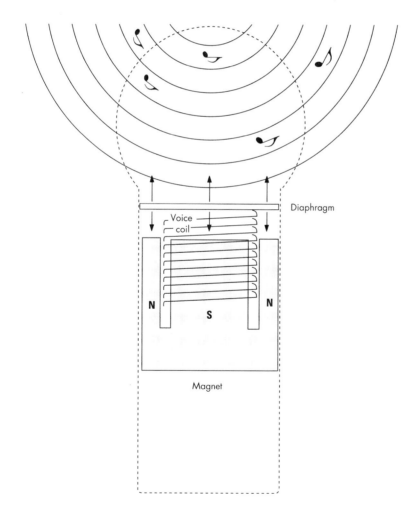

FIGURE 1.23
The inner workings of a dynamic microphone.

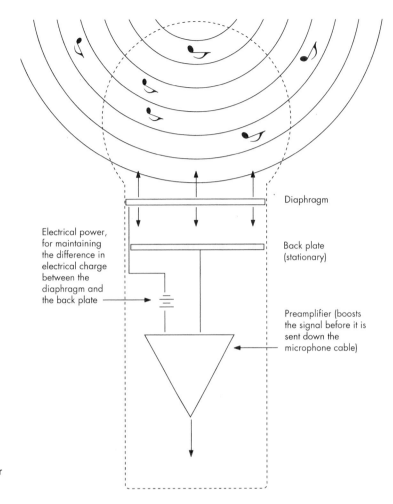

FIGURE 1.24
The workings of a capacitor microphone.

Diaphragm

Electrical power, for maintaining the difference in electrical charge between the diaphragm and the back plate →

Back plate (stationary)

Preamplifier (boosts the signal before it is sent down the microphone cable)

the capacitance (that is, the ability of the plates to maintain their difference in electrical charge) decreases, and the voltage applied between the plates rises. As the gap narrows, the capacitance increases, and the voltage drops. Thus again, acoustical vibrations can be transformed into electrical ones (see Figure 1.24).

Dynamic microphones tend to be robust and relatively inexpensive. Their quality is likely to be adequate for most recording or sound-reinforcement situations. Capacitor microphones tend to be somewhat more delicate and expensive. They also tend to respond more nimbly to rapid transients—the attacks of drum sounds and piano chords are crisper, for example, when recorded with a capacitor microphone. Capacitor microphones are usually of very high quality and are used in the most critically demanding recording environments.[7]

The electrical signal generated within a capacitor microphone is such that it is usually necessary to have an output preamplifier included inside the microphone itself. The electrical power for this, as well as the power needed to maintain the electrical charge between the diaphragm and the back plate of the microphone, can be provided by an installed battery or

---

7. A very cheap type of microphone, called the electret microphone, is also based on the capacitor principle. It is typically found in inexpensive cassette recorders, boom boxes, and telephone answering machines.

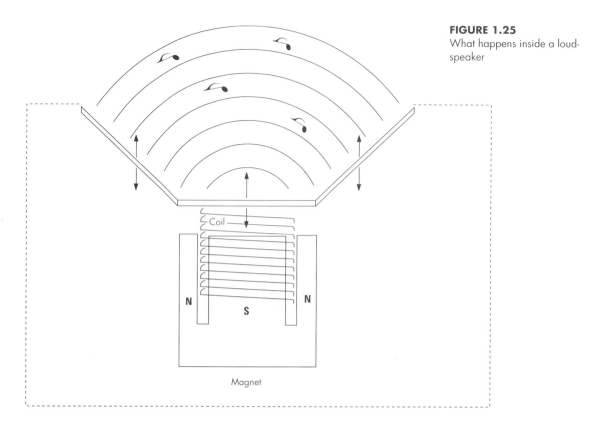

FIGURE 1.25
What happens inside a loudspeaker

Coil

N   S   N

Magnet

by an external power pack. Most often, the power is supplied through the microphone cable from the mixing console, as phantom power.

At the other end of the chain of audio devices is the loudspeaker, which transforms electrical waves to acoustical waves. The principal parts of a loudspeaker are a cone attached to a coil of wire, and a strong, permanent magnet that surrounds the coil. As the electrical signal from the power amplifier flows through the coil, there is an interaction between the electrical field of the coil and the field of the magnet. This causes the coil to move back and forth as the electrical signal rises and falls. The loudspeaker cone, being attached to the coil, also moves back and forth, alternately pushing and then pulling the air in front of it, thus creating waves of sound. A loudspeaker, in fact, is essentially a dynamic microphone in reverse (see Figure 1.25).

GETTING CONNECTED

The right connections are vital when working with the many different instruments found in a studio for electroacoustic music. Given that electricity has a demonstrable preference for complete circuits, only one improper connection or faulty cable is sufficient to stop a show or a recording session.

A cable used to connect electronic musical instruments contains one or two wires (and sometimes more) to carry the electrical signal. Wrapped around the wires is a shield made of metal foil or braided wire. The pur-

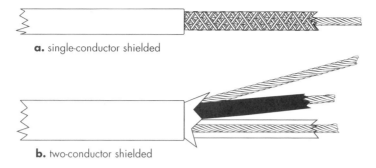

FIGURE 1.26
Standard cables.

a. single-conductor shielded

b. two-conductor shielded

pose of the shield is to isolate the conducting wires from external sources of electrical interference, such as local radio transmissions, noise from electric motors, or the 60-Hz oscillation in power cords. In a **single-conductor shielded cable** the signal will pass down the wire to the input of the destination device and then return through the shield to complete the electrical circuit. In a **two-conductor shielded cable** the signal will travel down one wire and return through the second wire (see Figure 1.26).

Although the shield can protect the signal in a cable from much of the electrical interference that comes from external sources, it does not provide complete isolation. With a single-conductor shielded cable, any interference that is induced in the wire will travel to the input of the next device and be accepted as part of the signal. This type of signal path is called an **unbalanced line.**

In a two-conductor shielded cable, the signal can be balanced electrically so that external signals or noise will be picked up by both conductors and will meet and cancel at a suitably designed input at the destination device. Such a **balanced line** is particularly beneficial if the desired signal is relatively weak. Microphones, for instance, are virtually always connected to other devices by balanced lines. Even when the desired signal is not so weak, balanced lines might nonetheless be used because of their superior ability to reject unwanted signals. Most professional-quality equipment is designed for connection to other equipment by balanced lines only.

If the connector at the end of a cable is designed to be inserted into another connector, it is called a **plug.** The connector that receives the insertion is called a **jack.** For reasons that may or may not be obvious, these are also referred to as male and female connectors, respectively.

The **RCA plug,** consisting of a center pin in a circular shell (see Figure 1.27a), is used with single-conductor shielded cables to connect consumer-quality audio equipment, such as turntables, cassette tape decks, compact-disc players, and stereo receivers. It is also known as a phono plug.

There are a variety of **phone plugs,** so called because they were initially used with telephone switchboards. The most common has a ¼"-diameter pin divided into a "tip" and a "sleeve" (see Figure 1.27b) and is used with single-conductor shielded cables. The tip is wired to the conductor, and the sleeve is wired to the cable shield. A variant of this has a shorter pin, ⅛" in diameter, and is called a mini phone plug (see Figure 1.27c). Another type of ¼" phone plug includes a middle segment on the pin (see Figure 1.27d)

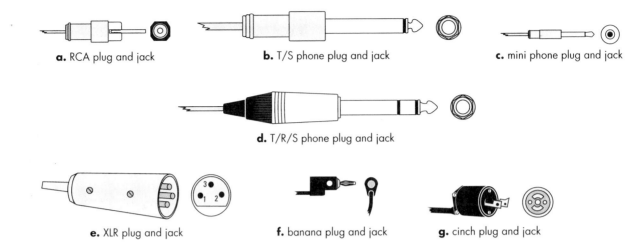

a. RCA plug and jack **b.** T/S phone plug and jack **c.** mini phone plug and jack

d. T/R/S phone plug and jack

e. XLR plug and jack **f.** banana plug and jack **g.** cinch plug and jack

FIGURE 1.27
Common connectors.

and is used with two-conductor shielded cables. The middle segment, called the ring, is wired to the second conductor in the cable. Such a phone plug, also called a T/R/S plug (for tip/ring/sleeve), is used with balanced-line connections or with stereo headphones.

Most professional equipment, including virtually all microphones, uses two-conductor shielded cables and **XLR connectors** (also called **Cannon connectors,** after the company that introduced them). The XLR male connector consists of three pins arranged in a circular shell (see Figure 1.27e). The longest pin is connected to the shield of the cable, and the other two pins are wired to the two conductors. A channel in the shell of the male XLR connector is matched to a ridge on the shell of the female connector so that the pins are properly aligned. A simple locking mechanism holds the two connectors in place, thereby helping to prevent accidental disconnection of the equipment. However, it is important to remember always to push the locking tab when releasing the connectors!

Banana plugs (see Figure 1.27f) are occasionally used with audio equipment. They are similar to RCA plugs except that the sides of the "banana" squeeze into the jack, thus providing a more secure connection.

A cinch plug, consisting of two rounded prongs (see Figure 1.27g), is inserted and then twisted into the corresponding receptacle. Cinch connectors are used for loudspeaker lines because they provide a connection that is secure and unlikely to be confused with other types of audio connections.

With such a variety of connectors in use on audio devices, it is often necessary, in order to connect various pieces of equipment, to make or purchase cables with different types of connectors at each end, or to purchase connector adapters. (Be aware that there are likely to be additional complications when attempting to connect consumer- and professional-quality equipment. See "Setting Up a Small Studio," later in this chapter, for further information on this subject.)

In many studios, cables are run from the inputs and outputs of all the devices in the room to a central location, called the **patch bay** (or patch-field or jack bay). The patch bay, which is mounted in an equipment rack, consists of rows of phone jacks that can be connected by patch cords—

short cables with a phone plug at each end (occasionally patch bays with RCA or XLR connectors are encountered as well). This provides a convenient and flexible way to make connections among any combination of electronic instruments and devices in the studio.

For particularly frequent connections (for example, the connection of synthesizers to the mixing console), it is possible with some patch bays to wire the connection internally, avoiding the necessity of using a patch cord. This type of connection, called a **normal,** can be interrupted when necessary by inserting a patch cord into one of the two jacks that are wired together (or "normaled").[8]

A **multiple** is a set of four or more adjacent jacks in a patch bay that are wired together in such a way that a signal patched into one of the jacks becomes available as output at the other jacks. In this way, a single signal can be split and routed to multiple destinations.

Here are a few very important things to remember when using patch cords to connect audio devices (whether directly or through a patch bay):

1. Turn down the levels on both devices before making the connection.
2. Do not try to connect an input to an input, or an output to an output.
3. When removing a patch cord from a jack, *do not* pull on the cord itself. Grab the metal or plastic jacket or the molding around the plug. Hold the molding, then tug the plug. Otherwise, the wire will expire.

This, then, concludes an introduction to a few of the essential facts regarding transducers, connectors, and common studio practices. In the next chapter, this knowledge will be applied to the task of learning the musical potential of the tape recorder.

---

8. Occasionally the output jack can be wired in such a way that its normal connection can be maintained even when the signal is connected to another device by a patch cord inserted in the jack. This is known as a half-normal connection and provides a way for an output signal to be split to two inputs (one of them being the normal input).

SETTING UP A SMALL STUDIO

The assortment of devices in a particular studio for electroacoustic music is determined by the financial resources and aesthetic preferences of the musician who establishes it. Some studios will be well equipped for recording and processing acoustically produced sounds; other studios will emphasize the use of synthetically produced sounds. A few general considerations, however, apply to virtually all small studios (and often to many larger ones as well).

It is important to have electrical power that is both stable and "clean." The devices in the studio should be on a separate power circuit, with its own circuit breaker in the circuit box in the utility room. If the small studio were to share a circuit with large home appliances, office machines, or other big consumers of electrical power, there would be frequent power surges or power sags as these appliances power up or shut down, and the lifetime of studio equipment could be shortened (or even terminated). In addition to providing power on a separate circuit, it is also advisable to acquire one or more "power conditioners" (such as those manufactured by Furman or Tripp-Lite). These relatively inexpensive devices provide further protection against power surges and also clean up the power signal by filtering from it most radio waves and other forms of electrical interference.

Audio cables should be kept well separated from the power cords of devices. If it is necessary to cross an audio cable and a power cable, then they should cross at a right angle. Audio cables and connectors should be of the highest quality (although gold-plated connectors may seem a bit extravagant, their defiance of oxidation and corrosion are much appreciated after a few years of use). Also, label the ends of all cables. Cable tags for this purpose can be purchased from most businesses that sell professional audio supplies.

Hums and similar unwanted signals tend to infest a studio, but there are ways to minimize or even eradicate them. The shield of a two-conductor shielded cable used for a balanced line between devices should be connected only at one end of the cable. In this way, stray electrical signals that are picked up by the shield have only one path through which they can be drained to the ground. If such interference signals are able to find a path to ground through either the preceding device in the connection or the device at the other end of the cable, then the potential for a "ground loop" is established. This is a major source of unwanted hums and buzzes in an audio signal. Single-conductor shielded cables must have both the conductor and the shield connected at each end, and therefore cannot so readily avoid the possibility of a ground loop. For this reason, single-conductor shielded cables should be as short as possible—six feet or less.

One of the more vexing tasks of setting up a studio arises from the significant differences between the signals expected for the inputs and outputs of "professional" audio equipment and the signals used with "consumer" equipment. The signals used by professional devices are at a higher level, referred to as +4 dBm, and are therefore less likely to be affected by sources of electrical interference. The signals are also carried through balanced lines (with two-conductor shielded cables). By contrast, the signals used by consumer devices are at a lower level, referred to as –10 dBu, and are carried through unbalanced lines (with single-conductor shielded cables). With such a lower signal level, the requirements of circuit design and isolation are less stringent and the devices can be offered at significantly lower prices. However, the signals that enter and emerge from these devices are much more vulnerable to electrical interference.

If every piece of equipment in the studio is consumer grade, or if every piece is professional grade, then difficulties of connecting devices are minimized. In reality, however, most studios include both kinds of equipment. It will therefore be necessary to acquire interface boxes (such as those manufactured by Aphex, Fostex, or Tascam) that can convert unbalanced signals at −10 dBu to balanced signals at +4 dBm, and vice versa.

Most of the equipment available today can be mounted in standard, 19-inch equipment racks or equipment cases. This facilitates the accessibility of equipment in the studio, as well as general tidiness. To avoid possible problems with ground loops and such, however, it is a good idea to insulate the rack screws by including nylon washers between the screw heads and rack ears on the equipment, and between the rack ears and the rails of the rack itself.

Given the particular sensitivity of digital equipment to dust, the studio should be kept as dust-free as possible. Furthermore, dust covers should be obtained and used for all devices. The plugs of patch cords should also be routinely polished now and then with an emery cloth to remove oxidation that can cause intermittent electrical contacts. An alternative is to purchase nickel-coated plugs, which do not require polishing.

These are just a few suggestions of what can be done when establishing and maintaining a studio to minimize future aggravations with disrupted projects or compromised results. Extra care taken at the outset will be amply rewarded later.

IMPORTANT TERMS

electroacoustic music
decay
compressions
rarefactions
frequency
period
cps
A-440
hertz (Hz)
subsonic, or infrasonic
ultrasonic
oscillation
amplitude
intensity
decibel (dB)
attack time
decay time, or release
transients
acoustics
psychoacoustics
equal loudness countour
sustain, or steady-state

envelope
phase
constructive interference
destructive interference
beating
interval
octave
fifth
fourth
third
consonance
dissonance
timbre, or tone color
transducer
line level
preamplification
field pattern
omnidirectional
cardioid
bidirectional
frequency response
presence peak

proximity effect
pop filter, or windscreen
shock mount
feedback
impedance
direct box
phantom power
contact microphone
dynamic microphone
capacitor microphone
single-conductor shielded cable
two-conductor shielded cable
unbalanced line
balanced line
plug
jack
RCA plug
phone plugs
XLR, or Cannon, connector
patch bay
normal
multiple

FOR FURTHER READING

ACOUSTICS

Backus, John. *The Acoustical Foundations of Music*. New York: Norton, 1969.

Hall, Donald E. *Musical Acoustics*. 2d ed. Pacific Grove, CA: Brooks/Cole, 1991.

Pierce, John R. *The Science of Musical Sound*. New York: Scientific American Books, 1983.

Rossing, Thomas D. *The Science of Sound*. 2d ed. Reading, MA: Addison-Wesley, 1990.

Scientific American. *The Physics of Music*. San Francisco: Freeman, 1978.

TRANSDUCERS AND STUDIO PRACTICES

Alten, Stanley R. *Audio in Media*. 2d ed. Belmont, CA: Wadsworth, 1986. This is a superb text, well illustrated, and enormously useful.

Bartlett, Bruce. *Introduction to Professional Recording Techniques*. Carmel, IN: Howard W. Sams, 1987.

Bartlett, Bruce. *Stereo Microphone Techniques*. Boston: Focal Press, 1991. This presents material of interest to the more advanced student.

Benson, K. Blair, ed. *Audio Engineering Handbook*. New York: McGraw-Hill, 1988.

Borwick, John, ed. *Sound Recording Practice*. 2d ed. Oxford: Oxford University Press, 1980.

Borwick, John. *Microphones*. London: Focal Press, 1990.

Davis, Gary, & Jones, Ralph. *The Sound Reinforcement Handbook*. Milwaukee: Hal Leonard, 1987. This is an excellent reference guide, particularly for field work.

Eargle, John. *Sound Recording*. 2d ed. New York: Van Nostrand Reinhold, 1992.

Giddings, Philip. *Audio Systems Design and Installation*. Howard W. Sams, 1990. The material will strike many readers as highly technical.

Nardantonio, Dennis N. *Sound Studio Production Techniques*. Blue Ridge Summit, PA: TAB Books, 1990.

Thom, Randy. *Audio Craft*. Washington, DC: National Federation of Community Broadcasters, 1982.

Wadhams, Wayne. *Sound Advice: The Musician's Guide to the Recording Studio*. New York: Schirmer Books, 1990. This text is quite thorough, and a useful guide for specific recording situations.

Woram, John M., & Kefauver, Alan P. *The New Recording Studio Handbook*. Commack, NY: ELAR, 1989.

CHAPTER 2

MUSIC FROM TAPE RECORDERS

The first magnetic sound recorder, called the Telegraphone, was developed in 1898 by the Danish inventor Valdemar Poulsen. Sounds were picked up by a telephone mouthpiece and recorded on a length of piano wire that was wrapped around a brass cylinder. The recorded sounds could then be played back through a telephone receiver. Total recording time was 30 seconds, and the audio quality was not quite as good as that of today's battery-powered talking toys. But it was the beginning of a series of developments that would lead to a radical transformation of the ways in which music is created and recreated.

Steel ribbon was used as the recording medium on many European machines before 1940. These reels of steel were bulky, heavy, and terribly awkward to handle (and there was a certain amount of danger to the machine operator if the ribbon broke during recording or playback!). Magnetic sound recording on piano wire continued to be the prevailing technology into the 1950s, however, during which time wire recorders were even widely available for home use.

In addition to the disadvantages associated with the storage and handling of reels of steel ribbon or spools of piano wire, it was completely beyond contemplation to attempt to edit a ribbon or wire recording (one can imagine a bold but crazed engineer attempting a splice with metal cutters and a soldering iron, or perhaps an arc welder). By 1935, a group of German scientists developed a recording medium that addressed many of these and other problems associated with the use of steel ribbon or wire: they coated a plastic tape with magnetic particles. Shortly after the invention of this magnetic recording tape, another group of Germans introduced the first magnetic tape recorder, called the Magnetophon.

It was not until 1945, however, when Germany was defeated and the Second World War was over in Europe, that magnetic tape recorders became more widely available. In the half-century since, these devices have come to be found everywhere: installed in cars, carried down streets and in subways, and placed in every recording studio and broadcast facility in the world.

THE OPERATION OF A TAPE RECORDER

Magnetic tape is available in ready-to-use cassettes and on open reels. Because open-reel tapes are much easier to edit (and because the recorded information can be arranged in a greater variety of formats on an open-reel tape), the preferred recording machine in a recording studio is an open-reel tape recorder (also called a **tape deck**).[1] Figure 2.1 identifies many of the controls and other parts of practical interest to the operator of a typical open-reel recorder.

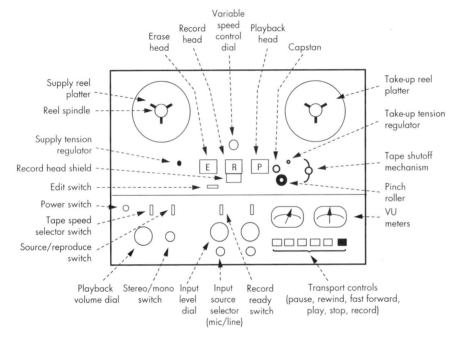

FIGURE 2.1
Typical parts and controls on an open-reel tape recorder.

To make a tape recording, a source must first be patched into the tape deck. If the deck does not include preamplification circuits for microphone signals, then there will be no input jacks for microphones. It will be necessary first to patch the microphone into a mixing console or some other device that can preamplify the signal to line level (see Chapter 1). The outputs of synthesizers, mixing consoles, and other tape decks provide line-level signals that can be patched without preamplification into the tape deck. (Note: on some tape decks the inputs for line-level signals may be

---

1. Generally, the sound quality of a recording on an open-reel deck is superior as well.

labeled as "auxiliary" or "aux" inputs.) If the deck can accept either microphone or line-level signals, then there will be an "input select" switch that should be set to the appropriate position.

THE TAPE PATH

Next, a reel of tape is fastened to the supply platter. The tape is then threaded past the supply tension arm. Next, the tape is threaded under a series of three electromagnets, called the **erase head,** the **record head,** and the **playback head.** A time-honored way to remember the order of these heads is to memorize the acronym formed by the first letter of each: **ERP.**

During the process of recording, the alignment of the magnetic particles on the tape is scrambled by the erase head first (even if the tape is already completely blank, fresh out of the box). Any information that may have been previously recorded on the tape is now irretrievable. The tape next passes under the record head. The fluctuating electrical signal that comes to the tape recorder from the microphone (or from some other source device, such as a synthesizer) will pass through the record head, creating a fluctuating magnetic field around it. As the tape travels under the record head, the magnetic particles on the tape, called **domains,** align themselves in response to the fluctuations of this magnetic field. Thus, the information becomes recorded as a pattern of magnetic fluctuations on the tape.[2]

During the playback of a tape, the erase and record heads are automatically switched off. As the tape passes under the playback head, the fluctuating magnetic field that is recorded on the tape induces a correspondingly fluctuating electrical signal in the playback head. This signal will be amplified and ultimately passed on to a loudspeaker (by way of an amplifier and other audio components, most likely). Thus, a sound that is recorded one day can be heard again (and again) the next. (This bit of magic is only the beginning, however, as will be seen in the second part of this chapter.)

The tape is kept in its path and in good contact with the machine, particularly with the tape heads, primarily because the electric motors for the supply and take-up platters continuously and gently tug the tape in opposite directions at the same time. The amount of force required from each motor depends on how much tape is on each reel; the supply tension regulator and the take-up tension regulator sense this and adjust the motors accordingly. The size of the reel is also a factor. Somewhere on the front panel of the tape deck will be a switch or button that enables the operator to select tape-tension regulation that is appropriate for either large reels or

---

2. Helpful hint: On many tape decks there is a hinged shield beneath the record head. Always check to be certain that you have threaded the tape between the record head and the shield. The function of this shield is to confine the magnetic field of the record head. If you inadvertently thread the tape beneath this shield, and if the shield works as it should, then the tape will never have the opportunity to be recorded upon and will continue to be blank.

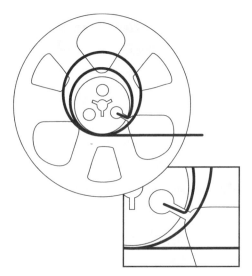
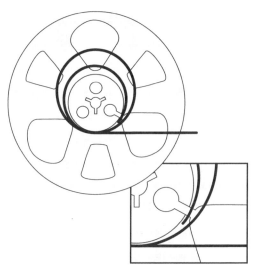

FIGURE 2.2
Unacceptable and acceptable methods for attaching tape to a tape reel.

a. Folding the tape into the notch in the hub of the reel can cause problems later.

b. A more considerate method of attaching tape to the reel is to lay it flat and secure it in place with additional layers of tape.

small reels. Manufacturers of tape decks generally recommend that the supply and take-up reels be the same size.

After the tape has passed the erase, record, and playback heads, it goes between a rotating metal cylinder, called the **capstan,** and a large rubber wheel, called the **pinch roller** (or capstan roller). It is the capstan motor that actually moves the tape during recording and playback—not the take-up motor, which (as described previously) only provides a gentle tug to keep the tape in its proper path. If the take-up motor is turned off (a feature that can be engaged on some tape decks), then the tape, which is still being pulled by the capstan motor, will dump over the edge of the tape deck and onto the tabletop or floor (or into a wastebasket—perhaps an appropriate destination for some of the worst takes of a recording session). Because the capstan has such a critical role in keeping the tape moving, always check to be certain that the tape is threaded between the capstan and its pinch roller.

Most machines have some type of mechanism for stopping the motors if the tape is broken or is finished playing or recording. On some tape decks, the tape is threaded under a weighted switch called the take-up idler. When there is no longer any tape under the take-up idler, it falls and switches the motors off. On other machines, a beam of visible or infrared light is directed toward a photocell across the tape path. When there is no tape in the path to block the light, then the motors are switched off.

It is a common, but not necessarily good practice to attach tape to the take-up reel by bending back the leading inch or so of tape and inserting this into a notch in the hub of the reel before spinning the reel around a few times (see Figure 2.2). This can be a problem when rewinding if the tape is not stopped in time. The inch or so of tape that is folded into the notch of the hub will be caught, and this can cause a momentary but hefty jerk of the works inside the tape deck. Not only is this unpleasant for the motors and other parts of the tape deck, but it can also cause the tape to stretch. A highly recommended alternative procedure for attaching a tape to the take-up reel is simply to lay the tape on the hub, then hold the tape in place with your fingers while turning the reel around (you will occasionally need to change fingers) until there are sufficient layers of tape on the reel to hold the tape in place by the friction between the layers and the hub. It may take a few days of practice to acquire this technique, but it is worth the trouble.

MAKING TRACKS ON THE TAPE

Virtually all tape decks in use today can record and play back at least two signals, or **channels,** of information at the same time. Different bands on the tape, called **tracks,** are used to record these channels. The structure of a record head (as well as the accompanying erase and playback heads) is determined by the number and width of the tracks that will be recorded on the tape. Figure 2.3 illustrates some common record-head formats and the pattern of the tracks they make on tapes.

One of the most common recording formats presently in use is the half-track stereo format. Two tracks are recorded on a tape that is ¼" wide, and each track nearly covers half the width of the tape. Stereo recordings in this format are made in only one direction on the tape (if, when the supply of tape is finished, the supply and take-up reels are switched and recording is resumed, then the previously recorded material will be erased as new material is recorded on the two tracks).

At one time, the quarter-track stereo tape deck was a popular component of home stereo systems, and a few such decks continue to be in use. Again, two tracks are recorded on a tape that is ¼" wide, but each track covers just less than one-fourth the width of the tape. All other things being the same, the quality of a quarter-track stereo recording is inferior to that of a half-track stereo recording. The magnetic field from a narrower track is weaker, so there is less difference in level between the signal and the background noise on the tape. Also, because there are imperfections in the size and distribution of the magnetic particles on even the highest-quality recording tapes, the larger the area used for each track on the tape, the better the recording. If the information is recorded over a wider area, then the particular imperfections on the tape will have a much less significant effect on the quality of recording.

The use of wider tapes makes it possible to place wider tracks on a tape, thus enabling the recording of multiple tracks of high quality. For example, a four-track recording on ½" tape is likely to be superior in quality to a four-track recording on ¼" tape (all other factors being the same). In fact, the quality of a four-track recording on ½" tape should be nearly as good as that of a half-track stereo recording on ¼" tape, because the tracks

FIGURE 2.3
An assortment of tape track formats.

a. Half-track stereo on ¼" tape: Two channels recorded in one direction, or one channel recorded one direction and one in the opposite direction

b. Quarter-track stereo on ¼" tape: Two channels recorded in one direction (on tracks 1 and 3), and two in the opposite direction (on tracks 2 and 4)

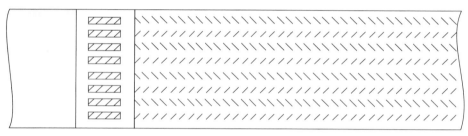

c. Four-track on ¼" tape: Four channels recorded in one direction, or two in each direction (as in (b)), or three in one direction and one in the opposite direction

d. Four-track on ½" tape

e. Eight-track on 1" tape

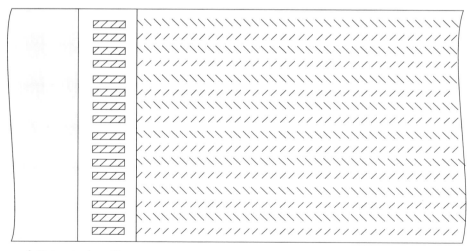

f. Sixteen-track on 2" tape

themselves have essentially the same width. Similarly, the quality of an eight-track recording on 1" tape should be nearly as good as that of a four-track recording on ½" tape or a half-track stereo recording on ¼" tape.

Another way to increase the area of tape on which a sound is recorded, in addition to using wider tracks (and wider tapes), is to increase the speed at which the tape passes the heads. Common tape speeds are 7.5, 15, and 30 inches per second (abbreviated **ips**). If a sound is recorded at 15 ips, then its information will cover twice as much area on the tape as it would if it were recorded at 7.5 ips, because the length of tape used to record the sound at 15 ips is twice as great. Also, the ability to record higher frequencies is enhanced at higher tape speeds (because the wavelengths of the magnetic fluctuations are longer relative to the size of the magnetic particles on the tape). The cost of this improvement in quality is that the total recording time is shortened. For instance, a typical 7-inch reel holds 1200 feet of recording tape, which at 7.5 ips can record 30 minutes of music. At 15 ips it can record 15 minutes of music, and at 30 ips (not an unusual speed in professional recording situations) it can store only 7½ minutes of material! Such trade-offs must often be considered.

Occasionally sounds that are recorded on one track are also somewhat audible on adjacent tracks. This apparent leakage of the signal, called **crosstalk,** can also occur between adjacent channels of mixing consoles, amplifiers, and other devices. Sounds that are loud and crisp, such as drum sounds or piano chords, are especially likely to be noticed when they cross to an adjacent channel. Therefore, it is best to record such sounds on an outside track so that there is one less track for them to cross to (see Figure 2.4). It is a common practice, for example, to record drums on track 1.

On many recordings one can often hear a faint premonition of a sound just before the sound itself is heard. This ghostlike phenomenon is particularly noticeable in the silences that precede the entrances of loud instruments, such as drums or trumpets. Such a premonition is called a **pre-echo** and is caused by **print-through.**

Print-through occurs after a section of a tape upon which a strong sound has been recorded is wound on the take-up reel. The strong magnetic patterns of the recorded sound will affect the magnetic particles on the preceding layer of tape and those on the layer of tape that is taken up next (sometimes several layers in each direction, in fact, if the recorded sound is especially strong). The pattern that prints through to the preceding layer will be heard upon playback as a pre-echo, and the print-through to the following layer will be heard as a post-echo. A post-echo is generally a natural-sounding phenomenon, and will probably blend in nicely with any reverberation that follows the sound (or the post-echo may print through to a layer of tape that contains the middle or end of the sound itself, and may not be heard at all).

A pre-echo, however, is a quite unnatural thing, so a number of measures should be taken to minimize it. First, only recording tape of high quality

FIGURE 2.4
Dealing with crosstalk between tracks.

a. A strong signal recorded on track 2 can affect both track 1 and track 3, thus potentially spoiling two tracks.

b. If the strong signal is recorded on track 1, then only one other track (track 2) is potentially affected. Recording a milder instrument with a similar rhythmic pattern on track 2 would effectively cover the crosstalk.

should be used. Print-through is largely the result of the presence on the tape of significantly smaller magnetic particles that respond much more readily to more distant magnetic patterns. On better recording tapes, the magnetic particles are much more uniform in size. Second, tapes that have thinner plastic backings should be avoided. Most recording tape is .0015 of an inch thick (that is, one-and-a-half thousandths of an inch, or 1.5 mils). If the tape is thinner (for example, .001 inches, or 1.0 mil), then more tape can be fit on a reel (for instance, 1800 feet of 1.0-mil tape can be wound on a 7-inch reel, for 45 minutes of recording time at a tape speed of 7.5 ips). However, the possibility of print-through is considerably greater. Third, tapes should be stored in rooms with temperature and humidity levels that are even and moderate (a temperature of between 60° and 75°F and a relative humidity of 40–60% are considered good).

Finally, and this is most important of all, a tape should not be rewound immediately after it has been recorded or played. It should be left with the end of the tape, called the tail, out. There are several advantages to storing a tape **tail-out.** Print-through is reported to be stronger on outer layers than on inner layers. Thus, if the tape is rewound to the supply reel, the pre-echo will be stronger than the post-echo; if the tape is left on the take-up reel, the pre-echo will be the weaker (see Figure 2.5).

Furthermore, when a tape is quickly rewound, the layers of tape pile up unevenly, a phenomenon called scattered wind (this also happens when a tape is fast-forwarded). With a scattered wind, the edges of individual layers of a tape are exposed and can be damaged. Also, the tension on the tape

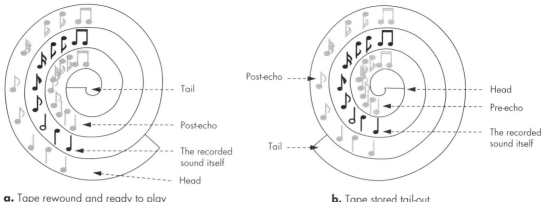

a. Tape rewound and ready to play

b. Tape stored tail-out

FIGURE 2.5
The pre-echoes and post-echoes caused by print-through. The pre-echoes, which tend to be more objectionable, are less noticeable if the tape is stored tail-out and rewound just before playback. (Tape thickness is greatly exaggerated for purposes of illustration.)

is irregular when it is wound quickly onto the reel; as a result, some layers may stretch a bit, thus distorting the recording. However, when a tape winds onto the take-up reel during recording or playback, the layers of tape move onto the reel at an even speed and with even tension.

Finally, when a tape is rewound, the smaller particles on the tape that are responsible for most of the print-through will rather quickly become disoriented as the relative position of the strong patterns on the adjacent layers is changed. Thus, for a few minutes at least, much of the print-through is dissipated. For several reasons, then, it is best to simply leave the tape on the take-up reel. Mark the box with a label "Stored Tail-Out," and rewind the tape only when you are ready to play it back. Indeed, some things are better put off until later. Rewinding tapes is one of those things.

SETTING LEVELS

Setting a good level is critical to making a high-quality tape recording. With any piece of audio equipment, the range of intensities that can be handled is determined at least in part by characteristics of the circuitry. All circuits are vulnerable to some degree of electrical interference, including 60-Hz hum and radio interference. Some amount of low-level noise caused by random straying of electrons in the circuits is also present. At a minimum, the intensity of the desired signal must be greater than the total intensity of these background electrical noises. At the other end of the range, the maximum intensity of the signal is limited by the capacity of the circuits to represent the signal without distorting it. The range of intensity that can be handled by an audio device is represented by a specification called the **signal-to-noise ratio,** or **SNR.** This is approximately the range, in decibels, between

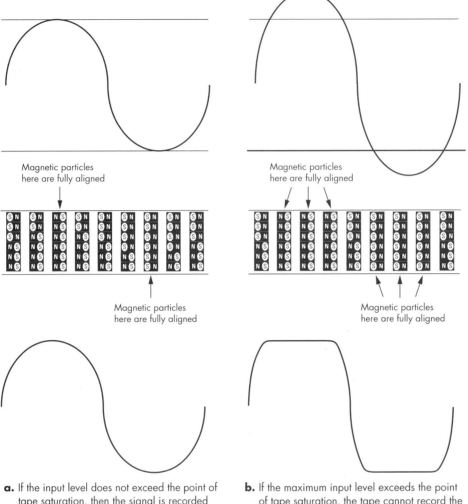

FIGURE 2.6
Tape saturation.

Magnetic particles
here are fully aligned

Magnetic particles
here are fully aligned

Magnetic particles
here are fully aligned

Magnetic particles
here are fully aligned

a. If the input level does not exceed the point of tape saturation, then the signal is recorded without distortion.

b. If the maximum input level exceeds the point of tape saturation, the tape cannot record the higher amplitude segments of the wave. The waveform is "clipped."

the softest signal that can be detected above the background noise and the strongest signal that can be represented without distortion.

With tape recorders, further limitations on the level of a signal are determined by characteristics of the recording tape. Random irregularities in the size and distribution of the magnetic particles on a tape are audible as a continuous noise in the background of a recording. This noise, called **tape hiss,** combines with low-level noise caused by interference or randomly straying electrons in the circuits of the machine. Any recorded signal must be significantly greater in level than this combined background noise, called the noise floor, if the recording is to be of good quality. If the record level is set too low, then the signal most likely will require amplification during playback so that it can be heard at a suitable level. This, of course, will also amplify the tape hiss and other background noises. Care must be taken, then, to avoid "underrecording" the signal; it should be recorded at as high a level (as "hot") as possible.

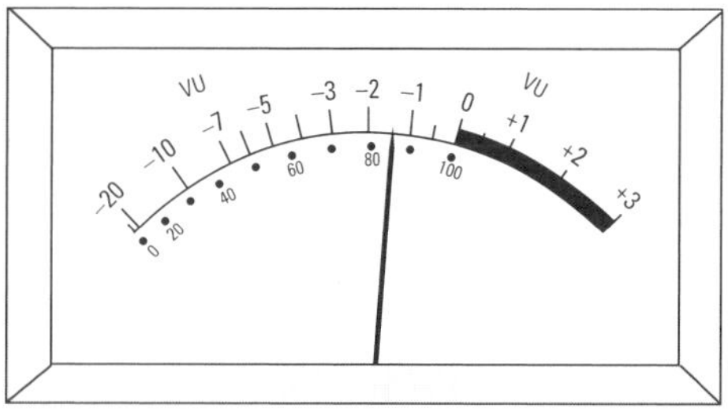

FIGURE 2.7
A VU meter.

The limit on how high the level can be set is determined by the point of **tape saturation** (assuming, of course, that the distortion limit of the circuitry of the tape deck is not reached first). Generally speaking, the stronger the signal, the greater is the number of magnetic particles on the tape at that point that are realigned by the magnetic field. Since there are a finite number of these particles on the tape, there is a level at which all the particles will become aligned and further increases in signal strength cannot be recorded. Attempting to record a signal that is stronger than the level of tape saturation will result in a recording that is distorted—much of the information will be missing (see Figure 2.6).

A meter on the tape deck, called a **VU meter,** provides an indication of where to find an optimal recording level. A VU meter is labeled with two sets of marks along an arc (see Figure 2.7). The lower set runs from 0, at the left end, to 100, at the boundary between black and red markings. These marks indicate the percentage of modulation, a value that is of interest to radio and television broadcasters. The upper set of marks denote volume units (VU). For steady, continuous signals, the number of volume units corresponds approximately to the intensity of the signal in decibels. Therefore, this upper set of marks is labeled in decibels. It typically begins around –20 dB at the left end, goes to 0 dB where the black marks meet red marks, and continues to +3 dB or so at the right end. The optimal recording level for the tape is indicated when the needle of the meter moves near the 0 dB mark. The tape approaches saturation when the needle of the meter moves above the 0 dB mark.[3] Signals that result in a reading greater than 0 dB can be recorded up to a point—the point at which the tape becomes saturated magnetically.[4] The number of decibels above 0 dB to the point of saturation is referred to as the **headroom** of the tape.

The mechanism of a VU meter is relatively delicate, so it is important to take considerable precaution not to pin the needle against the right side of the meter by setting the input to an excessively high level. The sound of a

---

3. Please note that 0 dB here refers to a high signal level; however, 0 dB is used elsewhere to refer to a level of acoustical power—the threshold of hearing, or the minimum level of intensity the average person can hear! Life, unfortunately, abounds with inconsistencies such as this, but it is at least a good idea to be aware of them.

4. Since different brands of tape have different levels of tape saturation, it is important that the circuits of the tape recorder be adjusted, or calibrated, to match the characteristics of the tape you will be using. Otherwise, the meter may indicate an acceptable level even though the tape may be saturating. Calibration can be a fairly involved procedure, however, and should be done by the studio technician.

IS IT WRONG SIDE OUT?

*T*he tape is coated with magnetic particles on one side only, and this is the side that comes into contact with the erase, record, and playback heads. With most modern tapes, this is the lighter-colored side; thus, the darker-colored side is generally the one that should be visible as the "out" side. If the tape does somehow become threaded wrong side out (and this *does* happen to everyone sooner or later), then the magnetic fluctuations of the record head will have to pass first through the plastic backing of the tape before they can reach the magnetic particles on the other side. The recorded signal will be much weaker, particularly for high frequencies. It will seem as if the sound were recorded underwater. A properly recorded tape that is played back wrong side out will sound much the same. Not much can be done to save a tape that has been recorded with the wrong side out, but for a properly recorded tape that is merely being played wrong side out the solution is quite simple!

---

needle bouncing frantically against the side of a meter is the sound of a machine in pain.

Some changes in intensity, or transients, occur too quickly to be reflected in movements of the needle on the meter. The mass of the needle makes it relatively sluggish during the crisp beginnings of percussive sounds in particular. Thus, it is possible that the level at the beginning of a drum, piano, or guitar sound may momentarily exceed the level of tape saturation, even though the meter provides no indication of this. Many tape decks, therefore, also include a "transient response indicator" that lights up the instant the tape saturation level is reached. Some tape decks go a few steps further, entirely replacing the VU meter with a series of lights (called LEDs, for "light-emitting diodes") that indicate the different levels of signal intensity.

To find the best level for a recording, begin by identifying the loudest passage in the series of sounds to be recorded. Locate the Source/Reproduce switch on the tape deck (sometimes labeled Source/Tape) and set it on Source, so that you can monitor the level of the signal coming from the source without yet needing to roll the tape. As the loudest material is heard, turn up the input level until the meter indicates 0 dB. Now you are ready to record. Set the Source/Reproduce switch to Reproduce, press the Record and Play buttons, and roll the tape. As the recording proceeds, you may occasionally want to flip the Source/Reproduce switch to compare the signal as it comes from the source to the signal as it is recorded and monitored from the tape. If there is a radical difference in level or sound quality between what is heard on Source and what is heard on Reproduce, your tape deck may be in desperate need of maintenance, or your tape may be threaded wrong side out!

Most tape decks have Record Ready switches or buttons for selecting channels to be recorded (assuming that sources are patched to them so that there will be something to record). Almost needless to say, check before recording to be certain that the desired channels have been selected. Then, when the recording is accomplished, switch these Record Ready buttons off as soon as you can. People who do electroacoustic music tend to work long hours, and much of the work can be tedious. It is entirely possible to erase days of work by mindlessly pushing the Record button, even though all you really wanted to push was the Play button. Oh well. . .

SUMMARY OF THINGS YOU CAN DO TO MAKE BETTER TAPE RECORDINGS

1. Use only high-quality recording tape, preferably 1.5 mils thick.
2. Use tape decks that record wider tracks.
3. Record at the highest speed available.
4. Record loud, crisp instruments on outside tracks.
5. Store tapes tail-out.
6. Store tapes in rooms with constant and moderate levels of temperature and relative humidity.
7. Do not set the record level too low (lest it be necessary to amplify the recording, along with the background noise, on playback).
8. Do not set the record level too high (lest there be distortion caused by tape saturation). Be particularly careful when recording sounds with sharp transients.
9. Use noise-reduction features (for example, Dolby B, Dolby C, or dbx™) if available.

ÉTUDE 2.1

Spend a few minutes reading the operator's manual of the open-reel tape deck you will be using (or perhaps a summary of the operating instructions that has been prepared by your instructor). Then, combining what you have learned of microphone techniques from Chapter 1 with the knowledge of tape recorders gained from this chapter, record approximately one minute of (a) a brief passage of poetry or prose, or (b) a solo musical instrument.

A GENTLE STOP

In addition to the Record, Play, Pause, and Stop buttons on a tape deck, there are the Fast Forward and Rewind buttons for those occasions when you want to move ahead quickly or to go back quickly to an earlier time. As you reach the desired location on the tape, however, it may not be best with some tape decks simply to hit the Stop button. This practice can cause the brakes for the motors, as well as other parts of the mechanism, to wear prematurely. For such decks (consult the operator's manual if in doubt), it is recommended that the opposite mode be used to slow the tape down before the Stop button is pressed. When rewinding a tape, for example, when the tape has nearly wound back to the desired location, push the Fast Forward button. As the rewind and fast-forward motors (also referred to as the supply and take-up motors) work toward a tie in their gentle tug-of-war, the tape will nearly come to a stop. This is when the Stop button can be pushed to finish the job. As with other techniques described in this chapter, this will require a few days' practice. But it will contribute much toward a long and prosperous life for the tape deck.

ROUTINE MAINTENANCE OF OPEN-REEL ANALOG TAPE RECORDERS

*A*s with any fine musical instrument, a tape deck should be maintained in the best condition possible so that it can perform well over a long period of ownership. It is an enlightened practice to read very carefully the instructions for routine maintenance that can be found in the owner's manual (these should take precedence over anything else stated herein). Routine maintenance procedures for an open-reel analog recorder include frequent cleaning and demagnetization of the components in the tape path.

As tape passes from one reel to the other, oxide particles are loosened from the tape and accumulate on the tape heads, guides, capstan, and such. As a result, the tape does not maintain sufficient contact with the heads and the quality of the sound is degraded, particularly for high frequencies. Buildup elsewhere in the tape path can cause misalignments that result in excessive wear on the tape. To avoid such afflictions, the tape path should be cleaned *prior to the beginning of each day's work* (even every few hours, if use is heavy). Use paper-shanked, cotton-tipped swabs (such as Q-tips™) dipped in pure isopropyl alcohol or the head-cleaning fluid recommended in the owner's manual. Rub the heads, back and forth, in the same directions that the tape travels (not up and down, perpendicular to the tape path—this could scratch the heads). Then use a clean swab to dry the surfaces. Also scrub the tape guides, capstan, and any other parts of the tape path. For cleaning the pinch roller, use a rubber-cleaning solution in a well-ventilated space.

Demagnetization, or degaussing, is a procedure for removing any residual magnetism that builds up on the components of the tape path. Considering the intense, fluctuating electromagnetic activity associated with recording and playing a tape, it is not surprising that these parts become magnetized after even a few hours of use. As with particle buildup on the heads, the effects of such magnetism are most noticeable as the higher frequencies in the signal are smothered and the sound becomes less brilliant and clear. In fact, such magnetism can partially and permanently erase the higher frequencies of a recording even as it is played back.

To avoid this, obtain a demagnetizer (available from most businesses that sell tape decks) and use it *prior to the beginning of each day's work* (or more often, on exceptionally busy days). First turn off the deck. THIS IS IMPORTANT! Make certain that the deck is off; otherwise, the demagnetizer can cause serious damage to the recording and playback electronics. Next, switch on the demagnetizer when it is at least three feet away from the deck (and from other decks, tapes, and other devices). Move the demagnetizer slowly toward the deck. Sweep slowly over the heads (avoiding contact so as not to scratch them) and all other metal parts on the tape path. Then slowly remove the demagnetizer to a safe distance of three feet or more and switch it off.

Other maintenance procedures are somewhat more complicated. It is perhaps best to engage the services of a trained technician for such operations as calibration of the record and playback levels; calibration of the meters; adjustment of record and playback equalization settings; adjustment of bias frequency (this is done so that the operating characteristics of the deck are matched to the properties of the brand and type of tape selected for use on the machine); adjustments of head alignment (including azimuth, height, tangency, and so on); and adjustments of tape tension regulation.

FUN WITH TAPE RECORDERS

Not long after tape recorders became widely available, it occurred to a few brash, inquisitive souls that a tape recorder could be used to do more than simply make an aural record of passing events. Indeed, once sounds were captured on tape, it became possible to alter and transform them until the origin of the sounds became totally obscure. The result would be a recording of something that didn't happen, and couldn't possibly have happened perhaps, except in the imagination of the composer holding the tape.

TAPE EDITING

Of the techniques for transforming a recording, perhaps the most powerful is tape **editing**—cutting segments of tape and **splicing** them together. For example, in a recorded speech, or passage of poetry or prose, words can be removed, added, rearranged, substituted, or turned inside out. The meaning of the words might be changed completely, perhaps even obscured altogether (see Figure 2.8).

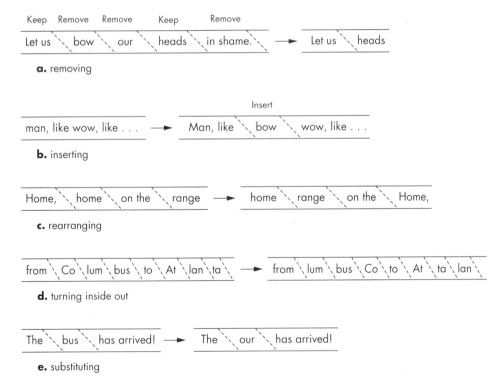

FIGURE 2.8
Various ways to edit a tape recording by cutting and splicing.

Material that is to be edited is usually recorded on ¼" tape in one direction only (if material is recorded in both directions, then a splice made in one passage will interrupt the material recorded in the opposite direction on that segment of tape). The following supplies are needed:

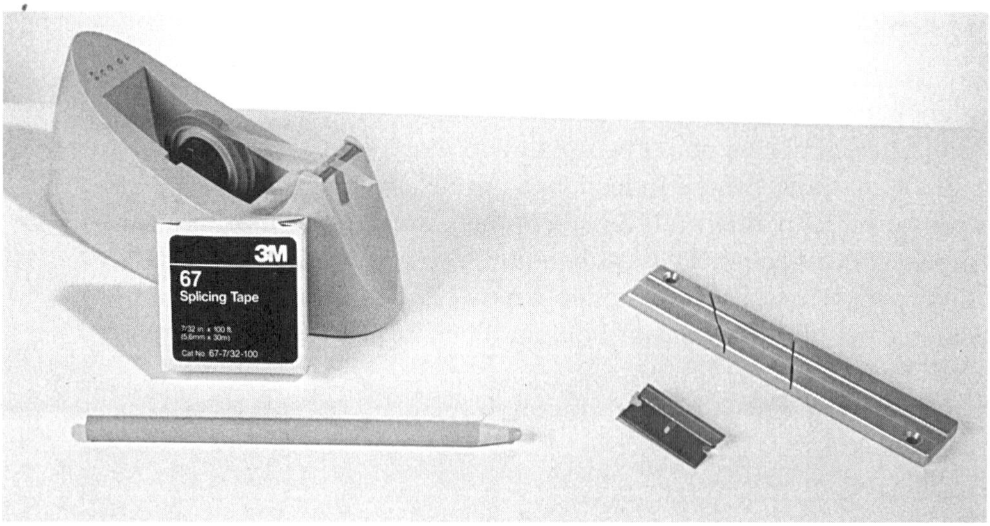

FIGURE 2.9
Splicing supplies.

- *A splicing block.* Selecting a high-quality splicing block can help avoid a significant amount of aggravation and tedium. The better splicing blocks are made of solid aluminum and have a shallow, $\frac{1}{4}$"-wide channel that holds the tape snugly in place (splicing blocks for other tape widths are also available). Two or three cutting grooves cross the tape channel at angles of 45° and 90° (see Figure 2.9).

- *Single-edged razor blades.* Use fresh blades. Blades that have made 20 or more cuts of tape will have become dull and will make an irregular cut. Also, there is a good chance that blades that have been around for a while will have become magnetized and will introduce a pop into a recording at the point where the splice is made.

- *Splicing tape.* For $\frac{1}{4}$" recording tape, splicing tape that is $\frac{7}{32}$" wide (such as Scotch™ 41) should be used. If the $\frac{7}{32}$" splicing tape is carefully centered when used to join two segments of tape, there should be a margin of approximately $\frac{1}{64}$" of recording tape visible on each side. As recording tape sits in storage, the glue on the splicing tape tends to ooze. If it oozes over the edge of the recording tape, it can cause several adjacent layers to stick together and may result in a permanent mangling of the recording. Leaving a margin of $\frac{1}{64}$" or so on each side of the splicing tape greatly reduces the possibility of this kind of damage.

- *A china marker.* Use a yellow or white grease pencil, or china marker, to mark the edit points on the back side of the tape (do *not* mark on the side coated with magnetic particles—that is, the side that passes the recorder heads). Because particles from the grease pencil can accumulate on the recorder heads and other parts of the tape path, it is important to clean these parts often.[5]

---

5. Some technicians recommend using a light-colored, fine-point, felt-tip marker or pencil to mark edit points on a tape. However, with a marker or pencil there is the danger of chipping at the protective material that coats the playback head, so care is advised.

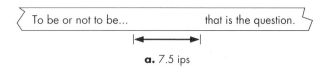

a. 7.5 ips

b. 15 ips

FIGURE 2.10
Wider spaces at higher speeds. A recording made at 15 inches per second provides double the margin for error when cutting a tape to make a splice edit.

FIGURE 2.11
Rocking the reels to locate a sound on tape.

Following is a step-by-step guide to the technique of tape editing:

1. Unless there is a good reason not to do so, record at the highest speed possible. In addition to the higher quality of recording at high speeds, there is also greater ease of editing. For example, a pause of one-tenth of a second between two sounds would be recorded on 1.5" of tape at a speed of 15 ips, but on only .75" of tape at a speed of 7.5 ips (see Figure 2.10). The higher recording speed literally provides a wider margin for error when the razor blade cuts through the tape.

2. Listen to the recording a few times. Note the pauses between sounds. Also, note any extraneous noises (clicks, pops, coughs, and the like) that could be distracting to a listener and might have to be removed. If the material is recorded speech, note the locations of sibilants, plosives, and other hard consonants—these can be important landmarks for you later as you attempt to locate edit points on the tape.

3. Plan the edits. Which segments of tape will be discarded? Which segments will be joined?

4. Engage the Edit button on the tape deck. This mechanism keeps the tape in contact with the heads but disengaged from the capstan. To hear what is recorded on the tape, you need to move the tape manually—to "rock the reels." Place a hand on each reel and turn (see Figure 2.11); do not pull the tape through by just turning the take-up reel (this could stretch the tape). Note that the pitch of the sounds varies with the speed at which you move the tape. If you move the tape too slowly, the pitch will be too low and you won't be able to hear the sounds very well; if you move the tape too quickly, you will not be able to locate the sounds with any precision. Locating sounds on tape will require some practice at first, but eventually there will come a time when you won't even remember how awkward this once seemed.

5. Mark the two segments of tape that are to be spliced together. Rock the reels to locate the end of the sound at the end of the first segment (if the recorded material is speech you might also want to include the space that comes after the last word). This edit point on the tape is now at the center of the playback head (at the gap of the magnet). Loosen the tape a bit, then take the china marker and draw a vertical line on the *back* side of the tape at this point. You may also want to write a label on the back of the tape here to help you identify later what is on this particular segment of tape (see Figure 2.12). Now rock the reels to locate the beginning of the sound at the beginning of the second segment of tape. Again, this edit point will be found on the tape at the center of the playback head. Draw a vertical line here, and perhaps write another label.

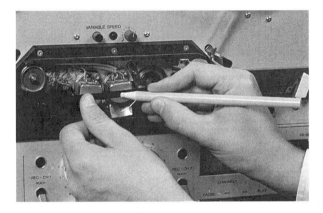

FIGURE 2.12
Marking an edit point on the back of a tape.

6. Loosen enough tape from the reels so that the first marked segment of tape can be placed down in the splicing block. Align the vertical mark on the tape on the 45° cutting groove. With your thumb and middle finger, grasp an upper corner of a single-edged razor blade. Extend your index finger to the top of the other upper corner to stabilize the blade, and then set it down at a 45° angle in the cutting groove of the splicing block (see Figure 2.13). Slowly pull the blade through the tape. If the blade is sharp, there should be no resistance and the cut will be a clean and even one. Next, cut the tape again at the vertical mark you made to identify the beginning of the second segment of tape. Do not discard the intervening tape yet: if you made a mistake, you will not want to rummage through hundreds of discarded tape segments in the wastebasket to find the one that can be used to correct the problem.

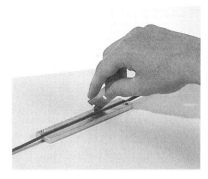

FIGURE 2.13
How to hold the single-edged blade used for tape editing.

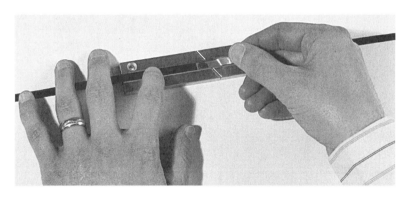

FIGURE 2.14
A piece of splicing tape in position to be applied.

7. Put the end of the first segment of tape and the beginning of the second segment of tape together in the splicing block. Be sure that the *outside* of the tape is facing up (not the side that passes next to the heads). The angle and smoothness of the cuts should match perfectly. Slide the two ends of tape together. They should not overlap, nor should there be a gap between them. Cut off about 1¼" of splicing tape. Place this at the tip of your index finger, extending the tape in the same direction as your finger points (see Figure 2.14).

8. Gently place the splicing tape over the two adjacent ends of tape to be joined. Center the splicing tape so that a slight margin of recording tape (approximately ¹⁄₆₄") is visible on each side of the splicing tape. Next, tamp down the splicing tape and carefully work out any bubbles. Hold the recording tape at each end of the splicing block and slide the tape until the splice is clear of the block. Then remove the tape from the block and rethread it on the tape deck. Wind the tape back a bit, push the Play button, and listen to what you have done.

Again, all of this will require some practice at first, but after you have made your first 50 splices or so, it will seem as easy and as instinctive as pushing the "snooze" button on an alarm clock at 6 A.M.

At the beginning of a recording, there are almost always a few extraneous noises—coughing and clearing of throats, feet shuffling, mike stands being bumped, musical instruments being picked up and tuned, switches clicking, and so forth. At the end of a recording, many of these same noises occur again. In a professional-quality recording, they are cut from the tape. A length of approximately five feet of **leader** tape is spliced to within two

inches or so of the first intentional sound on the tape, and another five-foot length of leader is spliced at the end of the tape, to within two inches or so of the end of the last intentional sound. Leader tape, which is essentially silent because it is not coated with magnetic particles, can also be used to separate different pieces of music stored on the same reel (see Figure 2.15). These bands of leader make it much easier to locate the beginning and ending of each piece of music. Avoid plastic leader because it can be more difficult to handle, and in dry climates it can build up electrostatic charge. Paper leader is preferred.

ÉTUDE 2.2

$\mathcal{R}$ecord a reading of a brief passage from your school catalog or from a magazine advertisement. Identify two or three words that, if moved or removed, will alter the meaning of the passage completely. Edit the passage by splicing these words out or into a new location, as necessary, to accomplish this alteration. Splice five feet of leader tape to the beginning of the recording and five feet of leader tape to the end. Then store this recording tail-out on an empty reel. On the tape box, make a note of the tape playback speed, the tape track configuration (such as half-track stereo or eight-track), and the fact that the tape is stored tail-out.

TAPE SPEED TRANSPOSITION

Normally a tape is played back at the same speed at which it was recorded. However, interesting things do happen when this practice is not followed. The techniques of **tape speed transposition** have proven quite valuable for the composer of tape music.

Tape speeds are normally related by a factor of two (for example, 15 ips is twice as fast as 7.5 ips). When a tape is played back at double speed, the durations of all sounds are halved. Rhythmic patterns become more crisp and precise because attack times are halved and because the small timing errors of the recorded performance have become too small to be heard easily. All frequencies are doubled, meaning that all pitches are transposed up an octave. Human speech sounds as if spoken by elves or small, furry rodents (in fact, this particular phenomenon is often referred to as the chipmunk effect, in honor of David Seville, who along with his pals Alvin, Simon, and Theodore, the singing "chipmunks," did commercially successful work with the technique of tape speed transposition in the late 1950s and 1960s). To maintain a sufficient degree of intelligibility of speech while employing this effect, it is important when recording to prolong the vowels somewhat and to exaggerate the consonants.

When a tape is played back at half speed, all durations are doubled and all frequencies are halved. This means that all pitches are transposed down an octave. The reverberation time is doubled (something like changing the room into a cavernous hall). The tempo becomes twice as slow. Within the sounds themselves, details that normally occur too quickly to be noticed are now much more apparent, and on occasion can sound positively Tibetan.[6] Ordinary, mundane sounds can be transformed into something monstrous, magical, surreal.

Some tape decks include a variable speed control. Normally this might be used, for example, to correct minor problems with intonation on a recording of a musical solo. However, it can also be used somewhat more dramatically to bend the pitch of a sound or to introduce a glissando (a continuous rise or fall of pitch across a relatively wide range) at the beginning or end of a sound. For example, this technique might be applied to create bells that swoop or ducks that quack up. Except when you definitely intend to use the technique of variable speed transposition, however, always check to be certain this control is off. If you inadvertently record some material off-speed, it can be very difficult later to identify and correct the problem.

ÉTUDE 2.3

*R*ecord a few sentences of a poem or a passage of prose. At a different speed, record a few musical tones from an acoustic musical instrument (this can include the singing voice, acoustic guitar, piano, or a woodwind, brass, or bowed-string instrument, but not a synthesizer). Splice a few sounds recorded at one speed into the passage of sounds that were recorded at the other speed. The finished product should be approximately one minute in duration—about the same length as a longer television or radio commercial. Splice five feet of leader to the end of this étude, and splice the beginning of this piece to the leader at the end of Étude No. 2.2. Store this on your project reel with Étude No. 2.2, and update the tape box with information about the tape speed, track format, and tape direction (should be tail-out) of this newly added band of tape.

---

6. A sustained low note sung by a bass, for example, can sound much like the drone of a Tibetan monk when played back at half speed.

On October 5, 1948, radio listeners in France were startled to hear a radical new music, composed of the sounds of such things as trains, children's toys, and pots and pans (along with a few sounds from pianos and other instruments). This event, billed as a "Concert of Noises," was the first public presentation of the work of Pierre Schaeffer, an engineer employed by the French Radio system, who had spent several years experimenting with recorded sounds.

The music that was the result of such experiments came to be known as **musique concrète,** or "concrete music." With the techniques developed by Schaeffer and his collaborators, a composer could work more directly with sound, without the intermediation of a performer.[a] Individual sounds could be treated as objects, or *objets sonores.*

Initially, Schaeffer worked with disc recordings of sounds, using several turntables and a record-cutting lathe to assemble his compositions. (Schaeffer's experiments with such equipment were preceded by those of other composers, including Paul Hindemith and John Cage.) His earliest experiments involved removing the attacks from sounds. Subsequently, he began to experiment also with changing the turntable speeds, reversing the direction of playback, and creating loops by cutting sounds into circular tracks (rather than the normally spiral tracks) on the discs.

In 1949 Schaeffer was joined at the studio by the composer Pierre Henry, and they collaborated on a piece entitled *Symphonie pour un homme seul* (translated liberally, the "One-Man Symphony"), created primarily from the sounds of a man breathing, speaking, shouting, humming, whistling, walking, knocking on doors, and such. In 1950–1951 Henry composed a work

[a]Music that was notated for subsequent interpretation by a performer was correspondingly labeled *musique abstraite,* or "abstract music."

TAPE REVERSAL

Sound recorded on a tape can be played back in its original order, as is the ordinary thing to do, or it can be played in reverse order, which can be extraordinary. When a recorded sound is reversed (something that is quite impossible to do, at least in the universe as we know it, when producing a sound live), the decay of the sound becomes its attack, and its attack becomes the decay. Sounds with short attacks and long decays, such as piano tones or cymbal crashes, are transformed into sounds with long, deliberate attacks and short, abrupt decays. As a result of **tape reversal,** spoken words become gibberish or take on the character of an unfamiliar foreign language, as the order of consonants and vowels (and even these phonemes themselves) is reversed.[7]

7. Incidentally, from time to time there arises a controversy about backwards messages recorded on rock albums. Retrograde in meaning and structure perceive to able is listener a that suggests that date to evidence scientific no is there. It is therefore not likely that such messages can in fact influence behavior in any way.

entitled *Le microphone bien tempéré* ("The Well-Tempered Microphone"), and in subsequent years he became the most prolific composer of *musique concrète.*

Among the composers working in the Paris group there was essentially no interest in electronically generated sounds. Schaeffer, Henry, and their colleagues were interested exclusively in the possible transformations of naturally produced sounds, including those of musical instruments. A particularly intriguing challenge for some of these composers has been the creation of an entire piece from a very few original sounds. One example is Henry's 1963 work, *Variations pour une porte et un soupir* ("Variations for a Door and a Sigh"). Another notable example is Hugh LeCaine's *Dripsody*, composed in 1955 on the sound of a single water drip.

On March 18, 1950, the first public concert of *musique concrète* was presented at the École Normale de Musique in Paris. This brave effort involved live performance with turntables, mixers, and other devices from the studio. A consequence of this concert was a heightened interest in the development of the technical means for controlling the apparent movement of sounds among several loudspeakers placed around the presentation space. This interest continues to be pursued by French-speaking composers in particular even now.

By 1951, the French Radio system decided to provide Schaeffer and his group with a reasonably well equipped space in which to pursue their work, and thus was established the first studio in the world for electroacoustic music. The equipment of the studio included several tape recorders, now available to Schaeffer and his colleagues for the first time. After some time, the composers in the Paris studio were able to adapt their techniques to these new instruments. In the ensuing years, several more fascinating and often magical works were created. As other studios became established around the world, the influence of the Paris group was strongly felt. It can still be discerned in the recent works of such gifted composers as Robert Normandeau, Jean Piché, Francis Dhomont, and others based in Montreal and in Paris.

To reverse a tape while maintaining the magnetic side of the tape as the one that still passes next to the heads, it is necessary to turn the tape upside down, so that the lower track becomes the upper track and vice versa (see Figure 2.16). This means, for example, that to create a sentence that has one or two words in reverse, it is necessary to record these words initially on the opposite track. When extracting the segments of tape on which these words are recorded, the segments are rotated and then spliced back into the recording, with the reversed words now joined with their companions on the same track.

ÉTUDE 2.4

𝓡ecord some familiar sounds on one track; record another set of familiar sounds on the next segment of tape, but on the opposite track. (Avoid synthesized sounds, because these tend to be novel and unfamiliar to begin with. Therefore, a listener can not readily discern if they are being played in reverse or at a different speed, and the effect is lost.)

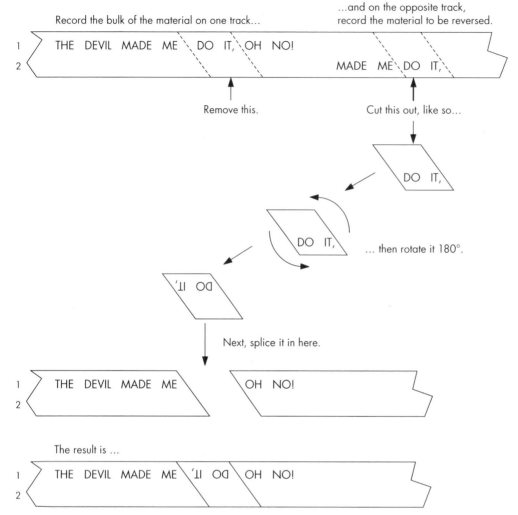

FIGURE 2.16
The evils of tape reversal.

Record the bulk of the material on one track...

...and on the opposite track, record the material to be reversed.

1 THE DEVIL MADE ME DO IT, OH NO!

2 MADE ME DO IT,

Remove this.

Cut this out, like so...

DO IT,

... then rotate it 180°.

DO IT,

DO IT,

Next, splice it in here.

1 THE DEVIL MADE ME   OH NO!

2

The result is ...

1 THE DEVIL MADE ME DO IT, OH NO!

2

Select a few of the sounds from the second group, cut them from the tape, reverse them, and splice them into the first passage of sounds. This should result in a one-minute series of sounds, all of which play back on the same channel but with some of them sounding in reverse.

Splice five feet of leader to the end of this étude, and splice the beginning to the leader that is at the end of Étude No. 2.3. Store this on your project reel with Études 2.2 and 2.3. Be sure to update the tape box with information about the tape speed, track format, and tape direction (should be tail-out) of this added band of tape.

TAPE LOOPS

If the end of a segment of tape is spliced to its beginning, a **tape loop** is formed. To play back a tape loop, first remove any reels of tape from the machine and replace them with empty reels, which can then be used as

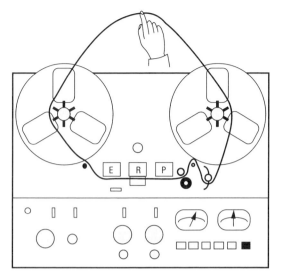

FIGURE 2.17
A tape loop, threaded and ready to play.

guides for the loop. Thread the loop through the tape path on the tape deck, and it can now be played repeatedly (see Figure 2.17).

Some planning will be necessary to ensure that the loop can be handled without too much trouble. If the loop is recorded at a low speed and is too short, it may be difficult to thread it around the head assembly. If the loop is recorded at a high speed and is too long, it may not be easy to maintain sufficient tension on the tape to keep it in the tape path. It may be necessary to use a pen or the boom of a microphone stand as an additional tape guide to hold up the tape loop.

ÉTUDE 2.5

The following line is taken from the text to a madrigal by the 14th-century composer Guillaume de Machaut: "My end is my beginning, and my beginning is my end." (Or you may prefer the original: "Ma fin est mon commencement, et mon commencement ma fin.")

Record this sentence. Then, with a sharp blade, cut off the last two words. Next, cut the tape again, just before the beginning of the sentence. Take the segment of text that remains, and splice the ends together. Thread this through the machine, and play it until you can no longer bear the repetition.

After a loop has repeated a few times, it quickly loses its ability to hold a listener's attention. People give their attention to the things around them that change. Therefore, it is a musical necessity to find ways to vary a repeating pattern that has become well established. Perhaps the volume of the loop can be faded in and out, or the variable speed control can be used to alter the pitch and tempo of the loop. Change is a fact of the natural world, and listeners have learned to expect it in music as well.

In 1951 Columbia University obtained some tape-recording equipment, reportedly for the purpose of recording concerts presented by its Department of Music. However, the equipment immediately provoked the curiosity of its custodian, Vladimir Ussachevsky, a composer and pianist who was serving at the time as a junior member of the music faculty at Columbia. He began to experiment with the recorded sounds of musical instruments, changing their playback speed, overdubbing them with other sounds, adding echoes through feedback techniques, and using other, by now familiar forms of manipulation.

In May of 1952 he presented some of the preliminary results of his explorations at a Composers' Forum at Columbia. Here he caught the interest of his faculty colleague, Otto Luening, and the two began to collaborate on several short pieces during the summer of 1952.

The principal sources of the sounds used by Luening and Ussachevsky in this work were the sounds of musical instruments and of the voice. Luening, an accomplished flutist, was a particularly busy source of sounds for the tape recorder. At this point, the composers were not especially interested in sounds produced electronically or, for that matter, in sounds produced naturally by objects other than musical instruments.[a] Luening and Ussachevsky were primarily interested in pursuing their "desire to extend the resonances of existing instruments."[b]

On October 28, 1952, at the Museum of Modern Art in New York City, the two Columbia composers presented "the first public concert of tape-recorder music in the United States."[c] The presentation received a great deal of attention in the press and was one of the most significant events in the establishment of electroacoustic music as a form of art in the United States. The concert included Ussachevsky's "Sonic Contours," based on piano sounds, and Luening's "Low Speed," "Invention," and "Fantasy in Space," all constructed from recorded sounds of Luening's flute.

These pieces, as well as two later pieces, "Incantation"[d] and "Moonflight," can be heard on an LP recording entitled *Tape Music: An Historic Concert* (DESTO DC6466), issued some years later. The pieces have been released more recently on a CD recording by Composers Recordings, Inc. (CRI CD 611). For an exercise in close listening, it may be useful, as the recording plays, to speculate on the sources of the sounds in these works and on the techniques of transformation that were applied by the composers to the recorded sounds. For example:

■ At what point in "Sonic Contours" does the use of tape echo techniques become particularly evident? Are these single echoes or multiple ones?

■ The title "Low Speed" clearly suggests a particular technique of tape manipulation. Is this expectation borne out?

---

[a] These latter sounds, however, were of particular interest to the composers of musique concrète, who were contemporaneously at work in their Paris studio.

[b] Otto Luening, "Origins," in Jon H. Appleton and Ronald C. Perera, eds., *The Development and Practice of Electronic Music* (Englewood Cliffs, NJ: Prentice-Hall, 1975), p. 17.

[c] Ibid.

[d] "Incantation," composed in collaboration by both Luening and Ussachevsky, was commissioned by Leopold Stokowski for broadcast on his CBS program, "Twentieth-Century Concert Hall." Ibid.

- Note the contrast of reverberant and nonreverberant sounds of the flute in "Fantasy in Space." Toward the end of the piece, a folklike tune is heard. Is it reverberated or not? How would its significance be changed if the opposite were true?
- "Incantation" is based on the sounds of woodwind instruments, bells, and the voice. Is tape reversal a significant technique employed in this piece? If so, the sounds of which source are more noticeably affected by this technique?
- Note the similarities between the opening and closing passages of "Incantation" (including the descending semitone motive). This simple but effective device rounds the form of the piece rather well. In many respects, "Incantation" is perhaps a miniature masterpiece—the piece on this recording that displays the most virtuosic use of the tape recorder as a musical instrument.
- Listen closely to how many elements are occurring simultaneously in "Incantation." Generally, only two things are part of the texture, occasionally three. Does this suggest that the limits of the technique of overdubbing are aesthetic, technical, or both?
- As you listen to this recording, you may perhaps share some of the astonishment of many in the audience at the first concert in 1952. Is this music? If so, why? If not, then what is it?

DUPLICATING A TAPE

By connecting the outputs of a tape deck to the line inputs (sometimes called the auxiliary inputs) of a second deck, it is possible to record a copy of a tape (see Figure 2.18). This technique is called **dubbing.** This ability to make copies of recorded sounds can greatly increase the opportunities for juxtaposing and manipulating sounds on tape. For example, a copy of a sound can be reversed and spliced next to its original. The repetitions of a tape loop can be recorded on another machine. An edited version of a recording can be compared to the unedited version.

When duplicating a tape it is especially important to set a good input level on the second machine. Not only will the original recorded sound be copied, but so will the recorded background noise and tape hiss. The copy will have its own machine noise and tape hiss as well. Thus, there are now two layers of noise on the tape. The amount of background noise continues to accumulate with each new generation of copies. By the time you have made a copy of a copy of a copy of a copy of a copy (that is, six generations of recordings), the accumulated layers of the background noise and tape hiss can be stronger than the recorded material itself![8]

---

8. This can be improved somewhat by the use of noise reduction circuitry, if available, such as the Dolby B, Dolby C, or dbx™ system.

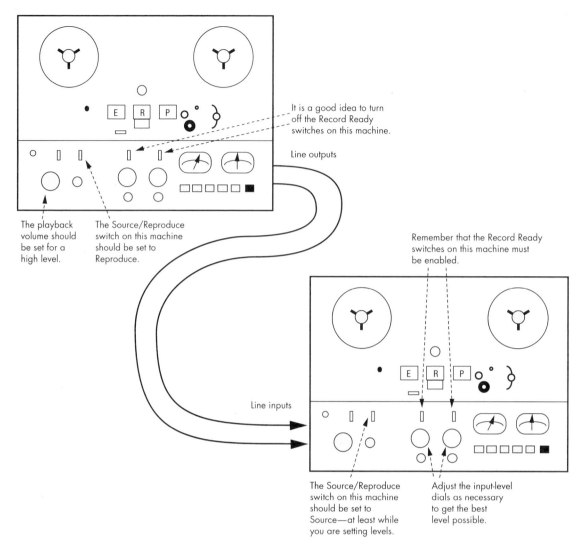

It is a good idea to turn
off the Record Ready
switches on this machine.

Line outputs

The playback
volume should
be set for a
high level.

The Source/Reproduce
switch on this machine
should be set to
Reproduce.

Remember that the Record Ready
switches on this machine must
be enabled.

Line inputs

The Source/Reproduce
switch on this machine
should be set to
Source—at least while
you are setting levels.

Adjust the input-level
dials as necessary
to get the best
level possible.

FIGURE 2.18
Patching two tape decks
together for dubbing.

ÉTUDE 2.6

Connect the outputs of one tape deck to the line inputs of a second tape deck. Make a tape loop (or use the tape loop you made for Étude No. 2.5), and thread it onto the first tape deck. As you play back your loop on the first tape deck, make a one-minute recording on the second tape deck. Find ways to vary the repetition of the loop. For example, use the playback volume control on the first tape deck to have the repetitions of the loop gradually fade in and out. Or use the variable speed control on the first tape deck to vary the playback speed of the loop. (Do not switch the setting of the regular tape speed switch. This may result in too abrupt a change in speed, or the electrical noise from the switch may affect the recording, most likely becoming audible as a click.)

Splice five feet of leader to the end of the recording that is made on the second tape deck, and splice the beginning of this recording to the leader at the end of Étude No. 2.4. Store this on your project reel with Études 2.2, 2.3, and 2.4. Be sure to update the tape box with information about the tape speed, track format, and tape direction (should be tail-out) of this newly added band of tape.

This has been only a brief introduction to the techniques of tape manipulation. Try experimenting with recording a variety of sounds. Play them back at different speeds, reverse them, loop them, edit them, and experiment with combinations of these techniques. Be sure to keep notes regarding how you have created sounds that are particularly interesting and that may be of potential use in the music you may soon want to write.

IMPORTANT TERMS

tape deck
erase head
record head
playback head
ERP
domains
capstan
pinch roller
channels
tracks

ips
crosstalk
pre-echo
print-through
tail-out
signal-to-noise ratio, or SNR
tape hiss
tape saturation
VU meter

headroom
editing
splicing
leader
tape speed transposition
musique concrète
tape reversal
tape loop
dubbing

FOR FURTHER READING

In addition to many of the sources cited at the end of Chapter 1, the following may be useful:

Griffiths, Paul. *A Guide to Electronic Music.* New York: Thames & Hudson, 1979.

Keane, David. *Tape Music Composition.* London: Oxford University Press, 1980.

Manning, Peter. *Electronic and Computer Music.* Oxford: Clarendon Press, 1985.

Schrader, Barry. *Introduction to Electro-acoustic Music.* Englewood Cliffs, NJ: Prentice-Hall, 1982.

CHAPTER 3

DIGITAL RECORDING

$\mathcal{M}$uch of the knowledge gained from the preceding chapter is doomed to become obsolete. With digital technology, sound can first be encoded in numerical form and then stored on tape. The result is a recording that is much more accurate, durable, and virtually free of noise. Also, most editing, as well as other techniques of manipulation, can be done electronically.

The technology for digital recording is still relatively young, but in time it will supplant most of the recording machinery in present use. In the following sections of this chapter, the techniques of digital recording are examined in greater detail.

FROM SOUND TO NUMBERS, AND BACK

A sound, as was described in Chapter 1, is produced when an object vibrates and creates fluctuations of air pressure that emanate from around the object. The primary function of a microphone is to sense these fluctuations of air pressure and to transduce these into a corresponding pattern of electrical fluctuations. If this pattern of electrical vibrations, which is considered to be an analog of the acoustical vibrations, is then recorded as a corresponding series of magnetic fluctuations on tape, the result is referred to as an **analog recording** (see Figure 3.1). This is the technology of recording that was described in the previous chapter. However, if the electrical signal produced by the microphone is instead measured repeatedly at equal intervals of time, and if it is this series of measurements that is encoded and stored, then a **digital recording** has been made (see Figure 3.2).

These periodic measurements of the instantaneous amplitude of the electrical signal are referred to as **samples.** The piece of equipment, or hardware, that takes these samples is called an **ADC,** or **analog-to-digital**

FIGURE 3.1
Making an analog recording
of a sound.

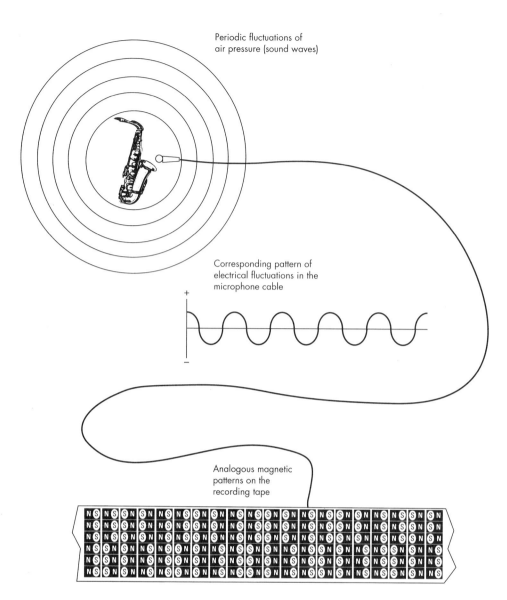

Periodic fluctuations of
air pressure (sound waves)

Corresponding pattern of
electrical fluctuations in the
microphone cable

Analogous magnetic
patterns on the
recording tape

converter. At the output of the ADC, these samples are represented in the form of binary numbers—numbers that include only the symbols 0 and 1—by rapid pulses of electrical current.[1]

The binary sound samples are then passed to the next component of the digital audio system. Here, the numbers may simply be stored, or they may be processed and manipulated in some way (or they may be processed first and then stored). One way in which the samples can be stored is in the form of a series of magnetic pulses on a computer's hard disk or floppy disk. Alternatively, the samples can be stored on magnetic tape, as will be described in this chapter. Yet another way to store digital sound samples is to etch a corresponding series of pits and ridges in concentric rings on a compact disc, or CD. When the time comes to retrieve the data, these successive pits and ridges are scanned optically by a laser.

---

1. A description of the binary system of numbering, and how it relates to the more familiar decimal system in everyday use by humans, can be found in Appendix B.

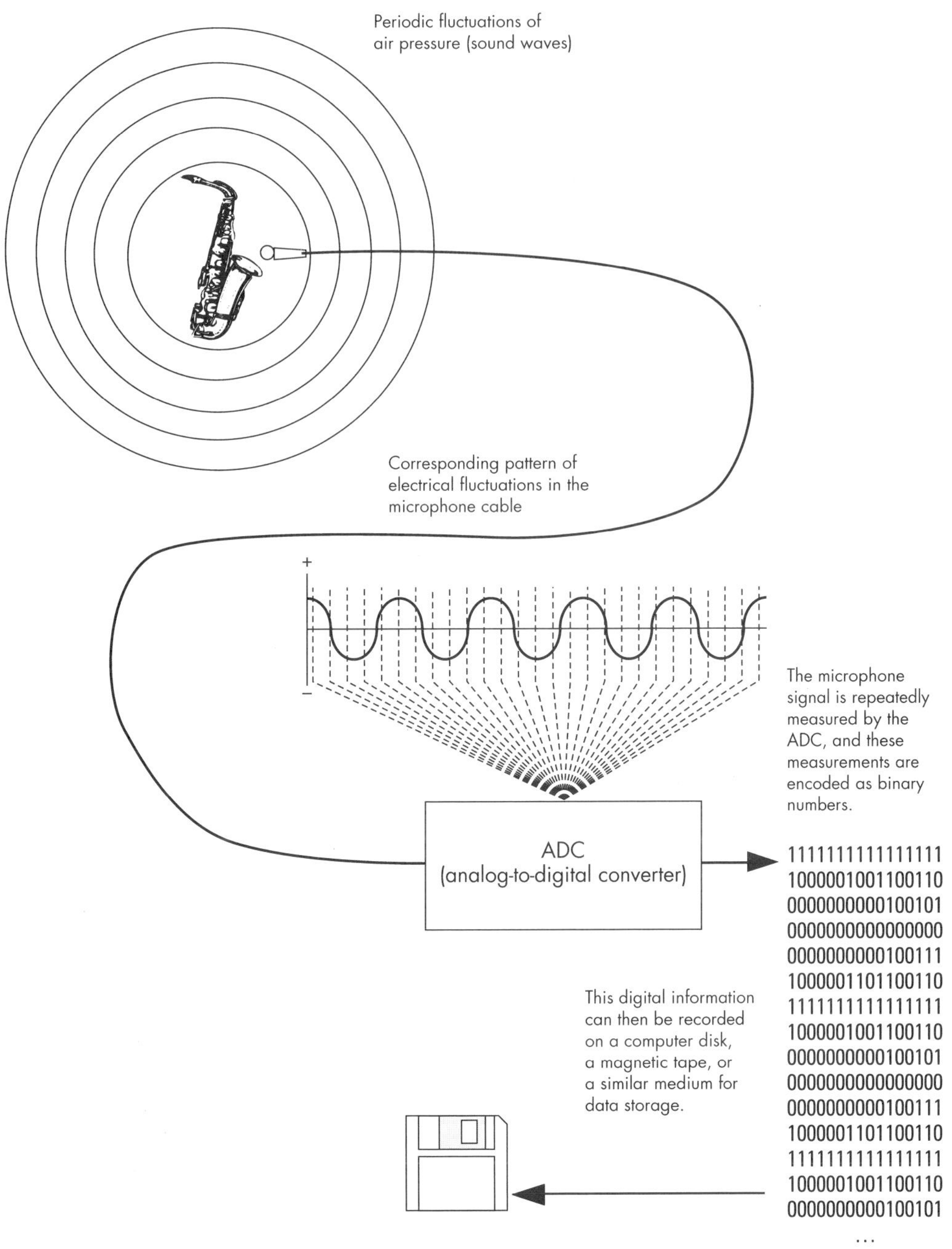

FIGURE 3.2
Making a digital recording of
a sound.

Periodic fluctuations of
air pressure (sound waves)

Corresponding pattern of
electrical fluctuations in the
microphone cable

The microphone
signal is repeatedly
measured by the
ADC, and these
measurements are
encoded as binary
numbers.

ADC
(analog-to-digital converter)

1111111111111111
1000001001100110
0000000000100101
0000000000000000
0000000000100111
1000001101100110
1111111111111111
1000001001100110
0000000000100101
0000000000000000
0000000000100111
1000001101100110
1111111111111111
1000001001100110
0000000000100101

...

This digital information
can then be recorded
on a computer disk,
a magnetic tape, or
a similar medium for
data storage.

One of the principal attractions of digital audio technology is the durability of digitized audio information. It can be stored for very long periods of time with no significant loss of quality. A pulse that represents the number 1 may weaken over time, but it will still be distinguishable from a representation of the number 0. Furthermore, if damage occurs to the storage medium (partial erasure of the magnetic disk, or abrasion of the surface of a CD, for example), it may still be possible to reconstruct the missing data. Thus, digital recordings of sound are virtually free of the hisses, pops, clicks, and dropouts that characterize analog recordings.

A second attraction of digital audio technology is that, as a series of binary numbers, the digital audio samples are readily amenable to computation, either by a general-purpose computer or by a computer dedicated to digital audio processing. This computation can take place before or after storage of the data. Or it can be done instead of storage, during a performance, as a form of live signal processing.[2]

Eventually, whether they are recomputed or merely stored for safekeeping, the samples will need to be reconstituted as sound so that the music or speech can be heard and presumably enjoyed. The hardware component primarily responsible for this is called a **DAC**, or **digital-to-analog converter.** For each sample in the signal, the DAC generates a corresponding level of electrical current. After a bit of smoothing, the signal can be sent to an audio amplifier and then to a loudspeaker. The numbers are once again sound—symbols have become reality.

DIGITAL RECORDERS

Many of the digital recorders now in use in professional recording studios have at least a superficial resemblance to the analog recorders that preceded them (see Figure 3.3). A ribbon of magnetic tape, stored on open reels of traditional sizes, passes by stationary recording and playback heads (now referred to as write and read heads, respectively). Among the speeds at which the tape may move past the heads are the traditional 7.5, 15, or 30 inches per second.

A digital open-reel recorder typically uses tape that is ¼", ½", or 1" wide and 1 mil (.001") thick. The formulation of the tape is quite different from that used on an analog recorder, however. A digital tape must be able to respond well to a dense stream of magnetic pulses that represent patterns of ones and zeros. Depending on the tape speed, tape width, and other factors, as few as two or as many as 48 channels of such digital audio signals can be recorded. Perhaps as many as four additional tracks may also be available for recording cues, time-code signals, and similar information.

Typically, the patterns of ones and zeros that represent digital sound samples are not recorded in consecutive order on the tape. Rather, they are divided into groups and then distributed about the area of the local segment of tape. This technique, called interleaving, makes it less likely that a group of samples will be completely disrupted by an imperfection of the tape or some other glitch. If there is a problem on the tape, and if some parts of the samples survive elsewhere on the recording, then it may be possible for the digital recorder to reconstruct the missing data during playback.

However, the technique of interleaving the data that are recorded on the tape makes it somewhat difficult to edit an open-reel digital recording by the traditional cut-and-splice method. Although some physical splices may

---

2. This application will be discussed in Chapter 4.

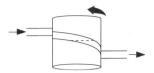

FIGURE 3.4
Helical scanning. The tape head is the rotating cylinder. Tape guides direct the tape down across the tape head. Consequently, the tape is recorded or scanned at an angle, as shown by the dashed line. In contrast to analog tape decks, and many digital decks as well, the information is recorded not on a set of parallel tracks that run the length of the tape, but on a layered series of oblique swaths.

FIGURE 3.3
An open-reel digital recorder.
(Courtesy of SONY.)

work (for example, during silent passages in a recording), it is more likely that different segments of the recording will be joined electronically. To accomplish this, the digital audio output of the deck is patched to the input of a second digital deck. The transport controls of both decks are linked by a device referred to as a synchronizer, or system controller. This device is programmed with a list of cues that corresponds to the desired sequence of recorded segments. The system controller then automatically controls the transport of the first deck so that it can locate and then play the segments in the desired order. The second digital deck records this new arrangement of the material, pausing as the first deck locates the various segments. This process is greatly facilitated by the use of a time-code signal that has been recorded on an auxiliary track of the first deck.[3] More advanced techniques of manipulating recorded material, such as pitch transposition, reversal, and looping, are extremely difficult, if not impossible to manage on an open-reel digital recorder.

Digital cassette recorders of two types have been widely used. Both of these employ rotating heads that scan the tape at an angle as it passes, a technique called helical scanning (see Figure 3.4).

Beginning in the late 1970s, digital audio signals could be recorded and played from a standard VHS or Beta™ videocassette. A device called a **PCM** (for Pulse Code Modulation) **processor** was used to convert the audio signal to a digital format that conformed to a standard format for video signals, such as the one used in North America and Japan (the NTSC format) or one used widely in Europe (the PAL format). This video signal, representing digital audio information, could then be recorded on a videocassette by a VCR. If the material recorded on the videocassette were viewed on a television monitor it would not be a pretty picture, but when decoded by a PCM processor the quality of the resulting sound was most

---

3. The time-code signal used for this purpose is one of the standard ones developed by the Society of Motion Picture and Television Engineers (SMPTE), and is described further in Chapters 4 and 6.

FIGURE 3.5
A DAT recorder. (Courtesy of Panasonic Professional Audio Systems.)

impressive. Editing a videotape by cutting and splicing was essentially impossible, however, although capabilities for electronic editing were provided on a few of the videocassette systems used for digital audio recording in professional studios.

Since the mid-1980s, another type of digital cassette recorder, called a **DAT** (for Digital Audio on Tape) **recorder,** has come into use (see Figure 3.5).[4] DAT cassettes are somewhat smaller (approximately 3" × 2" × 0.4") than standard, analog audio cassettes, but can record up to two hours of material with a quality of sound that approaches or even exceeds that of the compact disc (CD). A very useful feature of many DAT recorders is program numbering. Along with the audio data, there is a provision for recording "subcode data," including place markers that can be used to locate particular segments of the recording, such as the beginnings of songs. As with videocassette recordings of digital audio, however, it is impossible to edit a DAT recording by cutting and splicing, and very few, if any, DAT recorders provide for electronic editing.

Yet another digital recording system, referred to as **hard-disk recording,** has become more widely available since the late 1980s (see Figure 3.6). With this type of system, the digital sound samples can first be processed by a powerful microcomputer and then stored in a large file on the hard disk of the computer. Typically, the file will contain approximately ten megabytes of data for each minute of a stereo recording (by comparison, a standard floppy disk can hold only about 0.8 megabytes of data). Therefore, the hard disk must be one of very large capacity. It must also be able to gain access to data anywhere on the disk with sufficient speed (within 28 milliseconds, typically).

There is a significant advantage to using a hard disk as a storage medium for a digital recording. Unlike a digital tape, a hard disk is not a sequential-access storage medium that requires spooling through all of the data preceding the desired location on the recording. Rather, a hard disk provides

---

4. This is sometimes identified as an R-DAT (for Rotary-head Digital Audio on Tape) recorder.

FIGURE 3.6
A hard-disk digital recording system. (Courtesy of Digidesign, Inc.)

direct access to any passage of the recording. This greatly facilitates the process of editing. In fact, it has become a common procedure to copy a videocassette or DAT recording onto a hard disk for editing. Once the editing is complete, the recording is then copied back onto the cassette (which is, of course, a much more portable medium than the hard disk of a computer, and can be copied and distributed much more easily among friends and executives in the music industry!). Because of their powerful editing capabilities, hard-disk recording systems are becoming very popular in small studios as well as large ones, even though the least expensive hard-disk systems are still somewhat more expensive than most DAT recorders.

One of the keys to this power, in addition to the provision of direct rather than sequential access to the data, is that selected segments of the recording on the hard disk can be displayed graphically on the screen of the microcomputer that serves as host to the hard disk. This display of the values of successive digital sound samples in the form of a graph provides a very useful image of the sound (see Figure 3.7). Editing decisions can be made on the basis of visual as well as aural cues, providing a tremendous advantage over strictly aural techniques of editing, such as those used with analog tape recordings. For example, with a visual editing system it is possible to locate much more precisely the beginnings and endings of sounds and the transitions within sounds.

More advanced techniques for manipulating sounds are also possible. The pitch of a sound can be transposed by changing the rate at which its sound samples are played. Or, if the rate at which the samples are played

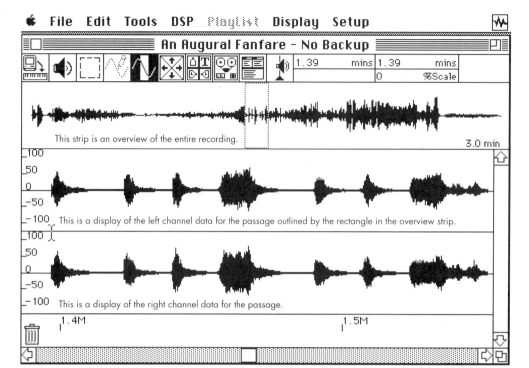

a. The samples as originally recorded.

b. If every other sample is removed, but the sample rate is maintained, then the frequency of the signal is doubled and the pitch is raised one octave.

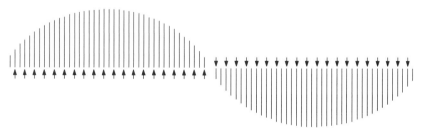

FIGURE 3.8
Pitch transposition of a digitally recorded sound.

c. If a new sample is interpolated between each of the samples but the sample rate is maintained, then the frequency of the signal becomes one octave lower.

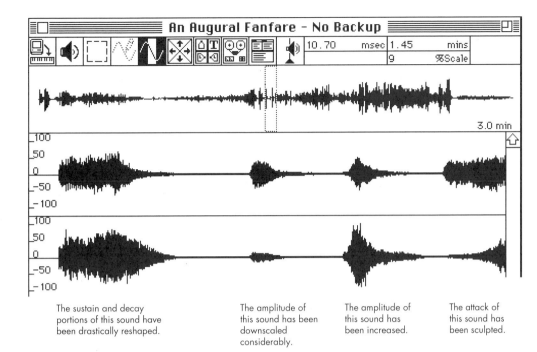

FIGURE 3.9
A few of the ways in which the amplitude of the samples in a hard-disk recording can be rescaled or contoured. (Courtesy of Digidesign, Inc.)

must remain fixed, then the pitch of a sound can be raised by selectively removing samples; for example, removing every other sample will raise the pitch one octave (see Figure 3.8a and b). The pitch can be lowered by interpolating new samples between the existing ones (see Figure 3.8c).

The volume of the sound can be adjusted simply by scaling the values of the digital samples that represent the sound. The volume can also be contoured (see Figure 3.9). A sound can be reversed quite easily by reversing the order in which its samples are stored (see Figure 3.10). A sound can be copied and then pasted repeatedly so that it becomes part of a series of duplicates, as with an analog tape loop (see Figure 3.11). Unlike analog tape operations, which involve physical manipulation of the recording medium, these digital techniques of *musique concrète* are "hands-off" procedures. They are more abstract, numerical operations.

When making any digital recording, it is important to be extremely careful not to set recording levels too high. When the digital data stream consists entirely of ones, it becomes impossible to represent samples that are any louder (see Figure 3.12). The optimal signal level, as shown on the LED meters of the recorder, should be around –12 to –15 dB.[5] This will allow a bit of headroom for transient peaks. Digital distortion, unlike other forms of distortion (some of which on occasion are even induced intentionally), is *never* pleasant to hear and is in fact quite intolerable to the ear.

Microphones that have a smooth response throughout the range of audible frequencies should be used. Many microphones have response peaks

---

5. The meters on many DAT recorders are quite helpful in this respect in that they show a change in color at this point.

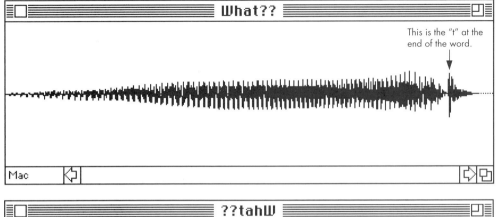

This is the "t" at the end of the word.

FIGURE 3.10
Reversal of the spoken word "What?" (Courtesy of Passport Designs, Inc.)

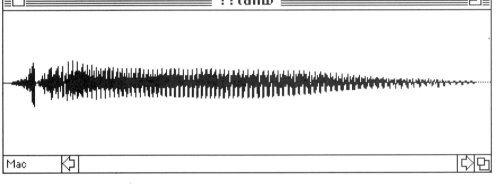

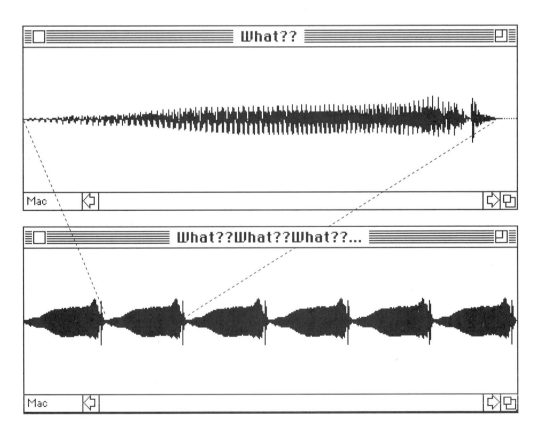

FIGURE 3.11
One way to simulate a tape loop in a digital recording is to append multiple copies of a sound to the file of sound samples. (Courtesy of Passport Designs, Inc.)

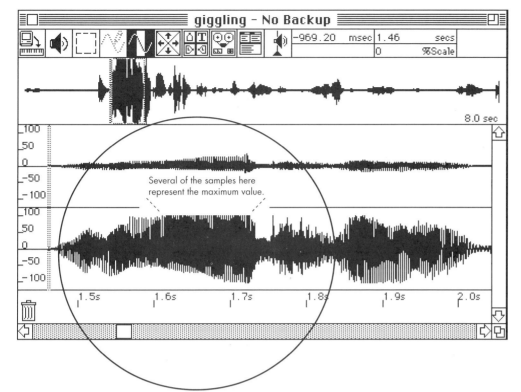

FIGURE 3.12
Digital distortion results when the maximum possible sample value is not sufficient to represent the amplitude of the input signal at that point in time. The signal becomes "clipped," as illustrated here by the flattened segment of the signal display. (Courtesy of Digidesign, Inc.)

that are readily concealed by the noise and uneven frequency response of analog recorders. Digital recorders are not so charitable, however. Everything is heard. For the same reason, the higher frequencies should not be routinely boosted while recording (as might be done with an analog recording to compensate for the partial masking of higher frequencies by tape hiss). Digital recordings can become rather shrill when this is done.

As much as possible, direct contact with the tape should be avoided. Digital equipment is especially sensitive to oils, body salts, dust, and other particles. Also, particular care must be taken to store digital tapes in a dust-free, temperate environment.

Most digital tape decks include connectors for transmitting or receiving a digital signal from another deck, so that a recording can be duplicated digitally. Digital duplication avoids many of the extraneous noises and errors that can be introduced as the digital samples of the original recording are converted to analog form by the digital-to-analog converter of the first deck and then converted back to digital form by the analog-to-digital converter of the second deck. For a digital duplication to be successful, however, the two decks must be compatible; that is, they must agree on the format for the digital information that is to be transmitted. Two principal formats are presently in use for the transmission of digital audio information. The **AES/EBU** (for Audio Engineering Society/European Broadcasting Union) standard is a professional-level format that uses XLR connectors or fiberoptic connectors. The **S/PDIF** (for Sony/Philips Digital Information Format) standard is typically found on consumer products, and uses RCA or fiberoptic connectors. It is essential that both decks recognize the same format. It is not possible to do a digital duplication from a deck that transmits in the AES/EBU format, for example, to a deck that recognizes only the S/PDIF format. It would still be possible, of course, to connect the analog audio outputs of the first deck to the analog audio inputs of the second deck to make a duplicate recording.

ÉTUDE 3.1

*S*pend a few minutes reading the operator's manual (or perhaps a summary of the operating instructions that has been prepared by your instructor) of the DAT recorder or PCM processor/videotape recorder system in your studio. Then record approximately one minute of (a) a brief passage of poetry or prose, or (b) a solo musical instrument.

ÉTUDE 3.2

*M*ake a recording on a hard-disk system of a brief passage of vocal sounds (unaccompanied song or speech). Using the visual display of the sound file of this recording, select three short sounds and copy them to a new sound file. In this new sound file, make multiple copies of the three sounds. Reverse some of the copies, blend others together, and rescale the amplitude of some of the copies, while arranging them into a composition of approximately two minutes' duration.

DIGITAL SAMPLERS

One other type of digital recorder has yet to be discussed—the **digital sound sampler.** This is indeed a special form of digital recorder. Typically, it is a keyboard instrument that resembles a sound synthesizer in appearance. Another type of sound sampler, called a **sampler module,** does not include a keyboard and can be installed in a standard equipment rack. In either form, the sound sampler is regarded as a musical instrument that can be performed onstage live or recorded in a studio.

A microphone or a line-level source can be patched to the audio input of the sampler.[6] Individual sounds, such as tones of acoustic musical instruments or sound effects, can then be converted to a stream of digital samples by an analog-to-digital converter circuit in the sampler. These samples are then stored in memory chips (called RAM, for Random-Access Memory) that are installed in the sampler.

---

6. On some models only a line input is available, in which case a microphone signal will require preamplification.

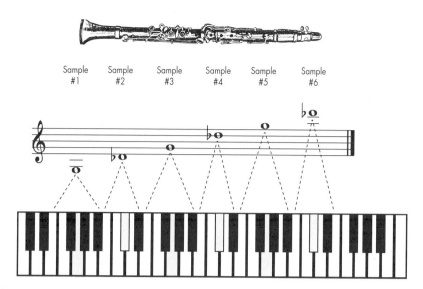

FIGURE 3.13
In multisampling, several distinct pitches are sampled, and each is used to represent a particular segment of the range of pitches that can be played by the instrument being sampled.

The playback of such a recorded sound is triggered by pressing a key on the keyboard.[7] The samples of different sounds—for example, the sounds of the various drums and cymbals in a standard drum set—can be assigned to different keys. This makes it possible to perform some intriguing (and occasionally amusing) juxtapositions and patterns of sounds.

Usually, the samples of a particular sound are assigned to a range of keys. One key, called the original key or base key, is designated to trigger the playback of samples at the same rate at which they were recorded. Keys above this will trigger playback at faster rates, meaning that the pitch of the sound will be transposed higher. Keys below the original key will trigger the playback of the samples at a lower rate, meaning that the pitch will be transposed down. With large intervals of pitch transposition, as with the techniques of analog tape speed transposition described in the previous chapter, the effects can be rather dramatic. Ordinary speech can be transformed into the babble of chipmunks or lowered to become the incantations of Tibetan holy men, for example.

Within the range of smaller intervals, however, the effects of this pitch transposition are not particularly noticeable. Thus, if the musician's goal is to emulate the sounds of an acoustic instrument, such as a grand piano or a clarinet, it is not necessary to sample the sound of each pitch produced by that instrument. Only a few pitches need be sampled, each representing the particular tone color of a segment of the range of pitches playable by the instrument (see Figure 3.13). This technique of sampling a small set of pitches to represent the complete range of an instrument is called **multisampling.**

Although the technique of multisampling makes possible a credible emulation of an acoustic instrument, it does not capture all the nuances of

7. Or, as in the case of a sampler module, the playback is triggered by the receipt of a MIDI Note message from another instrument, as described in Chapter 5.

instrumental technique of a professional performer of that instrument. Thus, a sound sampler is not an appropriate instrument to use in more subtle musical contexts. However, it is often quite sufficient for many commercial projects, such as film soundtracks and advertisement jingles. The effect this has had on many working musicians has been profound, to say the least. Often a group of professional players of instruments has found itself displaced by a solo keyboard player who has learned to be versatile with a sound sampler.

ÉTUDE 3.3

*S*pend a few moments reading the section on sampling in the operator's manual of the sound sampling instrument in your studio. Then sample two different sounds (for example, two words that are opposite in meaning, such as *yes* and *no,* or *right* and *left*). Assign these two samples to different halves of the keyboard. Then compose a rhythmic pattern of approximately 30 seconds' duration, consisting of a more or less regular alternation of these two sampled sounds. Record the pattern on tape.

A set of digital samples representing a sound can be edited in a variety of ways. Two or more sets of sound samples, for example, might be joined together into one set, either with an abrupt juxtaposition of sounds or with a cross-fade transition from one set to the next (see Figure 3.14). Computer-based, visual editing programs, similar to those used with hard-disk digital recording systems, can be particularly useful for such operations. Adjustments to the amplitude envelope of a set of samples or to the overall amplitude level can also be made with relative ease. A few visual editing programs even provide means to adjust the pitch envelope of a set of samples, or to make changes in the balance of frequencies represented. It is also quite easy to reverse the order of the samples of a sound, so that attacks become decays and decays become attacks.

Visual editing programs can be particularly helpful with the technique of **looping,** one of the more difficult, but necessary chores involved in working with a sampler. Typically, there are 44,100 or more samples taken of each second of an audio signal that is patched to the input of a sampler. At this rate, the internal memory of the sampler can fill rather quickly. There may be memory space for only one long, sustained tone from a clarinet or violin, rather than a larger set of tones. To provide for a more efficient use of memory, it is often possible to recycle continually just a portion of a digitized sound, a portion most likely selected from the sustain segment of the envelope of the sound (see Figure 3.15). To make this loop as smooth and inconspicuous as possible, great care must be taken to select a segment whose beginning and ending match closely in amplitude, pitch, and tone color. Otherwise, there will always be a click or thump whenever the loop

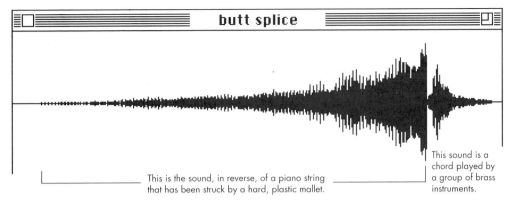

butt splice

This is the sound, in reverse, of a piano string that has been struck by a hard, plastic mallet.

This sound is a chord played by a group of brass instruments.

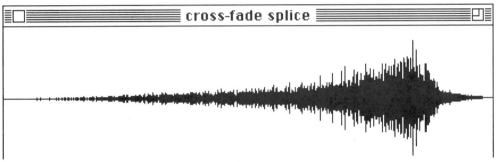

cross-fade splice

Here the end of the piano sound and the beginning of the brass chord overlap.

FIGURE 3.14
Two common ways in which two sample files can be spliced together. (Courtesy of Passport Designs, Inc.)

repeats. (A more detailed description of various techniques for looping is provided in Chapter 9.)

Not all loops need to be illusions of sustained, seamless purity, however. A pattern or phrase (such as a spoken phrase) can be looped as well. The effect is much like that of an analog tape loop. When the technique of creating such a loop of samples is combined with the versatility of a sampler for providing pitch transposition and reversal of sounds, then truly fascinating creative possibilities become apparent. As with many of the techniques of hard-disk digital recording, the potential uses of a digital sound sampler clearly indicate that many of the "classical" techniques of *musique concrète* continue to be available to the creative musician. A digital sound sampler, in other words, can do so much more than play back simple recordings of a variety of sounds.

ÉTUDE 3.4

*S*ample the sound of a bowed-string, brass, or woodwind instrument. Using either the available looping functions of the sampler itself or a computer-based, visual editing program, find a good loop for the sound. Then, sample a pattern of sounds (instrumental, sung, or spoken) and loop this as well, so that it can be used in the manner of a tape loop. Compose a one- or two-minute work that uses both of these sample files, in combination or in succession.

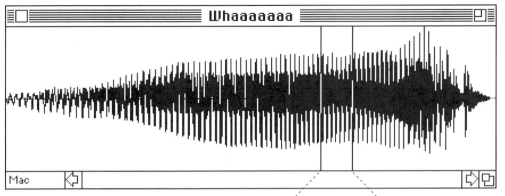

This is the looped segment.

a. an overview of the entire sound

FIGURE 3.15
A sustain loop in a set of digital sound samples: (a) an overview of the entire sound; (b) a closeup view of the transition from the end of the loop segment to the beginning of the loop. This transition needs to be as smooth as possible so that unwanted thumps and clicks are not heard as the loop begins to repeat. (Courtesy of Passport Designs, Inc.)

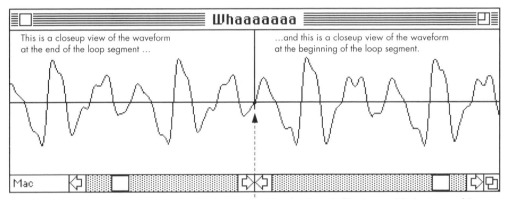

This is a closeup view of the waveform at the end of the loop segment ...

...and this is a closeup view of the waveform at the beginning of the loop segment.

Note that the end of the loop and the beginning of the loop meet at a point where the sample value is zero. Also note the similarity between the amplitude and waveshape at the end of the loop and at the beginning. This will be a very smooth-sounding loop point.

b. a closeup view of the transition from the end of the loop segment to the beginning of the loop

There are instruments called **sample players** for which such possibilities are somewhat more limited. On these instruments, the sets of samples are recorded permanently, probably at the factory, onto a different kind of memory chip, called ROM (for Read-Only Memory). Sample players are generally used simply as emulators of other instruments. They offer few, if any, opportunities to edit the sets of samples for use in a particular performance or recording project. The sample files have been prepared professionally and optimized for the instrument, and remain there until the ROM chip is replaced.

Storing a set of samples in the internal memory (RAM) of a true sampler is far from permanent, however. Such memory is volatile: when the electrical power to the sampler is switched off, the information evaporates. Therefore, a sampler provides for saving the information on a magnetic disk, typically a standard floppy disk. In a subsequent rehearsal, performance, or recording session, the samples can be loaded again from the disk into the internal memory of the sampler. Some instruments even provide for the storage of sample files on a hard disk that can be dedicated to the instrument. This greatly simplifies the task of managing the large collection of sample files that can accumulate rather quickly, often in just the first few months of playing with a sampler. This collection of home-made sample files can be supplemented by the purchase of professionally prepared sample files available on floppy disks. Once again, it is important to emphasize, however, that a sampler should be regarded as much more than a simple device for playing brief, digital recordings of sounds, whether recorded professionally or not. The sampler invites creative play with sound itself.

This has been only a brief introduction to digital sampling instruments. More advanced topics in sampling are discussed in Chapter 9. Meanwhile, the operator's manual of the sampler in your studio will include the specific information you need to commence your own sonic adventures with sampling.

A FEW SUGGESTIONS REGARDING SOUND SAMPLING

As with all other forms of recording, both digital and analog, it is important to sample the sound at a sufficiently high level of amplitude. Otherwise, as the sound is played back it will be necessary to amplify it somewhat, and this will also boost the level of the background noise in the sample file. On the other hand, the recording level must not be set too high. If the amplitude of the signal exceeds the capacity of the samples to represent it, then digital distortion results. The sound of a dentist's drill can be more pleasant than this. Virtually all samplers have an LED meter or a peak light to indicate when this critical level is reached.

It is usually necessary to repeat a sound as adjustments are made to the level. It can be rather difficult, therefore, to sample a source that is live, such as a singer, instrument player, or house pet. Each time the sound is repeated, it will be somewhat different with respect to amplitude, pitch, duration, or tone color. A standard practice, therefore, is to record the sound first on an analog tape deck or a DAT recorder. If the tape player can then be programmed to repeat a segment of the recording automatically, the task of setting a level on the sampler can be much more accurate (and much less stressful than asking a live source to repeat the sound yet again "exactly the same way as before").

While recording a sound that will subsequently be sampled, it is important to be aware of any background noises, such as squeaking floorboards, electric fans, rattling snares on a drum, or electrical hum. These may not be so noticeable when the sound that is sampled from the recording is played back from the original key. However, these extraneous noises can become very obtrusive when heard in an altered context, such as a pitch transposition, a reversal of the sound, or a loop. To minimize such noises, try to turn off their sources, or place the microphone very carefully so that these sources are in less sensitive areas of its field pattern.

For a similar reason, avoid the temptation to enhance a sound with effects, such as reverberation or flanging, before it is sampled. When the samples are transposed, reversed, or looped, the effects are transposed, reversed, or looped as well. With reverberation, for

FIGURE 3.16
Unwanted sounds at the beginning and end of a sample file
can be removed through a
process called extraction, or
trimming. (Courtesy of Passport
Designs, Inc.)

The segment of the file that is to be kept is first selected ...

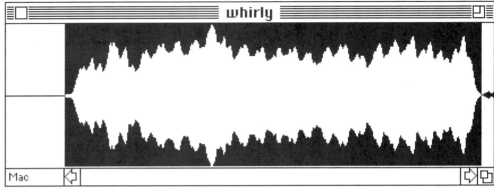

...and then extracted. The sample file, minus the unwanted material previously
found at the beginning and at the end, can then be saved to disk.

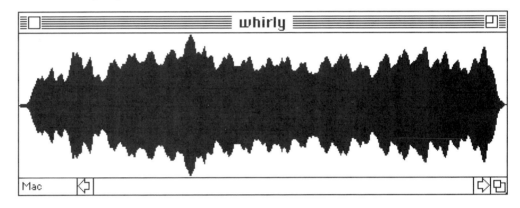

example, it may seem as if the size of the space in which the sound is placed shrinks as the pitch is transposed higher. Or it may seem that the room is turned inside out if the sound is reversed. Unless such unusual illusions are desired, it is better to add effects as the sounds are played back by the sampler, so that the effects are applied uniformly to each sound.

When a sound is sampled, it is quite likely that some of the silence that precedes and follows the sound will be recorded as well. To make more efficient use of the memory of the sampler, these "dead spaces" should be stripped from the file of samples. One way of accomplishing this, particularly with computer-based, visual editing programs, is to identify the boundaries of the sound and then to "trim" or "extract" it (see Figure 3.16). Or, the sensitivity of the sampler itself may be adjusted so that, when it is placed in record mode, it does not actually begin taking samples until it is triggered by a sound of sufficient amplitude, called the threshold level (see Figure 3.17). This prevents recording of the silence that precedes the sound. The silence that comes after the sound can then be eliminated by "truncating" the sample file—shortening it by designating a sample, generally the last identifiable sample of the sound itself, as the end of the file.

Finally, in addition to the technical concerns discussed here, there are a few ethical matters to consider when sampling sounds. It is unethical, for example, to sample someone without his or her knowledge and consent. It is important always to get, from the person whose sounds have been recorded, a signed release stating that permission is granted for the use of the sounds.

FIGURE 3.17

If a sampler is in trigger mode, it will continually sample sounds but will keep throwing the samples away until their amplitude reaches the trigger level. The sampler will then begin to store the samples, as well as the few samples from the signal it received a few milliseconds before the trigger level was reached. In this way, the sampler will ignore most background sounds that precede the wanted sound, but also will not forget to include the very soft sounds at the very beginning of the attack of the wanted sound. (Courtesy of Digidesign, Inc.)

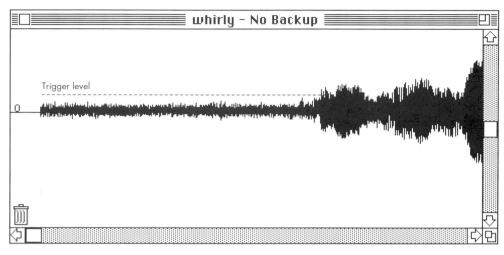

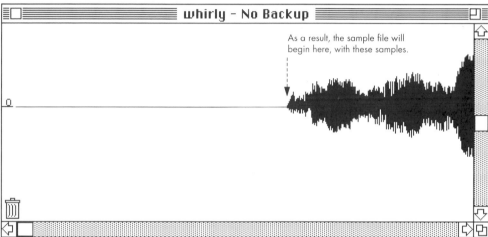

If the sounds that are selected for sampling are protected by copyright, as is the case with sounds on commercial recordings, film soundtracks, and radio or television broadcasts, it is not only unethical but also illegal to sample them without the written permission of the copyright owner. The process of identifying the owner begins with locating the copyright notice that is required to be included somewhere in the material (or on the packaging). Further assistance may be obtained from a reference librarian, audiovisual resource staff person, or from the office of a music industry association. When you become vastly rich and famous yourself, you will be glad that you have attended to these ethical concerns and have provided yourself with some degree of immunity from legal problems with major corporations in the entertainment industry (not to mention nuisance lawsuits from the envious, but clearly inferior musicians you encountered as you made your way to the top!).

IMPORTANT TERMS

analog recording
digital recording
samples
ADC, or analog-to-digital
  converter
DAC, or digital-to-analog
  converter
PCM processor
DAT recorder

hard-disk recording
AES/EBU
S/PDIF
digital sound sampler
sampler module
multisampling
looping
sample player

FOR FURTHER READING

de Furia, Steve, and Scacciaferro, Joe. *The Sampling Book*. Pompton Lakes, NJ:
  Third Earth, 1987.
Fryer, Terry. *A Practical Approach to Digital Sampling.* Milwaukee: Hal Leonard,
  1989.
Howe, Hubert S., Jr. *Electronic Music Synthesis.* New York: Norton, 1975.
Pohlmann, Ken C. *Principles of Digital Audio.* 2d ed. Indianapolis: Howard W.
  Sams, 1989.

CHAPTER 4

MULTIPLE-TRACK RECORDING AND MIXING

*M*any compositions of electroacoustic music include sounds from a variety of sources sounding together. The combination of these several sources into a single recording in the studio is usually accomplished by the use of multiple-track tape recorders and mixers. Many of the details and techniques of using these devices are described in this chapter. Because their most effective use depends upon an acquaintance with additional concepts of acoustics, however, it may be useful first to pursue a short review.

THE SCIENCE OF SOUND, PART II: MUSIC IN SPACE

Sound waves move through the air at a velocity of approximately 1130 feet per second. The length of each wave is the distance between one compression of air molecules and the next one. This **wavelength** can be determined by dividing the distance the sound travels each second by the number of waves generated each second to fill this distance (that is, the frequency of the sound):

$$\lambda = \frac{v}{f}$$

where λ (*lambda*) = the wavelength in feet
v = the velocity of sound in air ($\approx$ 1130 ft./sec.)
f = the frequency of the sound

The wavelength of a 30-Hz sound is approximately 37 feet 8 inches. A sound with a frequency of 13,560 Hz has a wavelength of 1 inch. A musical instrument producing a frequency of A-440 is generating waves of sound that are nearly 2 feet 7 inches in length.

The size of these waves has a great deal to do with the construction of musical instruments and the design of stereo components, among other things. For instance, the size of a piano's sounding board relates to its effectiveness as a radiator of low frequencies. Because the generation of a wave of low-frequency sound involves the motion of a relatively large volume of air, a piano with a larger soundboard, such as a nine-foot concert grand, will produce low tones of better quality than a piano with a smaller soundboard, such as a four-foot upright spinet.

When the cloth grille on the front of a loudspeaker is removed, two or three circular components of various diameters are revealed. The smallest of these, called the **tweeter,** is optimally designed for the reproduction of frequencies with short wavelengths. The largest component is called a **woofer** and is designed to push a much larger volume of air, as required for the reproduction of low-frequency sounds with long wavelengths.

In fact, most of the power of a stereo amplifier is used for the reproduction of low frequencies by the woofer of the loudspeaker. Thus, a more powerful stereo amplifier (one with a rating of hundreds of watts per channel) would be more likely to deal effectively with the reproduction of a recording of music performed on the grand piano; with an inadequate amplifier or loudspeaker, it would be just as well if the recording were made using an upright piano.

The size of the waves also has much to do with how sound interacts with the contents and boundaries of a given space. If the wavelength is greater than the size of an object, the sound will tend to bend around it, or diffract, much as an ocean wave washes around a swimmer. Low-frequency sounds, therefore, are more likely to find their way around the shadows and recesses of a space. Because of this **diffraction,** we are able to hear a sound even when we do not have a direct line of sight to the object producing the sound (see Figure 4.1).

Sounds that are not able to bend around an obstacle—for example, those in an enclosed space such as a room—are partially absorbed and partially reflected by the barrier. Thus, when a wave of sound encounters a wall, some of the energy of the wave will be absorbed by the wall, and the remainder will be reflected as a somewhat weaker wave traveling back from the wall. The amount of **absorption** and the amount of **reflection** depend upon the nature of the material on the wall. Hard surfaces, such as brick or polished stone, absorb little sound; most of the sound is reflected. Wooden panels absorb more sound, but nevertheless reflect most of the sound they receive.

Curtains, drapes, and carpets absorb quite a bit of sound, however. In particular, sounds with short wavelengths—higher frequencies—tend to become trapped or scattered by the fibers of carpets and the folds of curtains. Thus, when a loudspeaker is placed on the floor on a deep carpet, the bass frequencies become relatively more prominent as many of the higher frequencies are absorbed by the carpet.

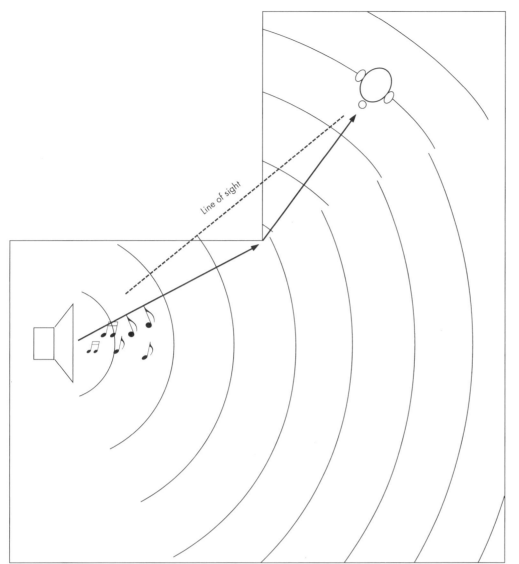

Line of sight

Because of their ability to diffract around obstacles and to avoid absorption, and because of the greater amount of energy often required to produce them, lower frequencies carry well over distance. The sounds heard from a faraway stereo system are those of the bass instruments—the kick drum and bass guitar (and maybe even a tuba or bass clarinet). The frequencies of the higher instruments do not survive the journey nearly as well.

RESONANCE

The frequencies at which an object is likely to vibrate are determined largely by the mass and the dimensions of the object. Such an object may be a piece of furniture, a part of a musical instrument, or even the air in an

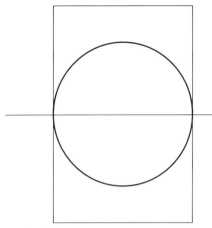

a. After the first quarter-cycle, a compression reaches the side walls and is reflected. Reflection shifts the phase of a wave by 180°, and the compression becomes a rarefaction.

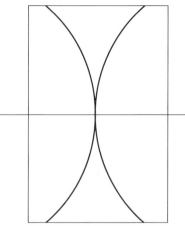

b. A quarter-cycle later, the two reflections are back at the center of the room, where they meet and interfere constructively with each other, and also with the rarefaction now being emitted by the original source of the sound.

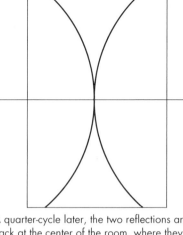

c. After a third-quarter cycle, the reflections reach the opposite walls and reflect again, shifting 180° and becoming compressions.

d. After one complete cycle, the reflections are back at the center of the room, where they again reinforce each other, and also reinforce the next compression being emitted by the source.

FIGURE 4.2
Establishment of a standing wave. When a wave is emitted with a length that is twice the width of the room, the points of constructive and destructive interference among the wave and its reflections appear to remain stationary. The balance of frequencies in a sound heard at such a point can be noticeably affected if the possibility of standing waves in a space is not recognized and acoustically remedied.

enclosed space (as in an organ pipe or a wind instrument). Whenever such an object is subject to externally produced vibrations at one of these frequencies, it will begin to vibrate sympathetically, thus reinforcing the vibration. This is the phenomenon known as **resonance.**

Related to the concept of resonance is the notion of a **standing wave.** After a sound has reflected from a wall or another boundary in an enclosed space, the wave is likely to be reflected again as it encounters the opposite boundary. This reflected wave will then pass by the source of the sound once again. If the compression of this reflected wave coincides with a compression currently being generated by the source (that is, if the reflected wave and the yet-to-be-reflected wave are in phase), then they will interfere constructively with one another and a standing wave is created (see Figure 4.2). The wavelength of this standing wave, a room resonance, is twice the distance between the two boundaries. All frequencies that are whole-number multiples of this resonant frequency will also be resonant.

The phenomena of resonance are very important to acousticians and architects as they design concert halls and studios that respond well to the frequencies of sound within the range of human hearing. The objective is to design rooms that do not "color" the sound by objectionably favoring or neglecting particular bands of frequencies.

Resonance is also important to understanding how the characteristic sounds of musical instruments (including the voice) are produced. For example, although the sound of a violin originates from the strings, the character, or "quality," of the sound is determined largely by the resonances of the body of the instrument. The cavities within the instrument have their own resonant frequencies. The wooden pieces of the instrument also have unique resonances (in fact, the resonances of the front and back are slightly different because the two pieces are made of different wood, meaning that the speed of sound within each of them will be slightly different).

The character of the sound of the human voice is substantially determined by the resonances of the vocal tract, including the throat, sinuses, and mouth. Lifting the jaw and tongue and spreading the sides of the mouth creates the high-frequency resonances necessary to produce the vowel sound *ee* (go ahead and try it—it works!). Dropping the jaw and tongue and rounding the mouth establishes the lower-frequency resonances necessary for the vowel sound *oh*.

Resonance, then, is a subject of great importance to understanding the behavior of sound in the small spaces of musical instruments as well as in the large spaces of concert halls. One of the most satisfying aesthetic experiences occurs when the characteristics of a fine musical instrument are matched by those of a superbly designed performance space.

REVERBERATION

The sounds produced by a musical instrument radiate in all directions (although high frequencies tend to radiate most strongly to the front of an instrument, whereas low frequencies, with their somewhat greater ability to diffract around the instrument, are more truly omnidirectional). Some of the sound will travel directly to the listener. The strength of this direct sound is inversely proportional to the distance between the instrument and the listener—the greater the distance, the weaker the direct sound will be.

Some of the sound from the instrument will reflect off one of the side walls before it reaches the listener. Other reflections will arrive from the other side wall, the rear wall, the ceiling, the floor, and the backside of the stage. Because these reflections have traveled greater distances, they will reach the listener somewhat later than the direct sound (see Figure 4.3). Such early reflections provide the listener with important clues about the location of the musical instrument on the stage. With several instruments

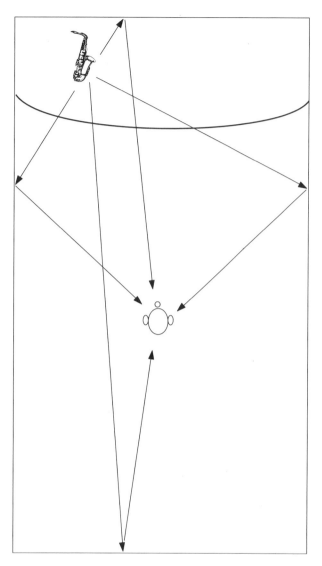

FIGURE 4.3
Paths taken by a few of the first reflected sounds to reach the listener. Note that each of these has been reflected only once. Next, the listener will begin to hear reflections of these reflections.

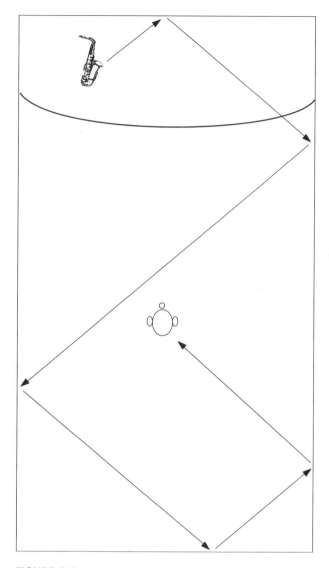

FIGURE 4.4
After many more reflections, this portion of the sound finally reaches the listener.

on stage, each providing clues to its location from its own unique set of direct sound with early reflections, it becomes possible for the listener to begin to appreciate the spatial depth and breadth of the musical ensemble. A good stereo recording will attempt to remain faithful to such subtle but crucial information in order to recreate the "ambience" of the performance space.

Meanwhile, the waves of early reflections continue to move across the room and are reflected again. Still other waves will reach the listener only after being reflected several times. For example, some of the sound of the instrument will reflect from the panel at the rear of the stage to the side wall, then to the opposite side wall, then to the rear wall, then to the side wall, and finally to the listener (see Figure 4.4).

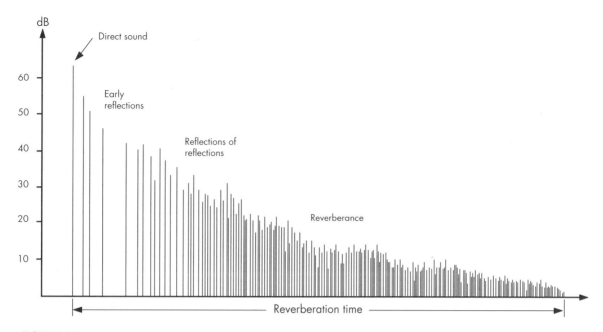

FIGURE 4.5

A typical pattern of sound reflections in a reverberation. Reflections of sound that are heard by the listener are represented by vertical bars on the graph. The intensity of the reflections is indicated by the height of the bars. The arrival time of the reflection is indicated by the position of the bar on the horizontal axis, from left to right.

Soon the room is filled with the sound of reflected waves and reflections of reflected waves. This is the **reverberation** of the sound. Each time a wave is reflected, however, some of its energy is absorbed by the reflecting surface. After several bouts of reflection, the energy of the waves will be greatly diminished. The interval of time during which the intensity of the reverberation drops to 60 dB below its initial level is called the **reverberation time** (see Figure 4.5).

The two most significant factors that determine reverberation time are the dimensions of the room and the amount of sound absorption by the surfaces in the room. In a very large room with hard, flat walls, such as the sanctuary of a cathedral, the waves have greater distances—and, therefore, take more time—to travel between reflections. Further, since very little energy is absorbed during each reflection, the waves can make many more trips before their intensity is finally extinguished. Such a room, with a long reverberation time, is often described as "wet." In contrast, a small room with thick drapes, deep carpet, and overstuffed furniture has a very short reverberation time. A room such as this is described as "dry"—even "dead"!

SOUND LOCALIZATION

A listener's ability to discern whether a sound is coming from the left, the right, or directly ahead derives primarily from the simple fact that people have ears on both sides of the head. Thus, for example, a sound coming

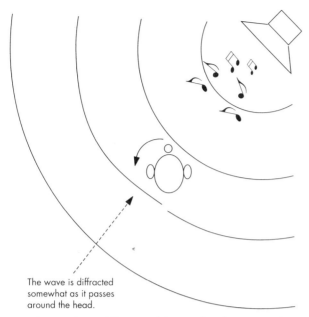

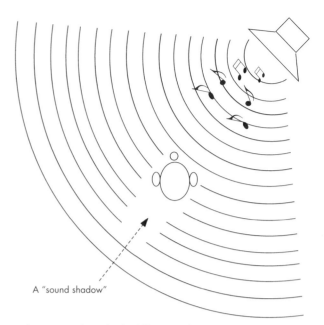

The wave is diffracted somewhat as it passes around the head.

A "sound shadow"

a. Interaural time difference: if the wavelength is greater than the size of the head, then a sound will be heard in the close ear before it is heard in the other ear.

b. Interaural amplitude difference: if the wavelength is less than the size of the head, then a sound will be heard as louder in the close ear because the head will block these higher frequencies from reaching the other ear.

from the right will first reach the right ear. If the wavelength of the sound is somewhat greater than the size of the listener's head (which is true for frequencies up to approximately 1000 Hz or so), the sound will diffract around the head until it reaches the other ear. It will take no more than .9 millisecond for the sound to travel this additional distance, but the brain nonetheless notes the difference in arrival times and from this information, called the **interaural time difference,** determines the angle from which the sound is coming (see Figure 4.6a).

For higher frequencies, with wavelengths considerably smaller than the size of the head (at least 2000 Hz), there is very little diffraction of sound around the head. If a sound is coming from one side, the head actually blocks much of the sound from reaching the other ear. This other ear is thus in a "sound shadow." The brain compares the higher intensity received by one ear to the lower intensity received by the other ear and again is able to determine, from this **interaural amplitude difference,** the angle from which the sound is coming (see Figure 4.6b).

Most sounds contain both low and high frequencies, enabling the ears and brain to use both techniques of lateral localization together. However, when music is reproduced through a pair of loudspeakers, it is difficult to maintain the interaural difference in arrival times of low frequencies unless the listener remains in place at a spot equidistant from the two speakers (the sweet spot). If the listener moves even a single head's width closer to one loudspeaker, this can offset any time difference between the sounds coming from the two speakers.

For this reason, the primary technique in studio music for creating or recreating the illusion of lateral sound placement is to adjust the amplitude

FIGURE 4.6
Perceptual techniques for the lateral localization of the source of a sound.

balance between channels, thus simulating the interaural amplitude differences that occur with high frequencies. If it is desired that an instrument seem to be placed to the left, for example, then more of the amplitude of the signal for that instrument will be directed to the left loudspeaker, and much less to the right loudspeaker. If it is desired that the instrument seem to be placed halfway between the loudspeakers, then the amplitude of the signal for this instrument will be distributed evenly to each loudspeaker. Further description of this particular technique for sound placement is provided later in this chapter, in the section on mixing.

As described previously, the early reflections of a sound provide the listener with important clues about the location of the source of the sound in the room. The directions from which these early reflections arrive, as determined from interaural time and amplitude differences, as well as their arrival times, provide additional information about the lateral placement of the sources (that is, whether they are to the left, to the right, or directly ahead of the listener). This information can also provide significant clues regarding the distance between the listener and the source of the sound.

Perhaps the most important clue for judging the distance to the source of a sound, however, is the balance between the direct and reverberant sound that is heard. While the intensity of directly received sound decreases with increasing distance, the level of reverberation, which is fairly uniform throughout a space, remains the same. Thus, a person seated close to the stage in a concert hall will hear a higher proportion of direct to reverberant sound, while a person seated near the back of the hall will most likely hear more reverberant than direct sound. In a recording studio, where a number of devices are available to simulate reverberation, the engineer takes great care when adjusting the mix of "dry" (direct) and "wet" (reverberant) sound so that a satisfactory illusion of the depth of the performance space is maintained (this technique is described in greater detail later in this chapter).

The distance to the source of a sound can also be judged by the apparent loudness of the sound, particularly if the sound is a familiar one. A musical instrument played loudly tends to sound brighter—the higher frequencies in the sound are more prominent. For example, imagine being in a room with a saxophone being played loudly; in addition to a high level of intensity, the sound is rather bright. Next, imagine that the saxophone is being played softly; it produces a sound that is less intense and somewhat more mellow. Now imagine a distant saxophone being played loudly; the sound will be less intense but will still be bright (even allowing for the relative attenuation of higher frequencies over distance). Because of the relative brightness of the distant sound, few listeners will confuse the distant saxophone with the close but mellow saxophone, even though the received levels of intensity may be the same for both. We know that the distant saxophone must be loud because it is bright; but because it does not sound very loud to us, we conclude that it must be far away.

Changes in the distance between a source of sound and a listener can be cued by a subtle change in the frequency of the sound. As a source of

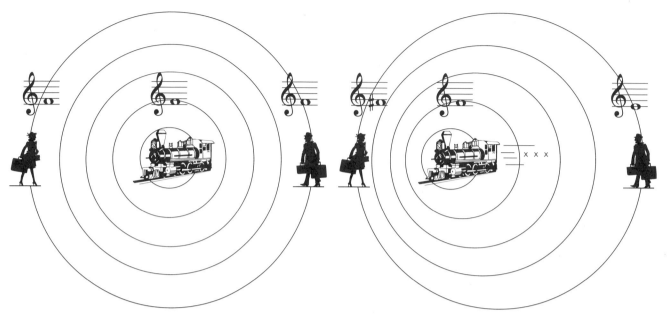

a. When a train at rest blows its whistle, the same pitch is heard by a person ahead of the train, on the train, and behind the train.

b. When the train is in motion, the wavelengths of the sound that travel ahead of the train are shortened, and the wavelengths that travel away to the rear of the train are lengthened.

FIGURE 4.7
The Doppler effect.

sound moves toward a listener, the distance between the wave currently being emitted and the wave previously emitted will be shortened by the distance the source has moved during that period of time. Thus, the wavelengths are shortened. The listener will hear these shorter wavelengths as being of a somewhat higher frequency. If the approaching source of sound then moves past the listener and recedes into the distance, the wavelengths will be lengthened by the increase of distance during the time each succeeding wave is emitted. As a result, the apparent frequency will be lower than what would be heard if the source were stationary (or if the listener were traveling along with the source).

This apparent change in frequency, resulting from the relative motion between a source and a receiver, is called the **Doppler effect** (see Figure 4.7). It is not normally a factor in performances with conventional, acoustic instruments (even a marching band careening at top speed cannot produce a noticeable Doppler shift in pitch), but it can become a significant element with synthesized or electronically manipulated sound that is distributed among loudspeakers. The Doppler effect can be simulated in this type of situation to create an illusion of movement by the sounds.

By noting the difference in the time a sound arrives at each ear or the difference in intensity of a sound as heard by each ear, by noting the directions from which early reflections come and their arrival times, by noting the balance between direct and reverberant sound, and by comparing the intensity of a sound with an estimate of its actual loudness—from all of this information, combined with that provided by our eyes, we are able to judge fairly accurately the location of a source of sound. In addition, subtle changes in pitch due to the Doppler effect can tell us if the location is

STEREO RECORDING

A stereo recording is in fact two recordings of the same source that differ in ways that correspond to the subtle differences in how each of our ears hears a sound. To recreate successfully a sense of the breadth of a sound field there will necessarily be differences in intensity, and perhaps even differences in phase, between how the sound is recorded on each of the two tracks.

If the capsules of the two microphones (most likely cardioid microphones) are placed together and aimed in directions that are between 90° and 135° apart, then differences in intensity will account for all of the stereo differences between channels. Phasing will not be a problem, because waves of sound arrive at both microphones at the same time (see Figure 4.8a). This technique is called X-Y coincident miking.

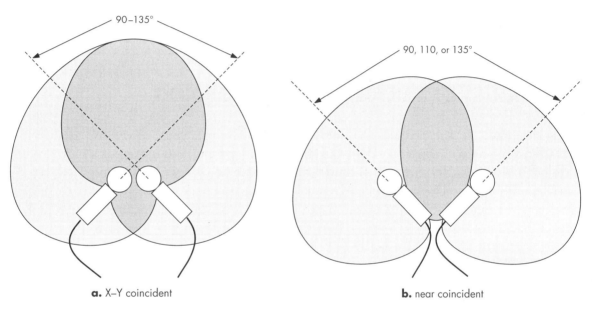

a. X–Y coincident   **b.** near coincident

FIGURE 4.8
Common microphone position-
ing for stereo recording.

However, if the capsules of the two microphones are separated by a few inches, and the two microphones are aimed in directions that are typically 90°, 110°, or 135° apart, then some phase differences will also be detected, because of the separation of the two microphone capsules. Waves of sounds originating from the left or the right will arrive at each microphone at a slightly different time. As a consequence, the stereo image will be somewhat more spacious. This technique is described as near-coincident miking (see Figure 4.8b).

In stereo recording it can be somewhat problematic to separate the microphones by more than 12 inches. First, there may be difficult phasing problems, as sounds reach each microphone at different times and the resulting signals manifest noticeably destructive interference at particular frequencies. Second, there may be a problem with detecting a sufficient level of amplitude from the middle of the musical group being recorded, in the region where the field patterns of the two microphones are weaker. A good, well-trained pair of ears is needed to make such wide microphone spacing successful.

becoming closer or more remote. This perceptual process is going on every waking moment and has been in place since the earliest months of our lives; research suggests that by the age of 12 months an infant has already acquired much of this repertoire of techniques for discerning the direction and distance of sounds. The "computer between our ears" is quite remarkable in its ability to handle these tasks.

The challenge for an electroacoustic musician is to preserve or recapture the marvelous and complex behaviors of sound in space that are perceived so effectively by the human ears and mind. This must be done while recording and mixing music that will be reproduced by a fixed pair of somewhat less than perfect loudspeakers. Illusion becomes an inevitable and indispensable part of this task. But before there can be illusion, there must be its prerequisite—technique. Success depends upon thorough familiarity with the tools being used to produce and reproduce the music.

TECHNIQUES OF MULTIPLE-TRACK RECORDING

Many tape recorders are capable of recording and playing several channels of audio signals from separate tracks on the recording tape. The more common of these **multiple-track,** or **multitrack, recorders** are four- or eight-track machines, but 16- and 24-track recorders are also fairly prevalent, particularly in larger studios. Digital multiple-track recorders that are relatively affordable and easy to use (such as the one shown in Figure 4.9) have recently become available as well.

The multiple-track recorder is one of those technological developments that has had a radical effect on the production of music in our culture. With the multitrack recorder, it is no longer necessary that all of the parts of a composition be performed by a group of musicians gathered together. Instead, different parts can be recorded at different times, with individual musicians scheduled to come to the studio on different days (even different weeks) to record their individual tracks. Or an individual artist, working alone, might record all of the tracks, one or two at a time—with the combined result of such an effort being the illusion of a group of musicians playing together.

FIGURE 4.9
A relatively affordable digital multiple-track recorder. (ADAT is a registered trademark of and is used with the permission of Alesis Corporation.)

Even when a group of musicians is actually brought together in the same place at the same time to play the same piece of music, multiple-track recording offers creative possibilities. If the work of these musicians is stored on separate tracks, there will be further opportunities to shape and combine their performances in a variety of ways even after they have finished their work and left the studio. Several techniques have been developed over the years to facilitate such wizardry.

If more than one musician is being recorded at the same time, it is desirable that the sound of each be isolated as much as possible. Particularly loud instruments, such as drums, might be placed in a different room entirely, or in an isolation booth. For instruments that can be placed in the same room, microphones with cardioid or bidirectional field patterns are likely to be selected, and each musician is positioned so that he or she is in the less sensitive areas of the fields of the other microphones nearby. Placing the microphones close to the instruments also makes it easier to maintain a degree of isolation between different musicians.

Whenever more than one microphone is being used in the same space, it is important to consider the possible phase relationships that might be established as a sound reaches each microphone. As illustrated in Figure 4.10, some frequencies in a sound might arrive out of phase at a more distant microphone, and if this signal is ever combined with the signal from the closer microphone, destructive interference will result in at least partial cancellation of these frequencies. Of course, the more distant the other microphone, the weaker will be the sound that reaches it, and the cancellation will be correspondingly less serious. A common guideline, called the 3:1 rule, is that a microphone intended for another instrument should be placed no closer than three times the distance between the first microphone and its intended source (see Figure 4.11).

Because the instruments are intentionally isolated from one another in a multitrack recording session, it will be necessary to mix the microphone signals together so that the musicians can monitor one another through headphones. In this way, each musician can receive the necessary cues from the other musicians so as to know what and when to play. The operation of such a cue monitor system is described more completely later in this chapter, in the section on audio mixing.

When more than one musician is being recorded at a time on separate tracks, sound isolation among the instruments is perhaps the biggest problem to be addressed. However, if the musicians record their tracks at different times, or if an individual musician records each track one at a time, then sound isolation is not a problem at all. The technique of recording new tracks while monitoring material recorded previously on other tracks is called **overdubbing.** This process, of course, presents its own set of challenges.

For example, musicians who play together in a group can observe one another's physical movements in order to anticipate entrances, chord changes, and similar events. Such visual cues are missing when the other

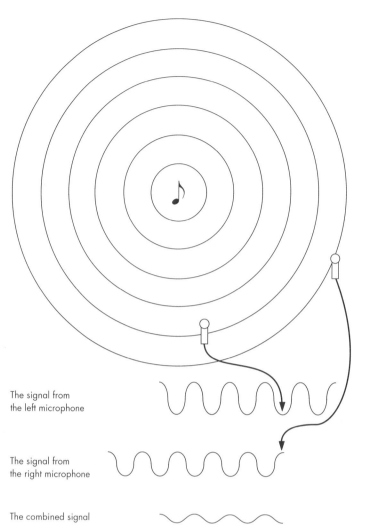

FIGURE 4.10
Two microphones, placed apart, will most likely produce phase cancellation of some frequencies. (Because the right microphone is slightly farther from the source, the amplitude of its signal is slightly smaller; therefore, the phase cancellation is not total.)

The signal from the left microphone

The signal from the right microphone

The combined signal

sounds are coming from prerecorded tracks. Several techniques can be used to compensate for this loss, at least in part, and to facilitate the synchronization of the material on different tracks.

If the music has parts that have a strong pulse, or beat, it is advisable to record these first so that they can serve as a reference for the rhythms of the later tracks. For instance, with a jazz or rock piece, the drums might be recorded first. The string bass or bass guitar might be recorded next (or might even be recorded at the same time, but on different tracks from the drums), followed by other "rhythm" instruments, such as the piano or guitar.

Sometimes a **click track,** or cue track, is recorded first to provide a rhythmic reference. This track might consist of a recording of a metronome, a drum machine, or someone clapping hands at regular intervals. It is probably a good idea as well to record a count-off (such as "one, two, ready, go!") on the cue track to indicate to the musician in the studio when the music is to begin on the recorded tracks. Similarly, it is recommended

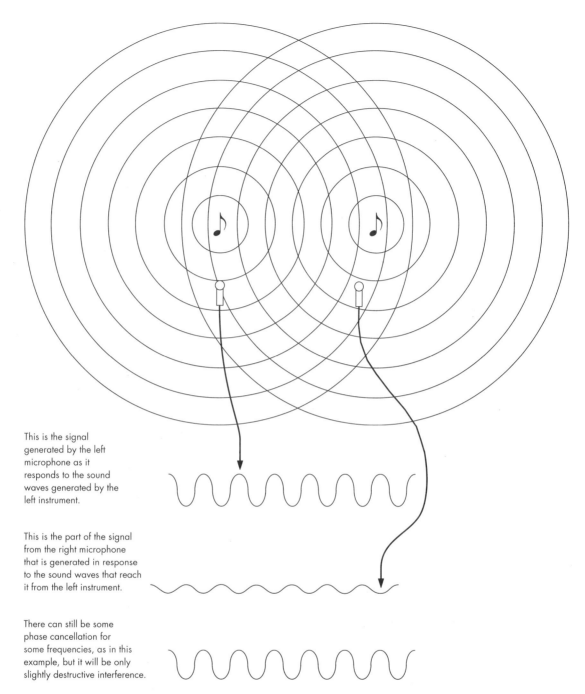

This is the signal generated by the left microphone as it responds to the sound waves generated by the left instrument.

This is the part of the signal from the right microphone that is generated in response to the sound waves that reach it from the left instrument.

There can still be some phase cancellation for some frequencies, as in this example, but it will be only slightly destructive interference.

FIGURE 4.11
Placing two microphones according to the 3:1 rule. The amplitude of the second signal is much weaker because the right microphone is more than three times farther from the left instrument than the left microphone is. Some phase cancellation of some frequencies is still possible, but it will be slight.

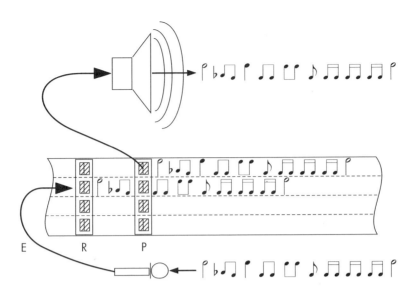

FIGURE 4.12
Recording out of sync. Here the material previously recorded on track 1 is being played from the playback head. A musician is monitoring this playback and is singing along into the microphone. The microphone signal is then recorded on track 2. Even though the sing-along may seem to the musician to be in sync, it is actually being recorded a bit later on the tape than the corresponding material on track 1.

that a reference pitch (most likely A-440) be recorded so that the instruments used on various tracks can at least begin in tune with one another.

Another potential problem for overdubbing derives from the fact that a tape is recorded by one head but usually played back by another head that is at least an inch farther down the tape path. If a musician monitors a previously recorded track from the playback head while recording a new track through the record head, there will be a lag of at least an inch or so on the tape between corresponding rhythmic points on each track. This will be heard as a delay in the second track when both tracks are played back later (see Figure 4.12).[1]

To solve this problem, virtually all multiple-track tape decks include a **sync** feature that enables those portions of the record head used to record previous tracks to be used temporarily to play back those tracks. Meanwhile, another portion of the record head simultaneously records the new track. Thus, the previous tracks are monitored from the record head while a new track is being recorded at the same point on the tape (see Figure 4.13). This feature is known as **selective synchronization,** or Sel-Sync™ (a registered trademark of the Ampex Corporation).

Crosstalk can be a particular problem with multiple-track recorders, since there are many tracks side by side on a given width of tape. Loud sounds with sharp transients, such as drum hits, are especially prone to leak into adjacent tracks. The potential damage can be minimized by recording such sounds on an outer track of the tape (see Figure 2.4). Drums, for example, are usually recorded on track 1.

On 16- and 24-track recorders, it is often possible to record several versions of a musical part. For example, alternate versions of an improvised solo might be recorded on several different tracks, and the final version of

---

1. For some applications, however, this delay is regarded not as a problem but as an opportunity (see "Tape Echo Techniques," later in this chapter).

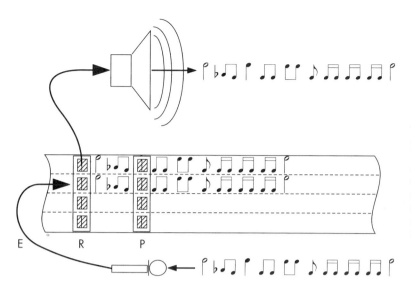

FIGURE 4.13
Selective synchronization. Here the part of the record head that is designated for track 1 is temporarily being used to play back the material previously recorded on track 1. A musician is monitoring this playback and is singing along into the microphone. This time, however, not only does the sing-along sound in sync to the musician, but it is also being recorded on track 2 on a segment of tape that corresponds exactly to that of the recording on track 1.

the solo might be a composite of the best passages from each. This is quite a luxury, however. More often the problem is what to do as the number of empty tracks begins to run out. One solution to this scarcity is the technique of **bouncing,** or ping-ponging. Material on several tracks can be mixed down to one track, thus freeing the other, previously used tracks for new material. Later, as the tracks begin to fill up again, the previously bounced material can be bounced again, together with the newly recorded tracks, so that even more new material can be recorded.

There are a couple of disadvantages to this technique, however. Once tracks have been bounced together, it is impossible to separate them for the final mixdown. The relationships of signal level can no longer be changed. Furthermore, every time tracks are bounced together, the tape hiss on each of them is also bounced. Thus, a significant amount of noise can begin to accumulate.[2]

Editing a multiple-track tape by cutting and splicing is difficult, and probably not even feasible if there is recorded material on one or more tracks that cannot be disturbed or interrupted. Nonetheless, it may be desirable to alter or correct a passage on one of the tracks. One way to do this, without resorting to the use of a razor blade that will cut across all tracks, is simply to re-record the passage without disturbing the passages that immediately precede it and follow it on the track.

However, when the machine is switched into the record mode so that a passage on a previously recorded track can be re-recorded, there will be a short segment of tape, between the erase and record heads, that will not have been satisfactorily treated by the erase head. Likewise, at the end of the passage that has been re-recorded, where the record mode is switched off, there will be a short segment of tape that has been erased but has not

---

2. Also, when bouncing a track to an adjacent track, there is the possibility of feedback caused by crosstalk from the newly recorded track to the adjacent track being bounced.

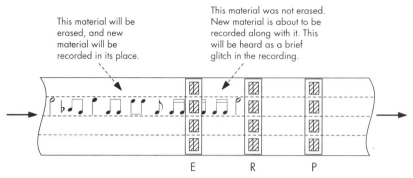

This material will be erased, and new material will be recorded in its place.

This material was not erased. New material is about to be recorded along with it. This will be heard as a brief glitch in the recording.

E   R   P

a. Beginning of a passage being re-recorded

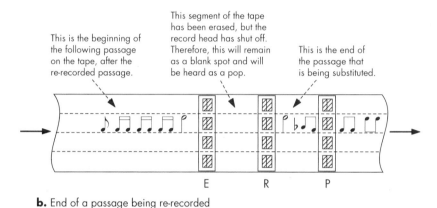

This is the beginning of the following passage on the tape, after the re-recorded passage.

This segment of the tape has been erased, but the record head has shut off. Therefore, this will remain as a blank spot and will be heard as a pop.

This is the end of the passage that is being substituted.

E   R   P

b. End of a passage being re-recorded

FIGURE 4.14
Re-recording a passage can result in glitches and pops at the beginning and end. Punch-in/punch-out techniques have been developed to avoid these noises.

yet been affected by the record head (see Figure 4.14). These brief segments that have been incompletely erased or recorded are often heard as clicks or pops in the recording.

To address this problem, many multiple-track tape decks include a feature called insert recording, or **punch-in/punch-out.** The beginning of the passage to be re-recorded is electronically marked as the punch-in point; the end of the passage is marked as the punch-out point. The tape is rewound and played, so that the musician can hear and perhaps even play along with the previously recorded track. In this way, the musician is better prepared to jump in with the new material for the passage to be re-recorded (also, this gives the motors of the recorder a chance to stabilize so that the new material will be recorded at the proper tape speed).

Just before the punch-in point, the erase head smoothly switches on. At the punch-in point, the record head switches on, and the old material is replaced by new material. At the punch-out point, the erase head smoothly switches off, followed by the record head. Thus, a seamless insertion of newly recorded material is made on a previously recorded track.

Often, at the initial stages of a multiple-track recording project, a track is used to record a synchronization signal that can later be used to provide extended capabilities. The most common type of synchronization signal is the one that represents **SMPTE time code.** SMPTE (pronounced "simpty") is an acronym for the Society of Motion Picture and Television Engineers, an organization that developed this form of time coding to facilitate the production of television and other video programming. A SMPTE time code signal is an audio signal, so that it can be magnetically recorded, that provides a continuous stream of information marking the passage of time on the tape. The information includes, among other things, the hour, minute, second, and frame (a subdivision of the second).

One application of such a signal is to facilitate synchronizing an audio recording to a video recording. The SMPTE signal can also be used to synchronize two multiple-track recorders, thus nearly doubling the total number of tracks available for a recording. Synchronization signals recorded on one track on each machine are compared by a device called a synchronizer. If deviations are detected, the tape speed on one or both machines can be adjusted, if the decks are suitably equipped, until the recordings are again synchronized.

Perhaps the most common application of a synchronization signal in a smaller studio is to synchronize a drum machine or MIDI sequencer to a multiple-track tape machine. Material generated by the drum machine or by synthesizers controlled by the sequencer can be synchronized with material previously recorded on tracks of the tape recorder, thus increasing the apparent resources of the studio. A more detailed description of this application is provided in Chapter 6.

A synchronization signal is comprised of high frequencies recorded at high levels. Therefore, to minimize the potential for crosstalk, the signal is usually recorded on the highest-numbered track of the recorder, and often the next-to-highest track is left blank to function as a buffer.

Here are a few additional hints and suggestions for multiple-track recording in general:

1. Record each track at an optimum signal level. The balance among the tracks can be adjusted later, during the mixdown. If a track should have to be boosted at that time, then the noise associated with that track (and the noise of the mixer input channel as well) will also be boosted. On the other hand, if a track should have to be reduced in level at the mixer, then the noise will also be reduced. Less noise is always a good thing; you can never get enough of less noise!

2. Do not add reverberation or other effects to a track as it is being recorded. Once such effects have been added, they cannot be removed. Just as with level balancing, the addition of effects and other signal processing is more appropriately a part of the mixing process.

3. Musical parts that are particularly important should be recorded on middle tracks. If recorded on outer tracks, at the edges of the tape, they could be damaged by a misaligned tape transport or by improper storage and handling.

TAPE ECHO TECHNIQUES

The distance that separates the record and playback heads provided the principal opportunity for the creation of echo effects in the earlier years of electroacoustic music. If the output of one channel on a tape deck was monitored from the playback head and patched to the input of another channel, the material from the first track could be re-recorded, with a delay, onto the other track (see Figure 4.15).

A series of echoes could be established if the output of this second track were monitored from the playback head and patched into and recorded on yet another track, and if the output

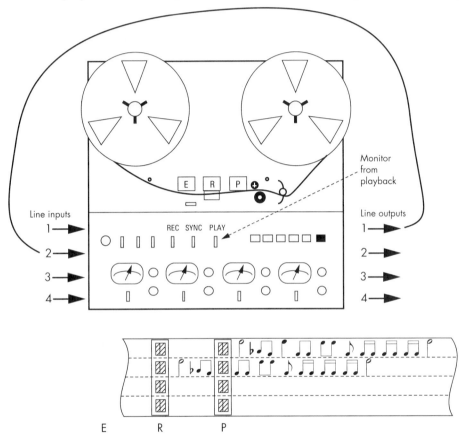

FIGURE 4.15
Recording a single echo.

ÉTUDE 4.1

Record a pattern with a strong beat (for example, hand-clapping or drumming) on one track of a four-track recorder. On the other three tracks, record patterns that are based on the same beat and synchronized to the beat track. Use a different source of sound on each track (for example, singing on one track, an instrument on another, and spoken words on another). This piece should be approximately one to three minutes in duration.

---

of this third track were patched into and recorded on a fourth track (see Figure 4.16). When these four tracks were subsequently played back, the sounds on the first track would be accompanied by three equally spaced echoes.

Figure 4.17 illustrates a technique for creating an endless series of echoes, at least in theory. The signal recorded on track 1 is monitored from the playback head and copied onto track 2. The echo on track 2 is monitored from the playback head and copied onto track 3. The echo on track 3 is monitored from the playback head and copied onto track 4. The output of track 4 is then mixed with the input to track 1, and the series of echoes moves once again across the tracks. The practical limitation of this technique is that each echo also includes the tape hiss

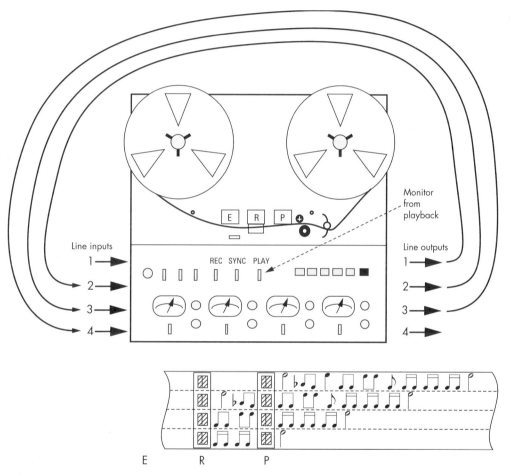

FIGURE 4.16
Recording a series of echoes.

ÉTUDE 4.2

Prepare four different tape loops. Play back each one separately, and record each of these on a separate track of a four-track recorder. Try to find ways to introduce slight variations to the repetitions of each loop (for example, volume fades or playback speed adjustments) as it is copied to the four-track tape. This piece should be approximately two to three minutes in duration.

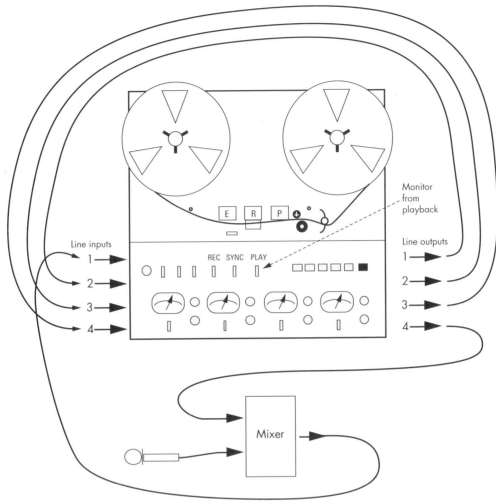

FIGURE 4.17
A recirculating series of echoes. The initial input
to this system is provided by a microphone.

copied from each of the preceding tracks, in addition to its own tape hiss. Eventually, the accumulated tape hiss overwhelms the sound itself.

The applications of these tape echo techniques, as they are called, have in recent years been largely taken up by digital echo devices, called digital delay lines. The tape techniques described here are nonetheless great fun, and should be tried at least once or twice.

MIXING

A piece of music produced in a studio for electroacoustic music might include sounds from several different sources—synthesizers, samplers, acoustic instruments, and voices—each recorded on a separate track of a multiple-track recorder. However, most studios have no more than four

FIGURE 4.18
A medium-sized audio mixer for a studio for electroacoustic music. (Courtesy of JBL Professional.)

loudspeakers (and probably no more than two in use at any particular moment) through which the music can be monitored. Consumer playback systems, including car and home stereos, can only monitor one or two channels of recorded music. Therefore, it is necessary to find a means by which the many channels of source material can be combined into one or two channels that can be heard through loudspeakers. This task is the basic function of an audio **mixer.**

Devices that are called mixers (or mixing consoles, or mixing boards) range in size and complexity from the microphone mixers used in PA systems to the room-size consoles installed in major, commercial recording studios. This discussion will focus on the functions and features of an intermediate-sized mixing board typically found in a studio for electroacoustic music.

Such a mixer includes input jacks for perhaps 8, 12, 16, or 24 different signals from microphones, synthesizers, tape recorders, and such. These inputs are then combined into 2 or 4 main outputs. A mixer with 16 inputs and 2 main outputs is described as a 16×2 mixer (this is read as "16 by 2"); a mixer with 24 inputs and 4 main outputs is described as a 24×4 mixer. Some mixers first combine the inputs into 4 or 8 group outputs, which are then combined into the 2 main outputs. A mixer with 24 inputs, 4 group outputs, and 2 main outputs is described as a $24 \times 4 \times 2$ mixer.

The jack for each input channel, together with the associated controls on the front panel, is referred to as an input module (see Figure 4.19). If the signal is coming from a microphone or direct box, then as it enters the input module it is first likely to encounter a preamplifier, which is used to boost the signal to line level. If the input signal is already a line-level signal—coming from a synthesizer or tape deck, for example—then it may first be necessary to attenuate it so that the preamplifier circuit does not overload. An input attenuation pad can provide 10 or 20 dB (or more) of reduction in the signal level when it is engaged, usually by a push button or dial on the front panel of the input module.

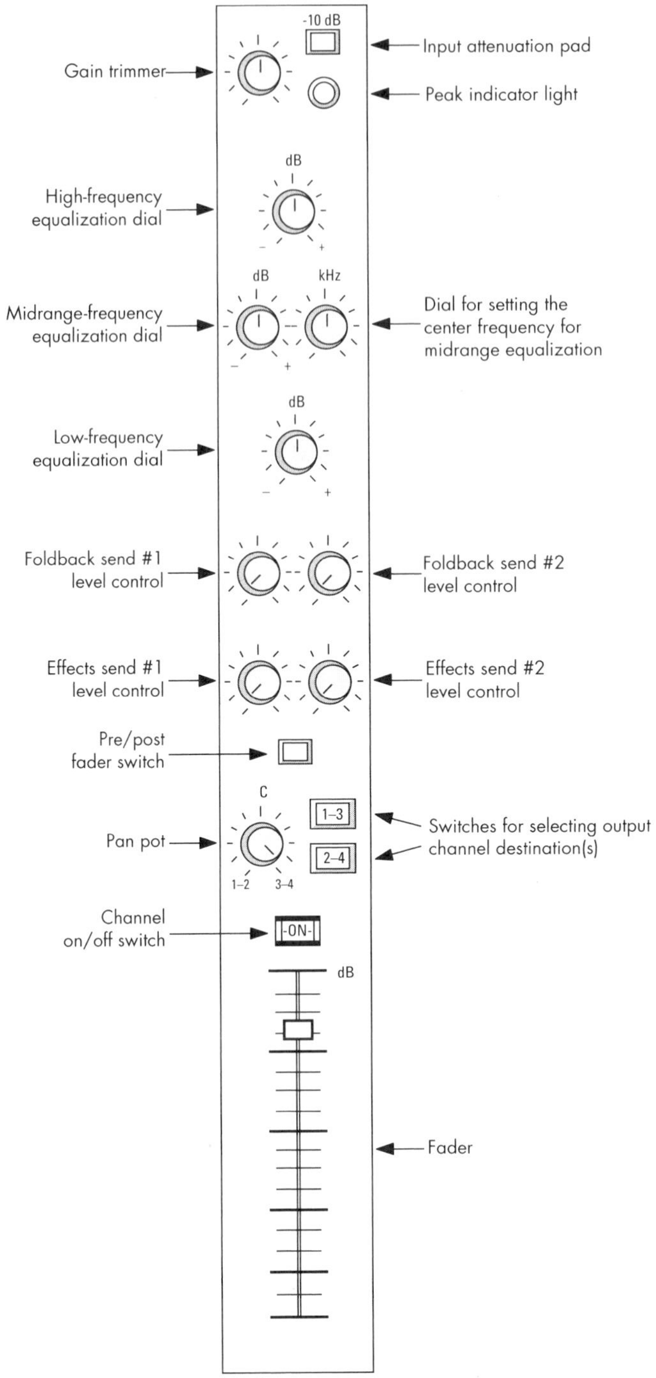

FIGURE 4.19
Typical controls on an input module of a mixer.

The gain of the preamplifier can then be adjusted by means of the gain trimmer dial (sometimes just called the gain or trim). Usually, a peak light is provided to indicate if the input signal is too strong. If the input signal overloads the preamplifier, then the signal will be distorted even before it gets very far into the mixing process. The gain trimmer should be turned down, therefore, until the peak indicator no longer lights. If the gain trimmer is then turned down just a bit more, this will be the optimal level of the input signal.

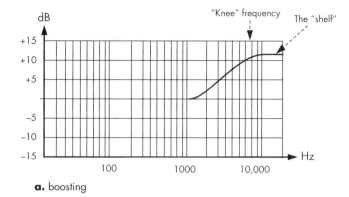

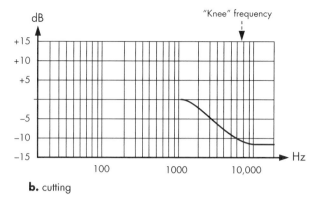

a. boosting

b. cutting

The next set of controls are used to adjust the relative strengths of the low, midrange, and high frequencies that make up the signal. The process of making these adjustments is called **equalization,** or **EQ.** A typical control for high frequencies can either boost them or attenuate (cut) them by as much as 15 dB. When high frequencies are boosted, the sound may become brighter or clearer; or the sound may seem raspy or shrill. Tape hiss and other noises may become unduly noticeable as well. The proper setting of the high-frequency equalization control is ultimately a matter of taste and judgment; it must be made in the context of any other adjustments made to the signal, as well as any adjustments made to the other signals going into the mixer.

It is helpful for the operator of a mixer to be aware of the pattern of the changes made by an equalization control. With a typical control for high-frequency equalization, for example, the change might begin with frequencies around 1 kHz, then slope to full effect at around 10 kHz or so, and flatten out with a more or less constant level of adjustment for still higher frequencies (see Figure 4.20a). Such a pattern of equalization is called **shelving.** Regardless of whether the frequencies are boost or cut, the same range of frequencies will be affected (see Figure 4.20b).

The equalization of low frequencies generally has a shelving pattern as well (see Figure 4.21). The slope may begin around 1 kHz, but the greatest effect will be heard with frequencies below the "knee" frequency of 100 Hz, where the "shelf" flattens out. These low frequencies can be boost or cut by as much as 15 dB. A boost to low frequencies can result in a warmer, more mellow sound; or it can give the sound a tubby, unfocused character. Furthermore, the rumblings of foot-tapping, microphone stand adjustments, and wind noises can become much more noticeable (as well as any 60-Hz electrical hum that finds its way into the signal). Again, taste and judgment are required to find the proper level of adjustment (if any) for the low-frequency contents of the signal.

The midrange equalization control most likely will affect the signal according to a pattern somewhat different from that of the controls for low- and high-frequency equalization. The boost or attenuation of a midrange control will slope to a frequency where the effect is greatest and then

FIGURE 4.20
Typical effects of a high-frequency equalization control.

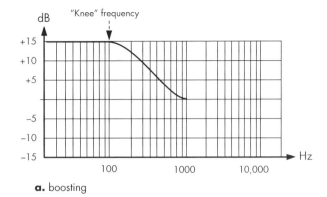

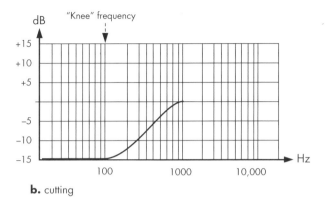

a. boosting

b. cutting

FIGURE 4.21
Typical effects of a control for
low-frequency equalization.

FIGURE 4.22
Midrange frequencies can be
boosted or attenuated, just as
low and high frequencies can.
The greatest effect occurs at
the "peak" frequency, which
can be adjusted by means of
the midrange-frequency dial.

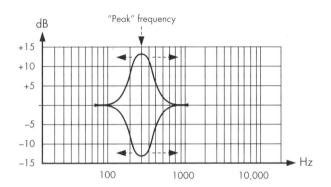

slope back to a point where there is no longer an effect. Such a pattern is
called **peaking** equalization (see Figure 4.22). In addition to the dial that
determines the amount of boost or cut at the peak frequency, many mixers
have a dial that makes it possible to adjust the location of the peak frequency itself. In this way, the peak can be tuned to the frequency where the
greatest effect is desired.

It is somewhat more difficult to generalize about the effects of equalization adjustments to midrange frequencies. One common technique with
musical textures that include a singing or speaking voice is to boost the frequencies that are produced by the voice between 2 kHz and 5 kHz in order
to enhance the clarity and intelligibility of the lyrics or text. Other input
channels that are receiving signals from instruments that produce frequencies in this range may have their midrange EQ cut correspondingly to give
further prominence to the "presence peak" of the vocal line. This is one
example of how the controls of a mixer can be used to enhance the textural
design of a passage of music: those musical elements with the greatest significance are brought a bit further into the foreground, while others are
nudged further into the background.

The overall level of the signal that goes from the input module to be
mixed with other signals is determined by the position of the fader on the
front of the module (or a rotary dial, as on many rack-mounted mixers

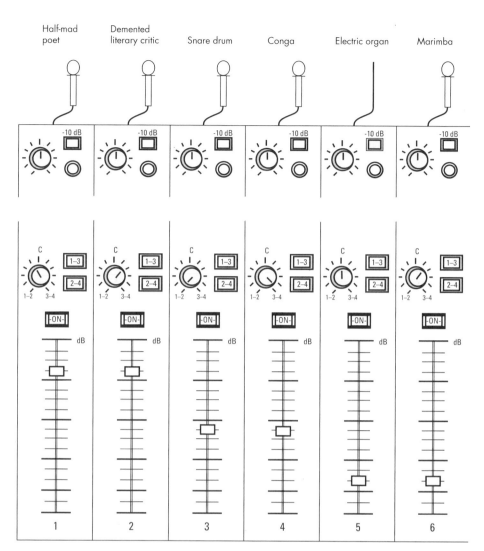

FIGURE 4.23
Setting fader levels helps determine the balance among the elements in a sonic texture.

Half-mad poet · Demented literary critic · Snare drum · Conga · Electric organ · Marimba

intended primarily for keyboard instruments). The balance of the intensity of this signal and the intensities of the signals that are processed by the other input channels on the mixer is determined by the relative positions of the faders on these modules. This provides a very important means to project the textural design of the music.

In Figure 4.23, for example, the chords played by the electric organ and the marimba are intended to serve as a background layer; therefore, the faders for these channels (numbers 5 and 6) are set relatively low. The incessant drumming of the conga and the snare drum is intended as a middle-ground layer, so the faders for these channels (numbers 3 and 4) are set a bit higher. The voices of the half-mad poet and the demented literary critic are the foreground of the texture, so the faders for these channels (numbers 1 and 2) are set at a level higher than those of the other four channels.

The signal from each input module is assigned a destination in one or more of the output channels (or output buses) of the mixer. This assignment is accomplished by the signal-routing controls on each input module. If there are only two output channels, then the signal-routing control is most likely to be a single dial called a **pan pot** (for "panoramic potentiometer"). If the pan pot is turned all the way to the left, fully counterclockwise, then the signal will be directed entirely to the left output channel. If the pan pot is turned all the way to the right, the signal will be directed fully to the right output channel. Intermediate settings of the pan pot will send proportionate amounts of the signal to each output. For example, if the pan pot is set at its midpoint, then the signal will be distributed equally between the two output channels. The sound will seem to come from a point midway between the two loudspeakers of a monitor system to which these output channels are connected.

Careful decisions are made regarding the setting of the pan pots for each input channel. In this way, the stereo image—the sense of lateral space of the music—is established and controlled. For example, bass instruments are usually placed in the center of the stereo field. One reason for this is that low frequencies, which diffract very easily, are more difficult for the ears to localize than high frequencies; therefore, there is not much point in trying to place them in the left or right loudspeaker exclusively.

Drum sets are usually recorded in stereo. The signal from the left microphone is directed to the left output channel of the mixer, and the signal from the right microphone is directed to the right, thus maintaining the stereo image that is picked up by the microphones. Pianos are also likely to be recorded in stereo and placed in the stereo field in the same way during a mixdown. The signal from a lead singer or instrumentalist is likely to be placed slightly off-center, while the signals from backup singers and instruments are likely to be placed more off-center and to the opposite side from the leader.

A special effect can be obtained by adjusting the pan pot while the mixdown is under way. The result is an illusion that the sound is moving, or **panning,** from one output channel to the other. This technique works best with high-frequency sounds (or sounds with significant high-frequency content, at least), because it depends on the listener's ability to detect changes in the differences in the amplitude of the sounds that reach each ear.

If the mixer has more than two output channels (or if the mixer has group outputs that are in turn mixed to a pair of main output channels), then the signal-routing controls on each input module will also include two or more push-button switches. These push buttons engage pairs of output channels, with the distribution of signal between the pair being determined by the setting of the associated pan pot (see Figure 4.24). This selection of output paths is sometimes referred to as busing.

Besides the main outputs, each input can also provide its signal to some other types of outputs on the mixer, called **auxiliary outputs,** or **aux sends.** For example, many mixers include one or two **foldback outputs.** In a recording studio, these can be used to provide signals to the headphones that musicians use to monitor previously recorded tracks, so that

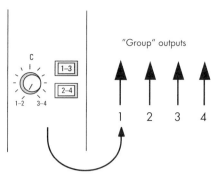

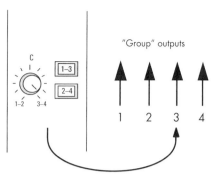

FIGURE 4.24
When a mixer has four or more output channels (called output groups), the pan pot is used in conjunction with channel push buttons to determine the output destination of the signal in a particular input module.

a. If the 1–3 button is pressed and the pan pot is turned to the left, then the signal is directed to output channel 1.

b. If the 1–3 button is pressed and the pan pot is turned to the right, then the signal is directed to output channel 3.

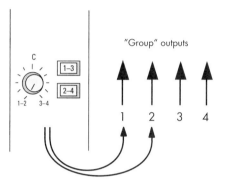

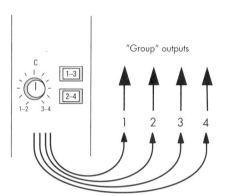

c. If both the 1–3 and the 2–4 buttons are pressed, and the pan pot is turned to the left, then the signal is directed to output channels 1 and 2.

d. If the pan pot is moved to the center position, then the signal is directed to all four output channels.

they can hear what other musicians in the studio are playing or receive other types of cues, such as a click track. In a live performance involving electronic amplification and sound reinforcement, the foldback outputs of a mixer can be used to send signals to amplifiers for loudspeakers, called foldback speakers or stage monitors, that are placed on stage. These stage monitors provide the musicians with some indication of how they sound to the audience (which is hearing sound from a main loudspeaker system, or house system, that usually receives its signal from the main outputs of the mixer). This onstage monitor system also provides each musician the cues needed to play together and in tune with the other musicians onstage.[3]

Each input module of the mixer will have for each foldback output a dial that determines how much signal will be passed along from the module to that output. Thus, a mix of input signals can be made to the foldback outputs that is different from the one sent to the main outputs of the mixer.

The auxiliary outputs of most mixers also include **effects outputs.** These outputs, also called **effects sends** or **echo sends,** can be patched to the inputs of an external audio signal processor, such as an artificial

---

3. This is described in further detail in Chapter 11.

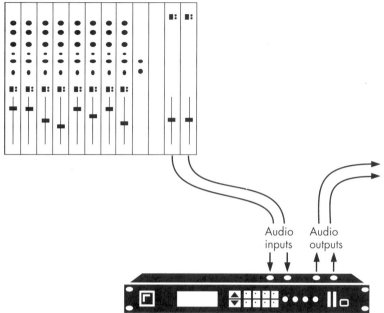

FIGURE 4.25
A simple but very limiting way to add special effects, such as artificial reverberation, to a mix would be to connect the main outputs of the mixer directly to the inputs of the signal-processing device, in a series connection, as shown here. However, because the special effect is applied after the mixing has occurred, all instruments will be affected to the same degree. It will not be possible to differentiate among the various elements of the musical texture. Furthermore, the mixed signal will be fully processed. The result could be a signal entirely drenched with reverberation, for example. Some effects processors, however, do provide a control for adjusting the balance between affected and unaffected signal.

reverberation device, a pitch shifter, flanger, or compressor (these and similar processing devices are discussed in greater detail in the concluding section of this chapter). The output signals of the external processing devices are then patched back to inputs on the mixer that are marked as **effects inputs, effects receives, effects returns,** or **echo returns.** The processed signals that are thus returned to the mixer are then mixed to the main outputs, along with the signals that come directly to the main outputs from each input module. There will usually be a pan pot and maybe a set of push buttons to determine the distribution to the main outputs of the signals returned from the external processor. There will also be a dial or fader that sets the level of returned signal to be mixed in.

Each input module will have for each effects output a dial that determines how much signal is to be sent from the module to the external processor. In this way, the degree to which each input signal is "effected" can be adjusted relative to that of the other inputs to the mixer. (For an alternative method, and its limitations, see Figure 4.25.) For example, the sounds of a background instrument or singer can be processed with more reverberation to give the illusion that they are coming from behind the other, more "foreground" instruments or singers. This provides yet another technique by which the intentions of the composer or arranger regarding the design of the texture—the relative prominence of the musical parts—can be supported and projected to the listener.

The path a signal takes from a mixer to an external processing device and back is called an **effects loop,** or echo loop (see Figure 4.26). In addition to the controls already mentioned, there is a dial to regulate the overall level of the signal that is mixed from the input modules and sent to the external device. Proper setting of this dial ensures that the input of the external device is not overloaded with too strong a signal from the mixer, nor provided with a signal that is too low in level to process satisfactorily.

Each input module shown in Figure 4.19 also includes something called a Pre/Post switch. This determines whether the signal is sent to the effects output before it is affected by the main fader on the input module (a pre-fader send) or after it has been adjusted by the main fader (a post-fader send). If the signal is sent pre-fader, and the main fader is turned all the way down, then none of the direct, unprocessed signal will be heard from the main outputs, although the effects processor will receive the signal. The signal that is returned from the processor (to the effects receive jacks) and mixed to the main outputs will be heard, however. Thus, a piano sound can be fully flanged, or a flute sound can be completely reverberant, or the drum sounds heard can be only the echoed or compressed ones, so long as the main fader on the input module is kept down to prevent any unprocessed signal from entering the mix. This should suggest some of the possibilities for creative, dynamic mixing techniques that are available even on many of the less expensive mixers found in studios.

A particular mixer is likely to have many other functions and features in addition to those that have been described here. It is highly recommended that the operator's manual for the mixer you will be using be studied carefully and consulted often as you begin to learn how the mixer can be used to help produce the music you want to create. Here are a few more hints regarding helpful mixing habits and customs:

1. Begin each mixdown session by "normalizing" (or at least checking) each control setting. Equalization controls should be set so that there is neither boost nor cut in any range of frequencies (this is described as a flat equalization setting). Foldback send dials and effects send dials should be turned all the way down (at least for the time being, until deliberate, intentional adjustments need to be made to them).

2. Turn down all faders for unused channels. Better yet, if each mixer input module includes a Channel On/Off button, switch off these unused channels. This will reduce the amount of noise that appears at the outputs of the mixer.

3. If the instrument patched to an input is primarily a high-pitched instrument, then turn down the low-frequency equalization for this channel. This will roll off any unwanted low frequencies, such as those caused by 60-Hz electrical hum, rumble and stumble noises, and the like. Similarly, if the

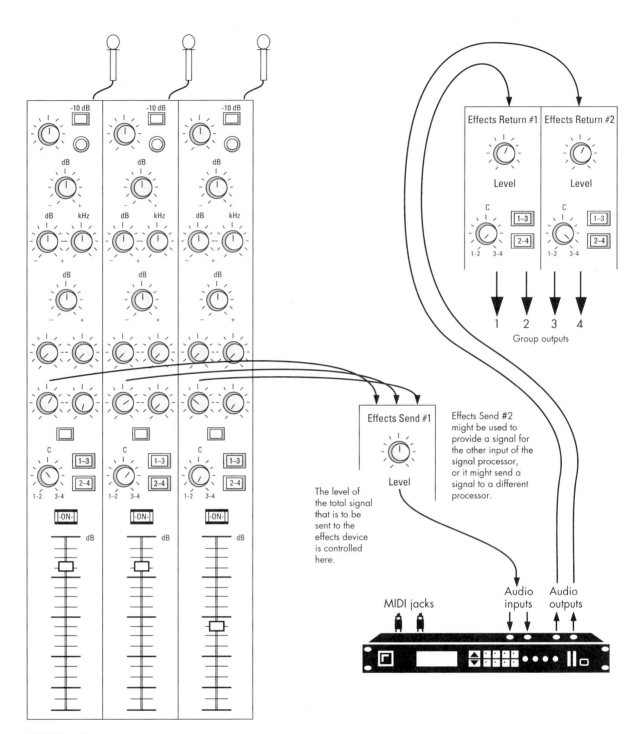

FIGURE 4.26

An effects loop creates an opportunity for part of the input signals to digress through an external signal-processing device before being passed on to the output channels of the mixer. In contrast to the connection shown in Figure 4.25, the effects device here is connected in a signal path that is parallel to the main signal path through the mixer. This is a much more flexible arrangement. The degree of effect applied to each signal in the mix can be controlled by adjusting the effects send level controls on each input module. The relative prominence and placement of the processed signal in the final mix can be adjusted by the effects return controls.

instrument is primarily a low-pitched instrument, then turn down the high-frequency equalization control.

4. Always take whatever time is necessary to set the gain trimmer and input attenuation pad for each channel to provide the best input levels for the signals patched into the mixer.

SIGNAL-PROCESSING DEVICES

Signal processors—or effects devices, as they are sometimes called—are used to enhance or otherwise transform a sound in ways that can be quite subtle, or quite radical. The effects these devices have on a sound should perhaps be thought of in the same way as that of spices in cooking, or makeup in the theater. Too much artificial reverberation in a recording, for example, can have just as unsatisfactory a result as an excess of oregano in a pasta salad, or too much powder on King Lear's face. It is important to begin with a good understanding of the essential characteristics of the sound itself, and only then proceed to explore what a signal-processing device can do with the sound.

ARTIFICIAL REVERBERATION

While the techniques of multiple-track recording make it possible to record several musical parts independently and to control very precisely how these parts will be combined, there is one vital element that is absent from the mixdown of these separate tracks. The reverberation that would have been created if the musicians had performed together as a group in a concert hall, or similar performance space, is missing from the mix and must be created artificially if the illusion of group performance is to be maintained. A recording that is made in the acoustical dryness of a recording studio will probably require some degree of **artificial reverberation.**

A variety of techniques have been used over the years to create artificial reverberation (see "Classic Reverbs"). In recent years, however, the digital reverberation device has become the preeminent means for simulating reverberation. The audio signal from the mixer is measured, or sampled, thousands of times per second, a process similar to that described in Chapter 3 (see Figure 3.2). These samples are converted into digital numbers and then stored temporarily in the memory of the device. After a delay period (simulating the time required for a wave of sound to traverse the room), the numbers are called from memory and converted back to an audio signal. The numbers will be called back several times, in fact, simulating the multiple reflections of a sound around a room. The resulting

CLASSIC REVERBS

On many early recordings, the effect of reverberation was achieved by playing the tape through a loudspeaker placed in a small but highly reverberant room and recording the sound again from a microphone placed in the same space. Rooms especially designed for this purpose, called reverberation chambers, could be found at many recording studios, and were characterized by highly reflective surfaces (for example, ceramic tile, as in bathrooms). Although this provided for a thick set of reflections, the very close arrivals of the early reflections was particularly problematic. This was due to the small size of the chamber, relative to the dimensions of a typical performance space, and provided the listener with a clear cue that the reverberation was artificial.

Another early technique for creating artificial reverberation involved the use of metal springs, normally in pairs, with transducers at each end. The audio signal from the effects send of the mixer would be converted into mechanical vibrations by the transducer at one end of the spring. These vibrations would then traverse the spring and be reflected, thus simulating the reflection of sound waves in a room. The transducer at the other end of the spring would sense these reflected vibrations and convert them to an electrical signal that could be returned to the mixer.

A related technique involved placing a transducer, called an acoustic driver, on a metal plate. This transducer would convert the audio signal from the effects send of the mixer into mechanical vibrations on the plate. A set of pickup transducers, positioned at various places on the plate, would sense these vibrations and their numerous reflections from the edges of the plate. The signals from the pickup transducers would then be combined and returned to the mixing console.

Plate reverberation units tended to be much more expensive that spring reverb devices (some "plates," in fact, were sheets of gold foil). For the extra expense, they returned a much less noisy reverberation, with much better response to rapid transients (spring reverbs would tend to "ping" on sounds with rapid attacks, for example). However, both spring and plate reverberation devices produced a distinctive coloration of the sound—metal springs and plates tend to favor a different mix of low-, middle-, and high-frequency reflections than is heard in natural reverberation—again providing the listener with an unmistakable cue that the reverberation was artificial.

audio signal is then returned to the console and mixed in as artificial reverberation.

In essence a small computer, the digital reverb can be programmed to recreate a variety of reverberant environments, from small rooms—with their own characteristic mix of early reflections and low-, middle-, and high-frequency reverberation times—to large concert halls. A digital reverberator can also be programmed to recreate ancestral forms of artificial reverberation, if desired, such as that produced by reverb chambers, spring reverbs, or plate reverbs. Although there may be situations in which it is

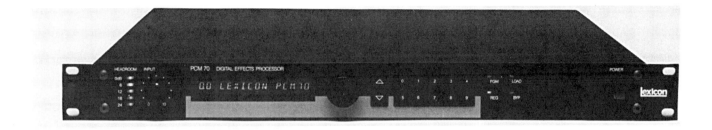

FIGURE 4.27
The Lexicon PCM 70, a digital signal processor well known for its very good artificial reverberation. (Courtesy of Lexicon, Inc.)

desirable to recreate the distinctly artificial character of these earlier devices, the reverberation that is typically provided by a digital reverb is of very high audio quality and can sound quite convincingly natural.

Before adding artificial reverberation to a recording or to a mixdown of live music, it is important to consider the character of the music that is going to be reverberated. Rapid, intricate rhythmic patterns can get lost in thick reverb. Similarly, the clarity of speech or of lyrics can be compromised by excessive reverberation. On the other hand, music that consists of very long, sustained sounds is unlikely to be much affected regardless of how much signal is passed through the processor. Reverberation is most likely to be noticed only when there are at least small changes in sound that can be reflected around the simulated space.

It may be recalled from the discussion of reverberation near the beginning of this chapter that the mix of reverberant to direct sound is a primary cue for a listener's ability to judge the distance of a source of sound. Therefore, it may often be appropriate when mixing a recording to add a greater portion of reverberation to background instruments than to the more active, foreground elements of the musical texture.

"Gated" reverb is a special effect noticeable on many recent popular recordings, particularly with snare drums. The digital reverberation, which is typically that of a large and lively space, is prematurely dampened, or gated off. The result is a big, spacious sound without the muddiness that often results from the overlapping reverberations of a train of loud sounds with rapid transients.

ÉTUDE 4.3

*R*ecord a passage of speech. Remove the reels of tape from the machine, and reverse them. Next, patch the output of the tape deck to the input of an artificial reverberation device. Connect the output of the reverberation device to the input of a second tape deck. While playing in reverse the recording on the first deck, record a copy (with the added reverberation) on the second deck. Now reverse the reels on the second deck, and play back the new recording. The speech, no longer reversed, is once again intelligible, but the words are preceded by reversed reverberation. This effect is called "preverb." Enjoy.

ECHO EFFECTS

If a sound is repeated after a delay of less than 40 thousandths of a second, the ear is not able to identify the repetition as a separate event. However, if the delay is approximately 40 milliseconds or longer, then the repetition can be heard as an echo.

Early in the history of electroacoustic music, composers were able to create echo effects with tape recorders. Such effects, as we have seen (pp. 100–102), were made possible by the physical separation of the record and playback heads, which meant that there would be a delay between the time when a sound was recorded and the time when the recorded segment of tape would reach the playback head. If the delayed playback was at least partially fed back to the record head, then an echo would be recorded. If the level of feedback to the record head was sufficiently high, a series of multiple echoes could be created. The delay time, however, was determined by the tape speed. On most tape decks, this meant that only two or three delay times were available.

With **digital delay lines,** a much greater variety of echo effects is possible. Delay times can range from a few milliseconds to several seconds. With "multi-tap" delay settings, a series of multiple echoes can be created easily. When the echoes are assigned alternately to the left and right output channels, a "ping-pong" echo effect is heard. Similarly, a series of echoes can be panned from one channel to the other, or combined with reverberation and other delay effects.

It is important to remember, however, that echo effects are somewhat unusual, rarely heard when music is performed in the usual spaces. Therefore, they should be used judiciously, as punctuation perhaps, rather than be permitted to run persistently. When echo effects are employed in popular music, for example, they are often heard only on the final notes of musical phrases. In this way, they do not obscure the pulse and do not fatigue the listener, but they do have meaning and do make an impression (impression, impression, impression).

DOUBLING, AND RELATED EFFECTS

When two or more musicians play or sing the same thing at the same time, there is not a significant difference in the total intensity of the sound. Although two instruments can have twice the power of one instrument, a doubling of the power will only result in a 3-dB increase in intensity.[4] There is no readily apparent difference in loudness. However, two or more musi-

---

4. The combined intensity of the two instruments is a doubling of the power in watts. The difference in intensity in decibels is derived as follows:

$$dB = 10 \times \log(I_1/I_0) = 10 \times \log(2/1) = 10 \times .301 \approx 3dB$$

where I_1 = the power in watts of two instruments playing together
I_0 = the power in watts of one instrument playing alone

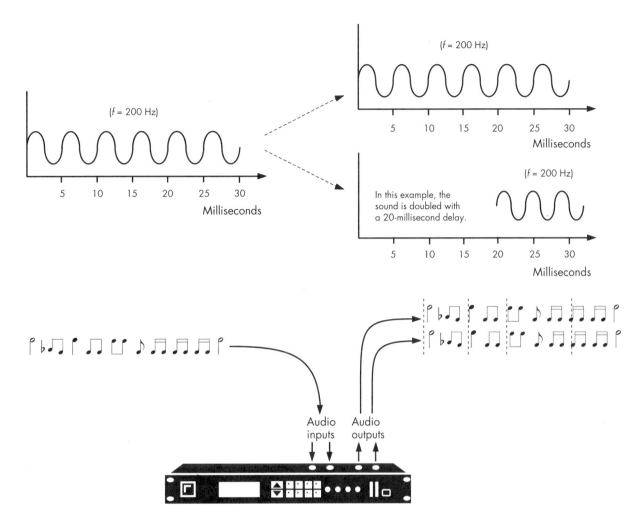

FIGURE 4.28
Doubling.

cians who are playing the same thing will never play exactly in tune with one another, except for an occasional instant, and will never begin and end their tones at exactly the same times, even if they are professional musicians with the finest training. These subtle differences, which taken together comprise something called the **chorus effect,** are readily detected by the ear and cue the listener to the fact that more than one musician is playing the musical line. They also give the musical line a richer, deeper texture.

A digital delay line can be used to mimic the chorus effect. Delaying a signal between 15 and 40 thousandths of a second and combining this with the original signal creates the impression that there are two musicians singing or playing the same thing (see Figure 4.28). This technique, called **doubling,** is particularly effective if the delayed signal is panned to the opposite channel from the original sound in the stereo field, thus creating a greater sense of spaciousness. Doubling is often used to enliven a relatively plain singing voice or to enrich the steady, relatively simple tones of a synthesizer line.

If the signal is processed into four or more different doubling patterns at the same time, with different delay times, signal levels, and independent

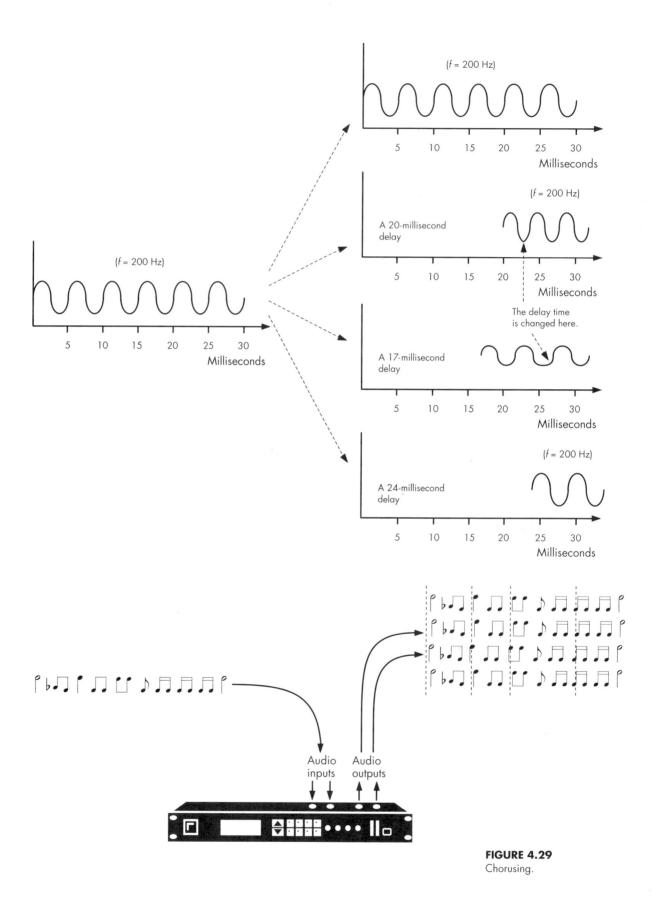

FIGURE 4.29
Chorusing.

fluctuations of delay time, then a more realistic simulation of the chorus effect results (see Figure 4.29). This technique is most commonly identified as **chorusing,** in fact, and is especially useful when applied to sustained, synthetic tones and chords.

FLANGING AND PHASING

A delay technique called **flanging** can have a particularly dramatic effect on a sound. To understand flanging, it is helpful first to consider what happens when a sound is combined with a copy of itself that has been delayed by two milliseconds. A frequency with a period of vibration that is two thousandths of a second—that is, a frequency of 500 Hz—will be reinforced by constructive interference with its delayed copy. So will all other frequencies in the sound that are whole-number multiples of 500—that is, all sounds that complete in two milliseconds a whole number of cycles of vibration, including 1000 Hz, 1500 Hz, 2000 Hz, 2500 Hz, and so on. However, a frequency that is only able to complete a half-cycle of vibration in two milliseconds, such as 250 Hz, will be at least partially canceled when combined with its delayed copy. The same will be true at 750 Hz, 1250 Hz, 1750 Hz, 2250 Hz, and so on. Figure 4.30a is a graph of the frequency response that results from a two-millisecond delay. This contour, because of its appearance, is often described as a comb-filter response.

If the delay between a sound and its copy is increased to five milliseconds, then a different set of frequencies of reinforcement (200 Hz, 400 Hz, 600 Hz, 800 Hz, and so on) and frequencies of cancellation (300 Hz, 500 Hz, 700 Hz, 900 Hz, and so on) will result, as illustrated in Figure 4.30b. If the shift in delay time from two to five milliseconds is relatively smooth and gradual, then the pattern of reinforcement and cancellation of frequencies will interpolate between that shown in Figure 4.30a and that seen in Figure 4.30b. The sound acquires a very dynamic quality as frequencies that are fed into the process are alternately reinforced and canceled as they appear in the output.

Flanging occurs when the delay time is periodically shifted in this way, over a range perhaps as great as from 0 to 20 milliseconds, at a rate of once per second or so.[5] The effect is particularly strong if the level of the delayed signal is nearly as great as the level of the original signal, or if some of the output of the process is fed back to the input. The sound acquires a sweeping, swooshing, or twanging character. Flanging is most likely to be noticeable with sounds that have a rich content of frequencies, such as those of the guitar, piano, or cymbals and other "noisy" instruments.

---

5. Originally, flanging was accomplished by playing back two identical copies of a recording simultaneously on two tape recorders. The necessary delay was introduced by intermittently pressing against the sides, or flanges, of the supply reel on one of the recorders. As the outputs of the two recorders were mixed, the effects of the flanging could then be heard.

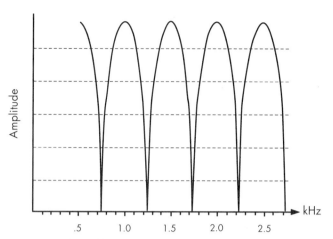

FIGURE 4.30
Flanging involves a changing
pattern of constructive and
destructive interferences.

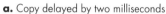

a. Copy delayed by two milliseconds

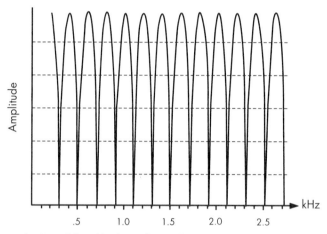

b. Copy delayed by five milliseconds

Phasing, a delay technique similar to flanging, was especially popular in the 1960s and 1970s. The devices that accomplished this technique were known as phasers. The most significant difference between flanging and phasing is that with phasing the frequencies of reinforcement and cancellation are not necessarily evenly spaced, as they are with flanging (see Figure 4.31). Most digital signal processors now available can simulate either effect.

PITCH SHIFTING

In the earlier days of electroacoustic music, the pitch of a recorded sound could be changed by playing the tape at a different speed from that at which it was recorded. However, as may be recalled from Chapter 2, the duration of the sound would also change as the tape was played faster or slower. Many digital signal processors now available are capable of transposing the pitch of a sound without changing its duration. One common

FIGURE 4.31
A typical pattern of cancellation and reinforcement in the frequency response of a phaser at a particular instant. The pattern will change as the time delays produced by the device change. Contrast the irregular spacing of the response peaks here to the regular spacing of the response peaks of a flanger, as shown in Figure 4.30. [Based on Stanley, Alten, *Audio in Media*, 3rd ed. (Belmont, CA: Wadsworth, 1990), Figure 8.25, p. 231].

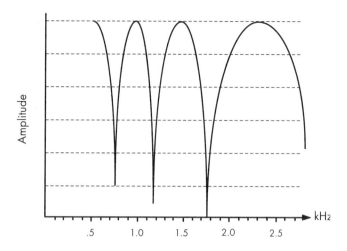

application of **pitch shifting** is to "fatten" the sound of a synthesizer or vocalist by mixing it with a duplicate that has been very slightly shifted in pitch.

With wide shifts in pitch it becomes possible to create a harmonizing part—using a pitch a third or sixth above or below the melody, for example. In fact, pitch shifters are often referred to as Harmonizers™ (a registered trademark of Eventide Inc.), and many are even able to adjust the size of the pitch shift so that the harmonizing melodic line remains in the same musical scale as the melody being processed.

Wide shifts in pitch can noticeably alter the character of a sound, as with tape speed transposition techniques. Vocal lines that are shifted higher in pitch, for example, can become dominated by the "chipmunk effect." In some situations this would be quite a distraction, but in others it might be regarded as a creative opportunity.[6]

COMPRESSION

Some signals have a wide dynamic range: occasionally the signal is rather low in level, and at other times quite strong. The total dynamic range of the signal may exceed the range of signal levels that can be handled by the tape deck. A recording engineer can attempt to compensate for this by boosting the level during the soft passages and pulling it back during the loud ones (a technique called "riding the gain"). The same thing can be done more or less automatically, however, by means of a **compressor.**

Up to a specified level, called the threshold, the signals pass through the compressor unaffected. With any increase in level above the threshold, however, there is a smaller increase in level at the output of the compressor

---

6. Another signal-processing device often used with vocal sounds is the vocoder, described in Chapter 8.

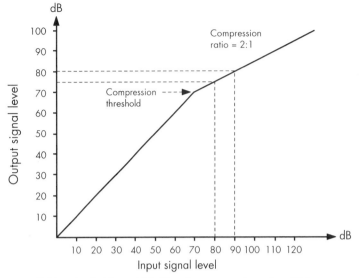

FIGURE 4.32
Compression.

a. With a threshold set at 70 dB and a compression ratio of 2:1, an 80-dB input signal is squeezed down to a 75-dB output signal; a 90-dB input emerges as an 80-dB output.

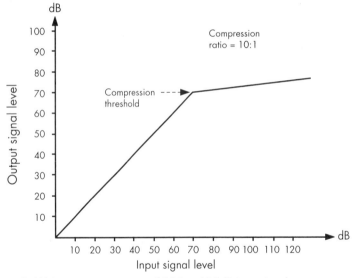

b. With a compression ratio of 10:1, a 120-dB input signal emerges as a 75-dB output; thus, the compressor becomes a limiter.

(see Figure 4.32a). The ratio between the increase in input level, above the threshold, to the corresponding increase in output level is called the **compression** ratio. A typical compression ratio is set between 2:1 and 6:1.

"Squeezing" the gain of the stronger signals in this way reduces the overall dynamic range. This is often helpful when recording a vocalist unfamiliar with the techniques of handling a microphone or when recording an acoustic guitar, which can have a wide variation in dynamic levels. Compressors are also used to reduce the dynamic range in voice-overs for television and radio commercials—thus making it possible to boost the average level of the voice-overs and ensuring that they can be heard over everything else, even from other rooms in the house.

A compressor with a compression ratio of 10:1 or higher is called a **limiter.** Essentially, any increases in level at the input that are above the threshold level are not passed through to the output (see Figure 4.32b). This is particularly useful when it is necessary to protect loudspeakers or other audio components from excessive signal levels.

EXPANSION

An **expander** is used to increase the dynamic range of a signal by making the sounds that are softer than a set threshold level even softer (see Figure 4.33a). The ratio between the level of an input signal, below the threshold, and the level of the corresponding output level is called the **expansion** ratio, and is typically set between 1:2 and 1:6.

An expander with a ratio of 1:10 or less is called a **noise gate.** Sounds that are below the threshold level are essentially reduced to extinction (see Figure 4.33b). This is especially useful in quieter passages of music where tape hiss or other noises may be otherwise obtrusive.

Another type of signal-processing device is an outboard equalizer, which is likely to have a greater number of controls and capabilities than the equalization functions provided on the input modules of a mixer. Many studios also have a device called an exciter, which adds brilliance to a recording by boosting the relative prominence of certain frequency components.

Most effects devices, such as reverberators, digital delay lines, pitch shifters, and outboard equalizers, will receive their input signals from the Effects Send jack on the mixing console. The outputs of these devices will usually be patched to the Effects Return jack on the mixer (as shown in Figure 4.26).

All effects devices add a certain amount of noise to a signal. If the signal sent to the effects device is weak, then the signal returned to the mixer will also be weak. When this weak signal is boosted to a suitable level, there will be a corresponding increase in the level of noise contributed by the effects device. Therefore, it is best to send as strong a signal as possible to the effects device (but not so strong as to overload it and cause distortion). The signal returned to the mixer can then be reduced in level, if necessary. This will result in a corresponding reduction in the level of noise that has been added to the signal by the processor.

Some effects devices, particularly compressors or expanders, are often used to process the signal even before it gets into the mixer. Many mixers have, on each input module, an insertion jack. From this jack, the signal

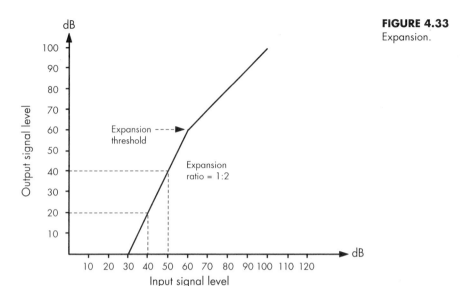

FIGURE 4.33
Expansion.

a. The threshold is set at 60 dB, and the expansion ratio is 1:2.

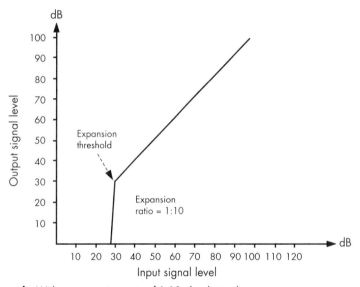

b. With an expansion ratio of 1:10, the device becomes a noise gate.

can be diverted to a processor and then returned to the input module, ready to be mixed.

Signal-processing devices can do much to enhance the quality and character of sounds that exist in electronic form. In a sense, the techniques of signal processing can be regarded as extensions of *musique concrète*—the music of tape manipulations. As with all techniques that have such great potential, however, it is important to employ them thoughtfully and with premeditation.

IMPORTANT TERMS

wavelength
tweeter
woofer
diffraction
absorption
reflection
resonance
standing wave
reverberation
reverberation time
interaural time difference
interaural amplitude difference
Doppler effect
multiple-track, or multitrack,
　recorder
overdubbing
click track
sync

selective synchronization
bouncing
punch-in/punch-out
SMPTE time code
mixer
equalization, or EQ
shelving
peaking
pan pot
panning
auxiliary outputs, or aux sends
foldback outputs
effects outputs, or effects sends,
　or echo sends
effects inputs, or effects receives,
　or effects returns, or echo
　returns

effects loop
artificial reverberation
digital delay lines
chorus effect
doubling
chorusing
flanging
phasing
pitch shifting
compressor
compression
limiter
expander
expansion
noise gate

FOR FURTHER READING

In addition to many of the sources cited at the end of the preceding chapters, the following may be useful:

Anderton, Craig, *The Digital Delay Handbook.* New York: Amsco, 1985.
Milano, Dominic, ed. *Multi-Track Recording.* Milwaukee: Hal Leonard, 1988.

CHAPTER 5

THE MUSICAL INSTRUMENT DIGITAL INTERFACE

The previous chapters in this text describe techniques by which electroacoustic music can be made from natural, or "acoustic" sounds. Such sounds are converted, by means of microphones or other transducers, into fluctuations of electricity, which can then be mixed or otherwise processed before being recorded as magnetic patterns on tape. These recorded patterns, in turn, can be manipulated further, so that the sounds that finally emerge from the loudspeakers will often be radically transformed from those that were initially picked up by the microphone.

Fluctuating patterns of electricity can also be generated within electronic circuits. These patterns, too, can be mixed, processed, and recorded (and can also be edited and otherwise manipulated while on tape). When they emerge as sound from a loudspeaker, however, they are heard for the first time. They have not had a prior existence; they are newly formed, "synthetic" sounds. A **sound synthesizer** is the musical instrument designed especially for the task of generating, processing, and controlling the electrical oscillations that become these sounds.

TYPICAL FEATURES OF A CONTEMPORARY SYNTHESIZER

During the 1950s and 1960s, electronic sound synthesizers and related devices were somewhat rare, found only at research facilities, university studios, and a few advanced commercial studios. Progress in electronic technology, however, made possible the development of successive models of sound synthesizers that were increasingly affordable, portable, and easy to use. By the late 1970s, synthesizers had become well established as musical instruments, particularly for such popular musical styles as "progressive" or "art rock." By this time, certain features had also become

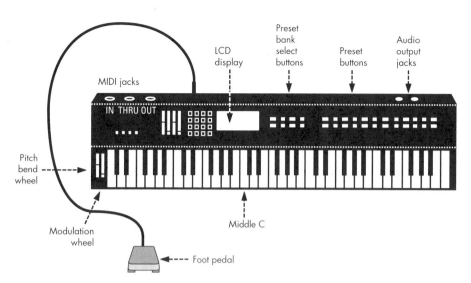

FIGURE 5.1
Features of a typical contemporary sound synthesizer.

established as fairly standard, at least for synthesizers used in live performance. Other features have since become quite common as well.

A typical synthesizer, as illustrated in Figure 5.1, is a keyboard instrument.[1] The keyboard usually includes at least 61 keys, spanning a range of five octaves. Many early synthesizers were **monophonic**: they could sound only one pitch at a time, regardless of how many keys were pressed on the keyboard. The contemporary synthesizer, however, is **polyphonic**: it can produce as many as 16 (or even more) tones as the corresponding number of keys is pressed. Whereas the older, monophonic instruments were primarily restricted to solo lines, instruments since the late 1970s have been capable of sounding different musical parts, including chords, simultaneously.

Many instruments provide for **keyboard splitting.** The keyboard is divided into two (or more) sections, and each section is assigned a different instrumental sound. Thus, for example, a solo line can be played with a flute-like sound by the keys on the upper half of the keyboard, accompanied by a bass line played with a guitar-like sound by the keys on the lower half of the keyboard. The boundary between these sections, called the **split point,** can be set by the performer (according to the procedure described in the owner's manual of the instrument).

On all but the least expensive instruments now available, the keyboard is **velocity sensitive.** This means that the synthesizer can sense the velocity at which a key is pressed—that is, how "hard" the key is played. On an acoustic piano—the model for this notion of a velocity-sensitive keyboard —the faster a key is played, the louder and brighter is the tone that is produced. Similarly, a synthesizer with a velocity-sensitive keyboard can be programmed to respond to various keystrokes with corresponding shadings of loudness, brightness, or perhaps gradations of some other attribute of the sound.

---

1. Alternatives to the keyboard as the means of playing a synthesizer are described in the next chapter.

Some synthesizer keyboards are sensitive to further pressure on a key that is already pressed down. This feature is called **aftertouch sensitivity.** The aftertouch information generated by a keyboard can be used in a variety of ways by a synthesizer—for example, to change the brightness of the timbre or the level of amplitude over the course of a tone as the performer applies varying degrees of pressure to the depressed keys, or to create or regulate inflections of the pitch. The type of change and the range over which it can operate are determined by the control settings, or programming, of the receiving synthesizer.

At the left end of the keyboard of a typical synthesizer are two control wheels (or similar controls). One of these, the pitch wheel or **pitch bender,** is used to introduce relatively small inflections of pitch. The pitch of a tone can be raised or lowered by perhaps as much as an octave by rotating the pitch bender in one direction or the other. The wheel is usually spring-loaded so that when released it returns to its center position, and the pitch of the subsequent tone is therefore unaffected.

The other control wheel is called the **modulation wheel.** It is normally used to regulate the amount of periodic fluctuation that can be introduced to the pitch of a tone. This is similar to the vibrato technique used by a player of a bowed-string instrument or by a singer. Such modulation is most often applied to tones of longer duration, to give them a more lively, more interesting character.

Additional, foot-operated controllers can be plugged into jacks on the back of the synthesizer. A foot pedal is usually provided to regulate the volume of the sound produced by the synthesizer. Yet another foot pedal, called the foot controller, may be available for controlling the brightness of the tone color or some other aspect of the sound (as determined by the programming of the synthesizer). A foot switch is typically used as a sustain pedal, enabling the performer to sustain tones even after the keys are released—much like the function of the damper pedal on an acoustic piano.

Perhaps the most significant capability of the sound synthesizer is that it can generate and shape electrical oscillations in an enormous variety of ways. Thus, it can more or less successfully emulate the sounds of many different instruments or, more interestingly, can create the sounds of previously unimagined instruments.[2] Even slight changes to the settings of the dials and switches on the control panel of the instrument can result in very different sounds.[3]

By the late 1970s, it became possible for a synthesizer to scan internally the settings of the dials and switches on its front panel and to encode them

---

2. The details of the methods by which sound synthesizers accomplish this are described in Chapters 7, 8, and 9.

3. On many contemporary instruments, it should be noted, these dials and switches for programming a sound may not exist as actual objects on the control panel. They may exist instead as virtual dials and switches on the display screen of a computer that is connected to the synthesizer.

digitally. This set of data, which specifies how the circuitry of the synthesizer is configured to produce a particular instrumental sound, can then be stored in a memory section of the synthesizer, along with other sets of data created in the same way.

These memorized sets of control settings are referred to on some synthesizers as "preset instruments," or just **presets,** and on other synthesizers as "programs" or "patches." Typically they are stored in memory in groups, called banks, that may include eight or more presets each. To recall a particular sound, its bank is first selected by pressing the appropriate bank button. Then the preset button corresponding to the memory location of the sound is pressed. As the memorized control settings are recalled, the circuitry or programming of the synthesizer is reconfigured almost instantaneously so that it can once again produce that particular sound. For example, pushing the Bank A button and then the first preset button may call up the dial and switch settings for preset 1, an instrumental sound labeled Buffalo Bells. Then, later in the piece of music, the Bank B button and then the fourth preset button might be pushed to recall preset 12, a patch called Bass ShoeHorn, or whatever else happens to be stored in memory at that location.

Typically there are 32, 64, or 128 different presets stored in banks in the internal memory of a synthesizer. These can be supplemented by additional banks of presets stored on a memory cartridge or memory card that can be inserted into a memory port on the synthesizer. A button on the control panel enables the performer to choose between the internal memory banks of the synthesizer and the external banks on the memory card.

Additional switches and controls, perhaps labeled Increment/Decrement and Data Entry, can be used for making adjustments to preset instruments and to other aspects of the programming of the synthesizer. Information relevant to these tasks is displayed on the LCD (liquid crystal display) panel on the instrument.

This introductory survey has described most of the more common features of a contemporary synthesizer. The most significant feature of such an instrument, however, is the subject of the remainder of this chapter (and the next chapter). This powerful feature is the compatibility of the instrument with virtually all other contemporary electroacoustic instruments by virtue of something called the Musical Instrument Digital Interface, or **MIDI.**

THE BIRTH OF MIDI

By the late 1970s, as synthesizers became more widely used as musical instruments, performers quickly came to appreciate the strengths and weaknesses of the various instruments made by different manufacturers. The synthetic string sounds of one instrument, for example, might be particularly impressive, while the filter effects of another synthesizer might be uniquely appealing. Yet another synthesizer might have a keyboard that felt especially comfortable and responsive, while the programmability of a different synthesizer might be a feature of great value for the onstage performer. Thus, there was considerable motivation for a musician to have more than one kind of synthesizer available, in order to meet the demands of various musical situations as effectively as possible.

Another motivation for acquiring diverse synthesizers resulted from a common weakness among synthesizers at the time. Because electronically synthesized timbres could be quite static and plain-featured by comparison to those produced on natural instruments, melodic lines from a synthesizer often had a thin, artificial quality. To overcome this deficiency, at least to some extent, synthesizer players in the 1970s developed a technique of playing the melody simultaneously on two or more synthesizers (or, in a recording, of overdubbing it on several tracks). These combined layers of tone provided for a much richer, "fatter" melodic line.

The multitude of live-performance synthesizers onstage (or in the studio) was enriched further as manufacturers introduced a variety of auxiliary devices. One of these was the synthesizer expander, which increased the number of tones that could be produced at one time from a synthesizer keyboard. Another was the sequencer, which generated programmed series of control voltages that, when applied to the oscillator of a synthesizer, for example, could generate patterns of accompaniment—thus freeing the musician to concentrate on the melodic line or other elements of the music. At about the same time, the first, primitive drum machines also became available.

There were many good reasons to have a variety of synthesizers and auxiliary devices and to try to use them together to produce music. However, the difficulties of synchronizing or otherwise coordinating such a collection of gadgets were nearly insurmountable. Virtually every device was designed independently, based on unique assumptions regarding how it would be used. Also, different manufacturers had different preferences regarding electrical levels, connectors, and other aspects of equipment design. Thus, an electroacoustic musician required an assortment of interface boxes, most of them custom-made, even to begin to use two or more instruments together.

Some manufacturers began to develop a more uniform approach to the design of their own products, and to work on means by which control signals could be readily exchanged among their devices. A synthesizer, sequencer, and expander module produced by Oberheim, for example, could be easily combined into a system of reasonably compatible devices. A synthesizer by Roland or Korg, however, still could not be integrated into this system without great difficulty. A more complete solution to the problem—a solution inclusive of all manufacturers—was needed.

The notion of a standard interface for electroacoustic musical instruments appears to have emerged first from informal conversations among representatives of Japanese and American companies at the June 1981 convention of the National Association of Music Merchants (NAMM). In October of that year, representatives of six companies—Kawai, Korg, Roland, and Yamaha from Japan, and Oberheim and Sequential Circuits from the United States—met to discuss the idea further. The following month, the president of Sequential Circuits, Dave Smith, presented a description of a "universal synthesizer interface" to a meeting in New York of the Audio Engineering Society. A larger group of manufacturers subsequently met at the January 1982 NAMM convention. Despite this larger turnout, the interest of many manufacturers wavered considerably over the ensuing months, and it was still not clear that a standard for synthesizer interfacing could be successfully established.

In December of 1982, the Sequential Circuits Prophet 600 was introduced as the first synthesizer to include this new standard interface—by then called MIDI, for Musical Instrument Digital Interface. At the January 1983 NAMM show, the Prophet 600 and a Roland Jupiter-6 were successfully interconnected in the first public demonstration of this new interface. Representatives of Kawai, Korg, Roland, Sequential Circuits, and Yamaha next met in Japan in August of 1983 to agree upon a document, called the "MIDI 1.0 Specification," that described the requirements of the interface in detail. This specification was then made freely available to all other interested manufacturers.

By the summer of 1984, the Musical Instrument Digital Interface was well established, as indicated by its inclusion on dozens of new products. It has continued to thrive since, and has proven to be a splendid example of the results of successful international cooperation. Both musicians and musical instrument makers, as well as many others, have benefited enormously from this determined effort by individuals on both sides of the Pacific.[4]

MIDI CONNECTIONS

The Musical Instrument Digital Interface is actually no more than a set of suggestions regarding the design and manufacture of instruments to make them capable of working together in certain ways with other instruments. Manufacturers can ignore these suggestions (and often do), but by doing so they risk irritating a significant number of their customers, who have come to appreciate the ways in which MIDI has extended the capabilities of their studios.

---

4. As the MIDI specification continues to evolve, changes are ratified by both the Japan MIDI Standards Committee (JMSC) and, for the United States and Europe, the MIDI Manufacturers Association (MMA). Authoritative information regarding the Musical Instrument Digital Interface is then disseminated exclusively by the International MIDI Association (IMA), a not-for-profit organization based in Los Angeles.

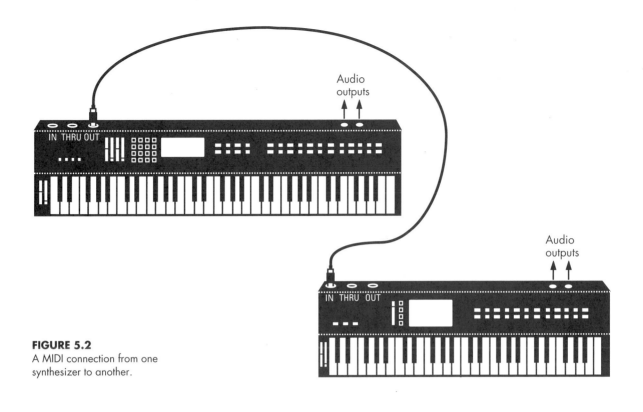

FIGURE 5.2
A MIDI connection from one
synthesizer to another.

FIGURE 5.3
MIDI connector

All instruments designed for MIDI should have at least two MIDI connectors, labeled **MIDI IN** and **MIDI OUT,** in addition to the usual jacks for audio signals, electrical power cords, and such. Information that originates on a device—for example, performance information that is generated on a keyboard synthesizer as keys are pressed and released, foot pedals are pushed, and controller wheels are moved—is passed through a cable that connects the MIDI OUT jack of the device to the MIDI IN jack of a second device (see Figure 5.2). This cable should be no longer than 50 feet. The connector at each end of the cable is a DIN-type male plug (a connector widely used in Europe and Japan) with five pins arranged in a semicircle (see Figure 5.3). The MIDI connectors to which the ends of the MIDI cable are connected are female DIN-type jacks with a corresponding arrangement of five holes.

In addition to MIDI IN and MIDI OUT connectors, many devices have a third connector, labeled **MIDI THRU,** that provides a copy, or echo, of any data that arrive at the MIDI IN connector. The uses of the MIDI THRU connector are discussed in further detail later in this chapter.

MIDI CHANNEL MESSAGES

The physical means by which information is moved from one device to another has just been described. Next it is time to examine more closely the structure and content of the information itself. This information is encoded in MIDI messages that consist of patterns of electrical pulses representing a variety of combinations of the numbers 1 and 0 (as described in Appendix B). Each 1 or 0 is referred to as a **bit**. During each second, 31,250 of these bits of information are transmitted in series—that is, one at a time—through the MIDI cable that connects one device to the next.

The bits of information that form this parade of data through a MIDI cable are organized into **bytes** of eight bits each.[5] These bytes are grouped to form messages that can signify various musical events, such as performance gestures, or can provide other kinds of data relevant to the operation of a device. A MIDI message begins with a **status byte,** which indicates the kind of musical event or function of operation to which the message pertains. Following the status byte there may be one or more **data bytes** that provide the details of the message. The first bit of a status byte is always a 1; data bytes begin with 0.

A performance gesture is generally represented by one of the category of messages referred to as **channel messages,** which include Note On, Note Off, Key Pressure, Channel Pressure, Control Change, Pitch Bend Change, and Program Change messages. In the simple MIDI network shown in Figure 5.2, the synthesizer on the left is functioning as the source of MIDI messages and the synthesizer on the right is the intended recipient of the messages.[6] Pressing a key on the left synthesizer, for example, will cause the right synthesizer to sound a tone. As this chapter proceeds, equipment will be added to this network, and the range of the capabilities of the Musical Instrument Digital Interface will become increasingly apparent.

NOTE ON MESSAGES

When a key is pressed on the synthesizer shown at the top in Figure 5.4, a MIDI message called a **Note On message** is created.[7] The first data byte in a Note On message indicates which key has been pressed. There are 128 possible keys, numbered from 0 through 127, that can be transmitted or recognized by a MIDI instrument. As points of reference (particularly

---

5. For transmission there are also a "start" bit and a "stop" bit, as described in Appendix C: Further Details of the Musical Instrument Digital Interface.

6. In some writings, the source device is identified as a "master" and receiving devices are referred to as "slaves." It should be noted, however, that many musicians are uncomfortable with this terminology.

7. A note, of course, is nothing more than a round mark on a page of notated music. A more appropriate name for this kind of MIDI message might be Tone On. Alas, it is too late now, as the Musical Instrument Digital Interface enters its second decade of use, to correct this problematic usage.

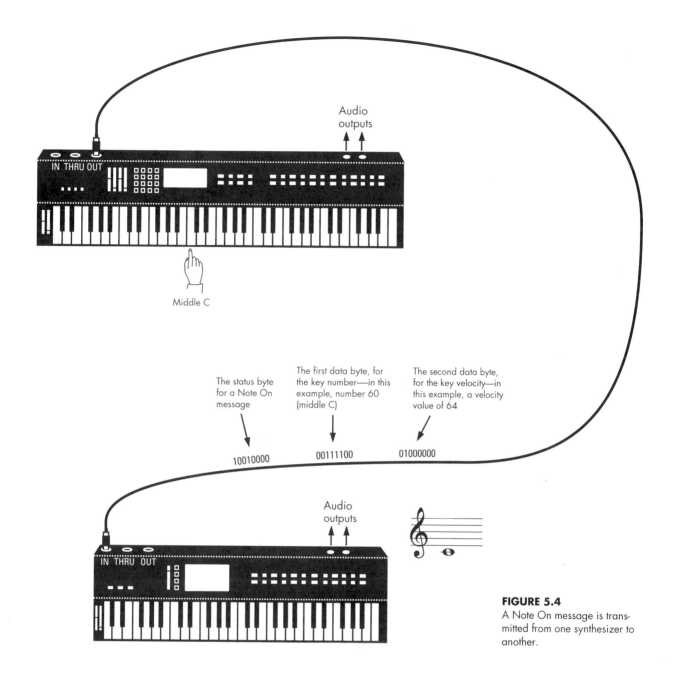

The status byte for a Note On message

The first data byte, for the key number—in this example, number 60 (middle C)

The second data byte, for the key velocity—in this example, a velocity value of 64

10010000   00111100   01000000

FIGURE 5.4
A Note On message is transmitted from one synthesizer to another.

for those whose earlier experience with keyboard instruments was acquired from piano lessons), the lowest and highest keys of a piano keyboard are key number 21 and key number 108, respectively. Middle C is key number 60.

The second data byte is used to indicate the velocity at which the key is pressed (as described earlier, this corresponds more or less to how hard the key is played). If the source keyboard in Figure 5.4 is velocity sensitive—that is, if it is capable of generating velocity information—then the key velocity value is scaled to a range of 0 to 127. Some keyboards are not velocity sensitive, in which case a default value of 64 is assigned as the velocity for each Note On message triggered when a key is pressed.

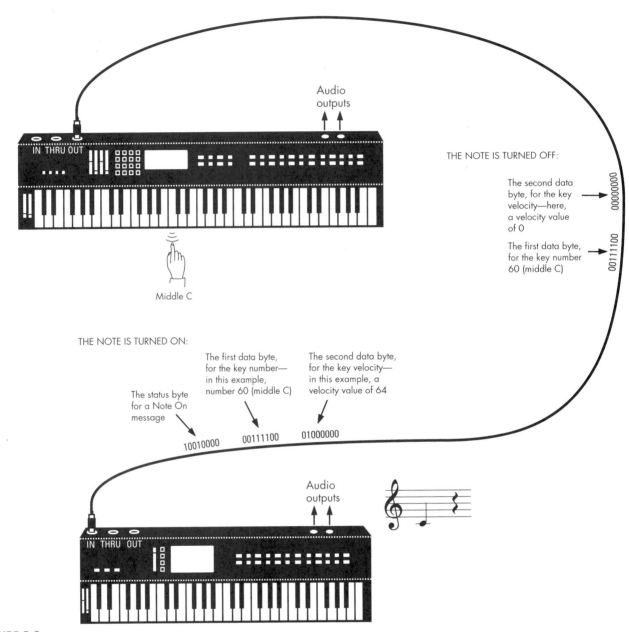

THE NOTE IS TURNED OFF:

The second data byte, for the key velocity—here, a velocity value of 0 → 00000000

The first data byte, for the key number 60 (middle C) → 00111100

Audio outputs

Middle C

THE NOTE IS TURNED ON:

The status byte for a Note On message

The first data byte, for the key number— in this example, number 60 (middle C)

The second data byte, for the key velocity— in this example, a velocity value of 64

10010000   00111100   01000000

Audio outputs

FIGURE 5.5
A Note On message is followed by a Note On message with a velocity of zero, to turn off the note. A status byte is not necessary for the second message because no other messages have intervened since the first Note On message.

A velocity of zero implies that the key has not moved and, therefore, that no sound should be produced for that key. Many keyboards will generate a Note On message with a velocity of zero whenever a key is released. This, in effect, turns the note off (see Figure 5.5).

For velocity values greater than zero, the way the information is used depends on the design of the particular instrument that receives it. Synthesizers that are velocity sensitive are able to respond to this information by scaling the loudness of the tone according to the value of the velocity, or by adjusting the brightness of the timbre in some corresponding way. However, if the tone generator of the receiving instrument is not velocity sensitive, the velocity information will be ignored (unless the velocity is zero, in which case the instrument will respond by turning off the tone).

NOTE OFF MESSAGES

Some synthesizers will produce a Note Off message (rather than a Note On message with a velocity of zero) when a key is released. This message begins with the unique status byte that is assigned for Note Off messages, followed by two data bytes. The first data byte indicates which key has been released, and the second indicates the velocity at which the key was released. Very few devices use this release-velocity information, however.[8]

For that matter, very few devices actually use Note Off messages, nor do they generate them. Most often, when a key is released, a Note On message with a velocity of zero is created. Thus, a single status byte, the one for the Note On message, can be used for an entire series of tones (provided there is no interruption from another type of message). This procedure is referred to as **running status** (see Figure 5.6). Without it, two status bytes would be required for each tone—one for the Note On, and one for the Note Off. Thus, running status provides for considerable economy in the transmission of MIDI data.

For every Note On message, there must be a subsequent Note On message for that same key but with a velocity of zero (or possibly a Note Off message instead). Failure to acknowledge this essential symmetry will result in stuck notes! If a MIDI cable gets pulled before a key is released, or if the electrical power to the source of MIDI data goes off before a key is released, then the receiving devices will continue to sing, waiting in oblivion for the message that tells them to stop. Some computer programs are known to be careless about such things—occasionally transposing a Note On message without also transposing the message that turns the note off, for example. For such occasions, many commercially available accessory boxes include a "panic button" that will transmit all known forms of messages that can turn notes off.

AFTERTOUCH

Some synthesizer keyboards generate MIDI messages in response to further pressure on a key that is already pressed down. There are two types of aftertouch sensitivity and, therefore, two forms of aftertouch messages:

---

8. It was initially intended that release-velocity information be used to scale the final decay time of a tone, thus providing for a variety of effects of musical articulation, such as staccato and legato.

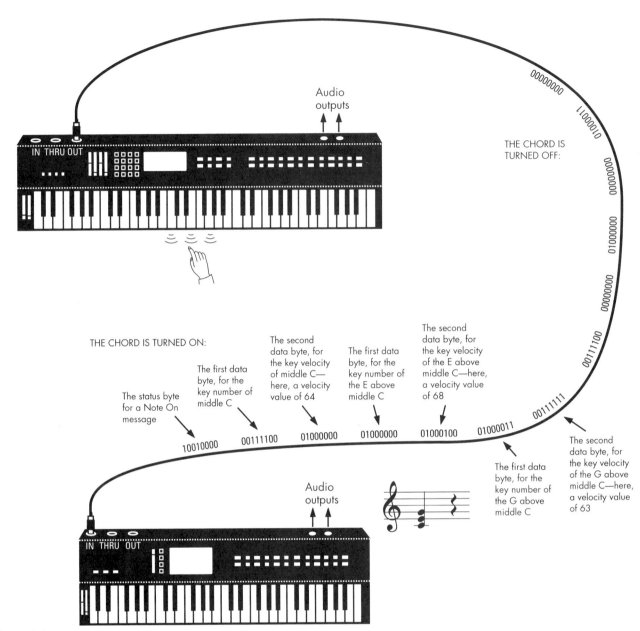

FIGURE 5.6
An example of running status. A series of Note On messages is transmitted to turn on a C-major chord played by the second synthesizer. Then another series is transmitted to turn off the chord. Since all of these are Note On messages, only one status byte is necessary.

polyphonic, or key pressure, aftertouch, which is usually found as a feature of more expensive instruments, and **monophonic, or channel pressure, aftertouch,** which is much more common. The term *aftertouch,* used without qualification, generally refers to channel pressure aftertouch.

The complexity of the effect that can be produced by a synthesizer in response to aftertouch messages is related to the type of aftertouch data being used. A polyphonic aftertouch message includes a status byte followed by two data bytes. The first data byte is the key number of the key being pressed; the second is a reading of the current level of aftertouch pressure on that key. Thus, on a keyboard that is capable of sensing different levels of pressure on different keys at the same time, it may be possible to generate a series of aftertouch messages by holding down the keys of a chord and applying different pressures from the fingers on each key. A synthesizer that is capable of responding to these polyphonic key pressure messages might then, for example, sound a chord with an independent level of vibrato or rate of vibrato for each tone, or with different pitch inflections for each tone.

With channel pressure aftertouch, also occasionally referred to as monophonic aftertouch, the situation is somewhat simpler (see Figure 5.7). A channel pressure message consists of two bytes: a status byte followed by a single data byte. The data byte represents the total of the pressures applied by all fingers that are holding down keys at that moment. All the tones being produced by a device that receives this message will most likely respond in a uniform way to this single value. For example, all tones will experience the same change in vibrato, brilliance of timbre, volume level, or pitch. Polyphonic key pressure messages are ignored by a device that is only prepared to respond to channel pressure messages.

Although aftertouch messages can potentially provide a means to achieve very subtle effects, in practice this has been difficult. Most keyboard players have not developed a technique for controlling precisely the pressure applied to keys (this is particularly true with polyphonic aftertouch). Furthermore, the response of most keyboards is quite uneven. Many of the more expensive keyboards, however, provide the musician with controls or commands for shaping the contour of the aftertouch response (and also for key velocity response), or for selecting from a programmed set of response contours.

CONTROL CHANGE MESSAGES

An instrument that serves as a source of MIDI data, such as a synthesizer, often includes a wide assortment of accessories, such as foot pedals and foot switches, as well as sliders and control wheels installed on the panel of the instrument. These are often used to generate what are called **Control Change messages.** The MIDI specification provides for as many as 121 different types of controllers that can create such messages. In practice, however, only a few of these are used regularly (others are cited in Appendix C).

Controllers 0 through 63 (inclusive) are defined as **continuous controllers.** Whenever a foot pedal, control wheel, control slider, or similar continuously variable control is moved, a corresponding Control Change message is created, with a value between 0 and 127 (inclusive), to represent the new position of the controller.

Controller 1 is designated for the modulation wheel (or, with some synthesizers, a modulation control stick), found on most synthesizers at the

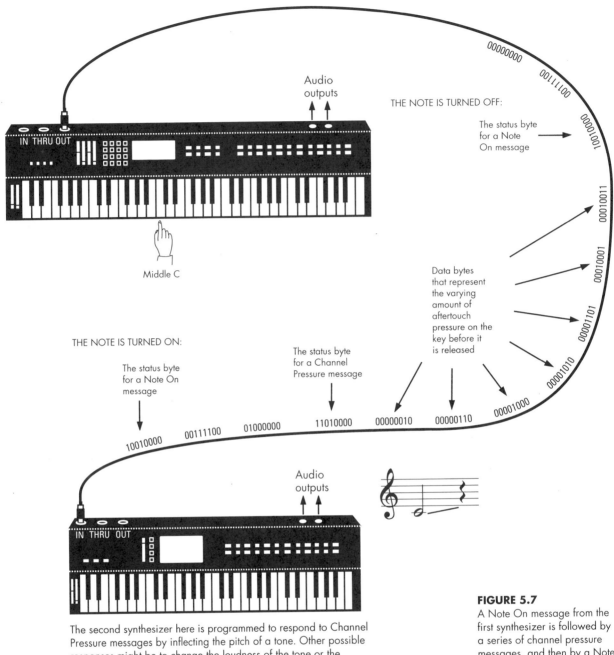

Audio outputs

THE NOTE IS TURNED OFF:

The status byte for a Note On message → 10010001

00000000
00111100
10001000
00010011
00010001
00001101
00001010
00001000

Data bytes that represent the varying amount of aftertouch pressure on the key before it is released

THE NOTE IS TURNED ON:

The status byte for a Note On message

The status byte for a Channel Pressure message

10010000   00111100   01000000   11010000   00000010   00000110

Middle C

Audio outputs

The second synthesizer here is programmed to respond to Channel Pressure messages by inflecting the pitch of a tone. Other possible responses might be to change the loudness of the tone or the brightness of the timbre of the tone. The extent of the change is determined by control settings on the second sythesizer.

FIGURE 5.7
A Note On message from the first synthesizer is followed by a series of channel pressure messages, and then by a Note On message with a velocity of zero.

left end of the keyboard. As described earlier, it is most typically used to control the width of the vibrato of the tone being synthesized (although other aspects of the sound may be controlled by the information instead, as determined by the patch programming of the receiving synthesizer).

Controller 7 is designated for the volume pedal. A synthesizer that recognizes Control Change messages from a volume pedal (and most now do) will usually respond by adjusting the amplitude level of the tone it is producing (see Figure 5.8).

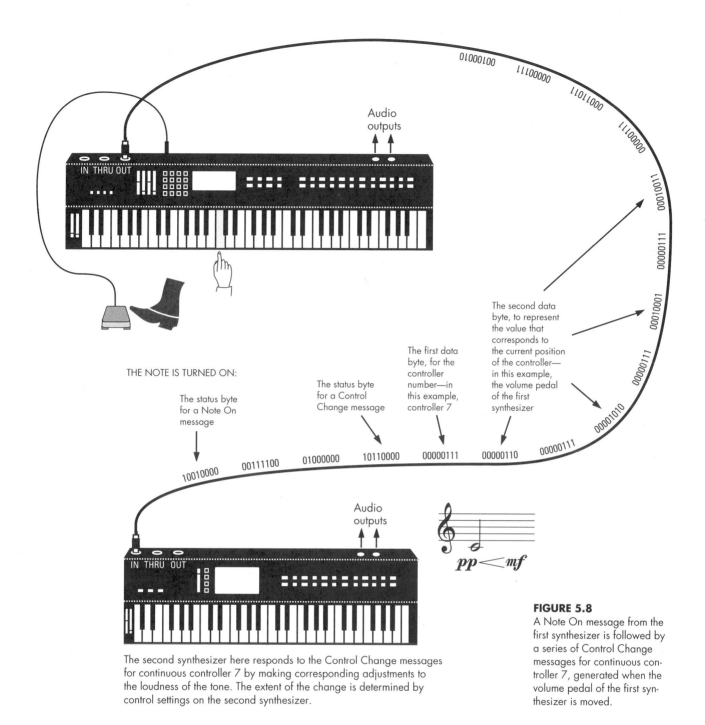

THE NOTE IS TURNED ON:

The status byte for a Note On message

The status byte for a Control Change message

The first data byte, for the controller number—in this example, controller 7

The second data byte, to represent the value that corresponds to the current position of the controller—in this example, the volume pedal of the first synthesizer

Audio outputs

The second synthesizer here responds to the Control Change messages for continuous controller 7 by making corresponding adjustments to the loudness of the tone. The extent of the change is determined by control settings on the second synthesizer.

FIGURE 5.8
A Note On message from the first synthesizer is followed by a series of Control Change messages for continuous controller 7, generated when the volume pedal of the first synthesizer is moved.

Another standard continuous controller is the foot pedal, which is desig-nated as controller 4. Messages from the foot pedal can be used to control the brightness of timbre, the width of vibrato, or some other aspect of the sound, again as determined by the patch programming of the receiving synthesizer.

Controllers 64 through 120 (inclusive) are reserved for **switch con-trollers.** If the value generated by one of these controllers is between 64 and 127 (inclusive), then the switch is considered to be in the On position.

A value between 0 and 63 (inclusive) signifies that the switch is off. As described earlier, a foot switch (or piano-type pedal) is often used much like the damper pedal on a piano, to sustain the tones being produced even after the keys are released. Controller 64 is reserved for this function.

Controller 65 is used as a switch for **portamento.** When this switch (normally a foot switch) is on, the pitch produced by the receiving synthesizer shifts smoothly and continuously (unless programmed otherwise) through the intervening frequencies between that of the first key played and that of a new key. The duration of this glide between pitches can be determined, on many instruments, by the setting of continuous controller 5.

Controller messages are useful for shaping a tone and creating nuance. A variety of computer programs and accessory devices can enhance this power by making it possible to translate one type of controller message into another, to scale the values of controller messages, or even to invert their values (so that, for example, turning up the modulation wheel decreases the vibrato). However, controller messages can become rather profuse. With several controllers in action at the same time, it becomes possible to generate MIDI messages faster than they can be transmitted— to oversaturate the capacity of MIDI to move data (a situation often described as "MIDI clog"). A transmission rate of 31,250 bits per second may seem very generous, but it is surprising how soon this limit can be reached by an ambitious composer or busy performer. Strategies for dealing with this limitation will be described later in this chapter.

PITCH BEND CHANGE MESSAGES

While the resolution of Control Change messages into 128 possible values (from 0 to 127) is sufficient for such things as changes in amplitude or width of vibrato, it is often not satisfactory for changes in pitch. The ear is sensitive to very small differences in pitch. If a pitch bend wheel is programmed with a range of two octaves (that is, the pitch can be bent as much as one octave up or one octave down), and if this range were to be represented by a controller message of only 128 steps of resolution, then the pitch bend would most likely be heard as a series of small, but discrete, changes in pitch.

Therefore, **Pitch Bend Change messages** consist of a unique status byte followed by two data bytes (see Figure 5.9). The two data bytes, identified as the least significant byte (LSB) and the most significant byte (MSB), together provide a total of 16,384 steps of resolution—much more than adequate to represent inflections of pitch that can be heard to be continuous.

PROGRAM CHANGE MESSAGES

As described earlier, virtually all live-performance synthesizers produced since the early 1980s have been programmable, in the sense that the set-

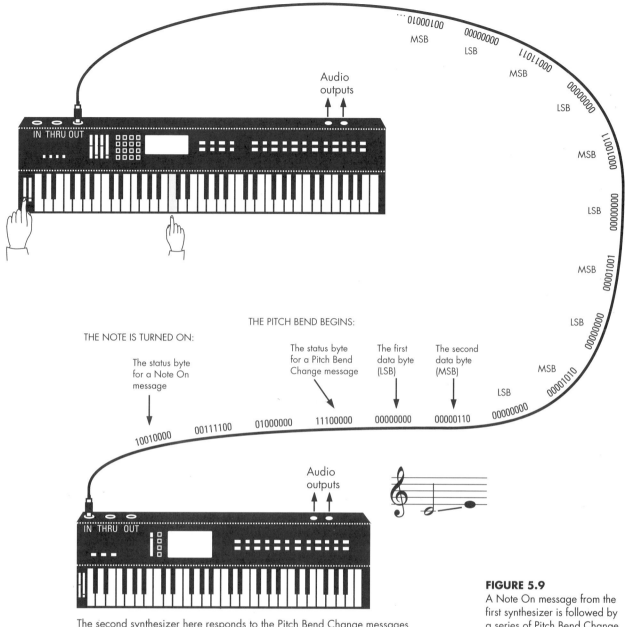

FIGURE 5.9
A Note On message from the first synthesizer is followed by a series of Pitch Bend Change messages that are being generated as the pitch bend wheel is moved.

The second synthesizer here responds to the Pitch Bend Change messages from the first synthesizer by making corresponding adjustments to the pitch of the tone. The extent of the change is usually determined by control settings on the second synthesizer.

tings of the dials and switches can be scanned and digitally encoded for storage in the memory of the synthesizer.[9] Several of these sets of control settings are typically stored together in memory banks. An individual set can be recalled by pushing the appropriate bank button and then the

9. Many synthesizers, beginning with the Yamaha DX7 in 1983, have dispensed with most of the dials and switches on the front panel, however, in an effort to simplify the mass production of these devices and lower costs. The buttons and dials that remain typically have multiple functions. This greatly complicates a musician's efforts to create original sounds (although, as will be described in Chapter 6, a small computer can be used to ease this task considerably).

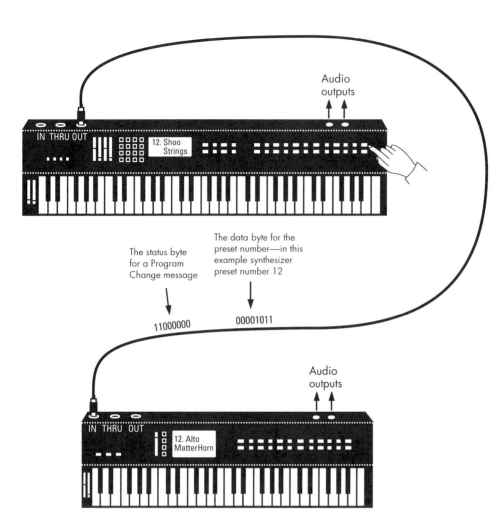

FIGURE 5.10
A Program Change message is transmitted from the first synthesizer to the second one.

desired "preset" or "program" button on the control panel of the synthesizer.

These preset changes can also occur in response to **Program Change messages** received from another device in a network of MIDI instruments. For example, when preset button 12 is pushed on the first synthesizer in Figure 5.10, it may call up a patch called Shoo Strings on that synthesizer, while simultaneously generating a Program Change message. When the second synthesizer receives this message, it will respond by calling up the corresponding preset in its memory, perhaps something called Alto Matter-Horn.[10] The precise nature of the corresponding presets in the memory banks of each synthesizer is determined by the tone-generation programming capabilities of each synthesizer, and by the particular set of presets currently stored in the memory of each.

---

10. Note that although Program Change values range from 0 to 127, the presets on most synthesizers are numbered from 1 to a maximum of 128. On some synthesizers, they are numbered according to a variant of the octal numbering system (see Appendix B). Therefore, it is often necessary to offset or translate the values provided by a Program Change message.

Performance Action	Resulting MIDI Message(s)
Playing a key	A Note On message
Releasing a key	A Note Off message or, more typically, a Note On message with a velocity of zero
Pressing harder on a key that is already pressed down	A series of channel pressure ("mono" aftertouch) messages or, on more expensive instruments, a series of key pressure ("poly" aftertouch) messages
Moving the modulation wheel	A series of Control Change messages (controller 1)
Pushing the volume pedal	A series of Control Change messages (controller 7)
Depressing the sustain pedal	A Control Change message (controller 64)
Moving the pitch wheel	A series of Pitch Bend Change messages
Pressing a preset button	A Program Change message

It is relatively easy to replace the presets of most synthesizers with another set. On many synthesizers, banks of preset information can be stored on memory cards or cartridges that can be easily inserted and removed from data ports on the front or back panels. Preset information can also sometimes be transmitted from one synthesizer to another as part of a MIDI message called a System-Exclusive message (described in detail in Chapter 6). As a result, it is often difficult to know, at an intuitive level at least, which sound color will be called forth by a given Program Change message. A Program Change message for preset 12, for example, may call up the patch called Alto MatterHorn, but if a different bank of presets has been loaded into the synthesizer that receives the message, a patch called Bass ShoeHorn or Anti-MatterHorn may turn up instead!

Thus, while one of the most powerful features of a modern sound synthesizer is its capacity to produce a range of perhaps thousands of different sound colors, it can often be exasperating to figure out precisely which 32 (or 64 or 128) of those possibilities presently reside in the preset memory banks of the synthesizer at hand. As will be described later, a small computer with a MIDI interface can be of great value in the management of these "libraries" of possible sounds.

EXTENDING THE MIDI NETWORK

The connection of two synthesizers by a MIDI cable makes possible a number of useful and interesting techniques. For example, it becomes rather easy to "layer" a melody—to enrich its timbre by doubling it with the different tone color of a second synthesizer. If the velocity sensitivity of the tone generators of each instrument is adjusted so that, for example, the second synthesizer is more responsive to higher velocity values, and if the second synthesizer uses a preset voice that is brighter or louder, it becomes possible to create more realistic rhythmic accents and other dynamic effects.

FIGURE 5.11
A Yamaha DX7 and its corresponding expander module, the TX7.

The second synthesizer provides the added punch on notes with accents. Similar effects of tonal shading or relative loudness can be achieved if aftertouch information is used differently by each instrument to control the timbre or amplitude of sustained tones.

For techniques such as these, the set of keys on the second synthesizer is superfluous. For some of their more popular instruments, therefore, many manufacturers offer models without keyboards. These **tone modules,** or **expander modules** (see Figure 5.11), can be played only by connecting them to a source of MIDI messages, such as a synthesizer with a keyboard (or to one of the alternate controllers described in Chapter 6, such as a guitar controller or wind controller). Typically, expander modules are somewhat less expensive than the corresponding models of the instruments with keyboards. Thus, they provide a more economical alternative for a musician seeking to expand a studio.[11]

The repertory of techniques possible with two synthesizers, or a synthesizer with an expander module, is relatively limited, however. When a third synthesizer is added to the network, the possibilities are vastly increased.

In the network of synthesizers shown in Figure 5.12, the MIDI data generated by the first synthesizer can control the production of sound by the second synthesizer, and the MIDI data generated by the second synthesizer can control the sounds of the third instrument, a synthesizer expander module. However, the data that originate with the first synthesizer do not pass through the second synthesizer and go on to control the third instrument. The data that reach the last instrument are those transmitted from the middle synthesizer. The MIDI data that appear at the MIDI OUT connector of a particular device—in this case, the middle synthesizer—are only

---

11. From the manufacturer's point of view, this correspondingly represents a significant opportunity for expansion of the market. It is one of the significant attractions the Musical Instrument Digital Interface has had for manufacturers, and one of the reasons it has enjoyed the degree of success that it has.

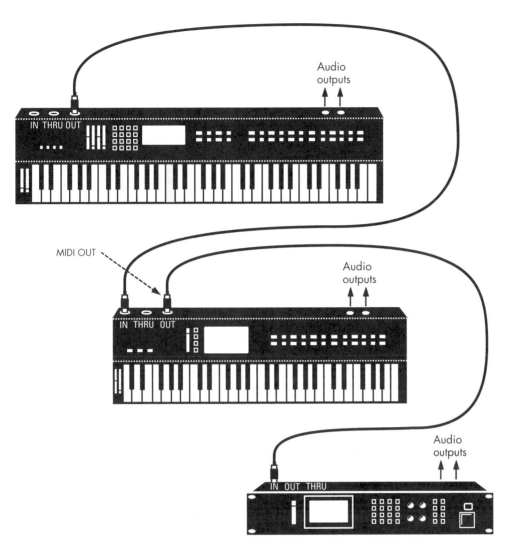

FIGURE 5.12
A limited way to connect more than two MIDI devices. The MIDI messages from the first device in the chain are not passed along to the synthesizer expander module at the end of the chain.

those that are generated within the device itself. To reach the expander module with messages from the first synthesizer requires a different MIDI jack on the middle synthesizer. The MIDI specification, therefore, provides for a third MIDI connector—the MIDI THRU jack. This jack provides a copy of any data that arrive at the MIDI IN connector.

The MIDI THRU jack makes possible a slightly different configuration of devices, as illustrated by the network of synthesizers shown in Figure 5.13. MIDI data that originate with the first synthesizer can control the production of sounds by the second synthesizer and are also passed through the MIDI THRU jack of the second synthesizer to control the sounds of the synthesizer expander module. Any MIDI data that might be generated by the second synthesizer or the expander module have no effect, however, because the MIDI OUT jacks of these instruments are not patched to the MIDI IN jacks of any other devices. Many devices connected in a network such as this can receive MIDI data, but normally only one device will serve as the source of MIDI data.

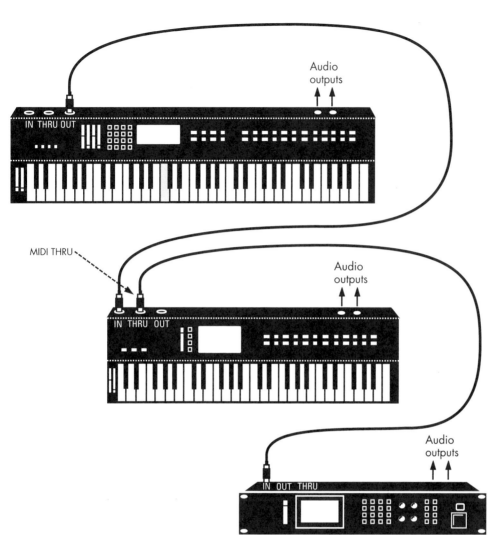

FIGURE 5.13
A "daisy chain" of MIDI devices. The MIDI messages from the first device in the chain are passed through the MIDI THRU connector of the second synthesizer to the synthesizer expander module at the end of the chain. Both the second synthesizer and the expander module can now be controlled by the first synthesizer.

This **daisy-chain network** of receiving devices can be extended even further if a MIDI cable is connected from the MIDI THRU jack of the third instrument to the MIDI IN jack of a fourth device. A MIDI cable can then be connected from the MIDI THRU jack of the fourth device to the MIDI IN jack of a fifth device, and so forth. There are limits to the number of devices that can be chained in a network of this sort, however. First, every time the MIDI signal that originates from the first synthesizer is retransmitted from the MIDI THRU jack of a subsequent synthesizer, there is some degradation of the quality of the signal. By the time the signal reaches a sixth or seventh device in the chain, it will be difficult to read without significant errors (for example, some notes might not play, while others might not stop). Second, many instruments do not have MIDI THRU jacks, which limits them to being placed at the beginning or at the end of the chain.

A more satisfactory arrangement of devices uses an accessory called a **MIDI THRU box.** This is a relatively simple box that receives MIDI data at

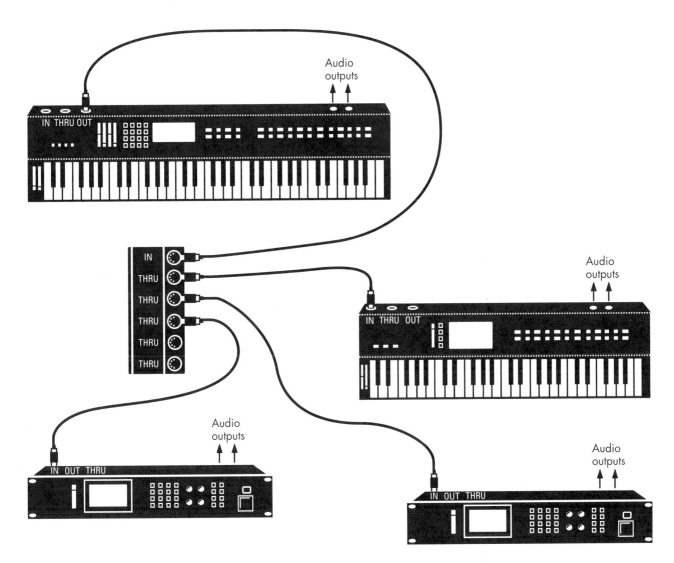

a single MIDI IN jack and then copies it to two or more parallel MIDI THRU jacks. Figure 5.14 illustrates a configuration of devices, called a **MIDI star network,** that uses a MIDI THRU box. Each device that receives MIDI data in this network will receive a relatively fresh copy of it, since the signal will have been retransmitted only once, by the MIDI THRU box, after leaving the source device.

FIGURE 5.14
A "star" configuration for a MIDI network. The MIDI THRU box makes copies of the MIDI messages from the first keyboard synthesizer, then passes them on not only to a second synthesizer but also to a couple of tone modules.

MIDI CHANNELS AND MODES

One of the principal motivations for assembling a network of MIDI devices (apart from the sheer joy of acquisition) is that it makes possible a distribution of musical tasks among several instruments. For example, one synthesizer might be dedicated to playing bass lines, another might provide a series of chords for accompaniment, while a third might carry the melody. Different instruments can be controlled differently as well. At the

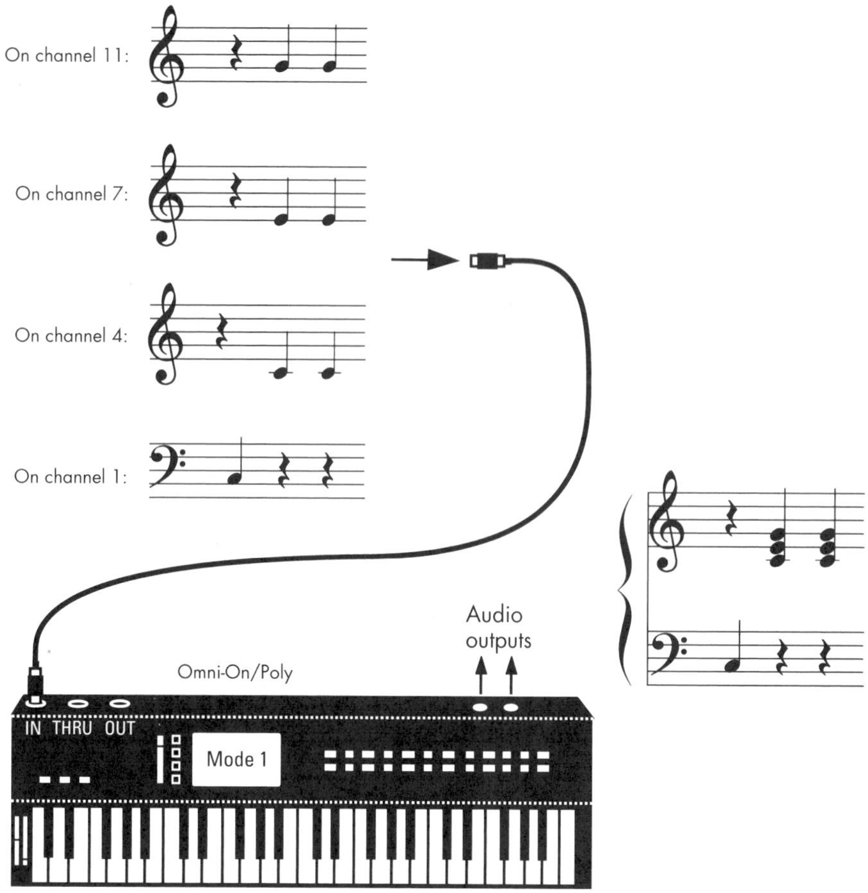

FIGURE 5.15
The response of a synthesizer in Mode 1 to a set of Note On messages on various channels.

beginning of the composition, for example, it may be desirable to set the balance of volume among the instruments by sending to each instrument a unique Control Change message for controller 7. At some point later in the composition, it may be desirable to send a particular Program Change message to each synthesizer.

MIDI messages such as those discussed in this chapter are marked with "channel" information, so that they can be ignored by some instruments while being accepted by others.[12] MIDI data can be transmitted on as many as 16 channels through a single cable or data path. Some messages, encoded for a particular channel, can be intended for one particular synthesizer, while other messages in the data stream, encoded for other channels, can be designated for one or more of up to 15 other instruments. The devices in the network must be prepared to receive and respond to these messages as intended, however. For a receiving instrument, according to the MIDI specification, there are four possible modes of responding to channel information.

Mode 1 is identified as **Omni-On/Poly.** In this mode, the instrument will disregard the channel designations in the status bytes of the messages and

---

12. Specifically, the final four bits of the status byte of such a MIDI message are used to represent a number from 1 to 16. This denotes the channel on which the message is being transmitted.

will attempt to respond to all MIDI messages on all channels (this is what is meant by Omni-On). The device will play as many simultaneous tones as it is called upon to play and is able to play (Poly denotes the word *polyphonic,* meaning "many-voiced"), as illustrated in Figure 5.15. Often Mode 1 is referred to as the "Midiot" mode, because it seems as though its primary purpose is to ensure that an instrument fresh from the store and out of the box will be prepared to respond immediately to MIDI messages. Although this may reassure the new owner that "the MIDI part works OK," it also places a severe limitation on the versatility of the instrument in a network with other MIDI devices.

Mode 2, referred to as **Omni-On/Mono,** is of even less practical value. An instrument in this mode will attempt to respond to all MIDI messages on all channels, but will play only one tone at any particular moment (see Figure 5.16). This mode is reported to have come into existence by mistake when one very important manufacturer of synthesizers apparently misunderstood the terms of an early draft of the MIDI specification.

Mode 3, on the other hand, is of absolutely crucial value. In this mode, identified as **Omni-Off/Poly,** a receiving instrument is programmed to respond only to MIDI messages whose status bytes signify a particular channel. The status bytes of all received MIDI messages will be examined, but the only messages that will be acted upon are those whose channel

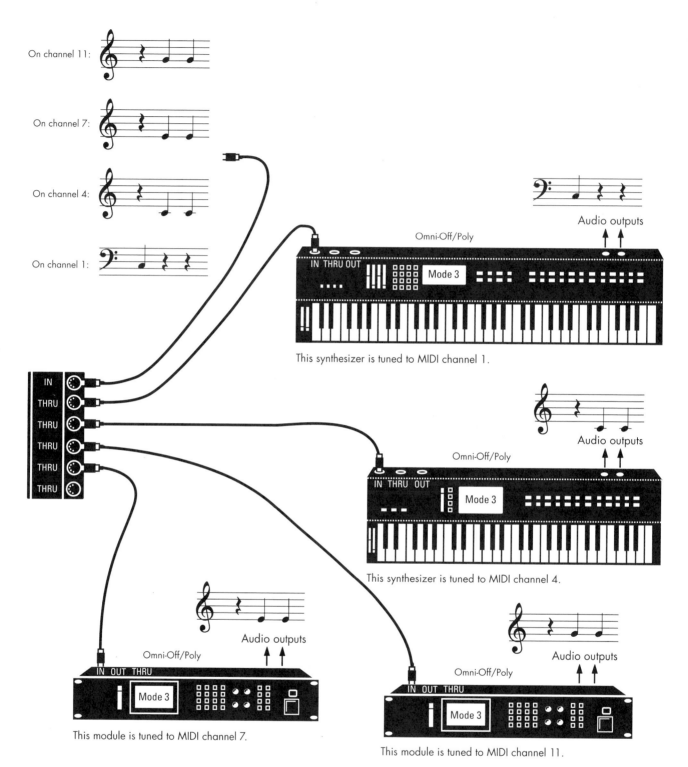

On channel 11:

On channel 7:

On channel 4:

On channel 1:

Omni-Off/Poly

IN THRU OUT

Mode 3

Audio outputs

This synthesizer is tuned to MIDI channel 1.

IN
THRU
THRU
THRU
THRU
THRU

Omni-Off/Poly

IN THRU OUT

Mode 3

Audio outputs

This synthesizer is tuned to MIDI channel 4.

Audio outputs

Omni-Off/Poly

IN OUT THRU

Mode 3

This module is tuned to MIDI channel 7.

Audio outputs

Omni-Off/Poly

IN OUT THRU

Mode 3

This module is tuned to MIDI channel 11.

FIGURE 5.17
The response of a network of synthesizers in Mode 3 to a set of Note On messages on various channels.

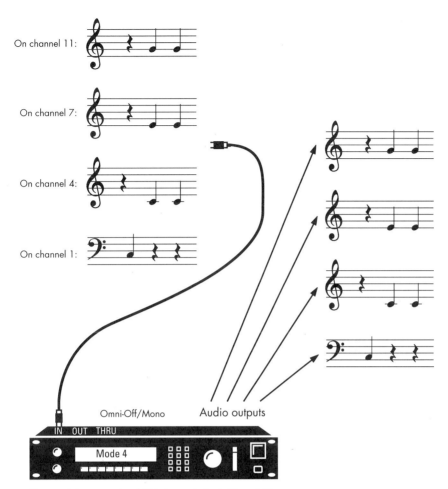

On channel 11:

On channel 7:

On channel 4:

On channel 1:

Omni-Off/Mono   Audio outputs

IN OUT THRU

Mode 4

This module is tuned to MIDI channels 1, 4, 7, and 11.

information matches the channel number to which the instrument is tuned (hence, Omni-Off). The instrument will play as many tones for that channel as it is called upon to play and is able to play (hence, Poly). The various devices in a MIDI network can each be placed in this mode and programmed to different MIDI channels, as illustrated in Figure 5.17. In this way, messages from the source device can be targeted for particular instruments. It is conceivable, therefore, that MIDI messages traveling through a single cable can result in as many as 16 different, simultaneous musical parts being sounded by as many as 16 different instruments.

Mode 4, described as **Omni-Off/Mono,** is similarly useful. An instrument can be tuned to respond to MIDI messages on a range of channels. The device will typically assign a different preset sound for each channel. Thus, different parts of a composition can be played with different timbres at the same time on the same instrument (see Figure 5.18). A synthesizer in this mode is functioning as if it were several synthesizers, and is described as a **multitimbral** instrument.

a. With programmable voice allocation, three voices must be set aside ahead of time to accommodate all of the notes in the melody. Five voices must be reserved to cover all of the tones used at any one time in the chords. Only one voice needs to be set aside for the bass line. If the tone module is capable of producing a total of 16 voices at a time, then only seven unassigned voices remain for use in parts that can layer the melody or the bass line—or for new parts, such as a countermelody.

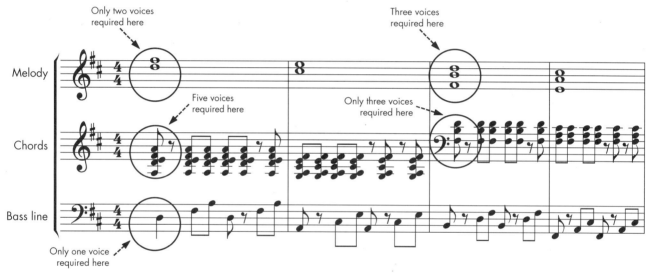

b. With dynamic voice allocation, voices are reassigned as needed. At any particular moment in this example, no more than eight voices are being used; in measures 3 and 4, only seven voices are in use. If the tone module is capable of producing a total of 16 voices at a time, then as many as eight or nine unassigned voices remain for use in other musical parts.

Normally a synthesizer in Mode 4 will sound only one tone at a time per channel (hence, the descriptive label Mono). However, some multitimbral instruments have gone somewhat beyond this, and are able to respond polyphonically on each channel. The total number of simultaneous tones is limited to the total number of "voices" the device is designed to generate, however.

A limited number of voices can be allocated among the channels being used in one of two ways. With **programmable voice allocation,** the number of voices available for each channel is determined by the user before the music is played (Figure 5.19a). Other, more recent instruments are

FIGURE 5.19
Programmable versus dynamic methods of voice allocation in a multitimbral tone module.

designed for **dynamic voice allocation,** in which the device reassigns the number of voices in use for each channel as requirements change during the performance of the music (Figure 5.19b). For example, at the beginning of the music, one voice may be required for the bass part being played through channel 1, five voices may be required for the chord on channel 2, and two voices may be required for the melody on channel 3. Later, only three voices may be required for the chord on channel 2, while two more voices may be required for the melody on channel 3. The device will freely trade voices as required, without requiring the ongoing attention of the performer.

ÉTUDE NO. 5.1

Connect two synthesizers with a MIDI cable (or find two that are already connected). Check to be certain that the second synthesizer is set to MIDI Mode 3, and that it is prepared to receive messages on the same channel as the one on which the first synthesizer is prepared to transmit messages.

On the keyboard of the first synthesizer, play a brief melody (or, if your keyboard skills are not quite ready for this, try a rhythmic pattern that can be played on just two keys).

Now, experiment with the preset buttons on the first synthesizer to call up different presets on it and the second synthesizer at the same time. Note the response of the second synthesizer (it should respond as if by remote control). Are the numbers of the presets called up on the second synthesizer the same as those on the first? If not, then perhaps the presets of the second synthesizer are numbered by a different system (such as the modified octal numbering system described in Appendix B).

Once you have found a combination of presets that you find appealing, connect the audio outputs of the two synthesizers to the inputs of a multiple-track tape recorder. Play the melody (or rhythmic pattern) again, and record it.

MIDI SEQUENCING

Our MIDI network now includes a keyboard synthesizer that functions as a source for MIDI messages, a second keyboard synthesizer, a synthesizer expander module, and a MIDI THRU box. We might also have decided by now to include a multitimbral tone module, such as a sampler module, as shown in Figure 5.20.

The ability to "channel" many MIDI messages means that it is possible to denote particular messages for particular instruments in a MIDI network (or for particular voices in a multitimbral tone module). Typically, however, a keyboard synthesizer can be configured to transmit MIDI messages on only one of the 16 MIDI channels that share a MIDI data path. This, of

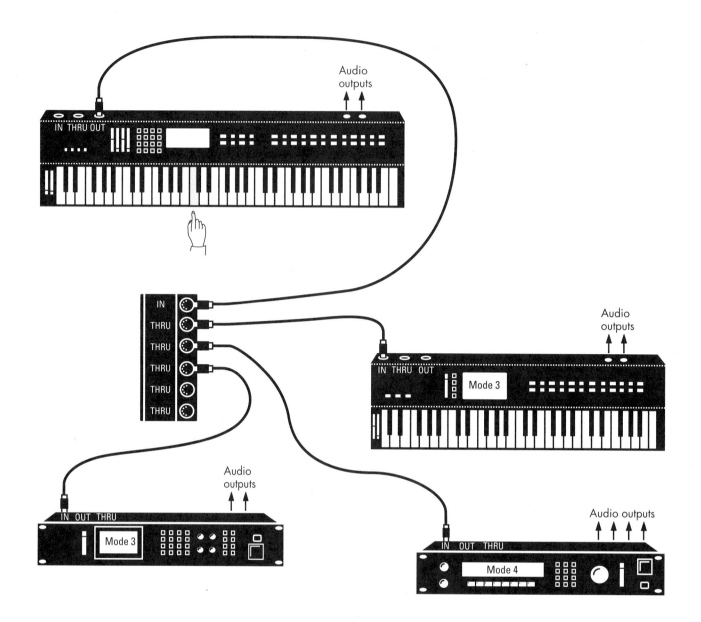

course, rather severely limits the potential for controlling various instruments and devices independently. However, the addition of a **sequencer,** a device that can record MIDI data and transmit it on many channels simultaneously, makes possible a more complete realization of the power and versatility of a multiple-channel MIDI network.

The concept of sequencing first became widely known as a technique of analog synthesis in the late 1960s. As described in Chapter 8, these early sequencers were control-voltage source modules on analog instruments such as the Buchla, Moog, and ARP synthesizers. Rows of dials on these modules provided the means to program carefully one or more series of as many as a few dozen control voltages. These control voltages could then be patched to an oscillator to create a series of pitches, to a filter to produce a series of tone colors, or to the sequencer's own clock to create a pattern of durations. By the mid-1970s, a second generation of sequencers, capable of

FIGURE 5.20
Our MIDI network now includes a keyboard synthesizer that functions as a source for MIDI messages, a MIDI THRU box, a second keyboard synthesizer, a synthesizer expander module, and a new addition—a multitimbral sampler module.

FIGURE 5.21
The Roland MC-50, a hardware sequencer popular in recent years. (MC-50 is a registered trademark of and is used with the permission of Roland Corporation US.)

recording in digital form as many as a thousand or so control voltages, was introduced. Many of these devices also provided a means for storing the information on a data cassette.

With the widespread acceptance of MIDI by the mid-1980s, however, the techniques of sequencing have become much more sophisticated. The contemporary sequencer is now essentially a MIDI data recorder. It includes hardware connectors for MIDI cables (and perhaps connectors for other types of control signals as well), digital memory, a floppy-disk drive (or a hard-disk drive) so that the information can be stored and retrieved when needed, and a data processor. With many sequencers, the programming instructions for the data processor are stored on a permanent memory chip that is installed internally. Such sequencers are called dedicated, or hardware, sequencers (see Figure 5.21).

Other sequencers, called software sequencers, consist of the programming instructions themselves. These programs are intended to be operated on general-purpose microcomputers, such as the Macintosh, the Atari, or IBM-compatible computers. These computers can be easily connected to an interface box that can receive and transmit MIDI messages; or, as in the case of the Atari computer, the MIDI connectors might be installed on the computer itself.

Hardware and software sequencers each have distinct advantages and disadvantages. Hardware sequencers tend to be more rugged and easier to set up, and are therefore particularly well suited to the requirements of live performance. In fact, some keyboard instruments that are popular now among synthesists who perform live include an on-board hardware sequencer.[13] However, hardware sequencers, including those installed on keyboard instruments, usually have small display screens, making it difficult to gain access to the information stored in the memory of the device and to make changes to it. An attempt to edit a sequence on a hardware sequencer

---

13. If the instrument also has readily accessible drum sounds, as well as the sounds of other percussive instruments, then it is often advertised as a workstation.

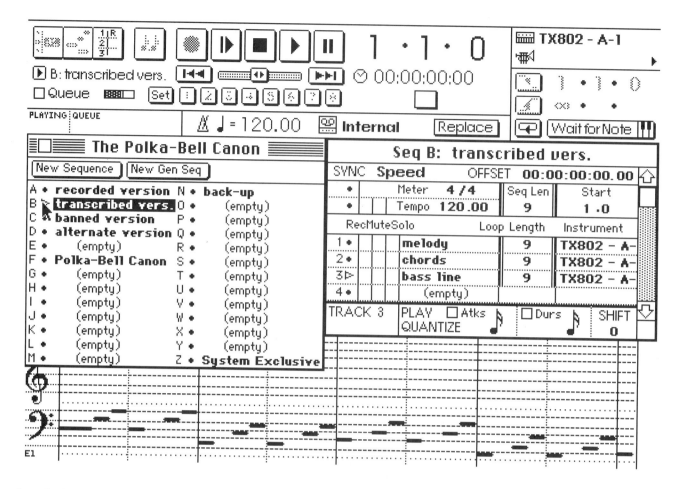

shortly before a performance can jeopardize not only the success of the performance, but also the esteem and affections of one's friends and fellow performers!

Software sequencers tend to be somewhat easier to work with, because a much greater amount of information can be displayed on a computer screen (see Figure 5.22). Because software sequencers essentially reside on computer disks, it is relatively easy to obtain a frequent series of updates and improvements from the software designer. Changes to the programming instructions of a hardware sequencer are provided on a replacement memory chip that must be installed by someone with the appropriate skills and tools. Software sequencers, therefore, tend to have more operating functions, and these are also likely to be more sophisticated and versatile. On the other hand, running a software sequencer on an onstage microcomputer can be rather cumbersome. For this reason, the natural home of the software sequencer is the studio, not the stage.

RECORDING MIDI DATA

One of the most important functions of a sequencer is to relate the occurrence of MIDI events to timing information. MIDI messages received by the sequencer are recorded in the sequencer's memory along with informa-

FIGURE 5.22

A screen display from a micro-computer that is running a software-based sequencer. (Courtesy of Opcode Systems, Inc.)

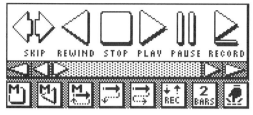

FIGURE 5.23

Screen display of the "transport control buttons" for a popular software-based sequencer. Note that the operation of this MIDI sequencer is modeled after the familiar techniques of multiple-track recording. (Courtesy of Mark of the Unicorn, Inc.)

FIGURE 5.24

A track list display for a software-based sequencer. Note that track 11 is "muted." An alternate version of the melody for the instrument assigned to MIDI channel 3 has been recorded on this track. (Courtesy of Opcode Systems, Inc.)

Seq A: recorded version			
SYNC Speed		OFFSET	00:00:00:00.00

		Meter 4 / 4	Seq Len	Start
•		Tempo 120.00	9	1 · 0

RecMuteSolo			Loop Length	Instrument
1 •		bass line	9	Channel 1
2 •		chords	9	Channel 2
3 •		melody	9	Channel 3
4 •		melody	9	Channel 4
5 •		melody	9	Channel 7
6 •		modulation	9	Channel 2
7 •		(empty)		
8 •		digital delay	9	Channel 9
9 •		reverb depth	9	Channel 9
10 •		(empty)		
11 ▷	M	melody bak	9	Channel 3

TRACK 3	PLAY ☐ Atks ♪	☐ Durs ♪	SHIFT
	QUANTIZE ♩	♩	0

tion pertaining to when the messages are received. This timing information is generated by the sequencer's internal clock, or it can be received from the clock of another device—perhaps a second sequencer or a drum machine.

A typical sequencer is programmed and designed to operate in ways that are quite familiar to musicians who have had some experience with the techniques of multiple-track recording and mixing. For instance, the operating controls of the sequencer generally include a row of buttons for record, playback, stop, and pause functions (see Figure 5.23). With a software sequencer, these may take the form of "virtual buttons" on the computer screen that are "pushed" by using a mouse to place the screen cursor on them, or by typing the appropriately designated keys on the computer keyboard. Some sequencers even have Fast Forward and Rewind buttons.

Streams of MIDI data from successive performances at the keyboard (or any other source of MIDI messages) are typically recorded in segments of memory referred to as tracks. Just as with a multiple-track recorder, a complete musical texture can be assembled by successively overdubbing each musical part on a separate track. Alternative versions of a part, such as a solo line, can be recorded on different tracks. When the sequence is played back, selected tracks can be muted or soloed, in a way similar to what can be done on most audio mixing consoles (see Figure 5.24). In this way, individual tracks or particular combinations of tracks can be auditioned more closely. This is particularly helpful to the musician who is trying to locate wrong notes and similar errors in a track.

A hardware sequencer typically provides 8, 16, or 32 tracks for recording MIDI data. A software sequencer, on the other hand, is limited only by the amount of free memory in the computer, and might therefore have as many as 99 available tracks. Some software sequencers, in fact, can accommodate immediate access to dozens of separate sequences, each of which might include as many as 99 tracks.

The most common way to create a sequence is to record the MIDI messages as they are being generated by a performance. This method is called **real-time recording.** To facilitate this, virtually all sequencers provide a means to produce a metronome sound, such as a click or a drum beat, so that the performer can maintain a sense of the tempo of the music. This feature also can provide for count-in beats (what a musician would refer to as "one measure for nothing"), so that the performer can establish a sense of the tempo by the time the first note is to be played.

Particularly difficult passages can be recorded at a slower tempo. When played back at the faster, intended tempo, they are usually much more precise rhythmically. With the analog recording of sounds (as you may recall from Chapter 2), as the playback speed is increased, the pitch rises as well. But when a MIDI sequence is played back at a faster tempo, the values of the MIDI key numbers remain unchanged, and the pitches are not transposed.

An alternative to the real-time recording of MIDI data is a technique of recording MIDI events one by one, called **step recording,** or step entry. For example, the duration of a note might be selected from a menu of note values (including whole notes, half notes, quarter notes, and so on), and the velocity of the note can be typed on a numeric keypad or computer keyboard. Then the key number is typed, or the corresponding key is played on a MIDI keyboard. The same values for duration and velocity will continue to be used for succeeding notes until different values are selected or typed. The step-entry method of recording has some appeal to those aspiring musicians who have limited abilities as performers of keyboard or other instruments. However, the technique does not produce the rhythmic subtleties and gestural nuances that can be captured with real-time recording. Step-entered tracks, being relatively untouched by human hands, typically have a lifeless, even robotic quality.

Yet another alternative to real-time recording is a technique called **loop recording.** A duration of several beats or measures is first defined as the length of the loop. Then, MIDI data are recorded in real time until the duration of the loop has passed. At that point, the clock resets to the beginning of the loop, and recording continues. Each time the clock passes through the loop, new MIDI messages can be recorded in addition to those that were recorded during previous passes. Complex patterns of pitch, timbre, and rhythm can be built up rather easily this way. For example, MIDI notes that trigger bass drum sounds can be recorded during the first pass through the loop, snare drum sounds can be added during the second pass, cymbal sounds can be added during the third, and so forth. As a matter of fact, the technique of loop recording is most commonly implemented in the sequencer section of digital drum machines (to be described in Chapter 6).

INPUT PROCESSING

Because MIDI messages are parcels of digital information, they can be easily modified—recomputed, as it were—by a small computer running a software sequencer program or by a hardware sequencer (which is essentially a special-purpose computer). In fact, some modifications can be made as the messages arrive at the sequencer, before they might be recorded. One of the most common forms of such input processing is data filtering. For example, many keyboard synthesizers generate quite a few aftertouch messages as the keys are played, and it may not be convenient or even possible to turn off the aftertouch sensitivity of the keyboard on those occasions when these messages are not needed by any of the other instruments in the MIDI network. If the sequencer can be programmed to ignore aftertouch information, then its memory can be used much more efficiently. Many sequencers can filter almost any kind of MIDI message in this way.

Another type of input processing is referred to as **rechannelizing.** In the MIDI network illustrated in Figure 5.25, the source of MIDI information is the keyboard synthesizer at the top. These messages are transmitted on MIDI channel 1. The intended recipients of these messages are the synthesizer expander module, set to channel 2, the second keyboard synthesizer, on channel 3, and the multitimbral sampler module, on channels 4, 5, and 6. The source keyboard is also prepared to respond to any MIDI messages it may receive that are on channel 7. If the sequencer is able to change the channel designation in the status bytes of the incoming messages—if it can "rechannelize" the data—then it becomes possible for the source keyboard to play any of the other instruments in the network. For example, if the messages from the source keyboard are "bumped" from channel 1 to channel 3, then the other keyboard synthesizer plays. If the messages are reassigned to channel 4, then one of the voices in the sampler module will sound. This capability of redirecting, or rechannelizing, MIDI messages, even when the sequencer is not in its record mode, is called **input thru.**

If the MIDI messages from the source keyboard in Figure 5.25 are rechannelized by the sequencer to channel 7, then there occurs a potentially troublesome situation. As the keys of the synthesizer are played, it produces the corresponding tones on that synthesizer. At the same time, the synthesizer is receiving messages from the sequencer that request it to play those same tones again. A four-tone chord becomes an eight-tone chord—four tones played directly, and the same four tones also played by "remote control." The synthesizer uses twice as many voices as are necessary, and the timbre is oddly doubled. To avert this situation, many synthesizers have a **local on/off** switch. This makes it possible to isolate the tone-generation circuitry of the instrument from the keyboard on that instrument. Although the keyboard can still generate MIDI messages for other devices, it cannot trigger the production of tones by its own tone-generation circuits whenever the local control is off, unless the messages are returned to the synthesizer from the sequencer.

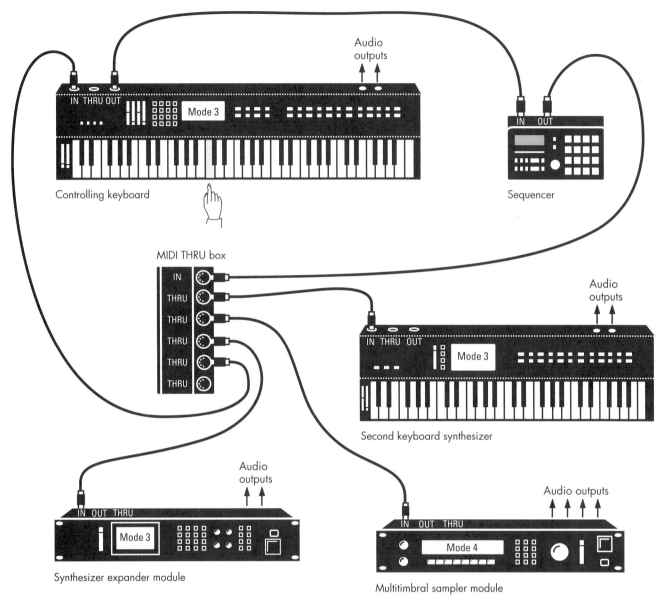

FIGURE 5.25
We have now added a hardware sequencer to our MIDI network. Note that the controlling keyboard can receive messages, via the MIDI THRU box, from the sequencer.

ÉTUDE 5.2

*T*ake some time to review the tutorial chapter(s) in the operator's manual of the sequencer you will be using. Then record a repeating pattern of notes on track 1 of the sequencer. The duration of the pattern should be approximately one or two minutes. Rechannelize the track as necessary so that the MIDI channel number of the information recorded on the track matches that of the synthesizer or sampler you decide upon to make those sounds.

Next, on track 2 record a complementary pattern of sounds, rhythmically synchronized to those represented on track 1. Rechannelize track 2 as necessary so that the information recorded there is sounded by a different synthesizer or sampler than that used for track 1.

Finally, on track 3 record a melody. Assign this track to yet another instrument. Mix the outputs of the three instruments. Add reverb or other effects as you wish. Make a two-track tape recording of the final result.

SEQUENCE EDITING

The capability of a sequencer to alter MIDI data as they arrive at the input is exceeded by the possibilities for processing the messages once they are recorded in tracks. For instance, once a series of MIDI messages is recorded into a track, it can be rechannelized by simply changing the channel designation of the track. A musical part, such as a melody or a chord progression that is recorded on a particular track, can be auditioned on several different instruments in the MIDI network by successively rechannelizing the track to the channels on which those instruments expect to receive data. More important, various musical parts, recorded on separate tracks, can be directed to different instruments at the same time, even though all of the data for these tracks originated from one instrument (see Figure 5.26).

It is this capability to record and then rechannelize MIDI data on several tracks that makes the sequencer such a critical component of any effort to realize more completely the potential of a network of MIDI instruments. By providing a means to coordinate closely the performance of music by several instruments, the sequencer makes possible a truly integrated system—in effect, an orchestra of electroacoustic musical instruments. Furthermore, this is an orchestra that is played by a solo musician, the composer of the music.

The fact that a sequencer can also provide powerful techniques for editing recorded MIDI data makes it still more attractive as an addition to the network. Software-based sequencers, which can make use of the larger display screens and more powerful processors of a general-purpose microcomputer, tend to have superior capabilities for the editing and manipulation of recorded MIDI data. With most software sequencers, the data can be displayed in at least two different forms: as a note list, as shown in Figure 5.27, or in graphical format, as seen in Figure 5.28.[14]

In either format, it is relatively easy to locate "wrong notes" and other performance mistakes. Such problems can be corrected by selecting these

---

14. The graphical format is sometimes referred to as a piano-roll display because of its resemblance to the rolls of punched paper used with player pianos during the earlier part of the 20th century. The location on such a roll of a punched hole, from left to right, corresponded to the key of the player piano that was to be played, and the length of the hole determined the duration of the tone. In a sense, the player-piano mechanism was an ancestral form of the contemporary sequencer.

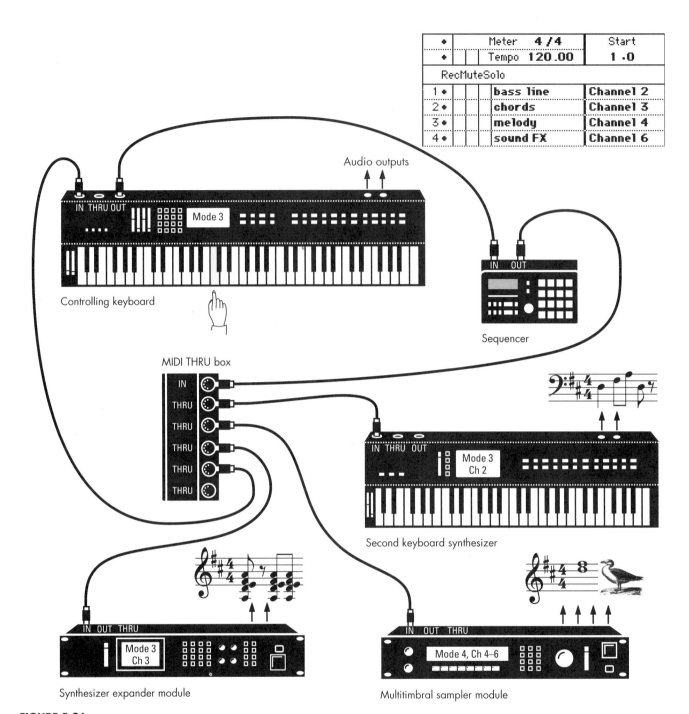

•			Meter	4 /4	Start
•			Tempo 120.00		1 .0
RecMuteSolo					
1 •			bass line		Channel 2
2 •			chords		Channel 3
3 •			melody		Channel 4
4 •			sound FX		Channel 6

FIGURE 5.26

In the sequence shown by the track list (upper right), the bass line was played on the source instrument (the keyboard synthesizer, upper left), then transmitted on channel 1 and recorded on track 1 of the sequencer. It was then rechannelized to channel 2, so that when the sequence is played back, the bass line will be sounded by the second keyboard synthesizer. The chords were played from the source keyboard, still transmitting on channel 1, and recorded on track 2. This track was then rechannelized to channel 3, so that when the sequence is played back, the chords will be sounded by the synthesizer expander module. Next, the melody was performed on the source keyboard (still transmitting on channel 1) and recorded on track 3. This track was then rechannelized to channel 4, so that when the sequence is played back, the melody will be produced by selected voices of the multitimbral sampler module. Another voice of the sampler module has been set to play sound effects (perhaps surf sounds or the cries of seagulls) whenever it receives Note On messages on channel 6. These messages have been recorded on track 4 of the sequence. (Courtesy of Opcode Systems, Inc.)

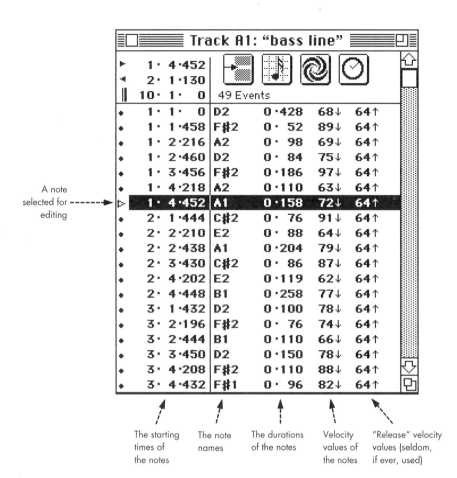

FIGURE 5.27
A "note-list" display from a software-based sequencer. (Courtesy of Opcode Systems, Inc.)

A note selected for editing →

The starting times of the notes

The note names

The durations of the notes

Velocity values of the notes

"Release" velocity values (seldom, if ever, used)

data and replacing them. It is also relatively easy to delete groups of messages, such as a series of extraneous notes or an errant pitch bend, and replace them with a more suitable set of messages.

The insertion of a new message (or series of messages) into a track is a fairly common editing operation. An extra note (including its initial Note On message as well as the corresponding message to end the tone) or any other kind of message can be inserted into any track. For example, while it may be possible to record Program Change messages by placing the sequencer in record mode and then pressing the corresponding preset buttons on the source keyboard, it is much more precise to insert these messages at the sequencer itself. Specific times and preset numbers can simply be typed in.

Similarly, series of Pitch Bend, Aftertouch, or Control Change messages can be added to a sequence. In fact, many software-based sequencers provide a limited set of graphics "tools" so that linear or curved progressions of such messages can be inserted by drawing them on the computer screen (see Figure 5.29). This enables the musician to specify with some degree of precision the musical nuances of pitch, timbre, and intensity that can be controlled by these messages. Also, it is relatively easy to redraw these message contours as the musician later revises and then polishes the musical composition.

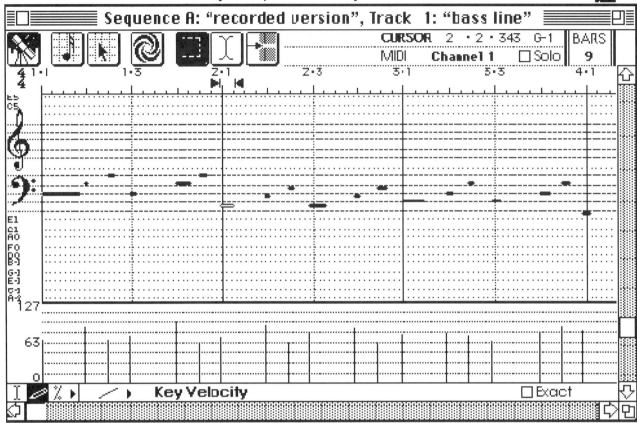

FIGURE 5.28
A graphic, "piano-roll" display from a software-based sequencer. (Courtesy of Opcode Systems, Inc.)

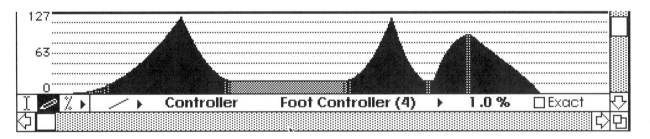

FIGURE 5.29
A graphic display screen, from a software-based sequencer, of contours of continuous controller values. In this example, data originating from a foot controller (continuous controller 4) are displayed.(Courtesy of Opcode Systems, Inc.)

Another important editing function, found on virtually all sequencers, is the ability to copy data. A series of notes can be copied to anywhere in a track, either as an insertion or to replace notes already there. A repetitive pattern of notes can be easily assembled by making multiple copies of the basic pattern of notes and arranging these copies in a series.

Data can also be copied from one track to another. In fact, an entire track can be copied into an empty track, and this makes possible several very useful techniques. For example, whenever a significant amount of editing of a particular track is contemplated, it is a good practice first to make a copy of the entire track as a backup (and then to mute this backup track). Then, should the editing of the original track go poorly, it will be possible to recover the data in its earlier form from the backup track.[15]

The ability to make one or more copies of an entire track greatly facilitates the technique of doubling, or layering, a musical part with the sounds of more than one instrument. The copy tracks are simply rechannelized, enabling one or more additional instruments to respond to the same previously recorded pattern of MIDI messages. The copy tracks can also be edited and embellished, as necessary.

Somewhat more sophisticated is a technique called track splitting. Essentially it involves removing selected data from one track and copying it into an empty track, where it can be edited independently. On many sequencers, track splitting is accomplished in practice by first making a copy of an entire track, then deleting the selected data from the first track. Then, the complementary set of data is removed from the second track. For example, all notes below middle C might be removed from the first track, and all notes above and including middle C might be removed from the second track. The second track might then be rechannelized so that these remaining notes (in this example, presumably those notes that were played on the source synthesizer by the performer's left hand) are sounded by a different instrument. The first track (in this example, only those notes played by the performer's right hand) might also be layered with rechannelized copies, or changed in some other way to suit the aesthetic purpose of the moment. The general procedure is illustrated in Figure 5.30.

Data copying can be a most helpful technique for musicians who compose music that is structured in sections. Blocks of data, including many measures of music on several tracks, can usually be duplicated without too much difficulty. Presumably, however, each repetition of the chorus or verse of a song (or analogous sections for some other form of composition) should not be identical. The editing capabilities of a sequencer make it possible to work relatively easily with each copy of a section independently to incorporate any variation or other adjustment that is required.

If data are copied into a place where other data already exist, the other data will be deleted and replaced. However, many sequencers provide a

---

15. For the same reason, it is always wise to make at least one backup copy of floppy disks that contain important work you cannot afford to lose.

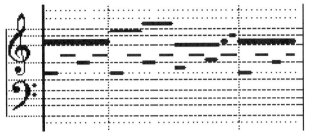

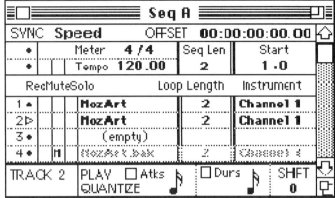

a. The recorded track (shown above in a graphic display) is copied to another track (as shown on the track list to the right). Note that a backup track has also been made, just in case something should go wrong with this procedure.

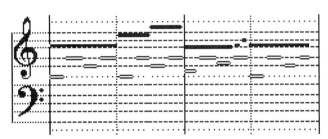

b. The notes to be removed from the first track are selected (as shown above) and then deleted (as shown below).

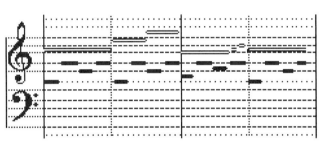

c. The notes to be removed from the second track are then selected (as shown above) and deleted (as shown below).

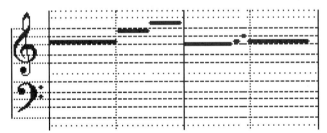

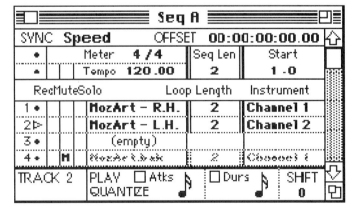

FIGURE 5.30
A technique for accomplishing "track splitting."(Courtesy of Opcode Systems, Inc.)

d. The tracks, now containing the separated notes, can then be rechannelized or copied for layering and embellishment.

means for **merging** new and old data so that both can coexist on the same track. For instance, a pitch bend contour can be copied from one note and then merged with the data for another, "unbent" note without writing over the data for the note itself. In fact, many musicians prefer to record Note On, Pitch Bend, Control Change, and Program Change messages on separate tracks at first, so that each of these kinds of information can be edited separately and more easily. Then, perhaps, all of these streams of data might be merged to a single track.

The process of transposition—of systematically shifting the pitches of a melody or a chord progression to a higher or lower level, perhaps to a different key—has exasperated musicians for centuries. Keyboard players practice diligently for years to acquire the skill to transpose music as they read it in order, for example, to find a key that is well suited to the singer, group of singers, or instrumental musicians with whom they are working. With a MIDI sequencer, however, the process of transposition is as simple as selecting the notes to be transposed and then specifying the direction and extent of the change in pitch. The sequencer then adds or subtracts the specified number to the key number values in the selected Note On messages (and the corresponding messages that turn the tones off, one hopes).

As mentioned previously, many software-based sequencers include the capability of using graphics tools to draw contours of Control Change, Pitch Bend, or Aftertouch values on the computer display screen. Contours of such messages that have been generated by operating the switches, dials, pedals, control wheels, or keys of a source keyboard can be displayed graphically as well. Often, the contour of velocity values of Note On messages can also be shown.

Whether these contours have been drawn or performed, it is generally possible to edit them in a variety of ways. A contour can be rescaled, for example, so that the range of the contour is decreased without changing its shape (see Figure 5.31). A fixed value can be added or subtracted from each of the values in the contour (provided that none of the new values exceeds 127 or is less than zero). The values can also be limited to a specified minimum or maximum value.

One particularly useful technique, called **controller thinning,** involves the systematic removal of messages represented in a contour—perhaps every other message, two out of every three messages, seven out of every eight, or some similar pattern. This technique can be used when an abundance of controller messages, together with Pitch Bend or Aftertouch messages, might exceed the capacity of the MIDI data stream. Such a situation is not likely to occur as a musician performs on a single instrument, but when several tracks, containing many different messages on many different channels, are assembled one by one and then played simultaneously, there is a genuine possibility that the MIDI data path can be oversaturated with information.

Many of these messages may be superfluous. For example, since the ear is relatively insensitive to small changes in loudness, it is probably not

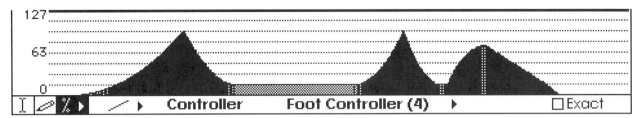

a. Starting with the contour of foot control values shown in Figure 5.29, have been rescaled so that all values are now 80% of their former values.

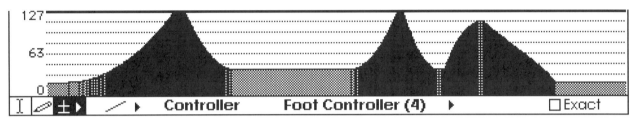

b. The values have all been increased by 20. Note that some of the peaks of this contour have been flattened out; if the sum exceeds 127, the value is limited to 127.

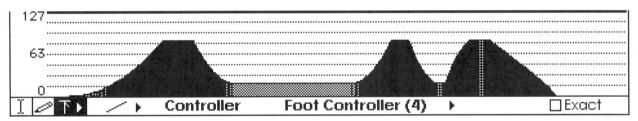

c. A limit of 84 has been placed on the values in the contour. All values originally greater than 84 are now just 84.

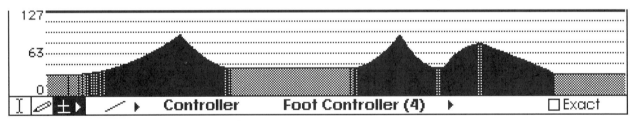

d. The values have been rescaled by 50%, and the resulting values increased by 32. This results in a compression of the range of the contour.

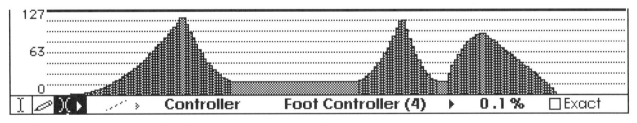

e. The values have been thinned. Only one of every ten previous values remains in the contour.

FIGURE 5.31
Various techniques for editing contours of controller information. These techniques can also be applied to aftertouch, pitch bend, or velocity data.(Courtesy of Opcode Systems, Inc.)

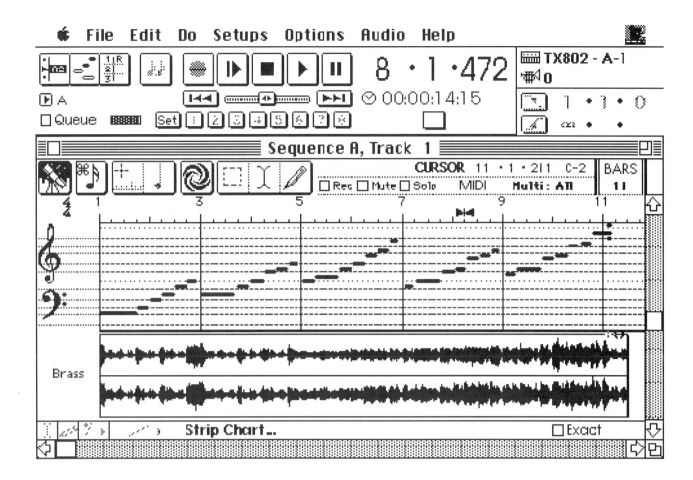

FIGURE 5.32

A screen display from a sequencer program that incorporates the ability to record and edit digitally recorded sounds. MIDI Note On messages are shown here in the piano-roll format. These MIDI notes are accompanied by a stereo digital recording of a brass ensemble, represented here by the parallel displays near the bottom of the window. (Courtesy of Opcode Systems, Inc.)

necessary to have hundreds of messages from controller 7 for each note. An adequate contour can be represented with far fewer values. Thinning the data contours recorded on several tracks can reduce the volume of messages to a manageable quantity without compromising the design or expressiveness of the music in any noticeable way.

The most powerful software sequencers now include the ability to edit and manipulate digitally recorded sounds along with MIDI data. If the computer on which the sequencing program is run is also equipped with the accessories required for hard-disk recording, then two or more tracks of a digital recording can be incorporated into the sequence (see Figure 5.32). This provides unprecedented opportunities for integrating acoustic, sampled, and synthetic sound sources in a single project.

ÉTUDE 5.3

Record a short melody, with some short notes and some notes of longer duration, on one track of a sequencer.

Rechannelize the track and play it a few times to explore how the melody sounds on different synthesizers (audition different presets on these synthesizers as well). Once you have found a synthesizer preset that sounds particularly fine for your melody, play the track again. As the track is playing, move the modulation wheel on the controlling synthesizer during some of the longer notes of the melody. Experiment with this for a while until you are satisfied that you have found some effective ways to use the effect of modulation with your melody.

Now, play the melody track yet again, while recording, on the second track of the sequencer, the modulation wheel movements. Then, call up a display of the modulation wheel messages (continuous controller 1) that have been recorded on track 2 (if your sequencer provides this capability). Edit the data if you think it should be modified.

Connect to the inputs of a multiple-track recorder the audio outputs of the synthesizer that is being played by the sequencer. Play the sequence a few more times as you set recording levels, and then roll the tape.

ÉTUDE 5.4

nce again, record a short melody, with some short notes and some long notes, on one track of a sequencer.

Rechannelize the track and play it a few times to explore how the melody sounds on different synthesizers. For this project, you may find that plucked-string sounds provide particularly interesting results. Once you have found a sound that seems well suited to your melody, play the track again. As the track is playing, move the pitch bend wheel on the controlling synthesizer during some of the longer notes of the melody. Experiment with this for a while until you are satisfied that you have found some effective ways to use the technique of pitch bending in your melody.

Now, play the melody track yet again, while recording, on the second track of the sequencer, the movements of the pitch wheel. Then, call up a display of the Pitch Bend Change messages that have been recorded on track 2 (assuming that your sequencer provides this capability). Experiment with different techniques for editing the data (make a backup track before doing this, however!).

Once you are satisfied with the pitch bend track, copy these data and merge them with the Note On messages on track 1. Make a copy of this track, which should now include Note On messages as well as Pitch Bend messages. Then rechannelize this copy track. Now, as you play the sequence, the melody should be layered by two synthesizers. (Note: The pitch bend range of the two instruments may differ, resulting in some amazingly bizarre and terrifying pitch effects as both instruments respond to the same contours of Pitch Bend messages, but to different degrees. Consult the operator's manual of one or both synthesizers to learn how to change the pitch bend range.)

Finally, connect to the inputs of a multiple-track recorder the audio outputs of the synthesizers that are being played by the sequencer. Play the sequence a few more times as you set recording levels, and then let the tape roll.

ÉTUDE 5.5

ℛecord these notes onto track 1 of a sequencer (if you do not have facility at the keyboard, recruit a friend who does, or try recording in step-entry mode):

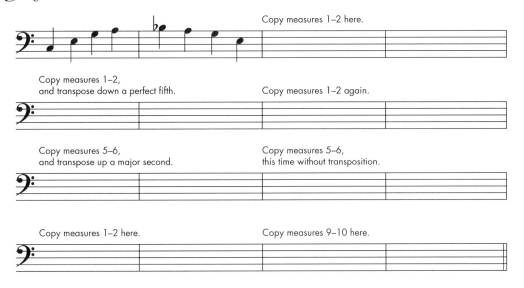

Record these chords onto track 2:

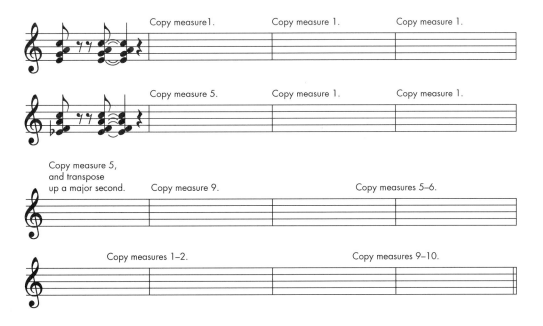

On track 3, improvise a melody above the patterns sounding from tracks 1 and 2. You now have one complete section, or chorus, of the *Rompin', Stompin', 'lectroacoustic Blues*.

Now, on track 4, improvise an alternative to the melody recorded on track 3. Mute track 3, and listen to the sequence. Then unmute track 3, mute track 4, and listen to the sequence again.

Make a copy of all four tracks of the entire chorus, and append it to the end. Select all the notes of track 3 or of track 4 in the *first chorus only,* and delete them. Select all the notes in the other melody track in the *second chorus only,* and delete them.

Add this note to the end of track 1 (at the end of the second chorus):

Add this chord to the end of track 2:

Add an appropriate note to the end of the melody track for the second chorus. Insert additional choruses, if you like. Experiment with variations of the suggested patterns of notes for tracks 1 and 2. Also experiment with inserting, between choruses, Program Change commands for the various tracks.

You are now a monster sequencer virtuoso.

QUANTIZATION

In this introduction to MIDI sequencing, there has been much discussion of how the messages recorded in a track can be edited. The timing information that is recorded with these sequenced events can also be manipulated in a variety of ways. For instance, the tempo of the music can be set to a higher or lower value by simply resetting the speed of the sequencer's clock. Many sequencers also provide a way to create a tempo track, so that changes in tempo, either abrupt or gradual, can be accomplished automatically as the sequence plays. The timing information that is recorded with each MIDI message is not altered by such tempo changes; what is affected is the rate at which this information is summoned from the memory of the sequencer.

The timing information itself can be edited with a set of techniques called **quantization.** A musical performance is never quite rhythmically precise. Musicians will generally play tones near the beat, for example, but never exactly on the beat. The most common technique of quantization is to shift the beginnings of notes and related events so that they begin precisely on the nearest beat or designated subdivision of the beat (see Figure 5.33). With some sequencers, the endings of notes may be left where they are, so that the durations of the notes will be somewhat lengthened or shortened (for a particular note, this depends on the direction in which the beginning of the note was moved). Alternatively, the ending times may also be quantized, especially if the musician intends eventually to export the note data of a sequence to a music transcription program (see Figure 5.34).

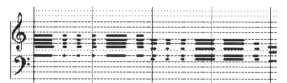

a. The recorded track shown above (in a graphic display) and to the right (as a note list) has not yet been quantized.

1·	1·	0	E3	0·310
1·	1·	0	F#3	0·310
1·	1·	0	A3	0·310
1·	1·	6	A2	0·304
1·	1·	12	D3	0·326
1·	1·464		E3	0·78
1·	1·464		F#3	0·78
1·	1·464		A3	0·78
1·	1·468		D3	0·84
1·	1·472		A2	0·56
1·	2·224		D3	0·94
1·	2·226		A2	0·64
1·	2·226		E3	0·80
1·	2·226		F#3	0·80
1·	2·226		A3	0·80
1·	2·468		E3	0·80
1·	2·468		F#3	0·80
1·	2·468		A3	0·80
1·	2·471		D3	0·93

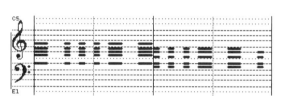

b. The beginnings of notes have now been quantized, to the nearest eighth-note value. In the piano-roll above, the beginnings of the notes in each chord are aligned, but the endings of the notes are still a bit ragged. In the corresponding note list to the right, the beginning times of the notes (in the first column) are now regular, but the durations (in the last column) are unchanged.

1·	1·	0	E3	0·310
1·	1·	0	F#3	0·310
1·	1·	0	A3	0·310
1·	1·	0	A2	0·304
1·	1·	0	D3	0·326
1·	2·	0	E3	0·78
1·	2·	0	F#3	0·78
1·	2·	0	A3	0·78
1·	2·	0	D3	0·84
1·	2·	0	A2	0·56
1·	2·240		D3	0·94
1·	2·240		A2	0·64
1·	2·240		E3	0·80
1·	2·240		F#3	0·80
1·	2·240		A3	0·80
1·	3·	0	E3	0·80
1·	3·	0	F#3	0·80
1·	3·	0	A3	0·80
1·	3·	0	D3	0·93

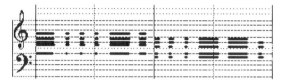

c. The beginnings of the notes are quantized to the nearest eighth-note value, and the durations of notes are quantized to the nearest sixteenth-note value. This represents perhaps the best idealization of the performance. Both the beginnings and endings of the notes of each chord are vertically aligned in the piano-roll display shown above. The corresponding note list (shown to the right) also indicates that both beginning times and durations are regularized.

1·	1·	0	E3	0·240
1·	1·	0	F#3	0·240
1·	1·	0	A3	0·240
1·	1·	0	A2	0·240
1·	1·	0	D3	0·240
1·	2·	0	E3	0·120
1·	2·	0	F#3	0·120
1·	2·	0	A3	0·120
1·	2·	0	D3	0·120
1·	2·	0	A2	0·120
1·	2·240		D3	0·120
1·	2·240		A2	0·120
1·	2·240		E3	0·120
1·	2·240		F#3	0·120
1·	2·240		A3	0·120
1·	3·	0	E3	0·120
1·	3·	0	F#3	0·120
1·	3·	0	A3	0·120
1·	3·	0	D3	0·120

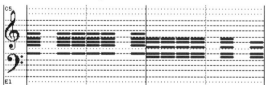

d. The beginnings of the notes are quantized to the nearest eighth-note value, and the durations of notes are also quantized to the nearest eighth-note value. Contrast this with the idealized version in **c.**, and also with the unquantized version **a.** This is a significant departure from what we may surmise to have been the intention of the musician who recorded the track. However, this quantization will give the most satisfactory results when transcribed by a music notation program (see Figure 5.34).

1·	1·	0	E3	0·240
1·	1·	0	F#3	0·240
1·	1·	0	A3	0·240
1·	1·	0	A2	0·240
1·	1·	0	D3	0·240
1·	2·	0	E3	0·240
1·	2·	0	F#3	0·240
1·	2·	0	A3	0·240
1·	2·	0	D3	0·240
1·	2·	0	A2	0·240
1·	2·240		D3	0·240
1·	2·240		A2	0·240
1·	2·240		E3	0·240
1·	2·240		F#3	0·240
1·	2·240		A3	0·240
1·	3·	0	E3	0·240
1·	3·	0	F#3	0·240
1·	3·	0	A3	0·240
1·	3·	0	D3	0·240

FIGURE 5.33
A few of the possible options for quantizing a recorded track. (Courtesy of Opcode Systems, Inc.)

FIGURE 5.34
The musical examples shown in Figure 5.33 are shown here as transcribed by a popular music notation program. The transcription of the unquantized track (a) is very difficult for a musician to read. The transcription of the track on which the beginnings of notes are quantized (b) is not much better. The most readable track is the one on which both the beginnings and the durations of the notes were quantized to eighth-note values (d).

The rhythmic value (such as half, quarter, eighth, sixteenth, or thirty-second note) designated as the reference for quantization must be chosen with some care. If the passage of music to be quantized contains only quarter notes, then the quarter note is certainly an appropriate choice as a quantization reference. If the passage also contains half notes, dotted half notes, and/or whole notes, then the quarter note is still the best choice. If the passage includes eighth notes, however, then quantizing everything to the nearest quarter-note value will result in eighth notes being piled atop other notes. If the shortest duration in the passage is a sixteenth note, as in Figure 5.35, then the eighth note will not be a good choice as a quantization reference either. The appropriate selection as a reference value for quantization in this case is the sixteenth note.

Because it is not always easy to determine the best choice of rhythmic value for a quantization reference, it is *always* a good idea to make a backup copy of a track before it is quantized. It is also wise to work with relatively short passages of music, not an entire track or group of tracks. Finally, each passage should be auditioned closely to detect any unintended coincidences or similar problems before proceeding to work on the quantization of another passage of music.

The techniques of quantization can be very powerful and should not be used thoughtlessly. It is important to realize that although musicians do not always play on the beat (or on precise subdivisions of the beat), this is not necessarily due to incompetence or inattention. To the contrary, often

FIGURE 5.35
The results of various decisions regarding the note value used as a quantization reference. (Courtesy of Opcode Systems, Inc.)

a. The original, unquantized track.

b. The beginnings and the durations of notes are quantized to the nearest quarter note. This is not a problem in the first measure; in the second measure, however, the dotted quarter is cheated of a third of its value, and the sixteenth notes are quadrupled in length. Also, the second sixteenth is piled atop the half note.

c. The beginnings and the durations of notes are quantized to the nearest eighth note. This is not a problem in the first measure, nor for the dotted quarter; however in the second measure the sixteenths are doubled in length and piled atop each other.

d. The beginnings and the durations of the notes are quantized to the nearest sixteenth note. This is not a problem in the first measure, nor in the second; it works.

there are expressive purposes to be served by playing ahead of a beat or behind a beat (or for favoring certain subdivisions of the beat, as with "swinging" styles of rhythm). Quantized music often sounds robotic by comparison. One of the principal criticisms of much contemporary, popular electroacoustic music can be attributed to the fact that it is overly quantized. Like orange juice made from frozen concentrate, much of the life has been squeezed from it!

Many sequencers offer means to attempt to compensate for this shortcoming. For instance, a controlled degree of randomness can be introduced (or reintroduced) into the determination of starting and ending times of notes and related events. This technique is often referred to as "humanization." Or a series of equal durations might be reshaped by a "swing factor," which typically means that the beginning times of alternating notes are

FIGURE 5.36
The "swing" factor. Observe
how the odd-numbered eighth
notes are somewhat lengthened, and the beginnings of
the even-numbered eighth
notes are somewhat delayed.
(Courtesy of Opcode Systems,
Inc.)

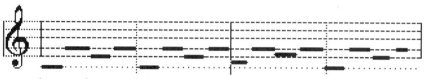

a. The original, unquantized track.

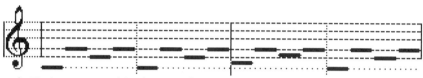

b. The beginnings and the durations of notes are quantized to the nearest eighth note.

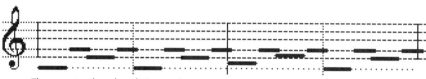

c. The quantized track with "swing."

delayed slightly (see Figure 5.36). Such techniques can help, but they don't fool everyone all of the time. (Always remember, "if you think, don't quantize"—or, at least, don't quantize too much.)

This brief overview provides a glimpse of the capabilities of a contemporary MIDI sequencer. For a more complete immersion, you should plan to spend some time working your way through the contents of the operator's manual of the particular sequencer that is available to you in your studio. Just as with any other musical instrument, making good music with a sequencer requires persistent and consistent practice, and then more practice.

GENERAL MIDI

A recent addition to the MIDI specification is a set of definitions and standard practices called **General MIDI.** This includes a table of 128 instrument sounds, grouped in families such as strings, brass, "ethnic," and such, that are assigned to specific preset numbers. There is also a table of percussion sounds assigned to specific MIDI note numbers (see Figure 6.2, in the following chapter).

A sound module that conforms to the General MIDI standard should include all of the presets in the table of instrument sounds. It should also respond with the appropriate percussion sounds when it receives Note On messages on MIDI channel 10. The module should have at least 24 voices that can be allocated dynamically, and should meet a variety of other requirements established by the MIDI Manufacturers Association and the Japan MIDI Standards Committee.

The purpose of General MIDI is to ensure that a sequence created on one MIDI network of instruments will sound pretty much the same when played back on another network, most likely at another location. The most significant applications of General MIDI are likely to be for multimedia commercial demonstrations and home entertainment systems. For such purposes, a number of small companies are now offering professionally prepared sequences of hit tunes for sale, in a generic format called the Standard MIDI File format. In many ways, this is reminiscent of the sale of performances of music on punched rolls of paper for player pianos nearly a century ago.

IMPORTANT TERMS

sound synthesizer
monophonic
polyphonic
keyboard splitting
split point
velocity sensitivity
aftertouch sensitivity
pitch bender
modulation wheel
presets
MIDI
MIDI IN
MIDI OUT
MIDI THRU
bit
bytes
status byte
data bytes
channel messages
Note On message

running status
polyphonic, or key pressure, aftertouch
monophonic, or channel pressure, aftertouch
Control Change messages
continuous controllers
switch controllers
portamento
Pitch Bend Change messages
Program Change messages
tone modules, or expander modules
daisy-chain network
MIDI THRU box
star network
Mode 1
Omni-On/Poly
Mode 2

Omni-On/Mono
Mode 3
Omni-Off/Poly
Mode 4
Omni-Off/Mono
multitimbral
programmable voice allocation
dynamic voice allocation
sequencer
real-time recording
step recording
loop recording
rechannelizing
input thru
local on/off
merging
controller thinning
quantization
General MIDI

FOR FURTHER READING

Anderton, Craig. *MIDI for Musicians.* New York: Amsco, 1986.

Casabona, Helen, and Frederick, David. *Using MIDI.* Alfred, 1987.

De Furia, Steve, and Scacciaferro, Joe. *The MIDI Book: Using MIDI and Related Interfaces.* Rutherford, NJ: Third Earth Productions, 1986.

Huber, David Miles. *The MIDI Manual.* Carmel, IN: Howard W. Sams, 1991.

Hurtig, Brent, ed. *Synthesizers and Computers.* rev. ed. Milwaukee: Hal Leonard, 1987.

Keyboard magazine, editors of. *MIDI Sequencing for Musicians.* Cupertino, CA: GPI, 1989.

Milano, Dominic, ed. *Mind over MIDI.* Milwaukee: Hal Leonard, 1987.

Pressing, Jeff. *Synthesizer Performance and Real-Time Techniques.* Madison, WI: A-R Editions, 1992.

Rothstein, Joseph. *MIDI: A Comprehensive Introduction.* Madison, WI: A-R Editions, 1992.

Rumsey, Francis. *MIDI Systems and Control.* London: Focal Press, 1990.

An interactive introduction to the Musical Instrument Digital Interface is: *The Book of MIDI*, a HyperCard™ stack (for the Macintosh™ computer) produced by Opcode Systems, Inc., Menlo Park, California.

CHAPTER 6

ADVANCED MIDI NETWORKS

By the end of Chapter 5, our MIDI network included a keyboard synthesizer used as a source of MIDI messages, a sequencer (which could actually be a microcomputer running a sequencer program), a MIDI THRU box, a synthesizer expander module, a second keyboard synthesizer, and a multitimbral sound sampler module. The development of our MIDI network now continues with the addition of a **drum machine** (see Figure 6.1).

A drum machine is, in part, a device dedicated to producing sounds of percussion instruments such as drums, cymbals, cowbells, and such. These sounds are most likely digital samples of the actual sounds of the instruments, and are stored permanently in ROM (Read-Only Memory) chips installed in the device.

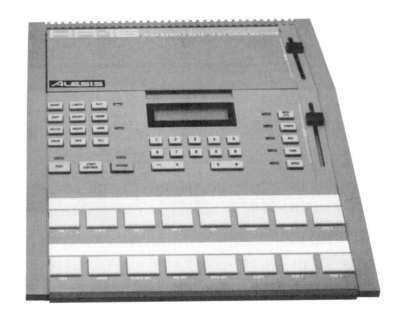

FIGURE 6.1
The Alesis HR-16, a drum machine quite popular during the late 1980s and early 1990s. (HR-16 is a registered trademark of and is used with the permission of Alesis Corporation.)

Typically, a drum machine has several push buttons, or keypads, on the front panel. These can each be assigned to a particular percussion sound, and can be reassigned to a different set of sounds as needs change. A percussion part can thus be performed by playing on these buttons. The drum machine is also likely to be able to respond to MIDI Note On messages, with each sound assigned to a specific key number (see Figure 6.2). Thus, percussion patterns can also be recorded and played from a sequencer.

A drum machine usually includes a few sequencer functions of its own. It has a clock and the ability to record and play back patterns that are performed on the keypads. It also has free memory to store these patterns, and some limited capabilities for editing them.

FIGURE 6.2
Percussion sounds of contemporary drum machines are generally assigned to MIDI note numbers as indicated here.

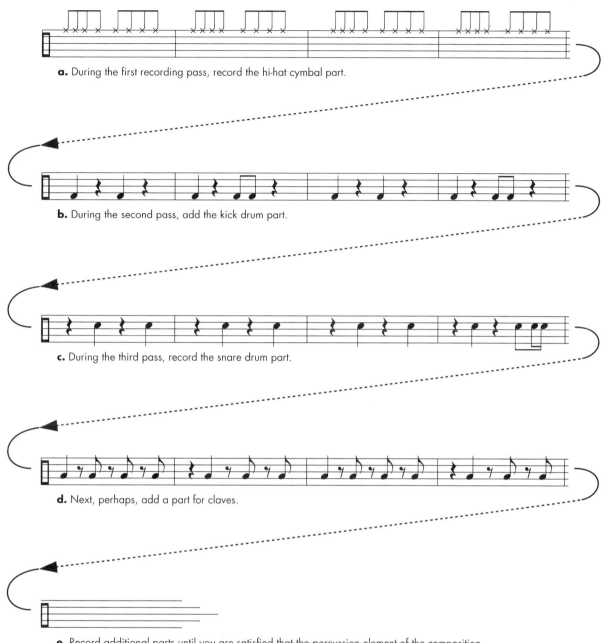

a. During the first recording pass, record the hi-hat cymbal part.

b. During the second pass, add the kick drum part.

c. During the third pass, record the snare drum part.

d. Next, perhaps, add a part for claves.

e. Record additional parts until you are satisfied that the percussion element of the composition is sufficiently active.

The technique for recording is loop recording, described in the previous chapter. The percussion part is organized into patterns, which are recorded one by one. First, the length of a pattern is defined in measures, or bars. Then the drum machine is placed in record mode, and instrumental sounds are added to the pattern each time the clock steps through it (see Figure 6.3). When all of the patterns have been recorded in this way, they are linked together in a higher-level structure usually called a "song." The "song" pattern represents the percussion part for the entire composition.

FIGURE 6.3
The technique of loop recording is used here to assemble a four-measure drum pattern.

SYSTEM MESSAGES

There is now a potential problem in our MIDI network, however: we now have essentially two sequencers, including the drum machine, and each has its own clock. This is something like the predicament of a person with two hearts—not a comfortable situation, to be sure. To keep all of the parts of the MIDI system synchronized, we need a way to designate one of the clocks as the official timekeeper of the system, and we need a way to share this timing information among the instruments that require it.

In an effort to address this situation (and a few others, to be described subsequently), the developers of the Musical Instrument Digital Interface defined a set of messages called **System messages.** Distinct from such Channel messages as Note On, Aftertouch, Pitch Bend, Control Change, and the others, these System messages are intended for any instruments in the network, regardless of the MIDI channel to which they are set. System messages may be of use to two or more instruments, even if these instruments are on different channels.

SYSTEM REAL-TIME MESSAGES

Many of the messages that can be used to synchronize the operation of two or more sequencers in a network fall into the category of **System Real-Time messages.** These messages, consisting of a status byte only, have priority over all other types of messages. Because these messages are used for synchronization, it is important that they be able to interrupt any other message at the necessary time (after which the other message can resume unharmed).

One of the primary agents of MIDI synchronization is a system real-time message called a **Timing Clock,** or **MIDI Clock message**. To configure the MIDI system so that this message can be used, one of the sequencers must be designated as the timekeeper of the network (see Figure 6.4). This can be any drum machine, hardware sequencer, or computer-based sequencer that is able to generate MIDI Clock messages (and most now do). The other sequencers in the network must be placed in "external sync" mode (sometimes called MIDI sync mode). This means that these other devices will ignore their internal clocks.

The timekeeping sequencer will produce Timing Clock messages at a rate of 24 for every quarter note. Thus, the other sequencers in the network can update their timing as often as 24 times for every beat.[1] It is important to recognize that this method of synchronization, sometimes called **MIDI sync,** is not directly related to the passage of absolute time, but rather is

---

1. This assumes that the quarter note represents the beat. If the meter of the music is 2/2 (also known as "cut time"), then there are 48 MIDI Clocks per beat. If the meter is 5/8, then there are only 12 MIDI Clocks per beat.

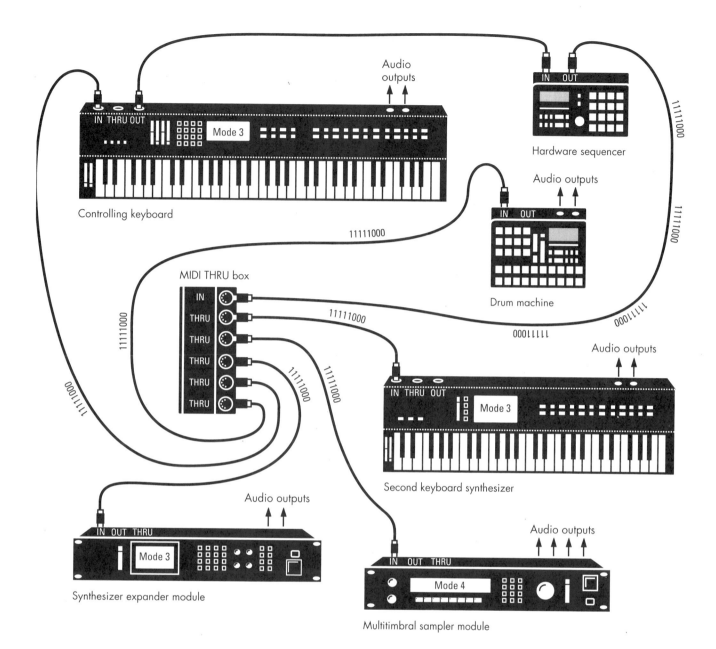

Audio outputs

IN THRU OUT
Mode 3

Controlling keyboard

IN OUT
Hardware sequencer

11111000

11111000

11111000

11111000

Audio outputs

IN OUT
Drum machine

11111000

MIDI THRU box
IN
THRU
THRU
THRU
THRU
THRU

11111000

11111000

11111000

11111000

00011111

11111000

Audio outputs

IN THRU OUT
Mode 3

Second keyboard synthesizer

Audio outputs

IN OUT THRU
Mode 3

Synthesizer expander module

Audio outputs

IN OUT THRU
Mode 4

Multitimbral sampler module

based upon tempo—that is, relative time. If the tempo of the music is 60 beats per minute, then there are 24 Timing Clock messages every second. If the tempo is 120 beats per minute, then 48 Timing Clock messages are transmitted every second. An alternative method of synchronization with MIDI messages, called **MIDI Time Code (MTC),** is based on the passage of absolute time and is independent of musical tempo. This latter technique is of particular value to those who work with film and video production and who must synchronize music or sound effects to visual cues. MIDI Time Code is described further in a later section of this chapter.

Three other system real-time messages that are used to synchronize two or more sequencers are the **Start, Stop,** and **Continue messages.** When the sequence on the timekeeping sequencer in a network starts to play, a

FIGURE 6.4
Our MIDI network now includes both a hardware sequencer and a drum machine. The hardware sequencer is the designated timekeeper of the network, transmitting Timing Clock messages 24 times a beat to the other devices in the network. However, these messages are only of interest to the drum machine as it endeavors to remain synchronized to the sequencer.

Start message should be transmitted so that the other sequencers can begin playing at the same time. Similarly, when the Stop button of the timekeeping sequencer is pushed, the other sequencers should stop as well. The Continue message causes the sequencers to resume playing from the location in their sequences that had been reached when the most recent Stop message was received.

ÉTUDE 6.1

*B*egin by studying the operating procedures of your drum machine, as described in the owner's manual. Then record a few patterns, and link them into a "song."

Now, put your drum machine into external sync mode, and make a MIDI connection to it from your sequencer. Record two or three tracks on the sequencer. The drum machine should play along. Record a few tempo changes into the tempo track on your sequencer. When you play the sequence again, the drum machine should be able to follow the tempo changes.

Connect the audio outputs of the drum machine and the synthesizers (and perhaps samplers) to an audio mixer. Then record the mixdown on a stereo recorder.

SYSTEM-COMMON MESSAGES

Another set of System messages falls into the category of **System-Common messages.** These messages, unlike System Real-Time messages, require data bytes and cannot interrupt other MIDI messages. One of the most common messages of this type is the **Song Position Pointer message.** This can be used—by a sequencer that can generate it, along with other sequencers that can recognize it—to set a group of sequencers to the same location in a piece of music so that playback can be started from a place other than the beginning. The data bytes of the Song Position Pointer message specify this location in terms of how many "MIDI beats" the desired location is from the beginning of the music; each "MIDI beat" is the equivalent of six Timing Clock messages. Since there are 24 MIDI Timing Clock messages for every quarter note, and therefore six MIDI Timing Clocks for every sixteenth note, the Song Position Pointer can accurately specify a location to a sixteenth-note value. After a Song Position Pointer message is transmitted to a group of idling sequencers, a Continue message from the timekeeping sequencer will cause playback to begin from the specified location.

Another System-Common message is the Song Select message. Some drum machines (and some sequencers) can have several different "song" patterns or sequences that are readily accessible from their memory at any

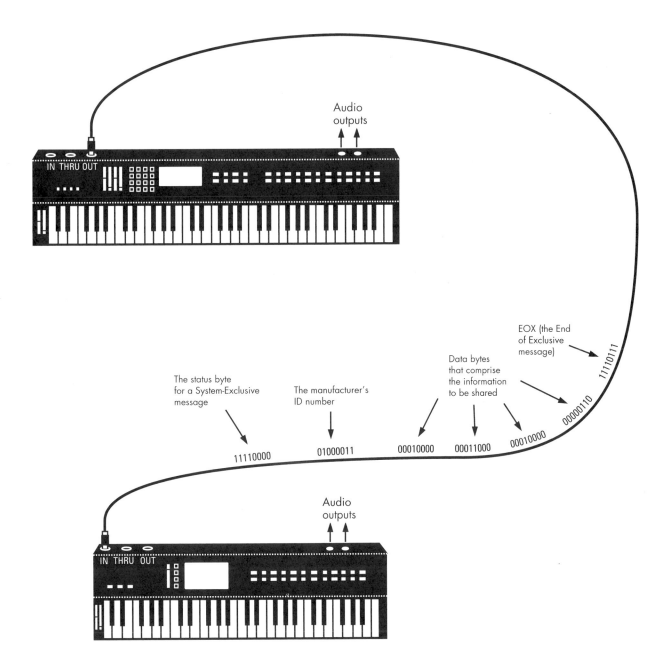

The status byte for a System-Exclusive message

11110000

The manufacturer's ID number

01000011

Data bytes that comprise the information to be shared

00010000   00011000   00010000   00000110

EOX (the End of Exclusive message)

11110111

given moment. A Song Select message can be used (assuming that the sequencer is designed to recognize it) to determine which "song" pattern or sequence will be played when a Start message is received.

SYSTEM-EXCLUSIVE MESSAGES

System-Exclusive (Sys-Ex) messages include some of the most important messages transmitted in a MIDI network. They typically contain data that are of particular relevance to a specific device. For example, information that can be stored in the preset memory of a synthesizer (information

FIGURE 6.5
A System-Exclusive message is transmitted from one synthesizer to another of the same make and model. This particular message, if received by a Yamaha DX7, would reset the pitch bend range to six semitones.

regarding the settings of the dials and switches that determine oscillator tuning, filter levels, envelope values, LFO waveform, LFO rate, and such) can be represented in the data bytes of a System-Exclusive message and then shared with other devices.

Since this type of information is germane only to the features and methods of operation of a device built by an individual manufacturer (as with, for example, the patch information of a Yamaha DX7), the first data byte in a System-Exclusive message will be a number that identifies the manufacturer of the device.[2] A System-Exclusive message, like any other MIDI message, can be transmitted throughout a MIDI network, but it will only be attended to by those devices that recognize the manufacturer's ID number at the head of the message.[3] Hence the message is "exclusive" to a particular product.

An obvious application for a System-Exclusive message is to copy preset data from one synthesizer to another of the same make and model (for example from one Yamaha DX7 to another Yamaha DX7, as shown in Figure 6.5). If the entire contents of the preset memory banks of a device are transmitted in a Sys-Ex message (or a series of Sys-Ex messages), this is called a bulk memory dump, or more simply, a **bulk dump.**

A bulk dump might also be transmitted to an inexpensive MIDI data recorder (essentially nothing more than a recorder for System-Exclusive messages and any other messages that are not time-dependent). In this way, the contents of the preset memory banks of a synthesizer or other device can be backed up on a floppy disk. Given that the on-board memory of a synthesizer can be rather volatile, it is prudent to maintain a backup copy of these data so that they can be restored fairly easily (particularly if the memory of the synthesizer should somehow get scrambled during an onstage performance!). A floppy-disk recording of a Sys-Ex bulk dump can also make it easier to share the data with other musicians.[4]

When working with a sequencer, many musicians often record a bulk dump of preset information from each device onto empty tracks of the sequence (then mute these tracks so the messages are not sent every time the sequence is played). This becomes, in effect, a set of snapshots of the current configuration of the operating parameters of the devices being used for that particular piece of music. If the project is interrupted for a few weeks or months, or if the musician later decides to make a few changes to the music, it becomes possible to restore the devices fairly quickly to the

---

2. Manufacturer ID numbers are assigned to companies by the MIDI Manufacturer's Association and the Japan MIDI Standards Committee. In some cases, the first three data bytes of a System-Exclusive message are required for the ID numbers of manufacturers who have only recently begun to develop MIDI products.

3. The end of a System-Exclusive message is signaled by a status byte of a System-Common message called an EOX (for "End Of eXclusive") message.

4. It is important to recognize, however, that many synthesizer presets are designed by people who do this work as a way of earning income to support themselves. The data are often registered for copyright protection in an effort to ensure that everyone who uses the presets provides a fair share of compensation to the designer.

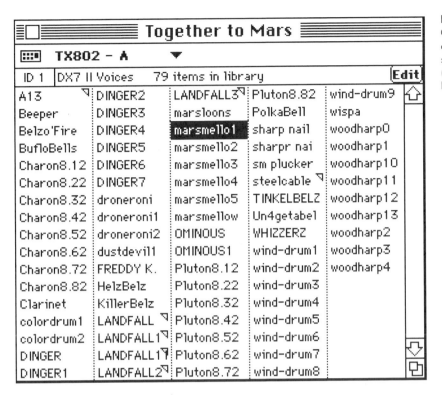

FIGURE 6.6
Computer screen display of the contents of a library file of presets for a synthesizer. (Courtesy of Opcode Systems, Inc.)

desired configuration. One-by-one, the Sys-Ex tracks are unmuted and played solo as the System-Exclusive information is transmitted back from the sequencer to the various devices from which it originated.

According to the specification of the Musical Instrument Digital Interface, manufacturers are expected to share with the public a description of the format of each of their System-Exclusive messages. With just a few, nefarious exceptions, this principle has been widely respected. The accessibility of such information has made possible the development, often by small, "third-party" companies, of a variety of inexpensive products that are quite useful to owners of synthesizers and other MIDI devices. Perhaps most notable has been the development of software to exploit the potential of the microcomputer for managing System-Exclusive data.

With a **librarian program,** for example, the System-Exclusive data for a synthesizer preset can be stored in a computer file called a library, along with the data for perhaps hundreds of other presets (see Figure 6.6). Presets can be added or removed from the library, or sorted within the library. Various presets within the library can be selected and copied into a bank file, which can then be transmitted as a series of System-Exclusive messages to the synthesizer to replace the bank of presets already there. (Presumably the musician has already copied the previous bank of presets into a library or bank file that has been saved to a computer disk.)

With a program called an **editor/librarian,** or **ed/lib,** the synthesizer parameters represented by the System-Exclusive data for any preset chosen from a library or bank file can be displayed graphically on the computer screen (see Figure 6.7). Any parameter that is displayed on the screen can

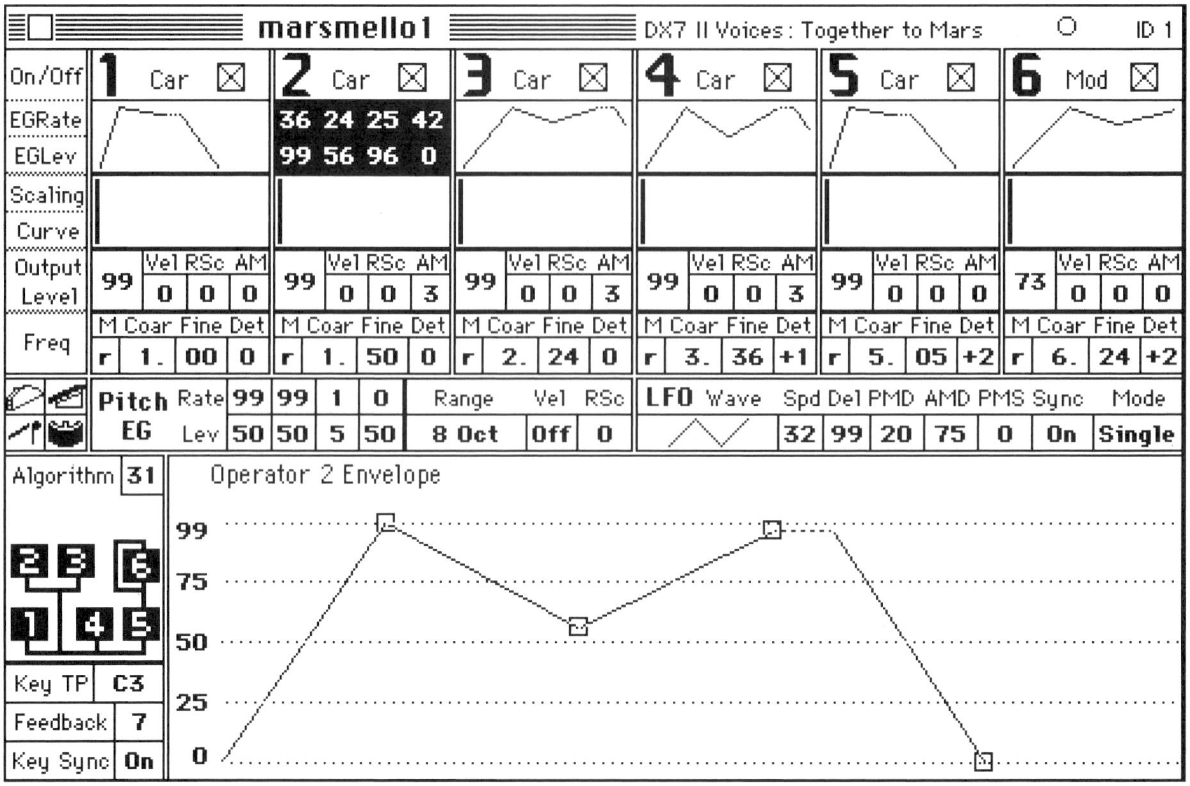

then be selected and altered. In a sense, the computer becomes a virtual control panel, providing graphic sliders, dials, and buttons for the dozens or even hundreds of variables that define the sound of a contemporary synthesizer. This has become particularly useful as manufacturers (with a few exceptions) now provide far fewer actual sliders, dials, and buttons on their devices, even though the techniques for producing and processing sounds are becoming increasingly complex.

FIGURE 6.7
Display screen of a typical patch-editing program running on a microcomputer. Virtually all of the parameters that define a synthesizer patch can be readily accessed with such a program. (Courtesy of Opcode Systems, Inc.)

ÉTUDE 6.2

For this composition, you will need a synthesizer, a microcomputer, and an editor/librarian program for the microcomputer. Begin by consulting the operator's manual of your synthesizer to learn the procedures for transmitting a bulk dump of the preset memories of the synthesizer. Then consult the manual of the editor/librarian program to learn the procedures for accepting a bulk dump from a synthesizer. Also review the procedures for transmitting a bank of presets in the opposite direction, from the computer to the synthesizer.

Next, make a backup file of the preset memories that already exist in the synthesizer. Transmit these from the synthesizer to the computer, store them in a bank file on a computer disk.

Now, open a library file on the microcomputer and explore the sounds of the presets that are stored there. Assemble the presets that seem most interesting and useful into a bank file, then transmit this bank file from the computer to the synthesizer. (Note: Most synthesizers have a memory-protect function. Either the synthesizer operator's manual or the manual of the editor/librarian program will provide the details of how to turn this function off.)

Compose and produce a short composition that uses the presets you have gathered together and placed in the memory of the synthesizer. As you produce the composition, you may wish to edit some of the presets. By doing so, you will truly begin to make the most of your synthesizer as a musical instrument of almost unimaginable ductility. Enjoy!

UNIVERSAL SYSTEM-EXCLUSIVE MESSAGES

Three manufacturer ID numbers for System-Exclusive messages have been reserved for general use. Messages that use one of these ID numbers are referred to (somewhat oxymoronically) as **Universal System-Exclusive messages.** One of the Universal System-Exclusive ID numbers is reserved for internal use at universities and other research facilities for projects that will not be made available on a commercial basis. The other two ID numbers are reserved for what are called Universal Real-Time System-Exclusive messages and Universal Non-Real-Time System-Exclusive messages.

An example of the latter is the set of messages that define the MIDI sample dump standard. These messages provide a format for transmitting through a MIDI cable the data that represent a digitally sampled sound. An instrument that recognizes these messages can accept a sound file that was created by another instrument that uses sampled sounds. A MIDI sample dump can also be used to transmit sample data to a microcomputer, where a sample-editing program can be used to make changes to the sound file (as described in Chapter 3).

Both Real-Time and Non-Real-Time messages are included in the set of messages that define MIDI Time Code (MTC). One of the principal functions of MIDI Time Code is to represent, in the form of various MIDI messages, the timing information found in **SMPTE time code,** a digital timing signal defined by the Society of Motion Picture and Television Engineers for use in the production of films, television programs, and other video projects. MIDI Time Code, therefore, can be a very useful tool for musicians who work in these media.

More recently defined Universal System-Exclusive messages include those for MIDI Show Control (MSC), which provides a way of using MIDI messages to control such things as stage lighting and the movement of hydraulic stage platforms. Also recently defined is the set of messages for MIDI Machine Control (MMC), used for the remote control of tape

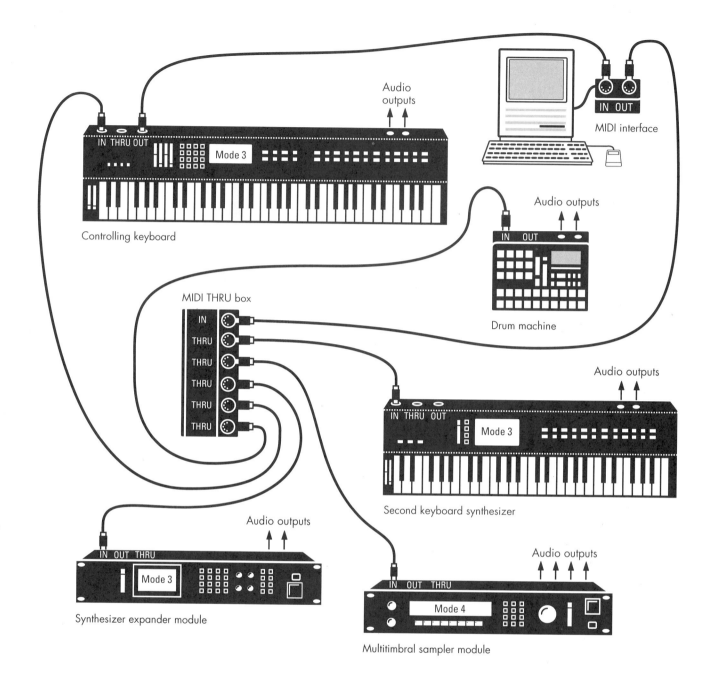

Audio outputs

MIDI interface

Controlling keyboard

Audio outputs

Drum machine

MIDI THRU box

Audio outputs

Second keyboard synthesizer

Audio outputs

Synthesizer expander module

Audio outputs

Multitimbral sampler module

recorders and other audio devices in a studio. Clearly, the provision for Universal System-Exclusive messages is a significant "loophole" in the MIDI specification that allows MIDI to continue to expand and adapt.[5]

FIGURE 6.8
We have now replaced the hardware sequencer (see Figure 6.4) with a micro-computer that can run a soft-ware-based sequencing program and other MIDI soft-ware.

5. Some would call it more of a rupture than a loophole. Most recent changes to the MIDI specification tend to involve definitions of new System-Exclusive messages (or new Registered Parameter numbers, described in Appendix C). Many musicians feel that, as a result, the coherence of the MIDI specification is weakening. Practically speaking, these recently defined messages also require a significant amount of overhead. For example, a typical Universal System-Exclusive message requires a System-Exclusive status byte, a Universal System-Exclusive ID number, perhaps a device ID number, perhaps one or two sub-ID numbers, the data themselves, and an EOX status byte. Just a few messages of this sort can quickly fill a significant portion of a MIDI data stream.

FURTHER EXTENSIONS AND VARIATIONS OF THE MIDI NETWORK

Our MIDI network now includes a keyboard synthesizer that serves as a source for MIDI messages, a MIDI THRU box, a synthesizer expander module, a second keyboard synthesizer, a sampler module, and a drum machine. Knowing what we now know regarding the usefulness of a microcomputer in a studio MIDI network, we may decide to replace our hardware sequencer, if that is what we have, with a microcomputer that can run a sequencer program and editor/librarian software. It may also be necessary to acquire a MIDI interface for the computer.

Sooner or later, many musicians who have been trained as pianists become dissatisfied with the "feel" and response of the keyboard on the synthesizer that serves as a source for MIDI messages in the network. At this point, it becomes appropriate to consider replacing the keyboard synthesizer with a **keyboard controller.** This instrument produces no sounds of its own; rather, it only generates MIDI messages. Whereas a typical keyboard synthesizer has 61 keys (covering five octaves), a typical keyboard controller has 76 or 88 keys (covering just over six or seven octaves, respectively). Of greater importance, the keys on a keyboard controller are weighted so that they respond in a way that is quite similar to the response of keys on a piano. Keyboard controllers are also likely to have several sliders and push buttons on the control panel that can be assigned to generate specific Control Change messages, and several jacks for foot pedals and foot switches that can be similarly assigned. There are also likely to be banks of push buttons on the control panel that can be used to trigger Program Change messages.

Most keyboard controllers provide a way to organize groups of keys into three or four zones. Each of these zones can be assigned to transmit on a different MIDI channel. Also, it may be possible to configure each zone so that velocity values of Note On messages and polyphonic aftertouch values can be scaled according to a linear or exponential contour (see Figure 6.9). In effect, the keyboard of the controller is split into three or four keyboards, a feature that greatly increases the versatility of the instrument for use in a MIDI network.

ALTERNATE CONTROLLERS

For musicians who have not been trained as keyboard players, there are a variety of **alternate controllers.** A MIDI **guitar controller** resembles a guitar in appearance and is played somewhat like a guitar. Some guitar controllers are, in fact, standard electric guitars with special pickups installed. Other models are a bit more esoteric (all six strings have the same diameter, for example) and require some adaptations of the musician's

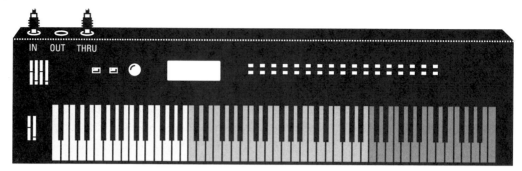

Keyboard controller

Zone A	**Zone B**	**Zone C**

Performed velocities of a pattern of notes played in Zone A:

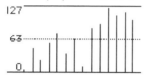

Performed velocities of a pattern of notes played in Zone B:

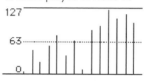

Performed velocities of a pattern of notes played in Zone C:

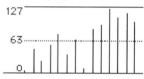

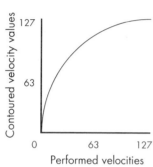

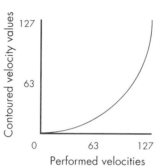

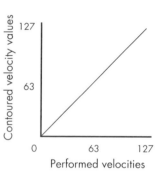

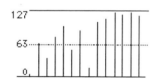

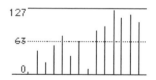

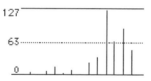

Key velocities in Zone A are rescaled according to an exponential contour. Small differences among low key velocities in the pattern of notes that were played become exaggerated in the velocity values in the corresponding Note On messages. Small differences among high key velocities become even smaller differences in the velocity values of the Note On messages.

Key velocities in Zone B are rescaled according to a different exponential contour. Small differences among low key velocities in the pattern of notes that were played become even smaller differences in velocity values in the corresponding Note On messages. Small differences among high key velocities become much greater differences in the velocity values of the Note On messages.

For Zone C, the velocity values in the Note On messages are unchanged from the performed values. This could be a problem if the performer's keyboard skills are not sufficiently accurate in the low or high ranges, or if the tone module that is destined to receive these messages is overly sensitive to small differences among key velocities in the low or high ranges.

FIGURE 6.9

Velocity contours. Many keyboard controllers, in addition to providing a selection of such velocity contours for each zone, provide a variety of aftertouch contours for rescaling polyphonic aftertouch information generated by a performance.

technique of guitar-playing. The information picked up from the guitar strings is generally transmitted through a cable to a rack-mounted module, where the data are converted into MIDI messages. Some of these modules also have the capacity to generate synthetic sounds; others do not, and require that the MIDI OUT of the module be connected to a synthesizer, sampler, or expander module. MIDI guitar controller systems typically can transmit MIDI data on several channels simultaneously (in MIDI Mode 4), with perhaps a separate channel assigned to each string of the guitar. Thus, a MIDI guitar controller might control as many as six different synthesizers, samplers, and/or expander modules.

A MIDI **wind controller** is designed for musicians who have been trained as players of woodwind or brass instruments. Typically, the pressure of the player's breath is converted to velocity, aftertouch, or continuous controller information. Lip pressure can be translated into pitch bend information. The fingering patterns, used to generate key values for Note On messages, are generally similar to the familiar patterns used on a woodwind or a brass instrument. However, it is important to recognize that a wind controller, like a guitar controller, is essentially a new instrument. Although many of the skills acquired from playing a traditional instrument can be transferred to the playing of a MIDI controller, a few adaptations and new skills are also required. It is wise to spend a few months in practice before venturing onstage.

A drum-pad controller resembles the practice pads used by student drummers. When a pad is struck with a drum stick or a mallet, a particular set of MIDI messages can be triggered. A MIDI percussion controller has several pads that are arranged in a pattern like that of the bars on a xylophone (see Figure 6.10).

Foot-switch controllers are often used as auxiliary controllers, particularly with MIDI guitar and wind controllers. By operating the foot switches, a performer can more easily trigger Program Change messages, short System-Exclusive messages, and the like. Another type of auxiliary controller is the MIDI data-fader controller, such as the Fadermaster™ by JL Cooper. This device consists simply of eight faders that can be configured to generate any set of continuous controller messages on any set of channels. It can also be programmed to produce series of System-Exclusive messages. These can be used to control in real time (as a performance is in progress) a synthesizer parameter, such as vibrato rate or oscillator tuning, that cannot ordinarily be affected by a continuous controller.

MIDI ACCESSORIES

While there may be many possible destinations for MIDI messages in a network, generally there can be only one source of MIDI messages. Therefore, if we attempt to add a MIDI guitar controller or wind controller to our network, we are confronted by the puzzle of how to patch it in. An accessory

a. The Roland A-80 MIDI keyboard controller (Roland A-80 is a registered trademark of and is used with the permission of Roland Corporation US)

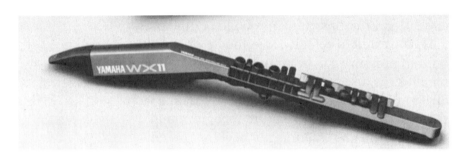

b. The Yamaha WX11 MIDI wind controller (courtesy of Yamaha Corporation of America)

c. The Yamaha G10 MIDI guitar controller (courtesy of the Yamaha Corporation of America)

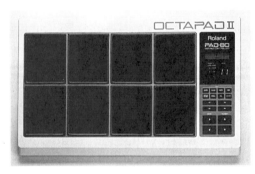

d. The Roland PAD-80 Octapad II drum-pad controller (PAD-80 Octapad II is a registered trademark of and is used with the permission of Roland Corporation US)

called a **MIDI merger,** or MIDI data mixer, can be used to blend and sort the data streams from two (or possibly more) sources so that the messages from one device do not intrude upon or interfere with the messages from another device. With a MIDI merger, it becomes possible for two or more musicians to play a MIDI network at the same time.

If the data from each source are on a different MIDI channel, and if each is being recorded simultaneously onto a single track on a sequencer, as is usually the case, then it may be convenient to "unmerge" the track after it has been recorded. This feature, found on most sequencers, makes it possible to split the data from each channel to a separate track. This greatly facilitates the editing of the data.

FIGURE 6.10 (continued)

e. The KAT MIDI mallet controller
(courtesy of KAT, Inc.)

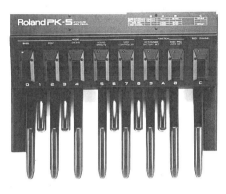

f. The Roland PK-5 dynamic MIDI pedal (PK-5
is a registered trademark of and is used with
the permission of Roland Corporation US)

g. The JL Cooper Fadermaster™ data-
fader controller (courtesy of JL Cooper
Electronics)

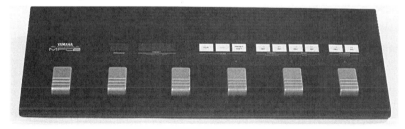

h. The Yahama MFC2 MIDI foot controller
(courtesy of the Yamaha Corporation of America)

Another MIDI accessory is the **MIDI data filter,** which can remove from the MIDI data stream selected types of MIDI messages, typically Aftertouch or Active Sensing messages. A **rechannelizer** can be used to change the channel of MIDI messages. Other special-purpose accessories are available for scaling or limiting key velocity, Control Change, or similar values in a message.

A device called a **mapper** has a variety of useful functions. In addition to many types of data filtering, it can reorganize the Note On messages of a

MIDI data stream into "zones," with each zone assigned to a different MIDI channel. Thus, the MIDI transmission of any keyboard instrument (or alternate controller) can be split into zones, much as can be done on some of the more expensive keyboard controllers described earlier. Within each of these zones, velocity values of Note On messages and polyphonic aftertouch values can be rescaled according to various linear or exponential contours.

A mapper can do simple transposition of the key values in Note On messages by adding or subtracting a specified value. A mapper might also be able to perform a somewhat more complex form of transposition, in which key values are reassigned according to values stored in a memory table called a transposition map. Thus, a piece of music in the key of C major, for example, might be transposed to A minor, or G mixolydian, or to some exotic scale pattern.

Program Change messages can be reassigned in a similar way, according to a table called a preset map. A related function of a mapper is to generate, upon receipt of a Program Change message from the source keyboard (or an alternate controller), an entire set of Program Change messages on different channels. The active presets of all the devices in a MIDI network can thus be changed simultaneously. This function is of particular value to a performing musician who will be presenting several different compositions in the course of a concert. At the press of a single preset button, all the presets in the network can be changed. The time required to reconfigure the instruments between compositions is greatly reduced (and the audience is much less likely to disappear between pieces or die of natural causes).

Finally, a mapper might also be used to reassign the controller number in a series of Control Change messages. This technique, called **controller mapping,** can be used to change foot controller messages into modulation wheel messages, or data slider messages into MIDI volume messages, for example.

It is very important to recognize that many, if not all, of the functions of a mapper—which is essentially a dedicated computer for the processing of MIDI data—can also be performed on a microcomputer equipped with a MIDI interface. Many sequencer programs, for example, can perform controller mapping, preset mapping, and transposition mapping (see Figure 6.11). With one particularly marvelous program called MAX (developed at the *Institut de Recherche et de Coordination Acoustique/Musique,* or IRCAM, and now offered commercially by Opcode Systems for use on the Macintosh personal computer), it is possible to do almost any form of MIDI data processing imaginable.

The most useful function of a device known as a **MIDI patch bay** is that it provides a place to connect MIDI cables for the MIDI IN and MIDI OUT connectors of every device in the network. Through the circuits of the MIDI patch bay, the MIDI OUT of any device can be connected to the MIDI IN of any other device in the network. By the same token, messages from the MIDI OUT connector of any device can easily be routed to the MIDI IN

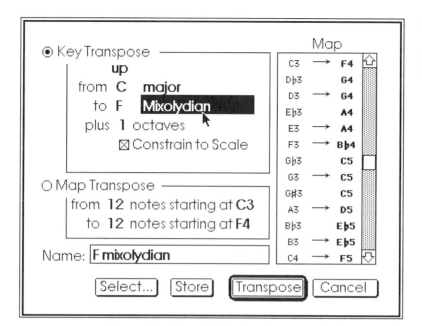

FIGURE 6.11
The transposition map display screen of a popular, software-based sequencer. (Courtesy of Opcode Systems, Inc.)

connectors of several devices. Thus, a MIDI patch bay can replace the MIDI THRU box in a network.

The use of a MIDI patch bay is much more convenient than the physical disconnection and reconnection of the MIDI cables whenever a reconfiguration of the roles of the devices in the network is desired. For instance, when recording tracks from a keyboard to a sequencer, MIDI messages originate with the keyboard, are then perhaps rechannelized by the sequencer, and then are passed on to the instrument that is intended to produce the sound in response to the messages. When the tracks are played later, the sequencer becomes the source of MIDI messages, and the connection from the keyboard to the sequencer is superfluous. When a bulk dump of System-Exclusive messages is to be recorded from an instrument onto a sequencer track, or is to be transmitted from one instrument into the memory of another, then neither the keyboard controller nor the sequencer rules the network; the device that is the source of the system-exclusive messages is acting as the controlling device in the network instead. Given that most devices are capable of bulk data dumps, at one time or another almost any device in the network can assume the role of transmitter. The various possible configurations of MIDI connections among devices can be stored as presets in the memory of a MIDI patch bay, then recalled at the touch of a button or two.

A MIDI patch bay can thus provide the flexibility needed to realize more completely the benefits of exchanging information among electronic musical instruments through MIDI. In addition to MIDI signal routing, many MIDI patch bays can merge MIDI transmissions from more than one source, rechannelize MIDI data, filter selected types of MIDI messages, and even perform some of the mapping functions previously described.

FIGURE 6.12
A MIDI patch bay. This model also can do MIDI merging, data filtering, and some mapping functions. (Courtesy of JL Cooper Electronics.)

EVEN FURTHER EXTENSIONS

Some digital effects devices have MIDI connectors and can be programmed to respond to some types of MIDI messages. For example, Program Change messages might be used to select among a bank of effects presets stored in the memory of the device. One Program Change message might call up an echo preset, another might activate a "large room" reverberation preset, and so forth. Control Change messages—from a foot pedal, for example— can be used on many of the more recent models of digital effects devices to adjust such parameters as echo delay time, reverberation time, flange speed, and chorus depth. Often, these messages can be written into a sequencer track that is designated for the control of the effects device. Many digital effects devices are also capable of transmitting and receiving bulk memory dumps in the form of system-exclusive messages. To assist in the management of the system-exclusive data, editor/librarian programs (or specific modules of the more generic editor/librarian programs) for several different models of digital effects devices have been developed to run on the microcomputers most commonly used by musicians.

A MIDI network can even be extended to include a multiple-track tape recorder. This requires, first, recording some type of synchronization signal (most likely a SMPTE signal) on one track of the tape (usually the highest-numbered track). As this track is played back, the synchronization signal is sent to a device that converts the timing information in the signal into MIDI messages, such as MIDI Timing Clocks or MIDI Time Code messages. These can then be used to drive the clock of the sequencer in the network. The other tracks of the tape recorder can then be used to record the sounds of synthesizers and samplers under the control of the sequencer. Acoustic sources, such as a vocalist or grand piano, might be recorded as well. When the multiple-track recording is played back, the same synthesizers and samplers can be used again, with different presets and sample files perhaps, to double the tracks already recorded or to add new parts to the mix. Unlike the process of simple overdubbing, however, this technique, called **virtual tracking,** provides a means of automatic rhythmic coordination of the new sounds and the previously recorded tracks by using the recorded synchronization tone on the tape as a common reference. If all goes well, the real-time tracks and the recorded tracks will start together, stay together, and end together. The technique of virtual tracking thus provides a relatively inexpensive but powerful way to expand the capacity of a MIDI network.

TAPE SYNCHRONIZATION TECHNIQUES

An early form of synchronization signal consisted of a tone that alternated between two pitches 24 times per beat.[6] This technique of representing a series of pulses with an alternating tone is called frequency-shift keying, and the tone is called an FSK sync tone. An FSK tone recorded on one track of a tape would provide the tempo reference for the other tracks on the tape and also for any drum machines and sequencers programmed to control the generation of additional musical parts.

Before the sync tone was recorded, however, a "tempo map" of all tempo changes in the music would be created, and the sync tone would then be generated according to this pattern of tempos. If the musician made any subsequent revisions to the pattern of tempos, a new tempo map would have to be made, and the sync tone on the tape would have to be replaced with a newly generated one. This procedure could become quite tedious. Another difficulty of using FSK sync derived from the fact that the tone consisted of nothing more than a simple alternation of pitches. Thus, it was impossible to begin the tape after the start of the sync tone and determine the precise location in measures and beats. For synchronization to occur, it was necessary always to start the tape from the beginning.

With progress in electronic technology, it became possible by the late 1980s for manufacturers to offer affordable devices that could generate a representation of SMPTE time code in the form of an audio signal that could be recorded on tape. The location of the tape at any given moment could be determined from the time code signal with great precision, in absolute time of hours, minutes, seconds, and "frames." The early devices that could generate and read a SMPTE time code signal could also be programmed with a tempo map. As a recorded time code signal was read from the tape, the SMPTE box would translate the readings of absolute time into the relative values of measures, beats, and parts of beats, according to the tempo map. The device would then generate the corresponding MIDI Sync messages, including the 24 Timing Clock messages per beat as well as Start, Stop, Continue, and Song Position Pointer messages. These would then be transmitted through a MIDI cable to the sequencer or drum machine in the network of MIDI instruments.

---

6. Devices by some manufacturers generated a tone that alternated 48 times per beat, and others created a tone that alternated 96 times per beat. A sync converter box was often necessary if devices by these different manufacturers were to be used together.

Subsequently, MIDI Time Code (MTC) was adopted as a means of representing, with specially defined MIDI messages, the absolute time code information contained in a SMPTE signal. Most devices that are currently available for the generation of SMPTE time code signals can also read these signals and convert them into a series of MTC Quarter-Frame messages. A set of eight successive Quarter-Frame messages will together convey the information regarding the current time reading of the SMPTE signal in hours, minutes, seconds, and frames. These Quarter-Frame messages are then transmitted through the MIDI cables to sequencers, drum machines, and any other devices able to use them.

A sequencer or drum machine that recognizes MIDI Time Code messages should be able to relate the absolute timing information they bear to the relative timing information entered in their own tempo tracks; a separate tempo map for the sync box is no longer necessary. Revisions to the pattern of tempos can be managed much more easily now by the programming of tempos in the sequencer or drum machine. Such machines are much more amiably disposed to tedious recalculations of this sort.

Some confusion often arises from the fact that there are five widely recognized variants of SMPTE time code: 24 fps, 25 fps, 30 fps, drop-frame, and non-drop-frame time code. Time code for motion picture film divides each second into 24 "frames." Time code for video in Europe counts 25 frames per second. For black-and-white video in North America and Japan, a frame rate of 30 per second was adopted (but not until after black-and-white video became obsolete!).

For color video in North America and Japan, however, a rate of 29.97 frames per second was established. Even so (and this is where the confusion begins), the time code counts 30 complete frames as if this were a second. Thus, one "second" of color video (counted at 30 frames per "second" even though the actual frame rate is only 29.97 frames per second) requires 1.001001 seconds in actual time to complete. At the rate of 29.97 frames per second (according to the clock), one "hour" of color video takes approximately one hour and 3.6 seconds of time as read from a clock. To reconcile this discrepancy and to eliminate the lag between SMPTE time and actual time, a variant of time code called drop-frame (or DF) was developed. As frames are numbered, the number of the first frame of every minute (except a minute that is a multiple of ten) is counted as frame number 2. There are no frames numbered 0 or 1 during these minutes. Two frame *numbers* are skipped at the beginning of every minute (except every tenth minute); no frames of information are actually dropped, however, despite what the term *drop-frame* might suggest. By skipping a couple of frame numbers now and then, the SMPTE count is able to keep up with the clock count. With drop-frame time code, the SMPTE time corresponds closely to actual time, most of the time.

For some applications, the use of drop-frame time code is not appropriate, however. When synchronizing music or sound effects to a videotape provided as a working copy of a film, it is less important that the indication of clock time be accurate and more important that the frame count be accurate. Therefore, yet another form of time code called non-drop-frame (or NDF) is used. The frame rate is 29.97 frames per second, and no frame numbers are skipped. For musical projects that do not involve synchronization to visuals, however, either drop-frame time code (sometimes called "30 DF") or the old black-and-white time code (sometimes called "true 30") can be used.

A procedure for virtual tracking with SMPTE time code and MIDI Time Code (along with a few other hints) is outlined below:

1. Configure the SMPTE time code generator/reader according to the instructions provided in the owner's manual. Select a time code format. The 30-frames-per-second format (black-and-white) is acceptable if the project will be done entirely in one studio. The 29.97-frames-per-second drop-frame format is also acceptable. If the time code information will be used for further production work in another studio or facility, however, then the 29.97-frames-per-second non-drop-frame format is recommended.

2. Connect the audio output of the SMPTE time code generator/reader to the input of the highest-numbered track on the tape deck. Also connect the output of the time code track to the audio input of the SMPTE generator/reader. Because the time code signal is highly prone to leak into adjacent tracks, an outer track such as the highest-numbered track is the recommended location for the time code signal so that the crosstalk only affects the next-to-highest track. It is also recommended that this next-to-highest track be left blank, as a "guard" track.

3. Use fresh, blank recording tape. Also be sure that the tape heads are well cleaned, demagnetized, and in good condition (not worn and not misaligned).

4. Place into Pause mode the track of the tape recorder selected as the time code track. Start generating a time code signal, and then set the recording level on the tape deck. If possible, any noise-reduction circuits on the time code track should be switched off (unless this means switching off the noise reduction for all of the other tracks as well). A signal level of –3 dB is often adequate. However, be prepared for the possibility that the level of the track will later prove to be too low or too high and the SMPTE reader will not be able to interpret it. A few rounds of experimentation with the signal level may be necessary.

5. With the time code track in record mode, start the tape. After the tape has been moving for a few seconds and has settled at its proper speed, start the SMPTE generator. The process of recording a track of time code is called "striping" a tape. Plan to stripe more of the length of the tape than is required for the duration of the music that will be recorded. Preferably, in fact, the entire length of the tape should be striped.

6. Play the time code track into the SMPTE generator/reader to be sure that the track has been recorded at a satisfactory level.

7. Connect the MIDI output of the SMPTE generator/reader to a MIDI input of the sequencer. Select the External Sync mode of the sequencer so that its internal clock is disengaged. Also select a SMPTE "offset time" on the sequencer. When this time is read from the time code track on the tape, the sequencer will recognize it as a cue to start.

8. Connect the outputs of the tape recorder (except those of the time code and guard tracks, of course) to the inputs of a mixer. Also, except for a few selected instruments as described in the next step, connect the outputs of the synthesizers, samplers, and drum machines to the inputs of the mixer. For each input, configure the mixer for the appropriate output assignments and EQ, effects, and pan settings.

9. Prepare to record on the multitrack deck at least one sequenced track. This should be one of the tracks of the sequence with the best-defined rhythmic patterning. Once this track is recorded on tape, it can be used as a reference track for any subsequent overdubs of vocals and other instruments that cannot be controlled by a sequencer, such as an acoustic guitar, piano, or real drums. To record this track, first connect to the appropriate tape recorder input(s) the audio output(s) of the instrument that plays this sequenced track. Place these channels of the tape deck in Record mode, and press the Start button of the sequencer. The sequencer will pause until it receives a message from the time code generator/reader indicating that the designated SMPTE offset time has arrived. Start the tape rolling, and if all goes well, the system will come to life and the track will be recorded.

10. Additional sequencer tracks may be recorded during this pass as well, or the remaining tracks may be filled with subsequent overdubs of vocals and acoustic instruments.

11. When the recording on the multiple-track tape deck is complete, prepare to play additional tracks of the sequence that can be sounded by the synthesizers, samplers, and/or drum machine. First, rewind the tape. Then press the Start button on the sequencer (remember, it will pause until it receives time code information indicating that the SMPTE offset time has arrived). Then start the tape. As the time code is read from the tape the sequencer will start, and the musical parts that have been recorded on the tracks of the tape deck will be joined by the additional, "virtual" tracks of the synthesizers and other devices playing in synchronization. A two-channel mixdown of all of this can be most impressive indeed.

FIGURE 6.13 (facing page)
Our MIDI network has now reached maturity. MIDI data usually originate from the keyboard controller, although occasionally the wind controller might be used instead. Our MIDI THRU box has been replaced by a MIDI patch bay. The MIDI OUT of each device is connected to one of the MIDI IN connectors on the patch bay, and the corresponding MIDI THRU connectors on the patch bay are connected to the MIDI IN of each device. The usual recipients of MIDI messages now include our synthesizer expander module, multitimbral sampler module, keyboard synthesizer, and also the keyboard synthesizer that we previously used as a keyboard controller. The network also now includes a digital effects device and a multiple-track tape recorder with a sync interface. The network does not include creativity, however. This contribution continues to be expected of the musician.

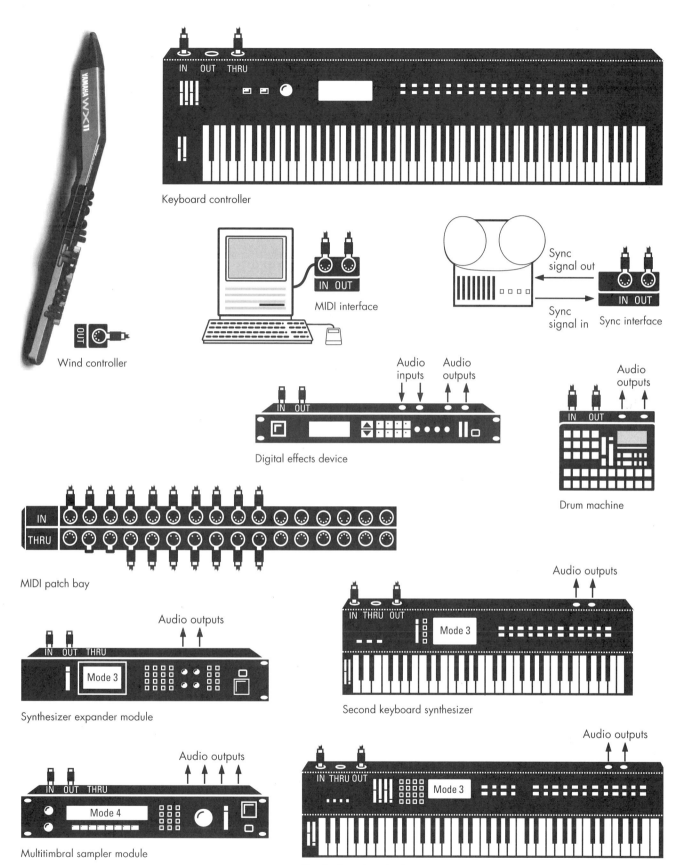

Keyboard controller

Wind controller

MIDI interface

Sync signal out

Sync signal in   Sync interface

Audio inputs   Audio outputs

Digital effects device

Audio outputs

Drum machine

MIDI patch bay

Audio outputs

Synthesizer expander module

Mode 3

Audio outputs

Second keyboard synthesizer

Mode 3

Audio outputs

Multitimbral sampler module

Mode 4

Audio outputs

First keyboard synthesizer

Mode 3

For additional information regarding these techniques, consult the works by Burger and Hall and by Rona that are cited at the end of this chapter. Also refer to the owner's manuals of the sync box, sequencer, and multiple-track tape recorder in the studio. These usually contain specific, quite helpful hints regarding synchronization techniques.

CONCLUDING THOUGHTS

As shown in Figure 6.13, our studio-based MIDI network has by now achieved a rather advanced stage of development. Even though such a network offers tremendous flexibility, it is often helpful to configure the network in a way that facilitates routine patterns of use. For instance, MIDI channel 2 might be regularly assigned to the synthesizer expander module; channels 3, 4, 5, and 6 might be reserved for the multitimbral sampler module; channels 7 and 8 might be regularly assigned to the two keyboard synthesizers; channel 9 might be designated for messages for the digital effects device; and so forth. These assignments can always be changed when required, but in general it is beneficial for the musician to form habits that foster a sense of familiarity with the network.

Similarly, it is important to resist the temptation continually to replace perfectly functional components of a network with the newest models of instruments. This syndrome, characterized by the desire to possess only the most recent, most technologically advanced equipment, is often referred to as "techno-lust." Given that a new generation of equipment has appeared every one to two years, on average, it is clear that this can be a very expensive habit to maintain. More important, this can lead to musical impoverishment as well. The creation of good music often requires the intimate familiarity with an instrument that can come only from use over an extended period of time.

The Musical Instrument Digital Interface is relatively inexpensive to implement in the design of a device, and is by now a nearly universal feature of electronic musical instruments (even including a few of those musical toys that can be purchased from retail chain stores). As an inexpensive control protocol, it is even beginning to find applications in such areas as the control of stage lighting.[7] However, the Musical Instrument Digital Interface itself does have some rather notable limitations. First, as noted earlier, the path for expanding and adapting the MIDI protocol is a somewhat awkward one. Most newly defined messages in recent years have been in the cumbersome form of Universal System-Exclusive or Registered Parameter messages (described in Appendix C).

---

7. Sleep-starved professionals occasionally joke about the possibility of MIDI alarm clocks, MIDI toasters, and even MIDI microwave ovens.

Second, the Musical Instrument Digital Interface was conceived to facilitate the production of music that is based on series of "notes" and combinations of "notes" (that is, more traditional music constructed of melodies and chords). Many musicians, however, believe that some of the more interesting and significant aspects of music occur *within* tones. Such musicians are intrigued, for example, by the evolution of timbre over the course of a tone, or by the beating of "mistuned" partial frequencies within a tone. Although such things can be influenced to a certain extent through the use of Aftertouch and Control Change messages, or bursts of system-exclusive messages, the techniques required to do so can be rather tedious and imprecise. Musicians who are inclined to experiment with sound, therefore, often find themselves at odds with the inherent bias of MIDI toward note-based music.

Finally, MIDI messages are transmitted one bit at a time at the relatively slow rate of 31,250 bits each second. Many musicians feel that the transmission of messages in a serial format, at this rate, is insufficient to accommodate the subtleties of a musical performance. Devices that transmit MIDI information usually set aside a portion of memory, called a buffer, to hold messages until the MIDI cable is clear to carry them. A performance that generates, on just a few channels, a data stream that includes polyphonic aftertouch, pitch bend, and even just a few continuous controller messages can saturate the transmission buffer relatively quickly.[8]

This is not always the most significant bottleneck in a MIDI network, however. Devices that receive MIDI messages typically also have memory buffers to hold messages until their circuits are ready to process them. It is not infrequent to see a message such as "MIDI Receive Buffer Full" on the screen of an instrument. This signifies that the rate of MIDI transmission has greatly exceeded the rate at which the instrument can handle the data. Even when a message is received and accepted, there is often a delay of several milliseconds before the instrument has finished its processing of the data and the result can be heard.[9] Contemporary microcomputers, operating sequencer programs or other MIDI software, can also be somewhat sluggish as they process the MIDI data they receive.

Eventually, digital technology will progress to the point where processing speeds in synthesizers, microcomputers, and other devices will become much faster. By then, it may also be possible to introduce a new form of MIDI that, while still inexpensive, can transmit information at a much greater rate—perhaps in the form of a "parallel" interface that can handle

---

8. The limited capacity of MIDI to carry messages is sometimes referred to as a problem of "limited bandwidth."

9. This should not be too horrifying a realization, however. After all, it was not so long ago that composers would have to wait hours, days, or even weeks before they could hear the results of their instructions to a computer that was programmed to synthesize sound. Modern digital synthesizers can be performed live, in real time, because they operate much more quickly than those older computers did. Real-time synthesis does not mean instantaneous synthesis, however. At least some amount of time will always be required to complete the processing. The real question is how much time is acceptable.

16 or even 32 bits of information simultaneously. So that instruments now in use are not doomed to instant obsolescence, it will be necessary to include the current form of MIDI as a subset of the new form. Perhaps "MIDI format converter" boxes will be needed to translate the new form of MIDI into the old form, and vice versa. For now, this can only be the subject of the wildest speculation.

Despite its limitations, both real and apparent, the Musical Instrument Digital Interface has done much in the past few years to give direction to the development of electroacoustic musical instruments. This is not to say that the purpose of MIDI should be to standardize electroacoustic musical instruments, in the same sense that the piano became standardized in more or less its present form by the middle of the 19th century. To be sure, standardization is not an appropriate goal for the development of a class of instruments whose ambition is to create or recreate any imaginable sound. However, a consistent means of control and interaction is desirable so that attention can be directed more toward the creation of the music itself. This is what MIDI has begun to provide, and as MIDI continues to mature and gain influence, increasingly subtle and masterful works of art will be created. It is indeed an exciting time to be an electroacoustic musician.

IMPORTANT TERMS

drum machine
System messages
System Real-Time messages
Timing Clock, or MIDI Clock,
    messages
MIDI sync
MIDI Time Code (MTC)
Start, Stop, and Continue
    messages
System-Common messages

Song Position Pointer message
System-Exclusive (Sys-Ex)
    messages
bulk dump
librarian program
editor/librarian, or ed/lib
Universal System-Exclusive
    messages
SMPTE time code
keyboard controller

alternate controllers
guitar controller
wind controller
MIDI merger
MIDI data filter
rechannelizer
mapper
controller mapping
MIDI patch bay
virtual tracking

FOR FURTHER READING

Burger, Jeff, and Hall, Gary. "Sync or Swim." *Electronic Musician,* January 1991, pp. 60–67.
De Furia, Steve, and Scacciaferro, Joe. *The MIDI Implementation Book.* Pompton Lakes, NJ: Third Earth, 1986.
De Furia, Steve, and Scacciaferro, Joe. *MIDI Programmer's Handbook.* Redwood City, CA: M&T Books, 1989.
De Furia, Steve, and Scacciaferro, Joe. *The MIDI Resource Book.* Pompton Lakes, NJ: Third Earth, 1987.
MIDI 1.0 Detailed Specification. Los Angeles: International MIDI Association, 1990.
Rona, Jeffrey. *Synchronization from Reel to Reel.* Milwaukee: Hal Leonard, 1990.

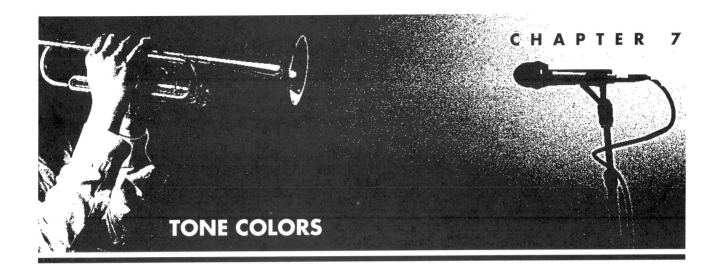

CHAPTER 7

TONE COLORS

*I*n an earlier chapter, a sound synthesizer was defined as a musical instrument designed especially for the task of generating electrical oscillations that can become sounds. In a limited sense, therefore, an electric organ or electric piano might be regarded as a sound synthesizer. However, instruments such as these are dedicated to the creation of particular sets of sounds, and the musician is not provided a means to alter them significantly. An instrument identified as a synthesizer is capable of a much broader range of sounds. More important, the musician has the opportunity to design these sounds by setting controls related to the various characteristics of sound.

This more general approach to the creation of synthetic sound has made it possible to set up a synthesizer so that it can emulate a great variety of instruments. Apart from certain commercial applications, however, it is almost always more musically satisfying simply to employ well-trained musicians to play the actual instruments. Just as real ice cream is preferred by discriminating taste buds to the cheap synthetic kind (that refuses to melt), so is the texture and body of the sound of a real instrument favored by a well-informed sense of hearing. Given the present level of the technology of electroacoustic instruments (including sampling instruments), it is not yet possible to create an entirely credible emulation that incorporates all of the vital subtleties of an acoustic musical instrument. Clever facsimiles of individual tones can be created, but entirely convincing musical passages remain beyond the capability of contemporary electronic instruments.

The synthesizer is, however, quite capable of creating hybrid sounds, or sounds and patterns of sounds that are very difficult to create otherwise and perhaps have never even been heard before. Effective use of such power, however, requires a very good understanding of the basic elements of sound so that these can be controlled intelligently. A rather thorough understanding of timbre is particularly important. Perhaps more than anything else, a synthesizer is a timbre machine. Therefore, this chapter presents an extended review of the subject of timbre. With this prerequisite knowledge, it then becomes possible to proceed to a more complete understanding of the methods of sound synthesis that will be described in the following two chapters.

THE SCIENCE OF SOUND, PART III: THE COLOR OF SOUND

When describing a sound, we refer to its pitch, loudness, duration, and perhaps even the apparent location of its source. However, there is yet another attribute of sound, one that is largely determined by the physical structure of a musical instrument and the means by which sound is produced on it. As described in Chapter 1, this attribute is referred to as the "color" of the sound, or its **timbre.**

Although it may often seem to be fairly simple, the sound of a voice or musical instrument is in fact quite complex, consisting of several simultaneous frequencies of periodic vibrations as well as some degree of noise contributed by nonperiodic vibrations. This teeming mixture, a fusion of many components, is what we perceive as the timbre of the sound.

OVERTONES

The frequencies of the periodic components of a timbre are usually related, as is illustrated by the behavior of an ideal stretched string as it produces a tone. The entire string vibrates at its primary resonant frequency, determined by the length, tension, and mass of the string. This frequency is called the **fundamental.** When we refer in a general way to the frequency of a tone, we are in fact referring specifically to the frequency of the fundamental. The string also vibrates in halves, at a frequency double that of the fundamental frequency. This frequency, produced by the vibration of the string in two parts, is called the second **partial** frequency (with the fundamental being the first partial), and is also known as the first **overtone.** Note that the frequency of the second partial (the first overtone) is one octave above that of the fundamental (see Figure 7.1).

Meanwhile, the string also vibrates in three parts, thus producing a third partial frequency, or second overtone. This frequency is a perfect fifth higher than that of the second partial. Vibrating in four parts, the string also produces a fourth partial, or third overtone, which is two octaves above the fundamental. Vibrating in five parts, the string produces a fifth partial (the fourth overtone) that is a major third above the fourth partial frequency. This series of partial frequencies, called the **overtone series,** extends theoretically to infinity. The amplitude of the higher partials tends

FIGURE 7.1
The overtone series.

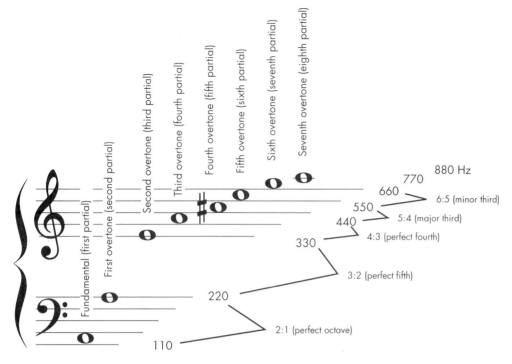

to be less than that of their lower neighbors, however, so that above a certain point the intensities become so low that further partials in the series are disregarded.

In the ideal overtone series, the frequencies of the overtones are related as whole-number multiples of the fundamental frequency (as shown in Figure 7.1). An ideal overtone series is produced by a string that is perfectly flexible. With actual string instruments, however, the stiffness of a string causes it to resist somewhat the vibrations in parts. Thus, the actual overtones are more likely to be *approximate* multiples of the fundamental frequency.

The **spectrum** (plural, **spectra**) of a sound is the distribution of energy across the range of audio frequencies at any given moment. This is analogous to a spectrum of light, in which the colors are separated in continuous bands starting from the longer wavelengths of red light, through the orange, yellow, green, and blue frequencies, to the short wavelengths of violet light. Figure 7.2 is a graph of the spectrum of a "sawtooth" wave, a timbre produced by many sound synthesizers. Each frequency in the sound is plotted as a vertical line on the *x*-axis, from left to right. The amplitude of a given frequency is indicated by the height of its line relative to the marks on the *y*-axis.

The sound illustrated by this graph has a fundamental frequency of 100 Hz. The relative amplitude of the fundamental is ten units. The frequency of the second partial (first overtone) is 200 Hz and its relative amplitude is five units. After examining the plots of a few more partials, two things become apparent. First, all frequencies in the spectrum of a sawtooth wave are related by a common factor: they are the whole-number multiples of the fundamental frequency (these are also referred to as integral

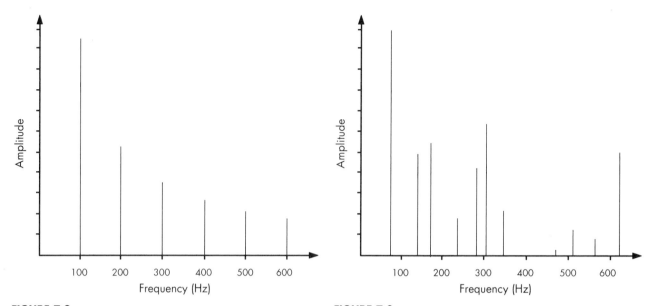

FIGURE 7.2
The spectrum of a sawtooth wave.

FIGURE 7.3
An inharmonic spectrum.

multiples). Second, the amplitude of a given frequency, relative to that of the fundamental, is inversely related to the partial number of that frequency. The spectra of other timbres commonly used in electronic music are defined in similar ways (as will be described in the next chapter).

If all the partial frequencies in a timbre are whole-number multiples of the fundamental frequency, as is the case with the sawtooth wave just described, then the sound is said to have a **harmonic spectrum.** On a graph of the spectrum of such a timbre, all the frequency lines will be spaced equally. Instruments with tones of relatively definite pitch, including the flute, clarinet, trumpet, violin, piano, organ, guitar, and their relatives, have spectra that are for the most part harmonic.

Conversely, if all the partial frequencies in a timbre are not related by a common factor, then the sound has an **inharmonic spectrum.** Figure 7.3 is a graph of such a spectrum; note the uneven spacing of the frequency lines. Instruments with tones of less definite pitch, such as bells, drums, and cymbals, are likely to have inharmonic spectra.

Each of the frequencies in the spectrum of a sound is a simple vibration. Plotted on a graph of amplitude over time, a wave of a simple vibration is identical to a graph of the sine function used in trigonometry (see Figure 7.4). For this reason, the wave produced by a simple vibration is called a **sine wave.**

Early in the 19th century, the French mathematician François Marie Charles Fourier proposed that any complex vibration can be analyzed as the sum of simple vibrations—sine waves—of particular frequencies, intensities, and phase relationships. This idea has come to be known as **Fourier's theorem,** and an analysis based upon this idea is called a

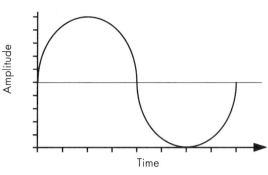

a. the amplitude of a simple wave through one cycle of vibration

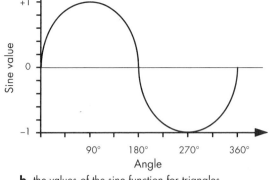

b. the values of the sine function for triangles formed with two radii of a circle

FIGURE 7.4
The sine wave—and how it came to be known as such.

Fourier analysis.[1] Figure 7.2 can be considered a representation of the results of such an analysis of a sawtooth timbre. Phase information has been disregarded in this graph, however, as research has demonstrated that the ears are generally oblivious of phase relationships among the partials within a sound.

Fourier's theorem can also be applied in reverse: sine waves of particular frequencies and intensities can be combined to form complex vibrations. This technique is called **Fourier synthesis,** or additive synthesis, and is very important to designers and programmers of electronic musical instruments, as will be described further.

In Figure 7.5, sine waves of various frequencies, all integral multiples of the lowest frequency, are added together one by one. Note that the amplitude of a particular sine wave is a fraction of the amplitude of the fundamental (the denominator of the fraction is the number of the partial—the integer by which the fundamental frequency is multiplied to determine the partial frequency). As partial frequencies are added, the shape of the wave, called the **waveform,** changes. As increasingly higher partials are added, this waveform begins to assume the characteristic appearance of a saw's tooth (a coincidence perhaps?), and is known as a **sawtooth wave.**

Note that all partials in this example are in phase with one another. If some partials had been added out of phase, the waveform would have assumed a somewhat different shape. However, the ears, being generally indifferent to phase relationships among partial frequencies within a sound, most likely would not detect the difference. Thus, the form of a wave, as it appears on an **oscilloscope**—an electronic laboratory instrument that displays waves on a cathode ray tube (CRT) screen—or in a textbook, may not be a particularly helpful indication of how the wave actually sounds.

---

1. The application of Fourier's theorem to describe the velocities of air molecules in a wave of sound is called Ohm's acoustical law.

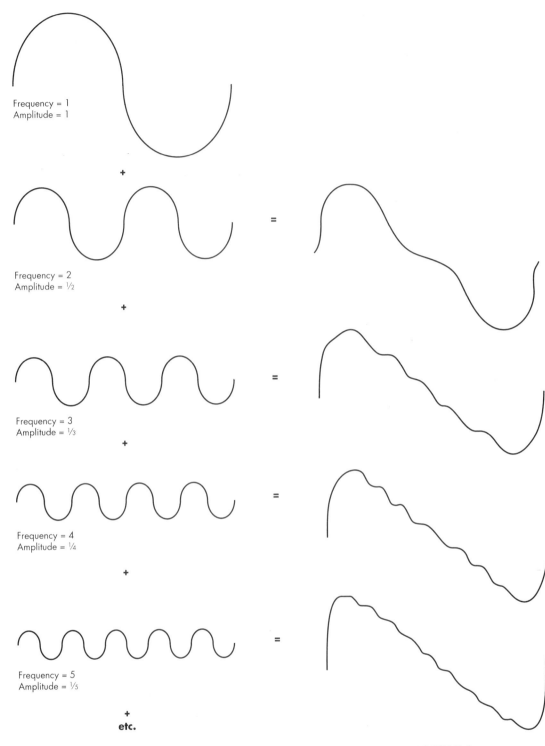

Frequency = 1
Amplitude = 1

+

Frequency = 2
Amplitude = 1/2

+

Frequency = 3
Amplitude = 1/3

+

Frequency = 4
Amplitude = 1/4

+

Frequency = 5
Amplitude = 1/5

+
etc.

=

=

=

=

FIGURE 7.5
The additive synthesis of a
sawtooth wave.

NOISE

Fourier's theorem provides a useful insight into the relationships among the periodic vibrations within a sound. But, as mentioned earlier, there are also nonperiodic vibrations that contribute to the color of a sound. These vibrations are largely random and do not convey a sense of definite pitch. Rather, they create the sound of **noise.**

The tone of a musical instrument of definite pitch, such as the clarinet, will include some degree of noise. This is created mostly by the clicking of the keys and the friction of the air as it rushes past the inside walls of the instrument. At one time it was thought that such **incidental noises** were undesirable components of the sound. One of the highly touted "virtues" of one of the earliest synthesizers, the R.C.A. Mark I, was its ability to eliminate such "unwanted noise" ("the clicking of keys, the rushing of wind, or the scratch of a bow").[2] While it is certainly true that, in the hands of an inexperienced performer, an instrument can produce an excruciatingly objectionable level of incidental noise, it is also true that some amount of such noise is present in the tone of even the very best performers. Listeners expect to hear such noises; removing them results in a tone that seems somehow lifeless and unnatural.

In fact, with many percussion instruments, such as the snare drum, cymbals, and tambourine, such noises are not incidental at all—they are the principal components of the sound. The few periodic vibrations that do exist in the timbre are the components that are "incidental" so far as these instruments are concerned.

On electronic sound synthesizers, two kinds of noise are commonly available. **White noise** (referred to by many writers as "white sound" to avoid the connotation of noise as unwanted or unintentional sound) has an equal distribution of random energy per band within the range of frequencies audible to the human ear (see Figure 7.6a). For example, there is the same amount of energy between 100 and 200 Hz as there is between 6100 and 6200 Hz or between 15,700 and 15,800 Hz. This is the sound of tape hiss, or the sound heard on a radio or TV channel after the station assigned to that channel has left the air (the random "snow" seen on the television screen can be thought of as the visual analog of the white noise being heard).

With **pink noise** (also called pink sound), there is an equal distribution of random energy per *octave* within the range of audible frequencies (see Figure 7.6b). For example, there is the same amount of energy between 100 and 200 Hz as there is between 200 and 400 Hz, 400 and 800 Hz, 800 and 1600 Hz, 1600 and 3200 Hz, 3200 and 6400 Hz, and 6400 and 12,800 Hz. Relative to white noise, the energy distribution of pink noise is more sparse

---

2. Harry F. Olson, "R.C.A.'s Electronic Music Synthesizer a Symbol of Things to Come," *Variety*, 19 October 1955, p. 46.

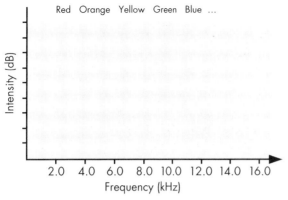

a. the distribution of energy in white noise

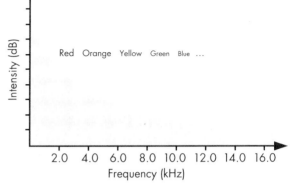

b. the distribution of energy in pink noise

in the higher frequency ranges and more concentrated in the lower frequencies (just as white light includes an even distribution of frequencies of visible light, whereas red light consists primarily of the lower frequencies of visible light). Examples of pink noise include the sounds of ocean waves crashing ashore, of distant thunder, and of bass drums.

FIGURE 7.6
The distribution of energy in white and pink noise.

FORMANTS

The sound of a violin originates in the vibration of a string as the bow is drawn across it. For the voice, the tone begins with the vibration of the vocal cords. With the clarinet and saxophone, the tone originates in the vibration of the reed in the mouthpiece. Taken at the point of origin, these sounds are remarkably wretched, thin, and puny (like the sound of an electric guitar that is disconnected from its amp). One of the most important facts about the structure of a musical instrument is that these vibrations are coupled to the resonances of the body of the instrument. This is how the tone becomes fuller and acquires its special character.

The timbre of the clarinet is shaped considerably by the resonances of the tube and bell of the instrument. The resonances of the throat, sinuses, and mouth determine the tone color of the human voice. The wooden pieces and enclosed spaces of the body of the violin are responsible for providing the resonances that make great bluegrass music possible (not to mention the Mozart string quartets).

These sets of resonances, called **formants,** affect fixed bands of frequencies on most instruments.[3] Any frequencies produced within these resonant bands by the instrument will be affected. Figure 7.7 shows two spectra of an instrument that has a single-band formant centered at 2000 Hz. The

---

3. A notable exception is the ability of the voice to adjust some formants. The fact that we can control the size and shape of some of the spaces in the vocal tract, such as the mouth, means that the resonances can be shifted to produce different timbres, thus making speech possible.

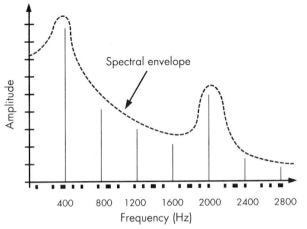

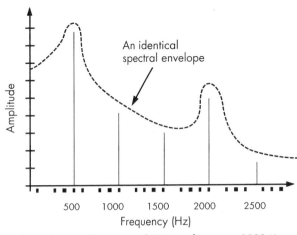

a. fundamental frequency of 400 Hz, formant at 2000 Hz

b. fundamental frequency of 500 Hz, formant at 2000 Hz

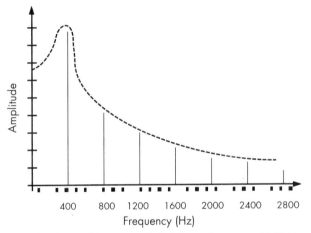

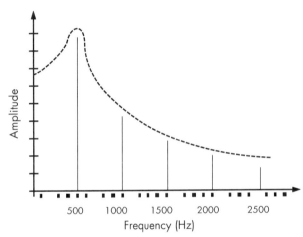

c. fundamental frequency of 400 Hz, no formant at 2000 Hz

d. fundamental frequency of 500 Hz, no formant at 2000 Hz

sound illustrated in Figure 7.7a has a fundamental frequency of 400 Hz. Its fifth partial (the fourth overtone) is relatively emphasized by the formant, as indicated by the bump in the spectrum at 2000 Hz. The sound illustrated in Figure 7.7b has a fundamental frequency of 500 Hz, with a fourth partial (the third overtone) that is relatively emphasized by the formant. For comparison, the spectra shown in Figure 7.7c and 7.7d are those of tones with fundamentals of 400 and 500 Hz, respectively, but without the formant in the region of 2000 Hz.

Thus, the presence of formants provides for a set of common elements between the shape of the spectrum of one tone produced by an instrument and the shape of the spectrum of another tone, with a different fundamental frequency, produced by the same instrument. This spectral shape, called a **spectral envelope,** can be envisioned as a contour that connects the top points of all the frequency marks in a graph of the spectrum of a tone. The relative constancy of the spectral envelope across a range of pitches is an important element in establishing the identity of a musical instrument.

FIGURE 7.7
The effect of a formant on the spectra of sounds.

TIME-VARIANT PHENOMENA

Yet another critical aspect of the behavior of the timbre of a sound produced by a musical instrument is that its spectrum is not static. Over the course of the duration of a sound, the spectral envelope will change. Some partials will speak more quickly than others. Some formants will take some time to stabilize. These phenomena impart a dynamic quality to the timbre.

In effect, each partial frequency has its own amplitude envelope. For example, with many tones of brass instruments, the lower partials are heard first, followed by the entrances of higher partials with shorter attack times. During the decay of some piano tones, a few partials actually increase in intensity for a few moments. Thus, the spectral envelope—a cross

FIGURE 7.8
The changing spectra of sounds as they begin. (Courtesy of Digidesign, Inc.)

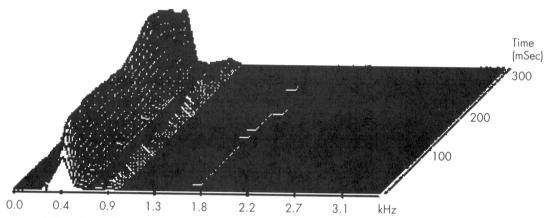

a. A flute playing the pitch A-440 at a dynamic of mezzoforte. Note the strength of the fundamental and the relative sparseness of overtones. This may account for the "pure" quality ascribed to the sound of the flute.

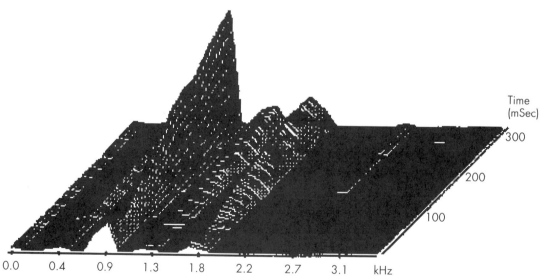

b. An oboe playing the pitch A-440 at a dynamic of mezzoforte. Note that the first overtone is much stronger than the fundamental. This may explain the common description of this sound as having a "nasal" quality. Despite the relative weakness of the fundamental, it is nonetheless perceived as such (and probably would be even if it were much weaker still) because it is recognized by the ear as the common factor in this overtone series.

section of the spectrum at any particular instant—will have a different shape at different stages in the life of a sound.

Figure 7.8 includes perspective plots of the beginning moments of the sounds of several common musical instruments, showing that their spectra do change through time. Frequency is plotted along the axis that runs from left to right, intensity along the axis that runs from bottom to top, and time along an axis that runs from front to back. When viewed in this way, each partial reveals an envelope of its own. This means that a successful Fourier synthesizer must not only be able to generate each of these frequencies, but must also be able to control their amplitudes independently.

FIGURE 7.8 (continued)

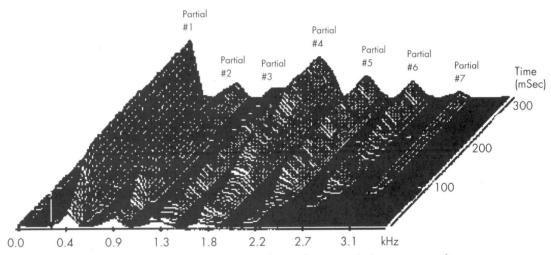

c. A trumpet playing the pitch A-440 at a dynamic of mezzoforte. Note the later entrances of the higher partials.

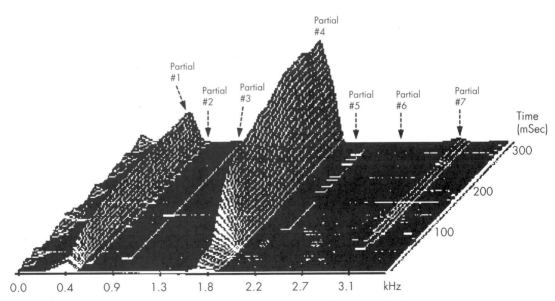

d. A trumpet wih a harmon mute, stem removed (Miles Davis's favorite mute), playing the pitch A-440 at a dynamic of mezzoforte. Compare this to the perspective plot of the unmuted trumpet **(c)**. Note that the second and third partials are greatly attenuated by the antiresonance of the mute (as if a great glacier had carved a wide valley down the spectrum of this sound). Note also that the fourth partial is much stronger; it has apparently found a friendly formant.

FIGURE 7.8 (continued)

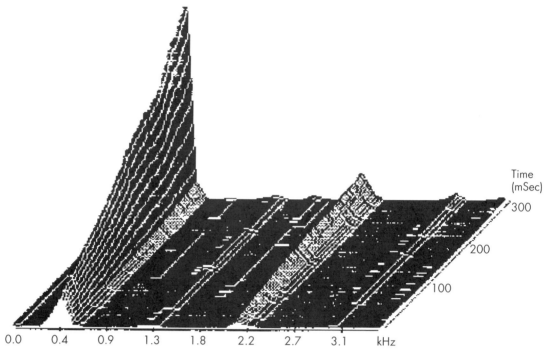

e. A violin playing the pitch A-440 (on an open string) at a dynamic of mezzoforte. Note the very smooth and gradual attack of the fundamental (at 0.44 kHz). Also note the relative strength of the fifth partial (near 2.2 kHz).

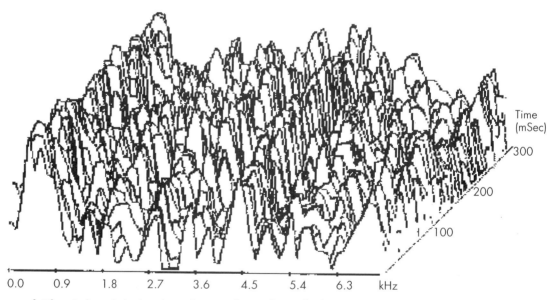

f. Fifteen-inch cymbals played at a dynamic of mezzoforte. Clearly, noise is the predominant element of this timbre. Periodic components (overtones, for instance) are not discernible in the spectrum.

The overall envelope, or "global" envelope of a sound, as described in Chapter 1, is simply the sum of the envelopes of each of the components of the sound. Nonetheless, it is often useful to refer to this global envelope. For example, differences among the timbres of a bassoon, 'cello, and trombone, each sounding middle C, are more easily attributed to differences among attack times than to differences among the spectra of these instruments. The more gradual, mellow attack of the 'cello, for example, makes its identity unmistakable when compared to the much quicker attack of the trombone.

Incidental noises during the attack of a sound can be especially significant. The onset of a tone is particularly noisy with many instruments. Eventually the frequencies that find resonances are the ones that survive. But in the meantime, the noises make their presence known as "chiffs," "dinks," "thumps," or similar rustlings that contribute indispensably to the identity and character of an instrument.

The perspective plots in Figure 7.9 illustrate a relationship between timbre and overall intensity. A louder sound tends to be a "brighter" sound because of the greater prominence of higher partials. A crescendo (a

FIGURE 7.9
The relationship between timbre and the overall intensity of a sound. (Courtesy of Digidesign, Inc.)

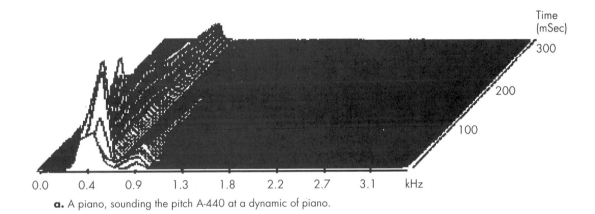

a. A piano, sounding the pitch A-440 at a dynamic of piano.

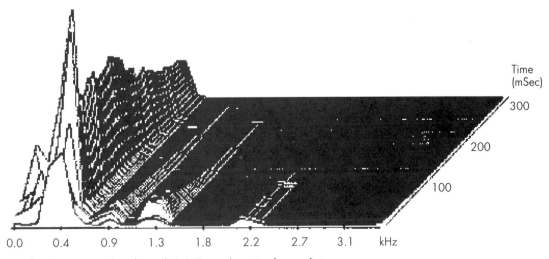

b. A piano, sounding the pitch A-440 at a dynamic of mezzoforte.

gradual increase in loudness over a passage of music) is as much a phenomenon of timbre as of intensity. This is particularly noticeable with trumpets and other brass instruments.

Audible, periodic fluctuations in the frequency or intensity of a tone—called **vibrato** and **tremolo,** respectively—are often regarded as phenomena of timbre. A natural vibrato is a typically narrow fluctuation, or **modulation,** of pitch at a rate of approximately six times per second. As the pitch fluctuates, so does the placement of the partial frequencies relative to formants. Thus, there is a subtle modulation of the spectral envelope that corresponds to the modulation of pitch.

A true tremolo—a fluctuation of intensity just a few times per second—is somewhat rare with acoustic instruments. Perhaps the best-known example is the vibraphone. When a tremolo does occur, there will most likely be a corresponding modulation of the strength of the higher partials in the spectrum. Therefore, as a by-product of the regular changes of intensity of a tremolo, there is a subtle fluctuation in tone color.

THE PERCEPTION OF TIMBRE

Without doubt, timbre is a complex element of sound—one with many dimensions indeed. A timbre includes periodic and nonperiodic vibrations. The periodic vibrations, if present, may be organized into spectra that are harmonic (or approximately so) or spectra that are inharmonic. The nonperiodic vibrations may consist of incidental noises, or they may be the primary components of the sound. The resonances of the instrument affect the balance of energy among the components—the spectral envelope. The overall intensity of the sound affects the prominence of the higher partials—the brilliance of the sound. Each of the components of the sound is likely to have its own attack, sustain, and decay patterns, meaning a lifetime of changes for the spectral envelope over the course of the tone. Even vibrato and tremolo can have subtle effects on the color of the tone.

Nonetheless, all of these elements fuse into a single perceptual object. Such an object, a timbre, can be very difficult to describe subjectively. We use adjectives such as *bright, dark, mellow, hollow,* or *pure* to refer to what we hear of particular constellations of overtones. Terms such as *raspy, buzzy, breathy,* or *harsh* refer in general ways to the noise content of a timbre. The attacks of sounds can be described as *smooth, abrupt, sharp, gentle,* or *easy.*

As with most complex phenomena, however, we attempt to categorize timbre mainly by relating what we hear to what we have seen and heard of other musical instruments. We have learned that certain modes of attack are related to certain ways of playing instruments. For example, a plucked string has an abrupt attack while a bowed string has a smoother, more gentle attack. We have also learned to associate spectra with certain kinds of instruments; for example, a full spectrum with staggered onsets of higher partials unambiguously denotes the sound of a brass instrument.

Part of this process of learning has also included becoming familiar with the kinds of musical patterns—riffs, licks, trills, easy leaps, arpeggios—that are characteristic of particular instruments. A guitar sound on a synthesizer is much more convincing, for instance, when the performer is rolling the keys E-A-D-G-B-E (the pitches of the open strings on a guitar) than when a Mozart piano sonata is played instead. Fanfares on a string bass type of sound are rather difficult to accomplish convincingly; with a brassy sound, however, they are somewhat more successful.

Our awareness of tone color seems to be inextricably linked to what we have learned from our experiences with musical instruments. It is important, however, not to confuse a function of timbre with its definition. Timbre does indeed provide the essential clues to the identity of instruments as we hear them. However, timbre is not "that quality of sound that enables us to identify instruments," as it is often defined; rather, it is the aggregate effect of the periodic and nonperiodic components of a sound and their envelopes.

This is not a particularly glamorous definition of timbre, but it is one that can well serve the musician who is about to explore the possibilities of sound synthesis. The techniques of electronic sound synthesis provide some degree of freedom from the structural constraints of musical instruments, so that patterns of thought acquired from prior learning no longer necessarily apply. As discussed previously, the primary function of synthesizers should not be simply to recreate the tones of natural instruments. However, a deep understanding of the models provided by natural instruments is essential if the tones of synthetic instruments are to be sufficiently detailed and credible as musical sounds. Such knowledge will prove its value as the great variety of analog and digital techniques of synthesis are examined in the next two chapters.

IMPORTANT TERMS

timbre	sine wave	incidental noises
fundamental	Fourier's theorem	white noise
partial	Fourier analysis	pink noise
overtone	Fourier synthesis	formants
overtone series	waveform	spectral envelope
spectrum (spectra)	sawtooth wave	vibrato
harmonic spectrum	oscilloscope	tremolo
inharmonic spectrum	noise	modulation

FOR FURTHER READING

Backus, John. *The Acoustical Foundations of Music.* New York: Norton, 1969.

Erickson, Robert. *Sound Structure in Music.* Berkeley: University of California Press, 1975.

Hall, Donald E. *Musical Acoustics.* 2d ed. Pacific Grove, CA: Brooks/Cole, 1991.

Pierce, John R. *The Science of Musical Sound.* New York: Scientific American, 1983.

Rossing, Thomas D. *The Science of Sound.* 2d ed. Reading, MA: Addison-Wesley, 1990.

CHAPTER 8

ANALOG SOUND SYNTHESIS

E lectronic sound synthesizers have been available to composers since the mid-1950s. Many synthesizers, particularly the most recent ones, deal primarily with numerical representations of electrical oscillations, and so are called **digital synthesizers.** These are described more completely in the next chapter.

Other synthesizers, generally older ones, work with the electrical oscillations themselves. These electrical waves are directly analogous to the vibrations of sound that are produced when the signal reaches the loudspeaker. For this reason, such synthesizers are identified as **analog synthesizers.** Although these are no longer in widespread use, many of the concepts of synthesizer operation introduced with them continue to be of great relevance.

The modern history of analog synthesis begins with the work of Herbert Eimert and his colleagues in the studio they established in 1951 at the station of the Northwest German Radio (or NWDR, for Nordwestdeutscher Rundfunk) in Cologne. The equipment in this studio included signal sources such as electronic oscillators and noise generators, and signal processors such as electronic filters, gates,[1] and related devices. Much of this equipment was generic test equipment that had been previously used elsewhere at the station. The essential equipment of the studio also included a variety of tape recorders. The signals that were generated and processed by the electronic equipment were recorded on tape, where they could then be edited, looped, mixed with other sounds, or otherwise manipulated.

---

1. A gate is an electronic device that regulates the passage of an electronic signal. When the gate is electronically open, the signal passes through; otherwise, it is blocked. By connecting the output of an electronic oscillator or noise generator (both of which produce a continuous signal) to the input of a gate device, it becomes possible to produce separate tones, with distinct beginnings and endings.

FIGURE 8.1
The RCA Mark II synthesizer. (Courtesy of the Electronic Music Center of Columbia University.)

The composers in the Cologne studio were attracted by the degree of control that these techniques provided (see the discussion in Chapter 10 of the *Gesang der Jünglinge* by Karlheinz Stockhausen). However, producing such ***elektronische Musik*** could be exceedingly tedious work. To record a simple series of pitches, for example, they had to tune the oscillator, record the tone, retune the oscillator, restart the recorder, and repeat the process until all the tones were on tape. Next, these separate tones had to be spliced together, with each segment of tape being measured carefully to ensure the accuracy of the rhythmic relationships among the tones.

The RCA Electronic Music Synthesizer, introduced in 1955, provided for the automation of many of these processes. The second model, called the Mark II, was built in 1957 at a cost of a quarter-million dollars; it was later placed with the Columbia-Princeton Electronic Music Center, jointly operated by Columbia and Princeton universities. The device, which included more than 1700 vacuum tubes, was housed in nine equipment racks, virtually covering an entire wall (and then some) in the studio in which it was located (see Figure 8.1). Needless to say, it was not an instrument intended for the onstage performances of an itinerant rock-and-roll band; it was most certainly a studio synthesizer.

Some rather remarkable claims were made at first regarding the capabilities of this synthesizer. It was said to be able to:

- "match the sound of any instrument or ensemble"[2]
- "project a speaking voice, even in familiar tones and accents"[3]

---

2. Howard Taubman, "Synthesized Piano Music Found to Have Tone Matching a Grand's: RCA Electronic Device Can Produce Ensemble and Voice Sounds Too—Musician's Role Still Important," *New York Times,* 1 February 1955, p. 35.

3. Ibid.

- "synthesize any human voice and any combination of words. That is, a speech that was never made might be synthesized. This feature, it is believed, might be of some value in psychological warfare."[4]
- "conjure up all sounds in nature"[5]
- "dispense with performing musicians. . . . Only the performer's unions would stand in the way."[6]

Nonetheless, it did provide composers with a powerful means to explore new ideas about music (see the discussion in Chapter 10 of the *Ensembles for Synthesizer* by Milton Babbitt). Precise instructions regarding the frequency, intensity, envelope, duration, and timbre of sounds (and the connections between sounds) could be encoded by punching holes in a paper roll, which was then scanned to activate controls within the synthesizer. The automation of such tasks, which had previously required considerable effort (tuning oscillators, splicing segments of tape, and so on), was facilitated by the fact that the various components of the RCA synthesizer were designed to be mutually compatible. Rather than being an eclectic assembly of assorted equipment found around a radio station or custom-built for particular applications, the RCA instrument was an integrated system dedicated to the synthesis of electronic sounds.

By the mid-1960s, a newer technique had been developed for controlling a sound synthesizer. An electrical signal called a **control voltage** could be used to regulate the operation of an audio device. At about the same time, the technology of electronic transistors was becoming widely available. The development of the technique of voltage control, together with the technological feasibility of replacing vacuum tubes with transistors, made it possible for musically inclined electrical engineers to design much smaller, and in many respects more powerful, synthesizers.

In 1964, Robert Moog introduced elements of one of the first of this new generation of synthesizers in New York. Donald Buchla, working with Morton Subotnick and other musicians in the San Francisco area, introduced a synthesizer at about the same time. In Rome, Paul Ketoff created a small synthesizer called the Synket that was particularly well suited to live performances of electronic music, such as those by the composer John Eaton. Within a short time, sound synthesizers were being produced commercially and were being used on some very successful LP recordings, such as Walter Carlos's *Switched-on Bach*. Dozens of new studios for electronic music were being established around the world. The great proliferation of electroacoustic music was underway.

---

4. David Sarnoff, chairman of RCA, quoted in Robert K. Plumb, "Electronic Device Can Duplicate Every Sound," *New York Times*, 1 February 1955, p. 1.

5. Taubman, op. cit.

6. Ibid; see also "How's Petrillo Gonna Collect AFM Dues from RCA's Electronic Tooter?" *Variety*, 2 February 1955, p. 55.

THE PREHISTORY OF ELECTRONIC MUSIC

The synthesizer was predated by dozens, if not hundreds, of electrical and electronic musical instruments. One of the most awesome of these was the Telharmonium (see Figure 8.2), developed around the turn of the century by the American inventor and lawyer Thaddeus Cahill. After working on some prototypes in the late 1890s, Cahill built the largest version of the instrument at the beginning of this century. It was a large instrument indeed. Reported to have weighed at least 200 tons, it required 30 railroad cars to transport it to New York City, where it was installed in 1906 in the basement and first floor of a building at 39th Street and Broadway called Telharmonic Hall. Its signal was sent out over special telephone lines and offered to subscribers for a monthly fee.

The vast bulk of the instrument was necessary because high voltages were required for its operation. It was not until 1906 that the triode, a vacuum tube that made electronic amplification possible, was invented—too late to be used in the Telharmonium. Although Cahill's New York Electric Music Company soon failed, many of his ideas were revived three decades later by Laurens Hammond and implemented with techniques of electronic amplification. By 1935 this new instrument, the Hammond organ, was introduced; it has since become a classic instrument of gospel music and rock-and-roll.

One of the most unusual instruments ever invented is the theremin (see Figure 8.3), introduced in 1920 by the Russian inventor Leo Theremin. It is unlike all other instruments in that it is played by *not* touching it. The performer waves hands around its two metal antennae—one for the control of pitch, and the other for amplitude. The pitch rises as the hand moves closer to the pitch antenna. A vibrato is produced if the hand is shaken. Moving from one pitch to another requires sweeping through all of the pitches in between. Thus, great skill is required to slight these swoops so that the listener does not tire of the sound too quickly.

A few people established reputations as virtuosi on the theremin, including Clara Rockmore, whose performances can today be heard and seen on recordings and film. Theremin spent some time in New York City during the 1930s and then returned to the Soviet Union, where he was soon arrested by the Stalin regime. During his imprisonment, he developed aircraft tracking instruments and eavesdropping devices for the Soviet government; he was awarded a technical prize for these "contributions" shortly after his release in 1947.

FIGURE 8.2
The dynamo room in the basement of Telharmonic Hall. This photograph (from the *Telharmonic Hall Program: Week of December 30th,* New York: Telharmonic Securities Co., 1907, p. 2) shows only a portion of Thaddeus Cahill's Telharmonium. (Copy photo courtesy of Reynold Weidenaar.)

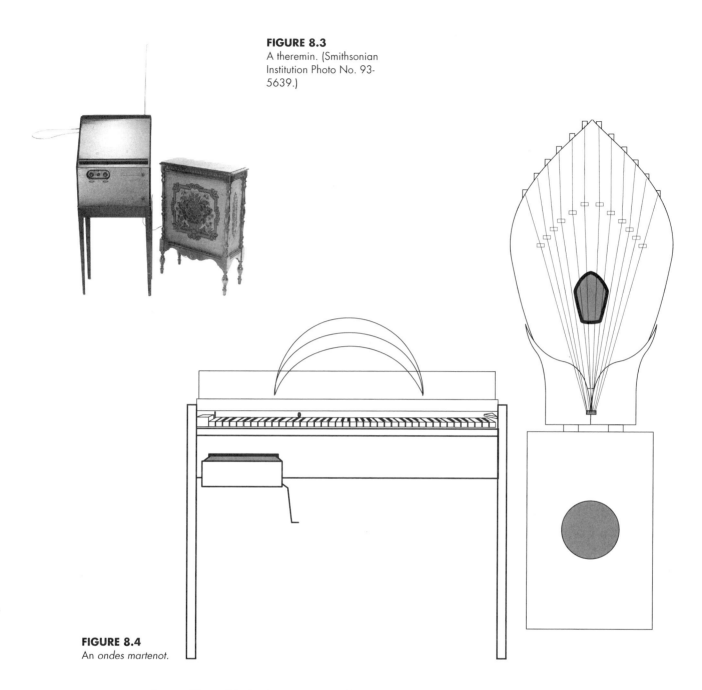

FIGURE 8.3
A theremin. (Smithsonian Institution Photo No. 93-5639.)

FIGURE 8.4
An *ondes martenot.*

Another well-established instrument from this period is the *ondes martenot* (see Figure 8.4), produced in Paris in 1928 by the French inventor Maurice Martenot. The instrument is based on the same principle of operation as the theremin, and sounds much the same, but is played by sliding a ring attached to a wire on a pulley. This mechanism is mounted over a painted keyboard to provide the performer with a reference for pitch (later versions of the instrument have had actual, working keyboards). Literally hundreds of pieces of music have been composed for the *ondes martenot,* including some excellent music by the eminent French composer Olivier Messiaen.

This provides only a glimpse of the early activities in this field. The reader is encouraged to explore many of the excellent writings and recordings cited at the end of this chapter.

FUNCTIONS ON A TYPICAL ANALOG SYNTHESIZER

The transistorized sound synthesizers that appeared in the 1960s were primarily studio instruments. Despite the reduction in size (at least in relation to the size of the RCA synthesizer) and the application of the concept of voltage control, they were still rather bulky and somewhat complicated to operate. Typically these instruments were designed as a collection of individual, electrically compatible components called **modules,** each dedicated to a specific function of sound synthesis, such as signal generation, gating, amplification, filtering, or control voltage generation. Thus, a particular sound synthesizer was likely to be a custom set of modules selected and arranged in the way considered best suited to the aesthetic aims of a particular studio.

The inputs and outputs of a module are connected to those of other modules by patch cords (or, on some models, a matrix switch arrangement.) Thus, different subsets of the modules on a synthesizer can be connected in a variety of ways to produce an enormous variety of sounds (many of which may even be genuinely new and interesting). A particular combination of modules such as this is called a **patch.**

A module in a patch performs at least one of three basic functions: (1) It may function as the source of the audio signal, providing an oscillation or a band of noise. (2) It may process or modify the amplitude, spectrum, or some other attribute of the signal in some way. (3) A module may function as a source of control voltages that can be applied to the other modules in the patch.

Figure 8.5 includes a block diagram of a common synthesizer patch that illustrates how these three categories of modules relate to one another. The audio signal originates at the oscillator, then passes through the filter and the amplifier before being sent from the synthesizer to the tape recorder. The pitch of the oscillator is controlled by a voltage provided from the keyboard, and the level of the amplifier is controlled by a voltage from the envelope generator. The signals from the keyboard and the envelope generator are themselves never heard, but their effects on the oscillator and the amplifier are heard as changes in the pitch and loudness of the audio signal, respectively.

AUDIO SIGNAL SOURCES

Three types of modules can function as audio signal sources on an analog synthesizer: voltage-controlled oscillators, noise generators, and interfaces for external sources (such as microphones). The **voltage-controlled oscillator (VCO),** illustrated in Figure 8.6, is found on all analog synthesizers. In fact, there will most likely be at least two or three of them.

FIGURE 8.5
A synthesizer patch.

a. A photograph of the actual patch

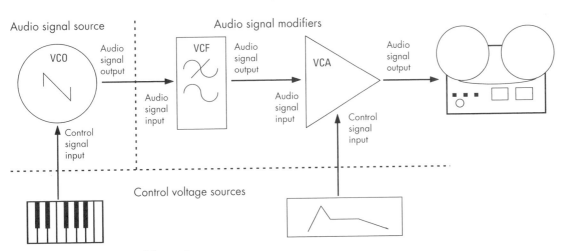

Audio signal source

Audio signal modifiers

VCO

Audio signal output

VCF

Audio signal output

VCA

Audio signal output

Audio signal input

Audio signal input

Control signal input

Control signal input

Control voltage sources

b. A schematic diagram of the patch

FIGURE 8.6
A VCO.

A typical VCO will have a dial for coarse adjustments to the frequency of the signal produced by the module. The range of this dial usually covers a major portion of the range of frequencies audible to humans. Another dial, with a much narrower range, is used to make finer adjustments to the frequency. Some VCOs have a frequency range switch that is labeled after pipe organ stops—for example, 16'–8'–4'.[7] Such a switch is used to shift the frequency of the VCO up or down one or more octaves.

A VCO usually offers a selection of common waveforms. Some synthesizers have an output jack dedicated to each available waveform. Others have a single output jack, and the waveform is selected by a switch. One commonly available waveform is the sine wave, which has no overtones—only a fundamental frequency.[8]

Virtually all VCOs can generate sawtooth waves (see Chapter 7), which have a spectrum that includes all partials. The amplitude of a particular partial, relative to that of the fundamental, is the inverse of its partial number ($1/n$, where n is the partial number). Thus, the amplitude of the second partial (the first overtone) is half that of the fundamental, the amplitude of the third partial (the second overtone) is one-third that of the fundamental, and so on (see Figure 7.5). The combined amplitude of the first three overtones is greater than that of the fundamental ($1/1 < 1/2 + 1/3 + 1/4$). Thus, most of the energy in the spectrum of a sawtooth wave is found in the overtones, making this a rather bright and penetrating timbre.

A **triangle wave** has a spectrum that includes only the odd-numbered partials. The amplitude of a particular partial, relative to that of the fundamental, is the square of the inverse of its partial number ($1/n^2$, where n is the partial number). Thus, the second partial is absent, the third partial has 1/9 the amplitude of the fundamental, the fourth partial is absent, the fifth partial has 1/25 the amplitude of the fundamental, and so forth. Most of the energy of a triangle wave is concentrated in the fundamental ($1/1 > 1/9 + 1/25 + 1/49 + . . .$), resulting in a relatively mellow tone color.

A **pulse wave** has a waveform that is positive at a constant level for the first part of the cycle, then instantly drops to a negative level for the remainder of the cycle. The proportion of the positive portion of the cycle to the total length of the cycle is called the **duty cycle** of the wave. A **square wave** is a pulse wave with a duty cycle of 1:2. This means that the wave is positive at a constant level for the first half of the cycle and negative at a constant level for the other half of the cycle. The spectrum of a square wave includes only the odd-numbered partials; the amplitude of a particular partial, relative to that of the fundamental, is the inverse of its

---

7. An organ pipe 16 feet long, open at each end, will produce a pitch three octaves below middle C. An eight-foot organ pipe, open at each end, will produce a pitch two octaves lower than middle C, and a four-foot organ pipe will produce a pitch one octave below middle C. A two-foot organ pipe will produce middle C itself.

8. The terms used here to refer to the constituents of a tone color—*overtones, fundamental frequency, noise,* and so on—were introduced and defined in Chapter 7. The reader may wish to review this material before proceeding.

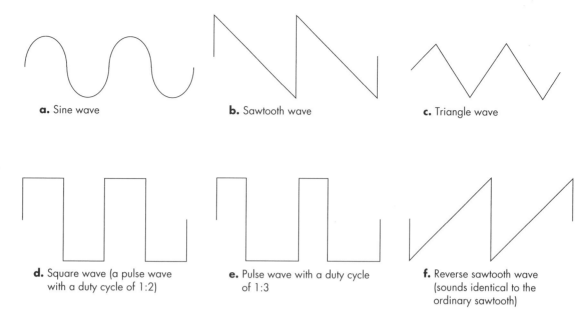

a. Sine wave

b. Sawtooth wave

c. Triangle wave

d. Square wave (a pulse wave with a duty cycle of 1:2)

e. Pulse wave with a duty cycle of 1:3

f. Reverse sawtooth wave (sounds identical to the ordinary sawtooth)

FIGURE 8.7
Common waveforms (two cycles of each), as displayed on the screen of an oscilloscope.

partial number ($1/n$, where n is the partial number). Thus, the second partial (the first overtone) is absent, the third partial (the second overtone) has one-third the amplitude of the fundamental, the fourth partial is absent, the fifth partial has one-fifth the amplitude of the fundamental, and so forth. In the absence of even-numbered partials, which reinforce odd-numbered partials at the octave (see Figure 7.1), the timbre of a square wave sounds "hollow."

A pulse wave with a duty cycle of 1:3 has every third partial absent from its spectrum, thus presenting a somewhat different timbre from that of a square wave. If the duty cycle is 1:4, then every fourth partial is missing, and so forth. Many VCOs include a dial for adjusting the duty cycle, or pulse width, of the pulse waveform so that these subtle variations of timbre can be achieved. Some VCOs even have an input jack for control voltages that can automatically vary, or modulate, the duty cycle of the pulse waveform.

The geometric origin of the names of these waveforms can be discerned when the output of a VCO is viewed on an oscilloscope (see Figure 8.7). As described in the previous chapter, however, these particular shapes appear only if all the partial frequencies in the wave are in phase with one another. If some of the partials are out of phase, the shapes will turn out somewhat differently. Nonetheless, the timbre will still be perceived as the same.

The audio signal output of a VCO is usually patched to an audio signal input on a voltage-controlled filter, voltage-controlled amplifier, mixer, or some other modifier module. The VCO module will also have at least one input for control voltages that might come from the keyboard, envelope generator, or some other source of control voltages.

Noise generator modules are typically very simple. As audio signal sources, they do not have inputs for an audio signal—they only have outputs. Separate outputs for white and pink noise may be available, or there may be a single output jack with a dial to adjust the coloration of the noise. The audio signal output of a noise generator is normally connected to the audio signal input of a voltage-controlled filter, voltage-controlled amplifier, mixer, or some other modifier module. Input jacks for control voltages are normally not provided on noise generator modules.

Some analog synthesizers include microphone preamplification modules so that a microphone signal can be boosted to the level expected by the filter and other modifier modules. There may also be input jacks for audio signals from tape recorders, mixing consoles, and other external, line-level sources. The capability to modify and control signals from such external sources greatly enriches the musical possibilities of an analog synthesizer.

SIGNAL MODIFIER MODULES

The function of a modifier module is to shape in some way the raw audio signal provided by a VCO, noise generator, or external source. As the audio signal passes through the module (on its way to its ultimate destination, the loudspeaker), the amplitude, timbre, or some other aspect of the signal will be modified or contoured in ways that result in a tone more appropriate for the musical context. This is similar to the way in which the vocal tract shapes the sound produced by the larynx, or the body of a guitar modifies the tone produced by the vibrating strings.

A **voltage-controlled amplifier (VCA)** modifies the amplitude, and therefore the intensity, of the audio signal. It has at least one input jack for an audio signal and at least one output jack, from which the signal can be connected to the audio signal input of another modifier module (or to the output lines of the synthesizer). Often there is a dial for adjusting the base amplitude level. Normally the base amplitude level of a VCA is set to zero so that the audio signal does not pass through the module until a control voltage is applied. There will always be at least one input jack on a VCA for control voltages. The most common source of control voltages for a VCA is an envelope generator (to be described soon).

Most voltage-controlled amplifiers do not actually amplify the signal— they attenuate it. If the dial for adjusting the base amplitude level is turned fully open, then the audio signal passes through at full strength. Lower settings represent the corresponding attenuation of the signal. The variations in amplitude that result from the application of a control voltage will build upon this base amplitude level, but the peak amplitude level will not likely exceed the original level of the signal at the audio input.

A **voltage-controlled filter (VCF)** can shape the timbre of a signal provided by a VCO, noise generator, or external source. "Active" filters accomplish this either by boosting the intensities of frequencies within a set

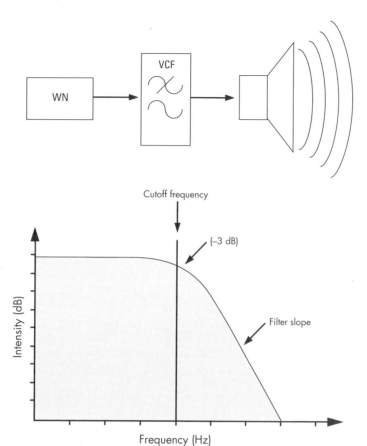

FIGURE 8.8
The effect of a low-pass filter on white noise.

range of the spectrum or by attenuating the intensities of frequencies within a range. "Passive" filters only attenuate frequencies within a range. Both types of filters can be found on analog synthesizers.

A **low-pass filter** is one that passes frequencies below a selected **cutoff frequency,** while filtering out the frequencies above the cutoff. Although the term *cutoff frequency* implies a distinct and perhaps even abrupt boundary between the range of frequencies that pass and the range of frequencies that do not, a graph of the response of a typical low-pass filter, shown in Figure 8.8, reveals that this is not necessarily the case. The cutoff frequency is simply the point at which the effects of the filter begin to be noticed. With a typical low-pass filter, the amount of attenuation increases gradually with frequencies above the cutoff frequency. This **filter slope** (or **roll-off,** as it is sometimes called) is usually expressed in decibels of attenuation per octave. For example, a low-pass filter with a roll-off of 12 dB per octave reaches the point at which attenuation is considered complete (signal strength is reduced by 60 dB) for frequencies that are five octaves above the "official" cutoff frequency. The cutoff frequency is set with a dial on most filter modules. An input jack is provided for control voltages that can vary the cutoff frequency above or below the point set manually with the dial.

The design of many low-pass filters provides for an internal path to feed some of the output of the filter back into the input. This recirculation of

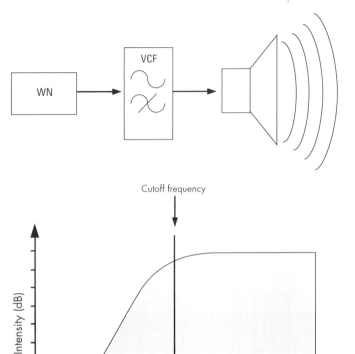

FIGURE 8.9
The effect of a high-pass filter on white noise.

Cutoff frequency

Intensity (dB)

Frequency (Hz)

part of the signal results in a resonance peak for any frequencies that happen to be near the cutoff frequency. The sharpness of this resonance peak is called the **Q** of the filter. Low-pass filters with this feedback capability have a dial that regulates the amount of the feedback and thus determines the Q of the filter. Such a dial is labeled Feedback, Q, Resonance, Emphasis, Regeneration, or something similar.

If a signal with a rich spectrum, such as a sawtooth wave, is patched into a filter tuned to a high Q, and if the cutoff frequency dial is swept across a broad range of frequencies, then each partial in the spectrum will be resonated in turn. This shimmering, even ethereal sound has become one of the classic sounds of analog synthesis. Another popular, and probably overused, technique is to patch white noise into such a resonating filter and then to sweep the cutoff frequency of the filter, thereby synthesizing the sound of a howling wind.

A filter that passes frequencies above the cutoff frequency, while filtering out the frequencies below, is called a **high-pass filter.** The effect of a high-pass filter is illustrated in Figure 8.9.

A **band-pass filter,** illustrated in Figure 8.10, removes frequencies above an upper cutoff frequency and also filters those frequencies that are below a lower cutoff frequency. The distance between the two cutoff frequencies is the width of the band of frequencies that passes (referred to as the **bandwidth**). A band-pass filter module may have separate dials to set the upper

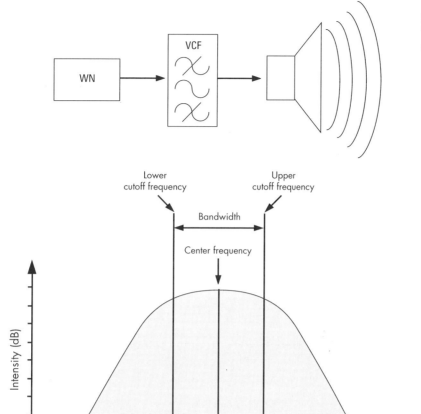

FIGURE 8.10
The effect of a band-pass filter on white noise.

and lower cutoff frequencies, or it may have a dial to set the bandwidth and another to set the center frequency of the band. An input jack for control voltages may be provided so that the center frequency can be shifted (meaning that the upper and lower cutoff frequencies are moved in tandem) in accordance with the pattern of voltage from a control voltage source, such as an envelope generator or keyboard. A control voltage input for the bandwidth of the filter may also be provided.

A **band-reject filter,** also known as a **notch filter,** is the obverse of a band-pass filter. Frequencies above the upper cutoff frequency are permitted to pass. So are frequencies below the lower cutoff frequency. The frequencies that fall between the two cutoff frequencies, however, are removed (see Figure 8.11). A band-reject filter will have a set of controls and control inputs similar to that of a band-pass filter.

A low-pass filter and a high-pass filter can be patched together to function as a band-pass or band-reject filter. If a signal is first filtered by a low-pass filter and then filtered by a high-pass filter with a lower cutoff frequency, then only a band of frequencies will remain, as illustrated in Figure 8.12. If the signal is split and one part goes through a low-pass filter and the second part goes through a high-pass filter that has a higher cutoff

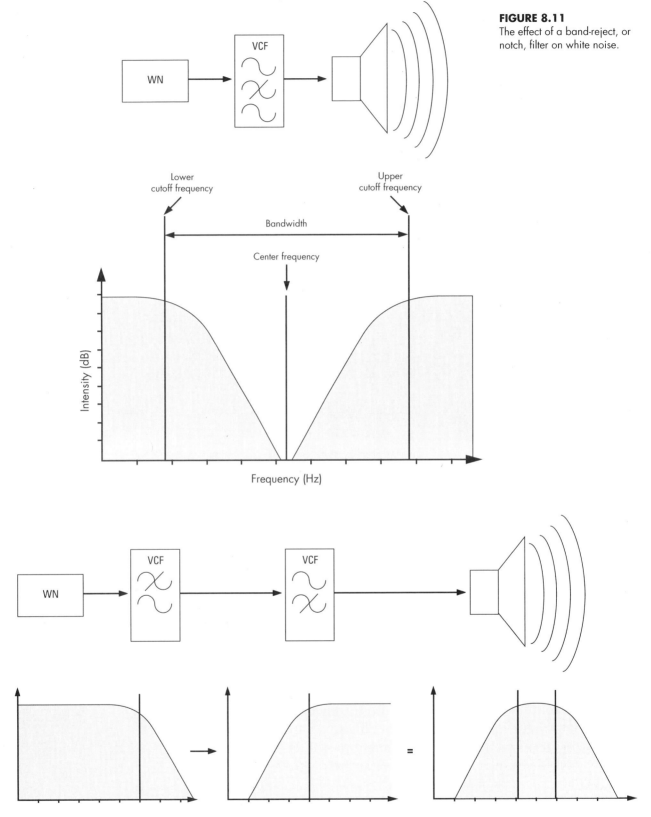

FIGURE 8.11
The effect of a band-reject, or notch, filter on white noise.

FIGURE 8.12
Creating a band-pass filter with a low-pass filter and a high-pass filter in series. The audio source signal is first sent through the low-pass filter. It is next sent through the high-pass filter. The frequencies that survive emerge as a band, as illustrated in the graph at the right.

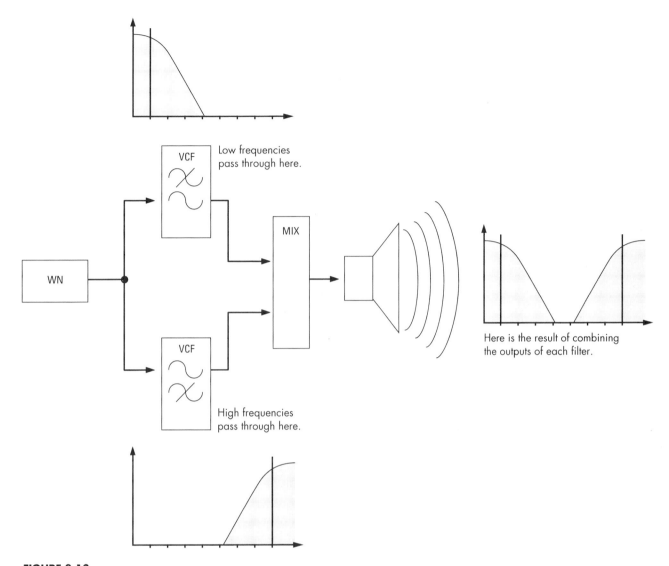

FIGURE 8.13
Creating a band-reject filter with a low-pass filter and a high-pass filter in parallel signal paths. The audio source signal is split. One part of the split is sent through the low-pass filter, and the other part of the split is sent through the high-pass filter. The signals from these two paths are then reunited by a mixer module.

frequency and if the two parts are then mixed back together, a band of frequencies will be discovered to be missing (see Figure 8.13). Because of the flexibility of techniques such as these, it is common with larger analog synthesizers to find low-pass, high-pass, band-pass, and band-reject filters conveniently located together in the same module, which might be called something like a "multi-mode filter."

A filter module can receive an audio signal from a VCO, a noise generator, or an external source, or it can receive the signal from the output of another modifier module. The output of the filter module can be patched to an audio signal input on another modifier module, or it can be connected to an output line of the synthesizer to become the signal that is monitored or recorded.

The technique of using filters to remove frequencies selectively from the standard timbres produced by VCOs and noise generators (or external sources) is called **subtractive synthesis.** It is an especially important and powerful technique of analog sound synthesis, particularly when a control voltage is used to change the effect of the filter over the duration of a sound. The synthesis of brass sounds provides an example of such dynamic filtering (in contrast to static filtering, in which the cutoff frequency is set and remains unchanged). As stated previously, an important characteristic of the timbre of a brass instrument is that the higher partials enter progressively later than the lower ones. This effect can be synthesized by patching a sawtooth wave through a low-pass filter. At the beginning of the tone the cutoff frequency is set relatively low, but it is swept up during the attack so that increasingly higher overtones can also begin to pass through the filter. Just as with a trumpet or trombone, the listener can hear the timbre brighten as the tone proceeds to develop. If the Q of the filter is high, the effects of such dynamic filtering can be especially dramatic.

ÉTUDE 8.1

Tune the frequency of a VCO to a bass pitch between two and three octaves below middle C. Select a sawtooth waveform. Patch the audio output of the VCO to the audio input of a low-pass filter. Then patch the audio output of the filter to an audio output line of the synthesizer. Connect the output of the synthesizer to an input of a multiple-track tape deck.

Adjust the Q of the filter so that it is set just below the point at which the filter oscillates on its own. Slowly sweep the cutoff frequency setting of the filter so that great arcs of overtones can be heard. Record approximately three minutes of arcs such as these on a track of the tape deck. Then record three more tracks with similar patterns of slowly unfolding arcs. If possible, monitor the four tracks with a quad speaker system (that is, with a loudspeaker in each corner of the room) for the greatest effect.

A mixer is a modifier module that simply combines audio signals from different sources. The mixer module is also used to recombine different branches of a patch (as, for example, in Figure 8.13). Typically, four audio signal inputs can be mixed to one audio signal output. A dial is provided with each input so that adjustments to the levels of each can be made. On some of the more advanced modular synthesizers, a control voltage input jack is also provided with each audio signal input so that the input level adjustments can be controlled simultaneously and independently by envelope generators or other sources of control voltage (essentially, each mixer input is functioning as an independent VCA). The output of a mixer module is generally connected to an audio signal input of another modifier module, or to an output line of the synthesizer.

Figure 8.14 shows a patch in which a mixer module is used to accomplish the **additive synthesis** of a timbre. Several independent VCOs pro-

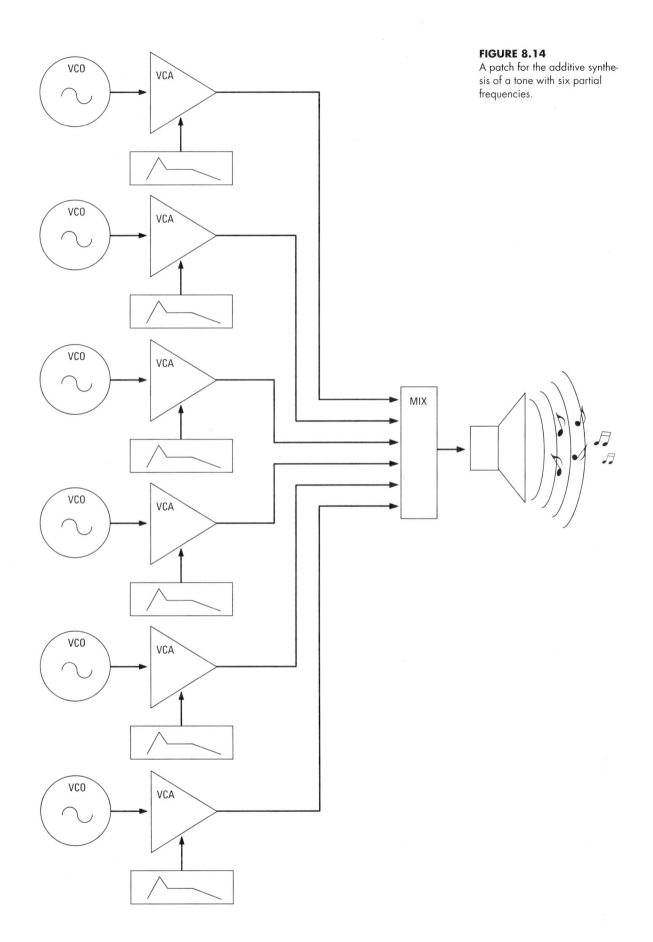

FIGURE 8.14
A patch for the additive synthesis of a tone with six partial frequencies.

vide the sine waves for the fundamental and the first few overtones. The output of each of these is first passed through a VCA controlled by an envelope generator. In this way, each partial frequency can have a unique envelope, as is the case with naturally produced timbres. The outputs of the VCAs are then connected to the audio signal inputs of the mixer (if the level of these inputs can be voltage-controlled, then the VCAs are not needed; the envelope generators can be patched to the control voltage inputs of the mixer module itself).

Unfortunately, this is not a very satisfactory way to synthesize a timbre on an analog synthesizer. First, a great number of modules are necessary, meaning that the synthesizer would have to be a large and probably expensive one. Second, it is doubtful that the VCOs can be tuned as precisely as required to simulate a gang of overtones; even if such precise tuning could be achieved, it is unlikely that the VCOs would stay in tune for very long. The successful implementation of the techniques of additive synthesis requires digital hardware, and this has become a realistic possibility for most electroacoustic musicians only relatively recently (more on this in the next chapter). For this reason, subtractive synthesis has been the main game in analog synthesis for some time.

CONTROL VOLTAGE SOURCES

The concept of voltage control is the key to the power of an analog synthesizer as a musical instrument. As stated earlier, control voltages themselves are not heard. They do not enter the audio signal path that leads to a recorder or loudspeaker. However, the effects of control voltages are most certainly heard as they are applied to the modules that generate audio signals or to the modules that subsequently modify the audio signals. Details of the structure of a sound, or of a group of sounds in a musical passage, can be shaped with some degree of precision and can be replicated fairly easily through the use of control voltages. By programming the production of sound in this way, a composer is able to work with sound in ways not readily achieved with other musical instruments.

One of the most important sources of control voltage on an analog synthesizer is a device called an **envelope generator.** This module creates a contour of voltage that is usually applied to the control input of a VCA to shape the amplitude envelope of a sound. Typically this contour has four stages: the **attack,** during which the voltage rises from zero to a peak value; the **initial decay,** during which the voltage falls off from the peak to the sustain level; the **sustain**; and the **release,** or **final decay,** during which time the voltage falls from the sustain level back to zero. Such an envelope, a very common one on analog synthesizers, is often referred to by the acronym **ADSR** (see Figure 1.8e).

An envelope generator usually includes four dials for setting the attack time, initial decay time, sustain level, and release time. Some of the more advanced systems also have input jacks for control voltages. These control

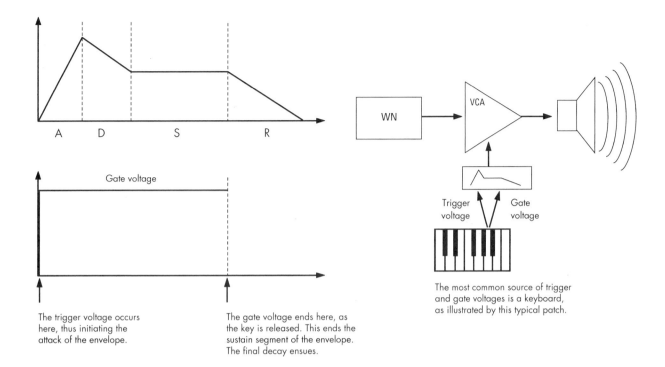

The trigger voltage occurs here, thus initiating the attack of the envelope.

The gate voltage ends here, as the key is released. This ends the sustain segment of the envelope. The final decay ensues.

The most common source of trigger and gate voltages is a keyboard, as illustrated by this typical patch.

FIGURE 8.15
Trigger and gate voltages.

voltages can be used to adjust (or to override) the values set manually with each of these four dials.

A signal called a **trigger** is required for an envelope generator to commence its operation. Such a trigger may be provided by a push-button circuit on the envelope generator itself, by a keyboard when a key is depressed, or by a dedicated trigger-generator module.

Another signal, called a **gate** voltage, determines the duration of the envelope. Gate voltages are typically generated by the same mechanisms that produce triggers. Thus, for example, when a key on a keyboard is played, a trigger voltage is sent to the envelope generator. As long as the key is held down, the gate voltage is also present. The envelope proceeds through the attack and initial decay stages to the sustain level. The sustain *time* is determined by how much longer the key continues to be held down. When the key is released, the sustain time is over and the final decay gets underway (see Figure 8.15).

Although the output of an envelope generator is most commonly connected to the control voltage input of a VCA, it can just as easily be connected to the control voltage input of a VCO. This results in a sound with a pitch envelope: at first the pitch rises, then it falls back a bit, and at the end of the sound the pitch falls the rest of the way back to its initial level.

Often, an envelope generator is patched to a control voltage input on a VCF. As a result, a timbre envelope is formed as the cutoff frequency of the filter rises, falls back, holds steady for a while, then returns to its initial level. If the filter is resonant at the cutoff frequency, then a "wow" or "wa-wa" effect is heard. Unfortunately, this sort of sound is one that rather quickly became one of the clichés of analog synthesis. It is best approached with care if it is used at all.

*P*atch the output of a white noise generator module to the audio input of a band-pass filter. Then patch the audio output of the filter to an audio output line of the synthesizer, and connect the output of the synthesizer to an input of a two-track recorder. Tune the upper and lower cutoff frequencies of the band-pass filter so that only a narrow band of frequencies passes. Also, set the center frequency to a relatively low part of the audio range.

Next, patch the output of an envelope generator to the control voltage input for the center frequency of the filter. Patch a trigger/gate voltage source, such as the keyboard, to the trigger/gate input of the envelope generator.

Trigger an envelope, and listen to how the signal passing through the filter is changed. Experiment with different settings of the attack time, initial decay time, sustain level, and release time of the envelope. Record a passage, of approximately one or two minutes' duration, that consists of a series of such enveloped noise patterns. Then, on the other track of the tape deck, record a similar series as a counterpoint to the patterns recorded on the first track.

Another control voltage source on an analog synthesizer is the keyboard. It provides a discrete, sustained voltage whenever a key is pressed (along with trigger and gate voltages that may be of use to an envelope generator). A quite ordinary application of the keyboard control voltage is to patch it to the control voltage input of a VCO. The VCO frequency is thus set according to which key has been pressed. This patch, illustrated in Figure 8.16, brings an analog synthesizer perilously close to being not much more than a mutant electronic organ. In fact, many analog synthesizers, such as those by Buchla, have been designed to avert this situation by providing only a rudimentary keyboard, or none at all. A great variety of modules have been developed as alternatives to the keyboard for the generation of control voltages. If the habits of thought associated with keyboard playing hinder the exploration of some of these other possibilities, and thereby limit the range of expression of the medium, then perhaps the keyboard is best avoided. Or, if it cannot be avoided, then at least it should be approached with a certain amount of circumspection.

The keyboards of early analog synthesizers were **monophonic**—capable of producing only one control voltage at a time (apart from the trigger and gate voltages). This in itself is not a particular disadvantage, since many of the world's great musical instruments—clarinets, saxophones, trumpets, and kazoos—are also monophonic. On a monophonic keyboard, some sort of priority scheme must be engaged to determine which control voltage is produced when more than one key is pressed. Usually the lowest key is given priority, although alternative systems assign priority to the highest note, the first note, or the last note played. Performers who had developed their keyboard skills on pianos and organs were rather unnerved by this,

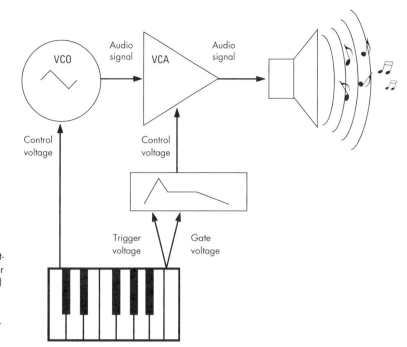

FIGURE 8.16
A very ordinary patch. The keyboard generates control voltages that determine the frequency produced by the VCO. The keyboard also generates trigger and gate voltages for the envelope generator. The envelope generator produces a control voltage that determines the gain level of the VCA. The amplitude of the audio signal produced by the VCO is shaped by this VCA. The signal is then passed to the external output line and to the studio monitor system.

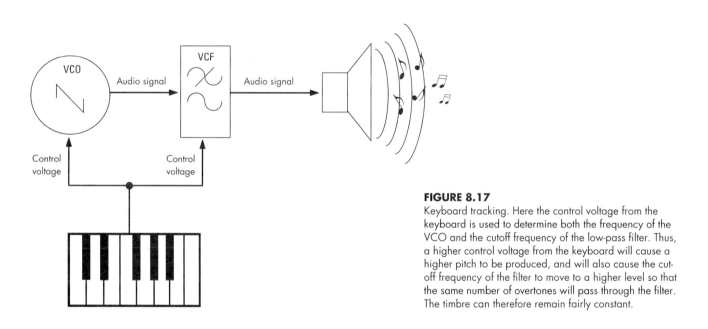

FIGURE 8.17
Keyboard tracking. Here the control voltage from the keyboard is used to determine both the frequency of the VCO and the cutoff frequency of the low-pass filter. Thus, a higher control voltage from the keyboard will cause a higher pitch to be produced, and will also cause the cutoff frequency of the filter to move to a higher level so that the same number of overtones will pass through the filter. The timbre can therefore remain fairly constant.

however, and pressed for the development of keyboards that were **polyphonic.** These could provide up to eight independent voltages that could be patched to several different VCOs or other modules.

A control voltage output from a keyboard can be patched into the control voltage input of a VCF so that the cutoff frequency of the filter can be moved in tandem with the pitch changes of the VCO, as illustrated in Figure 8.17. This **keyboard tracking** by the filter ensures that the waveform remains unchanged, regardless of the frequency of the sound. If the

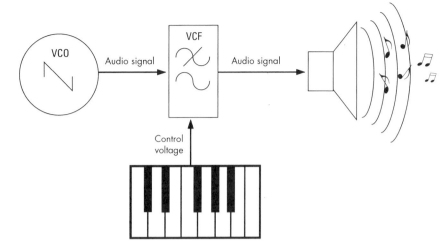

FIGURE 8.18
A synthetic jaw harp. The control voltage from the keyboard is connected only to the low-pass filter. Thus, the cutoff frequency of the filter rises and falls to discrete levels, determined by the key that is being played, while the frequency of the sound remains constant. For best results, a bright waveform, rich in overtones, should be used. Also, it helps if the resonance setting of the VCF is turned up to at least a moderate level.

cutoff frequency of the filter were to remain stationary, then many of the overtones of the higher pitches would fall above the cutoff frequency and would be filtered out. This would result in a more rounded waveform with a more mellow, perhaps somewhat dull sound.

A more interesting sound, perhaps, is produced by a patch in which the control voltage of the keyboard is connected to the filter, but is *not* connected to the VCO (see Figure 8.18). The pitch of the oscillator remains constant, but whenever a different key is pressed, the timbre of the sound changes as the cutoff frequency of the filter is set to a different level by the control voltage. The sound that results is much like that of a jaw harp or of the Australian aboriginal instrument, the didjeridu.

Control voltages can themselves be modified, usually by modules such as **control voltage attenuators** or **control voltage inverters** (often the functions of these two are combined in a single module). For example, if the control voltage output of a keyboard is passed through an attenuator with its dial set at midpoint, then the keyboard voltages will be halved (see Figure 8.19a). If these reduced voltages are patched to a VCO, then the intervals of pitch will also be halved. A major second (a "whole step") played on the keyboard will thus sound a minor second (a "half step"); a minor second played on the keyboard will sound a **quarter tone.** This creates an opportunity to explore systems of tuning other than the currently extant system of 12 equal steps per octave.

If the control voltage of a keyboard is passed through an inverter, and the output of the inverter is patched to the control voltage input of a VCO (as in Figure 8.19b), then the higher voltages produced by playing higher keys will be inverted to lower voltages, and lower pitches will be sounded. Likewise, if lower keys are played, the lower voltages that are thus generated will be inverted to higher voltages, and the VCO will respond by producing higher pitches. Ascending scales played on the keyboard will be heard as descending scales, and vice versa.

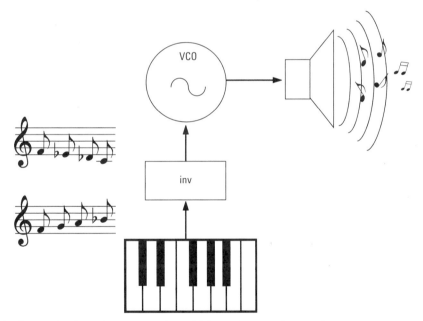

FIGURE 8.19
Two common techniques of control voltage modification.

a. With a control voltage attenuator inserted between the keyboard and the VCO, the voltage generated by the keyboard is halved, and the intervals of pitch produced by the VCO are halved as well—in this example, from whole steps to half steps.

b. A control voltage inverter transforms higher voltages to lower voltages, and vice versa. In this example, playing an ascending series of keys on the keyboard produces a descending series of pitches from the VCO.

ÉTUDE 8.3

𝒫atch the voltage output of the keyboard to the input of a control voltage attenuator. Then patch the output of the control voltage attenuator to the control voltage input of a VCO. Patch the audio output of the VCO to the audio input of a VCA, and patch the audio output of the VCA to an output line of the synthesizer. (You may also want to patch the output of an envelope generator, perhaps triggered by the keyboard, to the control voltage input of the VCA, so that each tone is shaped with an amplitude envelope.)

Alternately play these two keys on the keyboard, and adjust the level of the control voltage attenuator until the interval of pitch heard is a perfect octave:

You have now tuned your synthesizer to a 19-tone-per-octave scale. This particular tuning is noted for the purity of its minor thirds and major sixths, which come very close to their ideal ratios of 6:5 and 5:3, respectively (you may want to review the description of interval ratios provided in Chapter 1). Experiment with other tunings by adjusting the control voltage attenuator level. (Be aware, however, that the stability of pitch from an analog oscillator is usually not too great; the oscillator is likely to drift out of tune within a few minutes.)

A **low-frequency oscillator (LFO)** is one with a frequency that is usually below the range of human hearing. Since it cannot be heard, its only use is to function as a control voltage source. When the output of an LFO is patched to the control voltage input of a VCO (see Figure 8.20a), the audio frequency of the VCO will begin to fluctuate up and down at the rate of the frequency of the LFO. The extent to which the audio frequency is raised and lowered is determined by the amplitude of the signal from the LFO. This amplitude can be regulated if a control voltage attenuator is patched in between the LFO and the VCO (see Figure 8.20b).

The periodic fluctuation of an audio frequency at a rate less than 20 times per second (so that the ear can follow the individual changes of frequency) is called a vibrato. The rate of the vibrato is the same as the frequency of the LFO. The width of the vibrato is determined by the amplitude of the LFO signal.

If the output of an LFO is patched to the control input of a VCA (as illustrated in Figure 8.21), then a similar modulation of amplitude, called tremolo, is produced. A "wa-wa" effect is produced if the cutoff frequency of a filter is controlled by an LFO (as depicted in Figure 8.22).

Such subtle modulations of pitch, amplitude, or timbre are often applied to longer tones, much as a trained singer, violinist, or woodwind player shapes long tones. For example, the tone begins without vibrato, but will begin to vibrate after it is about halfway through its duration. This gives

FIGURE 8.20
The use of a low-frequency
oscillator (LFO) to create a
vibrato in the audio signal.

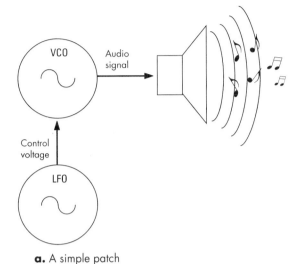

a. A simple patch

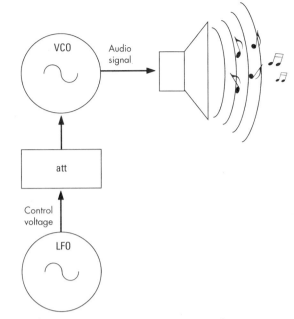

b. With a control voltage attenuator used
to regulate the width of the vibrato

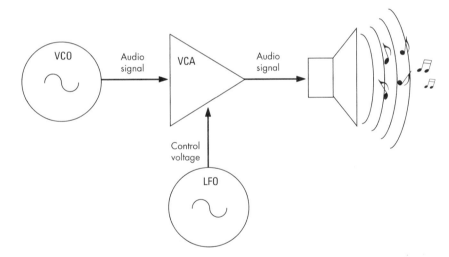

FIGURE 8.21
The use of a low-frequency
oscillator (LFO) to create a
tremolo in the audio signal.

direction to the tone by drawing the attention of the listener forward into
the next sound. The result is a warmer, more expressive, and more lifelike
sound. To facilitate this technique, many LFOs have a dial for setting a
delay time for the onset of the low-frequency oscillation that controls the
modulation.

ÉTUDE 8.4

Tune the frequency of a VCO to a bass pitch between two and three octaves
below middle C. Select a sawtooth waveform. Patch the audio output of the
VCO to the audio input of a VCF. Then patch the audio output of the VCF to an

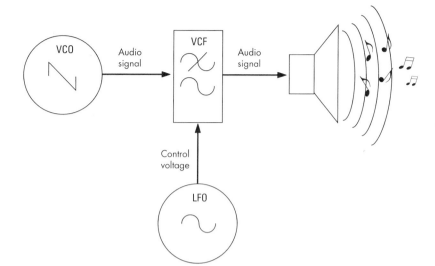

FIGURE 8.22
The use of a low-frequency oscillator (LFO) to create a "wa-wa" effect. The rising and falling voltage produced by the LFO causes the cutoff frequency of the filter to rise and fall accordingly, thus producing a slow undulation of the timbre of the signal that originated in the oscillator.

audio output line of the synthesizer. Connect the output of the synthesizer to an input of a two-channel tape deck. Adjust the Q of the filter so that it is set just below the point at which the filter oscillates on its own.

Patch the control voltage output of the keyboard to the control voltage input of the VCF. Play a random assortment of keys in a markedly rhythmic pattern. Record approximately two minutes of this synthetic didjeridu.

Now remove all the patch cords and start a new patch. Tune the frequency of a VCO to a pitch in the octave above middle C. Select a sine waveform. Patch the audio output of the VCO to the audio input of a VCA. Patch the audio output of the VCA to an output line of the synthesizer, and connect the output of the synthesizer to the input of the other track of the tape recorder.

Next, patch the output of an envelope generator (to be triggered by the keyboard) to the control voltage input of the VCA. Set a long decay time for the envelope.

Patch the output of an LFO to the input of a control voltage attenuator (if available), and patch the output of the control voltage attenuator to the control voltage input of the VCO. Select a square waveform on the LFO, and set the frequency of the LFO in the range of 4–10 Hz. Adjust the level of the control voltage attenuator so that the audio frequency produced by the VCO is alternated no more than a major third or perfect fourth by the control voltage originating from the LFO. Also, if possible, try to delay the arrival to the VCO of the control voltage from the LFO to coincide with the beginning of the final decay of the envelope of the tone.

Record a series of a few of these tones on the second track of the tape recorder. Perhaps, for variety, reset the frequency of the LFO for each tone recorded on this track.

An audio frequency oscillator, a VCO in fact, can also be used as a control voltage source, and this can produce some very unusual effects. If an oscillating voltage with a frequency greater than 30 Hz is patched to the

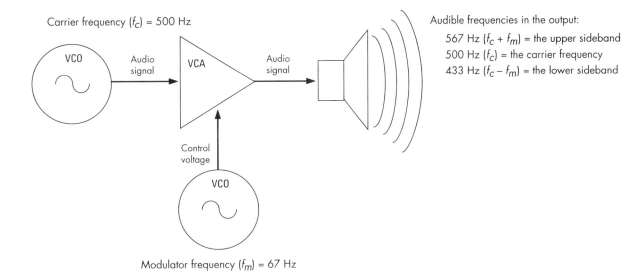

Carrier frequency (f_c) = 500 Hz

VCO

Audio signal

VCA

Audio signal

Control voltage

VCO

Modulator frequency (f_m) = 67 Hz

Audible frequencies in the output:

567 Hz ($f_c + f_m$) = the upper sideband
500 Hz (f_c) = the carrier frequency
433 Hz ($f_c - f_m$) = the lower sideband

FIGURE 8.23
The use of an audio frequency oscillator as a control voltage source to modulate the amplitude of the audio signal produced by the first VCO. As a result of the rapid fluctuations of the amplitude of the audio signal, additional frequencies called sidebands become audible.

control voltage input of a VCA that is passing an audio signal, then additional frequencies, called **sidebands,** will be heard around the frequencies in the audio signal. For each of these frequencies in the audio signal, there will be an upper sideband with a frequency equal to the sum of the audio frequency, called the **carrier** (f_c), and the controlling frequency, called the **modulator** (f_m). There will also be a lower sideband, with a frequency equal to the difference between the carrier and the modulator frequencies (f_c-f_m). This technique of producing sidebands by causing the amplitude of a signal to fluctuate periodically at a rate greater than 30 times per second is called **amplitude modulation,** or **AM** (in contrast to tremolo, the fluctuation of amplitude at a rate less than the lower limit of the range of audible frequencies—approximately 20 Hz).

In Figure 8.23, a sine wave with a frequency of 500 Hz is produced by the VCO and patched to the audio input of the VCA. A sine wave with a frequency of 67 Hz is produced by another VCO and patched to the control voltage input of the VCA. One audio frequency goes into the VCA, but three audio frequencies are present in the audio signal output: 433 Hz, the lower sideband; 500 Hz, the carrier frequency; and 567 Hz, the upper sideband.

If the carrier waveform is a sawtooth wave, as in Figure 8.24, or any other complex waveform, then sidebands around the overtones also appear in the output. If the modulator waveform is a sawtooth, as in Figure 8.25, then each overtone in the modulator will also act as a modulator and produce sidebands in the output. If carrier and modulator frequencies do not have an obvious, common arithmetic factor (for example, a sawtooth wave with a frequency of 100 Hz for the carrier and a sine wave with a frequency

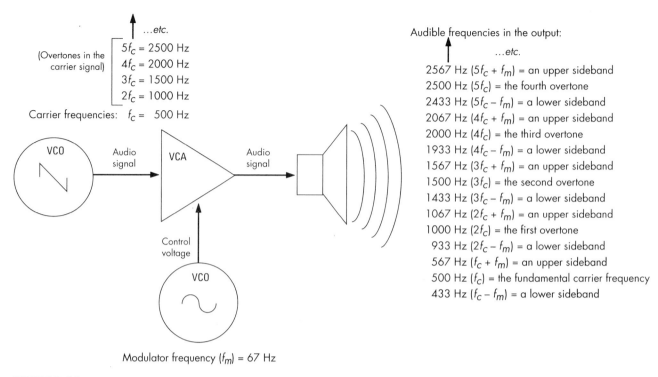

FIGURE 8.24
The use of a sawtooth wave as a carrier signal results in a more complex output signal, as sidebands are produced around each overtone of the sawtooth.

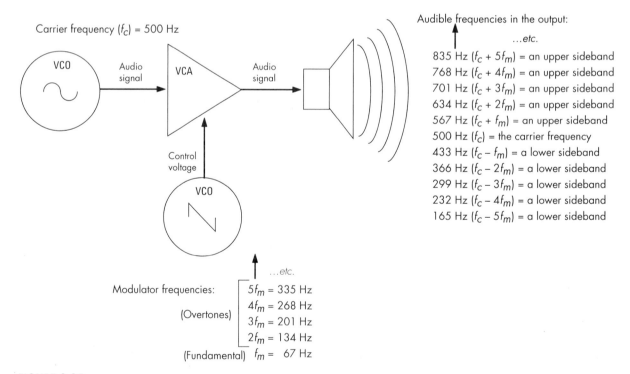

FIGURE 8.25
The use of a sawtooth wave as a modulating signal also results in a more complex output signal, as each overtone of the sawtooth creates sidebands around the carrier frequency.

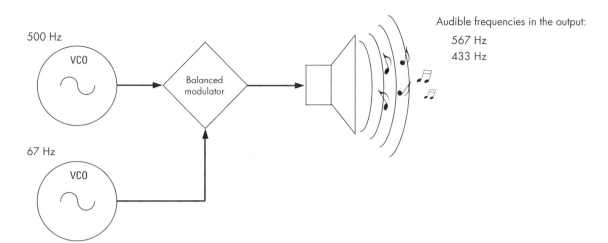

FIGURE 8.26
A balanced modulator. Note that neither of the input frequencies is audible in the output. The two frequencies that are heard at the output are the sum of the input frequencies and the difference between the input frequencies.

of 43 Hz for the modulator), then fairly complex, inharmonic spectra, like those of bells, can be created with relative ease.

A **balanced modulator,** also called a **ring modulator,** is a modifier module found on many larger analog synthesizers. Its operation is based upon a special application of the technique of amplitude modulation. The module has two inputs and one output. The signal that is available at the output consists exclusively of the upper sideband and lower sideband frequencies produced by the modulation of the amplitude of one of the input signals by the other input signal (see Figure 8.26). The carrier frequencies themselves are blocked and so are not present in the output. The effect of a balanced modulator module is particularly striking when one of the input signals is patched from an external source—a microphone that is picking up a speaking voice or a tape recorder playing prerecorded music. The radical transformations performed by a balanced modulator can even do justice to some such sources, such as political speeches or dull classroom lectures.

Frequency modulation, or **FM,** is the technique of producing sideband frequencies by modulating the frequency of an audio signal at a rate greater than 30 times per second (a sort of super-vibrato). Figure 8.27 illustrates a patch for frequency modulation. As with the production of a vibrato (illustrated in Figure 8.20a), the output of a controlling oscillator is connected to the control voltage input of the audio frequency oscillator. The difference with FM is that the frequency of the controlling oscillator is greater than the lower limit of the range of audible frequencies. We are unable to hear the individual fluctuations of frequency; instead, we hear sidebands.

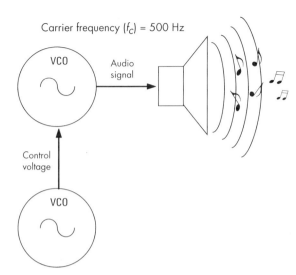

Carrier frequency (f_c) = 500 Hz

VCO

Audio signal

Control voltage

VCO

Modulator frequency (f_m) = 67 Hz

FIGURE 8.27
The use of an audio frequency oscillator as a control voltage source to modulate the frequency of the audio signal. This is frequency modulation, or FM.

FURTHER DETAILS OF FREQUENCY MODULATION

*W*ith AM there is only one upper sideband and one lower sideband per carrier frequency, but with FM there can be many more upper and lower sidebands per carrier. The approximate number of upper sidebands (and also lower sidebands) is found by first dividing the range of the deviation of the carrier frequency (Δf_c) by the frequency of the modulator (f_m). This value ($\Delta f_c/f_m$) is called the **modulation index** (*I*). Generally, the number of upper sidebands (and the number of lower sidebands) is two more than the value of the modulation index.

If the amplitude of the modulator is increased, then the amount of change in the frequency of the audio oscillator (that is, the deviation of the carrier frequency) is also increased. The modulation index in this case has a greater value, indicating that more sidebands are likely to be audible. If the *frequency* of the modulator is increased (while its amplitude remains the same), then the modulation index has a lower value, signifying that fewer sidebands will be heard.

Figure 8.28 illustrates a collection of sidebands created by the modulation of a 500-Hz audio signal by a 67-Hz control signal. The modulation index in this example is 3, meaning that one may expect to hear five upper sidebands and five lower sidebands. The waveform produced by both oscillators is a sine. If the carrier has a more complex waveform, then five orders of sidebands will also be created on both sides of each overtone (an even more complex result than that illustrated in Figure 8.24 with the amplitude modulation of a sawtooth). If the *modulator* has a more complex waveform, then each of its overtones will create five sidebands on each side of the carrier (likewise an even more complex result than that illustrated in Figure 8.25 by the simple amplitude modulation of a sine wave by a sawtooth wave).

If the carrier and modulator frequencies are related by a simple ratio, then a constellation of sidebands is created that looks suspiciously similar to an overtone series (see Figure 8.29). Thus, the result of the additive synthesis of a timbre using several VCOs (as in Figure 8.14)

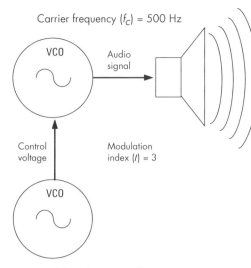

Carrier frequency (f_c) = 500 Hz

VCO

Audio signal

Control voltage

Modulation index (I) = 3

VCO

Modulator frequency (f_m) = 67 Hz

Audible frequencies in the output:

835 Hz ($f_c + 5f_m$) = the 5th-order upper sideband
768 Hz ($f_c + 4f_m$) = the 4th-order upper sideband
701 Hz ($f_c + 3f_m$) = the 3rd-order upper sideband
634 Hz ($f_c + 2f_m$) = the 2nd-order upper sideband
567 Hz ($f_c + f_m$) = the 1st-order upper sideband
500 Hz (f_c) = the carrier frequency
433 Hz ($f_c - f_m$) = the 1st-order lower sideband
366 Hz ($f_c - 2f_m$) = the 2nd-order lower sideband
299 Hz ($f_c - 3f_m$) = the 3rd-order lower sideband
232 Hz ($f_c - 4f_m$) = the 4th-order lower sideband
165 Hz ($f_c - 5f_m$) = the 5th-order lower sideband

FIGURE 8.28
The sidebands that can be created from just two sine waves by using frequency modulation techniques. The value of the modulation index in this example is 3. This means that there can be a total of five upper sidebands and five lower sidebands.

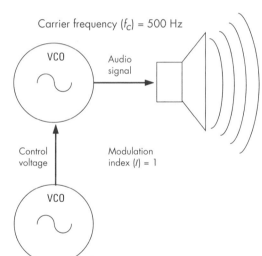

Carrier frequency (f_c) = 500 Hz

VCO

Audio signal

Control voltage

Modulation index (I) = 1

VCO

Modulator frequency (f_m) = 100 Hz

Audible frequencies in the output:

800 Hz ($f_c + 3f_m$) = the 3rd-order upper sideband
700 Hz ($f_c + 2f_m$) = the 2nd-order upper sideband
600 Hz ($f_c + f_m$) = the 1st-order upper sideband
500 Hz (f_c) = the carrier frequency
400 Hz ($f_c - f_m$) = the 1st-order lower sideband
300 Hz ($f_c - 2f_m$) = the 2nd-order lower sideband
200 Hz ($f_c - 3f_m$) = the 3rd-order lower sideband
100 Hz = implied fundamental

Note: If the modulation index is increased to a value of 2, then the "fundamental" frequency of 100 Hz will actually be present in the signal, as the 4th-order lower sideband.

FIGURE 8.29
A harmonic series of sidebands can be created if the carrier frequency and the modulating frequency are related by a simple ratio.

can be approximated fairly closely with the use of only two oscillators—one to produce a carrier frequency, and one to produce a modulator frequency. Because of the instability of the tuning of analog oscillators, this is not an easy technique to implement. However, FM synthesis has become an extremely important technique of digital sound synthesis (and will be described more completely in the next chapter).

ÉTUDE 8.5

*une the frequency of a VCO to a pitch in the octave above middle C. Select a sine waveform. Patch the output of the VCO to the audio input of a VCA. Set the dial for base amplitude on the VCA to approximately the midpoint. Patch the audio output of the VCA to an output line of the synthesizer.

Tune the frequency of a second VCO to a pitch an octave below that of the first VCO, and select a sine waveform. Patch the output of this second VCO to the audio input of a second VCA. Set the base amplitude of this second VCA to zero. Patch the output of an envelope generator to the control voltage input of the second VCA. Patch a trigger source to the envelope generator, and set the envelope for long attack and decay times.

Patch the output of the second VCA to the control voltage input of the first VCO. The sustained tone being produced by the first VCO will then blossom into many colors whenever an envelope is applied to the second VCA. The passage of the signal through the second VCA permits modulation of the frequency of the first VCO by the frequency of the signal originating from the second VCO.

GUIDE FOR LISTENING
THE WILD BULL, BY MORTON SUBOTNICK

Among the most highly regarded compositions realized on an analog synthesizer system are those of Morton Subotnick. Born in Los Angeles in 1933, Subotnick joined Pauline Oliveros, Terry Riley, Ramon Sender, and others around 1962 in establishing the San Francisco Tape Music Center. By 1965 Don Buchla, an engineer, had become involved at the center. In particular, he collaborated with composers Subotnick and Sender in the development of a solid-state, modular, analog synthesis system. This was subsequently introduced commercially, in 1966, as the Buchla Modular Electronic Music System.[a]

Unlike the Moog synthesizer and other instruments that were introduced contemporaneously, the Buchla system did not include a traditional keyboard as a source of control voltages. Instead, it had a set of 16 touch-sensitive plates that could be used primarily to generate trigger voltages. However, the most important source of control voltages in the system was the control voltage sequencer, the first of its kind to be included on a synthesizer. On receiving a trigger from one of the touch-sensitive plates, or a similar source, the sequencer could begin to generate a repeated pattern of events, or with more sophisticated programming and occasional manual control, it could create a complex and richly varied series of events. Sounds triggered by the sequencer could be shaped with a variety of pitch contours, amplitude envelopes, and filter contours through the use of several envelope generators. As an instrument without a keyboard, the

---

[a] Buchla continues to develop marvelous instrument systems—most recently, a powerful alternate MIDI controller called Lightning™.

Buchla system encouraged composers to explore more boldly and to rely less on familiar patterns and techniques. It was indeed a terrific "toybox" for composers.

Shortly after the introduction of the Buchla synthesizer, a classical-music record label, Nonesuch Records, commissioned Subotnick to compose a piece for the instrument. This composition, entitled *Silver Apples of the Moon,* was released in 1967 (Nonesuch H-71174) and was expressly intended for the record medium—a piece to be heard on a stereo system at school or at home rather than for concert presentation or broadcast. *Silver Apples* was a great success, and a second piece was subsequently commissioned by Nonesuch and released in 1968 (Nonesuch H-71208). This piece was *The Wild Bull,* with a title inspired by a Sumerian poem from about 1700 B.C. Like the earlier Nonesuch release, this work is a masterful excursion through rich and exotic worlds of sound evoked by the Buchla instrument.

Side 1 begins with lengthy sounds of descending pitch and inharmonic spectrum that pan gently from one side of the stereo field to the other. The texture is very sparse here, with much silence. Unlike the compressed compositions of Stockhausen and Babbitt (described in Chapter 10), the compositions of Subotnick convey a much more expansive sense of time; they unfold rather gradually, and the total duration of this piece is about 28 minutes.

At around 1:29, the first sequenced pattern makes a clear appearance as a background textural element. Generally, the stratification of texture is fairly clear throughout the work. From 2:22 to 4:44, the warblings of an oscillator controlled by a low-frequency square wave become an important element of the texture. At 4:44, a sequence with a strongly defined rhythmic pattern and a variety of percussion and metallic timbres commences. The machine seems to acquire a life of its own as it proceeds to generate a succession of patterns. This passage could perhaps be described as the stirrings of a demented drum kit accompanied by a surreal bass soloist. The pace accelerates subtly and the texture gets busier until there is an abrupt change of texture at around 8:23. From here to the end of side 1, the texture consists predominantly of more delicate timbres, including some ethereal contours created by the play of resonating low-pass filters.

Many of the same techniques are in evidence on side 2 of the recording. The timbres here seem to be somewhat harsher, however, and very "metallic." The spectrum of the sounds is often inharmonic, or if harmonic, the high, closely spaced partials are extraordinarily prominent and therefore noticeably dissonant. The listener familiar with the ways in which rich spectra can be sculpted with filters may want to listen with particular closeness to the virtuosic use of these modules here by Subotnick.

The sequencer is also quite busy on side 2. A notable sequence, consisting of repeated notes descending three steps and then rising in pitch, first appears at 5:49 on side 2. At 6:55, the pattern also appears in inversion (rising three steps, then descending in pitch). This may be the result of applying the technique of control voltage inversion to the output of the sequencer. This inverted form recurs at 12:20, and the original form of the pattern makes a brief subsequent reappearance at 12:48, shortly before the end of the work. A listener will want to study closely the ways in which this and other sequenced series of events are altered upon successive repetitions. These patterns provide just one illustration of the fact that, as an expressive instrument at the hands of a gifted composer, the Buchla synthesizer has rarely been matched as a source of sonic wonders.

A **sequential controller,** also known as a **sequencer,** is a module that can produce a programmed series of discrete control voltages. Connecting the main output of the sequencer to a control voltage input on a VCO makes it possible to produce a repeatable series of pitches. A series of timbres is created if the output of the sequencer is patched to the control voltage input of a VCF. Each control voltage in the series is referred to as a step, or stage, in the sequence. The number of stages in a sequence is typically 8 or 12, but can range from 2 to 256.

The voltage produced at each stage is usually preset by means of a dial. A 12-stage sequencer would typically feature a row of 12 such dials. Some sequencers that can produce three or more control voltages simultaneously might have several rows of dials, called banks.

A pulse generator functions as the sequencer clock, and advances the sequencer from one stage to the next. If a control voltage is applied to the control voltage input of the clock, the duration of each stage can be adjusted automatically. Thus, if a sequence of control voltages is applied to the input of the clock, then rhythmic patterns that are varied and repeatable can be established.

As even this brief description might suggest, a sequential controller can be a complex device, and there are significant differences in design among the many models that have been built and sold. If you should encounter one on an analog synthesizer, you should plan to spend more than a few moments reading the appropriate sections of the operator's manual so that you can make the most effective use of this module.

A variant of the sequential controller is a controller known as an **arpeggiator.** The purpose of this module is to generate control voltages that can be used to produce an arpeggio—a rolling chord, much like that produced by a harp (*arpa,* in Italian). When the arpeggiator is engaged, it will scan the keyboard to identify which keys are being pressed. It will then produce their corresponding control voltages in a sequential fashion. There will probably be a switch on the arpeggiator to determine if this pattern of sequenced voltages is to be confined to its original range or extended to the other octaves covered by the keyboard. Another switch will determine if the pattern begins from the lowest voltage and proceeds to the highest (an ascending arpeggio), if it begins at the top and goes to the bottom (a descending arpeggio), or if it will move up and then back down. Other features may be available as well. Again, it is wise to refer to the operator's manual for a complete description of the capabilities of the arpeggiator on a particular synthesizer.

A fine assortment of even more esoteric controllers has been developed over the years. One of these, called a **ribbon controller** (see Figure 8.30), produces a control voltage that is proportionate to the point along its length at which the ribbon is pressed. Moving the finger up or down the ribbon generates a continuously changing control voltage. This can be patched to a filter to create a smoothly changing timbre; to a VCA to

FIGURE 8.30
A ribbon controller.

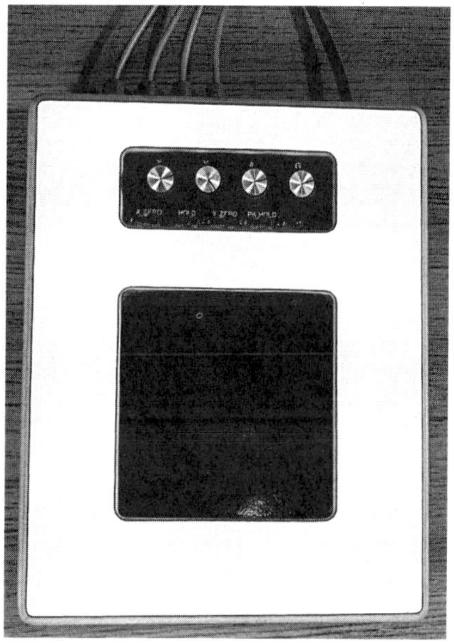

FIGURE 8.31
A touch-sensitive plate

achieve an even, gradual crescendo or diminuendo; or to a VCO to bend the pitch.

An **X-Y controller** (also known as a **joystick**) is operated by moving a stick left and right, and front and back. Two control voltages are generated—one that is proportional to the position of the stick to the left or right (the X axis), and the other determined by the position of the stick to the front or back (the Y axis). Each of these voltages, like that of the ribbon controller, is continuously variable and can be put to many of the same uses as that of the ribbon controller.

A **touch-sensitive plate** (see Figure 8.31) can produce up to four independent control voltages. One is determined by the position, on a continuum from left to right, at which the plate is touched. Another is determined by the position, on a continuum from front to back, of the point of contact on the plate. Yet another is proportional to the pressure applied by the finger to the plate. And yet another is proportional to the surface area of the plate that is covered by the contact.

An **envelope follower** produces a control voltage with a contour that is proportional to the intensity of an external signal patched into the module. Typically, an external source of audio signals, such as a microphone or tape player, provides the original signal. The control voltage that results from following the fluctuations in the intensity of this original signal—in effect, the envelope of the original signal—can then be patched to the control input of a VCA or VCF. An electronic sound being processed by the VCA or VCF can thus be shaped by envelopes modeled after those of the external sounds (see Figure 8.32).

A **sample-and-hold unit** (or **S/H controller**) also requires an input signal. This input signal is measured, or sampled, from time to time. The level of the input voltage at the moment of sampling is then "held" until the next sample is taken. Thus, a continuously variable input voltage can be con-

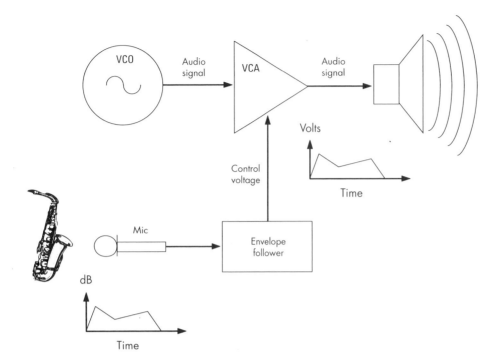

FIGURE 8.32
One potential application of an envelope follower. Here the amplitude envelope of the saxophone tone is converted into a control voltage envelope. This can then be applied to the VCA to shape the amplitude of the audio signal produced by the VCO.

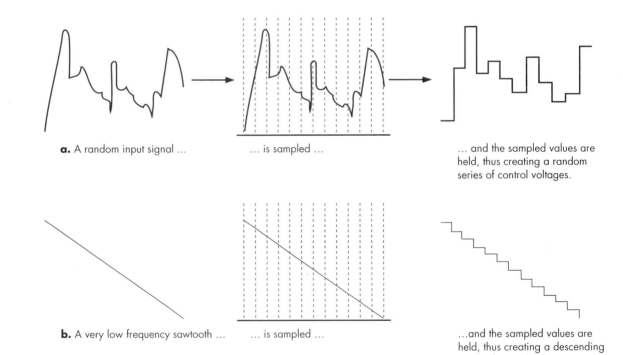

a. A random input signal …   … is sampled …   … and the sampled values are held, thus creating a random series of control voltages.

b. A very low frequency sawtooth …   … is sampled …   …and the sampled values are held, thus creating a descending series of control voltages.

FIGURE 8.33
Two examples of series of control voltages that can be created by a sample/hold unit.

sample is taken. Thus, a continuously variable input voltage can be converted into a series of discrete voltage levels (see Figure 8.33). If the input signal is random, as is the case with white or pink noise (illustrated in Figure 8.33a), then the output signal will be a series of random voltages that can be patched to the control input of a VCO, for example, to produce a random series of pitches. If the input signal is a periodic waveform of very low frequency, then the output signal will be a patterned series of voltages (as in Figure 8.33b). Some sample-and-hold units provide for voltage control of the sampling rate, so that durational patterns can also be created.

THE DEMISE OF ANALOG SYNTHESIZERS

At first, nearly all analog synthesizers were studio instruments (with the notable exception of the Synket). Though certainly not as bulky as the RCA synthesizer of the 1950s, they were nonetheless rather large compared to most musical instruments and rather difficult to pack and transport for a performance tour. They were also complicated to set up and operate on stage. The modular design facilitated great flexibility in the production of sounds, but required the proper connection of numerous patch cords and the correct setting of dozens of dials and switches. Only the bravest of electroacoustic musicians would attempt these things while in the presence (and under the pressure) of an eager and expectant audience.

By the early 1970s, however, manufacturers began to introduce analog synthesizers that were specifically designed for live performance. Not only were they more compact, but they were also somewhat less complicated to operate. Many of the most common connections among modules were wired internally, and other connections could be made by pushing switches on the front panel. Thus, it became possible for a performer to set up the patch for a sound while onstage. The gain in relative ease of operation meant somewhat less flexibility in the design of sounds, but this loss was considered an acceptable trade-off by electroacoustic musicians who aspired to get onstage.

The Mini-Moog, introduced in 1970, was one of the first performance synthesizers. Its controls included two wheels at the left end of the keyboard for bending the pitch and for regulating vibrato. These controller wheels have since become standard equipment on performance synthesizers. Other performance synthesizers introduced at about this time were the ARP 2600, the ARP Odyssey, and the Synthi AKS.

While the elimination of most patch cords certainly made the task of live performance much easier, it was still necessary to change manually the settings of the dials and switches when moving from one kind of sound to another. By the late 1970s, however, so-called programmable synthesizers were developed that made it possible to change a patch at the press of one or two buttons. The settings of the dials and switches could be scanned and digitally encoded for storage until needed later. Entire banks of control

THE VOCODER

In the 1930s, researchers at the Bell Telephone Laboratories, searching for a more efficient way to transmit telephone messages, developed a device called a **vocoder** (for VOice enCODER). It was found to be of limited use to the telephone company, but in the 1950s the composers in the studios for electronic music in Cologne and New York became interested in the device as a way to transform sounds.

The basic function of a vocoder is to model the spectral characteristics of one sound after those of another sound. Or, to put it another way, the spectral characteristics of a sound are superimposed from a different sound. Figure 8.34 is a diagram of a network of analog circuits designed to accomplish this. The sound to be modeled is provided as an input to a bank of band-pass filters, each covering perhaps only one-third of an octave within the range of audible frequencies. An envelope follower circuit for each frequency band then detects the amplitude envelope of the output from each of the filters. In this way, the amplitude changes within each frequency band of the input sound are analyzed.

The sound upon which this spectral information is to be superimposed is provided as an input to a second bank of band-pass filters, covering the same frequency bands as those in the analysis filter bank. Each band of frequencies in the target sound is then passed to a voltage-controlled amplifier. The control voltage for each VCA is provided by the corresponding envelope follower in the analysis bank. In this way, the amplitude envelopes from each frequency band of the model sound are used to shape the amplitudes of each band of frequencies in the target sound. The output of each VCA is then passed to a mixer and the target sound is reassembled, now with new spectral patterns.

For the technique to provide satisfactory results, the second sound should have at least as rich a spectrum as the first sound. Noisy sounds, or sounds with sawtooth waveforms, are typically effective. Common examples of vocoding include robotic voices in grade-B science fiction films, or talking windstorms and other such special effects in similar films. Many artists, such as Laurie Anderson, have made much use of the vocoder in very effective ways in their music.

The functions of a vocoder circuit can now be emulated digitally, and a vocoder function is found on many commercially available effects devices. Such digital signal processors, described in Chapter 4, are esteemed as especially versatile and useful devices in the studio.

FIGURE 8.34 (facing page)
A schematic diagram of an analog vocoder.

settings could be stored in this way. Any of the patches required during a performance could then be recalled, virtually in an instant. The first performance synthesizer to implement this technology was the Sequential Circuits Prophet-5, introduced in 1978. Other popular programmable synthesizers were the Korg Polysix (1982), shown in Figure 8.35, and the Roland Jupiter 8.

Analog synthesizers have other limitations that have not been so easy to address. For example, subtractive synthesis is a relatively crude way to specify and shape a timbre. The technique of biting away chunks of the

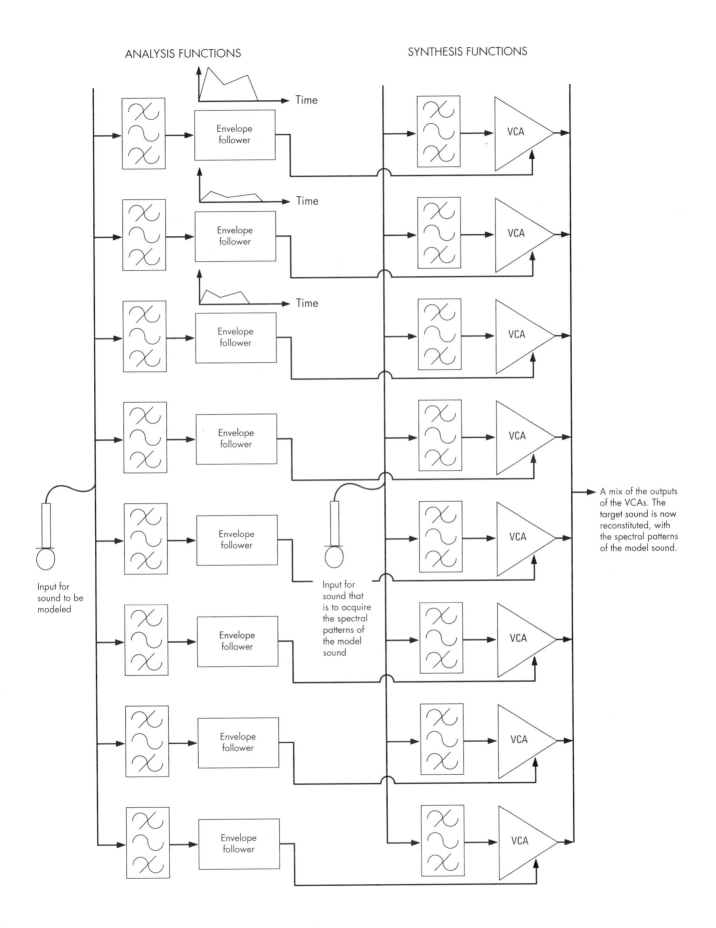

ANALYSIS FUNCTIONS

SYNTHESIS FUNCTIONS

Time

Envelope follower

Time

Envelope follower

Time

Envelope follower

Envelope follower

Envelope follower

Envelope follower

Envelope follower

Envelope follower

VCA

VCA

VCA

VCA

VCA

VCA

VCA

VCA

Input for sound to be modeled

Input for sound that is to acquire the spectral patterns of the model sound

A mix of the outputs of the VCAs. The target sound is now reconstituted, with the spectral patterns of the model sound.

FIGURE 8.35
The Korg Polysix synthesizer.
(Courtesy of Korg USA, Inc.)

spectra of fixed waveforms by using relatively imprecise filters does not permit a great range of subtlety.

Amplitude envelopes tend to be similarly crude. Rather than an individual envelope for each frequency component of a timbre, as research has indicated to be the case with natural sounds, the VCA superimposes a single envelope over the whole sound, as illustrated by the perspective plots in Figure 8.36 (contrast these to the perspective plots in Figures 7.8 and 7.9).

Furthermore, analog electrical circuits tended to be rather unstable over the duration of a performance or a studio session. This is particularly noticeable as VCOs drift in and out of tune. Finally, there was the problem that synthesizers made by different manufacturers were almost totally incompatible with one another. Without a satisfactory way to connect synthesizers of different manufacturers, there was no practical way to integrate the strengths of one synthesizer with the strengths of the other synthesizers in the studio or onstage. Setups involving several instruments could be very difficult to manage.

By the end of 1983 there were two significant developments that would eventually lead to the near extinction of analog synthesizers. Yamaha introduced the first commercial digital synthesizer, the DX7. At the same time, a group of manufacturers announced their agreement on a set of digital messages and the corresponding hardware requirements that would enable control information to be exchanged among synthesizers. This, of course, was the introduction of MIDI, the Musical Instrument Digital Interface.

By the time of this writing, the techniques of analog synthesis have been almost entirely supplanted by those of digital synthesis. Even so, it is important that everyone who is interested in electronic music find an opportunity to spend at least some time with an analog synthesizer. Many of the concepts and paradigms that were introduced with analog synthesis continue to be important. Perhaps of the greatest importance, however, is the sense of extended musical possibilities that these machines fostered. The modular design of analog synthesizers virtually invited experimentation with sound and form. Modern, digital synthesizers seem to be much more tightly locked into the "normal" 12-equal-tone-per-octave paradigm. Some of the most fascinating sounds produced by analog synthesizers—the grand sweep of a resonant low-pass filter, or the truly random series of pitches produced by a VCO controlled by a sample-and-hold unit—have yet to be satisfactorily recreated by even the most modern digital machine. This belies the notion (to be discussed further in Chapter 12) that progress is an inseparable companion to technological change.

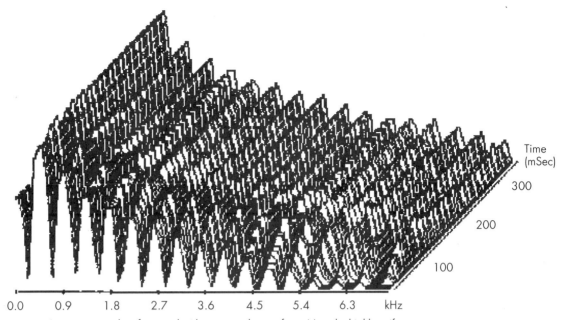

a. A perspective plot of a sound with a sawtooth waveform. Note the highly uniform distribution of partial frequencies and the flatness of their envelopes relative to those of acoustic instruments (compare Figures 7.8 and 7.9).

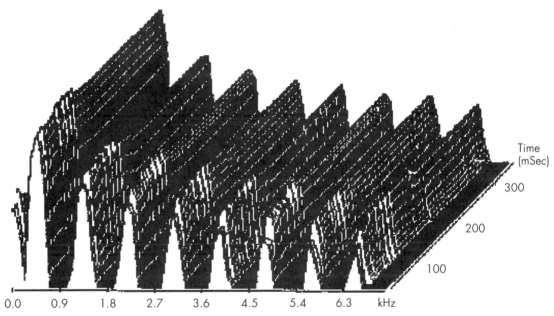

b. A perspective plot of a sound with a square waveform. Again note the very regular spacing of the partials and the extreme uniformity of their envelopes. Incidentally, observe also that in the square-wave timbre, every other overtone is absent (compared to the sawtooth-wave timbre shown in (a).

FIGURE 8.36
The uniformity of spectral characteristics of simple, electronically synthesized tones. A major challenge of synthesis is to create tones with much less regimented patterns of activity. (Courtesy of Digidesign, Inc.)

IMPORTANT TERMS

digital synthesizer
analog synthesizer
elektronische Musik
control voltage
modules
patch
voltage-controlled oscillator
  (VCO)
triangle wave
pulse wave
duty cycle
square wave
noise generator
voltage-controlled amplifier
  (VCA)
voltage-controlled filter (VCF)
low-pass filter
cutoff frequency
filter slope, or roll-off
Q

high-pass filter
band-pass filter
bandwidth
band-reject filter, or notch filter
subtractive synthesis
additive synthesis
envelope generator
attack
initial decay
sustain
release, or final decay
ADSR
trigger
gate
monophonic
polyphonic
keyboard tracking
control voltage attenuator
control voltage inverter
quarter tone

low-frequency oscillator
  (LFO)
sidebands
carrier
modulator
amplitude modulation, or AM
balanced modulator, or ring
  modulator
frequency modulation, or FM
modulation index
sequential controller, or
  sequencer
arpeggiator
ribbon controller
X-Y controller, or joystick
touch-sensitive plate
envelope follower
sample-and-hold unit, or S/H
  controller
vocoder

FOR FURTHER READING

Adams, Robert Train. *Electronic Music Composition for Beginners.* Dubuque, IA: Brown, 1986.

Appleton, Jon, and Perera, Ronald C., eds. *The Development and Practice of Electronic Music.* Englewood Cliffs, NJ: Prentice-Hall, 1975.

Barbour, J. Murray. *Tuning and Temperament.* 2d ed. East Lansing: Michigan State College Press, 1953.

Darter, Tom and Armbruster, Greg, eds. *The Art of Electronic Music.* New York: GPI, 1984.

Holmes, Thomas B. *Electronic and Experimental Music.* New York: Scribner, 1985.

Howe, Hubert S., Jr. *Electronic Music Synthesis.* New York: Norton, 1975.

Naumann, Joel, and Wagoner, James D. *Analog Electronic Music Techniques.* New York: Schirmer, 1985.

Strange, Allen. *Electronic Music: Systems, Techniques, and Controls.* 2d ed. Dubuque, IA: Brown, 1983.

Trythall, Gilbert. *Principles and Practice of Electronic Music.* New York: Grosset & Dunlap, 1973.

Weidenaar, Reynold. *Magic Music from the Telharmonium.* Metuchen, NJ: Scarecrow, 1993.

Wells, Thomas, H. *The Technique of Electronic Music.* New York: Schirmer, 1981.

Wilkinson, Scott R. *Tuning In: Microtonality in Electronic Music.* Milwaukee: Hal Leonard, 1988.

CHAPTER 9

DIGITAL SOUND SAMPLING AND SYNTHESIS

$\mathcal{A}$s digital hardware and its associated software have become increasingly fast, sophisticated, and affordable in recent years, the techniques of digital sampling and synthesis have become increasingly preeminent. This chapter begins with a closer look at some of the concepts of digital audio technology that were introduced in Chapter 3, followed by a more detailed examination of the principles involved in the operation of digital sound sampling instruments. Finally, a number of techniques by which sounds can be synthesized digitally will be discussed. Along the way there will be occasional glimpses of future possibilities as well.

SOUND BY THE NUMBERS

As stated previously, the pattern of electrical oscillations in a microphone cable (or in a cable from a line-level source) is considered to be an analog of the acoustical vibrations that constitute a sound. The process of digital recording begins with periodic measurements, called **samples,** of the instantaneous amplitude of such an electrical signal. The hardware component that performs this sampling is called an **ADC,** or **analog-to-digital converter.**

SAMPLING RATE

To represent accurately a frequency that is present in the signal, at least two samples must be taken during each cycle of vibration (see Figure 9.1). In other words, the number of samples per second, called the **sampling rate,** must be at least twice the number of cycles of vibration per second of

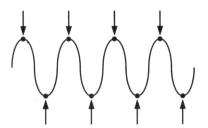

FIGURE 9.1
At least two digital samples per cycle—one during the positive portion of each cycle and one during the negative portion—are required to represent the essence of the vibration.

the highest desired frequency component in the sound.[1] It may be recalled that the very highest frequency that is reported to be audible to humans is 20,000 Hz. To represent this accurately (and therefore all lower audible frequencies as well) requires taking, at a rate of two samples per cycle, a total of at least 40,000 samples each second.

Many sounds include frequencies that are higher than 20 kHz, however. Although these sounds are inaudible, their presence can result in undesirable artifacts in the digital representation of the sound if the sampling rate is maintained at 40,000 samples per second. To remove these ultrasonic frequencies, the signal is usually passed through a low-pass filter before it is sent to the ADC.

The notion that the sampling rate must be at least twice the value of the highest frequency to be represented is called the **sampling theorem.** It is also sometimes called the **Nyquist theorem,** after Harry Nyquist, who developed much of the theoretical basis for these concepts in the 1920s. The highest frequency that can be adequately represented at a given sampling rate—that is, the frequency whose value is half that of the sampling rate—is often referred to as the **Nyquist frequency.** So long as the Nyquist frequency is greater than or equal to the highest audio frequency to be represented, the signal will be reasonably accurate and free of misleading information.

Figure 9.2, for example, shows a signal that includes two frequencies, 100 Hz and 400 Hz. If this signal is sampled at a rate of 800 samples per second, then the Nyquist frequency is 400, which coincides nicely with the highest frequency to be represented. A sampling rate of 800 is therefore sufficient.

However, if the pitch of the signal is transposed up a perfect fifth, so that its constituent frequencies are now 150 Hz and 600 Hz, a different situation exists, as shown in Figure 9.3. To represent this signal accurately would require a sampling rate of at least 1200 samples per second. But if the sampling rate is maintained at 800 samples per second, then each suc-

---

1. A good illustration of this principle can be found in the weather. To represent the annual fluctuation of the temperature outdoors, for example, it is necessary to record a thermometer reading once each January or so, and again exactly six months later, in July. At this sampling rate of two "samples" per year, however, the daily fluctuation of temperature would not be detected. To represent this additional fluctuation of temperature, it is necessary to record the thermometer level twice each day—once at midday and again exactly 12 hours later, in the middle of the night. To represent both the annual and the daily temperature frequencies, then, requires a sampling rate of at least 730 temperature readings per year (732 for leap years!).

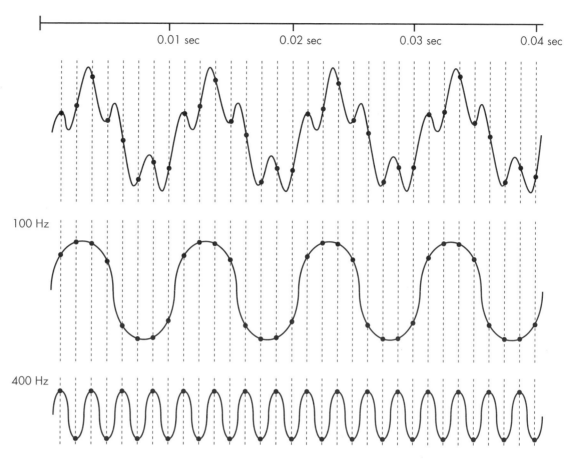

FIGURE 9.2
The waveform shown at the top includes a fundamental frequency of 100 Hz and an overtone with a frequency of 400 Hz. A sampling rate of 800 samples per second is more than adequate to represent the fundamental frequency and is also sufficient to represent the frequency of the overtone.

cessive sample would lag further and further behind the pattern of 600 vibrations per second. The frequency pattern that would be implied by a series of samples taken every 1/800 of a second would not be that of a vibration of 600 cycles per second. The highest frequency that can be represented at a sampling rate of 800 is 400 Hz. A frequency of 600 Hz cannot be represented. The frequency that takes shape instead is something other than 600 Hz—an **alias.**

The creation of such artifacts due to an insufficiently high sampling rate is called **aliasing,** or **foldover.** If an analog-to-digital converter is sampling a signal at a rate of 40,000 samples per second, any frequencies in the input signal that are higher than 20,000 Hz will be represented as "aliases," and these will likely fall within the range of audible frequencies. (These alias frequencies are often heard when the highest keys are played on a sampler or digital synthesizer. Most likely, overtones of these sounds have frequencies that exceed the Nyquist frequency of the instrument.)

To avoid these aliases, the cutoff frequency of the input filter is typically set to the highest frequency in the signal that is to pass undisturbed.

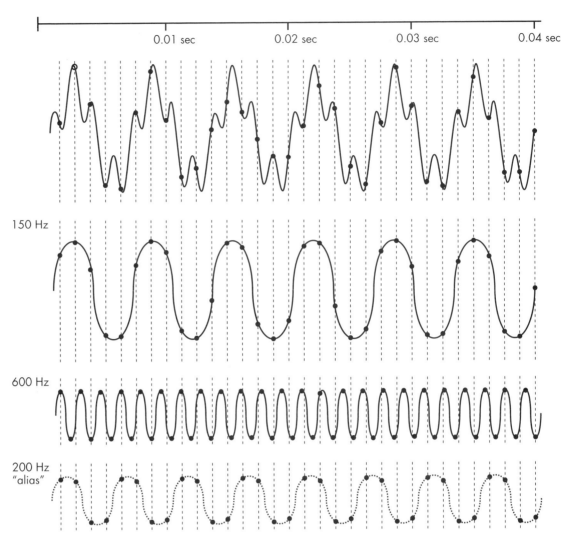

FIGURE 9.3
The waveform shown at the top includes a fundamental frequency of 150 Hz and an overtone with a frequency of 600 Hz. A sampling rate of 800 samples per second is more than adequate to represent the fundamental frequency, but is not sufficient to represent the frequency of the overtone. Instead, the pattern formed from the samples of the overtone is that of a sound with a frequency of 200 Hz. This is called an alias, or fold-over, frequency. As is usually the case, this alias frequency is not a harmonic overtone of the given fundamental.

However, as may be recalled from the description of low-pass filters in Chapter 8, the cutoff frequency is not an abrupt boundary between frequencies that pass and those that do not. The cutoff frequency simply represents that point at which the effect of the filter begins to be noticeable. Frequencies that are higher than the cutoff frequency can still pass, although somewhat reduced in level. Therefore, to accommodate this slope in the cutoff action of the input filter (as well as other factors), the sampling rate of a digital system is usually set somewhat higher than the required value of twice the highest desired signal frequency. The sampling rate of a compact disc (CD) system, for example, is 44.1 kHz; that of a digital audio tape (DAT) system can be 44.1 kHz or 48 kHz.

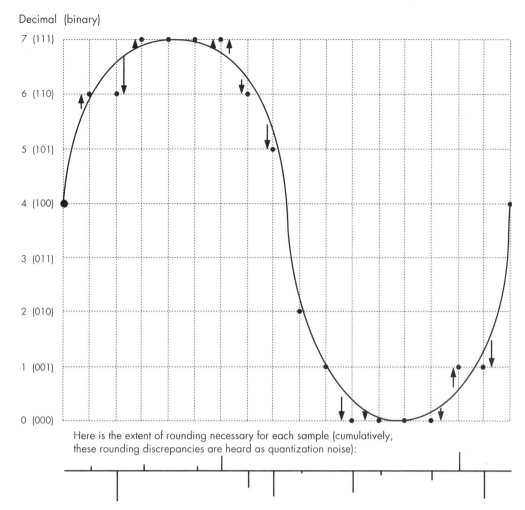

FIGURE 9.4
The curved line represents the ideal signal. The dots represent the actual sample values that are available when the quantization resolution is only three binary bits. Because the rounding errors that result are a significant portion of the signal, the digital background noise will be quite noticeable.

Here is the extent of rounding necessary for each sample (cumulatively, these rounding discrepancies are heard as quantization noise):

QUANTIZATION

A sample begins its existence as the measurement of the amplitude of a signal at a given instant. The analog-to-digital converter must then encode this measurement as a binary number, a process called **quantization** (see Appendix B for a review of binary numbers).[2] The precision of this quantization is very much affected by the limitations of the digital circuitry. It is necessary that the amplitude be represented as a finite, binary number. But, for example, if the circuits can only accommodate 8-bit numbers (00000000 to 11111111 binary, equivalent to 0 through 255 decimal), then only 256 different levels of amplitude can be represented. If the actual amplitude reading falls between two of these levels, it must be rounded off. The difference between the actual amplitude of a sample and the rounded value of the amplitude is called **quantization error.** It represents, in effect, a distortion of the actual signal (see Figure 9.4).

2. Note that this use of the term *quantization* is distinct and independent of the one in the section of Chapter 5 that refers to techniques for editing rhythm on a MIDI sequencer.

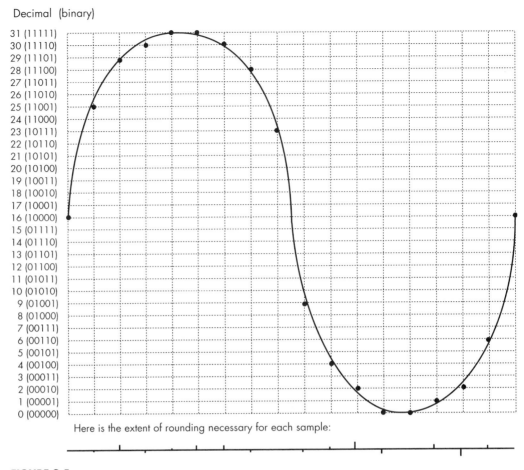

Decimal (binary)

Here is the extent of rounding necessary for each sample:

FIGURE 9.5

Again, the curved line represents the ideal signal. The dots represent the actual sample values that are available. Here the quantization resolution is five binary bits. As a consequence, the rounding errors are much smaller than those shown in Figure 9.4. The digital background noise, therefore, is much less noticeable.

The quantization error of one sample is not likely to be the same as the error of the next sample, or of the sample after that. These seemingly random variations in the degree of quantization error will cumulatively become noticeable as a background noise in the digital signal. This **quantization noise** is one of the most significant sources of noise in a digital audio system.

The amount of quantization noise can be reduced if the digital circuitry can employ a greater range of numbers to represent the amplitude of a sample. A 16-bit analog-to-digital converter, for example, can represent 65,536 different levels of amplitude (from 0000000000000000 to 1111111111111111 binary). This permits a far greater degree of precision. While the actual amplitudes of most samples will still have to be rounded off, they will not have to be rounded off by so much. The quantization errors will be much, much smaller (as illustrated in Figure 9.5), and the

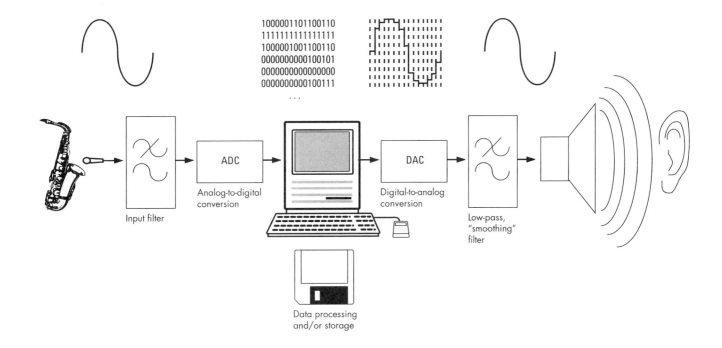

resulting background noise will be far less significant. With an 8-bit ADC, the best signal-to-noise ratio that can be obtained in theory is only 48 dB, but with a 16-bit ADC, the signal-to-noise ratio can theoretically be as good as 96 dB (and a 32-bit system, in theory, can achieve an SNR of 192 dB, a range that far exceeds the 130-dB range between the threshold of human hearing and the threshold of feeling).

After a good analog-to-digital conversion, the sound will now be adequately represented in both the frequency domain (by a sufficient number of samples per second) and the amplitude domain (by an adequate degree of quantization). The binary sound samples will now be fed to the next component of the chain of digital audio hardware. Here, the numbers may simply be stored (perhaps using one of the media described in Chapter 3), or they may be processed and manipulated in some way.

Eventually, it will be necessary to reconstitute the samples as an analog signal so that they can subsequently be heard as sound. This is the function of the **DAC,** or **digital-to-analog converter.** For each sample, the DAC generates a corresponding level of electrical current. This level is maintained until the next sample is read. Thus, the analog waveform initially has a jagged, "staircase" aspect (see Figure 9.6). For this reason, the analog signal is passed through a low-pass, "smoothing" filter to remove the ultrasonic frequencies represented by these edges on the waveform. Now the signal can be sent to an audio amplifier, and then to a loudspeaker. However, there are many, quite interesting things that can occur well before the signal reaches the digital-to-analog converter. These can now be described further.

FIGURE 9.6
The digital audio chain.

A CLOSER LOOK AT DIGITAL SOUND SAMPLERS

In Chapter 3, the digital sound sampler was described as a special form of digital recorder that is used as a musical instrument. It is also a small computer with relatively sophisticated programming for managing and manipulating the files of digital samples that represent sounds.

One of the first instruments to become available commercially that was capable of digital sampling was the Fairlight CMI. This instrument, introduced in 1979, was a very expensive device that also functioned as a digital synthesizer. In 1981, the first instrument dedicated exclusively to digital sound sampling, the Emulator™ by E-Mu Systems, appeared on the market. This was a somewhat less expensive instrument, but still beyond the means of most studios. By 1985, the costs of designing and manufacturing digital hardware had declined to a more attainable level, and this made possible the introduction of the Mirage™ by Ensoniq. The Mirage was just the first of a series of increasingly sophisticated, relatively inexpensive sampling devices by Ensoniq, Roland, Akai, Casio, E-Mu, Kurzweil, and others.

MEMORY ALLOCATION

A major constraint in the design and operation of digital sound samplers has been the limited amount of memory in the instrument to contain the digital samples. Given a finite amount of memory, the total available sampling time is determined by the sampling rate. If the memory of a sampler has a capacity of 1,000,000 samples, for example, then at a rate of 32,000 samples per second (a standard sampling rate), the maximum available sampling time is just over 31 seconds. However, the Nyquist frequency at this sampling rate is only 16 kHz. Any audible frequencies above this cannot be accurately represented in the set of digital samples. At a higher sampling rate of 48,000 samples per second (another standard sampling rate), the Nyquist frequency of 24 kHz is well above the upper limit of audible frequencies. However, the total sampling time—again assuming that the memory of the sampler is sufficient to contain 1,000,000 samples—is reduced to less than 21 seconds.[3]

---

3. The term *sample* has been used here to refer to an individual, binary-coded measurement of the instantaneous amplitude of an audio signal. A group of successive samples that represent a sound is referred to in this text as a set of samples, a file of samples, or a sound file. However, in common usage, the term *sample* is often used to refer to the group as well as to the individual. For example, an advertisement for "great drum samples" or "realistic piano samples" is referring, in fact, to sets of digital measurements of the sounds of drums or pianos. In this text, the term *sample* will continue to be used only in reference to individual measurements of an audio signal. Thus, "the memory of a sampler has a capacity of 1,000,000 samples" does not mean that the sampler can contain information about the sounds of as many as 1,000,000 different instruments! It will be perhaps a few more decades before samplers have such a capability.

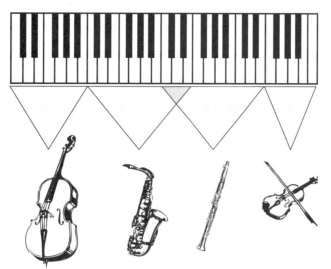

FIGURE 9.7
Specified segments of the keyboard can be assigned to play individual sample files. Some sample files can be assigned, or "mapped," to overlapping ranges of keys, as shown here with the saxophone and clarinet sample files. Keys played in this overlapped range will sound a mixture of the two instruments.

The memory of the sampler must be allocated to provide the maximum possible variety of sounds to the musician. At a rate of 44,100 samples per second (yet another standard sampling rate), the maximum available sampling time is approximately 24 seconds (once again, assuming that the memory of the sampler can contain as many as 1,000,000 samples). This amount of time can be used to sample one sound that is 24 seconds long. Or, it can be used to sample two different sounds that are each 12 seconds long; three sounds that are 8, 11, and 5 seconds long, respectively; or any other set of sounds whose combined durations equal approximately 24 seconds. These can be entirely different sounds, or similar sounds sampled from different ranges of pitches produced by a single instrument. The latter situation, of course, is the technique of multisampling, first described in Chapter 3.[4]

The assignment of sample files to the keys, or ranges of keys, that will trigger their playback is a process called key mapping (see Figure 9.7). On some samplers it is possible to overlap the ranges assigned to adjacent files, gradually fading out one sample file and fading the next one in. For multisampling, such cross-fading greatly facilitates a smooth transition from the sound associated with one range of pitches of the original instrument to the sound of the next one.

With most samplers, it is possible to assign two or more sample files to the same range of keys—a technique called **layering** (see Figure 9.8). Each sound might be heard together with the others, or different sample files might be heard in response to differences in key velocity. With this latter technique, called velocity switching, the sample file from one layer is

---

4. Because there is no limit to the number of sounds a musician would like to have immediately accessible—"at the fingertips," as it were—the issues of the availability and allocation of memory are likely to be of great significance for some time to come to musicians who use digital sampling instruments.

Layer 1

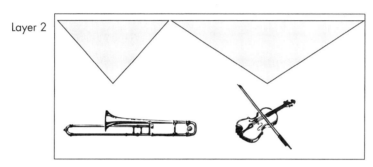

Layer 2

Layer 3

FIGURE 9.8
Different sets of samples, called layers, can be independently mapped to the keyboard. The sample files in these different layers can then be called forth by assigning them to different ranges of key velocity (shown in Figure 9.9) or by programming the sampler to switch among layers in response to messages from foot pedals or similar controls.

assigned to respond to one range of key velocities, while a sample file in another layer mapped to that same key will respond to key velocity values in a different range. For example, the sound of a horn played softly can be assigned to a layer that is heard when the key velocity is less than 64, and the sound of a horn played loudly can be assigned to a layer that will be heard if the key velocity is 64 or greater. The transition between these two layers may be abrupt, or it may be a cross-fade (as shown in Figure 9.9). Besides the assignment of different layers to different ranges of key velocity, many samplers provide for access to different layers through differences in key aftertouch values or continuous controller values. Foot

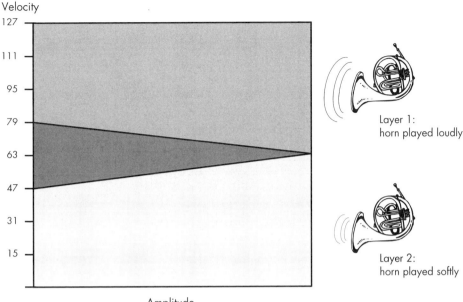

FIGURE 9.9

The technique of velocity switching provides a way to approximate the timbre changes that are associated with differences in loudness among tones produced by an instrument. In this example, the sample file of a horn played softly is heard whenever the key velocity is less than 79 (although the amplitude of this sample file tapers away for velocities between 64 and 79). For key velocities greater than 47, the sample file of a horn playing loudly is heard, tapering in gradually between 48 and 63 and reaching full strength at velocities greater than 63. Thus, there is a smooth cross-fade between the velocity regions dominated by each sample layer. For a more unorthodox application, the technique of velocity switching might just as easily be used to switch between two entirely different sample files.

switches or panel switches might also be used to call forth the sound files assigned to various layers.

ÉTUDE 9.1

Spend a few moments reading the sections of the owner's manual for the sampler in your studio that deal with the subjects of mapping sample files to keys and establishing layers of sample files. Then choose six sample files of short, distinct sounds (perhaps those of various percussion instruments, or the sounds of barnyard animals).

Create three layers of sample files, with two files assigned to each layer. Map one of the sample files in each layer to the lower half of the keyboard, and map the other sample file to the upper half of the keyboard. Program the sampler to play each of the three layers in response to different ranges of key velocities or different settings of a control pedal.

Compose and then perform a two- to three-minute piece for the sampler that is now configured in this way. If possible, store on a disk the data for this performance configuration so that the performance can be repeated.

LOOPING TECHNIQUES

As mentioned in Chapter 3, one method for making the most efficient use of the available memory of a sampler is to loop a portion of the steady-state segment of a sustained tone. Much of the remaining part of the sound file can then be deleted, thus freeing some memory for another sound file to be recorded or loaded into the memory.

A variety of techniques can be used for looping sounds. The most common type of loop is the "forward" loop, in which the playback of the sound file proceeds to the end of the loop segment, skips back to the beginning of the loop segment, proceeds again to the end of the loop, skips back, and so forth (see Figure 9.10). The challenge of creating a successful forward loop is to identify points for the beginning and ending of the loop that match closely, if not identically, with respect to amplitude, pitch, and tone color. If this is not accomplished, a click or a thump will be heard each time the ending and the beginning of the loop come together. With a computer-based visual editor program, the task of finding satisfactory loop points is eased considerably (see Figure 3.15).

Another type of loop is the "reversing" or **mirror loop.** In this type of loop, the playback of the sound file proceeds to the end of the loop segment, then reverses direction and continues through the loop segment back to the beginning (see Figure 9.11). This pattern then repeats through the remainder of the sustain time. An advantage of this method is that the beginning and ending of the pattern are matched quite precisely in amplitude, pitch, and tone color, as the loop gradually returns to its beginning. However, with some sounds, such as vocal sounds, the reversed portion of the loop cycle may seem quite odd. Also, if there is a significant difference in amplitude, pitch, or tone color between the beginning and the end of the

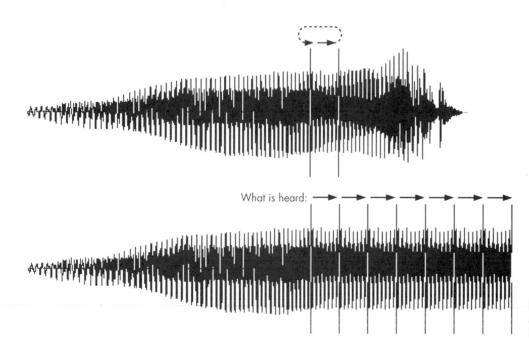

What is heard:

FIGURE 9.10
A forward loop. (Courtesy of Passport Designs, Inc.)

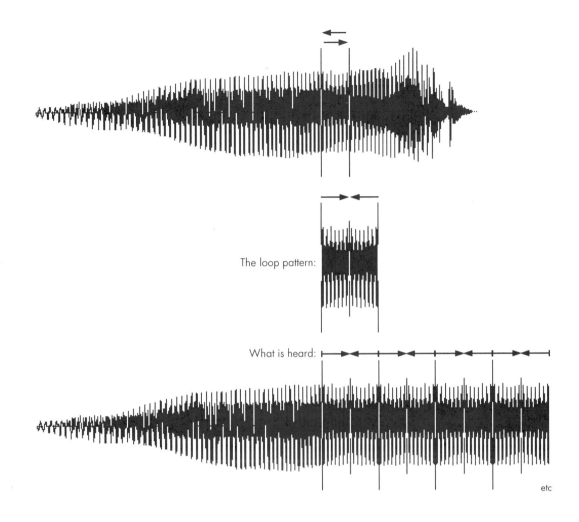

The loop pattern:

What is heard:

etc

loop segment (or between any other points in the loop segment, for that matter), there will be a noticeable, unnaturally regular fluctuation in the sound as the loop repeatedly cycles back and forth across these differences.

Yet another type of loop is the **cross-fade loop.** With this technique, a portion of the sample file that precedes the beginning of the loop segment is cross-faded with the samples at the end of the loop segment, as shown in Figure 9.12, so that any potential discontinuities between the ending and the beginning of the loop segment are faded away. This truly does minimize the potential for thumps and clicks at the point where the ending and the beginning of the loop segment are joined. However, as with other types of loops, there may still be a problem with audible, regular fluctuations in amplitude, pitch, or tone color as the loop is repeated. If there are significant changes in any of these qualities within the loop segment, then such fluctuations are likely.

One way to deal with this problem is to loop a much shorter segment of the sound, presumably because any changes in amplitude, pitch, or tone color are not likely to be so large over such a short span of time. A short loop such as this may include only the samples that represent a single cycle of vibration, or perhaps up to 16 cycles (see Figure 9.13). The sustained

FIGURE 9.11
A mirror loop. (Courtesy of Passport Designs, Inc.)

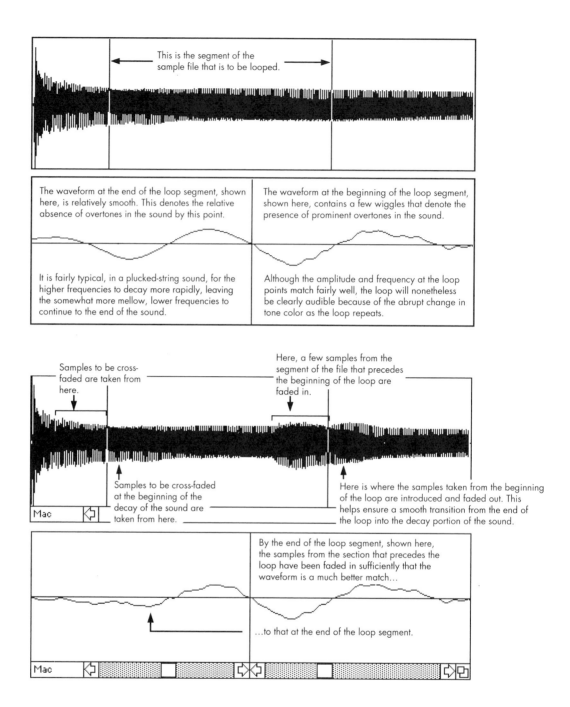

This is the segment of the sample file that is to be looped.

The waveform at the end of the loop segment, shown here, is relatively smooth. This denotes the relative absence of overtones in the sound by this point.

The waveform at the beginning of the loop segment, shown here, contains a few wiggles that denote the presence of prominent overtones in the sound.

It is fairly typical, in a plucked-string sound, for the higher frequencies to decay more rapidly, leaving the somewhat more mellow, lower frequencies to continue to the end of the sound.

Although the amplitude and frequency at the loop points match fairly well, the loop will nonetheless be clearly audible because of the abrupt change in tone color as the loop repeats.

Samples to be cross-faded are taken from here.

Here, a few samples from the segment of the file that precedes the beginning of the loop are faded in.

Samples to be cross-faded at the beginning of the decay of the sound are taken from here.

Here is where the samples taken from the beginning of the loop are introduced and faded out. This helps ensure a smooth transition from the end of the loop into the decay portion of the sound.

Mac

By the end of the loop segment, shown here, the samples from the section that precedes the loop have been faded in sufficiently that the waveform is a much better match...

...to that at the end of the loop segment.

Mac

portion of tones that have short loops tend to have a flat, almost synthetic quality, precisely because significant changes in amplitude, pitch, or tone color are deliberately kept to a minimum. To a certain extent, one of the principal advantages of sampling over synthesis—the ability to capture the liveliness of acoustic sounds—is being sacrificed.

As with analog synthesizers, one way to compensate for this regularity is to shape the playback of the samples with envelopes for amplitude or tone color. A sampler may include circuits for voltage-controlled amplifiers

FIGURE 9.12

A cross-fade loop. The sound file being looped here is that of a plucked guitar string. (Courtesy of Passport Designs, Inc.)

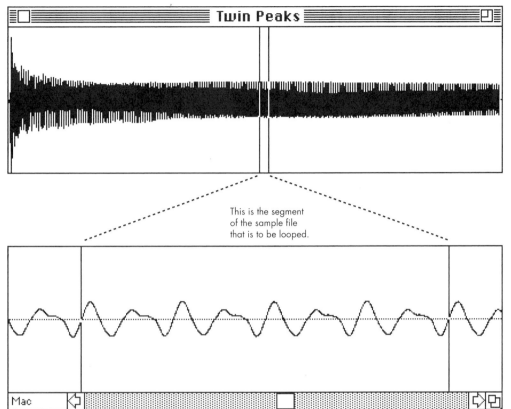

FIGURE 9.13
A short loop of eight cycles of vibration. Again, the sound file being looped is that of a plucked guitar string. (Courtesy of Passport Designs, Inc.)

This is the segment of the sample file that is to be looped.

(VCAs) and voltage-controlled filters (VCFs) such as can be found on an analog synthesizer. More likely, these are circuits for digitally controlled amplifiers (DCAs) and digitally controlled filters (DCFs). Even more likely, a sampler that is a more recent model will be programmed with computer instructions to emulate the functions of such circuits. In addition to the capability of applying envelopes for amplitude and tone color, it is also likely to have the capability of applying an envelope to the pitch of a sample file as it plays back.

Typical samplers also include the capability to modulate the pitch (and probably also the amplitude and tone color) of the sample file, as it is played back, with a low-frequency oscillation (LFO). Just as with analog synthesis, this is used to animate the tone with vibrato or tremolo effects. A low-frequency oscillation with a rate that is carefully chosen can also be used to camouflage or confound a regular fluctuation of amplitude, pitch, or tone color in a long loop that includes noticeable changes in these qualities. For this application to be successful, the period of the low-frequency oscillation should be related to the period of the loop by a value that is not a ratio of small numbers. For example, a ratio of 4:3 between the period of the LFO and the period of the loop is not likely to be as satisfactory as a ratio of 19:14. The goal is to have the two rates of fluctuation be out of synchronization as much as possible.

SAMPLE-PROCESSING TECHNIQUES

Artificial envelopes for amplitude, tone color, and pitch, as just described, can be used to sculpt a sampled sound as it is played back. However, a visual editing program, such as one used to assist in the creation of successful loops, can also provide powerful techniques for sculpting the sample files themselves. Typically, the computer that is running the visual editor software is linked to the sampler through a MIDI interface and MIDI cable, or through a cable with many parallel conductors that are used to transmit data at a much higher rate.

Sound samples can be transmitted through a MIDI cable in the form of Universal System-Exclusive messages defined by the MIDI Sample Dump standard. Because MIDI is a serial interface, transmitting data one bit at a time, it can take quite a while (often several minutes) to transfer a complete sound file from the sampler to the computer, or vice versa. Using a parallel interface, such as the Small Computer Systems Interface (SCSI, pronounced "scuzzy"), can reduce considerably the time required to transfer the data. However, such parallel interfaces can be tricky to operate satisfactorily, particularly if three, four, or more devices are involved (such as external hard-disk drives for the computer or the sampler). The reader is advised to examine closely the operator's manual of each device, but also to be prepared to telephone the technical support staff of the manufacturers of the hardware and software being used. As this description is being written, a new standard, the SCSI Musical Data Interchange standard (SMDI, pronounced "smiddy") is being developed to address many of the problems associated with SCSI transfers of sample files.

Once the samples have been transferred to the computer, by whatever means, they can then be subjected to relatively intense varieties of recomputation. For instance, the amplitude envelope of the sound—its natural envelope—can be traced by the visual editing program and then altered. The natural envelope of one sound can be superimposed on the amplitudes of the samples of another sound. For example, the amplitude envelope of a flute tone might be superimposed on that of a piano, as shown in Figure 9.14. Similar operations with the natural pitch envelopes of digitized sounds can be executed as well.

The balance of frequencies in a sound can be adjusted with software that is capable of digital equalization. An even more sophisticated operation than digital EQ begins with an analysis of the frequency content of a selected segment of a sample file (a Fourier analysis). The information that results from this analysis is displayed graphically on the computer screen (see Figure 9.15). The frequency content can then be redefined by manipulating the display, and the samples in the segment recomputed according to these new specifications for energy distribution among the various frequencies in the sound. This technique, which will be revisited in the next section as a technique of digital sound synthesis, is called **resynthesis.**

This is a sample file of a flute-like sound,

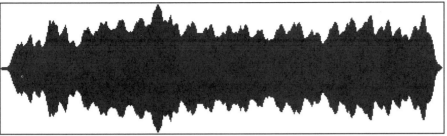

and this is a sample file of a piano sound.

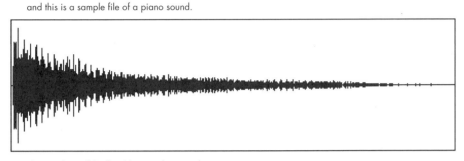

The envelope of the flute-like sound is traced,

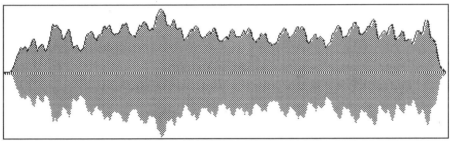

and then copied over the sample file of the piano tone.

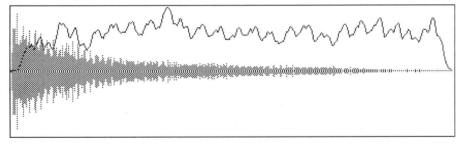

The samples of the piano tone are then rescaled to fit the superimposed envelope.

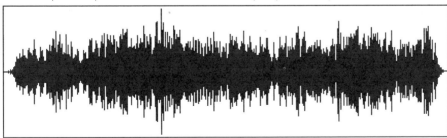

FIGURE 9.14
Envelope superimposition.
(Courtesy of Passport Designs,
Inc.)

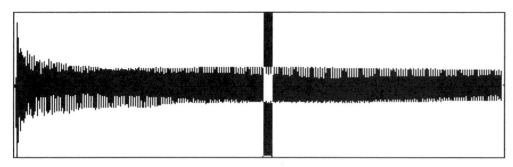

FIGURE 9.15
The graph displays the results of a Fourier analysis of the selected region of this sample file of a guitar tone. (Courtesy of Passport Designs, Inc.)

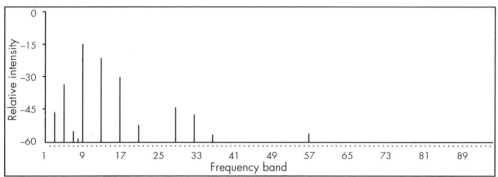

A technique called **time scaling,** or **time compression,** is used to change the duration of a sample file without changing the pitch of the digitized sound. Individual samples are interpolated or deleted as necessary to lengthen or shorten the file. Similar operations can be used to raise or lower the pitch of a sample file without changing its duration. This technique, known as pitch shifting, is helpful when it is necessary to compensate for small problems with the tuning of the natural sound used as the source of the sample file.

The computer that is linked to a sampler can also be used to run programs that can themselves create the samples needed for sample files. Programs such as Softsynth™ or Turbosynth™, developed by Digidesign, Inc., in the late 1980s, have this powerful capability. The sample files that are generated in this way are functionally indistinguishable from sample files of acoustic origin. They can be layered, looped, shaped by envelopes, and modulated by LFOs. The sampler, together with the computer to which it is linked, has in effect become a digital synthesizer. Many of the techniques of digital sound synthesis, to be described in the next section of this chapter, can easily be emulated on a digital sound sampler in this way.

Without doubt, a digital sampler is a device with much potential—an instrument that can do much more than simply record relatively short sounds in digital form and then play them back. It invites creative approaches to sound and the exploration of new ways to shape it into musically expressive works of art.

LOOPING THE IMPOSSIBLE LOOP

The author was able to use successfully many of the techniques of sample processing described here in order to loop the sound of a tam-tam—a gong of indefinite pitch. This sound is a challenge to loop, not only because its spectrum is inharmonic, but also because the sound decays exponentially, with high frequencies decaying much more rapidly. Therefore, the beginning of a loop segment is louder and also brighter in color than the end of the segment.

The first step in creating a loop for this sound was to make a copy of the loop segment, reverse it, invert it, and then mix it with the original. The result, shown in Figure 9.16, was a saddle-shaped loop segment. Next, the amplitude envelope of the segment was redrawn so that the amplitude maintained a more constant level, as shown in Figure 9.17. This eliminated any

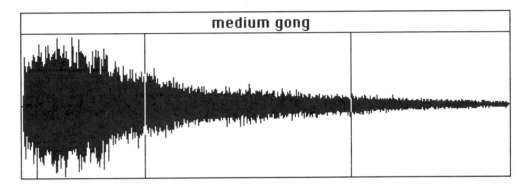

A copy of the loop segment is created, then reversed, and the phase is inverted.

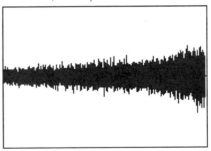

This modified copy is then mixed into the loop segment (in effect, creating a special form of a mirror loop).

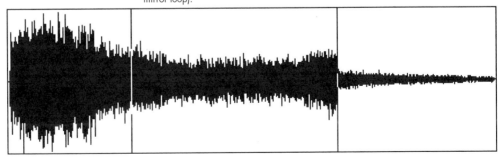

FIGURE 9.16
Courtesy of Passport Designs, Inc.

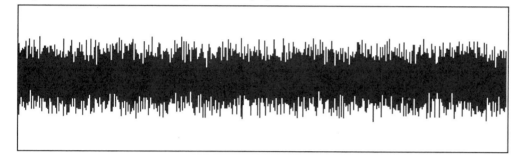

FIGURE 9.17
Courtesy of Passport Designs, Inc.

The amplitude envelope during the loop segment is then leveled as much as possible to minimize fluctuations of amplitude as the loop repeats.

FIGURE 9.18
Courtesy of Passport Designs, Inc.

After the amplitude envelope of the loop segment has been modified, two copies of the sound file are created. With the first copy, the duration of the loop segment is expanded by a factor of 1.43 (without alteration of the pitch).

The duration of the loop segment in the other copy is expanded by a factor of 1.13 (again, without alteration of the pitch).

These three sound files are then assigned to different layers of a sampler so that they are sounded together whenever the designated key (or key within the designated range) is played. The unnatural quality of repetition associated with the playback of a single one of these files is obscured by the asynchronous repetitions of the loops among the three files together.

major fluctuations in amplitude as the loop recycled, but the tone color of the loop still fluctuated because of the presence of higher frequencies near the boundaries of the loop segment.

To address this fluctuation of tone color, two copies of the sample file were made. The duration of one of these copies was rescaled, without altering the pitch, by a factor of 1.43; the duration of the other copy was rescaled by a factor of 1.13 (see Figure 9.18). The original sound file and these two copies were then assigned to three different layers of the sampler so that they sounded together whenever a key was played. The result was a turbulence of tone color that seemed natural, with no discernible pattern of repetition, because the loops of the three layers rarely came into synchronization. With the assistance of these powerful techniques of sample processing, it had become possible to loop the impossible loop.

ÉTUDE 9.2

Select two sounds of medium duration and sample them. Transfer the sample files to a computer-based visual editing system. Make several copies of each file. To each copy apply a different sample-processing technique, such as envelope superimposition, time scaling, pitch transposition, or resynthesis. Or apply to each copy a different amount of sample processing by a single technique.

Arrange the original sample files and their variants into a brief composition of one or two minutes' duration. Apply reverberation or other effects as desired. Then, record the finished work on a two-track tape machine.

DIGITAL SOUND SYNTHESIS

A digital synthesizer is defined as one that deals primarily with numerical representations of vibrations. In essence, a digital synthesizer, like a digital sampler, is a computer in the guise of a musical instrument. One of the principal attractions of digital audio technology, as mentioned previously, is the great variety of opportunity it offers for manipulating sound samples through computation. The series of computational procedures involved in accomplishing such a task is called an **algorithm.** Some algorithms can delay a series of samples that represents a signal and then perhaps combine these delayed samples with a series that has not been delayed in order to create a variety of special effects, such as echo, reverberation, and flanging (as described in Chapter 4). An example of a more complex algorithm is one that is used by digital audio specialists to analyze the samples that represent an old phonograph recording, identify and remove the pops and scratches on the recording, and then interpolate computed estimates of the signal in place of those imperfections.

Of particular interest here, however, are algorithms that actually compute the series of samples itself, thus dispensing with the microphone, analog-to digital converter (ADC), and any other devices that generally precede the computer or storage medium in the chain of digital audio components. With an algorithm of sufficient complexity, it is theoretically possible for a computer to synthesize a series of samples that is indistinguishable from one that can be provided by an ADC. Over the years, this has been a major goal of research in digital sound synthesis.

Much of the early work in the development of digital audio technology, and of digital synthesis techniques in particular, was done by Max Mathews, John Pierce, and others at Bell Laboratories (the principal research facility of AT&T). The initial objective of their work, in the 1950s, was to develop a computer simulation of a telephone system. For the telephone company, this has facilitated such practical achievements as touch-tone telephone service, automated directory assistance, and transmission of telephone messages by earth satellite. However, the Bell researchers were interested in the broader musical implications of their work as well, and they attracted the attention of a number of musicians interested in the potential of the computer as a musical instrument.

In these early years, computer sound synthesis could be very tedious work for the aspiring computer musician. The computation of sound samples was done by large, general-purpose computers (called mainframe computers) that were usually located only at major universities or research facilities. A composer could spend hours, days, or even weeks punching holes in paper cards to encode instructions and information for the computer. Typically, one set of cards described the characteristics of the instruments to be simulated—the "orchestra." Another set of cards comprised the list of notes these instruments would play—the "score." The composer would then submit these cards as a job for the computer. It might take several hours for the computer to generate all the samples required. The composer would then pick up the data tape on which all of these samples were stored and take it to a studio equipped for digital-to-analog conversion. (For some composers, working at smaller universities, it might be necessary to mail their data tapes to a larger facility and hope that it would not be too many days or weeks before they received in return an audio tape recording of the converted samples.)

With a piano, one can press a key and immediately hear sound. But during the first decades of computer music, there was a lengthy series of enormous delays between imagining a sound and hearing the result produced by the computer. If the result was not quite satisfactory, the composer would have to endure the long process again to achieve a revision. This made the computer a most excruciating instrument to play. From virtually the beginning of experimentation and composition with digital sound synthesis, therefore, the ambition has been to develop a computer-music instrument that could be played in **real time,** just as any other instrument is played.

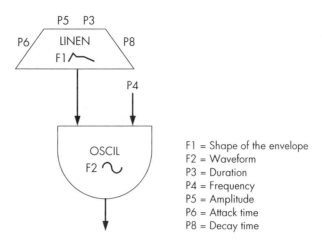

FIGURE 9.19
A flow chart of a simple computer instrument algorithm.

F1 = Shape of the envelope
F2 = Waveform
P3 = Duration
P4 = Frequency
P5 = Amplitude
P6 = Attack time
P8 = Decay time

Over the years, computers increased tremendously in power while decreasing in size and cost to the point where it became possible, by the early 1980s, to build a computer that could accomplish digital sound synthesis in real time. Within a short period, these computers were packaged with piano-type keyboards, mass-produced, and marketed in music stores just about everywhere on earth. In politics, this would be described as a revolution.

WAVETABLE SYNTHESIS

Although digital sound synthesis in real time has now become both technically and commercially feasible, there are still limitations of computer memory and computational power. Most techniques of digital synthesis specifically attempt to deal with these limitations by economizing the resources necessary to produce a satisfactorily complex sound.

A series of computer programming instructions that produces a stream of digital sound samples is often referred to as an instrument algorithm. This is typically organized as a group of shorter algorithms, called unit generators, that are responsible for particular functions of digital sound synthesis, such as generating the frequency of the sound or its amplitude envelope.

Figure 9.19 is a flow chart that indicates the organization of unit generators in a simple computer instrument algorithm. The unit generator labeled OSCIL has the basic task of producing a series of numbers (the digital sound samples) with an oscillating pattern. Although the value of each sample could be computed directly according to a formula that describes the pattern, this would require a very large amount of computing capability. A more efficient approach, sometimes referred to as **wavetable synthesis,** is to compute one cycle of the pattern and then store this in the memory of the computer as a function table, or waveform table. The unit generator OSCIL simply refers to this table to find the value that it requires (see Figure 9.20).

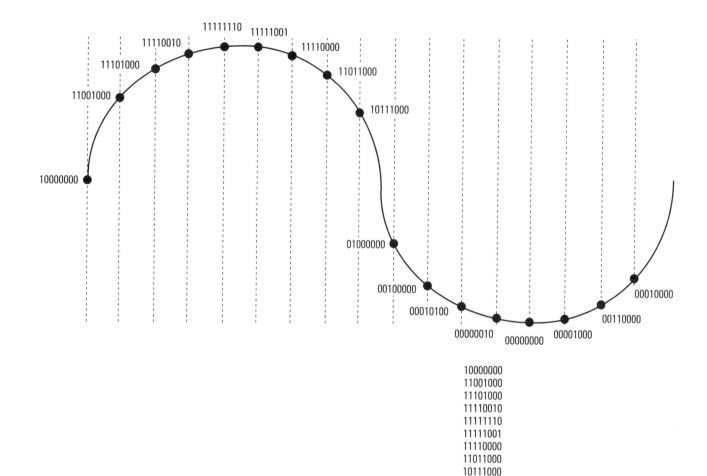

FIGURE 9.20
The genesis of a waveform table. Sample values for one complete cycle of the wave are computed and then stored as a table of binary numbers (far right). An OSCIL unit generator can then refer to this table each time it needs to produce a sample. NOTE: The wavetable shown here, consisting of a mere handful of 8-bit numbers, is a highly simplified example. In practice, a wavetable will consist of 512, 1024, or even 2048 numbers that are quantized as 16-, or even 32-bit numbers.

The frequency of the pattern generated by the OSCIL is determined by how fast the unit generator looks through the numbers in this waveform table. If the sampling rate is 48,000 samples per second, for example, then this is the number of times per second that the OSCIL will have to get a value from the table. If the table consists of 1024 values, and if the OSCIL reads each of them in order, then at a sampling rate of 48,000 it will read through the table 46.875 times each second. At the output of the digital-to-analog converter (DAC), this pattern will become audible as a frequency of 46.875 Hz. If the OSCIL skips over every other number in the waveform

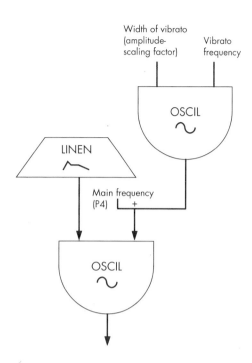

table, then it can read through the table twice as fast, and it will generate a frequency of 93.75 Hz. If the OSCIL skips over eight numbers at a time, it will produce a frequency of 375 Hz. The number of values in the function table that are skipped in this way is called the **sampling increment.** The value of the sampling increment is one of the necessary pieces of information provided as an input, or "argument," to the unit generator OSCIL; it is represented in Figure 9.19 by the symbol P4.

Another important piece of information that must be passed to the OSCIL is a factor for scaling the amplitude of the pattern of vibration. This information makes it possible to generate an oscillating pattern that will be heard, upon digital-to-analog conversion, as a tone that is soft, loud, or at an intermediate level of dynamics. If the amplitude-scaling factor is increased over the duration of a tone, then a crescendo is produced; conversely, if the scaling factor is decreased over the duration of a tone, a diminuendo results.

The unit generator LINEN in Figure 9.19 produces a series of amplitude-scaling factors that describes an amplitude envelope.[5] The unit generator is provided with information regarding attack time, peak amplitude, total duration of the envelope, and decay time (represented in Figure 9.19 by the symbols P6, P5, P3, and P8, respectively). From this information, it generates the correspondingly contoured series of scaling factors that shape the amplitude of the signal computed by the unit generator OSCIL.

An only slightly more complicated instrument algorithm is illustrated in Figure 9.21. Here a second OSCIL is used to alternately increase and

---

5. The name LINEN for this unit generator is a concatenation of the words LINear and ENvelope. The set of programming instructions that constitutes a LINEN unit generator can generate a series of numbers that represent straight lines that can be linked to form an envelope.

decrease the value of the sampling increment provided to the primary OSCIL. The result is a fluctuation in the frequency of the pattern produced by the primary OSCIL, and is heard at the output of the DAC as a tone with a vibrato (or perhaps some more extreme form of frequency modulation, as described later). The rate of the vibrato is determined by the sampling increment provided to the second OSCIL, and the width of the vibrato is determined by the amplitude-scaling factor specified to the second OSCIL. The configuration of analog synthesis modules that corresponds to this instrument algorithm is illustrated in Figure 8.20. The second OSCIL in Figure 9.21 is essentially functioning in the same way as the LFO in Figure 8.20.

FOURIER SYNTHESIS

The simple computer "instruments" that have just been described are capable of generating an enormous variety of timbres. To enable the computer instrument to create a specific timbre, it is only necessary to generate a series of sample values for one cycle of the waveform that represents the timbre (for example, a sine or a sawtooth) and then to store these values in a function table, where they can be "looked up" by the instrument. In fact, a single cycle of vibrations (perhaps more) from a digital recording of an acoustic instrument can be stored and used in this way as well. This latter technique, which of course is very closely related to the basic principle of the digital sound sampler, is often referred to as "PCM-based" synthesis.[6]

However, by repeatedly referring to the same waveform pattern for each cycle of vibration, the computer instrument produces a signal that has a lifeless, static timbre. Such a timbre may be useful as a dial tone, microwave beep, or elevator chime, but it is of limited musical interest.

By comparison, a timbre produced by natural means, on an acoustic musical instrument, is likely to change quite a bit from the beginning through to the end of a tone. Tones that change in timbre over the course of their duration in this manner are said to have time-variant spectra. Another major goal of research in digital sound synthesis has been to develop computer instruments that produce tones whose timbre evolves, or "blossoms," in a way similar to that of naturally produced tones—that is, to create instruments that can synthesize tones with time-variant spectra.

Figure 9.22 is a flow chart of a computer instrument algorithm that can produce such time-variant spectra quite effectively. In this example, the frequency produced by each OSCIL is a multiple of the lowest frequency, as in the overtone series. Also, each frequency component has its own amplitude envelope, so that the balance of intensity among the frequency components can change over the course of the duration of the tone. Furthermore, each

---

6. PCM stands for "pulse-code modulation," an expression used by engineers to refer to the process of digital sampling.

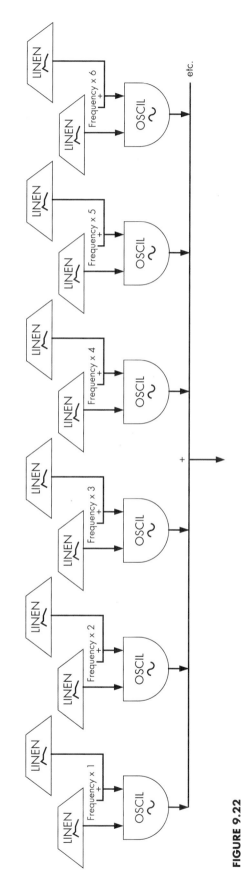

FIGURE 9.22
A computer instrument designed for additive synthesis.

frequency component has a unique frequency envelope, to simulate the subtle changes in frequency that are characteristic of the individual frequency components in a naturally produced sound.

This instrument algorithm is an implementation of the concept of additive or Fourier synthesis, described in Chapters 7 and 8. On an analog synthesizer, Fourier synthesis is very difficult to accomplish successfully, primarily because there are usually too few oscillators to produce a sufficient number of overtones. Also, the frequency produced by each analog oscillator will tend to drift somewhat unpredictably; thus, it is difficult to synthesize by analog means an overtone series that stays in tune with itself.

A digital synthesizer, however, can have hundreds of digital oscillators, since these exist as software (programming instructions) rather than hardware (circuits). Furthermore, the tuning of these oscillators is virtually perfect. Thus, Fourier synthesis is a much more feasible technique on a digital music system, and potentially can provide a means for the synthesis of any known or imaginable sound.

However, there are a couple of practical limitations to the power of additive synthesis. First, a rather large amount of information is required to define an instrument. It may be necessary to provide for the creation of at least 30 partial frequencies (for a satisfactorily complete overtone series), and the amplitude and frequency envelopes for *each* of these partials must be specified. Having thus defined the timbre for one tone, a different set of frequency and envelope values will probably be required for the next tone in the musical composition.

To say the least, it is tedious to specify all of this information. Furthermore, there is also an excellent chance that all of this information will be insufficiently coherent, resulting in a sound that is so much at variance from what we know or expect of the behavior of a musical instrument as to be completely implausible—unconvincing as a unified perception of a musical instrument.

Many composers and researchers, when working with computer synthesis instruments, therefore find it useful to work from a model. They first digitize a sound from a natural musical instrument and then analyze it to determine the content of partial frequencies and the associated amplitude and frequency envelopes. This approach is identified as **analysis-based synthesis** (or "analysis/synthesis" or "synthesis from analysis"). The synthesis of a sound on the basis of information derived from the analysis of another sound is called **resynthesis.**[7]

A second limitation of Fourier synthesis is that it is quite expensive in terms of the computational resources it requires. To calculate each sound sample involves a considerable number of arithmetic operations (a sound with 30 partial frequencies requires 60 multiplications per sample—one for each amplitude and frequency envelope—as well as 30 additions as the partial frequencies are combined). The processing hardware required for real-time Fourier synthesis must therefore be very fast, relatively powerful, and

---

7. This approach is reminiscent of the division of functions in the vocoder, described in Chapter 8.

consequently rather expensive. This situation, of course, is likely to improve with the continuing progress of the technology. In the meantime, however, the techniques of Fourier synthesis are not likely to be employed by real-time digital synthesizers, particularly those that are mass-produced.

VARIATIONS OF WAVETABLE SYNTHESIS

*B*ecause of the onerous demands of such techniques as Fourier synthesis, most real-time digital synthesizers that have made it to market in recent years rely on the relatively simple techniques of wavetable synthesis. As described earlier, these involve having the digital oscillator repeatedly refer to a function table, or wavetable, that contains the values for one cycle of the desired waveform. In its simplest form, wavetable synthesis does not provide a means of producing tones with time-variant spectra. However, several manufacturers have developed techniques that facilitate the creation of tones whose timbre does change over their duration.

One technique is to have the digital oscillator read from two wavetables at the same time and to interpolate between the values taken from each table. If the weighting of the interpolation is varied over the duration of the tone, then the timbre changes as the values from one table or the other predominate. For example, the digital oscillator in Figure 9.23 produces a waveform that varies between a sine and a sawtooth according to the interpolation function

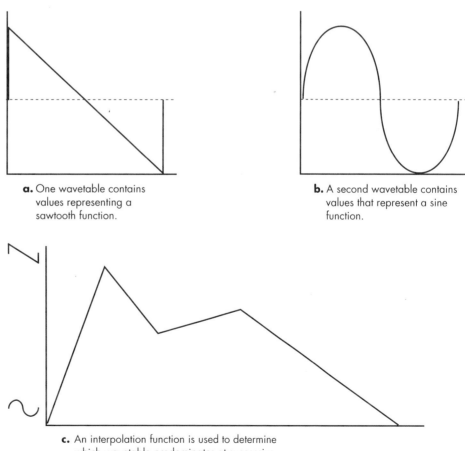

a. One wavetable contains values representing a sawtooth function.

b. A second wavetable contains values that represent a sine function.

c. An interpolation function is used to determine which wavetable predominates at successive moments over the course of the sound.

FIGURE 9.23
Interpolation between wavetables.

FIGURE 9.24

A Korg Wavestation™ module. On the left side of the front panel is a small X-Y controller for "vector" control of the tone color of the sound produced by the instrument. (Courtesy of Korg USA, Inc.)

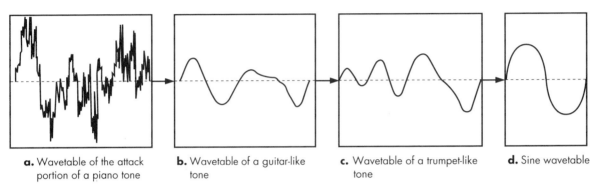

a. Wavetable of the attack portion of a piano tone

b. Wavetable of a guitar-like tone

c. Wavetable of a trumpet-like tone

d. Sine wavetable

FIGURE 9.25

Some synthesizers create tones with changing tone color by successively reading through a series of wavetables.

shown. The timbre begins as a pure sine wave and then adds overtones as the values of the sawtooth function begin to make a presence. By the end of the tone, the waveform has returned to a simple sine pattern.

A related technique, called **vector synthesis,** involves the interpolation of values from at least four wavetables. The interpolation factors can be controlled in real time by an X-Y controller, or joystick, on the control panel of the synthesizer.

Some synthesizers, such as the Korg module shown in Figure 9.24, store a series of wavetables in memory. The digital oscillator then reads through a programmed selection of these wavetables, usually cross-fading from one table to the subsequent one. The amount of time the digital oscillator spends with each table in the sequence, as well as the durations of the cross-fade transitions, can usually be programmed, but might be controlled in real time by the performer. At least a few of the wavetables in the instrument may be excerpted from digital recordings of tones produced by acoustic instruments. In particular, the attack segments of natural tones are commonly used as initial wavetables (see Figure 9.25). This is an especially important aspect of the so-called Linear Arithmetic, or LA synthesis, techniques employed by the Roland D-50 and related synthesizers.

Finally, there still exist a few hybrid synthesizers that combine digital and analog circuitry. For example, the signal produced by a digital oscillator might be immediately converted by a DAC to an analog voltage. This analog signal can then be shaped over the duration of the tone by an analog voltage-controlled amplifier and an analog voltage-controlled filter. This hybridization takes advantage of the stability and purity of the digital oscillator while relying on the relative ease and economy of analog signal processing by the VCA and VCF. As digital signal processing becomes more powerful and economical, however, the attractions of hybrid designs diminish.

FM SYNTHESIS

One of the most ingenious techniques devised for the digital synthesis of tones with time-variant spectra is **FM synthesis.** This is one of a class of techniques called nonlinear, or distortion, synthesis. The signal that is generated by such a technique is "distorted" in the sense that it contains frequencies in addition to, or instead of, those that were initially specified as inputs to the algorithm. With FM synthesis, the frequency of a signal is fluctuated, or modulated, at least 30 times per second to create a cohort of additional frequencies called sidebands. This technique can be realized on an analog synthesizer (as discussed in Chapter 8) by using an audio frequency signal from one oscillator as a control voltage source for a primary audio oscillator. (For a review of some of the concepts of frequency modulation, see pages 000–000.) FM synthesis is much more practical and precise on a digital music system, however, particularly as a result of the pathbreaking work done by John Chowning since the 1960s at the Center for Computer Research in Music and Acoustics (CCRMA) at Stanford University.

A simple computer instrument, containing the components that are essential for FM synthesis, is illustrated in Figure 9.26 (note the similarity to the simple instrument, shown in Figure 9.21, for producing a tone with a vibrato). The frequency of the signal produced by OSCIL1— the carrier frequency (f_c)—rises and falls as the sampling increment is alternately increased and decreased by OSCIL2. If the modulator frequency (f_m) produced by OSCIL2 is greater than approximately 30 Hz, so that it is no longer possible to follow the individual fluctuations of the carrier frequency, then sideband frequencies appear along with the carrier frequency in the output signal produced by OSCIL1.

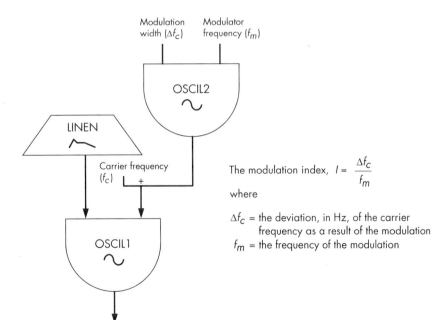

The modulation index, $I = \dfrac{\Delta f_c}{f_m}$

where

Δf_c = the deviation, in Hz, of the carrier frequency as a result of the modulation
f_m = the frequency of the modulation

FIGURE 9.26
A flow chart of a simple computer instrument algorithm that performs FM synthesis.

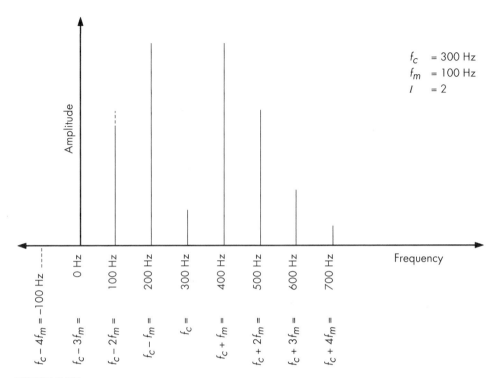

FIGURE 9.27

Spectrum of a tone produced by digital FM synthesis. Because the frequencies of the carrier and modulator in this example are related by a simple ratio of whole numbers, this will be heard as a tone with a harmonic spectrum and a fundamental frequency of 100 Hz. (Note: The frequency component at –100 Hz is heard as a frequency of 100 Hz, but is 180° out of phase with respect to the +100-Hz component. The two components interfere destructively, as indicated by the broken lines, to produce the spectrum indicated by solid lines.)

The number of noticeable sidebands, as reported in Chapter 8, is determined by the modulation index (I). If the amplitude of the modulator (the signal produced by OSCIL2) is increased, then the deviation of the carrier frequency (produced by OSCIL1) is increased as well. The value of the modulation index is greater, meaning that more sidebands are likely to be audible in the signal (after it has been converted to analog form by the DAC, of course).

The frequencies of the upper sidebands are found by adding whole-number multiples of the modulator frequency to the frequency of the carrier. The frequencies of the lower sidebands are determined by subtracting whole-number multiples of the modulator frequency from the carrier frequency. If the result is less than zero, the frequency is represented by the absolute value of the result, but with a phase shift of 180°, as shown in Figure 9.27. This figure also illustrates that if the carrier and modulator frequencies are related by a simple ratio (in this example, 3:1), then the carrier and sideband frequencies together resemble an overtone series (in this case, an overtone series with a fundamental frequency of 100 Hz). Similar examples are shown in Figure 9.28.

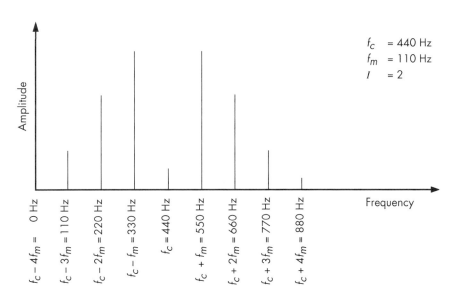

f_c = 500 Hz
f_m = 200 Hz
I = 2

$(f_c - 3f_m)+(f_c - 2f_m)$ = 100 Hz
$(f_c - 4f_m)+(f_c - f_m)$ = 300 Hz
f_c = 500 Hz
$f_c + f_m$ = 700 Hz
$f_c + 2f_m$ = 900 Hz
$f_c + 3f_m$ = 1100 Hz
$f_c + 4f_m$ = 1300 Hz

Amplitude

Frequency

a. This combination of carrier and modulator frequencies results in a tone with a harmonic spectrum, consisting of odd partials only and a broader bandwidth, and a fundamental frequency of 100 Hz.

f_c = 440 Hz
f_m = 110 Hz
I = 2

$f_c - 4f_m$ = 0 Hz
$f_c - 3f_m$ = 110 Hz
$f_c - 2f_m$ = 220 Hz
$f_c - f_m$ = 330 Hz
f_c = 440 Hz
$f_c + f_m$ = 550 Hz
$f_c + 2f_m$ = 660 Hz
$f_c + 3f_m$ = 770 Hz
$f_c + 4f_m$ = 880 Hz

Amplitude

Frequency

b. This combination results in a tone with a harmonic spectrum, consisting of all partials, and a fundamental frequency of 110 Hz.

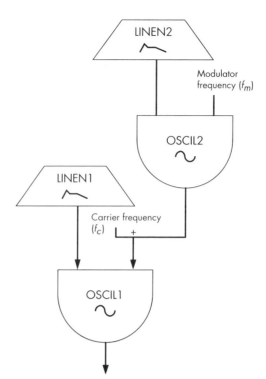

FIGURE 9.29
A flow chart of an FM synthesis instrument that, with relatively few calculations, can produce a time-variant spectrum.

If the amplitude of the modulator frequency is changed over the course of a tone, then the modulation index also changes, and this means that the number of noticeable sidebands changes too. As the spectrum changes, the listener hears changes in the timbre of the tone. In the computer instrument illustrated in Figure 9.29, a LINEN unit generator is used to create an envelope for the amplitude of the modulator frequency. In this rather elegant way, a time-variant spectrum can be created.

Both the Fourier synthesis instrument illustrated in Figure 9.22 and the FM synthesis instrument shown in Figure 9.29 generate a similar spectrum, but the FM algorithm requires far fewer calculations (although the Fourier instrument does provide a greater degree of control over the amplitude of each harmonic). For this reason, FM synthesis has been an enormously versatile and successful technique, both at large university facilities for computer music and on commercial real-time digital synthesizers, such as the Yamaha DX series of instruments introduced with the appearance of the DX7 in 1983.

EXTENDED TECHNIQUES OF FM SYNTHESIS

A few sample extensions of the techniques of FM synthesis can lead to even more complex results. In the computer instrument shown in Figure 9.30, the modulator frequency is itself modulated by a third OSCIL. This means that there will be sideband frequencies along with the modulator frequency itself. When applied to the carrier frequency generated by

OSCIL1, these sideband frequencies will act as additional modulator frequencies. The sidebands formed by these sidebands, together with the sidebands formed by the primary modulator frequency, form quite a busy spectrum, particularly if the modulator unit generator (OSCIL2) and the modulator of the modulator (OSCIL3) have different amplitude envelopes. Modulator unit generators that are patched in a series such as this are described as **cascade modulators.**

The computer instrument shown in Figure 9.31 is referred to as a **parallel carrier** instrument. The signal from a single modulator is used to establish a set of sidebands around two or more different carrier frequencies. The resulting spectrum can be broader in bandwidth (that is, it can include a broader range of frequencies) than that produced by simple FM synthesis.

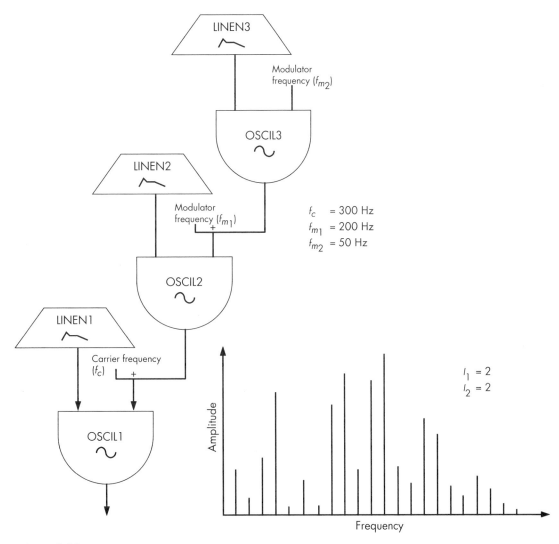

FIGURE 9.30

Cascade modulators. As a consequence of being modulated by OSCIL3, the primary modulator signal, produced by OSCIL2, will include sidebands. These sidebands will then act as additional modulator frequencies when the signal produced by OSCIL2 is used to modulate the primary carrier frequency produced by OSCIL1. The graph is a "snapshot" of the spectrum when the value of the modulation index of the FM at both OSCIL1 and OSCIL2 is 2.

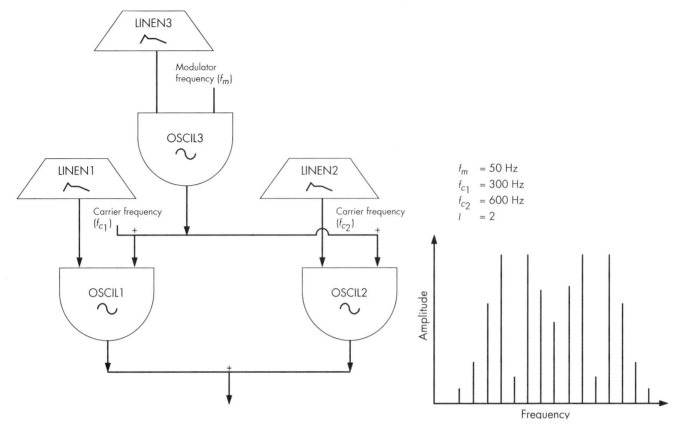

FIGURE 9.31
Parallel carriers. The resulting tone color includes the sidebands produced around two or more carrier frequencies by the same modulator frequency. The graph is a "snapshot" of the spectrum when the value of the modulation index of the FM at both OSCIL1 and OSCIL2 is 2.

Also, since different carrier frequencies are responsible for the formation of different parts of the spectrum, these parts can be controlled somewhat more independently.

A **parallel modulator** instrument, illustrated in Figure 9.32, employs two or more modulating frequencies on a single carrier frequency. Each modulator will create a set of sidebands around the carrier frequency. Also, each set of sidebands produced by one modulator will be treated as carrier frequencies by the other modulator. That is, each modulator will also create sidebands around the sidebands created by the other modulator. Needless to say, the spectrum can rapidly become quite thick and busy, even though the instrument design is relatively simple and involves few calculations.

A typical application involving parallel or cascade modulators is to place a quick, sharp amplitude envelope on the additional modulator to create a transient burst of sidebands that quickly dissipates—thereby simulating the noisy attack of an instrument. The remaining modulator is then used to shape the timbral evolution through the remainder of the duration of the tone. This technique of designing an instrument so that different portions of the algorithm are responsible for simulating the separate, distinguishable elements of the timbre of a sound has been called "component synthesis." This approach to computer instrument design is not unique to FM synthesis—it can be used quite readily with Fourier synthesis techniques, for example—but has most certainly been popular among programmers who design sounds for FM synthesizers.

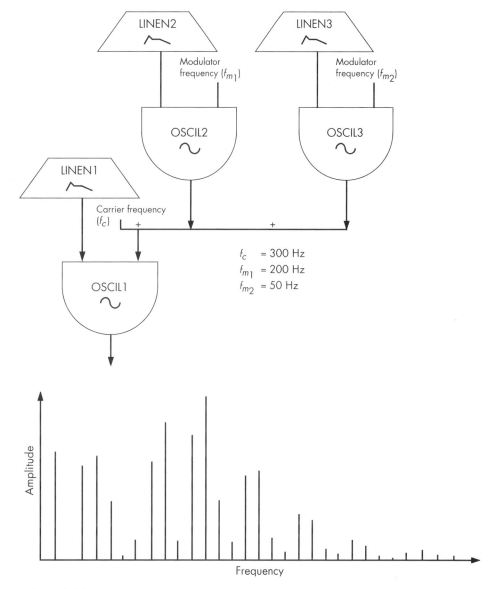

FIGURE 9.32
Parallel modulators. The sidebands created around the carrier frequency by OSCIL2 are treated as carrier frequencies by OSCIL3. Likewise, the sidebands created around the carrier frequency by OSCIL3 are treated as carrier frequencies by OSCIL2. The result is, to say the least, rather complex. Three frequencies are specified as inputs, while many, many more appear at the output. The graph is a "snapshot" of the spectrum when the value of the modulation index of the FM at OSCIL1 is 2 with respect to both OSCIL2 and OSCIL3.

ÉTUDE 9.3

𝓕or this composition you will need an instrument capable of FM synthesis, such as a Yamaha DX7, TX7, TX816, DX7-II, TX802, FB-01, SY77, TG77, or a related synthesizer. Highly recommended is a good editor/librarian program that enables you to edit patches for your synthesizer on a computer.

Design three instrument patches for your synthesizer. You may want to begin by viewing the details of the settings of the patches that were in your instrument as it left the factory (the so-called factory patches). There is much to be learned by studying these as models of how FM synthesis patches work. If you feel comfortable with your understanding of the extended techniques of FM synthesis described here, then perhaps one of the three instruments you design can be a cascade modulator instrument, one a parallel carrier instrument, and the other a parallel modulator instrument.

Compose and perform a two- to three-minute work that uses exclusively the three instruments you have designed.

WAVESHAPING

Waveshaping is another technique of distortion synthesis. It was first introduced commercially in 1987 on the Casio CZ101 and related synthesizers, and has since been employed by a variety of Korg synthesizers and other instruments. Figure 9.33 illustrates an algorithm for waveshaping. A digital oscillator produces a series of samples, usually one that represents a sine waveform. The amplitudes of these samples are then altered (or "distorted") by a unit generator called a waveshaper.

The waveshaper does not simply rescale the amplitudes in a linear fashion. Rather, the amount of alteration is usually different for samples of different amplitudes—the "distortion" is nonlinear. It is important to recognize that this is not the sort of misbehaved distortion that can be created by providing too great a signal to an amplifier, for example. Rather, it is carefully designed distortion with precisely intended consequences. The waveform is reshaped as a result of this distortion, and this coincides with the presence of additional frequencies in the spectrum. The content of the spectrum depends upon a formula called the **transfer function** that is specified to the waveshaper. This function describes the way in which the amplitude of the signal is to be distorted—that is, the relationship between the input and output amplitudes of samples that are processed by the waveshaper (see Figure 9.34).

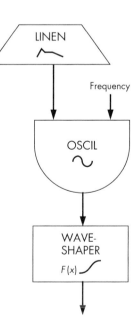

FIGURE 9.33
A flow chart of a simple computer instrument algorithm that can produce a complex spectrum by waveshaping. $F(x)$ is the transfer function, which is used as a reference by the WAVESHAPER to determine the appropriate modification of the amplitude of each sample that arrives from the OSCIL.

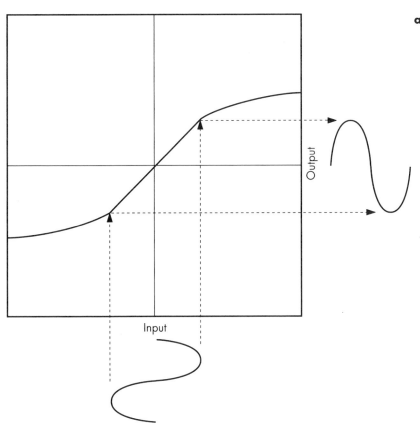

a. The midsection of the transfer function illustrated here is linear. If the amplitude of the input waveform remains within the range of this midsection, no distortion of the amplitude will appear in the output signal. Therefore, when the amplitude of the input signal is low—such as at the beginning of the attack or near the end of the decay—the spectrum will consist of a simple sine wave.

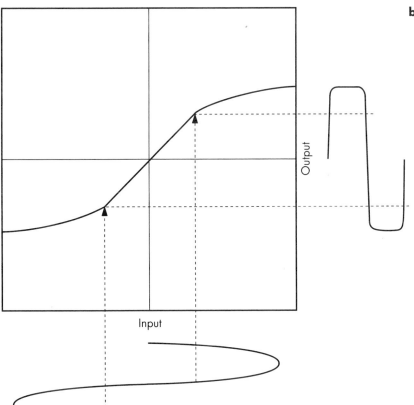

b. The outer sections of the transfer function, however, are not linear. If the amplitude of the input waveform exceeds the range of the midsection, then distortion of the amplitude will appear in the output signal, and the output waveform will be altered. When the amplitude of the input signal is high—such as at the end of the attack of a sound—the spectrum will become somewhat more complex, consisting of many partial frequencies, and the tone will be considered "richer." Thus, time-variant spectra can be produced relatively easily by means of waveshaping. Changes in amplitude over time will correspond to changes in timbre, just as is the case with tones produced by most acoustic instruments.

FIGURE 9.34
The transfer function describes the relationship between the input and output signals of the WAVESHAPER unit generator. More precisely, it describes the relationship between the amplitude of an input sample and the amplitude of the corresponding output sample. It is a "map" for transforming amplitude values.

DIGITAL FILTERS

*D*igital filters are computations that combine the values of current samples with those of previous samples. For example, modifying a signal according to the following formula will recreate the effect of a low-pass filter:

$$y(n) = .5\ x(n) + .5\ x(n-1)$$

where $y(n)$ = the value of the sample at the output of the filter
$x(n)$ = the value of the sample at the input to the filter
$x(n-1)$ = the value of the preceding sample provided as input to the filter

The output of this filter is the numerical average of the current and previous input samples to the filter. Large differences in amplitude between adjacent samples are likely to be due to the presence of higher frequencies in the signal. When these differences are averaged, the higher frequencies are "smoothed out."

If the large differences in amplitude between adjacent samples in a digital signal represent the presence of higher frequencies, then a formula that extracts and preserves these differences can be used as a digital high-pass filter:

$$y(n) = .5\ x(n) - .5\ x(n-1)$$

Because a digital filter involves the combination of values from a series of two or more adjacent samples, the operation of the filter cannot be instantaneous. The following formula is another example of a low-pass filter (but with a lower cutoff frequency, because more samples are averaged):

$$y(n) = .5\ x(n) + .3\ x(n-1) + .2\ x(n-2)$$

The first sample of the signal that is provided to the filter is scaled in amplitude but not yet filtered (there is no averaging until a second sample is provided). The second sample will be averaged with the first sample, so that some filtering begins to take place. It is not until the third sample, however, that the full effects of the filter are apparent. A similar tapering of the output of the filter occurs as the last samples in a signal are processed.

The pattern of the response of a filter over time—most noticeable, perhaps, at the beginning and the end of the signal—is called its impulse response. The filters described so far are called finite impulse response (FIR) filters. The output of such a filter will sooner or later reach zero after the conclusion of the signal being applied to the filter.

Other filters, sometimes called recursive filters, include previous output samples of the filter itself in the computation, as illustrated by the following formula:

$$y(n) = .5\ x(n) + .5\ y(n-1)$$

where $y(n)$ = the value of the sample at the output of the filter
$x(n)$ = the value of the sample at the input to the filter
$y(n-1)$ = the value of the preceding sample generated as output from the filter

The element of feedback in the design of such a filter can provide for a much sharper effect with much less computation. The feedback can also make the filter unstable, however, so the filter must be designed very carefully. Because some of the output of the filter is fed back to the input, the filter will continue to produce an output signal even after the primary input signal has ceased, and this will continue for an infinite period of time (although sooner or later, the feedback values will be scaled down to the point of relative insignificance). For this reason, such filters are called infinite impulse response (IIR) filters.

This discussion provides a mere glimpse of the arcane science of digital filter design. Much research in this very important field continues. For further information (including much more rigorous descriptions and mathematical treatments of this topic), you may wish to refer to the writings by Dodge and Jerse and by Smith that are cited at the end of this chapter.

SUBTRACTIVE SYNTHESIS

On analog synthesizers, filters can be used to alter the timbre of a sound by removing (or at least attenuating) one or more bands of the partial frequencies in the sound, as described in Chapter 8. A time-variant spectrum can be created by changing the cutoff frequency of the filter (or cutoff frequencies, in the case of a band-pass or band-reject filter) over the course of the duration of the tone. These are relatively crude techniques, however, for shaping the timbre of a sound. It is very difficult with analog filters to alter the relative amplitudes of individual partials rather than entire blocks of adjacent partials. Furthermore, the variation of timbre that results from sweeping the cutoff frequency of the filter over the duration of the tone tends to be crude and unnatural sounding. Unlike the behavior of partials in naturally produced sounds, the individual partials appear and disappear in strict succession, and each partial has an envelope that is nearly identical in contour to that of the other partials in the sound.

A computer music instrument can include algorithms that recompute the digital signal so that adjustments are made to the relative strengths and weaknesses of various frequencies represented in the signal. These algorithms, called **digital filters,** can be used to replicate the gross effects of analog filters, but they can also be used in much more subtle and precise ways.

As with digital additive synthesis, the composer or researcher who employs the techniques of digital subtractive synthesis may first turn to the analysis of a naturally produced sound in order to create a model for digital synthesis. A set of computations will then be devised to create the digital filter (or filters) needed to replicate the pattern of strong and weak frequencies heard in the spectrum of the natural sound.

Many composers and researchers go even further and take an approach referred to as **physical modeling.** They analyze the physical properties of the instrument that creates the natural sound—the resonances and antiresonances of its parts, and the mechanisms by which energy is transferred from one part to another (for example, from the bow to the string of a

In 1982, at the Center for Computer Research in Music and Acoustics (CCRMA) at Stanford University, the composer David Jaffe produced a composition entitled *Silicon Valley Breakdown*. It is a virtuoso demonstration of the uses of the Karplus/Strong algorithm, a technique that is modeled on the physical behavior of plucked-string instruments such as the banjo and guitar.

The Karplus/Strong algorithm begins with a series of samples with random values—digital noise. The number of samples in this series corresponds to the number of samples for one period of the vibration of the "string." This series of random numbers is then continually recirculated through a digital low-pass filter. Thus, as with most plucked-stringed instruments, the tone begins with a burst of noise, but with each additional cycle through the filter, the aperiodic elements in the signal become extinguished. What remains is the set of periodic patterns in the signal, most likely those corresponding to the resonances of the filter (like the resonances of the "string" and "body" of the instrument).

The Jaffe piece demonstrates a great variety of applications and extensions of this technique. For instance, in the passage of repeated tones at the very beginning, the effects of changing the point where the "string" is plucked are heard clearly. Shortly thereafter, in a brief passage beginning around 1:05, a giant instrument, with strings that have been likened to the cables of the Golden Gate Bridge, is simulated. Around 2:28, a very miniature mandolin begins strumming away. Such "instruments" are, of course, quite imaginary—if they were to be actually built of wood and metal, they would quite likely be physically impossible to play. Another example from the realm of impossibility is the passage that begins around 10:09, in which the instruments are played at tempos much faster than human players would even want to contemplate.

Remarkable as well are the harp-like strummings across large sets of strings, first heard at 1:55. The sympathetic vibrations among the strings and the ring-off after each strumming seem to be quite authentic.[a] In the harp-like passages that begin at 15:53 and 16:17, an exploration of alternate systems of tuning is perhaps most evident. Such digital "instruments," unlike the physical ones upon which they are modeled, can be retuned almost instantly, with nearly complete accuracy, and they do not subsequently slip out of tune.

Like the fantastical harps just described, many of the synthetic instruments heard in this piece evoke associations with more or less familiar acoustic instruments. The bending pitches in the passage that begins at 4:33, for example, resemble those of a "bottle guitar."[b] At 6:25, something like a Hungarian cimbalom can be heard, along with a brief hint of the Japanese koto. At 11:39, the sounds of chords on what could easily be taken to be a harpsichord are heard. Sometimes the strings on these digital instruments are metal, sometimes nylon, sometimes the strings are wound with wire, and sometimes they sound as if made from materials that have not yet been used on acoustical instruments.

---

[a] And unlike many synthetic sounds, which may sound equally unfamiliar whether played backwards or forwards, when these harp strums are reversed they do in fact sound reversed—an "acid test" of apparent authenticity!

[b] A "bottle guitar" is an ordinary guitar whose strings are plucked while a glass bottle is moved up and down the strings over the fingerboard.

However, the composition is not a mere effort to emulate a great variety of instruments and playing techniques. Rather, it reveals the capabilities of digital synthesis to extend the conceptual possibilities of instruments, to transmute them, and to transcend the limitations of physical construction and human dexterity. Such digital instruments can be continually reshaped, transformed, even mutated. This piece provides a glimpse of a very desirable future for digital synthesis in which the physical models of instruments, and the techniques for playing them, become more sophisticated while also becoming more accessible to more computer musicians.

The musicality of Jaffe's performance on his digitally imagined instruments is remarkable, particularly upon consideration that the piece was "played" as a lengthy series of sets of instructions typed on a computer terminal. Yet the piece sounds as if the instruments were touched in the way that conventional instruments are. To achieve this quality of tangibility, Jaffe was obviously able to draw upon his extensive knowledge of performance techniques gained from years of playing the mandolin and other stringed instruments.

Finally, the listener might also note that in this composition Jaffe juxtaposes and blends musical styles—particularly bluegrass and the academic avant-garde styles—as if they were musical objects themselves. People in contemporary society who are actively involved in music, as listeners, performers, or composers, share an awareness of a great variety of musical styles—undoubtedly a consequence of the ubiquity of sound recordings. Jaffe's stylistic pluralism is certainly not unique among contemporary composers, therefore. But in *Silicon Valley Breakdown*, it is presented with exceptional skill and thoughtfulness.

---

violin, and from the string through the bridge to the body of the instrument). This information is then used to guide the design of a computer instrument that emulates the behavior of the natural one.

Much work of this sort has been done in the area of voice synthesis, for example. There are two sources of sound in the vocal tract: the vibration of the vocal cords, and the turbulence that results as air moves past various surfaces and obstacles in the throat and mouth (as in *sh*). The frequencies that are produced by one or the other of these methods (or both) will then be resonated or attenuated in the various spaces of the vocal tract. The positions of the jaw and the tongue determine the size and shape of the mouth and can of course be adjusted, thus providing for a variety of sets of resonances. Particular vowel sounds are associated with particular sets of resonances and, therefore, with particular positions of the jaw and tongue (to test this, try speaking the word *meow* very slowly and think consciously of the positions of the jaw and tongue as you proceed through the sequence of vowels in the word). The vowel sound *uh*, for example, is characterized by resonances of frequencies in the vicinity of 640 Hz, 1190 Hz, and 2390 Hz.[8] Such resonances tend to remain fixed, regardless of fundamental frequency. Thus, it is possible to understand the vowel *uh*, or most any other

---

8. G. E. Peterson and H. L. Barney, "Methods Used in a Study of Vowels," *Journal of the Acoustical Society of America* 24 (1952): 183.

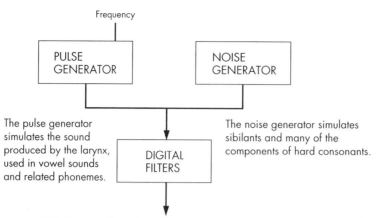

FIGURE 9.35
Flow-chart model (greatly over-simplified) of a computer instrument that can emulate the human voice.

Frequency

PULSE GENERATOR

NOISE GENERATOR

The pulse generator simulates the sound produced by the larynx, used in vowel sounds and related phonemes.

DIGITAL FILTERS

The noise generator simulates sibilants and many of the components of hard consonants.

With the signal from the pulse generator and with a set of filters tuned to the appropriate set of resonance peaks, around 640, 1190, and 2390 Hz, the instrument can produce the vowel sound *uh*. With a properly enveloped burst of noise at the beginning, from the noise generator, the instrument says "Duh."

vowel, whether it is uttered by a female or male voice, even though the latter is likely to have a lower fundamental frequency. Such resonances, described in Chapter 7, are called formants.

Figure 9.35 is a flow chart of a computer instrument algorithm based on the physical model of the human voice. The pulse generator simulates the production of tone by the vocal cords, and the noise generator provides the turbulent sounds associated with the passage of air. The filter unit generator in this example will boost frequencies in the vicinity of 640 Hz, 1190 Hz, and 2390 Hz. The tone that is produced should resemble that of the vowel sound *uh* as spoken by a male voice. This is an example of what is called formant synthesis.

If the set of resonant frequencies for the filter is shifted successively to other sets of resonances, then a crude form of speech might be synthesized. Many composers, such as Paul Lansky and Charles Dodge, have explored such techniques in detail and have developed them to a point of considerable sophistication. A particularly intriguing extension of the vocal model is known as cross synthesis. If, for example, the digitized sound of an orchestra is substituted for the samples produced by the pulse generator "voice box" in Figure 9.35, and passed through a digital filter that is shifting its resonances in response to speech cues, the result can be something like a "talking orchestra."

As the power and speed of digital signal-processing hardware have increased, it has become possible to attempt to resynthesize sounds from ever more complex physical models. Recent work at the University of California at Berkeley by Adrian Freed and others is leading to the development of sophisticated techniques for what is called resonance synthesis. The contributions of the individual parts of an instrument to the liveliness and richness of its tones, as well as the patterns by which the sound radiates from the instrument, are first analyzed extensively. For example, a tone from a piano is the result of the vibrations of the strings that are struck as well as the sympathetic vibrations of other strings, the resonances of the sound board, the thud of the keybed as it is struck by a pressed piano key, the resonances of the iron frame and the black wooden piano case, the rustling of the bushings in the key mechanism, the reflections of sounds from the piano lid, and many other sounds from other parts. After such an analysis, resonance synthesis involves attempting to recreate these complex interactions and then, perhaps, to alter or extend them. The model may also include the resonances and other characteristics of the acoustic environment of the instrument, and this information might become material for even further creative manipulation. For example, a synthetic trumpet might play a melody through a series of very different, imaginary rooms as it is stretched and reshaped to become a bass trombone (with a bassoon mouthpiece)!

GRANULAR SYNTHESIS

Although still regarded by some as a rather exotic technique, **granular synthesis** has been used quite effectively in several compositions. Other techniques of digital sound synthesis deal with apparently continuous signals—for example, repeating cycles of a sine pattern. The basic element of a sound produced by granular synthesis, however, is a short burst of a signal, on the order of 20 milliseconds in duration, called a **grain** (see Figure 9.36).

Hundreds, or even thousands, of these "grains" of sound are combined to form "events" of specified beginning times and durations. The composer configures each event according to the density of grains it contains, the frequency (or band of frequencies) represented by the grains, the net level of amplitude, and the waveform employed in the grains of the event. Any

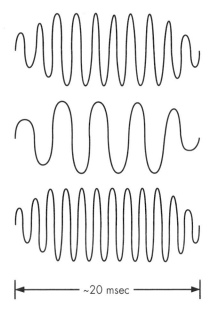

FIGURE 9.36
"Grains" of sound (also known as acoustical quanta) are used as the basic constituents of sounds produced by granular synthesis.

~20 msec

changes in these properties over the duration of the event can also be specified. A complete sound is likely to consist of a series of such events.

Sounds produced by granular synthesis typically have a busy, sometimes shimmering texture. The complexity and subtlety of changes in the timbre of these sounds cannot be readily matched by other techniques of digital sound synthesis.

ÉTUDE 9.4

*F*or this composition, you will need an instrument capable of a synthesis technique other than FM synthesis. Again, as with Étude No. 9.3, it is most helpful to have a good editor/librarian program that enables you to edit patches for your synthesizer on a computer.

Design three instrument patches for your synthesizer. Again, you may want to begin by viewing the details of the settings of the patches that were in your instrument as it left the factory—the so-called factory patches. These can be very helpful models for understanding how a technique of synthesis can be applied.

After you have designed your patches, compose and perform a two- to three-minute work that uses them exclusively.

IMPORTANT TERMS

samples
ADC, or analog-to-digital
　converter
sampling rate
sampling theorem, or Nyquist
　theorem
Nyquist frequency
alias
aliasing, or foldover
quantization
quantization error
quantization noise
DAC, or digital-to-analog
　converter

layering
mirror loop
cross-fade loop
resynthesis
time scaling, or time
　compression
algorithm
real time
wavetable synthesis
sampling increment
analysis-based synthesis
resynthesis

vector synthesis
FM synthesis
cascade modulators
parallel carriers
parallel modulators
waveshaping
transfer function
digital filters
physical modeling
granular synthesis
grain

FOR FURTHER READING

Chowning, John, and Bristow, David. *FM Theory and Applications: By Musicians for Musicians.* Tokyo: Yamaha Music Foundation, 1986.

Deutsch, Diana, ed. *The Psychology of Music.* New York: Academic Press, 1982.

Dodge, Charles, and Jerse, Thomas A. *Computer Music: Synthesis, Composition, and Performance.* New York: Schirmer, 1985. See especially the discussion in Chapter 5 of digital techniques for subtractive synthesis.

Mathews, Max V. *The Technology of Computer Music.* Cambridge, MA: M.I.T. Press, 1969.

Moore, F. Richard. *Elements of Computer Music.* Englewood Cliffs, NJ: Prentice-Hall, 1990.

Roads, Curtis, ed. *Composers and the Computer.* Los Altos, CA: Kaufmann, 1985.

Roads, Curtis, ed. *The Music Machine.* Cambridge, MA: M.I.T. Press, 1989. Advanced material.

Roads, Curtis, and Strawn, John, eds. *Foundations of Computer Music.* Cambridge, MA: M.I.T. Press, 1985.

Smith, Julius O. "An Introduction to Digital Filter Theory." In *Digital Audio Signal Processing: An Anthology,* edited by John Strawn, pp. 69–135. Los Altos, CA: Kaufmann, 1985.

Strawn, John, ed. *Digital Audio Engineering: An Anthology.* Los Altos, CA: Kaufmann, 1985.

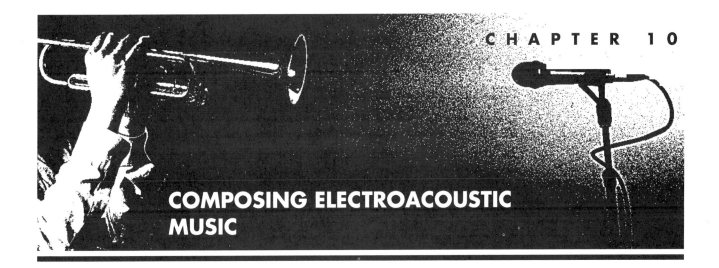

COMPOSING ELECTROACOUSTIC MUSIC

To write a poem, you need to have words—lots of them. What's more, you need to know what they mean—not only what they mean to you, but also what they might mean to your readers. You need to know how words work together in phrases. It is also good to know how the words sound as they are spoken, just in case someone reads your poetry out loud. (It is always helpful to know, too, how to spell the words correctly.)

To write a poem also requires a certain amount of experience. You need to nurture the ability to recognize apt and unique phrases as they occur to you. You need to become acquainted with a variety of poems by writers who have preceded you. In this way, you develop a sense of what a poem is—what qualities make poetry of a group of words, their rhymes and rhythms, how they sound when read aloud. You also need to learn to draw from your life experience, to impart to the words some of your own life's energy. You need to have something to write about, perhaps even the experience of words themselves.

This is not a chapter about how to write poetry, however.

To make a painting, you need paints, to be sure, and a blank canvas to which they can be applied. You also need brushes and a familiarity with a variety of appropriate strokes for using them to apply paint to the canvas. Such familiarity can come from studying paintings by other artists and from long, patient experience and experimentation.

You also need an awareness of how colors can be combined, juxtaposed, balanced, and blended. An understanding of the techniques by which three-dimensional objects can be represented on the two dimensions of the canvas may also be useful. The ability to recognize suitable subjects for a painting is also a good one to develop.

But this is not a chapter about making a painting, either.

To write a piece of music (yes, that's it) you should have:

- a familiarity with the tools that are used to make sound, and
- a familiarity with the ways sounds are formed into patterns that have meaning.

Without knowledge of the materials that are available, and how they are used, it is not possible to imagine a successful poem, or painting, or piece of music. The study of musical composition begins, therefore, with the study of the "tools" that are used to make sound—musical instruments (including the singing voice). Before writing music for an instrument, a composer needs to know the capabilities and limits of the instrument. What are its ranges of pitch and loudness? What are the diverse timbres it can produce? This information is readily available in textbooks of orchestration and such, but there is much more to it than this.

Music is an aural experience, to be sure, but for those who perform an instrument or sing, the experience of music is a tactile one as well. A pianist knows the feel of the keyboard and whether it has a light or heavy touch (how much of the weight of the hand and arm is required to depress a key). The pianist knows how far to extend the arm to the right to reach a key in the higher range, or how far apart the fingers are spread to play an octave with strength and security. A singer understands how to shape the throat and mouth to produce a good vowel sound on a particular pitch, and how to support the tone by involving the deepest muscles of the breathing system. And all musicians tap their feet (although some of the more high-brow types may not like to admit it).

By virtue of extensive rehearsal, these pianists, singers, and other musicians acquire a wealth of skill memories based on the tactile experiences of making music with the instrument in association with the aural experiences of the sounds produced by these movements. Often these experiences are linked further to the visual experience of reading musical notation.

Thus, a composer's knowledge of the capabilities of a musical instrument must also include an awareness of what it is like to play the instrument. Some patterns can be so awkward to play that they should be avoided completely (if the composer does not want to discourage performances of the music). Other patterns fall so naturally under the fingers, are so familiar to the player, that they become a part of the character of the instrument. Musicians particularly enjoy music that makes effective use of such patterns (and consider this to be one of the big payoffs for all those years spent in practice rooms!).

It is not coincidental that some of the finest composers in the history of music—J. S. Bach, Mozart, Beethoven, Chopin, and Liszt—were equally accomplished performers on one or more musical instruments. Thus, they were aware of the subtle capabilities of the instruments, how the instruments sound, and what it feels like to play them. Nearly all composers, in fact, have begun their musical lives as performers who subsequently developed an interest in composition. It is a natural step for those who have played an instrument for a while to want to begin to write their own material for it.

What are the implications of this for the composer of electroacoustic music? First, you need to approach the equipment in the studio as if it were a collection of musical instruments. Learn to play them. Develop the same sort of network of tactile, aural, and visual associations that performers on other musical instruments develop. Learn where the knobs, dials, and switches are and how to reach for them. Listen closely to how the sound is changed as they are moved.

Begin by reading the operator's manuals. Spend some time watching and working with someone who already has some knowledge of the instrument—a teacher, a tutor, or a studio engineer. Most important of all, *practice!!!*—every day, if possible.

How can one "practice" electroacoustic music? First, devise small, relatively simple tasks—études (the meaning in French is "studies"). For example, experiment with mixing various amounts of artificial reverberation in a recording, or with reversing some of the sounds. As you begin to feel more comfortable with the equipment, experiment with variations on these tasks. Devise bolder and more complex projects. (In an occasional spare moment, read the operator's manual again. As you gain experience with the equipment, the passages in the manual that made absolutely no sense to you the first time you read them may begin to make sense now.) Keep a notebook to record information about valuable techniques and interesting sounds you discover.

Do this for a long time. The process can certainly be tedious from time to time, but the results are worth the occasional exasperation. Learning to fly must be an awkward process at first as well. But with experience comes the willingness to take risks—flying faster, higher, upside down, sideways, or in small loops!—continually testing the limits. With experience comes an awareness of nuance and control. Greater facility with the instruments in the studio becomes audible as greater subtlety in the music. The technology does indeed become an extension of your ability to convey something about yourself, to express your aspirations, to project your thoughts.

But you must practice—every day.

In addition to a familiarity with the tools used to produce musical sound, a composer needs to acquire a familiarity with the ways sounds are formed into patterns that have meaning. A pattern of sounds has meaning by virtue of the relationships that exist among its sounds and by virtue of any relationships it may have with other patterns of sounds. For example, the seventh note of a major scale (do-re-mi-fa-sol-la-*ti*) is meaningful because it implies very strongly the imminent completion of the scale (Figure 10.1); it carries the expectation of the final tone—the pitch one octave higher than the pitch on which the scale began (do-re-mi-fa-sol-la-ti-*do*).

The chord comprised of the notes G, B, D, and F (a G^7 chord) becomes meaningful when it is recognized by the listener as a precursor of a chord comprised of the notes C, E, and G (a C-major chord; see Figure 10.2).

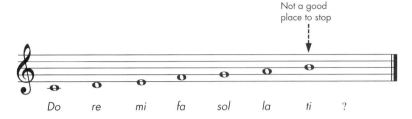

FIGURE 10.1

Not a good place to stop

Do   re   mi   fa   sol   la   ti   ?

Much better!

Do   re   mi   fa   sol   la   ti   do!

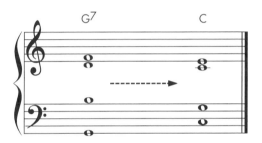

FIGURE 10.2
The sounding of a G⁷ chord means that a C chord is most likely not too far behind. (The C chord is the one voted "most likely to succeed.")

Progressions of chords are carefully crafted so that a particular chord will imply only a few other chords as possible successors, and each succeeding chord in turn will imply its own possible successors. The result is a chain of relationships of expectation and realization that links the opening chord of the progression to the closing chord.

A syncopated rhythmic pattern is meaningful in relation to the regular marking of the passage of time by a steady succession of beats. These may actually be heard, as performed by another instrument, or they may only be implied, to be imagined in the mind of the listener (see Figure 10.3).

The collected knowledge of the melodic, harmonic, and rhythmic relationships that give meaning to musical sounds is called the theory of the music. This knowledge may be consciously acquired through courses in music theory, or it may be intuitive knowledge gained through many years of less formal experience with music. Most likely (and most satisfactorily) it is a combination of the two. In any case, the success of a composer's effort depends on the extent to which there is a shared understanding with the audience of the theory of the music. The patterns should mean the same thing to both the creator and the "recreator" of the music.

This process is complicated (some would say enriched) by the plurality of contemporary culture. One does not have to go to a great deal of trouble to find bluegrass music, "newgrass" music, new age, country, any one of several varieties of rock music (heavy metal, soft, pop, progressive), any

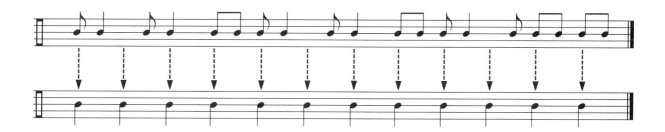

FIGURE 10.3
Rhythmic beats, as heard or imagined.

one of several varieties of jazz (New Orleans, Chicago, big band, bebop, fusion, free), any one of several varieties of European classical music (baroque, classic, romantic, modern, avant-garde), and an enormous range of classical and folk music from Asia, Africa, and Latin America. Each of these styles of music is characterized by relatively unique patterns of melody, harmony, rhythm, and choice of instrumentation—in a sense, each style has its own music theory. A composer who chooses to write for the audience for a given style of music needs to be familiar with the particular patterns that define that style. If the composer wants to work with more than one style, then the task becomes rather more complicated. For example, such a composer would need to know the differences between jazz drumming and rock drumming, or between country/western guitar playing and heavy-metal guitar work, or between bluegrass fiddling and classical violin technique. Such experience comes from hard listening and a great deal of playing. Like most other forms of growth, it is most likely a long, gradual, and irreversible process.

BEING CREATIVE

The prerequisites for musical creativity have already been described. To compose music that is regarded as creative and imaginative, you first need to know the sounds that are available and how they are usually used. If you have acquired an understanding of the ordinary ways sounds are used in music, then you will be prepared to consider ways that are different, unusual, extraordinary, perhaps even unprecedented.

Consider what knowledge is necessary to decide how to arrange the furniture in a room. You need to know where the windows are, the heaters, the electrical outlets, the dimensions of the walls. You also need to know something about the best place for the stereo system, the dimensions of the furniture, and the most likely location of paths to and from other rooms. Perhaps you have had the opportunity to study how other people have arranged similar rooms in the past, or perhaps you have gained a great deal of knowledge from your own previous experience with furniture arrangement. With all of this knowledge and experience, you are now prepared to do at least a competent, if uninspired, job.

Creativity begins from what is known, what is ordinary. To be creative and imaginative, you must first pause to reconsider the "usuallys," the "normallys," and especially the "almost always."

Then go on to imagine the "what ifs." "What if I extend the melody for an extra measure?" "What if I substitute this chord for that chord?" "What if we put the coffee table and the recliner chair on the ceiling, and then put the floor rug on the wall?" It is generally safe to experiment with music—apparently no one has ever been seriously hurt by this (the same can probably not be said of creative furniture arranging). Not all of the results of these explorations and experiments will necessarily be useful in the context of the piece of music you are trying to write, but there will be some discoveries that will make all the difference.

It is important to understand that being creative does not necessarily mean being totally, radically original. Creativity preys upon the familiar; it feeds upon a listener's expectations of what is normal and ordinary. Creativity can mean taking music just a bit further than it's been before, it can mean filling in a few more of the details, or it can mean transforming them. J. S. Bach, one of the most creative and imaginative composers in the history of music, did not need to invent the fugue. This was a compositional procedure he acquired from his teachers and colleagues and that he subsequently extended and enriched, to the delight of listeners for nearly two and a half centuries now.

Similarly, it was not necessary for Mozart or Beethoven to invent the sonata. If a form or style is well understood, then listeners can readily comprehend the significance of deviations or extensions. Apparently Mozart and Beethoven were quite aware of this as they proceeded to extend and transform the sonata form that was in wide use at the time. A successfully creative project is quite likely to contain a good balance of the familiar and the unfamiliar.

It should now be clear that creativity is not an "added special ingredient" or a commodity like a new suit of clothes. It is, rather, almost a way of life—of questioning, exploring, experimenting, inverting, thinking sideways some of the time rather than in a linear fashion all the time. As such, it requires a certain amount of discipline, of nurturing a mental climate conducive to creative thinking.

Many composers find it useful to work at composition at a regular time and place. This helps to minimize distractions and enables the composer to concentrate more quickly on the mental manipulations of musical ideas. Some composers work best in the morning, and others do their best work late at night—it really depends upon the rhythm of the composer's own nature.

Use some of the time you have set aside for composition to immerse yourself in the materials—listen to the sounds, play them, get a sense of their texture and character, get to know them on a first-name basis. The more familiar you are with the sounds, the easier it is to imagine them in a variety of different contexts and in different guises. The creative possibilities will begin to occur to you. For an occasional moment, now and then, it may seem that the music is writing itself.

At other times, it will seem as if the ideas are stubbornly refusing to reveal themselves to you. You have "composer's block." If you have already put many hours into this work—you have saturated your mind with information about the materials and have imagined them in innumerable contexts—and are not yet satisfied with what you have, then perhaps the best thing to do is simply walk away. Take a break of a few minutes or a few days. Even as you are attending to other business during this hiatus, the mind will continue to ruminate on the compositional problem. When a possible solution emerges, you will suddenly hear yourself say, "Ah HA! That's it! Of course! Why didn't I think of this before?" Rumination and subsequent insight are important parts of the creative process. By taking a break, you are allowing this process to take its course. Creativity is a natural process—it can be fostered, but it cannot be forced.

The foregoing discussion is applicable to musical composition in general, but there are particular ramifications and complications for the composer of electroacoustic music. Electronic musical instruments, being essentially creatures of the 20th century, are young relative to most other musical instruments, some of which have been around a thousand years or more. Being relatively young, electronic instruments are still undergoing rapid development. For example, a new generation of synthesizers, it seems, is introduced every two to three years. Furthermore, there are many different electronic devices that can be used musically—tape recorders, mixers, signal processors, as well as synthesizers—and a great variety of combinations of these devices. Finally, these musical machines can be quite powerful, producing a range of pitch, loudness, and tone colors that cannot readily be matched by older, more established instruments.

This expanded range of possibilities paradoxically makes it more difficult to establish a sense of the identity and character of an electroacoustic musical instrument. If a thorough familiarity with the capabilities of an instrument is one of the prerequisites for creative work with it, then composing for an electronic instrument can be exceedingly difficult indeed. Ten years hence, a guitar will still be a guitar, a piano will be a piano, and a singer will be a singer. But who can say with any certainty what a synthesizer will be after another decade has passed? Nonetheless, we work in the meantime with what we have, here and now, in the studio, even as we try very hard not to fall too far behind the leading edge of technological change.

The broad range of tone colors that an electronic instrument can produce is likely to include some fairly good imitations of those older, more established instruments. So it is quite possible—even commonplace, in fact—for sound synthesizers to be employed as substitutes for traditional instruments in the production of music in familiar styles. Thus, even though a composer may find it particularly challenging to acquire the requisite familiarity with electroacoustic musical instruments, once this is achieved composing for synthesizers should be no more difficult or complicated than writing for other instruments, one would think.

This is not quite the case, however. The relatively expanded capabilities of electronic instruments not only make possible a broad range of familiar, imitative sounds; they also make possible some very unusual sounds and textures, and odd hybrids of familiar sounds. These invite the composer to explore further and perhaps to push the stylistic boundaries—occasionally even beyond where the audience is prepared to go. In this respect, too, composing for electroacoustic musical instruments is on a wondrous and perilous frontier of contemporary musical activity.

THE "COMMISSION"

Within the universe of possible sounds and possible patterns of sounds, a single utterance, a specific musical composition, takes shape. In the face of an abundance of musical resources, limits become opportunities to focus and direct sounds (and patterns of sounds) so that they can be meaningful. What considerations help narrow a composer's choices from the broad range of possibility to the particular materials that are used? What are some of the factors that define the limits of a composition?

One factor is the social context. Who is the intended audience—a group of friends, a few commercial clients, young listeners to morning radio, worshippers at a religious service, an international circle of intellectuals, connoisseurs of rare and unusual music, or just yourself? Will the music be performed by amateurs or by professional musicians, perhaps even virtuosos? Will the composition be intended as music for dancing, background music for working or shopping, as accompaniment to film or video imagery, or as music to be heard for its own sake, perhaps as concert music—a purely listening experience requiring close attention? The answers to these and similar questions will go far toward defining the nature of an incipient musical work.

Based partly on considerations of social context is the determination of an appropriate musical style. People who are relatively new to composing music should work first in a style with which they are comfortable and familiar. As described earlier, traditional musical styles, such as the many forms of jazz, blues, gospel, pop, hard rock, modern classical, and so forth, are largely defined by characteristic melodic patterns, chord structures and progressions, rhythmic patterns, textures, and instrumentation.[1] These the composer can use as the basis of the composition.

---

1. For example, rock is generally characterized by the use of four-beat measures with strong accents on the second and fourth beats, called backbeats. The typical instrumentation includes electric guitars, singers, a set of drums, and probably a synthesizer or two. By contrast, the four-beat measures generally used in classic jazz are more evenly accented, and the typical instrumentation might include a saxophone, trumpet, piano, string bass, and a drum kit (similar to, but not quite the same as that used in rock).

A more experimental approach to musical style would take advantage of the extended capabilities of the electronic medium—for example, the ability to execute rapid patterns of pitch that are impossible to perform on a traditional instrument, complex patterns of rhythm that are extremely difficult for groups of performing musicians to keep together, or tones of such long durations that they are impossible to sustain on instruments that require bowing or blowing. Music that uses such sounds and patterns can often be described as "sound collage" or, as the composer Edgard Varèse called it, "organized sound." Whether the style is traditional, experimental, or some of both, a conscious awareness of the possibilities and expectations of the style will help give shape to the music.

A factor related to the choice of musical style is the selection of musical instruments. As suggested earlier, the limits and capabilities of an instrument can most certainly define the range of possible ideas and textures in a composition. For example, it may be possible to compose a brash, vitally rhythmic piece for solo snare drum, but a lyrical or melancholy piece is not likely to work so well. For an electronic composer, the choice of which instruments or techniques to use, or which to avoid, can be similarly decisive. For instance, a piece that relies on tape-manipulation techniques is likely to be quite different from one realized on an analog synthesizer or one that is based on signal-processing techniques.

The prospective duration of the piece is also a limiting factor. If the piece is going to be relatively short, on the order of three to five minutes, then there will be different expectations and challenges than would be the case with a composition of much longer duration. The latter, which might extend across two sides of a record, across an entire CD, or through an entire afternoon or evening, is likely to be articulated in smaller sections— "acts" or "movements." It is a challenge to maintain the sense that all of these musical ideas belong together—that they are to be associated in a single musical work.

Finally, what is the impetus, or "inspiration" for the piece? What is the music "about"? Is it going to be a musical depiction of a poem? A mood? A memory? A photograph? Might it be an expression of political concern? A comment on recent events, global or personal? An interpretation of yesterday's weather map? An exhortation to purchase Sniffy laundry detergent? Or perhaps the music will be self-referential. It might be "about" a good tune, a catchy rhythmic pattern, a unique chord progression, or an exploration of the possible combinations of instruments in a small ensemble.

Often when a professional composer is asked to write a piece of music, many of the musical limits are specified as part of the commission—the contract with the composer. For example, a composer might be commissioned to write a string quartet of 10 to 20 minutes' duration that will be of interest to a typical Sunday afternoon audience for classical music. For this the composer will receive some money. The terms of the commission go far toward defining the corner of the musical universe in which the composer will work in creating this piece. For example, it is not likely that the string quartet will turn out to be very, very loud, or that people will want to dance to it.

Here is a commission for you:

ÉTUDE 10.1

 ompose a three- to four-minute piece for stereo tape recorder. Using tape speed transposition, tape reversal, tape loops, overdubbing, and/or editing techniques, construct the piece from the sounds of a paragraph of text read aloud and the sounds of various drums. You will receive no money for this, but you might receive a grade. Your instructor may provide further details of this commission regarding deadlines and such.

Once the limits of your composition have been more or less defined, it is time to explore ideas that seem appropriate to the social and stylistic contexts, the instrumentation, the durational frame, and the subject matter of the piece. Perhaps you might begin by improvising on the available musical instruments and electronic musical equipment. If you plan to do a sound collage, search for rich, sustained sounds, and for shorter sounds that might serve as background sounds. If you will be doing a more traditionally structured piece of music, look for tunes that have character and profile, distinctive rhythmic patterns, and interesting chord progressions.

Record your improvisation on cassette. Then take this recording with you as you leave the studio. While away from the studio, listen to the tape a few times. Be critical. Select the ideas that seem most promising.

Return to the studio and explore ways to vary these ideas: transposition, reversal, inversion, fragmentation, extension, looping, signal processing, and so forth. Search for contrasting ideas, and explore how these too can be varied.

FORMING THE MUSIC

Now we come to the heart of the process. The materials are at hand. It is now time to fashion them into patterns and textures that have meaning. As stated previously, the meaning or significance of a sound is derived from the relationships it has to other sounds in the music, including sounds that are occurring at the same time or sounds that are heard at other times in the composition.

Our brains are disposed—by instinct, habit, or training—to attempt to prioritize events that are perceived to be concurrent. There are things around us to which we pay little attention, some to which we give some attention, and some to which we provide close attention. At any particular

Allegro

Melody: the "foreground"

Accompaniment: the "background"

moment, we may be surrounded by the din of conversations, the whine of equipment fans and motors, rumblings of traffic outside, the humming of fluorescent lights, and such. We don't seem to pay much attention to all of this. We do, however, notice when someone new enters the room, or when cars collide outdoors, or when the walls of the building begin to creak and crack! Were we not able to organize in this way the events around us that we perceive, our brains would quickly become saturated by the flood of sights, sounds, aromas, and other sensations being detected by our eyes, ears, nose, and skin during every moment we are awake. Our survival depends on our ability to make distinctions of relative significance among the events in our surroundings.

Visual artists, particularly painters and photographers, are keenly aware of this phenomenon of perceptual stratification, and take some care to organize the most compelling elements of their work, the **foreground,** against a **background** of elements that are less vivid. Similarly, the concurrent elements of a passage of music, or the **texture** of the music, may be organized into foreground and background elements. A common example of this differentiation is the division of labor between melody and accompaniment. The accompaniment provides a background layer against which the melody can work its magic—as in the opening passage of a famous piano sonata shown in Figure 10.4. Significantly, the expression "melody and accompaniment" is never heard in the reverse order—"accompaniment and melody," or "accompaniment with melody."

What are the characteristics of a musical background? It is a layer of the texture that tends to be softer in intensity. It usually draws most of its pitches from the mid to low ranges. The most important trait, perhaps, is a considerable degree of rhythmic uniformity. For example, the accompaniment layer in Figure 10.4 consists entirely of notes of the same duration (eighth notes).

Conversely, a foreground tends to be louder. Its pitches usually come from the mid to high ranges, and literally ride atop the texture so that they can be more readily noticed. The melodic patterns are better organized (more "tuneful"). There is a much greater variety of rhythm (as illustrated by the melody in Figure 10.4). There may also be further details that draw attention, such as vibrato, ornamentation, or timbre changes.

FIGURE 10.4

Mozart, Piano Sonata in C Major, K. 545, first movement, measures 1–4.

a. A famous portrait

b. A detail

FIGURE 10.5
The significance of a detail has much to do with where it is placed, particularly when there is a clear differentiation of foreground and background.

c. Detail added to the background

d. Detail added to the foreground

The relative significance of details in the foreground and background of a painting is illustrated in Figure 10.5. Similarly, in music the foreground bears the richest, most interesting sounds and patterns, and carries most of the dramatic action. The background provides support through less intrinsically interesting sounds (such as a drum track, a series of chords, or a cloud of twinkling sounds); these serve to fill the musical space without drawing undue attention to themselves. In general, the foreground is much more active, changing constantly, while the background tends to change much more slowly and rather more reluctantly. Such is the hierarchy of musical texture.

The stratification of texture is quite clear in a typical contemporary pop song. The background is created by the drums and bass guitar, with their steady beats and lower pitches. A middle ground is provided by the strummed chords of the rhythm guitar, the rolled or struck chords on a keyboard instrument, and/or the subdued, sustained vowels of backup singers. The foreground material is usually delivered by the lead singer, whose melodic patterns are more active and rhythmically free, occasionally even contradicting the rhythmic patterns established by the background and middle-ground parts. The highest pitches in the texture are likely to be those of the lead singer, who is also most likely to be the loudest element in the mix. Most important, the lead singer conveys the text of the lyrics (not just simple vowels, as the backup singers are doing). The text itself presents a level of meaning that further draws the attention of the listener. Occasionally, perhaps as a break for the lead singer, the foreground is taken by a lead guitar or synthesizer for an instrumental solo (sometimes just called the instrumental). Meanwhile the drums and bass guitar keep providing a steady background.[2]

A rather different set of textural relationships is illustrated in Figure 10.6, the opening passage of a Bach fugue. This is described as a contrapuntal texture, the idea of counterpoint being that two, three, or more melodies compete for the foreground at the same time. The beginning of the Bach piece also illustrates a valuable technique called textural **layering.** By introducing the elements of the texture individually, in succession, the meaning of each layer is made clearer. An application of this technique to a pop song is observed when a song begins with a few bars of the bass line alone, followed by the addition of the drums, softly at first. Then the chords of the middle ground are added, and finally the texture is made complete by the entrance of the lead singer.

ÉTUDE 10.2

*U*sing a four-track recorder, assemble a layered texture of sounds. Begin with a few seconds or bars of a background sound—for example, the sound of ocean waves, a bass line, or a drum pattern. Then add another sound on another track— bird sounds, chord patterns, or the like. Then add a foreground pattern on the third track—the recitation of a poem, or the singing or playing of a melody. Use the fourth track if you think that the texture could use another element, but don't feel obligated to use the track just because it is there. Finally, mix this recording down to stereo, taking care to balance the foreground, middle-ground, and background ideas.

---

2. An exception that proves the rule can be found at the ends of musical phrases (a musical phrase is a passage that roughly corresponds to the duration of a part of a melody that can be sung or played in a single breath). Here, typically, the foreground and middle-ground elements are briefly less active. At such times, the drummer is likely to play a fill pattern, a quick cluster of sounds from the drums, thus taking advantage of a momentary opportunity for glory.

FIGURE 10.6

J. S. Bach, Fugue in C Minor, measures 1–9, from Book I of the Well-Tempered Clavier. The principal melodic idea, called the subject of the fugue, is first introduced alone by one of the voices of the texture. As this voice continues, a second voice enters and presents the subject, thus usurping the role of the first voice as foreground. The rhythm of the first voice becomes much more regular at this point. The second voice, after stating the subject, is then in turn displaced from the foreground as a third voice begins to sound the principal theme. Here the second voice takes on a more uniform rhythmic character, while the first voice becomes even less active. For the remainder of the piece, the three voices continue to exchange textural roles.

GUIDE FOR LISTENING

THE *POÈME ÉLECTRONIQUE* OF EDGARD VARÈSE

One of the boldest pioneers on the frontiers of music in the 20th century was the French-born composer Edgard Varèse (1883–1965). His *Poème électronique* is widely regarded as one of the first masterpieces of electroacoustic music.

Because his father had hoped that Varèse would become an engineer, much of his early schooling was in mathematics and science. When the time came to pursue professional training, however, Varèse enrolled at the Schola Cantorum, a music school. Nonetheless, he maintained a lifelong interest in scientific and mathematical subjects. Perhaps as a consequence of this, his conception of musical composition was a highly original one. Rather than imagining structures of melodies and harmonies as such, he conceived of music more in geometric, sculptural terms. Blocks of sounds could be treated as objects, to be turned, reshaped, and projected through space—something of a "plate tectonic" theory of music. In fact, Varèse preferred not to call his works "music," but rather "organized sound."

Varèse recognized that conventional musical instruments might not be particularly well suited to the realization of such ideas. As early as 1916 (having moved to America the preceding year), he was quoted in a New York newspaper article as expressing a need for new instruments. In a lecture given in 1936, he declared:

> When new instruments will allow me to write music as I conceive it, the movement of sound-masses, of shifting planes, will be clearly perceived in my work, taking the place of the linear counterpoint. When these sound-masses collide, the phenomena of penetration or repulsion will seem to occur. Certain transmutations taking place on certain planes will seem to be projected onto other planes, moving at different speeds and at different angles. There will no longer be the old conception of melody or interplay of melodies. The entire work will be a melodic totality. The entire work will flow as a river flows.[a]

In another lecture, three years later, he elaborated further on his hope for a new musical technology:

> Personally, for my conceptions, I need an entirely new medium of expression: a sound-*producing* machine (not a sound-*reproducing* one). Today it is possible to build such a machine with only a certain amount of added research. . . .
>
> And here are the advantages I anticipate from such a machine: liberation from the arbitrary, paralyzing tempered system; the possibility of obtaining any number of cycles or, if still desired, subdivisions of the octave, and consequently the formation of any desired scale; unsuspected range in low and high registers; new harmonic splendors obtainable from the use of sub-harmonic combinations now impossible; the possibility of obtaining any differentiation of timbre, or sound-combinations; new dynamics far beyond the present human-powered orchestra; a sense of sound-projection in space by means of the emission of sound in any part or in many parts of the hall, as may be required by the score; cross-rhythms unrelated to each other, treated simultaneously, or, to use the old word, "contrapuntally," since the machine would be able to beat any number of desired notes, any subdivision of them, omission or fraction of them—all these in a given unit of measure or time that is humanly impossible to obtain.[b]

During his first few decades in the United States, Varèse dedicated enormous energies to the task of finding the resources needed to bring such instruments into existence. He contacted

---

[a]Edgard Varèse, "New Instruments and New Music," in *Contemporary Composers on Contemporary Music,* eds. Elliott Schwartz and Barney Childs (New York: Da Capo Press, 1978), p. 197.

[b]Edgard Varèse, "Music as an Art-Science," ibid., pp. 200–201.

film studios, communications companies with extensive research laboratories, philanthropic foundations, and a variety of other possible sources of support, but was not very successful in attracting sufficient interest. Perhaps out of frustration, he essentially stopped composing during the 1930s and 1940s. Clearly, he was ahead of his time.

In 1953, he received a gift of a tape recorder for his New York studio, and he immediately began to experiment with recording and transforming the sounds of sawmills, foundries, and similar sources. In 1954, he was invited by Pierre Schaeffer to work in the Paris studio. There, continuing his work with tape recordings, he produced a piece entitled *Déserts* for orchestra and taped sounds. This led to his being invited to collaborate with the architect Le Corbusier, who had been commissioned by Philips, the Dutch electronics firm, to create the company's pavilion for the 1958 World's Fair in Brussels. It was through that collaboration that the *Poème électronique* was composed.

The Philips pavilion was truly a multimedia work of art. The building itself was a startlingly modern structure, perhaps best described as a mutant circus tent with three steeples. The interior of the building has been described as resembling the walls of a cow's stomach. On these walls were projected moving colored lights and a variety of images selected by Le Corbusier, including fragments of text. The contribution of Varèse to this project, his "organized sound," was recorded on a three-channel tape in a studio in the Netherlands that had been established and fully equipped by the Philips company for the purpose. In the pavilion, this eight-minute tape was played through an impressive system of 425 loudspeakers distributed throughout the space and powered by 20 amplifier systems. This sound system made it possible to project the sounds of the piece in trajectories and other patterns among the array of loudspeakers. As Varèse said later, "For the first time I heard my music literally projected into space."[c] During the six-month duration of the fair, thousands of people each day experienced the "electronic poem."

The pavilion is now long gone, unfortunately, but recordings of Varèse's piece of the project are available (on two LP recordings from Columbia, MG 31078 and MS 6146, and a recently issued CD recording, Neuma 450-74).[d] Even when removed from its native, multimedia habitat and heard in a stereo reduction (for two loudspeakers rather that 425!), it remains a hauntingly powerful piece.

In realizing the composition, Varèse used sounds that were generated electronically as well as those produced acoustically, including the sounds of bells, drums, and other percussion instruments, a pipe organ, a singing voice, sirens (a signature of many pieces by Varèse, such as his *Ionisation* for percussion ensemble), and a jet airplane. The texture tends to be rather sparse, and only occasionally thickens with a burst of active sounds. Rather than articulating long, phrase-like structures, the piece consists largely of fragmentary, brief snatches of sounds—successions of groups of sounds that Varèse referred to as "sound-masses." These sometimes overlap, but more often are juxtaposed as startling contrasts.

---

[c]Edgard Varèse, "Spatial Music," ibid., p. 207.

[d]The CD recording is recommended, not only because it restores some of the dynamic range that had to be compressed for the LP issues, but also because, for some reason, the Columbia recordings were heavily processed by artificial reverberation, which noticeably colors the sounds and obscures many of the significant spatial relationships in the piece. Listening to the CD, by comparison, is like seeing a great painting that has been restored and has had numerous layers of shellac removed from its surface.

What makes this composition distinctively the work of Varèse, however, is its rhythmic vitality. Within groups of sounds there is a clarity of rhythm arising from well-defined patterns of accents, as can be heard, for example, in the "wood-block" motive that occurs at 6:20 (and in several instances before and after this). Each group of sounds has an unmistakable character.

At a broader level, there is a sense that the rhythmic proportions among the different groups of sound, and the timing of their appearances, have been carefully considered as well. Particularly noteworthy in this regard is Varèse's use of silence, as with the long, dramatic pause that begins around 5:35.

The overall impression of the piece is that it is a work conceived for a superset of percussion instruments. For example, in a passage that begins at 5:57, recordings of a percussion ensemble (perhaps taken by Varèse from a recording of an earlier work) are treated as objects, faded in and out. They appear as brief splashes of sound, as if the recordings themselves were percussive objects. The recorded sounds of a pipe organ are similarly treated in a passage that begins near the end of the piece, at 7:08. Listeners who are familiar with other compositions by Varèse will realize that this is not so different from these other works; the style of Varèse is readily apparent in any medium for which he has chosen to write.

The importance of the spatial placement of sounds in this work has already been noted. Clearly this was an aspect of the composition that received much conscious attention from the composer. The panning of sounds from one speaker to the other is frequently evident on the Neuma CD recording, and this provides at least a hint of the spatial richness of the presentations in the Philips pavilion. Elsewhere in the piece, there are occasions where gestures are divided spatially, as in the passage beginning at 3:24, where the antecedent of the gesture occurs in one speaker and the consequent in the other.

Some groups of sounds are treated as motives and recur in the piece. The gong-like bell sounds at the beginning, for example, recur at 2:33. Of more significance is the three-note motive of rising semitones that first appears at 0:55 and is immediately repeated twice. The listener will notice that each time it recurs, Varèse has added a bit more reverberation, giving the illusion that the sound is receding in space.[e] Somewhat later, at 1:33, the motive is again stated, this time with even more reverberation. This particular statement of the motive is perhaps anticipated quite subtly by the "mocking" motive that appears at 1:29 and serves as the basis of the longer passage that begins subsequently at 1:45. The original three-note motive returns for two more occurrences, beginning at 7:25. Significantly, there is much less reverberation the final time. Similar examples of developments of other motives can also be recognized throughout the piece. At a basic level, such patterns lend a considerable degree of cohesion to the work.

The use of vocal sounds in the composition, first appearing at 3:37, is particularly startling and quite significant. Varèse is able to objectify successfully even such sounds of human origin. He creates the illusion of freely manipulating the location of these objects in space by introducing radical shifts in the amount of reverberation. Another example of this objectification of human sounds can be found in the vocal passage that commences at 4:13 with a loud, strident sound and is then accompanied by a textural layer of patterns originally performed on

---

[e]This effect is, unfortunately, scarcely noticeable on the LP recordings because of the cloud of artifical reverberation that has been superimposed, as noted in the previous footnote.

percussion instruments. At 4:38 this passage, again introduced by a clang, appears to be repeated. This time, however, the recorded voice is transposed down in pitch to a growl, and the percussive sounds are sparser (many of them also sound as if they have been reversed). To underscore the significance of this passage, it is followed by a long, dramatic pause.

The outline of the work provided here offers just a glimpse of the richness of detail in the piece. For further study, the listener may want to entertain the following questions:

- What two techniques of tape manipulation are most evident in the passage that begins at 1:45?
- Is there any significant difference in this composition between the way Varèse handles sounds of electronic origin and those originally sounded by acoustic instruments?
- Would this piece be substantially different if Varèse had been able to work with digital synthesis equipment (perhaps even a few samplers and a MIDI sequencer)?

UNITY AND VARIETY

Just as meaningful relationships can be established among concurrent sounds and patterns of sound—what musicians refer to as vertical relationships—so can there be meaningful relationships between sounds that are consecutive, or among sounds that are further separated in time. These relationships, described as horizontal ones, are particularly important because music is indeed an art whose principal dimension is time.

One of the most basic relationships that can be established among successive sounds is one of continuity. A steady beat, the ascent or descent of a series of pitches, even the relative constancy of tone color among successive sounds played by the same instrument—these are a few of the ways by which a sense of musical continuity is established.

At a more general level of the musical structure, the repetition of patterns is a powerful way to establish continuity. A short, distinctive pattern of pitch and rhythm, called a **motive,** can appear frequently in a musical passage, or throughout a work, as a means of unifying the music. For example, the four-note motive that begins Beethoven's Fifth Symphony pervades the first movement of the work, appearing in a number of slightly different forms but generally maintaining its characteristic rhythmic and melodic pattern (see Figure 10.7). Occurrences of the motive can even be traced in the third movement.

Without doubt, continuity can be a good thing in music, particularly in background layers of the texture, but there can also be too much of a good thing. As music proceeds through time, it seems to require change. Unless contrasting sounds and patterns are introduced to hold the listener's attention, the music will slip away into the background. Note that the motive identified in Figure 10.7 rarely recurs in exactly the same form. While the basic structure of the motive is retained as a unifying element, the details are varied to provide some degree of contrast. Another example of this

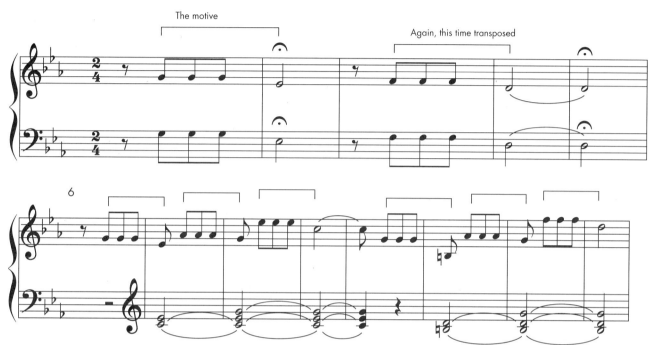

a. The principal motive of the first movement

b. The principal motive busily at work at the beginning of the first movement

c. The motive, hidden somewhat, in the third movement (measures 71–78)

FIGURE 10.7
A musical motive can do much to unify a composition, as shown in these examples from Beethoven's Symphony no. 5 in C Minor.

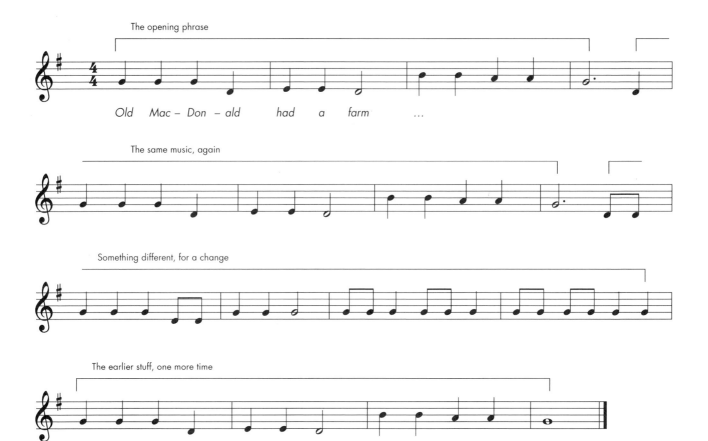

The opening phrase

Old Mac – Don – ald   had   a   farm   ...

The same music, again

Something different, for a change

The earlier stuff, one more time

FIGURE 10.8
The phrase structure of a familiar tune.

principle is the third phrase of the tune in Figure 10.8. Here the necessary contrast is introduced at just the right time to keep the tune alive.

A major task for a composer is to find and maintain a proper balance between elements of unity and variety, of continuity and contrast. Continuity in music, in fact, carries with it the expectation of change. A rich, busy timbre or texture may be capable of sustaining attention for quite a long time, but even with such rich sounds the composer must eventually do something before the attention of the listener drifts away. The challenge is to find the right moment for the right amount of change.

ÉTUDE 10.3

*U*sing a procedure similar to that described for Étude 10.2, assemble another layered texture of sounds. This texture should be in sharp contrast to that of Étude 10.2, however. The emotional, expressive, musical effect of this texture should be opposite to that of the earlier étude.

DIRECTION IN MUSIC

Many musical patterns develop more explicit expectations of change. These can provide a sense of direction to the music—more specifically, a direction of the listener's attention toward some future event in the music. For example, a dissonant combination of pitches is expected to resolve to a consonance. Certain chords can be expected to follow certain other chords—an E-major chord, for instance, is the usual consequent of a B^7 chord.

A rhythmically weak sound, an "upbeat," almost inevitably leads to a rhythmically strong sound, a "downbeat." The rhythmic ambiguity of the upbeat instills in the listener a desire for the closure and stability—the rhythmic completion—of the downbeat (see Figure 10.9).

A gradual increase or decrease in loudness (called a crescendo or diminuendo, respectively) can also create an expectation of change. The listener is aware that there is a limit to how loud or how soft the sound can get. Furthermore, the change in loudness itself becomes predictable and continuous. There is an element of suspense to the situation: When will this pattern of change in loudness cease? What exactly will be the nature of the change when it does occur? Informed and continuous speculation of this sort is what makes for an active listener—one who is a participant in the artistic experience.

A melody that gradually works its way to ever higher pitches can function in a similar way. Again, the listener is aware that there is a limit to how high the melody can go. As the instrument works closer to its upper limit, the pitches become increasingly difficult to produce with clarity and stability (imagine a singer at the high end of his or her range, or a violinist playing high on the string, near the end of the fingerboard). There is a certain amount of tension building in such a situation. Change must come; release is unavoidable. But when will the change occur, and what will it be? This instant of change can be a moment of dramatic importance. Often a composer will use such a moment, called a "structural downbeat" by the music theorist Edward Cone, as an opportunity to make a smooth transition to a highly contrasting texture, thus linking very different musical ideas.

Other techniques for creating musical expectations can involve gradual accelerations or decelerations of tempo, or changes in timbre, such as a slow brightening of the tone color. Perceptible changes in the speed of trills, or the rate or depth of vibrato, can also be used in this way. These techniques are particularly accessible on many electronic instruments,

FIGURE 10.9
Some familiar upbeat/down-beat patterns.

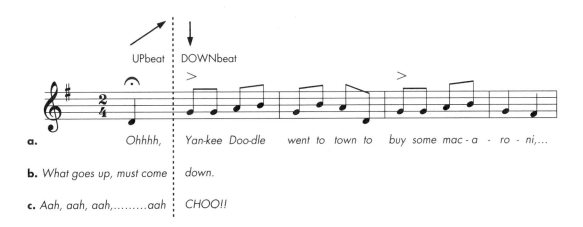

a. Ohhhh, | Yan-kee Doo-dle | went to town to | buy some mac - a - ro - ni,...

b. *What goes up, must come* | *down.*

c. *Aah, aah, aah,.........aah* | *CHOO!!*

particularly synthesizers. The composer's objective is to regulate changes such as these so that an appropriate sense of musical direction can be established and maintained. The important thing is not to allow the music to stop dead. While writing a piece of music, it may not be such a bad thing to pause now and then to ask, "Where is this passage going?"

The composition of much music is governed by alternating states: patterns of sounds that create expectations, followed by sounds that fulfill these expectations; elements of unity and elements of variety; continuity and contrast; passages of musical tension and moments of release; antecedents and consequents; upbeats looking for downbeats. This is how much music moves through time (two alternative approaches to the structuring of music are described later in this chapter). While a novice composer might be intimidated by some of the more abstruse aspects of this conceptual scheme, it may be helpful to consider that music in this sense is very much a mirror of the cause and effect, action and reaction, war and peace of everyday life.

ÉTUDE 10.4

*R*ecord a brief passage of sounds that collectively create a larger gesture, a sense of expectation and direction. For example, record a group of sounds that become louder and faster, or a melody that rises higher and higher in pitch. Conclude this brief passage with a sound that signifies the moment of arrival, the fulfillment of the musical expectation—a structural downbeat.

SIMPLE BUT EFFECTIVE MUSICAL FORMS

*S*ome pieces of music are organized into distinct sections that are articulated by clear contrasts of texture, instrumentation, rhythm, melody, harmony, or (most likely) some combination of these. You may find it useful to imagine the structure of your composition in one of the tried-and-true forms that are based on this principle.

A common sectional form is ternary form, also known as ABA form. The first, or A, section presents the best-defined, and perhaps most memorable, ideas of the piece. This is followed by a sharply contrasting middle, or B, section. Perhaps here there is a new tune, or the tempo is much slower, the music is softer, or is in a different key. The effect of this contrast is to inject new energy into the music. Then, after this middle section works itself out, the opening section is restated, thus rounding out the music and providing an effective sense of closure. Often this concluding A section will incorporate slight differences or variations with respect to the opening A section. Pieces in ternary form can be very short (such as "Twinkle, Twinkle Little Star") or quite long in duration (as in entire movements of symphonies).

Common song form, or AABA form, is related to ternary form. Here the B section is often identified as a "bridge." Familiar examples of music in this form include George Gershwin's

"I've Got Rhythm," "Old MacDonald Had a Farm," and the "Ode to Joy" theme of the final movement of Beethoven's Ninth Symphony.

Another useful sectional form is the theme-and-variations form. Here an idea is first presented in its simple, original form. Then it is repeated with one or two techniques of variation applied to it (for example, embellishment of the melody, or harmonization with a different set of chords). Then it is repeated again, this time varied in a different way (change of mode from major to minor, change of instrumentation, or change of textural structure). A series of four or five or more variations can be created in this way, with each variation usually separated from the others by a brief pause. The music is unified by the repetition of the same underlying musical idea, but is periodically refreshed by the contrasts introduced as new techniques of variation are applied.

The form of some pieces of music is less clearly sectional; the music seems to flow more continuously from one passage to the next. This might be described as a narrative form, in which the piece is the "story" of what happens to a main idea, or group of ideas. The first movement of a classical sonata can be described as a narrative, as can a fugue. The subject of the fugue, which functions as its principal theme or "main character," reappears in a number of situations throughout the piece (sometimes in the top voice, sometimes in the bottom, and sometimes in the middle) and in a number of guises (transposed, stretched, overlapped, inverted) before perhaps being stated once again in more stable form at the end. It is a "tune on the run"—metaphorically, a "fugitive." The narrative technique is also often successfully applied to the structuring of a sound collage.

ÉTUDE 10.5

Compose a theme and variations, using a familiar song as the theme. (Please note, if the song is protected by copyright, you will need to get written permission from the owner of the copyright to use the music. A reference librarian can help you determine if a particular song is protected by copyright or is in the public domain.) For each variation, use a particular technique of tape manipulation (splicing, speed transposition, reversal, overdubbing, signal processing, looping, and so on).

A FEW HINTS, SUGGESTIONS, AND OTHER MEDDLESOME BITS OF ADVICE . . .

As you begin to write a piece of music, perhaps you can imagine clearly a specific passage—the beginning, the ending, or something from in between. Next try to imagine a passage that could lead into this one, or a passage that might appropriately follow. Eventually the structure of the entire piece may coalesce around the passage that you were initially able to imagine in some detail. Alternatively, you may be able to build the piece around a well-defined texture, rhythmic pattern, melody, or chord progression you have discovered. Then find other patterns that work well, as variants of or contrasts to the one you have.

Be particularly thoughtful about how the piece begins. Does it begin softly, or with the fury of full forces? Will there be an introduction? The opening passages of the music are where the most important ideas are likely first exposed (in a traditional sonata form and in a fugue, the beginning section is in fact called the exposition). The beginning will establish the stylistic context of the piece for the listener, who will most likely form important judgments during these early moments about the quality of the music as well. First impressions do indeed matter.

How does the piece end—with a fade (implying perhaps, as the Beatles did with the ending of *Hey Jude,* that the music somehow will continue into eternity)? Or does it end with a crash and grand cadence? Will there be a coda—a brief passage at the very end that functions as something of a postscript? What is the outcome? Whatever the outcome, the piece must finish, not simply stop. For the sake of the listener, there needs to be some sense of conclusion, of closure, a release of the listener's attention. A considerate composer will give much thought to how this will be accomplished.

If the music has a text, as with a song, then find the melody and rhythm that are latent in the words themselves as you read them aloud—the rise and fall of inflection, the rhythm of accented and unaccented syllables. Use the text as a springboard for melodic and rhythmic ideas. In fact, if patterns of pitch and rhythm run counter to the natural patterns of the text, there is the danger that the music will be awkward or even unperformable. Careful study and acquaintance with the text is absolutely essential if literary and musical expressions are to be successfully merged into a single work.

As you compose, try at some point to develop a mental image of the entire piece so that you have a sense of how the sections balance, whether continuity is maintained, and whether there are sufficient contrasts. It may be helpful to draw a sketch of the piece. If you have had previous musical training, and particularly if you are doing a more traditional sort of piece, you might use conventional musical notation to outline the themes and chord changes. If you are doing a more experimental piece, it may be more appropriate to represent the elements of the music in a more graphic way, using pictograms, hieroglyphics, or other sorts of visual depictions (see Figure 10.10). Unless the music is intended to be performed or otherwise realized by another musician, the choice of symbols can be somewhat arbitrary, so long as *you* can remember the sounds that the symbols represent.

After you have drawn a rough sketch of the piece, begin to create a more detailed score, showing the relative pitches of sounds, the timing, the relative loudness, the choice of instruments or timbres, and the spatial placement of the sounds. As you begin to consider the details of the work, avoid the temptation to include too much. Do not place an undue burden on yourself or your listener by "overwriting" the music, overloading it with unnecessary details. Economize! Be ruthless! Throw away a few ideas now and then (or, if you're particularly fond of them, save them for another piece). A piece has greater continuity and cohesion—is more unified—the

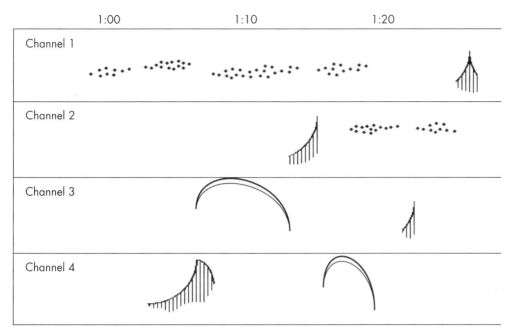

FIGURE 10.10
A graphic sketch of a passage of electroacoustic music.

more it can be focused on the varied musical exploits of a restricted number of ideas. Keep it simple and stupendous.

Use your detailed score to plan and prepare what you will be doing during your time in the studio. Think about what equipment will be needed to realize a particular passage: which tape decks will be used, what will be patched into what at the patch bay, how the mixer will be set up, which effects devices will be used, and so forth.

Be prepared at any time, however, for what the composer Daria Semegen has called a "happy coincidence." Some of the most interesting sounds in electroacoustic music are discovered as the composer is looking for other sounds, or while setting up a patch of equipment to do part of a piece. Be flexible enough to incorporate these new discoveries into the piece if they are appropriate and work well. Fresh ideas are usually good ones.

Do everything technically possible to achieve the highest-quality final recording. Record several takes of the source material, and carefully select the best. Splice out any clicks caused by tape machines starting and stopping. Keep tape hiss at a minimum. Splice out most of the blank tape at the beginning and at the end. Label the box clearly. Try to present your work in as professional a way as possible.

But most important of all, have fun!

ADVANCED TOPICS IN COMPOSITION

Creative minds, being restless as they are, eventually turn to the exploration of the frontiers of musical thought. This is generally motivated not so much by a desire to be perpetually novel, but rather often by simple curiosity. This section of the chapter examines a few of the more esoteric ways that have been considered as approaches to the composition of electroacoustic music.

CREATING MUSICAL PATTERNS OF TONE COLORS

As previous chapters have made clear, the synthesizer provides an impressive degree of control over the details of a sound, particularly its timbre. More than anything else, perhaps, a synthesizer can be regarded as a "timbre machine." In fact, in the early years of the sound synthesizer much was made, in magazine articles and advertisements, of the "infinite possibilities" of electronic music in this respect.[3]

To the extent that there are innumerable, infinitesimally different combinations of the settings of the dials, switches, and other controls on a synthesizer, then perhaps it is literally true that a synthesizer can produce a range of timbres that is infinite (just as there are, in theory, an infinite number of points on the short, horizontal line that crosses this letter *t*). In practice, however, the range of timbres available from a given synthesizer is limited to those permitted by the particular synthesis technique that is implemented on that synthesizer. For example, sounds that are produced by additive synthesis are likely to be extremely difficult, if not impossible, to replicate precisely by the techniques of FM synthesis (and vice versa). The range of timbres from a given synthesizer is likely to be further limited by the synthesist's understanding of the particular technique of synthesis involved and familiarity with the appropriate controls on the synthesizer. Or, put another way, the better a machine is understood, the greater the range of sounds that can be coaxed from it.

Even more significant limitations arise from the nature of timbre itself. As described in Chapter 7, timbre is a secondary parameter of a sound—a multidimensional composite of frequencies and noises of varying amplitudes. As a complex perceptual object, a timbre can be somewhat unstable. For instance, a group of simultaneous frequencies might be heard as a timbre, but there are also circumstances in which they might be heard as a chord instead. Research by John Chowning suggests that components fuse into a timbre when they share a common history—similar changes in frequency and amplitude (in particular, when they share such "global" characteristics as vibrato).[4] Stephen McAdams has reported that if the entrances of partial frequencies in a sound are offset from one another by 30 milliseconds or more, then the frequencies are much less likely to fuse into a tim-

---

3. Much has been made as well (although not nearly so much as with timbre) of the greatly increased accessibility to alternate systems of tuning made possible by many synthesizers.

4. John Chowning, "Computer Synthesis of the Singing Voice," in *Sound Generation in Winds, Strings, and Computers*, ed. Johan Sundberg (Stockholm: Royal Swedish Academy of Music, 1980), pp. 10–11.

bre and are more likely to be heard as a chord.[5] An awareness of these and related psychoacoustical principles is absolutely necessary for anyone who aspires to synthesize new, as yet unheard tone colors.

The complexity of a timbre as a perceptual object also means it is unlikely that, when heard for the first time, it will be accepted as a wholly new tone color. Rather, the listener will try to assimilate it, to relate it to timbres that are already known. A new timbre is very likely to be categorized as a variant of a similar, more familiar timbre, or as a hybrid of two or more such families of timbres. It is very common, for example, to find synthesizer patches with such names as "guitar-harp," "tromboon," or "drumbells."

For a variety of reasons, therefore, the range of possible timbres that can be produced by a synthesizer is a finite one. Still, the range is enormous, and requires that some thought be given to how such extensive timbral resources are to be applied.

One of the traditional uses of timbre in the design of a musical structure (that is, the composition of a piece of music) has been to contribute to the differentiation among the elements in a texture. Different textural roles are often assigned to different instruments—the melody to the flute, the chordal accompaniment to the piano, the bass line to the bassoon, for example. Competing melodies in a contrapuntal texture are more easily followed by the listener if each is carried by a distinct and contrasting instrument—trumpet and alto saxophone, for instance. The continuity of timbre provided by each instrument is what guides the listener through each melody.[6]

Another traditional use of timbre is to assist in the articulation of the segments of a musical form. For example, one of the characteristics that distinguishes the trio section from the minuet in a classical minuet-and-trio form is the greater prominence often given to the woodwind instruments in the trio section. Timbre is also used to articulate phrase structure. A melody stated by a violin in one phrase might be restated in the next phrase by a flute, for instance. In the 20th century, the use of timbral contrasts has been an important means of articulating the motive structure of a piece, with successive groups of tones being assigned to different instruments. The textural result is something of a kaleidoscope of tone colors (as illustrated by much of the music of Anton Webern).[7]

Timbre is also a significant source of nuance. Subtle inflections of tone color are often applied to the longer tones in a melody, at the high points of a melody, at the ends of phrases, or in the fill patterns between phrases.

5. Stephen McAdams, "Spectral Fusion and the Creation of Auditory Images," in *Music, Mind and Brain: The Neuropsychology of Music*, ed. Manfred Clynes (New York: Plenum Press, 1982), pp. 288–289.

6. Robert Erickson, *Sound Structure in Music* (Berkeley: University of California Press, 1975).

7. See Erickson, pp. 111–121.

Such nuances are not of particular structural significance; rather, they are surface details—embellishments and ornaments at the foreground of the music.

Tone color can also be a significant bearer of information regarding the loudness of a sound and the distance to its source. The association between dynamics and timbre has been described earlier in this text: louder sounds tend to have brighter timbres than those of softer sounds produced by the same instrument. The relative distance of the source of a sound can be judged by relating the brightness of the timbre of the sound to its apparent loudness, particularly if the listener has had previous experience with sounds produced by that source. For example, a gong struck vigorously may not seem very loud to a listener who is a half-mile away, but the timbral cues in the sound can be unmistakable indications of the violence that produced the sound.

A more radical role for timbre in a musical composition was foreseen by the composer Arnold Schoenberg, who wrote the following in 1911:

> The distinction between tone color and pitch, as it is usually expressed, I cannot accept without reservations. I think the tone becomes perceptible by virtue of tone color, of which one dimension is pitch. Tone color is, thus, the main topic, pitch a subdivision. Pitch is nothing else but tone color measured in one direction. Now, if it is possible to create patterns out of tone colors that are differentiated according to pitch, patterns we call "melodies," progressions, whose coherence evokes an effect analogous to thought processes, then it must also be possible to make such progressions out of the tone colors of the other dimension, out of that which we call simply "tone color," progressions whose relations with one another work with a kind of logic entirely equivalent to that logic which satisfies us in the melody of pitches. That has the appearance of a futuristic fantasy and is probably just that. But it is one which, I firmly believe, will be realized. I firmly believe it is capable of heightening in an unprecedented manner the sensory, intellectual, and spiritual pleasures offered by art. I firmly believe that it will bring us closer to the illusory stuff of our dreams.[8]

Klangfarbenmelodie—melodies of tone colors! An exciting possibility, but not without its difficulties. As the composer Robert Erickson has noted, in his pathbreaking book *Sound Structure in Music:*

> The analogy between klangfarbenmelodie and melody cannot extend very far. We have no intervals of timbre which correspond to pitch intervals. Pitches come in systems in Western music, and this is reflected in our scales and tuning systems. Intervals are carved out of the pitch continuum, stabilized by use and tradition, and they are transposable. These intervals and their relationships, a small selection from the infinity of those available in the continuum, provide the basic contrasts necessary for melodic construction and organization.[9]

Although a formal theory of tone color melody has yet to evolve, a few observations and speculations might be made. First, perhaps because we have learned as listeners to expect significant information to be found in

---

8. Arnold Schoenberg, *Harmonielehre*, trans. Roy E. Carter (Berkeley: University of California Press, 1978), pp. 421–422.

9. Erickson, op. cit., pp. 106–107.

pitch patterns—melodies and harmonies—it is difficult for us to attend to timbral patterns unless pitch activity is greatly subdued. Timbre melodies are most likely to flourish, therefore, among repeated pitches or within sustained tones, such as drones.

As with other musical structures, the formal design of a timbre melody is governed by considerations of contrasts and continuities. However, because of the complexity of timbre, these continuities and contrasts can operate through a multitude of dimensions. For example, the attack characteristics in a series of sounds may be held constant as the pattern of spectral contrasts unfolds. Conversely, the spectral content may be maintained through a series of sounds as the attack pattern shifts from an abrupt, percussive one to a smooth, gradual, woodwind-like attack.

A short pattern of timbres may be established as a motive, and then developed. For example, the timbral motive formed by the sequence of vowels in the word *why* ("oo-AH-ee") can be developed through truncation ("oo-AH"), extension ("oo-AH-ee-AH-ee"), as well as by several other means. This particular timbral motive, in fact, is used quite extensively by the composer Luciano Berio in the opening section of his 1966 composition for solo trombone, *Sequenza V.*

Timbre changes within a single tone are often called timbre modulations. Tones of very extended duration permit involved, even intricate, patterns of timbre change to develop. However, unlike the timbral nuances of more conventional melodies, these timbre patterns are essential and substantial material, perhaps even the heart of the music.

The concept of channeling, or streaming, is a notion of some importance in the organization of certain patterns of timbre. A channel, or stream, develops when some elements in a pattern present the illusion that they are a distinct and fairly continuous series of events that seem to emerge from a distinct source. For example, the pattern of pitches given in Figure 10.11 will organize into two apparently separate streams if the tempo is fast enough. If each succeeding pitch B in this example is sounded with a different timbre, then this upper stream can become, in effect, a tone color

FIGURE 10.11
If the tempo is fast enough, the notes of the melody shown at the top can segregate into two apparently distinct melodic patterns. These illusory "channels" or "streams" can be made even more distinct through sufficient contrasts of dynamics or timbre—for example, by accenting all of the B notes or by assigning a different instrument to them.

FIGURE 10.12
The repeating pattern of pitches suggests a quadruple metric pattern. Superimposed on this is the triple meter of the timbre pattern. The stream formed by the trumpet tones presents an illusory pattern of pitch at another level—in this example, an augmented version of the four-note pitch pattern.

melody.[10] Figure 10.12 illustrates another type of streaming.[11] Auditory streaming is far too involved a subject to be adequately described here, however. The reader is advised to refer for further information to the excellent materials cited in the bibliography at the end of this chapter.

The expanded range of timbral possibilities offered by digital synthesizers and sound samplers has made it possible to extend and enrich the traditional uses of tone color in music. But these devices have done significantly more than provide new clothes for old music; they have made it possible to imagine radically new forms of music as well. As the 21st century commences, it will be interesting to learn of the directions music has taken in response to this fascinating challenge.

ÉTUDE 10.6

Compose a *Klangfarbenmelodie* of approximately one minute's duration (perhaps a set of variations on the phrase "Yippee ti-yi, ti-yo!"). Use as many as 12 distinct timbres, but all should be on the same pitch. Create recognizable patterns that are subsequently repeated or are gradually developed.

Use rhythmic patterns as needed to help delineate the patterns of timbre. Make a stereo recording of the finished work.

ARNOLD SCHOENBERG'S METHOD OF COMPOSING WITH 12 TONES

As a medium for musical composition, the family of electroacoustic instruments has presented music in virtually all of the styles that have been extant during recent decades. One particular approach to composition that has been widely used by European and American composers (especially those posted at colleges and universities) during the second half of this

---

10. For further information, see Stephen McAdams and Albert Bregman, "Hearing Musical Streams," in *Foundations of Computer Music*, eds. Curtis Roads and John Strawn (Cambridge, MA: MIT Press, 1985), pp. 658–698.

11. David L. Wessel, "Timbre Space as a Musical Control Structure," in ibid., p. 650.

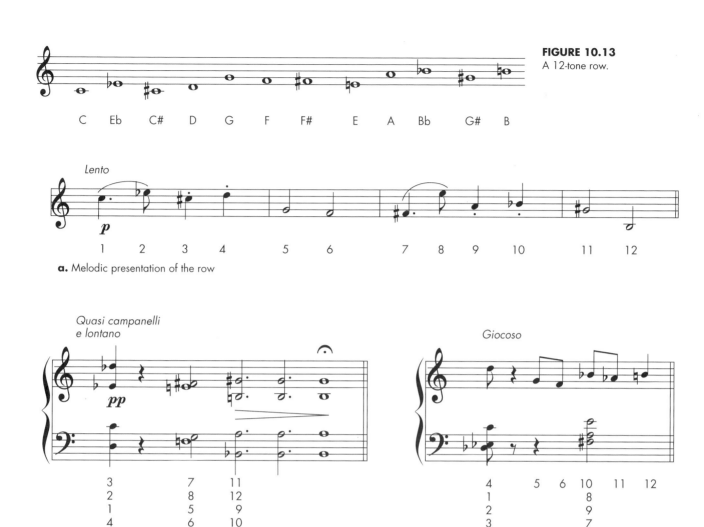

FIGURE 10.13
A 12-tone row.

a. Melodic presentation of the row

b. The row presented as a succession of chords

c. Melody, with accompaniment

FIGURE 10.14

The 12-tone row can be used in various ways to create a variety of textures.

century is based on a set of techniques introduced by the Viennese composer Arnold Schoenberg in the mid-1920s. These techniques are known as the **12-tone method** of composition.

Melodies composed by this method are not based on the familiar relationships among tones embodied in the venerable patterns known as scales. Nor are harmonies formed on the standard models provided by triads. Instead, with the 12-tone method, the melodies and harmonies are based on a series of pitches devised by the composer prior to the process of composing the music. Typically, the 12 pitches into which the octave is divided (at least in European music of the past two centuries) are arranged into a particular order, a pattern identified as a tone row (see Figure 10.13).

The order of pitches in the tone row is then used to determine the sequence of tones in a melody, the contents of a chord, or both. The musical passages in Figure 10.14 demonstrate just a few of the ways in which a tone row can be deployed to create a musical texture.

Notes are used in the order in which they appear in the series. Except for direct repetitions (as in Figure 10.14b), a note that is sounded cannot be

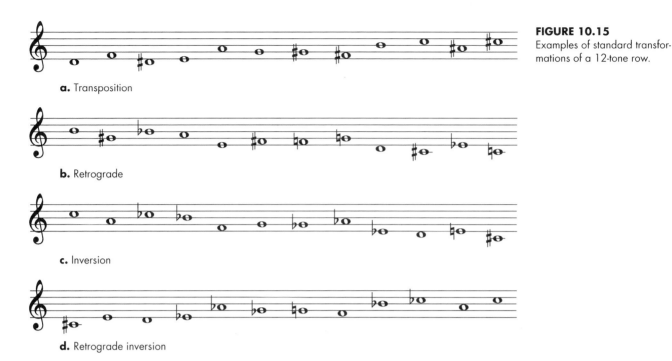

FIGURE 10.15
Examples of standard transformations of a 12-tone row.

a. Transposition

b. Retrograde

c. Inversion

d. Retrograde inversion

used again until all of the remaining notes in the row have been used. For variety, the pattern of pitches in the row can be transposed, reversed, inverted, or some combination of these techniques (see Figure 10.15).

Many composers have found it useful to display all of the possible forms of the row on a matrix, as shown in Figure 10.16. The original form of the row, and its transpositions, are read from left to right. Inverted forms of the row (and transposed inversions) are read in columns, from top to bottom. Retrograde forms are read from right to left, and retrograde inversions are read from bottom to top. This compositional aid is often referred to as a Babbitt square, in honor of Milton Babbitt, one of the foremost practitioners of advanced techniques of serial composition (and whose work is described in more detail later in this chapter).

Music composed by the 12-tone method is described as atonal—it is music that is not "in a key." Because each tone is sounded as often as any other tone, no particular tone can establish itself as the "keynote" or "tonic." There is no sense that dissonant combinations of pitches are obligated to resolve to consonant ones (Schoenberg described this as the "liberation of dissonance"). For people whose training and listening habits have been confined primarily to pieces written in major or minor keys, or simple modes, the first experience of a 12-tone composition can be disorienting, even distressing.

It is important to remember that the beauty of the composition may be found not so much in the play of melody and harmony, however, as in the abstract manipulation and exploration of certain possibilities suggested by the structure of the row. For example, the perceptive reader will have

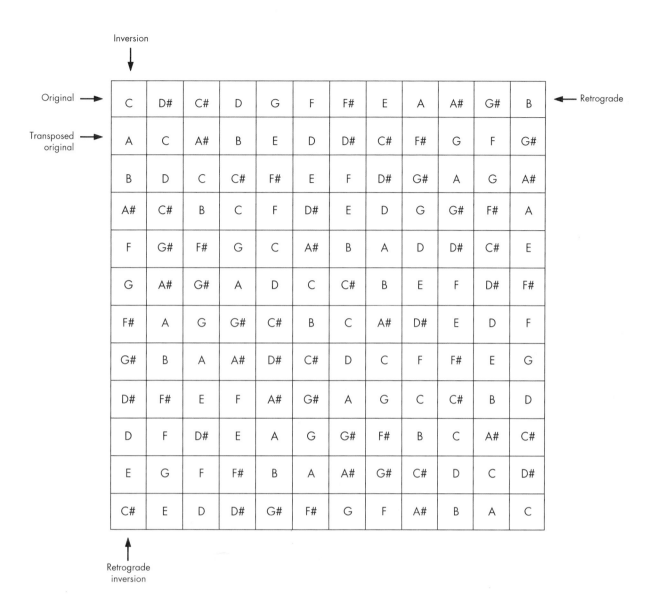

Inversion

Original →

Transposed original →

← Retrograde

Retrograde inversion

FIGURE 10.16
A Babbitt square.

noticed that the final six notes of the row shown in Figure 10.13 are a transposed, retrograde inversion of the first six notes of the row. This is particularly evident in Figure 10.15d: the retrograde inversion is also a simple transposition (up a semitone) of the original row. Similarly, if this particular row is segmented into three consecutive groups of four notes each, it will be observed that the interval between the highest and lowest note in each group is a minor third and that each segment accounts for one-third of the octave. Such interior symmetries in the structure of a row, or other obvious segmentations, are particularly attractive to composers who like to pose and solve musical puzzles. Metaphorically speaking, it is a music of crystal formations. The popularity of the 12-tone method is perhaps declining now among composers, but it has made possible the creation of works of great intellectual beauty, and its impact on the music of the 20th century has been enormous.

One of the most significant compositions to be realized in the Cologne studio that was established in the early 1950s for the creation of *elektronische Musik* (described in Chapter 8) was the *Gesang der Jünglinge* ("Song of the Youths") by Karlheinz Stockhausen (b. 1928). This piece, nearly 13 minutes in duration, reportedly took 18 months to complete, from 1955 to 1956.[a] Considering the richness of detail in the composition and the relative primitiveness of the techniques available at the time for its realization, it is not difficult to appreciate why such a long time was required to piece it together (needless to say, Stockhausen benefited enormously from the assistance of the very capable technicians assigned to the studio).

One of the most significant aspects of this composition is its use of both electronically generated and naturally produced sounds. Prior to this work, the composers in the Cologne studio were almost exclusively concerned with the manipulation of sounds produced electronically. The domain of naturally produced sounds was being explored elsewhere, in the Paris studio led by Pierre Schaeffer (described in Chapter 2) and in New York by Otto Luening and Vladimir Ussachevsky (also described in Chapter 2). The *Gesang der Jünglinge* was the result of Stockhausen's ambition to integrate and perhaps even reconcile these two apparent opposites.

The naturally produced sounds used in this work are taken from a tape recording of a solo boy soprano singing and speaking a biblical text. This text (in German) is the song of praise to God sung by the three young Jewish men who were thrown into a fiery furnace by the Babylonian king Nebuchadnezzar because they refused to worship him, as commanded, whenever music was sounded.[b] This composition is certainly nothing like a conventional song with a recognizably straightforward setting of the text. Stockhausen instead breaks the text into short phrases, single words, and individual sounds (phonemes) within words. There is rarely a sense of textural stratification—certainly nothing like a melody with an accompaniment. The texture might perhaps be described as an atomic soup of electronic tones and fragments of text.

In preparation for making compositional decisions for this work, Stockhausen imagined a continuum of sounds ranging from pure electronic tones at one end to sung tones at the other. In between are a variety of sounds that are more or less similar to each other and to the sounds at the ends of the continuum. For example, the rolled *rrr* heard around 8:56, perhaps extracted from the word *Herrn* ("Lord"), is noticeably similar to the pulsing, maraca-like rustlings of electronic noise heard at 8:20 (and many other places). In general, Stockhausen seems to be using filtered bursts of noise as consonants, as in a brief passage at about 9:15. Likewise, spoken consonants (such as the *d* at the end of the word *und*) are treated as if they are simply electronic noises. Occasionally there are tones of ambiguous origin, such as the very long, sustained tone that begins around 2:42—is it a sung tone (perhaps recorded as a tape loop?), or is it a sustained electronic oscillation? A similar passage begins at about 11:41.

---

[a]Paul Griffiths, *Modern Music* (New York: Thames & Hudson, 1978), p. 164.

[b]The text is an apocryphal one, and can be found in some Bibles in the third chapter of the Book of Daniel. The text is referred to as the "Benedicite."

Generally, both the phonemes and electronic sounds are manipulated as abstract objects of sound.[c]

Exceptions to this tendency to abstract and objectify the text occur with the words *preiset den Herrn* ("praise to the Lord"), first heard at about 1:09. As Stockhausen has written in his liner notes to the LP recording (Deutsche Grammophon DG 138811), this is an intentional effort to manipulate the degree of comprehensibility of the text. In an extended passage, from 3:01 to 4:45, several other brief words are also presented so as to be quite comprehensible: *den Herrn* ("the Lord"), *Sonne* ("Sun"), *und Mond* ("and Moon"), *Regen* ("rain"), *und Tau* ("and dew"), *Sterne* ("stars"), *ihr Winde* ("ye winds").

Sounds, such as those in the passage of relatively comprehensible words just cited, are often clustered in this way into *Gruppen* (groups), as Stockhausen refers to them. Besides being proximate in time, the sounds in these groups share one or more other characteristics, such as frequency range, timbre, duration, degree of comprehensibility, or loudness. For example, the piece begins with a group of electronic sounds. A group of vocal sounds appears after about 15 seconds from the beginning. Successive groupings of sounds are not at all difficult to discern.

For Stockhausen, however, an even more important structural principle is the extension of the 12-tone method of Arnold Schoenberg to include other aspects of the succession of sounds in addition to pitch. For example, Stockhausen regarded his arrangement of the continuum of electronic and vocal sounds to be a series of timbres that could be used in much the same way a 12-note row is used to determine the order of pitches in the composition. Similar series were employed by Stockhausen in this work to determine durations, loudness, textural thickness, the degree of comprehensibility of the text, the apparent placement of sounds among the loud-speakers, and other aspects. Such "total serialization," as this approach to composition is called, results in a composition with considerably fewer audible continuities than can be heard in music of more familiar styles. The musical texture truly does become "atomic." (Further description of techniques of total serialization is given later in this chapter.) Stockhausen believed that the apparent placement of sounds in space was a very important aspect of this composition. The technical capabilities of the electronic music studio made possible much more precise control of this. Stockhausen even claimed, in his liner notes to the LP recording, that "this work is the first to use the direction of the sounds and their movement in space as aspects of the form." The piece was originally conceived as a five-channel work for five clusters of loudspeakers distributed around the audience. The LP recording, of course, is a stereo reduction of this. Despite the limitations of the recording, it is still possible to hear (particularly when listening with headphones) the play of sounds around space, including panning, and the manipulation of reverberation to control the apparent distance of sounds. An especially effective passage in this regard begins around 8:20, in which the individual sounds in a group of phonemes seem to be emitted from a variety of spatial depths.

FOR FURTHER CONSIDERATION

■ Often in this work it sounds as if a boys' choir is singing. Given that the source is a solo boy soprano, by what technique or techniques might this effect have been accomplished?

---

[c]This approach is likely to have been influenced considerably by Stockhausen's studies in the early 1950s of phonetics and communication theory. Also, it is worth noting that Werner Meyer-Eppler, one of the founders of the Cologne studio, was a specialist in phonetics.

- What technique of tape manipulation is most in evidence in the passage that begins around 5:15, and is particularly noticeable with the vocal sounds at 5:38 and the electronic sounds at 5:55? How might this entire passage be described in relation to Stockhausen's concept of groups?
- In a brief passage that begins at about 10:19, there is a group of electronically generated chords of very short duration. These chords could have been generated by a device called a ring modulator, which accepts a single tone as an input and provides as an output a set of sideband frequencies on either side of the tone. Listen closely to the very brief setting of the word *dunkel* ("dark") that begins at 11:07. Is it possible that the same technique was applied here?

GUIDE FOR LISTENING

MILTON BABBITT AND HIS *ENSEMBLES FOR SYNTHESIZER*

A composer for whom the RCA synthesizer (described in Chapter 8) was an especially useful musical instrument was Milton Babbitt (b. 1916). In the late 1940s Babbitt, a professor of music at Princeton University, began to explore the possibilities of extending the 12-tone techniques developed by Arnold Schoenberg (and his pupils Anton Webern and Alban Berg) to other musical elements besides pitch. Just as a defined series of the 12 pitches could be used to determine the melodic and harmonic patterns of a piece of music, so could a defined series, most likely one derived from the pitch series, be used to determine patterns of duration, patterns of loudness, patterns of timbre, and other patterns in the music (see Figure 10.17). These patterns of duration, loudness, color, and such are thereby invested with an importance to be regarded as equal to that of the patterns of pitch.

A piece of music composed by the rigorous application of techniques for manipulating such series among several musical elements is called a "totally organized" or "serial" composition. As Babbitt was beginning to explore such techniques, similar procedures were coming into use by European composers such as Pierre Boulez and Karlheinz Stockhausen (as described earlier). Serial composition came to be regarded as an "international" style of music.

However, for Babbitt, who also taught mathematics at Princeton for a brief period in the early 1940s, these techniques had a particular fascination. By conceiving the series as a unique ordering of a set of integers (whose members include all the integers between 0 and 11, inclusive), it became possible to apply the mathematics of set theory to the process of serial composition. The standard transformations of the series (transposition, inversion, retrogression, and retrograde inversion) could be represented as a matrix (as illustrated in Figure 10.18). The quantities represented by the integers on such a matrix could then easily be interpreted as values for relative loudness, duration of attack, octave placement, tone color, or whatever other attributes define a musical tone.

Perhaps needless to say, music composed of such patterns applied in so many different ways requires special handling. It is simply not like more familiar music. As Babbitt has written,

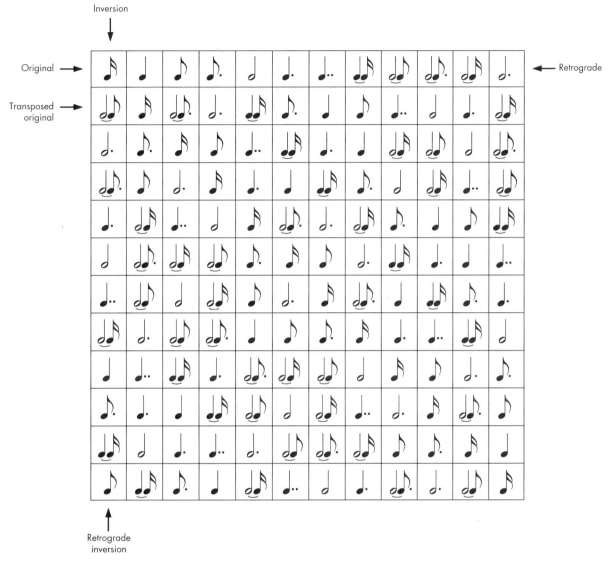

FIGURE 10.17
The Babbitt square shown in Figure 10.16 has here been transformed into an analogous matrix of durations.

the number of functions associated with each component of the musical event . . . has been multiplied. In the simplest possible terms, each such "atomic" event is located in a five-dimensional musical space determined by pitch-class, register, dynamic, duration, and timbre. These five components not only together define the single event, but, in the course of a work, the successive values of each component create an individually coherent structure, frequently in parallel with the corresponding structures created by each of the other components. Inability to perceive and remember precisely the values of any of these components results in a dislocation of the event in the work's musical space, an alteration of its relation to all other events in the work, and—thus—a falsification of the composition's total structure.[a]

---

[a]Milton Babbitt, "Who Cares If You Listen?" *High Fidelity 8*, no. 2 (February 1958), p. 39.

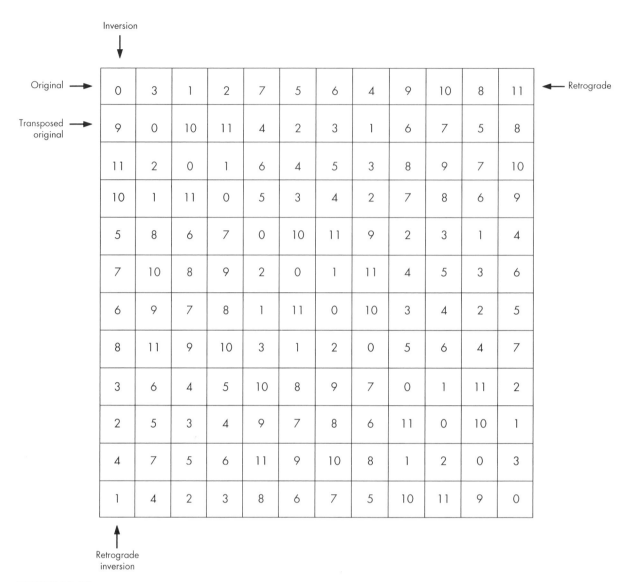

FIGURE 10.18

An integer matrix that corresponds to the Babbitt squares shown in Figures 10.16 and 10.17.

Such music is at least as difficult to perform as it is to comprehend when listening. Having endured quite a few flawed performances of his music, Babbitt was very interested to learn how to use the RCA synthesizer. The ability of the instrument to synthesize new tone colors was of no particular interest to him; rather, its appeal lay in precision of control—the ability to specify pitches, loudness, durations, attack times, and the like.

The *Ensembles for Synthesizer* (recorded on Columbia MS 7051 as a two-channel reduction of the original four-track version) is a ten-and-a-half-minute work composed by Babbitt from 1962 to 1964 that demonstrates his most impressive virtuosity with the RCA synthesizer. The synthetic tone colors—primarily tones like those of an electronic organ and a few splashes of filtered noise—are not particularly noteworthy. However, the patterns of the tones are quite dazzling—a kaleidoscope of patterns of pitch, rhythm, timbre, loudness, and related elements. A few similarities among these patterns are readily audible; many are not.

This is indeed extraordinary and difficult music. It is not music for everyone in the listening public. Indeed, Babbitt does not intend it to be. It requires a highly trained audience of people willing to study it with the scrutiny and patience of scholars. In a succinct manifesto published in *High Fidelity* magazine in 1958—an article Babbitt intended to title "The Composer as Specialist" but which the editor instead titled "Who Cares If You Listen?"—Babbitt raises the rhetorical question:

> Why should the layman be other than bored and puzzled by what he is unable to understand, music or anything else? . . . Why refuse to recognize the possibility that contemporary music has reached a stage long since attained by other forms of activity? The time has passed when the normally well-educated [person] without special preparation could understand the most advanced work in, for example, mathematics, philosophy, and physics. Advanced music, to the extent that it reflects the knowledge and originality of the informed composer, scarcely can be expected to appear more intelligible than these arts and sciences to the person whose musical education usually has been even less extensive than his background in other fields.[b]

For Babbitt, the question of whether or not the public likes this music is not a relevant one. The music simply is, it exists, and for those who take the time to seek it out and study it closely, the experience will be rewarding.

> I dare suggest that the composer would do himself and his music an immediate and eventual service by total, resolute, and voluntary withdrawal from this public world to one of private performance and electronic media, with its very real possibility of complete elimination of the public and social aspects of musical composition. By so doing, the separation between the domains would be defined beyond any possibility of confusion of categories, and the composer would be free to pursue a private life of professional achievement, as opposed to a public life of unprofessional compromise and exhibitionism.
>
> But how, it may be asked, will this serve to secure the means of survival for the composer and his music? One answer is that after all such a private life is what the university provides the scholar and the scientist. It is only proper that the university, which—significantly—has provided so many contemporary composers with their professional training and general education, should provide a home for the "complex," "difficult," and "problematical" in music.[c]

This is perhaps not so much a call for a retreat to an elitist, ivory tower as it is a recognition of many of the realities of contemporary musical life. Even today, as many music journalists who review concerts or recordings continue to decry the insularity of such "academic" music, they fail to recognize these simple facts of sociology expressed so eloquently by Professor Babbitt. The music is there for those who choose to learn about it.

---

[b]Ibid., pp. 39–40.
[c]Ibid., p. 126.

JOHN CAGE: COMPOSING BY CHANCE

A very different notion of musical composition is that espoused since mid-century by that marvelous virtuoso of musical innovation, John Cage (1912–1992). Cage, whose father was an inventor, was born in Los Angeles. From 1935 to 1937 he studied with Arnold Schoenberg, the composer who devised the 12-tone method of composition and who had recently emigrated to southern California. Not surprisingly, Cage's pieces from these years were relatively simple, 12-tone compositions. He soon became more interested in structures of rhythm than in patterns of pitch, however, and percussion instruments came to have an increasing significance in his compositions.[12]

In 1939 he composed his first piece involving electroacoustic media, a work entitled *Imaginary Landscape No. 1* for two variable-speed phonographs playing frequency recordings, muted piano, and a cymbal. He initiated the Project of Music for Magnetic Tape in 1952 in New York. Working at the same time as Otto Luening and Vladimir Ussachevsky were exploring the creative possibilities of their tape recorder, Cage went in a somewhat different direction. His tape composition from this period, *Williams Mix*, is an eight-track collage of recordings of sounds of the city, of the country, a few sounds of musical instruments, electronic sounds, quiet sounds that have been amplified, and others.

Around 1947 he began to study Asian philosophies and religions, particularly Zen Buddhism, and this was to have a profound effect on his musical concerns. At the risk of oversimplification, Western thinking has defined a role for humans as masters of the natural world, whereas Eastern systems of belief tend to regard humanity as a part of the process of nature. As Cage observed in a 1962 interview, "the philosophies that grow up in Europe are in opposition to Nature, and toward the control of Nature. Whereas, the philosophies that grow up in Asia and increasingly so toward the Far East, are concerned with the acceptance of Nature, not its control.[13] According to Zen teachings, a true state of peace can be attained as a person becomes less aware of self, relinquishing ambition to exert will over the environment, and becomes more conscious of the totality of all being in nature. The distinction between Self and Other dissipates.

For a composer in the Western tradition, the task is to assign meanings to sounds, to define relationships among them, and to arrange them into hierarchical structures. The shape of the music is determined by the taste and skill of the composer. For Cage, however, musical composition could

---

12. In 1938, while employed as a dance-class pianist in Seattle, Cage invented the "prepared" piano. This was a piano modified by the insertion of screws, bolts, rubber erasers, wooden sticks, coins, and similar items between the strings inside the piano. As a result of these modifications, the piano could produce a variety of percussive sounds even as it was played with conventional technique on the keys.

13. Roger Reynolds, "John Cage: Interview with Roger Reynolds, 1962," in *Contemporary Composers on Contemporary Music,* eds. Elliott Schwartz and Barney Childs (New York: Da Capo Press, 1978), p. 338.

no longer be an exercise in the expression of individual will. Instead, it became for him a search for ways to experience sounds that existed free of his preferences and determination. "I believe that by eliminating purpose, what I call *awareness* increases. Therefore, my purpose is to remove purpose."[14] This approach to composition is known as **indeterminacy.**

In 1951 Cage composed a piece for solo piano entitled *Music of Changes.* So that the pitches, durations, and loudness (as well as other aspects) of each sound could be discovered by a process free of his intention, he first prepared a series of charts. Each chart, modeled after the *I Ching* (a Chinese book of proverbs), included 64 possible choices. After tossing coins, Cage would consult each chart to identify the characteristics of each sound. After this painstaking process of innumerable coin tosses, the notation of the piece could be completed. It was a piece notated in the conventional way that could be presented in the traditional venue of the public concert, but as a result of the use of chance operations for decision making, it was largely free of the composer's impulse to impose structure. As Christian Wolff, an early associate of Cage has written, "Cage used chance as a way of liberation, both psychological and technical, from self, taste, imagination, musical tradition, and ingrained compositional habits."[15]

In the same year, Cage composed his *Imaginary Landscape No. 4* for 12 radios. Each radio is performed by two players, one for the volume dial and one for the tuning dial. Each pair of players reads from a musical part on which the volume changes are marked with crescendos, diminuendos, and other traditional notations for loudness. Changes of the tuning frequency (which could result in a change from monitoring one radio broadcast to the reception of a different broadcast) are notated as pitches and glissandi on a traditional five-line musical staff. A conductor marks the downbeats of measures and directs the frequent changes of tempo. Much of this, of course, seems quite conventional, except for the sound sources themselves. Since Cage cannot have known what would be broadcast at the time of any particular performance, or even what radio stations were transmitting in the area in which the performance site was located, the sounds that are heard are indeed indeterminate, quite free of the composer's will.

At one point in his career, Cage made a visit to the Bell Telephone Laboratories to listen in an anechoic chamber (a room virtually free of reflected sounds and insulated quite thoroughly from external sounds). He expected to experience total silence, but could nonetheless still hear the sounds of his heartbeat and the soft whine of his nervous system. He now realized there could be no such thing as silence, that the environment

---

14. Ibid., p. 341.

15. Christian Wolff, "John Cage," in *Dictionary of Contemporary Music,* ed. John Vinton (New York: Dutton, 1974).

would always include sound. In 1952 he composed a piece entitled *4′33″* in three movements (0'33", 2'40", and 1'20"). In the score for this piece, the performer (of "any instrument or combination of instruments") is instructed to produce no sounds, but simply to indicate through stage actions the passage from one movement to the next.[16] The sounds of the composition are those that happen to occur in and around the performance space (including from the audience) during the time of the performance. The "silence" is the piece.

In subsequent years, Cage devised many other ways to create "contexts in which sounds are allowed to happen." In his *Atlas Eclipticalis* for orchestra, composed in 1961–1962, he used star charts to help determine the attributes of sounds for the piece. Other compositions have exploited blemishes and other imperfections in sheets of paper, and random superposition of lines, graphs, and other drawings on transparencies.

Cage has been an active collaborator with other artists over the years, particularly with Merce Cunningham and his dance company. Largely as a consequence of such collaborative activity, Cage's later works have been even more theatrical and have made extensive use of live electroacoustic performance techniques. The range of Cage's work is simply overwhelming. Much of what he has done continues to be regarded as controversial by some, and his influence on younger generations of artists has been considerable. Without doubt, John Cage has been one of the major actors in the musical life of the 20th century.

IMPORTANT TERMS

foreground
background
texture
layering
motive
Klangfarbenmelodie
12-tone method
indeterminacy

---

16. In the premiere performance, performed at the piano, the performer lowered the key cover at the beginning, raised and lowered it between movements, and raised it again at the end.

FOR FURTHER READING

Austin, Larry, and Clark, Thomas. *Learning to Compose.* Dubuque, IA: Brown, 1989.

Brindle, Reginald Smith. *Serial Composition.* New York: Oxford University Press, 1966.

Cage, John. *Silence.* Middletown, CT: Wesleyan University Press, 1961.

Cope, David. *New Directions in Music.* 6th ed. Dubuque, IA: Brown & Benchmark, 1993.

Cope, David. *New Music Composition.* New York: Schirmer, 1977.

Erickson, Robert. *Sound Structure in Music.* Berkeley: University of California Press, 1975.

Griffiths, Paul. *Modern Music.* New York: Thames & Hudson, 1978.

Machlis, Joseph. *Introduction to Contemporary Music.* 2d ed. New York: Norton, 1979.

Perle, George. *Serial Composition and Atonality.* 4th ed. Berkeley: University of California Press, 1977.

Schwartz, Elliott, and Childs, Barney, eds. *Contemporary Composers on Contemporary Music.* New York: Da Capo Press, 1978.

CHAPTER 11

THE AUDIENCE FOR ELECTROACOUSTIC MUSIC

$\mathcal{P}$rior to the 20th century, there was simply no question that the presentation of music could take place only if performers and listeners were physically gathered together in the same space at the same time. Electronic technology, of course, has changed all this, making it possible for performers to reach an audience that may be dispersed in both space and time. Beginning in the 1920s, for example, performances by ballroom orchestras in the grand hotels of New York, Chicago, and other cities were broadcast live nationwide to millions of people who quickly became devoted fans of big band jazz as a result. Even decades later, recordings of many of these same performances continue to be broadcast by a few radio stations.

A more contemporary example can be found in the huge rock concerts of the 1980s that were organized to generate funding for famine relief and other causes. These events were not only enjoyed by thousands of people in the stands, but were also shared, via satellite, with a global audience of perhaps hundreds of millions of people. Subsequently, commercial recordings of these performances were made available as well. As these examples suggest, a composer of electroacoustic music (or of any other contemporary form of music, for that matter) must consider where the audience for the music will be and how it will be reached.

PRESENTATION TO A GATHERED AUDIENCE

Many of the early composers of electroacoustic music—Karlheinz Stockhausen, Milton Babbitt, Edgard Varèse, Otto Luening, and Vladimir Ussachevsky, for example—had been trained in the traditions of European concert music that reached maturity in the 19th century. A concert of European "classical" music was (and continues to be) a very formal event, and was as much a social occasion as an artistic one. The members of the audience were all likely to be of the middle or upper social classes. Many, if not all, members of the audience were likely to be acquainted with one another, perhaps through business or other social relationships. Dress and manners were important; members of the audience were present to "see and be seen." A "cultured" individual knew the appropriate moments for applause, for speaking with people in nearby seats, and for moving about the room.

Further aspects of the concert experience can be discerned from the architectural features of the performance space. Seats for the audience were fastened to the floor and all faced in the same direction, toward a raised platform or stage. Often the stage was framed by a proscenium, and it may have been set apart even further by a curtain suspended above the front of the stage. When a performance began, the lights on the stage were brightened as the other lights in the hall were dimmed. The clear implication was that significant activity, worthy of the attention of the eyes as well as the ears, was about to occur in this special portion of the room.

The members of the audience, fixed in their seats and with their attention directed to the stage, expected a spectacle. The response of composers and performers was to attempt to provide something sufficiently compelling to warrant such attention. Concert programs featured the presentation of works that were essentially dramatic in conception. The music would claim a passage of time and lead the listener through it. From the beginning of the work, the attention of the listener would be directed toward successive moments of significant action; then, with the narrative accomplished, the elements of music would collaborate to define the conclusion of the work, to achieve closure.

Because the social and architectural circumstances of presentation facilitated close listening, these works of art could become quite extended in time and very complex in structure and detail. For example, many of the symphonies of Anton Bruckner or Gustav Mahler are over an hour in duration. Listeners were also likely to have had some training as amateur performers, and this consequent degree of familiarity with the musical style and syntax also encouraged the creation and performance of works of greater expansiveness and subtlety.

Much of the excitement of attending a concert derived from the fact of being present as such "great works of art," the creations of "awesomely gifted intellects," were brought to life. Unlike a painting or a piece of sculpture, which can be touched and possessed, such a piece of music consisted only of the intangibles of tone and time. When the final reverberations subsided, it was gone once again. Therefore, it was important to the listener to be able to confirm the experience by observing clearly the gestures that gave rise to the sound. The ability to associate sight with sound was a vital part of the experience.

There may also have been, in the mind of the bourgeois concertgoer of the 19th century, a vicarious identification with the performer as an individual who was in command of the resources required to achieve such an impressive result. The independent shopkeeper or factory owner may have viewed this as an affirmation of the ideals of individualism. Certainly, on a more practical level, the social interaction in the concert hall was dominated by the performer. Particular gestures of the performer were understood by the members of the audience to mean that it was time for silence, while other gestures signaled the appropriate time for applause. A concert was, in a few respects then, a formal, ritualized event.

It was in this milieu that most of the early composers of electroacoustic music introduced their first works in the 1950s.[1] The relative crudeness of the available devices and the limitations of the techniques used to create music with them meant that the electronic instruments themselves could not be performed onstage. Rather, the actions that constituted the "performance" of such works generally took place beforehand, in the studio, over an extended period of weeks or months of tedious effort. The result of this effort was a tape, which could then be played for the audience.

This, of course, deprived the members of the audience of an essential part of the experience of being at a concert—the opportunity to witness the corporealization of a work of art. There was no special significance or magic to be found in the replay of past actions. Any particular hearing of the tape would be essentially identical to any other hearing. There would be no subtle differences of interpretation, no danger of mistakes, no apparent heroes with whom the members of the audience might identify.

Furthermore, despite the fact that all seats faced a stage, there was nothing there to watch, except perhaps for a few motionless loudspeakers and a tape machine with reels that rotated steadily and relentlessly. There was no opportunity for the listener to associate the sounds being heard with gestures that might have produced them. Few listeners were familiar with the techniques of tape music, so that few could even imagine the gestures that might have been responsible for the sounds. Thus, there was a distinct absence of visual cues that might otherwise confirm that the event was special. The architectural cues of the performance space were ignored, and the importance of the visual aspects of the concert experience were denied. This estrangement of sight from sound meant that even ordinary cues for silence and applause were absent, leaving the members of the audience feeling somewhat self-conscious and often perplexed.

The gradual realization that the concert hall was an inappropriate venue for tape music led composers to explore other means for the presentation of works produced in the studio. Given the continuing force of the institution of the public concert in musical life, however, it has taken many composers quite some time to come to terms fully with this realization. Even now an occasional concert of tape music is attempted in a hall somewhere. However, several other forms of electroacoustic musical activities have proven to be far more successful in recent years.

---

1. A notable exception was Pierre Schaeffer, who broadcast many of his early works over the French radio system, beginning with his *Concert of Noises* on October 5, 1948. The uses of radio as a medium for the dissemination of electroacoustic music are described later in this chapter.

LIVE PERFORMANCE WITH TAPED ELECTROACOUSTIC MUSIC

From very early on, there have been efforts to place tape music in the concert hall in a context that employs live performers as well.[2] The presence of one or more live performers onstage provides a sense of immediacy to the experience that is lacking when taped music is presented alone. Some degree of spontaneity is restored to the experience. There is significant activity onstage for the members of the audience to see, and the possibility of being able to associate at least some of the sounds heard with gestures.

The use of a prerecorded tape brings the carefully wrought results of studio techniques to the concert hall. But the hybridized form of live-with-tape music also offers special creative possibilities that derive from the combination of the two elements. There is, for example, the dramatic potential in the juxtaposition of the immediate and the nonimmediate, the present and the past. One often successful genre, the so-called live-ensemble piece, features a soloist performing along with a tape that includes sounds previously recorded by the soloist, as in Robert Erickson's *Ricercar à tre*, for two recorded contrabasses and one live contrabass. The soloist may alternately confront or collaborate with these unseen doubles. In a more general way, the tape may serve to extend the capabilities of the soloist, by sounding tones that are above or below the range of the instrument, or by executing patterns that are awkward for the instrument. Conversely, the performer can extend the material of the tape by providing a greater rhythmic flexibility or subtlety of articulation than the sounds on tape.

The tape part is capable of evoking the realm of the ethereal, the otherworldly, or the monstrous. This has inspired a number of live-with-tape pieces that to some degree manifest the concerto principle—the heroic live performer (or team of performers) in a contest with unseen forces, alternately competing with them, cooperating with them, or accommodating them. Different compositions may emphasize different aspects of such relationships. For example, Jacob Druckman's *Animus I*, for trombone and tape (recorded on Turnabout TV 34177), emphasizes the competitive possibilities of the combination, whereas David Cope's *Arena*, for 'cello and tape (recorded on Orion ORS 75169), expresses a more cooperative aspect. It is important to recognize that this sort of interaction is entirely illusory, but it can indeed provide a great sense of drama.

A more innocuous interaction between live performers and taped sounds can be characterized by a simple division of textural functions. The live elements typically assume a foreground role, while the taped sounds provide accompaniment. Occasionally the roles may be reassigned for variety.

A number of practical matters need to be considered when working with a combination of live performers and taped sounds. One is the challenge of

---

2. Perhaps the earliest of these efforts was a composition by the Italian composer Bruno Maderna in 1952 entitled *Musica su due Dimensioni* for "flute, percussion, and loudspeaker."

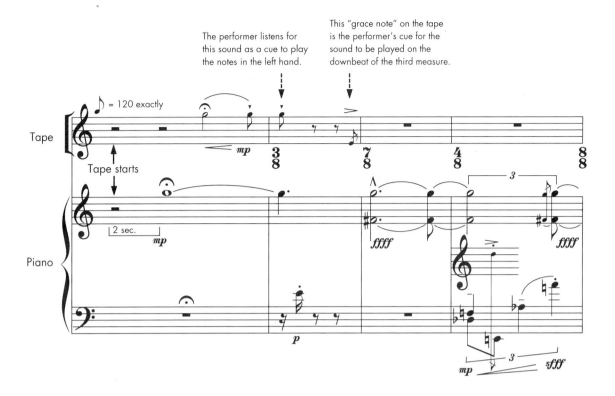

The performer listens for this sound as a cue to play the notes in the left hand.

This "grace note" on the tape is the performer's cue for the sound to be played on the downbeat of the third measure.

synchronization between the two elements. When performing chamber music with other live performers, a musician can generally depend upon the other players to provide a few subtle visual cues regarding the tempo, and the timing of entrances and cutoffs. Also, the performer can expect a certain amount of rhythmic flexibility among the members of the group. However, the tape recorder cannot provide any significant visual cues, nor does it accommodate any rhythmic flexibility, as it imperturbedly transports the tape from the supply reel to the take-up reel.

A variety of techniques have been developed in response to such difficulties. Some compositions incorporate passages during which the tape is stopped, allowing the performer to proceed more freely. The playback of the tape is then resumed when the performer arrives at a particular location in the piece (an assistant may be required to follow a copy of the musical score and stop and restart the tape recorder on cue). The occasions when the tape is stopped and then started again provide opportunities for the performer to remedy any lapses of synchronization with the tape part.

Other pieces may have an uninterrupted tape part that simply provides an "atmospheric" background element in the texture, with no sharply defined patterns that require precise synchronization by the live performer. Or there may be distinctive events and patterns in the tape part that anticipate actions by the live performer and can therefore be used as aural cues. Typically, these events are notated in the printed score used by the performer. Such notations may be relatively conventional, as when the electronic sounds have distinct patterns of pitch and rhythm (see Figure 11.1),

FIGURE 11.1

In this passage of music, the first four measures of Mario Davidovsky's *Synchronisms No. 6* for piano and taped electronic sounds, the cue sounds provided for the performer by the tape can be notated with standard musical symbols. (From Mario Davidovsky, *Synchronisms No. 6*. New York: Edward B. Marks Music Corporation, 1972.)

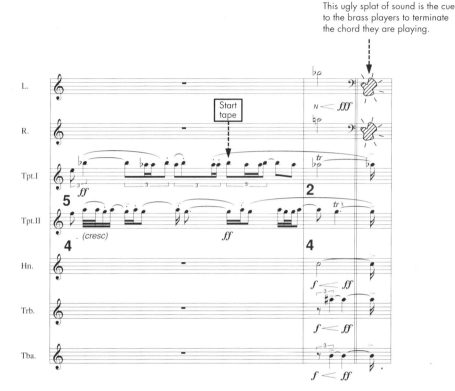

This ugly splat of sound is the cue to the brass players to terminate the chord they are playing.

In this musical excerpt, from the second movement of a composition by the author entitled *Sentinel,* for brass quintet and taped electronic sounds, the cue sound provided for the performers by the tape is most effectively notated in graphic form.

or they may be more pictographic, representing sounds for which no traditional notation exists (see Figure 11.2).

Such notated cues are especially important in compositions that involve more than one live performer. It can be fiendishly difficult to maintain synchronization between the members of a chamber ensemble and a prerecorded tape, even if a conductor is present to provide assistance. On a few occasions, performers have been fitted with headphones so that they could monitor a click track recorded on a spare track of the tape.

Another practical matter involved in the presentation of taped sounds with a live performer is the balance of intensity between the two elements. There is considerable anecdotal evidence that suggests that when a composer is consulted about the relative levels, during the sound check prior to a performance, the resulting balance tends to favor the electroacoustic sounds. Conversely, when a performer is consulted about the levels, the intensity of the electroacoustic sounds tends to be adjusted downward, to the benefit of the live performer onstage. Given the wide variety of acoustic conditions associated with different performance spaces, there is probably no satisfactorily objective way to specify the balance in advance (although a set of test tones recorded on the tape can certainly be most helpful). It is probably best to consult with several pairs of trained ears during the sound check.

ÉTUDE 11.1

Compose a brief piece, of approximately two or three minutes' duration, for a solo acoustic instrument (for example, guitar, piano, flute, or voice) and pre-recorded electroacoustic sounds. Consider the use of electroacoustic timbres and textures that sharply contrast with those created by the acoustic instrument. Alternately, consider textures and timbres that can match and extend those of the acoustic instrument. When you finish composing the piece, transcribe a musical score, in some form, for the use of the performer.

THE LIVE PERFORMANCE OF ELECTROACOUSTIC INSTRUMENTS

By the mid-1960s, electronic technology had become sufficiently sophisticated that it was now possible for composers to bring equipment onstage that could be used live to generate or process sound electronically. The ability of a composer to act as a performer of such equipment meant that many of the expectations intrinsic to the concert experience could be fulfilled much more satisfactorily than was the case with tape music. Members of the audience could witness the actions of performers as the sounds were formed. The immediacy and theatricality of the concert experience was reaffirmed. It could be a spectacle worthy of the attention of the eyes as well as the ears.

Many live-electronics pieces from this period (and since) feature the processing of sounds produced by acoustic instruments. These sounds are first picked up by either a conventional, "air" microphone or by a contact microphone fastened to the body of the instrument.[3] These signals might then simply be amplified. Some composers, such as John Cage (in such pieces as *Cartridge Music*), have been intrigued by the results of greatly amplifying a variety of very soft sounds, thus revealing small details of the sounds as if examining them through magnification. Other composers have experimented with feedback, from mild to extreme (as in Robert Ashley's notorious 1964 composition, *Wolfman*).

Echo techniques have long fascinated many electroacoustic musicians. Some of the earlier compositions that involved such techniques made use of the delay that occurs between the time a sound is recorded on tape and the time when the recorded sound passes the playback head. Feeding back some of the playback signal and mixing it with the input signal from the microphone resulted in a series of multiple echoes (see Chapter 4 for a more complete description of such tape echo techniques). Because the tape

---

3. Other transducers might be used as well, such as the guitar pickup.

speed was typically constant, and the distance between the record and playback heads was fixed, the echoes were spaced at equal intervals of time. Also, because of the limited number of tape speeds available, only a few delay times could be selected.[4] A few composers did experiment with techniques for creating much longer delay times by threading a tape from one machine, where the sounds were recorded, to another nearby machine, where the sounds could be played back from the tape.[5]

More recently, composers have used digital delay lines for such compositions. These devices can provide much greater flexibility than was possible with tape echo techniques. A great variety of delay times are available, ranging from a few thousandths of a second to several seconds. Furthermore, the delay time can be adjusted during the course of a performance. Multiple, repeated echoes can be created to produce a crowd of sounds around the performer. This becomes a special sort of live-ensemble piece, in which a performer (or group of performers) can play against sounds previously captured.

Another device that has been used widely as an instrument for live performance is the harmonizer. Composers who are performers, such as Laurie Anderson, Jon Hassell, and Dexter Morrill, use it to enlarge their solo lines into a thicker, richer texture. Spoken phrases acquire robotic, otherworldly companions (as can be heard on the Laurie Anderson album *Big Science,* as well as on many of her other albums). Solitary melodies become streams of chords.

In the 1960s and 1970s, the German composer Karlheinz Stockhausen made considerable use of the ring modulator as a device for processing the sounds produced onstage by musical instruments (the ring modulator is described in some detail in Chapter 8). For example, in his composition entitled *Mantra,* for two pianos and electronics, the tones produced by the pianos are enlarged into a great variety of esoteric harmonizations as they interact with a sine wave that is provided as the other input to the ring modulator, thus producing sum and difference frequencies. In each of the 13 sections of the piece, one particular pitch is matched by the frequency of the sine wave, and is therefore heard to be relatively unaffected. In a similar way, Stockhausen and his contemporaries also used a variety of audio signal filters, primarily low-pass and band-pass filters, to process the sounds produced by acoustic instruments such as the gong. Stockhausen's 1964 composition *Mikrophonie I* is particularly noteworthy in this regard.

None of this is likely to seem novel to performers of the electric guitar. Since the 1960s, electric-guitar players have used a variety of special effects, such as flanging, phasing, tremolo, reverb, and feedback, to modify

---

4. For example, on a tape deck with record and playback heads that are 1.5 inches apart, and with available tape speeds of 7.5 ips and 15 ips, the possible delay times are 0.2 second and 0.1 second, respectively.

5. Such a setup may entail mechanical difficulties, however. For example, the motors of the unused platters on each deck (the take-up platter of the first deck and the supply platter of the second deck) may begin to spin wildly. Or, if the tape speeds of the two machines are not identical, the tape may sag or stretch.

FIGURE 11.3
Composer Pauline Oliveros, with her accordion and electro-acoustic accessories. (Courtesy of Pauline Oliveros.)

FIGURE 11.4
Composer Dexter Morrill, with his MIDI trumpet and NeXT computer, which is used to process the messages generated by the trumpet. (Photo by John Hubbard, courtesy of Dexter Morrill.)

the signal produced by the pickup on the strings of the instrument. Many of the effects have been incorporated as functions of the guitar amplifier. Others are built into small boxes that are placed on the stage floor and operated by foot switches or foot pedals. The "fuzz box" (a limiter circuit that distorts the signal intentionally) and the "wa-wa" pedal (essentially a low-pass filter) are typical examples of such foot-controlled accessories.

The possibilities for the creative use of signal-processing devices in a live performance are apparently boundless. Such techniques also hold a special attraction for many musicians. Even as they explore the new possibilities uncorked by electronic technology, they can continue to make use of familiar skills acquired from their study of more traditional musical instruments. Laurie Anderson continues to play the violin, an instrument she learned to play at a much younger age. Dexter Morrill can continue an active acquaintance with the trumpet. Pauline Oliveros has found a fascinating new musical context for the accordion. This phenomenon illustrates an important, evolutionary aspect of musical change. More traditional skills can provide the basis for the development of powerful new techniques.

ÉTUDE 11.2

Compose a brief work in which the sounds of a solo acoustic instrument are processed during the course of the performance by a digital delay line, harmonizer, or similar digital effects device. Take care to avoid the overuse of a particular effect. Try to use different effects in different passages or sections of the piece to create a variety of textures. You may want to experiment with different combinations of effects as well.

Prepare a musical score by first transcribing the part to be performed by the solo instrument. Then provide copious technical information regarding the connections and settings of the effects devices used.

SYNTHESIZERS ONSTAGE

By the late 1960s, sound synthesizers began to appear onstage. Sounds of exclusively electronic origin could now be generated and processed live in a concert. The synthesizer might be used as a solo instrument, but more often it was played along with at least one other instrument (or perhaps a singer or narrator) or was one of a number of instruments in a chamber group or combo.

Although the relative portability of these transistorized, voltage-controlled, analog synthesizers made it possible to bring them onstage, they were nonetheless very challenging instruments in a performance. Because so many different elements of sound could be controlled by a synthesizer, a corresponding number of dials and switches had to be set prior to a performance. Many of these would then have to be adjusted during the course of the performance.[6] A few dozen patch cords (or matrix switches) generally had to be managed as well. A performance required careful planning and considerable preparation, and an onstage assistant was virtually always necessary.

These difficulties were compounded by a lack of design standardization among synthesizers produced by various manufacturers (note that this was well prior to the introduction of the Musical Instrument Digital Interface). A performer who became familiar with the features and the placement of controls on one synthesizer model could not readily transfer this knowledge to the task of performing on a synthesizer of a different make and model.

The development of so-called live-performance synthesizers helped to alleviate many of the challenges of live synthesis. The first of these, the Synket, built by engineer Paul Ketoff for composer John Eaton, was in use by 1965. Within a few years, commercial manufacturers introduced such models as the Mini-Moog and the ARP Odyssey. These synthesizers made minimal use of patch cords. Instead, internal wiring connected the circuits for voltage-controlled oscillators, voltage-controlled amplifiers, voltage-controlled filters, envelope generators, low-frequency oscillators, keyboard, and other typical modular functions (these, and others, are described in detail in Chapter 8). This greatly simplified the demands of live performance, but also limited the flexibility and power of the synthesizer to create unusual sounds.

---

6. The introduction of "programmable" synthesizers, such as the Prophet 5 by Sequential Circuits, in the late 1970s eased this difficulty somewhat.

This limitation, however, has not been regarded as much of a problem by musicians in the rock and jazz traditions, who tend to be less interested in the esoteric possibilities of sound synthesizers. They are perhaps more easily satisfied by the standard tuning systems and imitative timbres available on most live-performance synthesizer models. In fact, the most prevalent context by far for the live performance of a synthesizer has been the rock concert or recording session. By the early 1970s, such musicians as Keith Emerson of the group Emerson, Lake and Palmer, and Rick Wakeman of the group Yes were becoming pioneers of the live performance of synthesizers. The more esoteric German group Tangerine Dream was even making use onstage of a number of modular, studio-type synthesizer systems. Another notable crossover group from this time was Mother Mallard's Portable Masterpiece Company, based in Ithaca, New York, and led by David Borden.

Among composers in the "classical" music tradition, however, the pattern of use of synthesizers for live performance has been less clear. The lack of design standardization, even among live-performance synthesizers, has been regarded as a problem. Another perceived shortcoming has been the lack of a sufficiently rich and detailed system of notation. These factors, among others, have inhibited the development of a standard body of compositions that can be performed widely by performers who specialize in synthesizer techniques. Unlike the piano, violin, clarinet, or other established instruments, the synthesizer does not have a "standard repertory" of classical compositions.

PERFORMANCE GROUPS

The sounds that may result from some synthesizer patches can in fact be largely unpredictable, defying the intentions of performers to control them precisely in every detail, or of composers to notate them. For instance, many computer-based MIDI sequencer programs have the ability to generate a random series of MIDI Note On messages. This is reminiscent of an analog synthesizer technique that involves the use of a sample/hold module to produce control voltages that are essentially random. When applied to an oscillator, these random control voltages result in a patternless series of pitches. Some MIDI sequencers make it possible to loop individual tracks, or portions of tracks. By combining several simultaneous loops, of different tempos and lengths, a less random but still fairly unpredictable pattern can be produced. This, too, is reminiscent of an analog synthesizer technique that involves the combined use of several control voltage sequencer modules, with different clock rates and overlapping patterns, to control the production of pitches by an oscillator or the shaping of timbre by a filter.

Another analog synthesis technique involves connecting a microphone to a Schmitt trigger circuit to produce a trigger for the envelope generator whenever the amplitude of an ambient sound in the performance space exceeds a certain level. Thus, synthesizer sounds can be triggered by the sounds of other performers or even by sounds from the audience. Through the use of an envelope follower module (described in Chapter 8), the amplitude envelopes of the synthetic sounds can also be made dependent upon those of ambient acoustic sounds. The environment of sounds can indeed become highly interactive.

This potential for unpredictability inspired the formation, in the 1960s and 1970s, of a number of musical groups dedicated to live improvisation with synthesizers. One such group was *Musica Elettronica Viva*, founded in Rome in 1966 by composers Alvin Curran, Richard Teitelbaum, Frederic Rzewski, and others. Another prominent group was the Sonic Arts Union, initiated in 1966 in Ann Arbor, Michigan, by David Behrman, Alvin Lucier, Robert Ashley, and Gordon Mumma.

For an audience, the spectacle provided by a group improvisation can be especially rewarding. A member of the audience can be a witness to the spontaneous generation and transformation of musical ideas. The drama of the occasion is enhanced by the interaction among the musicians onstage as the ideas are shared. One of the musicians may fumble as the ideas are passed around, underscoring the element of risk in the endeavor, or there may be unprecedented moments of dazzling, brilliant musical intelligence. The sense of immediacy is heightened by the realization that the form, and most certainly the content, of the piece is not likely to be the same from one performance to the next.

Many composers have moved beyond the use of free and open musical forms to experiment with indeterminate methods of composition, first espoused by John Cage in the 1950s (and described in the previous chapter). The selection of sounds or the triggering of sounds is done by chance, not by design. The role of the "composer" is simply to create a context in which sounds can occur and be appreciated for themselves, and not for any imputed relationships they may bear to other sounds. Perhaps a random assortment of prerecorded tape loops is played, while sounds from the audience trigger random sounds from a synthesizer. Or perhaps the microphone signal produced by a speaking or singing voice is filtered, amplified, delayed, and otherwise processed in random ways by a synthesizer and a bank of effects devices.

Other composers have become interested in techniques for so-called algorithmic composition. A composer may describe the basic materials of a composition (such as the set of pitches, durations, timbres, and dynamic levels that can be used) and establish a set of "rules" or procedures to determine how these materials can be formed into patterns. These procedures might then be incorporated into a computer program to generate a musical score for live performers, or a synthesizer (or a more specialized network of devices) might be patched in such a way as to produce patterns of sounds that conform to the rules.[7]

---

7. For an excellent introduction to topics of "automated music," see Chapter 10 of David Cope's *New Directions in Music*, 6th ed. (Dubuque, IA: Brown & Benchmark, 1993).

The live performance of compositions based on indeterminate or algorithmic procedures have perhaps been less successful with concert audiences than pieces structured in more conventional ways. Members of the audience usually expect to be able to discern meaning in the sounds they hear, to be able to hear the relationships among the sounds, and to recognize the patterns they form. Even with a high level of musical education, or with lavishly detailed program notes in hand, it is rather improbable that a typical listener will be able to grasp quickly what is occurring in an indeterminate or algorithmic composition.

Most members of the audience have also learned to expect a directed movement of musical ideas through time. This is one element that normally compels their attention to the activity onstage. Without it, their attention is likely to lapse into an omnidirectional mode. However, concert manners inhibit looking about the room, and the lighting and the architecture continue to suggest that something of significance ought to be taking place up front. After several minutes, the audience is likely to become bored and impatient. It seems that indeterminate or algorithmic compositions may find a more hospitable context in gatherings that are less formal than a concert, or perhaps such works are better suited to media that reach a dispersed audience, such as recordings, broadcasts, and sound installations in museums (described in further detail later in this chapter).

ÉTUDE 11.3

*D*esign an improvisatory piece for a small ensemble of instruments, one of which is a live-performance synthesizer. Notate the basic melodic and harmonic patterns, along with a description of how these are to be used by the musicians. Also, describe how the piece might begin and how it might end. Provide a technical description, as necessary, regarding the patch settings and audio connections for the synthesizer.

MIDI NETWORKS ONSTAGE

Since the mid-1980s, composers have begun to make extensive use onstage of MIDI sequencers, digital synthesizers, and microcomputers. Live performers now have available to them an array of powerful techniques that formerly could be exercised only in the studio. Subtle textures of electronic sounds, carefully designed and intricately detailed, need no longer be prerecorded but can be generated live. Tape hiss, tape distortion, and other banes of recorded sound are gone.

In a few compositions that employ an onstage MIDI network, there is very little actual operation of the equipment. The composer relies on a

MIDI sequencer to execute the electroacoustic parts of the composition. The MIDI messages that have previously been recorded into the sequence are used to trigger and regulate the various events as they are generated. From the perspective of other performers onstage, however, this is essentially no different from the experience of performing with a tape. The potential of the MIDI network as an instrument for live performance can be more fully realized if a performer takes a more active role with the equipment. Changes in the tempo of the sequence can be made live as the performance progresses. Sub-sequences can be executed on cue, perhaps in response to a MIDI message from a MIDI keyboard or alternate controller. Settings of switches and continuous controllers can be adjusted in real time, perhaps from the controls of the sequencer.

The incorporation of a computer into the MIDI network creates an incredible domain of capabilities. A program developed at the California Institute for the Arts by Mark Coniglio and Morton Subotnick, called Interactor, can monitor a performance and respond when certain conditions occur. For example, when a MIDI keyboard player has struck a particular key a specific number of times, a designated sequence of electroacoustic sounds can be triggered. Or when the keyboard player strikes a specific key at a velocity greater than a specified threshold level, the electroacoustic sounds being generated might be panned around the performing space according to a designated pattern. An enormous variety of possible triggers and responses of this sort can be programmed.

At IRCAM, in Paris, a group led by Miller Puckette has developed a program called MAX (subsequently adapted for commercial release for the Macintosh computer by Opcode Systems, Inc.). MAX provides a vast set of computer routines, called "objects," that can be linked in order to process and respond to MIDI messages in an incredible variety of ways. Working with these program objects is in many ways reminiscent of work with the modular analog synthesizers of a few years ago. MIDI messages are accepted as input and then transformed by various objects into different MIDI messages for output. Or MIDI messages received as input can be used to trigger computations that can result in a cloud of MIDI messages that shape a complex event. The MAX program is not only of tremendous value as a MIDI processor but can also be used very effectively as a tool for algorithmic composition (see Figure 11.5).

A team led by composer Tod Machover at the Massachusetts Institute of Technology has begun to develop a series of networks called hyper-instruments, so far including a hyper-cello and a hyper-viola. The hands and arms of the performer, as well as the body of the acoustic instrument the performer is to play, are wired with a set of sensors. The messages from these sensors are interpreted by one or more microcomputers to direct the generation of sounds by a bank of digital samplers and synthesizers. Thus, the actions of the performer of the acoustic instrument are extended technologically into the realm of electronic musical instruments. The develop-

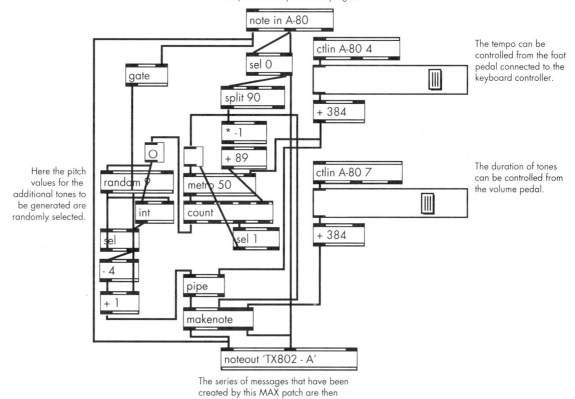

MIDI Note On messages (generated by a Roland A-80, in this Example) are received by the computer through a MIDI interface and then are processed by the MAX program.

note in A-80

The tempo can be controlled from the foot pedal connected to the keyboard controller.

Here the pitch values for the additional tones to be generated are randomly selected.

The duration of tones can be controlled from the volume pedal.

noteout 'TX802 - A'

The series of messages that have been created by this MAX patch are then passed back through the MIDI interface and on to a tone-generating module (in this example, a Yamaha TX802).

FIGURE 11.5
Screen snapshot of a MAX patch that executes an algorithmic compositional procedure to generate clouds of pitches as individual keys are played on a keyboard controller. When a Note On message is received by the computer running this MAX program, a series of pitches is generated. The number of pitches in the series is inversely proportional to the velocity value of the triggering note (if the velocity of the incoming note is greater than 90, however, then only one note is sounded). The pitches that are generated are randomly selected within a range of plus or minus four semitones of the value of the pitch of the triggering message. (Courtesy of Opcode Systems, Inc.)

ment of such networks, called "intelligent instruments," is currently one of the most vibrant areas of activity in the field of electroacoustic music.

COMBINED MEDIA FOR PRESENTATION TO A GATHERED AUDIENCE

Electroacoustic music, either prerecorded or live, is often presented in the concert hall in combination with other art forms that are typically experienced through the passage of time. These other media, including dance, theater, and visual media such as film, can provide an element for the attention of the eyes that seems to be such an essential part of the experience of a concert. The media can be combined so that the electroacoustic music is accompanied by the visual activity, or vice versa. Often, the balance among the elements may shift as the piece progresses.

The degree of relationship among the media is often described by the terms *multimedia, mixed-media,* or *inter-media.* In multimedia presentations, the various elements share the same performance space but proceed largely independently of one another. There is little effort to coordinate them beyond ensuring that they begin and end at more or less the same time. In mixed-media presentations, on the other hand, there is at least some degree of correspondence among the activities in different media. Changes in the texture of the music, for example, might be accompanied by changes in the size, shape, or color of the visual imagery. With inter-media pieces, there is an even greater integration of the various elements, perhaps even incorporating a division of the parts of individual artistic gestures. For example, a point of light may trace an ascending arc on a screen and then disappear, to be followed by the sound of a descending glissando, which then culminates in a burst of light at the bottom of the screen. In inter-media works, the sights and sounds cannot exist separately as works of art that are complete and comprehensible in their own right. The meaning of the patterns is to a large degree dependent upon the relationships that are established among the elements.

MUSIC FOR DANCE

The combination of electroacoustic music and dance has been notably successful for quite some time now. Several dance companies, in fact, have well-established affiliations with composers (such as the longstanding relationship that existed between the Merce Cunningham company and John Cage). The music is likely to be taped and is often intended to function in a subordinate, supporting role to the dance. The dancers provide the visual element of the experience and bring a sense of immediacy to the event. Their presence onstage also provides a point of focus for the social aspects of the gathering.

Occasionally the music may be presented live, by performing musicians rather than on tape, and the interaction between the elements of dance and music can become more dynamic, perhaps to the point of being characterized as an inter-media event. More often, however, such an event is a multimedia affair, in which the dancers and musicians coexist happily in the same space but proceed independently of one another. This is particularly likely in situations in which the music is created by indeterminate or algorithmic methods.

Even so, there may be close interaction of another sort, on another level. For instance, the stage may be set up with proximity sensors or with lights placed opposite photosensors, or the dancers themselves may be fitted with motion sensors. The signals generated by the sensors as the dancers move about the stage can be used to trigger and control the generation of sounds by nearby electronic musical instruments. Something of this sort was done by John Cage, with the assistance of David Tudor and Gordon Mumma, for his *Variations V*, presented in 1965 with the Cunningham Dance Company.

Most choreographers, however, are likely to be looking for music that is somewhat less esoteric. Perhaps a mere wash of sound, to fill what would otherwise be the silence, is all that is required. Or perhaps what is desired is a more thoughtfully constructed, formally structured piece, with clear counts, cues, and gestural groups of sounds. Close and continual consultation between the composer and choreographer is the key to achieving a satisfying result.

ÉTUDE 11.4

$\mathscr{F}$ind a friend who is a choreographer, and suggest the possibility of doing a piece together. Discuss the general character of the proposed piece and the general outlines of the form. Go to the studio and prepare a "demo" recording of the sort of music you think will be appropriate. Meet again with the choreographer to listen together to this "aural sketch." Revise plans as necessary, and proceed to work from there. Plan to meet again often with your collaborator.

MUSIC FOR THE THEATER

Often, electroacoustic music is used as incidental music for a theatrical production. Relatively short passages of music may be used to underscore the mood or setting at the beginning and end of various scenes in a play. Somewhat more extended music might be composed for the interval of time at the beginning or end of each act of the production. Other short bits of music, such as fanfares and other sound cues, may be needed for particular moments within the production. Generally, after the composer has read the play carefully, the director and composer will meet to "spot" those occasions when music is appropriate or helpful and to establish how much music is needed for each occasion. Most likely, they will also discuss the general character of the music required in each instance. The incidental music, which typically is prerecorded for the production, is then composed and produced. Eventually, much of this music may not be used, as the timing of the show is tightened or for a variety of other possible reasons. The composer must understand from the outset of the project that the purpose of the music is to support the production, and not to become the production.

In an opera or a musical, on the other hand, the music is not incidental, but essential. Live musicians are employed, with the most important of these being the singers onstage. Electroacoustic musicians are most likely to be found in the orchestra pit of a contemporary production.[8] With an opera or a musical, the composer has a much greater degree of control and responsibility for the shape and content of the production.

ÉTUDE 11.5

*I*ntroduce yourself to someone at your school who is producing a play, and offer to collaborate by providing incidental music. Obtain a copy of the script, and then prepare a "demo" recording of examples of possible music for the play. Get together with your potential collaborator again to listen to the sketches. If you decide the project is viable, establish a schedule of clear deadlines, and then get started immediately with your work in the studio. Plan to be involved in the technical rehearsals of the production.

MUSIC WITH PROJECTED IMAGES

The combination of electroacoustic music and projected images has been often captivatingly successful. The use of slide projections, laser-beam projections, film, or even video images can undoubtedly fulfill audience expectations of something to sustain visual attention. In an ordinary concert, of course, this is provided by live performers. But when visual media are combined with music (most likely prerecorded music), the need to have live performers is less urgent, and the social aspects of the situation are consequently somewhat less structured. The audience may become rather less formal, perhaps more relaxed in its behavior—in fact, more like a movie audience. The experience is a "cool" one, as media thinker Marshall McLuhan would have described it.

Slide projections have been used in combined-media works for several decades now. Slide projections accompanied the presentations of Varèse's *Poème électronique* in the Philips pavilion at the 1958 Brussels Exposition. John Cage has often included slide projections in multimedia works. During the 1960s in particular, live electroacoustic music was often presented along with dancers, actors, slide projections, special lighting effects, and other elements in multimedia events referred to as "happenings."

Some composers and artists have combined slide projections and electroacoustic music in ways that are more consciously structured, to create what can be described as mixed-media or even inter-media pieces. For some pieces, banks of slide projectors are controlled by devices called "dissolve units" that make it possible for one projected image to cross-fade to the next at a controlled rate. The music for these presentations is virtually

---

8. In many recent Broadway productions, in fact, many of the performers of acoustic instruments have been supplanted by electroacoustic musicians. This development has engendered considerable consternation and controversy, particularly among musicians' unions (understandably enough, perhaps).

always prerecorded (perhaps in the form of a MIDI sequence so that the sounds themselves can be generated live, unaccompanied by tape hiss). Synchronization of the elements in these productions can be rather difficult, however. The controls of dissolve units can be relatively imprecise, and there is no readily available, off-the-shelf interface device (at least none known to the author at the time of this writing) that can enable the control of slide projectors from a MIDI sequencer. Nevertheless, works of great beauty and expressive power have been created (by the composer Kristi Allik and others) for the equipment that is available.

Some composers, notably Ron Pellegrino, have experimented with the combination of electroacoustic music and images formed by projections of laser beams. The device that makes this possible is called a laser scanner; it directs the laser beam by means of small mirrors that are controlled electromagnetically by signals, such as audio-frequency signals, provided as inputs to the device. The patterns that can be formed range from relatively simple *Lissajous* figures[9] to remarkably subtle and exquisite patterns. Changes in the frequency, amplitude, waveform, and phase of the signals provided as input to the laser scanner result in dynamic, continually changing patterns in the projection. A sound synthesizer is a particularly versatile source of such signals for the scanner.

The use of electroacoustic music for film soundtracks has become virtually a standard practice in the filmmaking industry. Music has long been employed in a supporting role in the movies. Much like incidental music for the theater, the music is used to underscore the action or to help establish a sense of the mood or atmosphere of a scene. Only in more "experimental" films, generally, does the music assert itself in a more significant role, in works that can be characterized as inter-media creations.

In the early stages of the production of a commercial film, a composer is given a copy of the script and invited to produce a recording that demonstrates the kind of music the composer might write for the film. After this "demo," along with competing ones by other composers, has been auditioned by the producer of the film, a composer is hired. When the filming is completed and the visual editing begins, the composer may be asked to provide a temporary soundtrack to assist the editors in their work. Once the film is assembled, the composer meets with the producer, director, and others to view the film and decide where music will be used. After this "spotting session," the composer prepares a list of musical events with their timings, called a cue sheet. By this point, the composer is making extensive use of the timing reference provided by SMPTE time code. Most likely, the composer has been provided a working copy of the film on videotape that includes a continuous display onscreen of SMPTE time code values.

The music is then composed, performed, and recorded. Throughout this process, the composer consults frequently with the producer, director, and

---

9. Lissajous figures are named for Jules Lissajous, a 19th-century French physicist who was among the first to describe them.

others. The music is then transferred to film for editing, and any final adjustments required for synchronization with the images are made. Finally, the music is mixed with the dialogue and sound-effects tracks, and the film is then prepared for distribution to movie theaters.[10]

Until recently, the audio quality of film soundtracks did not compare well to that of other audio media. Limitations of dynamic range and frequency range, plus mechanical instabilities in the projector, compromised the clarity and dynamic range of the music. Many of these shortcomings could be attributed to the fact that the audio signal was encoded as an optical pattern near the edge of the film and was decoded by a photocell circuit in the projector. With the adoption of magnetic-stripe soundtracks, recorded on a thin band of magnetic material near the edge of the film rather than as an optical pattern, the audio quality was much improved. The subsequent development of a number of useful audio-processing devices for film soundtracks, by Dolby Laboratories and others, has contributed to an enormous improvement in the audio quality of recent films.

Occasionally there have been efforts to present video works along with electroacoustic music to a concert audience. The result is almost always less than satisfactory. If a standard-size video monitor is used, then the screen is probably too small for viewing by most of the audience. If a video projector is used to display the images on a large screen, their vividness and clarity are markedly inferior to what can be achieved with film projection. A possible alternative is a "video wall," with the image distributed among a bank of video monitors stacked onstage. However, this is logistically formidable, to say the least, and quite expensive. Works that involve video images are perhaps better suited to media of presentation that reach a dispersed audience—via broadcast, video installations in public spaces, retail sales demonstrations, and the like. Works involving video are described more completely in a subsequent section of this chapter in the context of dissemination to such a dispersed audience.

ÉTUDE 11.6

Explore the possibility of collaborating on a piece with a photographer (who can create slides for projection), a filmmaker, or a videographer. Discuss the degree of interaction that should take place between the music and the visual medium. Also, determine the extent to which synchronization is critical. Draft an outline of the project, and then proceed. Consult often with your collaborator as you develop your portion of the project.

---

10. This is a very cursory outline of the process of scoring music for a film. A more complete description can be found in Section 3, "Film and Video Scoring," of Jeffrey Rona's book *Synchronization from Reel to Reel* (Milwaukee: Hal Leonard, 1990).

FURTHER THOUGHTS

One of the greatest hazards for composers who are involved in combining various media is the temptation to try to do it all. To be successful at this, the composer must acquire mastery of all the media employed. It is not sufficient to be highly accomplished in one medium and have only mediocre ability in another. A piece, as the familiar expression goes, can only be as excellent as its weakest part.

A more fruitful approach is to collaborate with other artists. Musicians draw upon a wealth of experience—an awareness of traditions and techniques—from previous musical training. Photographers, videographers, filmmakers, choreographers, dancers, playwrights, and actors do the same. The combined strength of a team of like-minded artists creates the potential for truly strong results. It can also be tremendous fun. The figure of the heroic composer, struggling alone against the forces of philistinism and entropy, is not only anachronistic and banished to obsolescence by the technological art forms of the present, but it is also downright antisocial. The rewards of successful collaboration are too great to forego.

Apart from the creative challenges, perhaps the most significant deterrent to the creation of works that combine media is the ordeal of the logistics. Much equipment is required, and if some of it fails, the entire performance can be placed in jeopardy. Extensive rehearsal, careful prior testing of equipment and connections, and a rigorous preventive maintenance program can minimize the risks substantially. It is important to avoid the temptation to cut corners. Having witnessed and participated in many combined-media events over a number of years, the author concludes that a low-budget production can often be worse than no production at all. The artist should always obtain the best equipment possible, and the services of the most skilled technicians available. Insist on nothing less.

THE FUTURE OF THE CONCERT

There has been occasional speculation in recent years that the institution of the concert is becoming obsolete as a means for the dissemination of music. Certainly the financial circumstances of organizations that present "classical" music, such as symphony orchestras in many small and medium-sized cities, have become very tenuous in the past few years. Support for other sponsoring organizations, such as colleges and universities, has been attenuated as well.

Rock concerts apparently continue to thrive. These, of course, share many of the characteristics of the traditional concert as it evolved out of the 19th century. In many ways, in fact, the onstage spectacle can be much more overt, including dancing, special lighting effects, laser projections, pyrotechnics, and other special effects. Certainly the heroic figure of the

19th-century virtuoso performer finds a parallel in the contemporary rock star.

However, the principal medium for the distribution of rock music is the studio-produced recording, and many live acts do not always compare well to their studio products. In fact, a live rock concert is now often an illusory affair. Vocalists often lip-sync to previously recorded tracks, and many of the tracks of accompanying instruments are played from a MIDI sequencer. Only a few groups, such as the Grateful Dead and Phish, remain deeply committed to the ideal of live public performance.

The rewards of a live concert, including the opportunity to be present as highly accomplished artists make their music come alive, and the ability to share this experience with friends and many other people, are too great to be permitted to become extinct. Just as a salad becomes boring if fresh produce is allowed to be crowded out of markets by boxcar-ripened produce from thousands of miles away, recorded music can never be acceptable as a total substitute for the experience of live music. No compact disc can ever sound as good as the real thing can sound. It is important to continue to foster a diversity of means for the experience of music. This suggests that creative ways must continually be found to ensure that live performance does not become a rare experience that can only be enjoyed by a few.

ÉTUDE 11.7

*T*ogether with the other members of your class, organize a public presentation of works of electroacoustic music that you have created. First, select pieces to include on the program. Next, design a publicity effort for the event. Perhaps you may want to produce in the studio a few radio announcements for the campus station. You may also want to commission friends who are art students to prepare posters.

Make a list of technical requirements for the event. You may want to plan for backup equipment for essential components of the sound system. Make arrangements for a well-trained stage crew, and conduct at least one technical rehearsal.

Then, have a great show. May it be the kind of show that people talk about for a long while afterwards.

THE PRESENTATION OF ELECTROACOUSTIC MUSIC TO OTHER GATHERINGS

Besides the public concert, there are a few other situations in which electroacoustic music might be presented to a gathering of people. For example, at various festivals of electroacoustic music that have been held at colleges in recent years, "listening sessions" have been organized for the presentation in smaller rooms of prerecorded compositions. Listeners are free to come and go between pieces. No formal dress is required, no applause is expected, and seating is open. Slide projections may be used to announce the beginning and ending of the listening session and to announce the title and the name of the composer as each work is presented.

A somewhat more formal setting for electroacoustic music is a religious service. Here, such music might be used to evoke a sense of the spiritual dimensions of reality, to depict the supernatural, or to help sustain an ambience conducive to contemplation. Electroacoustic musical instruments such as synthesizers and samplers are also used extensively by rock groups with a religious identity, such as Christian rock groups and "praise bands."

A much less formal setting is the public dance. Many clubs present electroacoustic music as music to which people can dance. Several recent popular styles have in fact originated from this context. Such dance music provides a clear example of "functional" music, as distinct from "art" music. Art music is conceived as being the primary focus of attention, to be listened to closely and appreciated fully in its own right. Functional music is music used to facilitate other activities, such as working, shopping, or dancing. Clearly there are many potential contexts in contemporary culture for musical sounds produced by electroacoustic means.

SOUND REINFORCEMENT FOR LIVE PERFORMERS OF ELECTROACOUSTIC MUSIC

Electroacoustic music that is performed live is conveyed to the audience through a system of audio components called the house sound system (see Figure 11.6). The most prominent of these components are the house speakers, which typically include a set of loudspeakers at each side of the front of the stage or, preferably, a single cluster of loudspeakers suspended from the midpoint of the ceiling at the front of the stage. The house speakers receive the audio signal from a set of power amplifiers, which in turn receive the audio signal from the house mixing console. This mixer is placed in the seating area of the audience (it can be placed elsewhere, such as a sound booth, but with much less satisfactory results). If the speakers are placed on each side of the stage, then the house console should be placed at a point nearly equidistant from the house speakers and at a distance from the stage that is between one and two times the distance that separates the speakers.

The house mixing console receives signals from microphones and pickups that are placed onstage for the amplification of acoustic instruments. The outputs of onstage electronic instruments are usually patched into direct boxes there, and from those to the house mixing console. For neatness and convenience, individual microphone cables and cables from direct boxes may be patched onstage into a stage box, from which the signals are passed to the house mixing board through a "snake" trunk line (see Figure 11.7). Such snakes typically can carry perhaps 8 or 16 separate signals to the house mixer. Once the signals are brought to the house

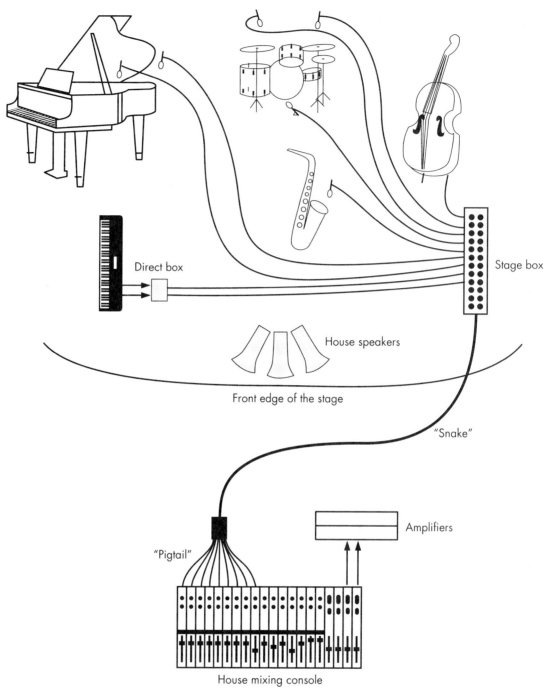

Direct box

Stage box

House speakers

Front edge of the stage

"Snake"

"Pigtail"

Amplifiers

House mixing console

FIGURE 11.6
A typical house sound system.

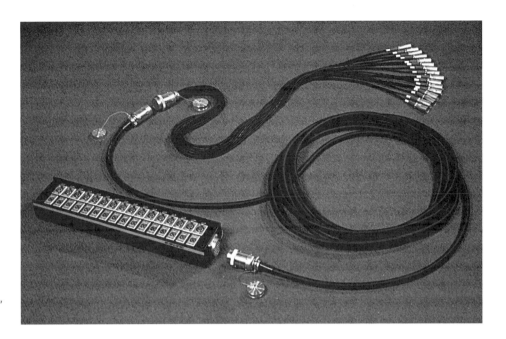

FIGURE 11.7
A stage box, with a "snake" and a "pigtail."

mixing console, the house sound engineer can regulate the balance of sound among the onstage musicians and the overall level of loudness on behalf of the listeners in the audience.

It is particularly important that the musicians onstage be able to hear themselves and each other. If the house sound system is applied to this purpose, then there is a great possibility that unpleasant audio feedback will become a great nuisance. Therefore, an additional "monitor" sound system is usually set up for the performers (see Figure 11.8). For this purpose, a stage box is essential. Most stage boxes include signal splitters, so that any signal patched to an input connector on the box can also be picked up from a corresponding output connector on the box, in addition to being passed along to the snake to the house mixing console. Thus, the signals that are patched into a stage box can also be connected to an offstage "monitor" mixer.

The operator of the monitor mixer typically can provide as many as four independent output channels that can be fed to the various onstage monitor speakers. Individual performers can thus receive a custom mix that emphasizes the instruments in the ensemble that are most important for them to hear. The monitor speakers are highly directional, thus providing fairly adequate separation from the monitor mixes being provided to other musicians from the other onstage speakers, and also reducing the possibility of feedback.

It may be possible to provide monitor mixes from the house console, thus avoiding the necessity of setting up a second mixer. However, the house sound engineer is often more than sufficiently busy with the house sound mix. It can also be somewhat more difficult for performers to communicate their wishes to a sound engineer out in the house; they often prefer to work with a monitor specialist who is just offstage. Contemporary musicians have come to expect a certain level of technical sophistication at performance venues, and it is wise to avoid cutting corners.

The widespread use of MIDI instruments has introduced a new element of complexity to onstage setups. Many performers would prefer not to share a stage with a multitude of keyboard stands and equipment racks. Also, technicians would prefer to have much of the MIDI

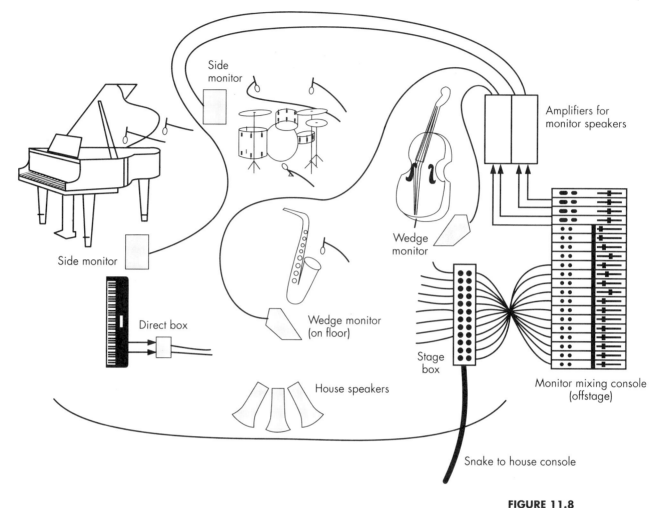

FIGURE 11.8
An onstage monitor sound system.

equipment offstage so that it can be more readily accessible in the event of a technical problem during a performance. Wireless MIDI systems have been developed that can transmit MIDI data several hundred yards, thus making it possible to keep the MIDI controllers onstage with the performers and to banish the rest of the equipment offstage.

THE PRESENTATION OF ELECTROACOUSTIC MUSIC TO A DISPERSED AUDIENCE

As described at the outset of this chapter, perhaps the most significant consequence for the musician of the development of electronic technology is the ability to reach an audience whose members are dispersed in several locations and who may come to the music at different points in time. The principal site for listening to music is no longer the concert hall. Rather, it is more likely to be the home, car, office, shop, store, or anyplace else where loudspeakers can be installed. As a result, the relationships between artists and listeners, and among listeners, are changed radically.

What are the consequences when performers and listeners are no longer in the same room together? Certainly this has a considerable effect on listening habits, and obviously it will have an effect on the social dynamics of musical activity. When music is distributed in the form of a recording or a broadcast, no social transaction occurs between artists and a group of listeners with a cohesive sense of social identity. The music reaches listeners as individuals, more or less isolated from one another, and there is virtually no opportunity for direct interaction between them and the artists. Instead, the experience is passed through a series of intermediaries, such as recording engineers, recording company executives, record store managers, radio station programmers, disc jockeys, and a variety of others. The unmistakable effect of this on how music is now experienced is described in the remainder of this chapter.

RECORDINGS

The ephemerality of a live performance, not to mention good manners toward the performers, dictates closely attentive listening at a concert. When listening to a recording at home, however, the listener is free to come and go, perhaps to do housework, or attend to the other distractions that can come up at home. An artist who reaches for a dispersed audience, and who is separated from that audience by a series of intermediaries, can never be quite certain of the circumstances under which the music will be heard. Not only will individual members of the audience bring different levels of attention to the experience, but the artist can never even be sure of the acoustic conditions under which the music will be heard.

Such uncertainties encourage a tendency toward moderation of musical contrasts (avoiding large differences in loudness or extremely high or extremely low pitches, for example). Lengthy pieces that require sustained attention are eschewed. Music that is less detailed, less intricately patterned, is regarded as more likely to succeed with a dispersed audience.

Paradoxically, recordings can also facilitate close listening. A recording, or a small section of it, can be repeated dozens or even hundreds of times. The listener will soon sort out all of the harmonic changes and melodic patterns—perhaps assisted by a printed musical score that can be viewed while listening to the recording. For some listeners, then, a recording can facilitate the understanding of very complex, richly detailed, or previously unfamiliar styles of music.

Some listeners still hear recordings as reminiscences, or "souvenirs," of the experience of live performance in a concert. The concert for them continues to serve as a point of reference. However, for most listeners today, the recording is an independent object, an experience in its own right. The sound becomes abstracted from its origins as performance gestures. For electroacoustic music, this can be fortuitous. The association of sound with gesture has always been somewhat problematic with electronic musical instruments. For example, playing middle C might produce first a trumpet tone, then a gong sound, later a sampled spoken word, and finally a filtered turtle burp. For a member of an audience at a concert, this ambiguity can be somewhat disconcerting (so to speak). But because a recording requires no such association of sound and gesture, the recording is quite a natural habitat for sounds of electroacoustic origin.

At present, there are two principal media for audio recordings: the compact disc (CD) and the analog cassette.[11] A CD can contain up to approximately 74 minutes of stereo music, digitally encoded for superb audio quality and durability. Homes and offices are typical sites for listening to compact discs. An analog cassette can satisfactorily contain up to 90 minutes of music. The audio quality is inferior to that of a CD, but cassette players are much more portable and can be found in such places as car interiors and at beaches.

A subject of much interest to electroacoustic musicians is the distribution of recordings to the dispersed audience. Major record companies are interested in music that conforms closely to one of the well-established styles that have demonstrated their appeal to mass audiences. New artists are typically brought to the attention of these companies by entertainment lawyers and others who specialize in scouting new talent.

Music that might appeal to smaller, more select audiences is often recorded by smaller, so-called independent record companies.[12] Even though the mass means of record distribution—through retail chain stores, for example—are somewhat inefficient and unresponsive to the needs of specialized audiences, a small "indy" record label is more likely to find creative means to reach such an audience (perhaps through direct-mail marketing). In this way, recordings of more experimental and esoteric music are more likely to find their way to a sympathetic audience (and much more likely to find a sympathetic audience in this way than in a concert arena).

Many artists begin by producing and distributing their own recordings. For just a few hundred dollars, a small business that specializes in duplicating recordings can produce a few hundred copies of a submitted master tape onto cassettes (be certain to request the highest quality blank cassettes for the project). They can also arrange for the printing of insert cards (from submitted copy), including color artwork. Cassette labels and shrink wrapping will also be included. For just a few times this cost, privately issued

---

11. Other media, such as the digital compact cassette (DCC) and the mini-disc (MD), are being introduced, but it is too soon to judge their success.

12. It has been said that the chances of getting a major company interested in music that might appeal to a smaller, but nonetheless well-defined audience are not much better than the chances of persuading General Motors to manufacture a limited-edition electric car for left-handed law school professors.

compact discs can also be produced. Friends and relatives always accept their copies graciously, of course, and the remaining copies can be used as "demos" to send to music industry executives and college radio stations.

BROADCASTS

Much of what has just been said regarding recordings applies also to broadcasting, the other principal means for disseminating electroacoustic music to a dispersed audience. As with recordings, members of this audience—in their homes, offices, cars, and elsewhere—can approach the experience provided by their radios or televisions at various levels of attention, and the degree of attention can vary in response to the distractions that are bound to occur in such places. The audience for a broadcast may tend to be even more passive than that for recordings, since the members of the broadcast audience are not directly involved in the decisions about what is to be played and are not required to become involved in actually loading and operating the playback equipment. Consequently, there is much less inducement for close listening.

Most of the material that is broadcast is recorded material. However, the broadcasting media do have one capability that recordings do not. Recorded performances are fixed, unchanging from one hearing to the next. Occasionally a broadcast performance can be of a live event, however. Some of the immediacy of a concert performance, some of the excitement and drama, can be conveyed through radio or television even to an audience whose members cannot be physically present at the event. Despite the expense and logistical difficulties associated with live broadcasts, it would be a very good thing if more of this were done.

The artist who produces electroacoustic music for broadcast needs to be aware that members of the audience are likely to tune in during the middle of a piece, or tune out before it is over. The subtleties of a complex, extended musical form would therefore be lost on most of the audience. Other subtleties are likely to be compromised as well. For example, very soft passages are likely to be masked by tire or wind noise in cars, fan noises from office machines, or the noises of appliances in the home. Very loud noises, on the other hand, are likely to irritate. Therefore, the dynamic range of the piece ought to be compressed (for a review of the functions of compressor/limiters, see the discussion in Chapter 4). Because some radio receivers (and most television receivers) are capable of producing only monaural sound, the producer of electroacoustic music for broadcast media must ensure that a stereo mixdown is "mono-compatible." When the two channels are combined, there should be no significant losses at most frequencies due to phase cancellations.

Also, it is important that the producer be aware of the limited frequency bandwidth of broadcast media. FM radio broadcasts, for example, absolutely cannot include any frequency content above 15 kHz. Higher frequencies are, of course, essential for the quality of the experience of listening to CD or cassette recordings, but they simply will not be missed from most of the musical material used for radio or television programs.

Electroacoustic music that is broadcast over the radio is most likely to be recorded on compact discs, cassettes, or even phonograph recordings. Electroacoustic music can also be heard as the functional music of jingles in commercial messages and "signatures" for news, public affairs, or sports programs. Such signatures are brief, very distinctive passages of music heard at the beginning and end of a program, and occasionally as interludes between segments of a program.

Electroacoustic music for commercial messages and program signatures is also heard extensively in television broadcasts. In addition, there is considerable use of electroacoustic music within programs. As with music for films, this music generally plays a supporting role to the visual aspects of the experience. However, with MTV and other cable channels such as VH-1 (Video Hits–One) and TNN (The Nashville Network), the music assumes a more substantial role.

As with the production of music for film, several decades' experience in combining visual and musical elements within the medium of television have led to the development of some highly sophisticated techniques. A complete description of such techniques is well beyond the scope of this text. The intensive use of particular forms of SMPTE time code, for example, is critical.

The general process of producing a sound track for a video production is similar to that for a film. After the visuals have been videotaped, on location or on a set, the project moves into the "postproduction" phase. During this part of the process, some editing of the visuals is completed and the composer receives a working copy of the show. A spotting session is held with the director and others, and a cue list is developed.

With a MIDI network of synthesizers, samplers, drum machines, and sequencers locked to the SMPTE time code on the videotape, the composer begins to put together the musical passages appropriate to the various cues listed for the program. Eventually these will be submitted for approval and then mixed with the dialogue or narration and with the sound-effects tracks (in many less expensive productions, the composer is responsible for the sound effects as well).[13]

Until recently, the audio quality of television and video productions was quite inferior to that of other media. However, high-quality stereo broadcasting and hi-fi stereo VCR equipment have done much to improve the situation. In the future, further improvements in audio quality are likely to be

---

13. This same process, more or less, is also used for the production of videos for private use rather than broadcast, such as industrial training videotapes and sales presentations. A few composers are able to find a fair amount of employment on such projects.

FIGURE 11.9
Still frame from *Love of Line, of Light and Shadow: The Brooklyn Bridge,* for clarinet, color video, and electronic sound, by Reynold Weidenaar. Courtesy of Magnetic Music Publishing Co. (ASCAP).

introduced along with high-definition television (HDTV), which presents a much better image than the video technology currently in use.

Other technological changes may include an increasing use of computer graphics and animated images to accompany the digitally generated music on soundtracks. More esoteric and experimental works of video art have featured this combination for many years (see Figure 11.9). Marvelous computer programs, such as the Producer software for the Macintosh by Passport Designs, have made microcomputer-based multimedia production much more accessible, however. With such software, computer graphics, including animated imagery, can be readily integrated with digitized sounds and MIDI sequences for playing digital sound samplers and synthesizers.

Another recent technological innovation is described as "interactive video." For instance, a relatively new compact disc format called CD-I (for "compact disc–interactive") allows the presentation of visual images along with music, but also provides a variety of programming paths for the consumer to explore. These are pursued by means of various commands transmitted from the hand-held remote controller for the CD player. Different versions of a performance might be recorded on the CD, for example, along with explanatory notes on the video monitor. The potential of this technology for education as well as entertainment is only beginning to be considered.

ÉTUDE 11.8

*W*rite and produce a 29-second public service announcement (PSA) or commercial message for possible radio broadcast. Begin by writing a script and sketching some appropriate music (you will probably want to use a MIDI sequencer to help you prepare a quick musical sketch without fussing yet over the details).

Consider the relationships among the narration, music, and any sound effects you may want to use. For example, the music should be more subdued during passages of narration (the "voice-overs"). This can be accomplished by simplifying the musical texture, reducing the intensity level of the music, using an equalizer to attenuate frequencies between 2 kHz and 5 kHz (the "presence peak" of the voice), or a combination of these techniques.

To get a better sense of how music is used in commercial messages, and a clearer idea of the form of a typical commercial, take an hour or two and simply listen closely to a local radio station. Then, design a commercial yourself!

INSTALLATIONS

Yet another way to reach a dispersed audience is to set up the equipment for presentation in a public space so that people can observe and hear the artist's work as they come and go. Such setups, called installations, may be encountered in museums, the lobbies of buildings, outdoor plazas, shopping malls, and similar spaces.

Installations are popular among artists whose work incorporates experimental or esoteric video imagery (see Figure 11.10). The ubiquity of video monitors in public spaces, such as airport terminals and shopping centers, helps make these spaces seem natural habitats for art installations of this sort. As mentioned previously, installations are also particularly suitable

FIGURE 11.10
Mary Ellen Childs, a noted creator of installations as well as a composer of music in a variety of more conventional media. (Photo by John Lovett, courtesy of Mary Ellen Childs.)

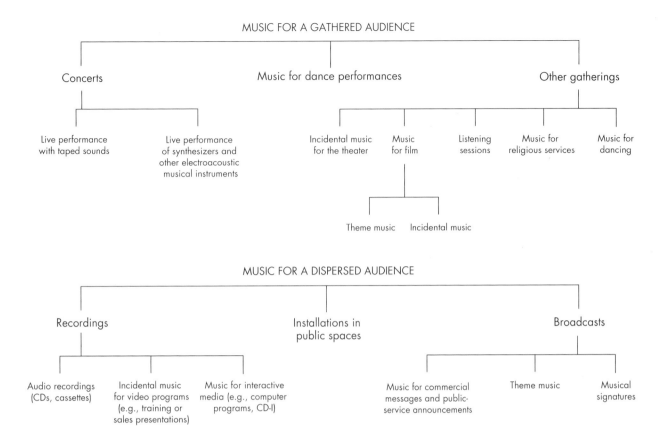

MUSIC FOR A GATHERED AUDIENCE

Concerts
- Live performance with taped sounds
- Live performance of synthesizers and other electroacoustic musical instruments

Music for dance performances
- Incidental music for the theater
- Music for film
  - Theme music
  - Incidental music
- Listening sessions

Other gatherings
- Music for religious services
- Music for dancing

MUSIC FOR A DISPERSED AUDIENCE

Recordings
- Audio recordings (CDs, cassettes)
- Incidental music for video programs (e.g., training or sales presentations)
- Music for interactive media (e.g., computer programs, CD-I)

Installations in public spaces

Broadcasts
- Music for commercial messages and public-service announcements
- Theme music
- Musical signatures

FIGURE 11.11
A variety of venues for electro-acoustic music.

contexts for musical works composed by indeterminate or algorithmic techniques. Unlike members of a concert audience, the individuals who hear an installed work are not constrained to remain any longer than their curiosity and fascination can sustain. Such "user-friendly" environments can enable works to thrive that would otherwise wilt in a concert hall.

An artist who plans an installation will need to consider several practical matters. An awareness of the acoustical conditions at the site is important. The availability of electrical power is, needless to say, an even more critical consideration. For outdoor installations, there may be a variety of weather conditions for which to prepare. Care must also be taken to secure the equipment from theft, vandalism, or even inadvertent tampering. If the concept of the installation is extended to include live performers, such as dancers, musicians, narrators, actors, or mimes, then their requirements must be accommodated as well. Despite all of this potential toil and trouble, however, the vitality of the installation as a contemporary artistic medium makes it very much worth the effort.

This concludes a brief survey of possible venues for electroacoustic music (Figure 11.11). It is likely, however, that others will be discovered or developed in response to further technological changes in the near future. The success of the efforts of a composer of electroacoustic music will nonetheless continue to depend on the extent to which the composer understands clearly where and how the audience for the music will be reached. Art is, after all, a social activity.

FOR FURTHER READING

Cope, David. *New Directions in Music*. 6th ed. Dubuque, IA: Brown & Benchmark, 1993.

Eisenberg, Evan. *The Recording Angel: Explorations in Phonography*. New York: McGraw-Hill, 1987.

Emmerson, Simon, ed. *The Language of Electroacoustic Music*. New York: Harwood, 1986.

Heifetz, Robin Julian. *On the Wires of Our Nerves*. Lewisburg, PA: Bucknell University Press, 1989.

Pellegrino, Ronald. *The Electronic Arts of Sound and Light*. New York: Van Nostrand Reinhold, 1983.

Pellman, Samuel Frank. *An Overview of Current Practices Regarding the Performance of Electronic Music*. Ann Arbor, MI: University Microfilms, 1978.

Rona, Jeffrey. *Synchronization from Reel to Reel*. Milwaukee: Hal Leonard, 1990.

Schwartz, Elliot. *Electronic Music: A Listener's Guide*. rev. ed. New York: Holt, Rinehart & Winston, 1975.

CHAPTER 12

TECHNOLOGY AND MUSIC: FROM THE PAST TO THE FUTURE

*I*n the past few thousand years, humans have shown a particular propensity for technology—the use of tools—to assist and expand their capabilities to do the things they need to do and those they want to do to make life more enjoyable. Although it might be argued that musical activities may be properly considered in the former category, it is indisputable that such activities as performing music, listening to it, collecting recordings of it, and even reading about it bring a measure or two of pleasure to the lives of many people. An impressive set of musical tools—a highly developed technology of music—now exists to facilitate and enhance this enjoyment.

We may not be accustomed to the notion of regarding our favorite musical instrument—our guitar, our piano, our clarinet—as a tool. This does not make it any less so, however, and it is readily apparent that without such assemblies of wood, wire, plastic, silicon, and other materials, our range of musical activities would be much narrower.

What determines the set of musical tools available? Does the acceptance of particular tools affect the development of the styles of music created and performed? Just as is the case with kitchen utensils and appliances, or tools in a woodworking shop, the development and acceptance of a musical instrument occurs in response to a perceived need. The same can be said for other tools with potential musical uses, such as the radio or the player of recordings. Changes in musical style, or changes in the social and economic circumstances of the audiences for music, have a direct effect on how music is produced and distributed, and therefore on the tools that are needed to accomplish these things. What is less obvious is the reciprocal influence that technology exerts on musical activity. Just as the availability of various cooking technologies—microwaving, boiling, broiling, or baking—determines the extent of the variety we find on our menu, the technology of musical instruments and related devices can affect, in ways that are subtle or not so subtle, the range and forms of expressions of what gets played and heard.

Of specific interest here is the role played in this interaction by the electroacoustic musical instruments and techniques described in this text. What is the significance of this technology in the present enjoyment of music? Might an understanding of this relationship provide some clues to the future of musical performance and listening?

A sense of the role of contemporary musical technology can perhaps be gained from a consideration of the history of one of the antecedents of the modern synthesizer—the piano. By the end of the 17th century, the technology existed to construct a keyboard instrument capable of expressive gradations of loudness, from soft (*piano*) to loud (*forte*). However, the musical style extant at that time did not require such a capability, and the instrument was for the most part ignored. By the middle of the 18th century, however, musical style had changed to one in which more subtle control of loudness was important, and the piano began to thrive.

By the end of the 18th century, as the social and economic group now known as the middle class grew in size and importance, a new audience for music developed. To reach this new audience, primarily in concert halls and other, larger performance spaces, pianists began to perform on pianos that were reinforced with iron and improved in other ways to strengthen the tone. The thrill of performing on such sturdy instruments before large crowds in turn inspired the development of an even more robust style of music, as exemplified by the works of Franz Liszt. (For a more detailed examination of the mutual influence of style and technology in the history of keyboard instruments, see the essay included at the end of this text as Appendix E.)

The history of the development of the piano has parallels in the history of other musical tools. A guitar-playing reader, for example, might reflect on the propitious coincidence of the electrification of the guitar (beginning in the 1920s) and the development of the mass audience through the electronic media of recordings and broadcasting. The effect of these developments on techniques of guitar playing and on styles of popular music has been immense. The reader may also be aware of fleeting developments that, while clever in themselves, never quite caught on. The need these developments attempted to address was apparently not felt to be sufficiently urgent by consumers of musical technology, or the development was not judged to be meeting the need sufficiently well.[1]

The success of the electronic sound synthesizer in the 1960s was the result of the confluence of the inventive impulse of Robert Moog and his contemporaries—their interest in the engineering challenge presented by the design of such a device—and the expressed need for such an instrument by many musicians (perhaps most notably, Edgard Varèse). The

---

1. An example of the latter is the ARP Avatar, an analog synthesizer system developed in the 1970s that was to be played with guitar technique rather than from a keyboard. The failure of this product contributed significantly to the demise of its manufacturer.

success of this development was later confirmed as the sound synthesizer came to be regarded, in the popular press and elsewhere, as the musical embodiment of the age of electronic technology.

More recently, the Musical Instrument Digital Interface has achieved a deep and widespread acceptance. This is primarily because it has met so many requirements for coordinated use of electroacoustic musical instruments, with a degree of success much greater than anyone could have dared to hope a decade ago. MIDI, particularly when used in a network of devices that includes a microcomputer, has facilitated the transcription of performed music into musical notation, the storage and recall of control data and timbre information, and an impressive array of other capabilities as well.

In particular, the success of MIDI sequencing has coincided with, and provided further impetus to, the development of personal studios—"electroacoustic cocoons." In these home studios, individual artists, whether amateur or professional, can toil in solitude, with the expectation of eventually reaching their audience through some medium of recording. It is vitally important, however, that the musicians who work in such studios continue to be explicitly aware of the limitations of the MIDI sequencer. For example, few sequencers yet provide adequately for a satisfactory degree of rhythmic suppleness—for music with fermatas, grand pauses, agogic accents, rubato, and similar rhythmic phenomena. Although this may not be considered a significant drawback by musicians who prefer hard-driving, mechanistic styles of rhythm, for other users the attractions of MIDI sequencing are offset somewhat by the difficulties of achieving expressive rhythmic flexibility. The danger is that the tool may discourage and eventually preclude such an interest to the extent that musical style and taste will have been shaped in a way that may not be desirable.

Similarly, it is argued by many electroacoustic musicians that the demise of analog synthesizers has resulted in a degree of musical impoverishment. With their hundreds of potential circuit paths, and dozens of control knobs and switches that could literally be grasped quickly and manipulated easily, analog synthesizers virtually invited a playful, experimental approach to creating sounds. Contemporary, mass-produced digital synthesizers, on the other hand, have eschewed such physical controls in favor of complex, internal programming. The tuning of such synthesizers is usually locked into the standard 12 tones per octave of equal temperament. The inherent bias of the Musical Instrument Digital Interface in favor of "note-based" music, as described near the end of Chapter 6, provides a further constraining factor. Great persistence and thorough familiarity with obscure passages in the owner's manual are required of the musician who desires to fashion truly innovative timbres and textures. Technological change, then, does not necessarily mean progress in every respect. Recent software packages, such as MAX and similar programs (described in Chapter 11) promise to mitigate this drawback somewhat and to restore some of the potential for freer exploration at the edges of stylistic possibilities. But there is still some way to go before the relative ease of programming familiar to those who worked with analog synthesizers is restored.

Indeed, there can often be unintended and unanticipated consequences —side effects—of the adoption of a new technology. The previous chapter included considerable discussion of the possible impact the availability of recordings may have already had on contemporary habits of listening—in particular, a tendency toward more casual listening. To this can be added a concern for the amateur live performer, who is forced to compete with an ideal, recorded performer whose efforts have been spliced and sweetened to virtual perfection in the recording studio.[2] Is it possible that live performance by amateurs will become nearly extinct? It is wise always to question what might be lost, as well as what is to be gained, by the adoption of new technology. An explicit awareness of the potential costs may inspire musicians to accept the new technology in a way that does not drive out the things of value that are already extant.

These cursory observations regarding the development of musical tools and the interaction of technology and music can be summarized as follows:

1. Musical technology changes as musical styles change. Newer instruments come into use to meet the requirements of newer styles of music. Older instruments may become obsolete.[3]

2. Musical styles change as audiences change, often in response to changes in social and economic conditions and relationships.

3. Musical styles also can change in response to changes in musical technology itself.

4. Musical technology, in turn, can change in response to more general changes in prevailing technology (for example, the pneumatic technology of organ-building was superceded by the mechanical technology of piano-building, which was supplanted by the electronic technology of analog synthesizers, which in turn is being replaced by the digital technology of contemporary devices). Musically curious engineers will always be interested in finding ways to apply the prevailing technology to the solution of current musical needs. Some of these applications will succeed.

5. Not all of the consequences of a new musical technology can always be anticipated.

With these principles in mind, it may be possible, with a requisite measure of timidity, to project some aspects of the mid-term future of electro-

---

2. Yet another side effect of the availability of recordings, however, is that young performers can learn much from listening to recordings of their predecessors, including those long since deceased. Certainly this is a vital part of the education now of most young jazz players.

3. Occasionally, however, older instruments may reappear as a need for them is again recognized. The harpsichord is a good example.

acoustic musical instruments and techniques. Perhaps the most widely recognized limitation of digital sound synthesizers and digital sound samplers at present is their homogeneity of timbre and articulation from one tone to the next, by comparison to the much more subtle differences in color and articulation among tones produced by an acoustic instrument. When a synthesizer takes a melodic line in an ensemble of instruments, for instance, it is identifiable as a synthesizer certainly by virtue of the novelty of timbre, but also because the range of timbral differences among various tones, whether high or low in pitch, is quite narrow. The primary restriction on the ability of a contemporary instrument to manifest a more natural range of subtlety and control of tone color is the relatively limited processing power available for real-time digital synthesis, or the considerably limited amount of memory for the storage of digital sound samples.

It is highly probable that this will change, as increasingly powerful, but inexpensive processing and memory circuits are developed. Eventually, the research now being done in physical modeling and other advanced techniques at CCRMA at Stanford, CNMAT at Berkeley, IRCAM in Paris, MIT, and other centers will be expressed in the design of commercially available instruments (as occurred with the Yamaha DX-7). The need for more natural sounding shadings of tone color among synthetic tones will be met much more satisfactorily than at present.

However, such subtlety is likely to be attained through techniques that involve far more complex sets of variables than is the case with current instruments. Patch programming is therefore likely to become even more the task of specialist "digital instrument makers" and "sound designers." Perhaps only at university studios will individual composers be likely to continue to design their own instruments (esoteric instruments with fantastical properties, such as the giant digital banjos of David Jaffe described in Chapter 9).

In a more general sense, it seems safe to predict that the tendency toward standardization that began with MIDI will continue. Even as the capabilities of devices increase, their user interfaces will become more standardized and refined. Manufacturers of instruments and recording equipment, and developers of software, have been listening very closely for many years now to their customers (sometimes receiving virtually immediate feedback over on-line, long-distance computer networks such as PAN). They do indeed respond to the suggestions and complaints that they receive.

As musicians in the next few decades become more familiar with their instruments, intriguing musical challenges (rather than irritating technical ones) will begin to occupy a greater portion of their attention. Perhaps a period of maturation for the medium of electroacoustic music, similar to that which occurred with the piano in the early decades of the 19th century, is about to take place in the first few decades of the 21st century. But then, perhaps something entirely different will take shape. It is not so much a matter of being certain of such things, but rather of being prepared for change and anticipating ways of making most effectively the music of the future.

KEEPING PACE WITH CHANGE

*T*he technology of electroacoustic music continues to change with daunting rapidity. A text such as this cannot possibly remain completely up-to-date with these changes or with the musical concerns that arise from such changes. However, a variety of excellent sources of relatively fresh information do exist. By consulting several of these sources regularly, the reader should be able to remain abreast of at least the most significant developments. These resources include:

Electronic Musician magazine is a monthly publication found at most retail news and magazine outlets. A typical issue includes articles related to techniques and technology. The equipment reviews are generally quite thorough and informative. Address: 6400 Hollis Street #12, Emeryville, CA 94608.

Keyboard magazine is another monthly that is available at most retail news and magazine outlets. A typical issue includes articles featuring contemporary artists in a variety of genres. The equipment reviews are generally very informative and helpful. Address: 20085 Stevens Creek Boulevard, Cupertino, CA 95014.

Mix magazine is a monthly publication that covers contemporary equipment and techniques for professional sound recording, sound production, live sound reinforcement, and related topics. Address: 6400 Hollis Street #12, Emeryville, CA 94608.

Mix Bookshelf is a service of *Mix* magazine that offers for sale a wide assortment of texts and other books currently in print that deal with audio technology. Address: 6400 Hollis Street #12, Emeryville, CA 94608.

The *Performing Artists Network* (PAN) is a commercial computer network that includes literally thousands of professional electroacoustic musicians, equipment manufacturers, retailers, music software programmers, and other people interested in electroacoustic music. Fresh information appears on virtually a daily basis. The service includes hotlines to well over a hundred different companies and organizations, and access to several well-stocked databases for computer utility programs, patch banks, and sample files (the sound file shown in Figure 9.12 and subsequent examples was downloaded from PAN, for example). A computer, modem, and communications software are required. For further information, write to The PAN Network, P.O. Box 162, Skippack, PA 19474.

The *International MIDI Association* (IMA) provides official information pertaining to the ever-changing MIDI specification. It occasionally publishes a newsletter that summarizes recent changes, along with a few helpful hints. For further information, write to the International MIDI Association, 5316 W. 57th Street, Los Angeles, CA 90056.

The *Society for Electro-Acoustic Music in the United States* (SEAMUS) is primarily an organization for composers working in college and university studios. It publishes a quarterly newsletter and a journal. Each year it sponsors an annual conference at which compositions by members are presented. For further information, write to SEAMUS, 2550 Beverly Boulevard, Los Angeles, CA 90057.

The *International Computer Music Association* (ICMA) brings together professionals from around the world who deal with advanced work in the uses of computers for musical composition and performance. It publishes a quarterly newsletter and sponsors an annual international conference that includes concerts of members' music, papers presented by members, and studio reports. For further information, write to the International Computer Music Association, Suite 330, 2040 Polk Street, San Francisco, CA 94109.

Inspired and initiated in the 1970s by Gil Trythall, Tom Rhea, and others, a series of festivals called *Electronic Music Plus* have been hosted by a succession of colleges and universities. In response to the visual deficiencies of earlier performances of electroacoustic music (as described in Chapter 11), this series has featured electroacoustic music presented with live musicians, dancers, projected images, or some combination thereof. Other notable annual festivals include those presented by the School of Music at Bowling Green State University in Bowling Green, Ohio, and by the Society of Composers, Inc. (P.O. Box 296, Old Chelsea Station, New York, NY 10113-0296).

HINTS FOR MICROPHONE PLACEMENT IN COMMON RECORDING AND SOUND-REINFORCEMENT SITUATIONS

There is a tremendous variety of successful techniques for placing a microphone near a given musical instrument, and every sound engineer has a unique set of ideas on what works well. The following suggestions should provide a general sense of how to think about this very important matter. For a more complete understanding, however, the reader is advised to consult many of the excellent writings cited in the bibliography at the end of Chapter 1.

Speech or singing   To minimize the effects of plosives and sibilance, place the microphone above, below, or to the side, but point it directly at the mouth (see Figure A.1). Be mindful of the boost of low frequencies that can occur with cardioid and bidirectional microphones that are placed

FIGURE A.1

close to the source (the "proximity effect"). This can be particularly notice-able if the microphone is placed within six inches of the source.

Grand piano (mono recording)   Place the microphone over the middle section of strings and right next to the lid (see Figure A.2), to minimize cancellation by sounds that are reflected from the lid and arrive at the microphone out of phase relative to those that reach the microphone directly from the strings.

Acoustic guitar   Place the microphone one to two feet away and point it at the center of the guitar hole (see Figure A.3). To reduce the prominence of string scrapes, use a cardioid microphone that is placed above the lower part of the fingerboard (but still pointed directly at the center of the guitar hole).

Woodwind instruments   Point the microphone at the fingerholes (see Figure A.4), since most of the sound of a woodwind instrument emerges from these, or from the bell at the end of the instrument. If the microphone is aimed at the mouthpiece, there will be an overbalance of breathing and hissing noises. (This is especially a problem at the headjoint of a flute, where the air passes over the mouthpiece, not into it.)

Brass instruments   These are powerful and highly directional. Generally, the microphone should be positioned somewhat off the center of the bell of the instrument, but still pointed directly at the bell (see Figure A.5), and should not be placed closer than one foot (unless a particularly close and "tight" sound is desired).

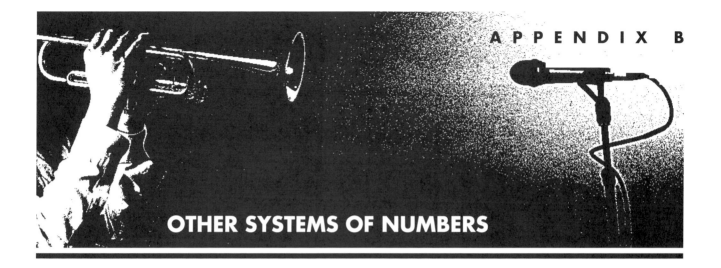

OTHER SYSTEMS OF NUMBERS

*I*n addition to the familiar decimal system for representing quantities, at least three other numbering systems—binary, hexadecimal, and octal—may be encountered from time to time by an electroacoustic musician. An adequate understanding of these systems can best be achieved by beginning with a review of the decimal system.

Perhaps because we have ten fingers (or digits), we are most comfortable with a system of numbering that includes ten symbols used to represent quantities: 0, 1, 2, 3, 4, 5, 6, 7, 8, and 9. To represent larger quantities, these symbols are placed together in combinations. The first place from the right in such a combination represents quantities of ones (10^0). The second place from the right represents quantities of tens (10^1). The third place from the right represents quantities of hundreds (10^2), and so forth. For example, the number 5247 is a four-place number that is understood to represent the sum of five thousands, two hundreds, four tens, and seven ones:

$$\mathbf{5247} =$$
$$\mathbf{5}\ (\times\ 10^3) + \mathbf{2}\ (\times\ 10^2) + \mathbf{4}\ (\times\ 10^1) + \mathbf{7}\ (\times\ 10^0) =$$
$$\mathbf{5}000 \qquad + \mathbf{2}00 \qquad + \mathbf{4}0 \qquad + \mathbf{7}$$

A computer, on the other hand, can only count on two digits, signified by the presence or absence of electricity in a circuit. For the convenience of humans, these states are represented by the symbols 0 and 1. A system of numbering that uses only two symbols to represent quantities is known as a binary numbering system. A single binary symbol is called a *bit* (a word formed by the collision of the words *binary* and *digit)*.

As with the decimal system, larger quantities are represented in a binary system by placing bits together in combinations. Each "place" in a binary number represents a quantity expressed in powers of two. Thus, the first place of the number (from the right) represents quantities of ones (2^0). The second place from the right represents quantities of twos (2^1). The third place from the right represents quantities of fours (2^2), the fourth place from the right represents quantities of eights (2^3), and so forth.

A binary number with eight places is described as an 8-bit number, and also is often called a *byte*. The binary number given in the example that follows is even larger, with bits in 13 places, and is described as a 13-bit number:

$$1010001111111 =$$
$$\mathbf{1}(\times 2^{12}) + \mathbf{0}\,(\times 2^{11}) + \mathbf{1}\,(\times 2^{10}) + \mathbf{0}\,(\times 2^{9}) + \mathbf{0}\,(\times 2^{8}) + \mathbf{0}\,(\times 2^{7}) + \mathbf{1}\,(\times 2^{6}) +$$
$$\mathbf{1}\,(\times 2^{5}) + \mathbf{1}\,(\times 2^{4}) + \mathbf{1}\,(\times 2^{3}) + \mathbf{1}\,(\times 2^{2}) + \mathbf{1}(\times 2^{1}) + \mathbf{1}\,(\times 2^{0})$$

The decimal equivalent of this binary number can be determined as follows:

$\mathbf{1}\,(\times 2^{12})$	=	$\mathbf{1}\,(\times 4096)$	=	4096
$\mathbf{0}\,(\times 2^{11})$	=	$\mathbf{0}\,(\times 2048)$	=	0
$\mathbf{1}\,(\times 2^{10})$	=	$\mathbf{1}\,(\times 1024)$	=	1024
$\mathbf{0}\,(\times 2^{9})$	=	$\mathbf{0}\,(\times 512)$	=	0
$\mathbf{0}\,(\times 2^{8})$	=	$\mathbf{0}\,(\times 256)$	=	0
$\mathbf{0}\,(\times 2^{7})$	=	$\mathbf{0}\,(\times 128)$	=	0
$\mathbf{1}\,(\times 2^{6})$	=	$\mathbf{1}\,(\times 64)$	=	64
$\mathbf{1}\,(\times 2^{5})$	=	$\mathbf{1}\,(\times 32)$	=	32
$\mathbf{1}\,(\times 2^{4})$	=	$\mathbf{1}\,(\times 16)$	=	16
$\mathbf{1}\,(\times 2^{3})$	=	$\mathbf{1}\,(\times 8)$	=	8
$\mathbf{1}\,(\times 2^{2})$	=	$\mathbf{1}\,(\times 4)$	=	4
$\mathbf{1}\,(\times 2^{1})$	=	$\mathbf{1}\,(\times 2)$	=	2
$\mathbf{1}\,(\times 2^{0})$	=	$\mathbf{1}\,(\times 1)$	=	1
				5247

People who program computers often use a system of numbers based on powers of the number 16. This system, called the hexadecimal system, uses 16 symbols: 0, 1, 2, 3, 4, 5, 6, 7, 8, 9, A, B, C, D, E, and F. In larger hexadecimal numbers, the symbol in the first place from the right represents the quantity of ones (16^0), the second place from the right represents the quantity of 16s (16^1), the third place represents the quantity of 256s (16^2), and so forth. Note that a letter h is often appended to signify that the number is hexadecimal.

$$\mathbf{147F}h =$$
$$\mathbf{1}\,(\times 16^{3}) + \mathbf{4}\,(\times 16^{2}) + \mathbf{7}\,(\times 16^{1}) + \mathbf{F}\,(\times 16^{0})$$

The decimal equivalent of this hexadecimal number can be determined as follows:

$$1 \, (\times \, 16^3) \quad = \quad 1 \, (\times \, 4096) \quad = \quad 4096$$
$$4 \, (\times \, 16^2) \quad = \quad 4 \, (\times \, 256) \quad = \quad 1024$$
$$7 \, (\times \, 16^1) \quad = \quad 7 \, (\times \, 16) \quad = \quad 112$$
$$F \, (\times \, 16^0) \quad = \quad F \, (\times \, 1) \quad = \quad \underline{15}$$
$$5247$$

An 8-bit binary number (or byte) can be converted rather easily to a two-place hexadecimal number. The right place of the hexadecimal number represents the last four bits of the binary number, and the left place of the hexadecimal number represents the first four bits of the binary number. The following table provides the hexadecimal and decimal equivalents of four-bit binary numbers:

Binary	Hexadecimal	Decimal
0000	00h	0
0001	01h	1
0010	02h	2
0011	03h	3
0100	04h	4
0101	05h	5
0110	06h	6
0111	07h	7
1000	08h	8
1001	09h	9
1010	0Ah	10
1011	0Bh	11
1100	0Ch	12
1101	0Dh	13
1110	0Eh	14
1111	0Fh	15

Thus, for example, the binary number 10011111 can be easily converted to hexadecimal form, as follows:

$$1001 \qquad\qquad = \quad 9h$$
$$\underline{\qquad\quad 1111 \quad = \quad Fh}$$
$$1001 \quad 1111 \quad = \quad 9Fh$$

As reported in Chapter 5, MIDI messages are encoded as sets of 8-bit binary numbers. It is often convenient for MIDI programmers (and others who use advanced MIDI programs) to represent MIDI messages as hexadecimal numbers according to the method just described. Sooner or later, therefore, an understanding of the hexadecimal system of numbering becomes quite useful to a MIDI musician who has advanced deeply into the programming of synthesizers, sequencers, and other devices.

Occasionally, numbers in an octal format are encountered in the studio. Many synthesizers, such as the Roland D-50 (and many other devices as well), organize presets into eight banks with eight presets in each bank. The presets are numbered 11 through 18, 21 through 28, 31 through 38, and so forth. Most synthesizers, however, number presets from 1 to 128 (inclusive), according to the more familiar decimal system.[1]

To determine the decimal preset number that corresponds to a given octal preset number, the value in the left place of the octal number is multiplied by 8, then added to the value in the right place of the octal number. The number 8 is then subtracted from this sum, as shown in the following example:

$$\text{preset \# } 42_{octal} = [(4 \times 8) + 2] - 8 = 26_{decimal}$$

Conversely, to convert a decimal number to the corresponding octal number, first add 8 to the decimal number, then divide the sum by 8. The result of this division becomes the first digit of the octal number, and the remainder becomes the second digit, as shown in the following example:

$$26_{decimal} = (26 + 8) \div 8 = 4 \text{ with a remainder of } 2 = 42_{octal}$$

Fortuitously, many software sequencers and similar programs are able to accomplish these conversions at the request of the user (perhaps even automatically). This, of course, is a particularly appropriate task for any device called a "computer"!

---

1. To confuse the situation further, MIDI Program Change values are represented by the decimal numbers 0 through 127 (inclusive). The MIDI Program Change value must therefore be increased by one to determine the corresponding decimal preset number. A MIDI Program Change message of 25, for example, corresponds to the decimal preset number 26.

FURTHER DETAILS OF THE MUSICAL INSTRUMENT DIGITAL INTERFACE

The information presented here may be useful to readers who are interested in the design of MIDI hardware and software or are simply curious to learn more about how it works.

This closer examination begins with the humble MIDI cable itself. Although the plug at each end of a MIDI cable includes five pins, only three are used. Pins 4 and 5 carry the signal, and pin 2 is connected to the shield of the cable. The other two pins are reserved for possible use in the future.

As mentioned in Chapter 5, different manufacturers of synthesizers and other electroacoustic musical devices may have different preferences regarding electrical levels, polarities, and other aspects of the design of electrical equipment. Therefore, running an electrical conductor, in this case a MIDI cable, from one product to the product of another company might create the potential (so to speak) for a great variety of electrical mischief. Problems with electrical grounding are likely to arise. There may be interference with the transmitted data so that they become garbled and impossible to decode. Possibly, circuit components in one or both of the devices could be overloaded and burn up.

To avoid these kinds of problems, the MIDI specification suggests that the MIDI IN connection on a device include a component called an opto-isolator. This is a sealed unit that includes both a light-emitting diode (LED) and a photo sensor. The electrical pulses that come in over the MIDI cable are converted into a corresponding series of bursts of light by the LED. The photo sensor, which is directly connected to the circuitry of the receiving device, converts these bursts of light back into a series of electrical pulses. Thus, there is no complete electrical connection between the two musical devices; instead, the data are transmitted via the pulsing beam of light in the opto-isolator.

MIDI messages are transmitted as groups of eight-bit binary numbers at a rate of 31,250 bits per second. A binary 0 is represented as a pulse of current, and a binary 1 is represented by switching off the current. During transmission, a "start bit" of 0 is prepended to each byte of MIDI data to signal its beginning. This is followed by the byte of data itself, beginning with the least significant bit (the bit that is in the first place from the right of the number). A "stop bit" of 1 is appended to each byte to signify the conclusion. Including start and stop bits, a maximum of 3,125 bytes of MIDI data can be transmitted each second through a single MIDI cable.

CHANNEL MESSAGES

Table C.1 presents a summary of the status and data bytes of MIDI channel messages. Table C.2 presents the same information in hexadecimal format. Note that all status bytes for channel messages are between 128 and 239 (80h and EFh), inclusive, and that all data bytes are between 0 and 127 (00h and 7Fh), inclusive. Note also that in the hexadecimal representation, in Table C.2, the MIDI channels are numbered 00h through 0Fh (and that the second digit of each status byte corresponds to the channel number). Although the decimal equivalents of these numbers are 0 through 15, the notion of a "channel 0" could be problematic for many users and designers of MIDI instruments. Therefore, the decimal numbering of MIDI channels is 1 through 16, as shown in Table C.1.

Following are a few examples of channel messages, in binary, decimal, and hexadecimal form.

NOTE ON (EXAMPLE: A SINGLE TONE)

10010000	(144)	(90h)	Status byte for a Note On message on channel 1
00111100	(60)	(3Ch)	Key number for middle C
01000000	(64)	(40h)	Key velocity of 64

Then later, to turn the note off:

| 00111100 | (60) | (3Ch) | Key number for middle C |
| 00000000 | (0) | (00h) | Key velocity of 0 |

Note that a status byte has not been provided for the message to turn the note off. Due to running status, a status byte is probably not required here, assuming that no other messages have intervened.

NOTE ON (EXAMPLE: A C-MAJOR TRIAD)

10010001	(145)	(91h)	Status byte for a Note On message on channel 2
00111100	(60)	(3Ch)	Key number for middle C
01000000	(64)	(40h)	Key velocity of 64
01000000	(64)	(40h)	Key number for the E above middle C
01000000	(64)	(40h)	Key velocity of 64
01000011	(67)	(43h)	Key number for the G above middle C
01000000	(64)	(40h)	Key velocity of 64

Channel #	1	2	3	4	5	6	7	8	9	10	11	12	13	14	15	16	Data Byte #1	Data Byte #2
Note On	144	145	146	147	148	149	150	151	152	153	154	155	156	157	158	159	Key number (0–127)	Key velocity (0–127)
Note Off	128	129	130	131	132	133	134	135	136	137	138	139	140	141	142	143	Key number (0–127)	Release velocity (0–127)
Key Pressure (poly aftertouch)	160	161	162	163	164	165	166	167	168	169	170	171	172	173	174	175	Key number (0–127)	Pressure value (0–127)
Channel Pressure (mono aftertouch)	208	209	210	211	212	213	214	215	216	217	218	219	220	221	222	223	Pressure value (0–127)	[not used]
Control Change	176	177	178	179	180	181	182	183	184	185	186	187	188	189	190	191	Controller number (0–127)	Controller value (0–127)
Pitch Bend Change	224	225	226	227	228	229	230	231	232	233	234	235	236	237	238	239	LSB (0–127)	MSB (0–127)
Program Change	192	193	194	195	196	197	198	199	200	201	202	203	204	205	206	207	Preset (0–127)	[not used]

Status Byte columns span Channel # 1 through 16.

TABLE C.1
Channel Messages in Decimal Format

	Status Byte	Data Byte #1	Data Byte #2
Channel #	00h 01h 02h 03h 04h 05h 06h 07h 08h 09h 0Ah 0Bh 0Ch 0Dh 0Eh 0Fh		
Note On	90h 91h 92h 93h 94h 95h 96h 97h 98h 99h 9Ah 9Bh 9Ch 9Dh 9Eh 9Fh	Key number (00–7Fh)	Key velocity (00–7Fh)
Note Off	80h 81h 82h 83h 84h 85h 86h 87h 88h 89h 8Ah 8Bh 8Ch 8Dh 8Eh 8Fh	Key number (00–7Fh)	Release velocity (00–7Fh)
Key Pressure (poly aftertouch)	A0h A1h A2h A3h A4h A5h A6h A7h A8h A9h AAh ABh ACh ADh AEh AFh	Key number (00–7Fh)	Pressure value (00–7Fh)
Channel Pressure (mono aftertouch)	D0h D1h D2h D3h D4h D5h D6h D7h D8h D9h DAh DBh DCh DDh DEh DFh	Pressure value (00–7Fh)	[not used]
Control Change	B0h B1h B2h B3h B4h B5h B6h B7h B8h B9h BAh BBh BCh BDh BEh BFh	Controller number (00–7Fh)	Controller value (00–7Fh)
Pitch Bend Change	E0h E1h E2h E3h E4h E5h E6h E7h E8h E9h EAh EBh ECh EDh EEh EFh	LSB (00–7Fh)	MSB (00–7Fh)
Program Change	C0h C1h C2h C3h C4h C5h C6h C7h C8h C9h CAh CBh CCh CDh CEh CFh	Preset (00–7Fh)	[not used]

TABLE C.2
Channel Messages in Hexadecimal Format

This series of messages will sound a C-major chord. Again, due to running status, only one status byte is required here. Until another type of message interrupts, it is assumed that all subsequent bytes are data bytes for Note On messages. Observe that the velocity of all three notes is 64. It is quite likely that the keyboard on which this chord was struck is not a velocity-sensitive one.

It may also be observed that because the data bytes are transmitted in a series, it will not be possible for the receiving synthesizer to begin sounding all three notes together, at exactly the same time. Simultaneous events cannot be transmitted as simultaneous messages through a single MIDI cable. Some messages must wait their turn. However, the delays are usually on the order of a few microseconds, well below the limits of perception. For that matter, it is extremely unlikely that all three fingers hit the keys at the same time!

Now, to turn off the notes of the chord:

00111100	(60)	(3Ch)	Key number for middle C
00000000	(0)	(00h)	Key velocity of 0
01000000	(64)	(40h)	Key number for the E above middle C
00000000	(0)	(00h)	Key velocity of 0
01000011	(67)	(43h)	Key number for the G above middle C
00000000	(0)	(00h)	Key velocity of 0

KEY PRESSURE (POLY AFTERTOUCH)

First, a chord must be sounded (otherwise there are no tones for the aftertouch messages to affect). For this example, the Key Pressure messages are preceded by a series of Note On messages that sound a C-major triad, as shown above. Then:

10100001	(161)	(A1h)	Status byte for Key Pressure messages on channel 2
00111100	(60)	(3Ch)	Key number for middle C
01000010	(66)	(42h)	Data byte representing a moderate amount of pressure
01000000	(64)	(40h)	Key number for the E above middle C
00011101	(29)	(1Dh)	Data byte representing a light amount of pressure
01000011	(67)	(43h)	Key number for the G above middle C
01110101	(117)	(75h)	Data byte representing a heavy amount of pressure

A series of additional pressure messages for each key may ensue, as the finger pressure on each key is adjusted. Eventually, there will be a series of Note On messages with a velocity of 0 to turn off the chord.

CHANNEL PRESSURE ("MONO" AFTERTOUCH)

First, a Note On message is sent to trigger a tone. Then:

11010000	(208)	(D0h)	Status byte for Channel Pressure message on channel 1
01010100	(84)	(54h)	Data byte for a moderately strong amount of pressure

. . .

A series of further data bytes may ensue, as the pressure of the finger on the keyboard is adjusted. Eventually, there will be a Note On message with a velocity of 0 to turn off the tone.

CONTROL CHANGE

In this example, the modulation wheel is the source of the messages.

10110000	(176)	(B0h)	Status byte for Control Change message on channel 1
00000001	(1)	(01h)	Controller number 1: the modulation wheel (see Table C.3)
00111011	(59)	(3Bh)	Controller value (the mod wheel is just below midpoint)

As the mod wheel is moved, further messages are transmitted.

00000001	(1)	(01h)	Controller number 1 (the modulation wheel)
01000000	(64)	(40h)	Controller value (the mod wheel is at the midpoint)
00000001	(1)	(01h)	Controller number 1 (the modulation wheel)
01000010	(66)	(42h)	Controller value (the mod wheel is above the midpoint)

. . .

CONTROL CHANGE

In this example, the volume pedal is the source of the message.

10110000	(176)	(B0h)	Status byte for Control Change message on channel 1
00000111	(7)	(07h)	Controller number 7 (the volume pedal)
01010000	(80)	(50h)	Controller value (the pedal is well past midpoint)

. . .

CONTROL CHANGE

In this example, the sustain pedal is the source of the messages.

10110000	(176)	(B0h)	Status byte for Control Change message on channel 1
01000000	(64)	(40h)	Controller number 64 (the sustain pedal)
01111111	(127)	(7Fh)	Controller value (the sustain pedal is down)

Later, the sustain pedal is released. Observe that the status byte is repeated, since presumably other messages (most likely, Note On messages) have intervened.

10110000	(176)	(B0h)	Status byte for Control Change message on channel 1
01000000	(64)	(40h)	Controller number 64 (the sustain pedal)
00000000	(0)	(00h)	Controller value (the sustain pedal is up)

PITCH BEND

11100000	(224)	(E0h)	Status byte for Pitch Bend message on channel 1
01111111	(127)	(7Fh)	LSB data byte
01111111	(127)	(7Fh)	MSB data byte (pitch is bent as high as it can be)
00000000	(0)	(00h)	LSB data byte
00000000	(0)	(00h)	MSB data byte (pitch is bent as low as it can be)
00000000	(0)	(00h)	LSB data byte
01000000	(64)	(40h)	MSB data byte (pitch is back to normal)

PROGRAM CHANGE

| 11000000 | (192) | (C0h) | Status byte for Program Change message on channel 1 |
| 00001011 | (11) | (0Bh) | Preset number |

For synthesizers that number presets from 1 to 128, inclusive, this Program Change message would call up preset number 12. For synthesizers that use an octal system for numbering presets, this Program Change message would call up preset number 24 (see Appendix B for a description of this octal numbering system).

Table C.3 lists standard controller numbers, as defined in the *MIDI 1.0 Detailed Specification,* published by the International MIDI Association. Note that continuous controllers 32–63 have been designated as LSB for Controllers 0–31. Initially it was intended that if the data provided by continuous controllers 0–31 were insufficiently precise, they could be supplemented by data from controllers 32–63. For example, if a range of values

TABLE C.3
Standard Controller Numbers

Decimal	Hex	Controller Name
0	00h	Bank Select
1	01h	Modulation Wheel or Lever
2	02h	Breath Controller
3	03h	Undefined
4	04h	Foot Controller
5	05h	Portamento Time
6	06h	Data Entry MSB
7	07h	Main Volume
8	08h	Balance
9	09h	Undefined
10	0Ah	Pan
11	0Bh	Expression Controller
12	0Ch	Effect Control 1
13	0Dh	Effect Control 2
14–15	0E–0Fh	Undefined
16–19	10–13h	General Purpose Controllers (Nos. 1–4)
20–31	14–1Fh	Undefined
32–63	20–3Fh	LSB for Controllers 0–31
64	40h	Damper Pedal (Sustain)
65	41h	Portamento
66	42h	Sostenuto
67	43h	Soft Pedal
68	44h	Legato Footswitch
69	45h	Hold 2
70	46h	Sound Controller 1 (default: Sound Variation)
71	47h	Sound Controller 2 (default: Timbre/Harmonic Content)
72	48h	Sound Controller 3 (default: Release Time)
73	49h	Sound Controller 4 (default: Attack Time)
74	4Ah	Sound Controller 5 (default: Brightness)
75–79	4B–4Fh	Sound Controllers 6–10 (no defaults)
80–83	50–53h	General Purpose Controllers (Nos. 5–8)
84	54h	Portamento Control
85–90	55–5Ah	Undefined
91	5Bh	Effects 1 Depth (formerly External Effects Depth)
92	5Ch	Effects 2 Depth (formerly Tremolo Depth)
93	5Dh	Effects 3 Depth (formerly Chorus Depth)
94	5Eh	Effects 4 Depth (formerly Celeste, or Detune, Depth)
95	5Fh	Effects 5 Depth (formerly Phaser Depth)
96	60h	Data Increment
97	61h	Data Decrement

continued on page 416

TABLE C.3 (continued)

Decimal	Hex	Controller Name
98	62h	Non-Registered Parameter Number LSB
99	63h	Non-Registered Parameter Number MSB
100	64h	Registered Parameter Number LSB
101	65h	Registered Parameter Number MSB
102–120	66–78h	Undefined

Courtesy of the MIDI Manufacturers Association.

from 0 to 127 was not sufficient to represent the desired control of the brightness of timbre by controller number 4, then more precise degrees of control could be indicated by also using the values of controller number 36 (provided that the receiving synthesizer is designed to use this information). To the knowledge of the author, this provision has rarely (if ever) been used, however.

REGISTERED AND NONREGISTERED PARAMETERS

The Registered Parameter Numbers, for which controller numbers 100 and 101 are reserved, are used (by synthesizers designed to respond to the information) for the adjustment of certain characteristics of synthesizer operation that are common to many devices. Characteristics of this sort that are presently recognized by the MIDI standards committees include Master Tuning control and pitch bend sensitivity (that is, the amount of pitch change that results when the pitch bend wheel is moved fully in one direction or the other). These characteristics have been assigned registered parameter numbers that are used as the final data bytes in messages for controllers 100 and 101. The actual adjustment of the characteristic is accomplished by the accompanying transmission of messages from controller numbers 96 and 97 (Data Increment and Data Decrement, respectively) or by messages from continuous controller numbers 6 (Data Entry MSB) and 38 (Data Entry LSB). The following series of messages, for example, would set the pitch bend sensitivity of the receiving synthesizer to one semitone:

10110000	(176)	(B0h)	Status byte for Control Change message on channel 1
01100101	(101)	(65h)	Controller number 101 (Registered Parameter MSB)
00000000	(0)	(00h)	Controller value (the MSB of the Registered Parameter Number for pitch bend sensitivity is 0)
01100100	(100)	(64h)	Controller number 100 (Registered Parameter LSB)

00000000	(0)	(00h)	Controller value (the LSB of the Registered Parameter Number for pitch bend sensitivity is 0)
00000110	(6)	(06h)	Controller number 6 (data entry MSB)
00000001	(1)	(01h)	Controller value (value of 1 semitone will be the gross range of the pitch bend wheel)
00100110	(38)	(26h)	Controller number 38 (data entry LSB)
00000000	(0)	(00h)	Controller value (value is 0; there are no further, finer adjustments to the range of the pitch bend wheel)

Messages from controllers 98 and 99 (Non-Registered Parameter Numbers LSB and MSB, respectively) can be used in a similar way for particular devices. The manufacturer of the device may select certain patch characteristics to be adjustable in real time by assigning nonregistered parameter numbers to them. These parameter numbers are then transmitted as data bytes for messages for controller numbers 98 and 99, and the characteristic itself is then adjusted by messages for controllers 96 and 97 or controllers 6 and 38, as described above.

Few devices are presently designed to transmit or receive registered or nonregistered parameter messages. However, this is very likely to change as increasingly sophisticated instruments become available. For further information regarding these messages, as well as other controller messages, request a copy of the *MIDI 1.0 Detailed Specification* from the International MIDI Association (at the address provided in Chapter 12).

CHANNEL MODE MESSAGES

Most synthesizers are capable of responding in more than one mode to channeled MIDI messages. The mode in which an instrument responds at any given time can be determined by buttons or switches on the control panel of the device. A few instruments can also change mode upon receiving a combination of Channel Mode messages on a designated MIDI channel.

Channel Mode messages have the same status byte as Control Change messages, and have two data bytes. The first data byte is a message number, between 121 and 127 (inclusive), and the second data byte is a value that signifies on (64–127) or off (0–63).

	Message Number
Reset All Controllers	121
Local Control[1]	122
All Notes Off	123
Omni Off	124
Omni On	125
Mono On (Poly Off)	126
Poly On (Mono Off)	127

If a synthesizer receives a series of messages that instruct it to change to a different channel mode, but the synthesizer is not capable of responding in that mode, then it will either ignore the messages or default to a designated mode. If the synthesizer is in fact able to change to the requested mode, it will first respond by turning off all tones that have been turned on by recent MIDI Note On messages, so that no tones are left stranded by the change of mode.

Again, not all instruments are designed to respond to all Channel Mode messages (some cannot respond to any, and so ignore them all). It is wise to read the owner's manual closely. Much of this information can be found by examining the MIDI Implementation Chart usually printed near the back of the owner's manual. For detailed guidance on how to decode a MIDI Implementation Chart, see Appendix B in David Miles Huber's *The MIDI Manual* (Carmel, IN: Howard W. Sams, 1991), or see Steve De Furia and Joe Scacciaferro's *MIDI Programmer's Handbook* (Redwood City, CA: M&T Books, 1989), pages 25–31.

SYSTEM MESSAGES

The most profuse system message is the Timing Clock (or MIDI Clock) message, a System Real-Time message. This message, as described in Chapter 6, is transmitted at a rate of 24 messages per beat by sequencers and drum machines that use MIDI sync. It can be represented as follows:

11111000   (248)   (F8h)   Status byte for Timing Clock message
                           No data bytes

---

1. On some synthesizers, it is possible to isolate the tone-generation circuitry of the instrument from the keyboard on that instrument. Although the keyboard can still generate MIDI messages for other devices, it cannot trigger the production of tones by its own tone-generation circuits. This situation is described as one in which Local Control is off. A Channel Mode message number 122, when recognized by such an instrument, can be transmitted from another device in the MIDI network, such as a computer or sequencer, to turn this Local Control switch on or off.

Other System Real-Time messages used for MIDI Sync are the Start, Continue, and Stop messages:

11111010   (250)   (FAh)   Status byte for Start message
                                    No data bytes

11111011   (251)   (FBh)   Status byte for Continue message
                                    No data bytes

11111100   (252)   (FCh)   Status byte for Stop message
                                    No data bytes

Two other System Real-Time messages are the System Reset message and the Active Sensing message. The System Reset message is a very rarely used message that is intended to cause an instrument to restore its control settings to the values that existed when the instrument was powered up. Very few instruments are designed to recognize this message. Active Sensing messages can be transmitted by a device at a rate of approximately three each second to reassure other devices in the network that it continues to function and that its MIDI cable has not been disconnected. Presumably if the stream of Active Sensing messages from the device is interrupted, the other devices will know to turn off any notes that were triggered by that instrument. Active Sensing is an optional procedure and was much more commonly implemented on early MIDI instruments than it has been on more recent ones. An Active Sensing message can be represented as follows:

11111110   (254)   (FEh)   Status byte for Active Sensing message
                                    No data bytes

Another prevalent MIDI sync message (in addition to the Timing Clock, Start, Continue, and Stop messages) is a System-Common message called the Song Position Pointer message. It includes a status byte followed by two data bytes. The two data bytes together point to a location in a sequence in terms of increments of six Timing Clock messages from the beginning of the sequence. For example, if 24 Timing Clock messages are represented by a quarter-note, then the Song Position Pointer would indicate a location in terms of the number of 16th notes from the beginning of the music. Here is an example of a Song Position Pointer message:

11110010   (242)   (F2h)   Status byte for Song Position Pointer message

01110000   (112)   (70h)   Least Significant Byte

00001011   (11)   (0Bh)   Most Significant Byte

The location pointed to is 2,938 (0B70h) 16th notes from the beginning of the sequence (assuming that a quarter-note is used to represent 24 Timing Clocks).

Other System-Common messages include the MIDI Time Code Quarter-Frame message, described briefly in Chapter 6, and the Tune Request

message, which is intended to be sent to MIDI-equipped analog synthesizers to instruct them to get their oscillators in tune. This is a very rarely
used message.

The following is an example of a System-Exclusive message. It represents
much of the data for the synthesizer preset selected for illustration in
Figure 6.7.

11110000   (240)   (F0h)   Status byte for System-Exclusive message

01000011   (67)   (43h)   Manufacturer's ID for Yamaha

This is then followed by a series of data bytes, shown here in binary
format:

```
00000000 00000000 00000001 00011011 00001101 00011110 00001010
00000101 01100011 01000111 01011111 00000000 00000000 00000000
00000000 00000000 00000000 00000000 00000000 00000000 01001001
00000000 00000110 00000100 00001001 01001011 00100100 01100011
00100000 01100011 01010111 01010111 00000000 00000000 00000000
00000000 00000000 00000000 00000000 00000000 00000000 01100011
00000000 00000101 00000001 00001001 00101000 00100011 00011001
00100011 01100011 00110100 01100011 00000000 00000000 00000000
00000000 00000000 00000000 00000000 00000001 00000000 01100011
00000000 00000011 00001100 00000100 00011001 00101001 00011100
00101000 01100011 01001100 01100011 00000000 00000000 00000000
00000000 00000000 00000000 00000000 00000001 00000000 01100011
00000000 00000010 00001100 00000111 00100100 00011000 00011001
00101010 01100011 00111000 01100000 00000000 00000000 00000000
00000000 00000000 00000000 00000000 00000001 00000000 01100011
00000000 00000001 00110010 00000111 01001011 00100100 01100011
00101101 01100011 01010111 01010111 00000000 00000000 00000000
00000000 00000000 00000000 00000000 00000000 00000000 01100011
00000000 00000001 00000000 00000111 01100011 01100011 00000001
00000000 00110010 00110010 00000101 00110010 00011110 00000111
00000001 00100000 00000000 00000000 00000000 00000001 00000000
00000011 00011000 01101101 01100001 01110010 01110011 01101101
01100101 01101100 01101111 00110001 00001011
```

Here is the same series of data bytes, shown in decimal format:

```
0  0  1  27  13  30  10  5  99  71  95  0  0  0  0  0  0  0  0  73  0  6  4  9  75
36  99  32  99  87  87  0  0  0  0  0  0  0  0  99  0  5  1  9  40  35  25  35  99
52  99  0  0  0  0  0  0  1  0  99  0  3  12  8  25  41  28  40  99  76  99  0  0  0
0  0  0  1  0  99  0  2  12  7  36  24  25  42  99  56  96  0  0  0  0  0  0  0  1  0
99  0  1  50  7  75  36  99  45  99  87  87  0  0  0  0  0  0  0  0  99  0  1  0  7
99  99  1  0  50  50  5  50  30  7  1  32  0  0  1  0  3  24  109  97  114  115
109  101  108  111  49  11
```

And here again is the same series of data bytes, this time in hexadecimal format:

```
00 00 01 1B 0D 1E 0A 05 63 47 5F 00 00 00 00 00 00 00 00 00
49 00 06 04 09 4B 24 63 20 63 57 57 00 00 00 00 00 00 00 00 00
63 00 05 01 09 28 23 19 23 63 34 63 00 00 00 00 00 00 00 01 00
63 00 03 0C 08 19 29 1C 28 63 4C 63 00 00 00 00 00 00 00 01 00
63 00 02 0C 07 24 18 19 2A 63 38 60 00 00 00 00 00 00 00 01 00
63 00 01 32 07 4B 24 63 2D 63 57 57 00 00 00 00 00 00 00 00 00
63 00 01 00 07 63 63 01 00 32 32 05 32 1E 07 01 20 00 00 00 01
00 03 18 6D 61 72 73 6D 65 6C 6C 6F 31 0B
```

The data bytes are then followed by:

| 11110111 | (247) | (F7h) | The EOX (End Of eXclusive) status byte |

New Universal System-Exclusive messages are continually being defined, although not so many are yet widely recognized by MIDI instruments. For the most recent information, contact the International MIDI Association (at the address provided in Chapter 12). Here is an example of a Universal System-Exclusive message, for setting the overall output volume level of a multitimbral instrument:

11110000	(240)	(F0h)	Status byte for System-Exclusive message
01111111	(127)	(7Fh)	Universal Real-Time System-Exclusive ID number
00000010	(2)	(02h)	ID number of instrument in network
00000100	(4)	(04h)	Sub-ID #1: signifies this as a Device Control message
00000001	(1)	(01h)	Sub-ID #2: specifically, a Master Volume message
00001101	(13)	(0Dh)	The LSB of the volume value
01001101	(77)	(4Dh)	The MSB of the volume value
11110111	(247)	(F7h)	The EOX (End Of eXclusive) status byte

In this example, the master volume setting, relative to a range of 0 to 16,383, will now be set to a value of 9869 $[(77 \times 128) + 13]$.

SUGGESTED LISTENING

**COMPOSITIONS REALIZED IN SIGNIFICANT PART
THROUGH THE "CLASSICAL" TECHNIQUES OF TAPE MANIPULATION**

Badings, Henk. *Evolutions—Ballet Suite.* Epic BC 1118.

———— . *Genese.* Epic BC 1118.

Bayle, François. *L'Oiseau-Chanteur.* Candide CE 31025.

Beatles. *Magical Mystery Tour.* Capitol 2835.

———— . *Sgt. Pepper's Lonely Hearts Club Band.* Capitol MAS-2653.

Berio, Luciano. *Thema (Omaggio a Joyce).* Turnabout TV 34177. This is one of the most powerful of the early works of electroacoustic music. It is based on the voice of Cathy Berberian, reciting a passage from James Joyce's *Ulysses,* along with electronically generated sounds.

———— . *Visage.* Turnabout TV 34046S and Candide CE 31027.

Ferrari, Luc. *Tête et queue du dragon.* Candide CE 31025.

Hambraeus, Brengt. *Transfiguration.* Swedish Society SLT 33 181.

Henry, Pierre. *Variations on a Door and a Sigh.* Philips DSY 836-898.

Henry, Pierre, and Schaeffer, Pierre. *Symphonie pour un homme seul.* Adès 14.122-2 and Philips 6521-021.

LeCaine, Hugh. *Dripsody.* Folkways FMS 33436.

Ligeti, György. *Artikulation.* Wergo 60059. See also the very beautiful "listening score" for this work that was prepared by Rainer Wehinger and published by Schott (Edition Schott 6378).

Luening, Otto. *Fantasy in Space.* Folkways Records FX 6160 and Composers Recordings, Inc. CD 611.

———— . *Low Speed.* Composers Recordings, Inc. CD 611.

Luening, Otto, and Ussachevsky, Vladimir. *Incantation.* Composers Recordings, Inc. CD 611. This, along with several other pieces listed here, is described in detail in Chapter 2.

———— . *Tape Music: An Historic Concert.* Desto DC 6466. The compositions on this disc, including "Sonic Contours," "Low Speed," "Fantasy in Space," "Incantation," "Invention in Twelve Notes," and "Moonflight," are described in detail in Chapter 2.

Mache, François-Bernard. *Terre de feu.* Candide CE 31025.

Malec, Ivo. *Dahovi.* Candide CE 31025.

Parmegiani, Bernard. *Danse.* Candide CE 31025.

Philippot, Michel. *Etude III.* Candide CE 31025.

Pousseur, Henri. *Scambi.* Philips 835 486.

Raaijmakers, Dick. *Contrasts.* Epic BC 1118.

Reich, Steve. *Come Out.* Odyssey 32 16 0160. This is a remarkable application of the technique of tape looping.

_____ . *It's Gonna Rain.* Columbia MS 7265.

Schaeffer, Pierre. *Objets liés.* Candide CE 31025.

Seville, David, with Alvin, Simon, and Theodore. *The Chipmunks Sing the Beatles Hits.* Liberty LST-7388.

Stockhausen, Karlheinz. *Gesang der Jünglinge.* Deutsche Grammophon 138 811. This is one of the early classics of electroacoustic music, and is described in detail in Chapter 10.

_____ . *Hymnen.* Deutsche Grammophon 139 421/22.

_____ . *Kontakte.* Deutsche Grammophon 138 811. This is another of the classics of electroacoustic music.

Ussachevsky, Vladimir. *Of Wood and Brass.* CRI 227 USD.

_____ . *Piece for Tape Recorder.* Composers Recordings, Inc. CD 611.

_____ . *Sonic Contours.* Composers Recordings, Inc. CD 611 and Folkways Records FX 6160.

_____ . *Wireless Fantasy.* CRI 227 USD.

Varèse, Edgard. *Déserts* for orchestra and tape. CRI SD 268.

_____ . *Poème électronique.* Columbia MG 31078 and Neuma 450-74. This is a masterpiece of electroacoustic music, and is described in detail in Chapter 10.

Xenakis, Iannis. *Bohor I.* Nonesuch H-71246. This monumental work was derived, according to the liner notes, from the sounds of "various Oriental bracelets and other jewelry, and a Laotian mouth organ."

COMPOSITIONS CONSISTING PRIMARILY OF ANALOG ELECTRONIC SOUNDS

Babbitt, Milton. *Composition for Synthesizer.* Columbia MS 6566.

_____ . *Ensembles for Synthesizer.* Columbia MS 7051. This piece is described in detail in Chapter 10.

Carlos, Walter (Wendy). *Switched-On Bach.* Columbia MS 7194.

_____ . *The Well-Tempered Synthesizer.* Columbia MS 7286.

Carlos, Wendy. *Digital Moonscapes.* M 39340 CBS Masterworks.

_____ . *Secrets of Synthesis.* Columbia KG 31234.

Cope, David. *Teec Nos Pos.* Folkways Records FTS 33869.

Eaton, John. *Concert Piece for Synket and Orchestra.* Turnabout 34428.

Erb, Donald. *In No Strange Land* for trombone, double-bass, and taped electronic sounds. Nonesuch H-71223. The electronic sounds for this piece were generated on a Moog modular synthesizer.

Fast, Larry. *Audion.* Passport Records PB 6005.

_____ . *Sequencer.* Passport Records PPSD-98014.

Holmes, Reed. *Nova.* Folkways Records FPX 6050.

Krieger, Arthur. *Theme and Variations.* CRI SD 483. The electronic sounds for this piece were generated on a Buchla synthesizer.

McLean, Barton. *Song of the Nahuatl.* Folkways Records FTS 33450.

_____ . *The Sorcerer Revisited.* Folkways Records FPX 6050.

_____ . *Spirals.* CRI SD 335.

McLean, Priscilla. *Dance of Dawn.* CRI SD 335.

_____ . *Invisible Chariots.* Folkways Records FPX 6050 and FTS 33450.

_____ . *Night Images.* Folkways Records FPX 6050.

Mother Mallard's Portable Masterpiece Company. Earthquack EQ 0001.

Oliveros, Pauline. *I of IV*. Odyssey 32 16 0160.

Rudin, Andrew. *Tragoedia*. Nonesuch H-71198.

Semegen, Daria. *Arc: Music for Dancers*. Finnadar SR 9020. The electronic sounds for this piece were generated on a Buchla 200 modular synthesizer.

_____ . *Electronic Composition No. 1*. Odyssey Y 34139.

_____ . *Spectra (Electronic Composition No. 2)*. CRI SD 443.

Smiley, Pril. *Kolyosa*. Composers Recordings, Inc. CD 611.

Subotnick, Morton. *4 Butterflies*. Columbia M 32741. As with Subotnick's other works listed here, the sounds for this piece were generated on a Buchla modular synthesizer, which was developed by Don Buchla in consultation with Subotnick and others.

_____ . *Sidewinder*. Columbia M 30683.

_____ . *Silver Apples of the Moon*. Nonesuch H-71174. As the liner notes state, "This album of electronic music represents a signal event in the related history of music and the phonograph: for the first time, an original, full-scale composition has been created expressly for the record medium."

_____ . *A Sky of Cloudless Sulphur*. Nonesuch N-78001.

_____ . *Until Spring*. Odyssey Y 34158.

_____ . *The Wild Bull*. Nonesuch H-71208. This work is analyzed in detail in Chapter 8.

Tangerine Dream. *Phaedra*. Virgin VR 13-108.

Tcherepnin, Ivan. *Electric Flowers*. CRI SD 467.

Wells, Thomas. *11.2.72, Electronic Music*. CRI SD 443.

Wuorinen, Charles. *Time's Encomium*. Nonesuch H-71225.

COMPOSITIONS CONSISTING PRIMARILY OF COMPUTER-GENERATED OR COMPUTER-PROCESSED SOUNDS

Ager, Klaus. . . . *Sondern die Sterne sind's*. Aulos FSM 53 544 AUL.

Appleton, Jon. *Brush Canyon*. Centaur CRC 2052 (CDCM Computer Music Series, vol. 6).

_____ . *Degitaru Ongaku*. Centaur CRC 2052 (CDCM Computer Music Series, vol. 6).

_____ . *Georganna's Farewell*. Folkways FTS 33442.

_____ . *Music for Synclavier and Other Digital Systems*. Folkways Records 33445.

_____ . *The World Music Theatre of Jon Appleton*. Folkways Records FTS 33437.

Austin, Larry. *Sinfonia Concertante: A Mozartean Episode*. Centaur CRC 2029 (CDCM Computer Music Series, vol. 1).

_____ . *Sonata Concertante* for piano and computer music on tape. Centaur CRC 2029 (CDCM Computer Music Series, vol. 1).

Bell Telephone Laboratories. *Music from Mathematics*, including short pieces realized on the computer at Bell Labs by Dr. J. R. Pierce, Dr. Max Mathews, Dr. Newman Guttman, David Lewin, Lejaren Hiller and Leonard Isaacson, M. E. Shannon, and Dr. David Slepian. Bell Telephone Laboratories 122227.

Berger, Jonathan. *Diptych*. Centaur CRC 2091 (CDCM Computer Music Series, vol. 8).

Boulanger, Richard. *from Temporal Silence*. Neuma 450-73.

Bresnick, Martin. *Lady Neil's Dumpe*. Centaur CRC 2039 (CDCM Computer Music Series, vol. 2).

Calon, Christian. *Ligne de vie: récits électriques*. Empreintes DIGITALes IMED 9001-CD.

Chadabe, Joel. *Modalities*. Centaur CRC 2047 (CDCM Computer Music Series, vol. 7).

Chafe, Chris, and Morrill, Dexter. *Duo Improvisation*. Centaur CRC 2133 (CDCM Computer Music Series, vol. 11).

Chowning, John. *Turenas*. Wergo WER 2012-50.

_____ . *Stria*. Wergo WER 2012-50.

_____ . *Phonē*. Wergo WER 2012-50.

Clark, Thomas. *Peninsula* for piano and computer music on tape. Centaur CRC 2029 (CDCM Computer Music Series, vol. 1).

Daoust, Yves. *Anecdotes*. Empreintes DIGITALes IMED 9106-CD.

Dashow, James. *In Winter Shine*. Massachusetts Institute of Technology Media Laboratory YHDS 16.

_____ . *Second Voyage*. CRI SD 456.

_____ . *Sequence Symbols*. Wergo WER 2010-50.

Dhomont, Francis. *Mouvances-Métaphores*. Empreintes DIGITALes IMED 9107/08-CD.

Dodge, Charles. *Any Resemblance Is Purely Coincidental*. Folkways Records FTS 37475. This piece is an excellent example of the technique of resynthesis. Here an operatic voice is resynthesized from an old recording.

_____ . *Changes*. Nonesuch H-71245.

_____ . *Earth's Magnetic Field*. Nonesuch H-71250.

_____ . *Profile*. Neuma 450-73.

Gressel, Joel. *Crossings*. CRI SD 393.

_____ . *P-Vibes: Three Canons*. CRI SD 393.

Heifetz, Robin Julian. *Heifetz Plays Heifetz*. Orion ORS 80366.

Hunt, Jerry. *Fluud* for dual Synclaviers. Centaur CRC 2029 (CDCM Computer Music Series, vol. 1).

Jaffe, David. *Silicon Valley Breakdown*. Wergo WER 2016-50. This piece is described in detail in Chapter 9.

Jones, David Evan. *Still Life Dancing*. Centaur CRC 2052 (CDCM Computer Music Series, vol. 6).

_____ . *Still Life in Wood and Metal*. Centaur CRC 2052 (CDCM Computer Music Series, vol. 6).

Lansky, Paul. *Idle Chatter*. Wergo WER 2010-50.

_____ . *just-more-idle-chatter*. Centaur CRC 2076 (CDCM Computer Music Series, vol. 5).

_____ . *mild und leise*. Odyssey Y 34139.

_____ . *Notjustmoreidlechatter*. Neuma 450-73.

_____ . *Six Fantasies on a Poem by Thomas Campion*. CRI SD 456.

Martirano, Salvatore. *Sampler*. Centaur CRC 2045 (CDCM Computer Music Series, vol. 3).

Mathews, Max. *Bicycle Built for Two*. Decca DL 79103.

Matthews, William. *Aurora, a Waltz*. CRI SD 483.

McNabb, Michael. *Dreamsong*. 1750 Arch Records S-1800.

Melby, John. *Chor der Steine*. Advance Recordings FGR-28S.

Moravec, Paul. *Devices and Desires*. Centaur CRC 2052 (CDCM Computer Music Series, vol. 6).

Morrill, Dexter. *Fantasy Quintet*. Redwood Records ES-13.

_____ . *Quartet*. Centaur CRC 2091 (CDCM Computer Music Series, vol. 8).

_____ . *Six Dark Questions* for soprano and computer. Redwood ES-10.

Normandeau, Robert. *Mémoires vives*. Empreintes DIGITALes IMED-9002-CD. A very strong example of contemporary, digital *musique concrète*.

Oliveros, Pauline. *Lion's Tale*. Centaur CRC 2047 (CDCM Computer Music Series, vol. 7).

Pellman, Samuel. *Foonly Tunes*. Redwood Records ES-24.

Pennycook, Bruce. *If Carillons Grew Wings.* Redwood ES-10.

_____ . *Speeches for Dr. Frankenstein.* Folkways Records FTS 37475.

Randall, J. K. *Quartersines.* Nonesuch H-71245.

_____ . *Quartets in Pairs.* Nonesuch H-71245.

Risset, Jean-Claude. *L'Autre face.* Neuma 450-73.

_____ . *Mutations.* Turnabout 34427.

Roads, Curtis. *nscor.* Wergo WER 2010-50.

Rolnick, Neil B. *Vocal Chords.* Centaur CRC 2047 (CDCM Computer Music Series, vol. 7).

Rosenboom, David. *Systems of Judgment.* Centaur CRC 2077 (CDCM Computer Music Series, vol. 4).

Scheidt, Daniel. *Action/Réaction.* Empreintes DIGITALes IMED 9105-CD.

Schindler, Allan. *Tremor of Night and Day.* Centaur CRC 2091 (CDCM Computer Music Series, vol. 8).

Spiegel, Laurie. *Unseen Worlds.* Scarlet IS-88802.

Sullivan, Timothy. *Luckeystone.* Redwood Records ES-13.

_____ . *Numbers, Names* for percussionist and computer. Redwood ES-10.

Teitelbaum, Richard. *Golem 1.* Centaur CRC 2039 (CDCM Computer Music Series, vol. 2).

Thibault, Alain. *Volt.* Empreintes DIGITALes IMED 9003-CD.

Todd, George. *Satan's Sermon.* CRI SD 443. This piece was realized on a Synclavier at Dartmouth.

Truax, Barry. *Arras.* Cambridge Street Records CSR-CD9101. This work was composed in 1980, as the techniques of FM synthesis were reaching a level of considerable maturity at many university facilities for computer music. Although many people now regard FM-synthesized sounds to be passé, this work demonstrates how a powerful piece of music can achieve a degree of musicality and expressiveness that endures well past the time of popularity of any particular technique.

_____ . *Riverrun.* Cambridge Street Records CSR-CD 8701. This piece provides an excellent illustration of sounds produced by the techniques of granular synthesis.

Vercoe, Barry. *Synapse* for viola and computer. CRI SD 393.

_____ . *Synthesism.* Nonesuch H-71245.

Warner, Daniel. *Delay in Glass.* Neuma 450-73.

White, Frances. *Still Life with Piano.* Centaur CRC 2076 (CDCM Computer Music Series, vol. 5). This is a very effective combination of live piano sounds with computer-processed piano sounds—a very strong piece.

Winham, Godfrey. *NP.* CRI SD 393.

Winsor, Phil. *Dulcimer Dream* for amplified piano. Centaur CRC 2029 (CDCM Computer Music Series, vol. 1).

Wolff, Christian. *Mayday Materials.* Centaur CRC 2052 (CDCM Computer Music Series, vol. 6).

Wyatt, Scott A. *Still Hidden Laughs.* Centaur CRC 2045. (CDCM Computer Music Series, vol. 3).

_____ . *Trans.* University of Illinois School of Music LC 84-743210.

Xenakis, Iannis. *Mycenae-Alpha.* Neuma 450-74.

RECORDINGS OF COMPOSITIONS THAT INVOLVE LIVE PERFORMANCE WITH ELECTROACOUSTIC SOUNDS

AMM Group of London. *Live Electronic Music.* Mainstream MS/5002.

Anderson, Laurie. *Big Science.* Warner Brothers Records 3674-2.

Ashley, Robert. *She Was a Visitor.* Odyssey 32 160156.

———. *Wolfman.* CPE-Source IV.

Babbitt, Milton. *Philomel.* Neuma 450-74.

———. *Vision and Prayer* for soprano and tape. CRI SD 268.

Berio, Luciano. *Sequenza VII* for oboe and oscillator. Philips 6500 202.

Bunger, Richard. *Mirrors* for pianist and tape recordist. Musical Heritage Society MHS 4187.

Cage, John. *Fontana Mix.* Turnabout TV 34046S.

———. *HPSCHD.* Nonesuch H-71224.

———. *Solos for Voice 2.* Odyssey 32 160156.

———. *Variations II.* Columbia MS 7051.

Cope, David. *Arena* for 'cello and tape. Orion ORS 75169.

Davidovsky, Mario. *Synchronisms No. 5* for percussion ensemble and electronic sounds. Turnabout TV-S 34487, CRI SD 268, and CRI CD 611.

———. *Synchronisms No. 6* for piano and electronic sounds. Turnabout TV-S 34487.

Dodge, Charles. *Extensions for Trumpet and Tape.* CRI SD 300.

Druckman, Jacob. *Animus I* for trombone and tape. Turnabout TV 34177.

Erb, Donald. *Reconnaissance.* Nonesuch H-71223. In this piece, two Moog synthesizers are performed live as part of a chamber ensemble.

Erickson, Robert. *Ricercar à 3.* CRI CD 616.

The Grateful Dead. *Aoxomoxoa.* Warner Brothers WS 1790.

Hanlon, Kevin. *Through to the End of the Tunnel.* Folkways Records FPX 6050. This piece is described as involving "live electronic performance, using tape delays."

Haynes, Stanley. *Prisms* for piano and tape. Folkways Records FTS 37475.

Kolb, Barbara. *Solitaire* for piano, vibraphone, and tape. Turnabout TV-S 34487.

Lucier, Alvin. *North American Time Capsule 1967.* Odyssey 32 160156.

Luening, Otto, and Ussachevsky, Vladimir. *Concerted Piece* for tape recorder and orchestra. CRI 227 USD.

Machover, Tod. *Valis.* Bridge Records BCD 9007. This is an opera based on a science fiction book by Philip K. Dick.

Martirano, Salvatore. *L's G A.* Polydor Stereo 24-5001.

McLean, Barton. *Dimensions I* for violin and tape. Advance Recordings FGR-25S.

———. *Dimensions II* for piano and tape. CRI SD 407.

Messiaen, Olivier. *Fêtes des belles eaux.* Musical Heritage Society 821. This piece was composed for an ensemble of six *ondes martenot.* It is truly an extraordinary sounding piece of music.

Morrill, Dexter. *Studies* for trumpet and computer (trumpet performed by Marice Stith). Golden Crest Records RE-7068.

Mumma, Gordon. *Hornpipe.* Mainstream MS 5010.

Musica Elettronica Viva. *Spacecraft.* Mainstream MS 5002.

Pousseur, Henri. *Rimes pour différentes sources sonores* for orchestra and taped electronic sounds. RCA VICS-1239.

Reich, Steve. *Violin Phase.* Columbia MS 7265.

Reynolds, Roger. *Ping.* CRI SD 285. This piece uses live electronic processing of sounds in the context of a multimedia presentation.

———. *". . . the serpent-snapping eye."* CRI SD 495.

———. *Traces.* CRI SD 285. This piece also features live electronics, as well as prerecorded tapes, in a multimedia context.

Riley, Terry. *Rainbow in Curved Air.* CBS MK 7315.

Rockmore, Clara (as performer of works by a variety of composers). *The Art of the Theremin.* Delos DCD-1014.

Schwartz, Elliott. *Cycles and Gongs* for organ, trumpet, and tape. CRI CD 598.

SUGGESTED LISTENING   **427**

_____ . *Extended Clarinet* for clarinet and tape. CRI CD 598.

Stockhausen, Karlheinz. *Kurzwellen.* Deutsche Grammophon 2707 045.

_____ . *Mikrophonie I* for tamtam, two microphones, two filters, and potentiometers. CBS 32 11 0043.

_____ . *Mikrophonie II* for choir, Hammond organ, and ring modulators. CBS 32 11 0043.

_____ . *Mixtur* for orchestra, sine-tone generators, and ring modulators. Deutsche Grammophon 137 012.

_____ . *Opus 1970.* Deutsche Grammophon 139 461 SLPM.

_____ . *Prozession* for tamtam, viola, elektronium, piano, filters, and potentiometers. Candide CE 31001.

Stokes, Eric. *Eldey Island* for flute and tape. Advance Recordings FGR-28S.

Subotnick, Morton. *After the Butterfly.* Nonesuch N-78001. This piece involves performers whose sounds are processed live by electronic devices—what Subotnick refers to as "ghost" electronics.

_____ . *Parallel Lines.* CRI SD 458. This piece also features "ghost" electronics.

FOR FURTHER LISTENING

Arel, Bülent. *Electronic Music No. 1.* CRI SD 356.

_____ . *Mimiana II: Frieze.* CRI SD 300.

_____ . *Music for a Sacred Service: Prelude and Postlude.* CRI SD 356.

_____ . *Stereo Electronic Music No. 1.* Columbia MS 6566.

_____ . *Stereo Electronic Music No. 2.* CRI SD 268 and CRI CD 611.

Austin, Larry. *Canadian Coastlines.* Folkways Records FTS 37475.

Avni, Tzvi. *Vocalise.* Turnabout TV 34004S.

Babbitt, Milton. *Phonemena.* Neuma 450-74.

Boretz, Benjamin. *Group Variations.* CRI SD 300.

Celona, John. *Music in Circular Motions.* Folkways Records FTS 37475.

Childs, Mary Ellen. *Standpoints.* University of Illinois School of Music LC 84-743210.

Davidovsky, Mario. *Electronic Study No. 1.* Columbia MS 6566.

_____ . *Electronic Study No. 2.* CRI SD 356.

_____ . *Electronic Study No. 3.* Turnabout TV-S 34487.

Eaton, John. *Mass.* CRI SD 296.

Gaburo, Kenneth. *Lemon Drops.* CRI SD 356 and Heliodor HS-25047.

_____ . *For Harry.* CRI SD 356 and Heliodor HS-25047.

Greenwald, Jan. *Duration 2.* CRI SD 443.

Grippe, Ragnar. *Capriccio.* Bis LP-74.

Hiller, Lejaren. *Machine Music.* Heliodor HS-25047.

Holmes, Reed. *Around the Waves.* Advance Recordings FGR-28S.

_____ . *Moire.* Folkways Records FSS 37465.

Ivey, Jean Eichelberger. *Pinball.* Folkways FM 3436.

Keane, David. *Elektronikus Mozaik.* Cambridge Street Records CSR 8502.

Korte, Karl. *The Whistling Wind.* Folkways Records FSS 37465.

Krieger, Arthur. *Dance for Sarah.* CRI SD 483.

_____ . *Variations on a Theme by Davidovsky.* CRI SD 495.

Lucier, Alvin. *Crossings.* Lovely Music LCD 1018.

_____ . *I am sitting in a room.* Lovely Music/Vital Records VR 1013.

Luening, Otto. "In the Beginning" from *Theater Piece No. 2.* CRI SD 268.

Machover, Tod. *Light.* CRI SD 506.

_____ . *Soft Morning, City!* CRI SD 506.

Martirano, Salvatore. *Underworld.* Heliodor HS-25047.

McLean, Barton. *The Last Ten Minutes.* Folkways Records FSS 37465.

Mimaroglu, Ilhan. *Agony.* Turnabout TV 34046S.

_____ . *Six Preludes for Magnetic Tape.* Turnabout TV 34177.

_____ . *Tract.* Folkways Records FTS 33441.

Pinkston, Russell. *Emergence.* Folkways FTS 33442.

Pousseur, Henri. *Trois visages de Liège.* Columbia MS 7051.

Powell, Mel. *Events* for tape recorder. CRI 227 USD.

_____ . *Second Electronic Setting.* CRI 227 USD.

Ross, Eric. *Electronic Études.* Doria Records ER-103.

Shields, Alice. *Coyote.* CRI SD 495.

_____ . *The Transformation of Ani.* CRI SD 268 and CRI CD 611.

Stockhausen, Karlheinz. *Sternklang.* Deutsche Grammophon 2707 123.

_____ . *Telemusik.* Deutsche Grammophon 137 012.

Tanenbaum, Elias. *Contradictions.* CRI SD 483.

Ussachevsky, Vladimir. *Metamorphosis.* CRI SD 356.

_____ . *Linear Contrasts.* CRI SD 356.

Weidenaar, Reynold. *The Tinsel Chicken Coop, for Your Usual Magnetic Tape* and *Wiener, Your Usual Magnetic Sequel.* Advance Recordings FGR-28S. This remarkable diptych is a powerful narrative for our times.

Wyatt, Scott. *Menagerie.* Ubres CS-303.

THE INTERACTION OF MUSIC AND TECHNOLOGY: A CASE STUDY

As mentioned in Chapter 12, a sense of the role of contemporary musical technology might be gained from a brief review of the history of a few of the keyboard instruments—in particular, the piano—that are among the direct antecedents of the modern synthesizer. Although the invention of the piano can be traced to the workshop of the Italian Bartolomeo Cristofori in the 1690s, the instrument was largely ignored for the first several decades of its existence. The prevailing musical style during these decades, now called the Baroque style, did not require such an instrument capable of fairly subtle and smooth gradations and shadings of the loudness of the tones in a musical line. Direct contrasts of loudness, instrumentation, and texture among successive sections of a composition were more the rule.

The principal keyboard instruments during the first half of the 18th century (the time of the great composer J. S. Bach) were the pipe organ, the harpsichord, and the clavichord. The pipe organ was a very public instrument, particularly well suited to religious services. It could provide a sustained harmonic background. In solo pieces, it could present dazzling patterns of simultaneous melodies, involving both hands and the feet. The organ was also capable of successive contrasts of tone colors, as different ranks of pipes were engaged to produce the sound (a characteristic that foreshadows the preset changes of modern synthesizers).

The harpsichord was a somewhat less public instrument, better suited to the performance of chamber music in the large rooms of aristocratic homes. Because the tone of a harpsichord is produced by plucking the strings, a sustained tone is not possible.[1] However, clear contrasts of volume or tone color can be achieved by engaging mechanisms inside the instrument that can muffle or mute the strings, or double them by also plucking the strings an octave higher or lower. This was perfectly satisfactory for the performance of music in the prevailing style.

---

1. Pressing a key causes a quill mounted on the other end of the key to rise and pluck the corresponding string (or set of strings).

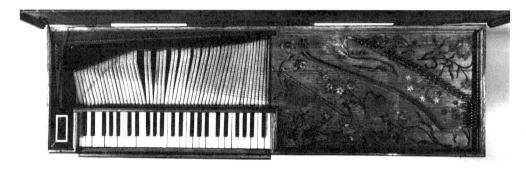

FIGURE E.1
A clavichord.
(Smithsonian Institution
Photo No. 83-4230.)

The clavichord was a much smaller instrument that produced its tone by the direct impact of the interior segment of a key on the corresponding string (see Figure E.1). So long as the key was held down, it maintained contact with the string, thus dampening the vibrations rather quickly. Before the tone could decay completely, however, the performer could shake the key (much like the vibrato technique of a stringed-instrument player) and produce a quivering of the pitch of the dying tone. This technique, called *Bebung* (literally, "quaking" or "trembling") might be regarded as an ancestral form of the aftertouch control capability of a modern synthesizer.

Because of the manner in which its tone is produced, the clavichord is a very quiet instrument. Within its limited range of amplitude, however, it is capable of quite delicate shadings of loudness. Consequently, it was a very private instrument and often played in a way that expressed shifting and deeply felt states of emotion. This latter characteristic was a harbinger of a significant change in musical style that took place around the middle of the 18th century—the development of what is now described as the Classical style.

The increasing significance of opera during this time meant that many composers were becoming interested in the musical depiction of dramatic gestures.[2] Music outside of the opera quickly began to be influenced by these ideas, and after 1750 music became increasingly dramatic in conception. Rather than the abrupt contrasts of loudness characteristic of the Baroque style, for example, music began to incorporate more gradual changes in loudness (crescendi and diminuendi), with their corresponding emotional implications.

The piano, which had languished for so many decades, had now, at last, found a reason for being. Since the end of the 17th century, the technology had existed for the construction of an instrument capable of considerable volume that was also readily capable of gradations of loudness (as Cristofori called it, a *gravicembalo col pian e forte*, or "harpsichord with soft and loud"). The musical reason for doing so, however, did not come until the middle of the 18th century. The change in musical style, from Baroque to Classical, was the engine that made the technological change desirable. By 1790 the harpsichord, incapable of the shadings of loudness required by the new musical style, was essentially obsolete. The clavichord,

---

2. See Charles Rosen, *The Classical Style* (New York: Norton, 1972).

while capable of some degree of dynamic subtlety, was insufficiently loud overall, and it too disappeared from active use.

The piano of the late 18th century, generally called a "fortepiano," was itself not particularly loud. During the first decades of the 19th century, however, a series of changes in design and construction made it a sturdier instrument capable of much greater volume. The primary motivations for these developments were social and economic. Up to this time, secular music had been supported primarily by the landowning, aristocratic class. But the American and French revolutions of 1776 and 1789 signaled a decline in the relative importance of kings, queens, princes, princesses, dukes, duchesses, and their pals. The development of steam-powered manufacturing and techniques of mass production, expansion of global trade, and improvements in transportation, constituting what is now referred to as the Industrial Revolution, led to the rise of the middle class. Not surprisingly, musicians began to shift their attention to the more numerous members of this flourishing class. After 1790, and particularly after 1820, musicians began to perform in large rooms before large groups of newly prosperous people in concerts announced to the public.

Income for the musicians from such events was generated by charging for admission, and larger performance spaces could generate proportionately more income. Larger rooms required louder instruments, however. In response, perhaps the most significant technological improvement to the piano was the introduction of iron reinforcement to the frame of the instrument by the 1820s. In the words of Arthur Loesser, in his masterful survey of the social, economic, and technological history of the piano, this improvement made possible a

> greater range of expression in the instrument, one more appropriate to the projection of its music into larger rooms and to more numerous and distant groups of people. The expression could only come from the musculature of a player; the problem consisted in strengthening the instrument so that its parts would respond to more forceful muscular impacts by emitting a greater volume of sound, without crumpling or breaking.[3]

By the middle decades of the 19th century, this obvious technological solution of using iron to reinforce the frame of the piano, together with other changes to the instrument, would rebound to engender changes in musical style. Loesser continues:

> The metal frame permitting a stronger blow and therefore greater volume, the rapid double-escapement action making for more delicate stroke-responsiveness combined with speed, the thickly felt-covered hammers giving a "rounder" tone than those formerly used—all these developments converged into one trend: the making of an instrument suitable for use by a person who could project music commandingly, fascinatingly, in a large room, a concert virtuoso in other words.[4]

---

3. Arthur Loesser, *Men, Women, and Pianos* (New York: Simon & Schuster, 1954), p. 302.

4. Ibid., p. 339.

FIGURE E.2
The von Jankó keyboard.
(Smithsonian Institution
Photo No. 56378B.)

Thus, Europe became infested for a few years by self-styled super-musicians who traveled from city to city to dazzle audiences with prodigious displays of pianistic gymnastics. Women were reported to swoon at the performances of Franz Liszt, perhaps the greatest of the virtuoso pianists. These proto–rock stars required music that incorporated stunning sonic effects and displays of dizzying technical dexterity. The piano became a vehicle for the projection and promotion of a heroic self-identity. Just a few decades earlier, the piano had become popular in response to changes in musical style. Now, ironically, technological changes to the instrument were contributing to further changes in musical style.[5]

The history of the development of the piano is relatively uneventful after this. Although there were many attempts to change the piano further, only a few were sufficiently compelling to be accepted. One particularly notable idea whose time never came was a reconfiguration of the keyboard proposed by Hungarian Paul von Jankó in the 1880s (see Figure E.2). Like the proposed Dworak arrangement of keys on the typewriter, it was ergonomically more efficient than the traditional pattern, but this was not a sufficient advantage to motivate thousands of piano players to learn "how to play the instrument all over again."[6] These pianists, both professional and

---

5. A perhaps more benign change in musical style in response to a technological change occurred as a result of the change in the covering of the hammer heads from leather to felt by French piano-builder Jean-Henri Pape in 1826. This change made possible the delicate and ethereal textures of piano sound in the compositions of Chopin and Debussy, for example.

6. Loesser, op cit.

amateur, had already invested a considerable portion of their childhoods in learning to play the piano on the traditional keyboard. The von Jankó keyboard illustrates the fact that the impulse to invent, while a necessary condition for change in musical technology, is not a sufficient condition for change to occur.

During the 20th century, composers have shown an interest in the insides of the piano. The American composer Henry Cowell composed several pieces, including *The Banshee* (ca. 1923), in which the hands of the pianist play the strings directly, with the sustain pedal down (in a different vein, Harpo Marx also did much of this sort of thing). In 1938, John Cage (himself the son of an inventor) developed the "prepared piano"—a piano with coins, wooden dowels, screws, washers, rubber erasers, and similar items inserted between the strings—in response to his need for a great variety of percussive timbres that could be played from an instrument by conventional keyboard technique. Subsequently, many other composers have also written for the prepared piano.

Also in the 20th century, the harpsichord has experienced something of a revival. Performers have become more interested in how the music of J. S. Bach, and other composers of the Baroque, sounded on the instruments for which they were composed. A more recent manifestation of this "authentic performance" movement is the use of replicas of fortepianos (those pianos, it may be recalled, that preceded the introduction of cast iron to the frame). A variety of insights has been gained from the use of such replicas in performance. For example, the psychological intensity of a Beethoven piano sonata, such as the first movement of the *Tempest* (opus 31, no. 2), is much more apparent in the stresses and groaning of a fortepiano (as demonstrated superbly by the Malcolm Bilson recording on Nonesuch H-78008) than in the ample headroom of a modern piano. In the lingo of the pilot of high-performance jet aircraft, Beethoven clearly was "pushing the envelope" when he composed the piece. The composition can now be understood somewhat differently. The return to the use of the harpsichord and the fortepiano by virtue of the efforts of the advocates of "authentic performance" illustrates that even instruments that have come to be regarded as obsolete may nonetheless reappear if they can once again meet a perceived need.

This brief account of the history of keyboard instruments illustrates a few of the ways in which music and technology have interacted in the past. These may perhaps suggest a few of the forces that are even now determining the future of musical technology.

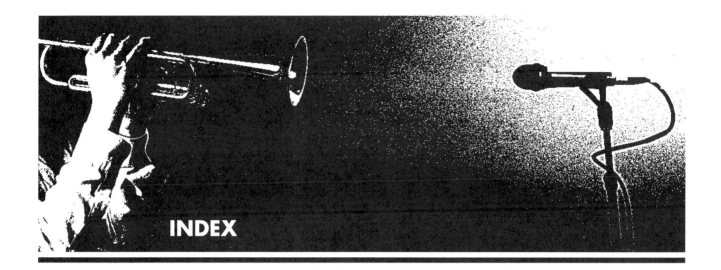

INDEX

Channels, 35
Childs, Mary Ellen, 390
Chipmunk effect, 51
Chorus effect, 117
Chorusing, 118, 119
Chowning, John, 340
Cinch plug, 26
Clavichord, 431
Click track, 94, 109
Color, tone, 13, 209–24
   musical composition and, 340–49
Coloration, off-axis, 16
Combined media for presentation to gathered audiences, 373–80
"Commission," 322–24
Compact disc (CD), 62
Composing by chance (John Cage), 353–56
Composing electroacoustical music, 315–57
Composition, advanced topics in, 339–56
   "serial," 354
   "totally organized," 354
Compression, 121–23
Compressions, 2, 3
Compressor, 121
Computer-generated sounds, suggested listening for, 424–26
Computer graphics and electroacoustical music, 389
Computer-processed sounds, suggested listening for, 424–26
Computer storage of digital sound, 62, 63, 64
Concert, future of, 379–80
"Concert of Noises" (Schaeffer), 52
Concrete music, 52–53
Condenser microphones, 22–23
Cone, Edward, 335
Cone, loudspeaker, 24
Coniglio, Mark, 372
Connecters, electrical, 24–27
Consonance, 13
Constructive interference, 9, 10
Consumer-grade audio equipment, 28–29
Contact microphone, 20
Continue message, 185
Continuous controllers, 139–41
Control Change messages, 139–42, 413–14
Controller mapping, 198
Controller numbers, standard, 415–16
Controllers, 139–42
   alternate, 193–95
   continuous, 139–41
   guitar, 193
   ribbon, 258
   sequential, 258
   S/H, 259–61
   switch, 141–42
   wind, 195
   X-Y, 259
Controller thinning, 169
Control voltage, 227
   sources of, 242–61

Control voltage attenuators, 246, 247
Control voltage inverters, 246, 247
Cope, David, 362
Copyright, 78–79
Cowell, Henry, 434
cps (cycles per second), 4
Creativity, musical, 319–22
Cristofori, Bartolomeo, 430, 431
Cross-fade loop, 279, 280
Crosstalk, 37, 38
Cunningham, Merce, 356, 374
Cunningham Dance Company, 375
Curran, Alvin, 370
Cutoff frequency, 235
Cutting tape, 45. *See also* Editing tape.
Cycles per second (cps), 4

D

DAC, 64, 273
Daisy-chain network, 148
Dance, electroacoustical music for, 374–75
Data bytes, 134
Data filter, MIDI, 197
DAT cassettes, 66
DAT recorder, 66
dB, 5, 41
Decay time, 3, 6
   final, 242
   initial, 242
Decibel (dB), 5, 41
Decimal number system, 404–7
Degaussing, 44
Demagnetization, 44
Déserts (Varèse), 330
Destructive interference, 9, 10
Dhomont, Francis, 53
Diabolus in musica, 13
Diaphragm, 22
Diffraction, 82
Digital delay lines, 116
Digital distortion, 69, 71
Digital filters, 306–7
Digital recorders, 64–72
   cassette, 65–66
   digital sound sampler, 72–79
   hard-disk, 67
   open-reel, 64–65
   videocassette, 65–66
Digital recording, 61–80
   analog versus, 63
   hard-disk, 66–69
   making, 63
Digital sound, computer storage of, 62, 63, 64
Digital sound samplers, 72–79
   closer look at, 274–87
Digital sound sampling, 267–87
Digital sound synthesis, 287–313
Digital-to-analog converter (DAC), 64, 273
Direct box, 20, 21
Direction in music, 334–36

Dispersed audiences, presentation to, 384–92
Dissonance, 13
Domains, 33
Doppler effect, 90
Doubling, 116–19
Dripsody (LeCaine), 53
Druckman, Jacob, 362
Drum machine, 181
Dubbing, 57–58
Duplicate recording
   analog, 57–58
   digital, 71–72
Dust covers, 29
Duty cycle, 232
Dynamic markings, 6
Dynamic microphones, 22, 23
Dynamic voice allocation, 154, 155

E

Eaton, John, 227, 368
Echo, tape, techniques for, 100–102
Echo effects, 116
Echo returns, 110
Echo sends, 109
Editing, sequence, 163–74
Editing digital recordings
   on computer hard disk, 66–67
   open-reel, 64–65
   visual, 67, 68, 74–75
Editing samples, 74–75
Editing tape, 45–50
   step-by-step guide to, 47–49
Editor/librarian, 189
Edit point, 48
Ed/lib, 189
Effects devices, 113. *See also* Signal processing devices.
Effects inputs, 110
Effects loop, 111, 112
Effects outputs, 109
Effects receives, 110
Effects sends, 109
Eight-track recording, 36, 37
Eimert, Herbert, 225
Electret microphone, 23 *n*.7
Electric guitar pickup, 20
Electroacoustic music, 1
   composing, 315–57
   recording, 385–87
Electronic music, prehistory of, 228–29
Electronische Musik, 226, 348
Emerson, Keith, 369
Emerson, Lake, and Palmer, 369
Ensembles for Synthesizer (Babbitt), 350–53
Envelope follower, 259, 260
Envelope generator, 242
Envelopes
   ADSR, 8, 242
   intensity, 5–9
   spectral, 217
EQ, 105